LIVED EXPERIENCE IN THE LATER MIDDLE AGES:

STUDIES OF BODIAM AND OTHER ELITE LANDSCAPES IN SOUTH-EASTERN ENGLAND

Edited by Matthew Johnson

HP

© Individual authors

ISBN 978-0-9926336-6-0

Published by The Highfield Press
75 Watson Avenue, St Andrews KY16 8JE
http://highfieldpress.org/

This book is available from
Oxbow Books Ltd, 10 Hythe Bridge Street, Oxford OX1 2EW or from
Casemate Academic, 1950 Lawrence Road, Havertown, PA 19083, USA
http://www.oxbowbooks.com/

Cover design: Camilla Lovell

Printed in Great Britain by The Short Run Press Ltd, Exeter

2017

Abstract

This edited volume sets out the work of a team of scholars from Northwestern University and the University of Southampton led by Matthew Johnson, in collaboration with the National Trust. Between 2010 and 2014, different members of the group carried out topographical, geophysical and building survey at four different late medieval sites and landscapes in south-eastern England, all owned and managed by the National Trust: Bodiam, Scotney, Knole and Ightham. Studies were also undertaken into documentary, map and other evidence. A particularly important element of the research was to synthesise and re-present the 'grey literature' at all four sites.

This volume seeks to present this work and discuss its archaeological and historical importance. It places the four sites and their landscapes in their setting, as part of the wider landscape of south-east England. It discusses the importance of these places in understanding later medieval elite sites and landscapes in general, and in terms of their long-term biographies and contexts. Central to the volume are the linked ideas of lived experience and political economy and ecology in presenting a new understanding of late medieval sites and landscapes.

Table of Contents

List of Figures.. vi

List of Tables... xi

Acknowledgements.. xii

List of Contributors.. xiv

Foreword... xvi

Chapter 1.   Introduction.. 1
              Matthew Johnson

Chapter 2.   Bodiam: Research prior to 2010.. 9
              Richard James, Casper Johnson, Matthew Johnson, David Martin, Matt Pope, Chris Whittick

Chapter 3.   Bodiam: a new survey of the interior... 25
              Catriona Cooper, Penny Copeland, Matthew Johnson

Chapter 4.   Bodiam as a landscape of work: topographical and geophysical survey....... 51
              Dominic Barker, Kathryn A. Catlin, Matthew Johnson, Timothy Sly, Kristian Strutt

Chapter 5.   The environment of Bodiam: land, vegetation, and human impacts....... 75
              Kathryn A. Catlin, Penny Copeland, Matthew Johnson, Rob Scaife

Chapter 6.   Scotney: archaeological survey and map analysis......................... 95
              Eric D. Johnson, Matthew Johnson, Timothy Sly

Chapter 7.   Knole: sport, labour, and social contest..................................... 106
              Dominic Barker, Ryan Lash, Kristian Strutt

Chapter 8.   Ightham: topographical and geophysical survey and 3D analysis of the landscape...... 129
              Matthew Johnson, Timothy Sly, Carrie Willis

Chapter 9.   Lived experience at Bodiam and Ightham.................................. 143
              Catriona Cooper

Chapter 10.   Moated sites in the Wealden landscape...................................... 158
              Eric D. Johnson

Chapter 11.   Publics, volunteers and communities: public engagement at Bodiam, Scotney, Knole, and Ightham.............. 171
              Becky Peacock

Chapter 12.   Discussion: elite sites, political landscapes and lived experience in the later middle ages... 183
              Matthew Johnson

Chapter 13.   Conclusion.. 202
              Matthew Johnson

TABLE OF CONTENTS

Appendix 1. Summary and guide to archaeological finds from Bodiam Castle............................ 206
Kathryn A. Catlin

Appendix 2. A layperson's account of survey techniques.. 212
Kathryn A. Catlin, Kristian Strutt

Appendix 3. Further details of environmental methods.. 218
Kathryn A. Catlin, Penny Copeland, Rob Scaife

Glossary.. 220
Bibliography.. 224
Index... 241

List of Figures

1.1: Location map of Bodiam, Scotney, Knole and Ightham.
1.2: The Royal Commission on Historical Monuments of England (RCHME) survey of Bodiam (after Taylor *et al.* 1990, fig. 4).

2.1: The site of Bodiam, in relation to the floodplain and Romney Marsh.
2.2: The property as it is today, with boundaries of the Trust property outlined.
2.3-4: Location of Burrin's transects, with long valley profile of the River Rother showing change in gradient and sedimentary regime at Bodiam.
2.5: Simplified diagram of the key features of the landscape around Bodiam Castle, as visible today.
2.6: The postulated access route from the south (after Everson 1996, fig. 1).
2.7: View of Bodiam Castle from the 'Gun Garden'/'Viewing Platform'.

3.1: Simplified plan of Bodiam Castle with key elements designated.
3.2: Faulkner's access diagram (after Faulkner 1963, fig. 11).
3.3: Students from Southampton and Northwestern Universities at work.
3.4: Bodiam Castle, basement plan.
3.5: Bodiam Castle, ground floor plan.
3.6: Bodiam Castle, upper floor plan.
3.7: Bodiam Castle, upper chambers plan.
3.8: Elevation of east curtain wall, as seen from the courtyard looking east.
3.9: Bodiam Castle, GPR results.
3.10: Bodiam Castle GPR results, with key added.
3.11: Evidence for inserted floors, western ground floor room of gatehouse.
3.12: One of Tavernor Perry's drawings, commissioned by Lord Curzon in the 1920s.
3.13: Curzon's render to the plinth or 'apron'.
3.14: Buttress against gatehouse, built up against stair to reach chamber.
3.15: Southern cross wall of western range showing relieving arch and flue or stoke holes.
3.16: West side of gatehouse showing the straight joint between the original and the southern sections.
3.17: Leafy boss in the first floor corridor of the gatehouse.
3.18: Plinth to the east of the gatehouse showing a slight misalignment reused to support a beam.
3.19: Window in north-east range of unusual design.
3.20: Straight joint in external wall to east of gatehouse.
3.21: Recess with lintel in wall of chamber floor of north-east tower.
3.22: Differences in floor levels in the chapel.
3.23: Straight joint and rebuilt walls in basement level of east tower, also showing cupboards where stair access would normally be.
3.24: Fireplace in main range that connects through to east tower recess.
3.25: Possible sites of mortices for drawbridge chain.
3.26: Window to basement of service range excavated by Curzon, also showing the substantial mortices for wall partitions.
3.27: Kitchen layout showing the unusual ledge at upper floor level for a possible partition of the well and staircase areas.
3.28: Double latrine and window at northern end of western range with inconsistent chamfers.
3.29: Change from corbel to string course on the north-west tower.
3.30: Possible straight joint between north-west tower and north wall.

LIST OF FIGURES

- 3.31: Southern section of the east curtain wall showing different building seasons.
- 3.32: Window seat and plinth in northern range often interpreted as stables.
- 3.33: Suites at the upper end of the hall, viewed from the summit of the southern gatehouse.
- 3.34: View down only narrow window jamb to west, and rebated door jamb to right.
- 3.35: Vaulted basement room of the south-east tower.
- 3.36: Interior of south-west tower, with two lodgings and a dovecote above, partially restored.
- 3.37: Stair turret and chimney of the north-west tower.
- 3.38: Floor joists with gap for trimmer and faint scar in surviving plaster for staircase from ground floor against the external northern wall of the kitchen.

- 4.1: Bodiam Castle in its landscape; photo facing south from the Gun Garden.
- 4.2: Map of the Bodiam landscape, showing survey areas, the National Trust property, and the Scheduled Ancient Monument boundaries.
- 4.3: Features in the Bodiam landscape.
- 4.4: Topographic survey of the Bodiam landscape (hillshaded Triangulated Irregular Network (TIN)).
- 4.5: A. Topography (TIN) of the Bodiam landscape. B. Exaggerated vertical profile of the Bodiam landscape.
- 4.6: Floodplain of the River Rother.
- 4.7: Location of augur tests in the cricket field, shown with magnetometry data.
- 4.8a: Floodplain: Magnetometry survey results.
- 4.8b: Floodplain: Magnetic susceptibility survey results.
- 4.9a: Dokes Field: Interpreted magnetometry and earth resistance survey results.
- 4.9b: Dokes Field: Magnetometry and earth resistance survey results.
- 4.10a: Gun Garden: Interpreted magnetometry and earth resistance survey results.
- 4.10b: Gun Garden: Magnetometry and earth resistance survey results.
- 4.11a: Castle West: Interpreted magnetometry, earth resistance, and GPR survey results.
- 4.11b: Castle West: Magnetometry, earth resistance, and GPR survey results.
- 4.12: Suggested path of mill leat.
- 4.13a: Cricket Field: Interpreted magnetometry, earth resistance, and GPR survey results.
- 4.13b: Cricket Field: Magnetometry, earth resistance, and GPR survey results.
- 4.14a: Castle East: Interpreted earth resistance and GPR survey results.
- 4.14b: Castle East: Earth resistance and GPR survey results.

- 5.1: Coring locations relative to the Bodiam grounds.
- 5.2: Key to stratigraphic diagrams.
- 5.3: Relative heights of the cores, facing east.
- 5.4: East range of castle, showing core locations relative to the groundwater level.
- 5.5: Pollen diagram from Profile A2.
- 5.6: 'A colored view of the interior of the east side of Bodiham Castle; drawn by S.H. Grimm, in 1784'.
- 5.7: Pollen diagram from Profile B.
- 5.8: Pollen diagram for Profile C1.
- 5.9: James Miles, Dominic Barker, and Victoria Stevenson coring on the south bank of the moat.
- 5.10: Pollen profile of section D.
- 5.11: The lowest 50 cm of Core F, in the east pond.
- 5.12: Pollen diagram from Profile F.

- 6.1: 2011-2012 Northwestern and Southampton Scotney Castle Landscape Survey extent.
- 6.2: General appearance of Scotney Park today, looking north from the valley bottom.
- 6.3: The inner court of Scotney Castle and moat, from the south-west.
- 6.4: Sunken approach to the castle, as viewed from the north-east looking up towards the higher ground.
- 6.5: Summary of the 2011-2012 Northwestern and Southampton Scotney Castle Landscape Survey results.

LIVED EXPERIENCE IN THE LATER MIDDLE AGES

6.6: Linear features identified in topographic survey and resistivity surveys.
6.7: Geophysical survey in the valley bottom, 2010.
6.8: Medieval administrative boundaries at Scotney.
6.9: 1757 William Clout map georeferenced and overlaid with topographic features identified in the 2011-2012 survey of Scotney Castle.
6.10: 1870 Ordnance Survey map georeferenced and overlaid with topographic features identified in the 2011-2012 survey of Scotney Castle.

7.1: The west frontage of Knole House dominated by the four turrets of the gatehouse tower of Green Court.
7.2: View of Knole House and surrounding garden wall from the north.
7.3: A simplified plan view showing the main courtyards of Knole House.
7.4: Plan of Knole landscape indicating the areas under the stewardship of the National Trust and the Sackville Estate.
7.5: Neolithic or Bronze Age worked flint uncovered at Echo Mount in 2015.
7.6: Detail of the folly ruins near the Birdhouse.
7.7: The extent of the house and gardens at Knole has changed little since Leonard Knyff and Jan Kip produced this engraving in 1698.
7.8: John Harris and Jan Kip produced this engraving for John Harris's History of Kent, published in 1716.
7.9: Conducting survey in the park meant interacting closely with inquisitive locals and day-trippers.
7.10: University of Southampton student Patrick Thewlis wearing the non-magnetic clothing required for magnetometry survey.
7.11: Team members conducting earth resistance survey.
7.12: Team members operate the GPR equipment.
7.13: Results of the topographic survey at Knole.
7.14: Results of the magnetometry survey.
7.15: Detailed view of the magnetometry around Echo Mount.
7.16: Results of the GPR survey.
7.17: Detailed view of the GPR survey results from the west front of the house and within Green Court and Stone Court.
7.18: Results of the resistance survey.
7.19: A group of fallow deer rest in the August sun, 2014.
7.20: One of four possible rabbit warrens located in the wooded area across the long valley south-west of the house.
7.21: The conversion of St Eustace from a wall painting along the north aisle of the choir of Canterbury Cathedral.
7.22: This rounded embankment, now part of a fairway in the golf course, may represent a former park pale.
7.23: Illustrations from The Penny Pictorial News and Family Story Paper 28th June 1884.

8.1: The inner court of Ightham Mote, from the south-west.
8.2: A simplified diagram of Ightham Mote as it exists today, with key features indicated.
8.3: Contour map of the area surveyed at Ightham Mote.
8.4: The wider landscape of Ightham Mote, with the location of possible sections of park pale and other substantial field boundaries indicated.
8.5: Ground plan of the inner court as it exists today.
8.6: Reconstruction of the inner court in the 14th century.
8.7: Possible layout of landscape and water features around the house in the 14th century, before the addition of the outer court.
8.8: Water features north of the house as they exist today, with valley sides and woods beyond, viewed from the gatehouse tower.

LIST OF FIGURES

8.9: Dam, of post-medieval form but possibly of medieval origin, between the two ponds north of the house, looking east.
8.10: An earthwork ditch, now used as a modern field boundary, 700 m south of the house.
8.11: Three-dimensional topographical model of the landscape at Ightham Mote, rendered in ArcGIS.
8.12: GPR results from survey in the orchard at Ightham Mote.
8.13: View north-west from the gatehouse tower towards the orchard, with modern reconstructed gardens in the foreground and the valley sides beyond.
8.14: The route of approach to Ightham Mote from the eastern side of the valley (blue line) and western side of the valley (red line), superimposed on the 1889 Sale Particulars map.
8.15: The outer court, probably added in the 1470s, as seen looking west from the summit of the gate tower.

9.1: This diagram shows how social ideas are linked to space.
9.2: The eastern elevation of Bodiam Castle, taken from the west.
9.3: The Arnolfini Portrait by Jan van Eyck.
9.4: Medieval chest, Chester Cathedral.
9.5: Dover Castle, reconstructed interior.
9.6: The Annunciation by Rogier van der Weyden.
9.7: Detail of a miniature of the birth of Alexander the Great, at the beginning of Book Five, from the Miroir Historial.
9.8: Lighting assessment of the modelled private apartments of Bodiam Castle.
9.9: An example of the modelled space.
9.10: Internal space which appears dark when printed without adjustments for lighting.
9.11: The same image lighted for printing.
9.12: Reading mood board.
9.13: Sound mood board.
9.14: The Great Hall at Ightham Mote from the courtyard.
9.15: The Great Hall at Ightham Mote looking towards the upper end of the Hall.
9.16: Minstrel carved into the beam ends.
9.17: Undertaking the acoustical survey at Ightham Mote.
9.18: Equipment setup for recording acoustical properties.
9.19: Model of Ightham Mote. Each colour represents a different surface property.
9.20: This graph shows the differences between the modelled and simulated Great Halls.

10.1: Selection of individual moated sites in south-eastern England.
10.2: Part of the ditch surrounding the moated site at Bodiam (East Sussex, TQ 784264).
10.3: Distribution of moats in south-eastern England, plotted against elevation.
10.4: Distribution of moated sites, plotted against underlying geology.
10.5: A representation of a moated manor house and park in the initial capital of the licence to crenellate the dwelling place of 'La Mote' granted to Sir Edmund de Pashley in 1318.
10.6: Density of mentions of places in Domesday 1086, plotted against distribution of moated sites.
10.7: Landscape context of The Mote, near Iden.
10.8: Moated sites in relation to parish boundaries. Above: inset of the Eastern Weald. Below: distribution of moated sites within parish boundaries.

11.1: Members of local archaeology societies inspect the GPR equipment at Bodiam, April 2010.
11.2: Becky Peacock interviews a dog walker at Bodiam, April 2010.
11.3: Cinderella Castle, Magic Kingdom, Tokyo Disneyland.
11.4: Charlotte and Davy Allen dig for artefacts at Bodiam; operations directed by Sarah Johnson.

12.1:   Geology of Britain, with position of section 12.2 indicated.
12.2:   Simplified section through the geology of Britain from Snowdon to Harwich.
12.3:   Geology of the Weald.
12.4:   Simplified section through the geology of the Weald, with vertical axis exaggerated.
12.5:   Bodiam, Scotney, Knole and Ightham, mapped against the underlying geology and the boundaries of Kent, Sussex and the rapes of Sussex.
12.6:   Mutilated tomb effigy of Sir John Dallingridge, on display at Bodiam Castle.
12.7:   The north-west tower and part of the surviving north range of Otford Palace, Kent.
12.8:   View south over the Weald, as seen from the top of the greensand ridge between Knole and Ightham.
12.9:   Tomb and effigy of Thomas Couen, died 1372, Ightham church.
12.10: Heraldry above the south gate, Bodiam Castle.
12.11: Heraldry above the north gate, Bodiam Castle.
12.12: Schematic representation of some of the activities and flows around Bodiam Castle.

A1.1:   Bodiam mortar, on a modern carriage at the Royal Artillery Museum.
A1.2:   Selection of pottery finds from Curzon's excavations.
A1.3:   Selection of Roman-period finds, now held at the Battle Museum.

A2.1:   Kristian Strutt engaged in topographic survey using RTK GPS at Bodiam Castle in 2010.
A2.2:   Peter Harris, Ceri Bridgeford, and Patrick Thewlis conduct topographic survey using a Leica TotalStation at Ightham Mote in 2013.
A2.3:   The basic four probe circuit of a resistance meter (after Clark 1996: 27).
A2.4:   Dominic Barker supervises earth resistance survey at Bodiam Castle in 2010.
A2.5:   Diagram of an Electrical Resistivity Tomography (ERT) survey.
A2.6:   ERT survey in progress at Bodiam in 2010.
A2.7:   The effect of the earth's magnetic field and the local magnetic field generated by buried material, measured during magnetometer survey.
A2.8:   Eric Johnson and Meya Kellala conduct magnetometer survey in Dokes Field at Bodiam Castle in 2012.
A2.9:   Diagram showing the footprint of a GPR antenna as the radar wave propagates through the ground, and the reflection caused by a circular or oval body located below the surface of the ground as the antenna passes over it.
A2.10: Katie Fuller and Helena Glover conduct GPR survey in the Green Court at Knole in 2013 using a 500 MHz Sensors and Software Noggin Plus.
A2.11: Ivan Yeh, Emily Pierce-Goldberg and Chen Xiaowen conduct GPR survey in 2012 at the Bodiam cricket field using a 200 MHz GSSI instrument.

List of Tables

2.A: Palaeoenvironmental Summary.

4.A: Summary of geophysical survey techniques. See Appendix Two for more details of the techniques.

5.A: Pollen count data from Profile A1 (north-eastern corner, castle interior).
5.B: Stratigraphy of Profile A2.
5.C: Stratigraphy of Profile B.
5.D: Stratigraphy of Profile C1.
5.E: Stratigraphy of Profile C2.
5.F: Stratigraphy of Profile D.
5.G: Stratigraphy of Profile F.

A1.A: Excavations, finds, and archived locations as of 2015.

Acknowledgements

Innumerable people have helped in different ways with this project since 2009 – colleagues and students at Northwestern University and the University of Southampton, National Trust staff and volunteers, local and amateur archaeologists, and members of the public. Academic colleagues at many different institutions, too numerous to mention here, have offered ideas, insights and informal feedback on presentations of the work in a variety of contexts.

Caroline Thackray, Regional Archaeologist for the National Trust, supported the work in its early stages; Nathalie Cohen took over from Caroline in 2012. Both Caroline and Nathalie have been tremendous friends and partners to the project. David Thackray, Head of Archaeology at the Trust until 2012, and his successor Ian Barnes gave consistent encouragement. In 2012, during site visits to Bodiam and Scotney, various members of the National Trust Archaeology panel made acute and incisive comments.

We thank the Bodiam site manager until 2016, George Bailey, and all the staff and volunteers at Bodiam Castle for all their patience and assistance during the survey. The Bodiam Advisory Group provided critical feedback on the progress of the project; we thank chairs Vivienne Coad and John Henderson in particular. We would also like to thank Dora Church, her family and other residents of Bodiam who were patient with our students in their houses and gardens, and provided coffee!

In 2015, Paul Drury and his team at Drury McPherson Partnership were commissioned to write a new Conservation Management Plan for Bodiam. We thank them for their willingness to share their data and for collegiate conversations, both by email and in the Castle Inn, over the understanding of the castle and its landscape.

The standing building survey and coring and pollen analysis at Bodiam were funded by the Engineering and Physical Sciences Research Council and Arts and Humanities Research Council (AHRC) as part of the Parnassus Project, under licence from the National Trust and with the consent of English Heritage (Scheduled Monument Consent S00044985). We also gratefully acknowledge the support of the Science and Heritage Programme at University College London, as well as the Universities of Southampton and Bristol. The AHRC also funded two Collaborative Doctoral Awards; the AHRC is thanked, as well as the anonymous referees for the application, who provided important input into the developing idea of lived experience. At Southampton, Anne Curry, Chris Woolgar, Alison Gascoigne and Graeme Earl acted as co-supervisors for Catriona Cooper and Gemma Minihan, with Caroline and David Thackray and latterly Nathalie Cohen and Emma Slocombe acting as co-supervisors on behalf of the Trust.

We thank Les Smith at the Royal Artillery Museum for information about the 'Bodiam Bombard'.

We thank the Scotney staff and volunteers, particularly Ross Wingfield, Caroline Binder and John Musgrave. Ross was especially helpful in assisting with our stay at the Scotney Base Camp in 2010 and 2011.

At Knole, Emma Slocombe, Helen Fawbert and many other Trust staff and volunteers were generous in providing accommodation, research and Internet facilities for the team, and invaluable logistical help in the 2013 and 2014 seasons. Alistair Oswald, formerly of English Heritage and currently a PhD student at the University of York, generously shared his research on the Knole landscape with us. We also thank Lord Sackville for giving permission to survey areas of Knole Park outside the area under Trust guardianship.

ACKNOWLEDGEMENTS

At Ightham, Bernadette Gillow, Adam Ford, Sarah Gaines, Lynne Antwis and all the other Trust staff and volunteers gave invaluable help. Susan Oosthuizen, Reader in Medieval Archaeology at the University of Cambridge, discussed her observations on the site, and both she and Adam pointed out the existence of the stretch of probable park pale discussed in Chapter Eight.

Around 100 Southampton and 12 Northwestern undergraduate students, too numerous to name here, took part in fieldwork at all four sites over the course of the five field seasons of the project. We thank everyone for their professionalism, hard work and good humour in varying weather conditions.

Colleagues and fellow faculty, staff and students at Northwestern University and the University of Southampton provided an intellectual and practical structure within which our work could flourish. Southampton graduate students involved in the work included James Cole, Meya Kellala, James Miles and Dave Underhill.

Penny Copeland thanks the Elias family for support and hospitality throughout the project.

A number of people reviewed parts or all of the final manuscript extensively and made invaluable comments. These included Tim Earle, David Hinton, Rebecca Johnson, David Martin, Susan Oosthuizen and Cynthia Robin. Additionally, during the research process, we conducted interviews with, picked the brains of, or otherwise encroached upon the time of, a large number of local scholars. Particularly important contributions made in this way include Casper Johnson, David and Barbara Martin, and Chris Whittick. Richard Jones directed us to the significance of the Bodiam place-name. Any errors and misconceptions that remain are the authors' responsibility.

Catriona Cooper thanks Filippo Fazi and Diego Murillo Gomez from the Institute of Sound and Vibration Research at the University of Southampton for their help with the acoustics project and Grant Cox from Archaeology for his technical support. Finally Sam Griffiths for constant edits and support in getting it together.

Carrie Willis thanks Mark Hauser for his advice and encouragement in the development of her senior thesis on Ightham Mote.

We thank the National Trust and Northwestern University for financial support towards the production costs for this volume. In addition to authoring and co-authoring several chapters, Kathryn Catlin worked as an editorial assistant on the project; without her work, the volume would still be at the concept stage. Lyn Cutler and Kat Cutler from The Highfield Press guided the manuscript through the final stages of production, and showed great patience with delays in its submission.

List of Contributors

Dominic Barker
Fieldwork Technician, University of Southampton
d.s.barker@southampton.ac.uk

Kathryn A Catlin
PhD Candidate, Northwestern University
kathryncatlin2012@u.northwestern.edu

Catriona Cooper
Formerly PhD Student, University of Southampton; now Heritage Research Supervisor, Allen Archaeology Ltd, and Visiting Fellow, University of Southampton
catrionaelizabethcooper@gmail.com

Penny Copeland
Research Fellow/Technician in Archaeology, University of Southampton
p.copeland@soton.ac.uk

Richard James
Senior Archaeologist – Historic Environment, Archaeology South-East
richard.james@ucl.ac.uk

Casper Johnson
County Archaeologist, East Sussex County Council
casper.johnson@eastsussex.gov.uk

Eric D Johnson
PhD student, Harvard University (former undergraduate at Northwestern University)
ericjohnson@g.harvard.edu

Matthew Johnson
Professor of Anthropology, Northwestern University and Visiting Professor, University of Southampton
matthew-johnson@northwestern.edu

Ryan Lash
PhD Candidate, Northwestern University
ryanlash2012@u.northwestern.edu

David Martin
Former Senior Historic Buildings Officer, Archaeology South-East (retired)
david.martin@ucl.ac.uk

Becky Peacock
Outreach and Interpretation Officer (Canadian Pacific Project) based at the Watercress Line; formerly PhD student, University of Southampton
outreach.mhr@hotmail.com

LIST OF CONTRIBUTORS

Matt Pope
Principal Research Associate, UCL Institute of Archaeology
m.pope@ucl.ac.uk

Rob Scaife
Visiting Professor of Palaeoecology and Environmental Archaeology, University of Southampton
r.scaife@soton.ac.uk

Timothy Sly
Senior Teaching Fellow in Archaeology, University of Southampton
tim.sly@soton.ac.uk

Kristian Strutt
Experimental Officer in Archaeology, University of Southampton, also Director, Archaeological Prospection Services Southampton
k.d.strutt@soton.ac.uk

Chris Whittick
Senior Archivist, East Sussex County Council
christopher.whittick@eastsussex.gov.uk

Carrie Willis
User Support Specialist, IT Technology Support Services, Northwestern University (former undergraduate at Northwestern University)
carrie.willis@northwestern.edu

Foreword

by
Ian Barnes, MCIfA, FSA, Head of Archaeology, National Trust

The National Trust is honoured to be the custodian of some of the United Kingdom's most magnificent and significant houses and landscapes *'for ever, for everyone'*. This is both a privilege and a daunting task requiring copious amounts of skill, knowledge, foresight and resources. It is a mission undertaken not only by the Trust's staff but one shared between a multitude of volunteers and partnerships dedicated to the understanding and conservation of our past. Academics and their students rate highly in this partnership: their studies of Trust properties in pursuit of their own research agendas simultaneously provide vital management knowledge for the Trust as well as a wealth of new stories to tell visitors.

Professor Johnson and the team of experts he brought together, from Northwestern University in the USA and the University of Southampton in the UK, is an excellent example of how well the Trust and academia work together. This work builds on the knowledge of generations of historians and archaeologists who have cared for and studied the properties. This model of collaborative working has resulted in a new depth of understanding of how these properties functioned.

Though the Trust has cared for Bodiam, Ightham, Knole and Scotney for many years it would not claim to fully understand how they functioned in their pomp. These are long-lived, multi-layered structures, that sit within a complicated and mostly vanished set of physical and social networks and ways of life. We can wonder at the physical intricacy of the building remains, but without the context of how they functioned within the rituals and politics of their day they remain curiosities. The work of Professor Johnson and his team, beautifully portrayed in this volume, brings these properties to life and illustrates how remarkable they were. This will allow the Trust to care for them in an even more sympathetic manner and, just as importantly, tell their authentic stories to the thousands of people who visit each year.

By attempting to explain how these great houses worked at a physical and social scale, Professor Johnson is continuing with the tradition in archaeology to move away from the study of sites as isolated places to the understanding of landscapes, societies, networks and connections. The Trust itself is doing the same with its landscapes; researching the human and natural connections that formed them, and that need to be understood in order to manage them in the future. The modern world is a complex place, but it is naive to think it was not always so. The relationship between people and the landscapes and buildings they construct is fundamental to who we are as a society and a nation, and to how we move forward.

As previously written, the Trust, wherever possible, is keen to share the responsibility to research and understand its properties as it cannot itself cover the vast range of expertise required to understand such complex entities. Professor Johnson's project has been a shining example of how this can work. The fieldwork facilitated by Trust staff has given many undergraduates the opportunity to work and learn on significant and spectacular sites, and has seen two students progress through to their Doctorates. This volume is a tribute to all of their efforts for which the Trust is extremely grateful.

Bodiam, Ightham, Knole and Scotney are four important properties of which we now have a much greater understanding, but the Trust never stands still. Undoubtedly this work is a landmark moment, but with many more properties still to research and techniques continually evolving, for the Trust, the work goes on.

1

INTRODUCTION

Matthew Johnson

Abstract. This chapter provides an introductory narrative of the work set out in this volume. It discusses the intellectual origins of the programme of research, how different members of the project became involved, and how the scope and aims of the work shifted and expanded as the project developed, starting with the castle and landscape of Bodiam and moving on to Scotney, Knole and Ightham.

This edited volume reports on and discusses the work of a team of scholars from Northwestern University and the University of Southampton. The team was led by myself, and the work was conducted in partnership with the National Trust. Between 2010 and 2014, different members of the group carried out topographical, geophysical and building survey at four different late medieval sites in south-eastern England, all owned and managed by the Trust: Bodiam, Scotney, Knole and Ightham (Fig. 1.1). Different members of the team also undertook research into documentary, map and other evidence. A particularly important element of the research was to synthesise and re-present the 'grey literature' at all four sites.

The volume reports on this work, and sets out a wider view of later medieval buildings and their contexts. It places the four sites and their landscapes in their setting, as part of the wider landscape of south-east England. It discusses the importance of these places in understanding later medieval elite sites and landscapes in general, and in terms of their longer-term biographies and contexts.

A key idea running through all this work is that of *lived experience*. Though the interests and backgrounds of the team members were and are very diverse, and ideas of lived experience can be very complex in theoretical terms, at its heart the focus is very simple: it is about understanding buildings and landscapes in terms of the different human experiences they afford. Its application to understanding later medieval building and landscapes will be expanded on in later chapters. Here, as an introduction, is a brief indication of some of the themes that lived experience refers to:

- A focus on the everyday – the ordinary routines of work: how people moved around and acted upon landscapes and buildings on a day-to-day basis.
- A focus on the local context – the immediate and regional landscapes around the different sites.
- Engaging with the subjective experience of different individuals and groups, both elite and commoner, women, men and children.
- A focus on practice – how the experience of places is bound up with what people do at those places.
- A focus on the senses: how places were experienced through the body.
- Cultural biography and the long term: how buildings and landscapes change through time, at a series of scales, from the daily, weekly and seasonal, to the millennia.

Our governing thesis is that late medieval buildings and landscapes can be better understood through a focus on these themes. We will present a view of Bodiam, Scotney, Knole and Ightham that places these sites in their local and regional context, but also does much more than this. We will situate these sites in their long-term histories and contexts, from prehistory to the present, and understand them as

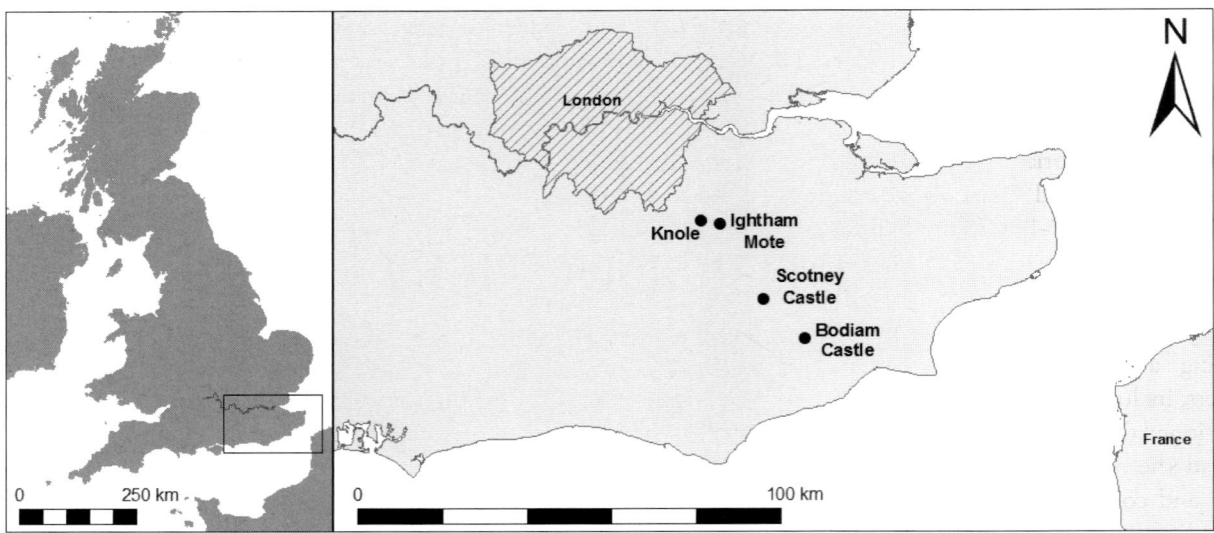

Fig. 1.1: Location map of Bodiam, Scotney, Knole and Ightham.

complex taskscapes and places of work rather than as architectural types or individual buildings.

Different elements of the themes that define lived experience are picked up in the chapters that follow. The concluding discussion will try to draw them all together into a fresh view of medieval buildings and landscapes. It will relate issues of lived experience to themes of political economy and ecology in a new understanding of these buildings that moves at a series of scales from the Weald and south-east England to the British Isles and beyond.

Narrative of the Project

Over the last thirty years, approaches to the study of late medieval buildings and landscapes have changed radically. Many of these changes have been practical in nature, as new survey technologies and methods have produced much more accurate and detailed representations of buildings and the landscapes around them. Other changes have been intellectual and theoretical in nature. Changes include: a rethinking of the relationship between archaeological and historical evidence, a growing stress on understanding meaning and lived experience, growing stress on the social and landscape context of buildings within the discipline of architectural history, and a changing understanding of the demands and issues of public engagement and community archaeology. (For a fuller account of these intellectual shifts in medieval archaeology, see Austin 1984; 1990; 2007; Gilchrist 1999; Moreland 2001; Gerrard 2003; Johnson 2007 and Johnson 2010a).

My own work has been part of these changes. My 1993 book *Housing Culture: Traditional Houses in an English Landscape* (Johnson 1993) was an early attempt to apply some of these ideas to the study of traditional houses between the 14th and 17th centuries. In *Housing Culture*, I explored the shift from the medieval hall to the early modern vernacular house in social and cultural terms, as part of a 'process of closure'. I asked what cultural meanings the open hall carried, and how and why those meanings shifted as the open hall was abandoned and houses became more segregated in the course of the 16th and 17th centuries. I amplified and broadened these ideas in my 2010b *English Houses 1300-1800: Vernacular Architecture, Social Life,* in which I took the story up to the segregated, symmetrical houses of the Georgian period. I also discussed the implications of new ideas for the traditional study of landscapes in *Ideas of Landscape* (2007).

I turned my attention specifically to the evidence of medieval and later castles and elite landscapes in my 2002 book *Behind the Castle Gate: From Medieval to Renaissance*. In this book, I showed how castles had traditionally been seen and interpreted in largely military terms, but that we needed to understand castles in social and cultural terms also. Castles were also stage settings, backdrops against which the identities and agencies of their builders and owners were played out. The landscapes around castles were part of these staged settings, controlling and delimiting views and the movement of people inwards and outwards. Having explored these themes for later medieval castles, I then traced how these views and settings changed at the end of the Middle Ages and through into the 16th and early 17th centuries.

A key case study in the changing interpretation of later medieval buildings was that of the castle of Bodiam, in south-east England, built in the 1380s and associated with Sir Edward Dallingridge[1] (Fig. 1.1). Chapter Two lays out the very long history of debate over the interpretation of this site, termed by the eminent architectural historian John Goodall the 'battle for Bodiam' (Goodall 1998b; see also Goodall 1998a & Goodall 2011: 307-19). Many traditional scholars have seen Bodiam as having been built near the south coast as a defence against the French at an historical moment during the Hundred Years War when the French were making attacks upon the southern English coast. Others, including myself in *Behind the Castle Gate,* have questioned this exclusively military view and emphasised instead the social and symbolic aspects of the castle's form and context. This latter view, as applied not just to Bodiam but to medieval castles in general, has been characterised by some as 'revisionist' (Platt 2007).

Three key pieces of work have been influential in so-called revisionist views. First, Charles Coulson wrote a series of articles reassessing the architecture of Bodiam in terms of what he saw as its lack of military effectiveness (Coulson 1992; 1996). Second, Coulson also reinterpreted Bodiam's 'licence to crenellate', a document dated to 1385 in the form of a licence issued by the king, suggesting that it and other such licences issued at the time were honorific in nature rather than transparent evidence of defensibility (1993; 1994). Third, a survey by the then Royal Commission on Historical Monuments of England (RCHME, or simply Royal Commission) of the immediate landscape setting led to their claim that the immediate landscape context of Bodiam could be understood as 'elaborate gardens' (Taylor *et al.* 1990; Everson 1996: 67).

The battle for Bodiam, and the broader debate over the meanings and functions of castles of which it was a part, stemmed in part from different disciplinary backgrounds, generational views and intellectual approaches to castles. Some elements of the 'debate' were frustrating. In particular, there was what I felt to be a false framing of the debate in terms of military *versus* social explanations of castles, and an assertion by some traditional scholars that I and others were claiming that castles had little or no military role to play (Platt 2007). The wrongly attributed view that castles were 'not defensive' (Thompson 2003: 621) could then easily be refuted by a long list of examples where castles could and did play a military role. There was a strong element of rhetoric here: military views were presented by their advocates as 'common sense' and the currency of the 'plain historian or archaeologist' (Thompson 2003: 621), and conversely 'social' interpretations were derided as 'imaginative flights' or as 'hostile to empirical research… never needing to put a spade in the ground' (Thompson 2003: 622; Platt 2010b: 431).

The mismatch between a rhetoric of empiricism and common sense, and the reality, was particularly apparent when one considered the previous history of field and archival research at Bodiam. I had taken care to examine closely the archive at Bodiam, and to talk to local archaeologists and historians such as Casper Johnson and David and Barbara Martin. One of the things that was striking about critical reactions to the battle for Bodiam was that they paid so little attention to the work of these and other local scholars and of the grey literature (research written-up and archived, but not fully published: see Glossary) on the site. In particular, as we will discuss at more length in Chapter Two, important grey literature research outlined in a 2000 Conservation Management Plan commissioned by the National Trust (Johnson *et al.* 2000) had placed Bodiam much more fully in its local and regional context, and raised a series of questions about the 1990 RCHME interpretation.

The battle for Bodiam, then, seemed to be going around in circles. Scholars were spilling a great deal of ink on the interpretation of the castle and its context, and sometimes getting quite cross with one another, without, it seemed to me, advancing to a better understanding of the site or what the evidence of the site might mean during the later Middle Ages. This lack of progress was frustrating, but it wasn't enough to just get cross. It occurred to me that as someone who had worked on 'theory' in archaeology (Johnson 2010a), it was incumbent upon me, not merely to be frustrated, but to ask the question *why*. Why was the debate going round in circles? How might we change the terms of the debate to make it more meaningful, and to move it forward – to enable different scholars to discuss and advance their understanding of the site with reference to evidence, rather than simply restating old views over and over again?

Towards 2010, I was developing two related answers to these questions. The first was that as framed, questions about the purpose or intent of the builder of Bodiam were unanswerable. Much of the debate concerned questions of individual intention – what did Dallingridge intend when he built this castle, to defend against the French or to express his social status? In general, scholarly arguments that appeal to the presumed intention of an individual in this way can be very difficult to resolve,

---

[1] Sir Edward Dallingridge's surname can be spelt several different ways; in this volume, we follow the place-name from which it was derived.

for the rather old-fashioned reason that we will never be able to directly observe what goes on between someone's ears, let alone someone who has been dead for over six centuries. Consequently, any piece of evidence could be marshalled to support either view, depending on one's prejudice – one person's defensive causeway was another person's processional routeway, one person's gunport was another person's fashion statement.

The debate was also framed around terms and concepts which appeared simple and straightforward but which, when examined more closely, were actually quite complex – defence, honour, status, display, conspicuous consumption… any student of social, cultural and political life in the later Middle Ages would readily affirm that defence, honour, status, display, conspicuous consumption were very complex and fluid ideas in the thought and conduct of the period. One might suggest that they need to be defined and dissected in anthropological terms, before looking for them in the archaeological and documentary record.

If it is to be a responsible and rigorous science, then archaeology must have at its centre the relationship between theory and evidence. The accumulation of vast amounts of evidence, in and of itself, leads precisely nowhere if it is not related in its turn to the evaluation of different ideas. We can look very hard at a castle, climb its stairs, stand in its ruins, and tramp across the surrounding landscape until our legs are heavy and our feet are cold and tired, but unless the observations we make are rigorously tied to the evaluation of different and often competing interpretations, such hard and back-breaking labour tells us nothing. What was needed, then, was more careful theoretical consideration of how arguments over Bodiam, and for that matter late medieval buildings and landscape generally, were framed in relation to the evidence.

The second answer was more prosaic, and was practical rather than theoretical: despite the huge literature on the interpretation of Bodiam, including my own contributions, much basic work at the site had yet to be done. First, there was no modern building survey of the castle. Plans of the building were direct or indirect copies of the drawings Sydney Toy made of the building during Lord Curzon's work in the 1920s. These drawings were outstanding for their time, but buildings archaeologists are very aware that time and again new surveys have thrown up fresh insights into buildings. For example, work at the Tower of London (Impey 2008), at Colchester (Drury 1982), and at Norham and Hedingham (Dixon & Marshall 1993a; 1993b) has shown how the popular image of the Norman stone residential tower-keep actually conceals a great variety of early forms and arrangements. Chapter Three, then, reports on our survey of the interior of Bodiam, the new observations arising from that survey, and their implications for the interpretation of that site.

There was, second, no systematic topographical survey of the Bodiam landscape, and a sustained programme of geophysical work had never been done. The famous Royal Commission survey (Fig. 1.2) was a hachure survey, with all the strengths and limitations of that method. Hachure surveys are a distinctive form of field practice and representation. They are national, in the sense that the drawing of hachures was developed within the 'English school' of landscape archaeology and direct equivalents are rare in other national traditions. Hachured plans draw on the immense and deep knowledge of their practitioners in making judgments about the form, nature and relative chronology of the humps and bumps being surveyed. The hachures or 'tadpoles' that appear on the final plan are the product of close observation of the land by experts in the craft, but they cannot be characterised as objective or neutral, as they always go hand-in-hand with a developing understanding of the site, as their own practitioners often affirm (Bowden 2000; Johnson 2007: 93-5).

In 2008-9, then, I was thinking about how frustrating it was that all sides in the battle for Bodiam had taken so little notice of the grey literature, and how so much work remained to be done. At the same time, I also became aware, both indirectly and directly, of the outlooks and views of local archaeologists and historians. These included Caroline Thackray, then the Regional Archaeologist for the National Trust, Casper Johnson, who at the time was working for Archaeology South-East and went on to be County Archaeologist for East Sussex, David and Barbara Martin, who had worked in the area for over forty years, knew the castle intimately and whose work there included a report on work on the bridge timbers and other features exposed during draining of the moat (Martin 1973), Chris Whittick, Senior Archivist at Sussex County Council, and George Bailey, who was Site Manager at Bodiam between 1992 and 2016.

Discussing Bodiam in 2008-9 with those who had a local and intimate knowledge and continuing engagement with its immediate landscape clarified several impressions. First, the information in the grey literature needed to be more widely disseminated. To that end, Chapter Two presents the key findings from past work since 1999 and in particular the surveys and interventions since 2000, including the key points

INTRODUCTION

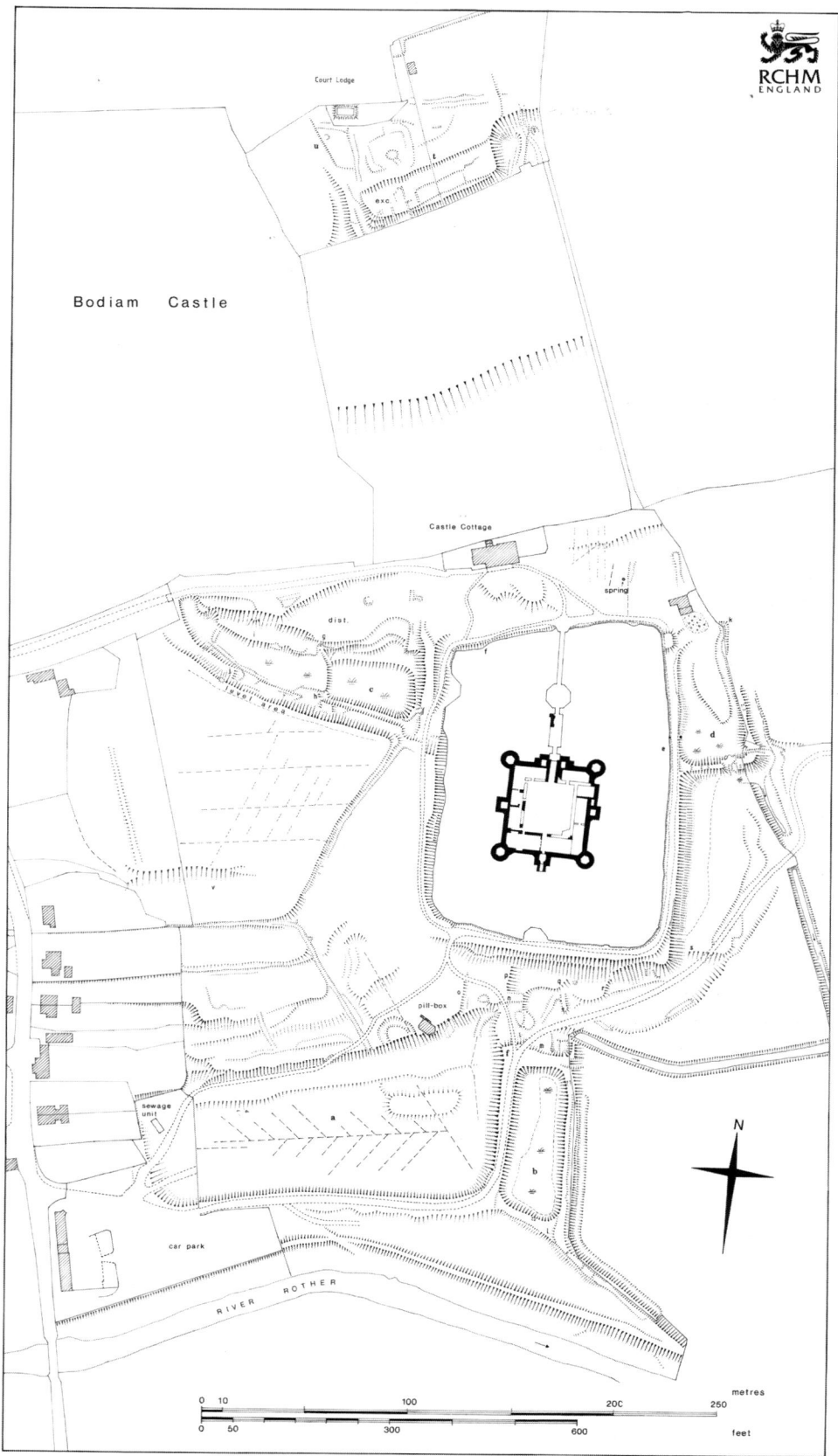

Fig. 1.2: The Royal Commission on Historical Monuments of England (RCHME) survey of Bodiam (after Taylor et al. *1990, fig. 4). The use of hachures will not be familiar to all members of an international audience: they are the 'tadpoles' indicating breaks and changes of slope. 810438 Bodiam Castle in AF0809527 RCHME survey 1988. © Crown copyright. Historic England Archive.*

from the observations in the 2000 Conservation Management Plan of Casper Johnson, David Martin and Chris Whittick. This chapter is the result of a very long gestation, going back to early discussions initiated with Caroline Thackray's encouragement in 2009 of what a paper on the grey literature might look like. Here, it forms an introduction to the rest of the work on Bodiam, a framing of questions which we have been able to partly answer through subsequent fieldwork.

Second, there was a need for more systematic survey of the Bodiam landscape using the latest technologies. Here, I turned to my colleagues at Southampton, Dominic Barker, Timothy Sly and Kristian Strutt. Tim, Dom and Kris were annually running two extremely popular survey courses in Archaeological Survey and Geophysical Survey for Southampton undergraduates. An integral part of both courses (and a key reason for their popularity) was a week's field experience on local sites, and it was imperative that the students get experience with as wide a range of up-to-date equipment as possible during that time. They expressed enthusiasm when I suggested that we work together at Bodiam; it has proved to be an ideal partnership. Dom, Tim and Kris work to the highest professional and technical standards; managing large programmes of systematic fieldwork has never been my strength, but I hope I have been able to engage with their work and facilitate the articulation of its results within a wider intellectual frame. The National Trust, thanks to the efforts of Caroline and George, were able to provide student accommodation at their Scotney Base Camp for two two-week spring field seasons at Bodiam, in March/April 2010 and 2011. During this time, a total of c. 80 Southampton undergraduates took part in the work, with c. 15-20 working on the project at any one time.

At the same time as the topographical and geophysical survey of the landscape was underway, we were able to undertake a new survey of the castle fabric. We were successful in obtaining Arts and Humanities Research Council (AHRC) funding through the PARNASSUS project (studying the impact of climate change of ancient monuments) for Penny Copeland, Research Fellow/Technician at Southampton, to work on the standing fabric of Bodiam as an example of a monument that rises from standing water. The AHRC was also able to fund a limited programme of coring. Penny Copeland and Catriona Cooper prepared a new survey which is presented and discussed in Chapter Three. Chapter Four presents the results of topographical and geophysical survey of the areas around the castle, and Chapter Five does the same for coring and environmental analysis.

In 2011, we extended the work to the nearby site of Scotney. Scotney is another later 14th-century castle with striking parallels to Bodiam; it is also owned and managed by the National Trust. It was always apparent that for all its fame as a particularly impressive site, Bodiam's significance was in part that it was representative of a group of late medieval buildings and landscapes, most of which, including Scotney, have been much less cited in the literature. Scotney is very similar to Bodiam in a number of ways – built by a contemporary and associate of Dallingridge's, Roger Ashburnham, in the 1370s, and also surrounded by an extensive, watery landscape including a mill and artificial moat or lake. The topographical and limited geophysical survey of the Scotney estate, extensively re-landscaped in the 19th century, was led by Tim Sly.

In the autumn of 2011, I moved from the University of Southampton to Northwestern University in the USA. For the three years of 2012, 2013 and 2014, we continued work as a three-week summer field season, involving a team of students from both universities in an Anglo-American collaboration that brought a new intellectual dimension to the project.

In particular, Northwestern graduate students Kat Catlin and Ryan Lash worked on different aspects of the material and played a key role in the move from fieldwork to publication, collating, processing and re-presenting the data from different sites. Eric Johnson, then an undergraduate at Northwestern, and at the time of writing a graduate student at Harvard, took the survey data from Scotney and related it to the map and documentary evidence presented in Chapter Six. Eric also conducted the survey and analysis of moated sites across the Weald that is presented in Chapter Ten.

In 2013, having concluded work at Bodiam and Scotney, we moved our accommodation and base of operations from the Scotney Base Camp 30 km northwest to the northern side of the Weald at the Base Camp at Outridge, and on to two further late medieval sites owned and managed by the National Trust: Knole and Ightham. Ightham developed from quite obscure origins in the 14th century as an 'unfortified' house, sited at the base of a narrow valley on the north edge of the Weald. Ightham is of comparable size to Bodiam and Scotney, and its owners, including Thomas Couen and the Haute family, were of a similar social class to the builders of Scotney and Bodiam. The landscape context of Ightham is a complex one, again with an intricate arrangement of watery features and routeways that speak to the wider debate about the meaning and interpretation of 'designed landscapes'. Chapter Eight discusses the results of the 2013 and 2014 survey at Ightham, and its relationship to the history of the house and the surrounding landscape.

Knole, by contrast, is a much larger residence; its present form owes its origins to its construction as a great house for the Archbishop of Canterbury in the later 15th century. Again, the landscape context of Knole is critical: it is sited within the largest surviving medieval deer park in England. Knole is still partly occupied by the Sackville family. Chapter Seven summarises our survey of that part of the Knole landscape owned and managed by the National Trust, and puts the survey in the wider context of the history and development of Knole and the meanings and practices of medieval deer parks in general.

In 2010, we were successful in obtaining funding for two AHRC studentships into lived experience at the sites we were studying, which were filled by Southampton students Catriona Cooper and Gemma Minihan. As the two projects developed, Catriona focused on digital visualisation of the private apartments at Bodiam, worked with Penny Copeland on the Bodiam building survey, and engaged in an aural study of the great hall at Ightham. Her work is presented in Chapter Nine. Gemma's study as it evolved became a more traditional historical study of the life and career of Thomas Couen, the later 14th-century owner of Ightham Mote. Catriona's PhD is available to download from Southampton University Library, at http://eprints.soton.ac.uk/377916/, and copies of both PhDs are on file in the National Trust archives.

Intellectual Basis of the Project

As the project has developed, our view of all these sites has changed, and the questions we have asked of these sites have evolved. Our ideas, as we express them in this volume, were not ones that were fully articulated at the start of our work. As outlined above, they were initially articulated out of a particular frustration with the perceived sterility of the battle for Bodiam and a desire to move thinking and research at that site forward in very general terms. So at the outset, the research aims of the project could be seen as quite limited and specific.

Rather, the intellectual basis of the project emerged incrementally and gradually through the process of research in the broadest sense – of talking to collaborators, National Trust staff and volunteers, and to other stakeholders, through formal and informal discussions between different members of the team, and through the changing field and intellectual setting of the work. An important element of this development was the commitment to public engagement – the work on all four sites was conducted in full view of visitors; students and staff wore project T-shirts and were expected to respond fully to enquiries from the public, even if it meant interruptions to their work. Southampton student Becky Peacock conducted a qualitative survey of public attitudes and opinions at all four sites and this public feedback was fed in to the project as it developed. Becky's work is reported in Chapter Eleven.

I would pick out several key elements in terms of the intellectual progress of the work. First, I was very struck in the earlier years of the project at the constant reference back to local and regional context in the comments of local archaeologists and historians. Many people, both professional and amateur, working in the region clearly felt that national and international scholarship had viewed these places in a rather disembodied way, set apart from local landscapes; they had tended to overlook the smaller scale networks and regional affiliations of which these four sites were a part. Of the four sites, Bodiam in particular had suffered from what I came to call the 'A21 syndrome' – national scholars and academics, including myself in my earlier work, had driven down the A21 road from London, spent a few days or even a few hours at the site, and then driven back again in short order.

Second, the field experience itself was distinctive. All four sites are located either in or on the edge of the Weald, a distinctive form of rural landscape found on either side of the Kent/Sussex border in south-east England. The Weald and adjacent areas have a particular quality all of their own, what the great landscape historian WG Hoskins would call a *genius loci* after the Classical idea of a spirit presiding over a particular locality (Hoskins 1955; Phythian-Adams 1992; Johnson 2007). The Weald is very different from the stereotype of the English village, with houses clustered round the church and manor house. By contrast, the Weald is a landscape of rolling hills, small fields, and patches of woodland, sandwiched between the more open ridges of the North and South Downs. Working in such a distinctive landscape, only 40-90 km from the very centre of London, and yet at the same time deep in the countryside, prompted further thoughts on the issue of place and space.

One of the most difficult things to communicate to an international audience is the way the English landscape can be so very particular – it has innumerable subtle variations and sudden changes over very short spaces, so that the landscape of Scotney, say, is very different from the landscape of Ashdown Forest 30 km away. Understanding these particularities, making sense of them, is a rational and empirically informed exercise in historical geography, but as I discussed in *Ideas of Landscape* (Johnson 2007), it is also in part about the bodily and sensory experience of 'being there', coming back to the place in different times of the day, weather conditions and seasons of the year. One of the most challenging parts of the project, but also the most enjoyable, was introducing students from a North American and urban background to these subtleties, seeing them grow to appreciate the texture and nuances of the Ordnance Survey map, variations in field and woodland, and uses and patterns of different building materials. As any teacher will affirm, the act and effort of explaining particular features and differences to an intelligent and inquisitive audience can also become a move towards a deeper personal understanding of them.

Third, discussions and interactions with Southampton and Northwestern colleagues, particularly research and graduate students, prompted the development of the idea of lived experience. Part of the utility of lived experience is as a bridging concept. It has the potential to bring together the stress on the local and regional with wider theoretical trends in the study of archaeology generally, the love of particular place in the Hoskins tradition, mentioned above and discussed in my *Ideas of Landscape*, with a wider need to situate scholarly findings within a broader, comparative context. Lived experience also bridges a series of disabling oppositions between function and aesthetics, practical and symbolic, utility and ornament, that were embedded into habits of thought in the 18th century and have impaired thinking about landscape ever since.

Fourth, the move to Northwestern and to a North American intellectual environment impressed on me that however attractive the understanding of a particular place was, it always had to be situated within a wider, comparative context of political economy and ecology. Describing the lived experience of a particular place is arguably a necessary first task. What one then needs to do is situate that understanding within a wider analysis of the context and affordances of the region, and more widely still in comparative context. Viewed in this light, 'subjective' and 'objective' approaches to landscape are complementary rather than competing approaches: if properly thought through, each enables the other, a point I will return to in the Conclusion.

In Chapter Twelve, and in the conclusion to this volume, I try to draw together some of the findings presented in the earlier chapters of the book. I discuss the idea of lived experience and relate it to the long-term histories and biographies of the sites. In particular, I stress how all four sites were elements of a distinctive regional landscape on the edges of the Weald of south-eastern England. I then try to work outwards to understand the four sites at a series of scales, from the most intimate and local, outwards through the landscape and region, to the widest of temporal and geographical scales.

This report is presented as an edited volume. Individuals or small groups of scholars worked within the project on particular pieces of work. Though the project as a whole was under my overall direction, this structure allows individual contributions to be properly foregrounded and acknowledged. The authors for each chapter are presented in strictly alphabetical order, rather than in order of academic or professional 'seniority', and each jointly-authored chapter includes, in the first footnote, a brief statement on who did what.

2

BODIAM: RESEARCH PRIOR TO 2010

Richard James, Casper Johnson, Matthew Johnson, David Martin, Matt Pope, Chris Whittick[1]

Abstract. This chapter reviews and summarises the 'grey literature' and other material relating to research into the history and archaeology of Bodiam in the decades prior to the start of the work of the Southampton/Northwestern team in 2010. It provides a general introduction and background to the landscape, history and archaeology of Bodiam and some of the different ideas and approaches that have been taken to the site.

Introduction

Bodiam Castle is in East Sussex, close to the border with Kent, and now 14 km from the coast (Fig. 2.1). Its initial construction is generally dated to the 1380s, though the building campaign may have lasted into the 1390s; the form of its standing fabric shows relatively little obvious evidence of later alteration and addition. Bodiam is one of the best-known castles in Europe, and arguably the most famous late medieval castle in England. It is certainly one of the most written about medieval sites in the country and indeed internationally. For a domestic structure in the countryside that is not of the highest rank or scale of medieval building, it has generated a vast scholarly literature over more than a century (Clark 1884: 239-47; Thompson 1912: 322-7; Simpson 1931; Hohler 1966; Turner 1986; Coulson 1992; Goodall 1998b and Johnson 2002: 19-33 are a very few examples).

Jacquetta Hawkes (1967: 174) famously wrote that 'every generation gets the Stonehenge it deserves – or desires'. The same is true of Bodiam. The interpretation of Bodiam provides a classic case study in archaeological and historical views of the Middle Ages. Prehistorians argue about the nature and function of Stonehenge, or about the interpretation of the Mousterian. In the process, they articulate their own theoretical ideas and positions; Stonehenge and the Mousterian become vehicles for a wider governing view of prehistory. Successive generations of scholars have seen in Bodiam, not just an assemblage of masonry and earthworks, but also a mirror, a reflection of their particular interests and concerns as archaeologists and historians. Bodiam has been, for scholars of different generations and outlooks, a defence against the French, an old soldier's dream house, a symptom of a desire for status, a complex statement of elite and masculine identity, a symbolic landscape.

All this scholarly attention on Bodiam has resulted in a fascinating body of literature that any student of medieval archaeology and history should familiarise themselves with. However, it has had unintended consequences. Like Stonehenge and the Mousterian, one sometimes gets the feeling that a full understanding of the particular context has been forgotten in the quest for a wider narrative about the nature of late medieval castles. Scholars rarely seem to pause to consider Bodiam

---

[1] This text was put together from specially written contributions and from the 'grey literature' referenced, particularly Johnson *et al.* 2000, by Matthew Johnson, who also drafted the introduction and conclusion. The text was then edited and approved by all the authors. Matthew Johnson thanks all the contributors for their openness and intellectual generosity, and their patience with delays in producing the final text.

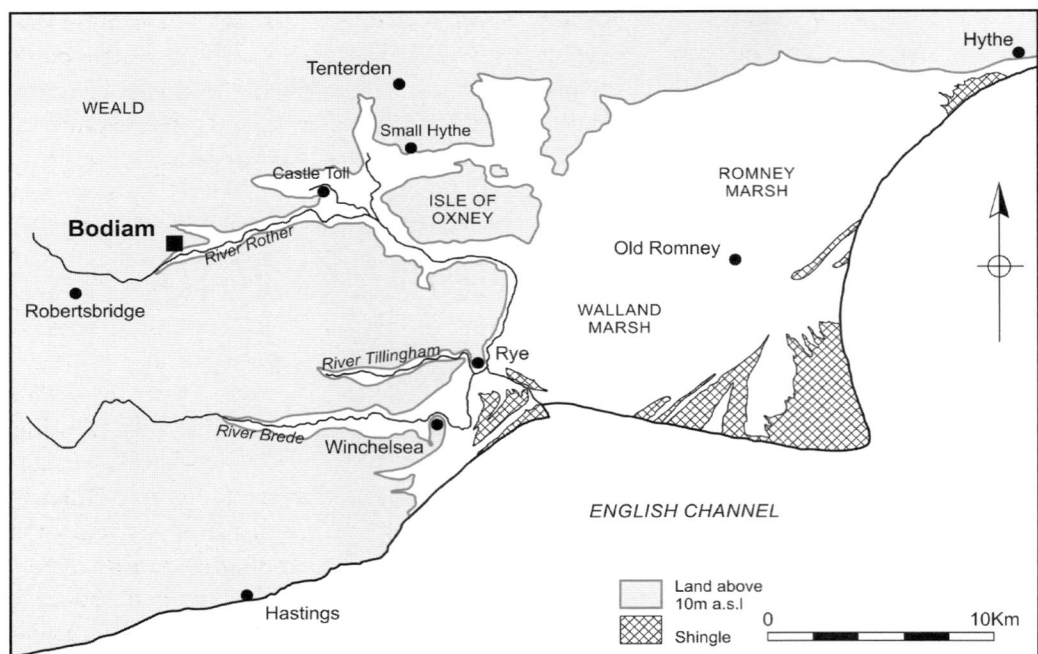

Fig. 2.1: The site of Bodiam, in relation to the floodplain and Romney Marsh.

dispassionately, in its local context. The temptation to immediately enlist particular details in the cause of a wider view -- the position of this gunport (it must be military!) or the siting of that mill pond (it must be aesthetic!) – has been too strong to resist.

One unintended consequence of the 'battle for Bodiam' (an apt phrase taken from the title of Goodall 1998b) has been that the development of different interpretations has outpaced the dissemination of primary research at the site. In what follows, we aim to correct this issue by reporting on a decade of archaeological findings and historical research on the landscape setting of the castle, from 2000 to 2010 (though we make reference to some earlier work also). Subsequent investigations at Bodiam by the University of Southampton and Northwestern University from 2010 onwards, including geophysical and topographical survey and analysis of the interior of the castle, are also reported on in later chapters.

Bodiam and its immediate landscape is a National Trust property with the challenge of c. 200,000 visitors a year and an ongoing programme of management and conservation. The origins of this chapter lie in the observation that while this activity has enhanced archaeological and historical understanding of Bodiam substantially, very little of it has been cited in recent published scholarly discussions. In particular, we draw on work by Johnson, Martin and Whittick (2000), and previous research including documentary work on the mill and mill leat (Whittick 1993) as well as more general work on the landscape of the River Rother and its catchment area (see below and Chapter Five).

The primary and guiding theme of this chapter in presenting the results of work before 2010 is not to argue for one narrow view or interpretation of Bodiam over another, but to present a series of findings that do suggest a more complex, multi-faceted and nuanced understanding of the site and its context. We do want to establish the more general point that there is much more to be said about this place. Oliver Creighton and Robert Liddiard have suggested that it is time to move on from the prominence of Bodiam in castle debates (2008) and Liddiard has added that 'Bodiam may well be 'old hat' to many researchers in the field' (Liddiard 2005b: 7). We understand their position, but respectfully dissent from the implication that Bodiam has been studied to death. A lot of powerful and occasionally intemperate views have been published on the site (cf. Platt 2007), but these tend to go over old ground in terms of the evidence presented rather than present original research incorporating new data.

It could be asserted, instead, that we are still in the process of scratching the surface of this very complex site. Before 2010, survey of the standing fabric using modern survey techniques had yet to be undertaken; much of the documentary record, particularly of Bodiam in the post-medieval period, had not been systematically gathered; and perhaps most surprisingly, a detailed topographical and geophysical survey of the Trust property had not been undertaken until the Southampton/Northwestern work of 2010-2012 (the famous Royal Commission survey [Taylor *et al.* 1990; see Fig. 1.2, this volume] was a hachured, not a contoured plan, and will be reinterpreted in what follows).

Specifically, this chapter will introduce a number of related themes that will be developed in the course of this monograph, at first in relation to Bodiam, and in subsequent chapters to the other sites of Scotney, Knole and Ightham. First, the local and regional context of Bodiam is too little appreciated or understood. As well as being an important monument in terms of national and international castle development, it occupies a place within a distinctive local landscape. That local landscape is an essential element in the understanding of Bodiam.

Second, there is much more to Bodiam than the story of the building of the castle in the 1380s alone. The surrounding landscape of Bodiam, inevitably, contains elements dating from early prehistory onwards. The most obvious of these elements was the preceding manorial site on the hill immediately north of the castle, but this is by far from being the only element; others include a Roman road and settlement on the riverside and earlier field systems. These elements structured the parameters of the site that was transformed in the later 14th century. The castle and its landscape, then, were not created on a *tabula rasa*. At the same time, there is a complex and meaningful history to the site subsequent to the Middle Ages that cannot be ignored.

No discussion of Bodiam can be innocent of this subsequent history. The most visible element today is the restoration and other work at Bodiam by the retired Viceroy of India, Lord Curzon, but this is only one element of many, for example, the landscaping of the site by John 'Mad Jack' Fuller in the early 19th century, discussed further in Chapter Twelve.

Our hope is that discussion will move beyond some of the rather tired and stale oppositions in some of the recent literature. This chapter, and this book as a whole, does not argue for a position in which Bodiam is either primarily defensive or about social emulation, either symbolic or functional, whether its features and surrounding landscape either are or are not militarily effective, or whether it is or is not a designed landscape. The six different scholars contributing to this chapter have six different viewpoints on how Bodiam should be understood. However, the agreed and guiding principle of this chapter is that Bodiam is a very complex and subtle landscape and monument that must first be considered on its own terms before any attempt can be made to assimilate it into wider arguments in castle studies and medieval archaeology.

We will first consider a variety of evidence for a complex and changing landscape prior to the building of the castle and landscape in the 1380s. LiDAR coverage exists for the land immediately south of the castle, though not for the castle itself, and the whole area of Trust property (indicated on Fig. 2.2) has been the subject of topographical and geophysical survey by the University of Southampton; this work from 2010 onwards, as well as work on the landscape south of the River Rother, is the subject of later chapters.

The Landscape Context: Geology and Palaeoenvironment

The first element we must consider is the long-term geological and palaeoenvironmental record of the site. Bodiam Castle lies just above the floodplain of the middle section of the Rother Valley, half way between Robertsbridge and the Isle of Oxney.

Bodiam is the site of a critical junction between two landscape types, the Weald and the floodplain leading eastwards to the wider Romney Marsh (Fig. 2.1). It is located at a point between the narrow and constricted upper regime of the river Rother with typically short, inorganic sequences, and the lower, deeper largely estuarine and marine sequences of the Romney Marshes. The valley bottom is formed of layers of peat interleaved with sands and silts. These have been

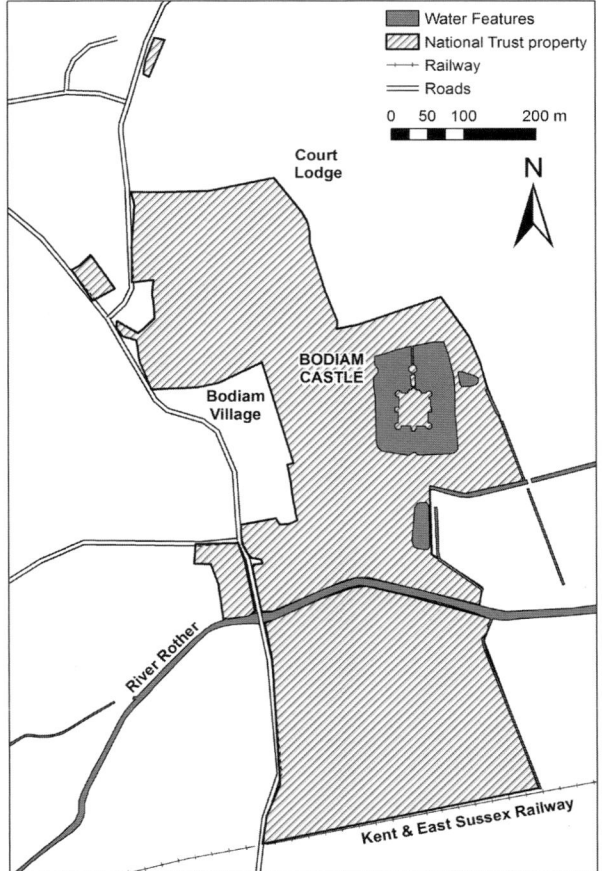

Fig. 2.2: The property as it is today, with boundaries of the Trust property outlined.

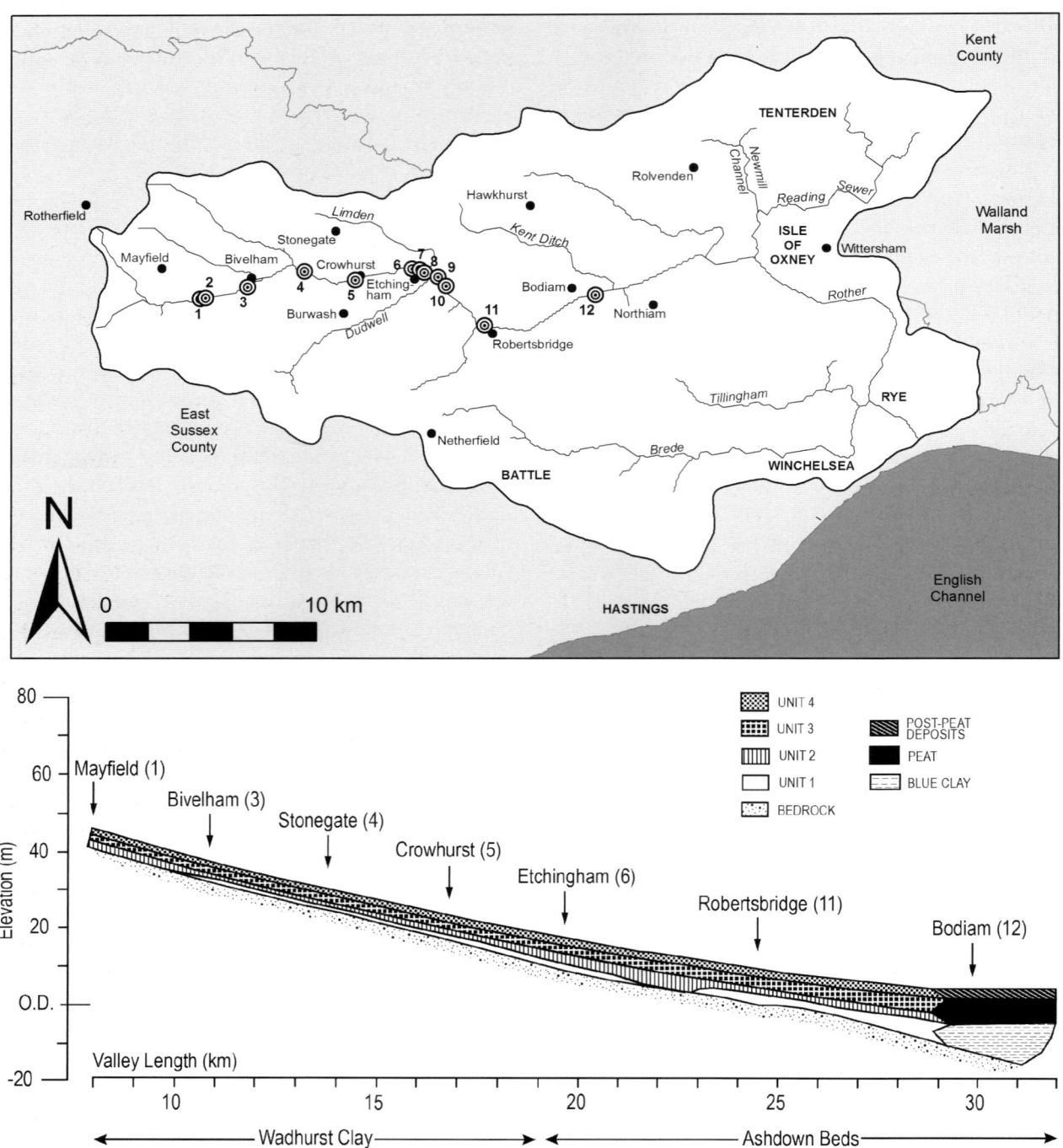

Figs 2.3 and 2.4: Location of Burrin's transects, with long valley profile of the River Rother showing change in gradient and sedimentary regime at Bodiam (after Burrin 1988, fig. 2.7).

observed in different locations including excavations in advance of new sewage works in the Rose Garden (Priestley-Bell & Pope 2009). At Bodiam, then, an extensive palaeoenvironmental sequence, of as yet unknown depth, is preserved, containing an extensive organic component that has already demonstrated the potential to deliver a detailed environmental history for the Holocene of the eastern Weald.

The Rother Valley drains the eastern and central Weald with a catchment area in excess of 700 km^2 (Fig. 2.3). Its floodplain sequences record long environmental histories encompassing tens of thousands of years: late Devensian marine transgressions, early Holocene climatic amelioration, to more recent de-vegetation and increased erosion. This record of de-vegetation and erosion may have its origins in the later Mesolithic period; its later stages can be associated with agricultural expansion, and may be an indication of Roman and post-Roman industrial expansion associated with the iron industry.

The river drains three distinct topographical zones (Fig. 2.4): Zone 1, an upper course from Rotherfield to Robertsbridge, Zone 2, a middle course from Robertsbridge to Bodiam, and Zone 3, a lower course from Bodiam to Rye. Each zone is characterised by a distinctive configuration of channel profile and provides palaeoenvironmental sequences of varying length, temporal and spatial inference. Bodiam itself sits at the interface between Zones 2 and 3 occupying a floodplain some 80 m wide at some 2.25 m OD (mean sea level). At this point the river valley appears to cross outcrops of the Wadhurst Clay, although it is unknown which of the Jurassic/Cretaceous geological layers comprise the sub-alluvial valley floor.

Prior to 2002, the only detailed profiling of the River Rother was undertaken a generation ago by Paul Burrin (1988); the pollen sequences were studied by Rob Scaife. This work, which incorporated the results of 134 boreholes across 12 separate transects between Rotherfield and Bodiam, provides a broad indication of variation in sedimentation and palaeoenvironmental history for this section of the eastern River Rother. The work has its limitations, notably incomplete sequences for the deeper alluvium indicated downstream from Udiam and including the Bodiam site. In this zone the sheer depth of the sub-alluvium valley bottom resulted in truncated sequences missing the very lowest elements, the key late glacial/early Holocene components. However, the borehole records from this pioneering piece of fieldwork are substantial enough for us to make a clear assessment of palaeoenvironmental potential of the Bodiam site.

Only two of the 12 cross-valley profiles were located in the Middle Zone of the River Rother's long-profile. These were sited at Robertsbridge (R11) and Bodiam (R12) (Figs 2.3 & 2.4), the latter being our area of interest. The R11 profile was superficially very similar to those of the Upper Zone with all four recognisable alluvial units overlying superficial high energy deposits on a flat-bottomed trough-like profile of Wadhurst Clay. At Bodiam, the fall of the river changes from 1:438 to virtually flat, the floodplain opens out to some 80 m in width and exhibits extensive inter-digitation with the valley side colluvial deposits.

The valley fill stratigraphy at Bodiam however is of a quite different character, indicating a palaeoenvironmental history of a different nature. Here the valley profile is neither relatively shallow, nor flat-bottomed. Up to 14 m of alluvium has been recorded at this site but only four of the 11 boreholes set across the profile here, those closest to the valley sides, fully bottomed the channel profile and these showed a trend for a more steeply shelving or even V-shaped profile developing here. The sedimentary sequence is consequently incomplete, preserving only the upper parts. These show a more complex sedimentary history with the lowest recorded sediment body being blue-grey silts similar in nature to the Unit 1 of the Zone 1 sequence but this is itself overlain by extensive (up to 6 m in thickness) peat deposits containing abundant plant macro-fossil remains including fragments of *Corylus*. Above the peat were further superficial alluvial deposits of grey and brown laminated silts and sands. These deposits included both a possible Romano-British occupation horizon and Wealden blast furnace slag, described further below.

No detailed pollen sampling was undertaken at the Bodiam site prior to the work described in Chapter Five. However the cross-valley profile at Robertsbridge was subject to pollen sampling and perhaps can be used to suggest the likely degree of potential at the Bodiam site. The Robertsbridge site 5 km upstream, falling in Zone 2, sits at the intersection between the more mineralgenic, inorganic deposits of the Upper Zone alluvial suite and the Lower, peat-rich deposits of the Rother Middle Zone described above (Scaife in Burrin 1988). While the absence of pollen in the upper reaches of the river matches observation from other Wealden river valleys (Scaife & Burrin 1985), and almost certainly resulted from a combination of sediment oxidisation and rapid accumulation of inorganic alluvium, these conditions do not seem to have pertained within the Middle Zone.

The Robertsbridge sequence showed an abundance of *Corylus* (hazel) throughout. This matches the observations of macro-fossil remains of the plant to suggest it was a locally growing species. *Alnus* (alder) and *Salix* (willow) are also important parts of the local plant community and both might be expected within the floodplain environment. Evidence for the vegetation of the interfluves comes from the dominance of *Tilia* (lime), *Fraxinus* (ash) and *Quercus* (oak). The abundance of these pollen types combined with low observed counts for *Betula* (birch) and *Graminae* (grasses) suggest very little woodland clearance close to the site, but cereal pollen and *Plantago* (plantain) within the pollen sequence suggest agricultural activity within the river catchment.

Between 2009 and 2011 a series of further investigations were carried out by Archaeology South East on the Rose

Table 2.A: Palaeoenvironmental Summary.

Context	Description	Pollen	Hydrology
[002]	Upper Weathered Alluvium	Some woodland regrowth (LPAZ3) followed by later renewed clearance towards top of sequence (LPAZ4)	Marginal, shallow water with periodic drying
[005]	Lower Blue Alluvium	LPAZ2 More open conditions and cereal growth	Clearance of floodplain margins and renewed deeper water flow
[012]	Organic Alluvium	LPAZ1 Tree and shrub dominated environment	Cut-off meander and floodplain margins fringed with woodland

Garden, situated just to the north of the National Trust car park, a position to the south-west of the castle but close to the road-bridge and high street. This location is a particularly important one in the Bodiam landscape, as it might have always represented the upstream limit of large river craft and therefore a water route-land route transfer zone. Three distinct phases of sedimentation were apparent within the sequence in this area, each relating to distinct alluvial depositional environments. These deposits and associated palaeoenvironmental evidence are summarised in Table 2.A.

The change in sedimentary regime seen at the junction between [012] and the subsequent switch to open, relatively deep river flow in [005] of medieval date, cannot at present be explained. It might be related to local channel migration or to a more systematic change in the flow regime of the river, leading to increased erosion, removal of alluvium and the formation of a large open channel. Investigations to date have certainly shown the existence of deep water close to areas of proven medieval occupation on the north side of the river crossing to the west of Bodiam. In the records of the Manor of Ewhurst, the valley as far up the river as Bodiam was stated to be 'under salt water' in 1388-1390, and the river east of the bridge is referred to as 'the salt stream' in 1476 (Johnson *et al.* 2000: 6 and vol. 2, 27).

Renewed woodland growth at the base of the weathered alluvium may relate to the marginalisation of this locale as the channel began to silt and water became shallower. The weathered, oxidised condition of the sediments here certainly indicates much shallower water conditions. The history and changing use of this area is discussed further in Chapter Five.

Bodiam before the 1380s

The palaeoenvironmental record discussed above, and the discovery of Mesolithic and Neolithic flint artefacts from the surrounding valley sides (Johnson *et al.* 2000: 26) indicates that the location of Bodiam, then, has been important since prehistory. In the Roman period, and probably from earlier periods, the river fording marked a critical crossing point between north-south communications and the east-west flow of the Rother Valley. The importance of this intersection continued through the medieval and modern periods.

The first direct archaeological evidence for settlement in the Bodiam area is Late Iron Age or Roman in date, in the form of a cinerary urn found in 1902 during the construction of the Bodiam rectory to the north-west of the castle. The Roman road running from Rochester to Ore (Hastings) crosses the River Rother at Bodiam; it then runs north from the ford/bridge at Bodiam before running north-west through Dokes[2] Field (as revealed by the 2011 geophysical survey; see Chapter Four). The location of the cemetery may be understood as located at the roadside.

As one would expect, the course of the River Rother has shifted during the prehistoric and Roman periods. Traces of Roman settlement have been excavated towards the southern edge of the present floodplain at a time when the river channel may well have been to the south of where it is now. The finds from this settlement included tiles with the *Classis Britannica* stamp, a trait that has been associated by some scholars with the presence of the Roman navy. This has led to the interpretation of this settlement as a port (Cleere & Crossley 1985: 65), probably for the purpose of shipping blooms of iron and/or other iron products out from the Weald (Johnson *et al.* 2000: 27).

The physical appearance and layout of settlement at Bodiam between ADE 400 and 1200 is unclear. No features of definite pre-Conquest date are known in the immediate vicinity of the castle. The earliest reference to a bridge at Bodiam is not until 1210 (Johnson *et al.* 2000: 30). The ladder-like form of the tenement boundaries to the west of the castle, characteristic of high medieval settlement across the country, suggests that they may well predate the castle itself, though by how long (a few years or centuries) is not certain.

---

2   Dokes Field can be spelled variously as Doke's, Dokes', Doakes Field or Doakes Meadow.

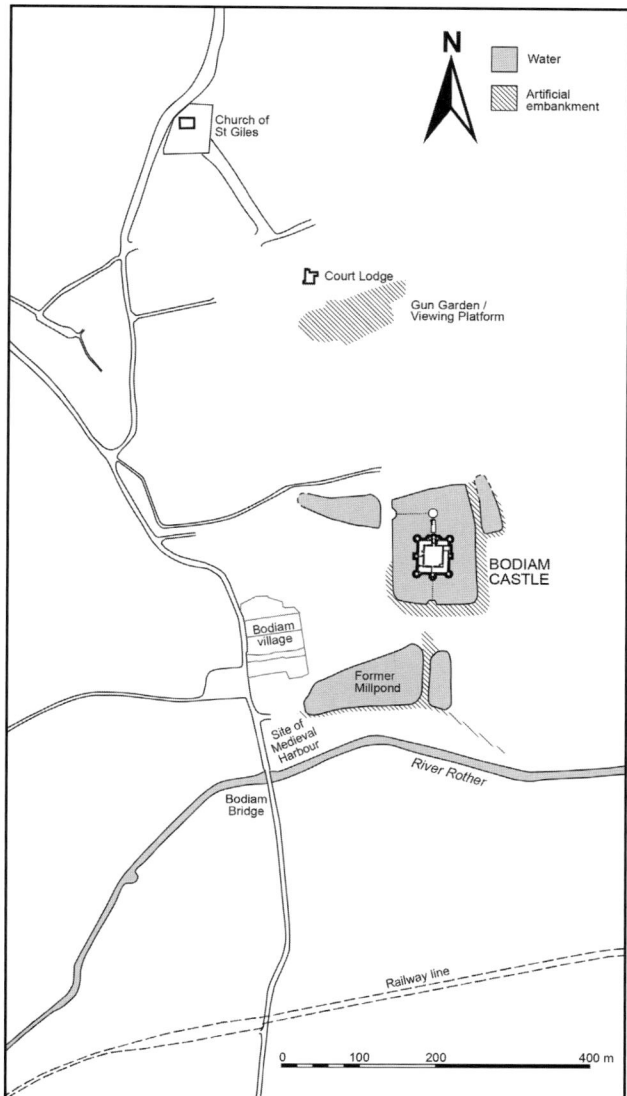

Fig. 2.5: Simplified diagram of the key features of the landscape around Bodiam Castle, as visible today.

The location of the medieval flote or harbour is indicated on Fig. 2.5. The flote probably existed prior to the 1380s, though it is probable that the facilities were further developed at that point as part of Dallingridge's development of the site. A series of archaeological interventions have identified possible evidence for its location, though its scale, form and appearance is not clear, in part because much of the relevant area underlies the modern car park and visitor facilities. The change in sedimentary regime noted above seems to bring the river close to the floodplain margins at the site, allowing for deeper navigable water and making the formation of the flote at this location viable. Occupation evidence from the base of the alluvial sequence recorded during excavations for a sewer trench and as discrete occupation horizons closer to the valley edge in the Rose Garden may all relate to activities taking place around or in the general vicinity of the flote (Priestley-Bell & Pope 2009).

The discovery of a possible revetment of 7th/8th-century date separating deeper alluvial sedimentation from occupation horizons flanking the line of the modern road may relate to river side settlement from the post-Roman period onwards (Priestley-Bell & Pope 2009).

The site of the earlier manor has sometimes been stated to be a moated site 500 m to the north of Bodiam, just south of the Kent Ditch (cf. Taylor *et al.* 1990). This attribution, derived from the account given in the Victoria County History, is unlikely. The site was excavated in 1961 and again in 1970 by the Robertsbridge and District Archaeological Society: it 'contains no periods which predated the late 13th century, whilst Bodiam manor is known to have [existed] before 1086' (Martin 1990: 97-8). The most likely location of the earlier manor is Court Lodge, c. 250 m to the north of the castle, as discussed further below and in Chapter Four.

It is difficult to give a clear chronology for the development of the demesne at Bodiam. It is clear that the demesne of the manor is unusually large for the region. The tenurial history of Bodiam before the 1380s is not as clear as the Victoria County History account suggests. The parish was probably formed in the 12th century (Rushton 1999). The church was extensively rebuilt in the later 14th century, but the location of the church is some centuries earlier, as is usual with medieval parish churches.

A more detailed analysis of the early medieval landscape of Bodiam can be found in the Conservation Management Plan by Drury McPherson Partnership, forthcoming at the time of writing (Drury & Copeman 2016). This thorough account deals in detail with the place of Bodiam within the developing early medieval landscape of Kent and Sussex, and in particular with the continuing importance of the river crossing after the Roman period, patterns of landholding and land division, the status and position of Bodiam as part of the late Saxon manor of Ewhurst, and the probable importance of Court Lodge as a place where local routeways intersect. Drury & Copeman go on to trace the development of Bodiam manor in the 12th century as the principal estate of the de Bodiam family; the emergence of the parish and parish church of Bodiam from its origins as a dependent chapel of Ewhurst; and the lands of Battle Abbey in Bodiam. Finally, Drury & Copeman also compile both LiDAR and documentary evidence for the shifting course of the River Rother across the floodplain prior to the 14th century, evidence for which will also be presented in Chapter Four.

For the purposes of this introductory chapter, it is important simply to stress that whatever the nature of the castle and landscape created in the 1380s, it was not created in a vacuum. The site had been important in terms of transport and communications for millennia. There were direct constraints on the site that was inherited in the 1380s, in terms of its physical topography, the earlier manor site and manorial structure, the medieval tenements to the west of the castle, preceding routeways including the River Rother and the Roman road, and the location of the church. Indeed, if it is the case that the medieval tenements do indeed predate the later 14th century, then the castle can be argued to have been 'squeezed in' to a relatively narrow and constrained space, between the rear of the tenements and the high ground to the west and undrained marshland to the east (Fig. 2.5).

Bodiam in the 1380s

Historical background to the castle

Bodiam Castle is associated with the name of Sir Edward Dallingridge. The manor of Bodiam was not the home of the Dallingridge family; rather, it came to Dallingridge from his wife Elizabeth Wardedieu. They married in 1363, and Sir Edward was in possession by 1378 following the death of Elizabeth's father. There is some evidence to suggest that building at Bodiam was underway in the early 1380s, perhaps following the death of Dallingridge's own father in c. 1380. The licence to crenellate was granted in 1385, but there are other cases where such licences were granted well after construction of a castle had commenced (Coulson 1993; 1994). Building work was going on at Bodiam church in 1382, and the work there shows very close stylistic parallels to the castle. Dallingridge began to sell his wife's midland property in 1381, possibly to fund building operations (Saul 1998: 127). The grant of a market and fair dates to 1383, and the licence to divert the course of the River Rother to power the watermill dates to 1386. However, the fabric of the castle strongly suggests a seven- to ten-year building programme, so it is very possible that building activity went on well into the 1390s.

What was created was a distinctive development of the entire village landscape of Bodiam. The houses and associated tenement boundaries may well have been earlier, as suggested above, or they may have been laid out at this point; the evidence can be argued either way. The end result, however, was a landscape with flote, mill, mill pond and mill leat, and water features: 'a planned, almost model village on the bank of the Rother – moated castle, mill, cottages and market-place' (Whittick 1993: 122).

Bodiam manor was not only distinctive in its form: it was an unusual manor for the Rape of Hastings in terms of the rights of its lord, being unusually 'strong', in respect of the terms and conditions under which land was held. No single tenant within the manor held particularly large areas of land. The overall numbers are not statistically significant, but it is nevertheless of note that only one medieval house has survived within the manor (Ellen Archer's, the northernmost of the tenements). The Rape of Hastings and East Sussex as a whole has an otherwise high rate of survival of medieval houses, and as will be discussed in the concluding chapters, this high survival rate may well relate to the distinctive form, affluence and security of peasant households in this region relative to others in England. In 1443 the manor had 570 acres plus a park, which probably lay to the north and west of the castle respectively.

Landscape context

Discussion of the immediate landscape around Bodiam Castle has been dominated by the results of the 1988 Royal Commission survey (Fig. 1.2; Taylor *et al.* 1990). This survey claimed to establish that:

> *without doubt that the majority of the extensive earthworks around the castle are the remains of elaborate gardens and water features all intended to enhance the visual appearance of the building… [which together formed] an elaborate modification of the whole landscape involving the creation of a number of ponds and sheets of water whose positioning has an ornamental impact… this modification was at least partly connected with the manipulation of visitors around the site to experience views whose components continually change.*
> (Taylor *et al.* 1990: 155)

Features that the Royal Commission identified included what they interpreted as a viewing platform to the north, a string of ponds with 'terraced walk-ways on both sides' to the north-west, and successive sheets of water surrounding the castle to the south and east. Paul Everson (1996) went on to suggest that the main approach to Bodiam was by means of a processional causeway that wound its way to the south and east of the mill pond, ascended the moat bank, and proceeded circuitously around the moat to south, east and north before entering the castle via the bridge, octagon and barbican (Fig. 2.6).

It is important to note that this interpretation was based on a hachured plan in the classic Royal Commission tradition of analytical fieldwork, based on close observation and interpretation of the humps and bumps on the ground, but without a full topographical survey or geophysical work. The interpretation was compromised by the presence of material dredged from the moat dumped in the 1970s, as well as known disturbance in several areas, particularly the area south of the postern bridge.

More recent work (in particular the 2000 report of Johnson, Martin and Whittick, confirmed by Drury & Copeman 2016) has raised issues with the specific interpretation of several of these elements. It suggested modifications to the Commission interpretation in three main respects: first, 'the manipulation of a principal access route from the south'; and second, 'the presence of a garden or pleasance at Court Lodge'. Third, across the site as a whole, Johnson *et al.* also drew attention to a number of later landscape changes that complicate interpretation.

Postulated access route from the south

The evidence for a manipulated access route from the south (Fig. 2.6) is not at all clear. First, the area to the south-west of the castle has been heavily altered and the ground level changed, most obviously in association with the modern car park. Second, the postulated causeway is held in the Commission account to have run east-west along the southern edge of the mill pond and then turned sharply north, between the mill pond to its west and a second pond to its east. However, there was probably no such eastern pond. The area immediately to the east of the mill pond dam has been variously and incorrectly interpreted as a harbour and/or water feature, following attributions given in Lord Curzon's account. In fact, this area became a pond/water feature only after Curzon's interventions, when he raised the level of the foreland to the south, thus cutting it off from the river (Curzon 1926). The bank on the eastern edge of this area may be a flood protection dam for the watercourse from the mill, though the precise position of the mill itself remains uncertain (see Chapter Four). Any visitor, having reached this point east of the mill pond, would have faced a steep 45 degree climb up the moat embankment. There is no evidence on the ground (or in the subsequent geophysical survey) for any causeway, stairway or other feature to facilitate such a climb at this point.

A more likely principal approach to the castle is from the north-west, along a route immediately to the south of the pond in this area. Again, the area has been subject to later alterations, but such a route would take a more direct course from the main north-south road and the

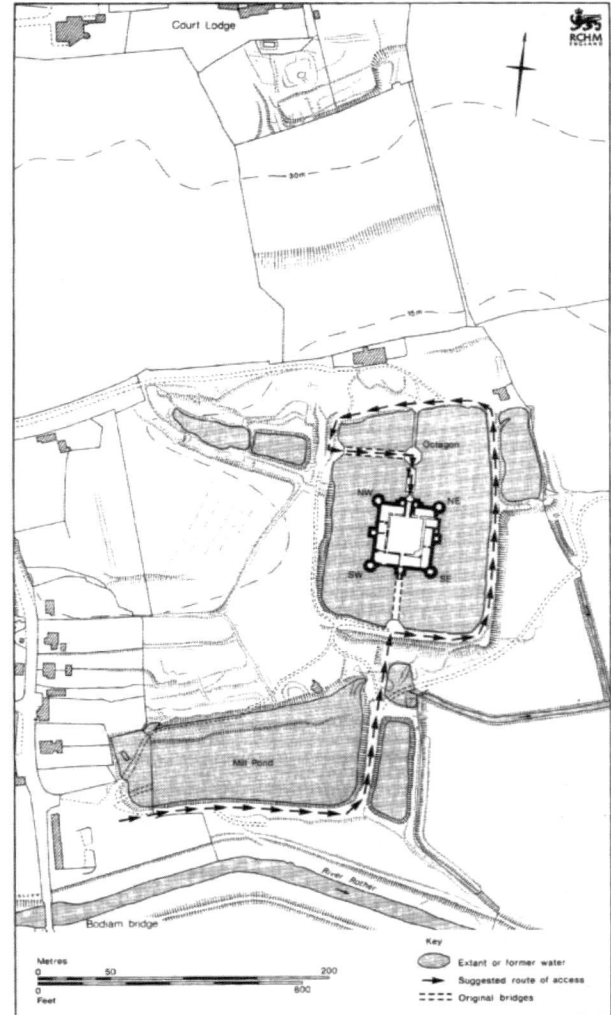

Fig. 2.6: The postulated access route from the south (after Everson 1996, fig. 1). © Crown copyright. Historic England Archive.

Wealden landscape beyond and lead directly down to the bridge abutment on the western side of the moat. The form of the series of ponds to the north-west of the castle, and the two ponds to the east of the moat, have again all been affected by the dumping of building waste and silt/vegetation from the moat during the 20th century; 20th-century material has also been dumped against the World War Two pillbox and at the west end of the mill pond (Johnson *et al.* 2000: 10).

It is, of course, entirely probable that there was more than one access route to the castle; even if the north-western route was the 'principal' one, it is still possible to argue in more general terms that the landscape to the south of the castle was carefully designed to maximise the number and visibility of water features and to delimit movement between them. It is also worth noting that the north-west access route is itself careful to present the castle to advantage, the descent of the slope being framed by the pond to the north of the routeway along with the appearance of the impressive northern façade with its angled entrance across the moat, barbican and main northern gate. The bridge abutment, timber bridge to the octagon, and causeway between octagon, barbican and north gate were all excavated by Curzon and re-excavated in 1970 (Martin 1973) and were all elaborate constructions; the causeway between barbican and north gate was modified shortly after initial construction.

The 'Gun Garden'/'Viewing Platform'

This earthwork, c. 250 m to the north of the castle and c. 30 m above it (Fig. 2.5), has been the subject of changing interpretations over the years. The area, outside the Trust property, is known as the 'Gun Garden', on the tradition that it is a Civil War gun emplacement. However, no Civil War activity in the area is known from documentary sources.

The Royal Commission survey suggested that the wide, curving southern edge of the earthwork was part of the designed landscape, functioning as a 'viewing platform' overlooking the castle to the south. It is certainly the case that the view of the castle from this earthwork is, today, an extraordinarily powerful and arresting one (Fig. 2.7). There are also parallels for 'pleasaunces' or other features deliberately placed some distance away from the main site, to afford spectacular views of other castles or medieval houses (Creighton 2009; see Liddiard & Williamson 2008 for a more sceptical view).

The broad, curving earthwork probably has a different significance, however. It does not stand in isolation; it marks and forms the apron for the southern edge of a complex set of earthworks. Small-scale excavations (Darrell Hill 1960-61) produced quantities of early 14th-century pottery and no later material. Given the date of the pottery, and the place-name Court Lodge, it is likely that these earthworks mark the site of the earlier manorial centre of Bodiam, the predecessor to the castle. This does not preclude their use as some kind of viewing feature in the 1380s, but it is at least equally possible that the Court Lodge complex continued as the centre of the manor's administrative and agricultural activities. In 1443

> *from the inquest on the death of John Dallingridge's widow Alice ... Bodiam Castle was identified separately from the site of the manor, implying that a viable manorial curia still existed on the site of the present Court Lodge.*

(Johnson *et al.* 2000: 32; TNA C139/111 no. 52)

The interpretation of the area, including evidence for the presence of a 17th-century garden, is discussed further in Chapter Four.

If the gun garden/viewing platform formed an element of a site which continued to have important manorial functions in the 1380s and after, then our view of the Bodiam landscape is radically changed. One of the puzzling features of Bodiam is its apparent lack of a lower or base court. However, it could be suggested that

Fig. 2.7: View of Bodiam Castle from the 'Gun Garden'/'Viewing Platform'.

Bodiam can be understood as a double-courtyard house, with the two courts separated and the functions of the lower court, as well as the functions of the manor, being carried out at Court Lodge. Such a wide separation (of c. 250 m) has no known parallels. However, seeing the Bodiam complex as two related courtyards, or at least two related complexes of buildings, would go some way to explain the northern aspect of the main gatehouse. There is an ongoing debate over whether later medieval houses generally possessed lower or base courts, with the West Country house of Dartington Hall, also built at the end of the 14th century, being the classic case study (Currie & Rushton 2004; Emery 2007). Contemporary and nearby structures of similar size and social standing generally have more than one court (Scotney, Westenhanger, and Cooling are definite examples; Iden and Ightham are likely).

The watermill, leat and wider landscape

An important element of the Bodiam landscape that has received little attention is the watermill. Dallingridge obtained a licence to divert the course of the River Rother to power a watermill in 1386. Whittick (1993) has traced the course of the leat for the mill through a combination of documentary and field observation. The leat was diverted some miles upriver from the lands of Robertsbridge Abbey, where there is a sharp break in alignment in the river as it crosses the floodplain. The leat ran to the north of the river before eventually feeding into the mill pond (misleadingly termed the Tiltyard by Curzon). The precise location of the mill is not certain; it is discussed further in Chapter Four.

The landscape beyond the immediate context of the castle has also received too little attention. As we have seen, the nature of the demesne and of the manor at Bodiam is distinctive. There was a hunting park in the parish, but it was not directly adjacent to the castle, as recorded in 1443 when the manor had 570 acres plus a park (Johnson *et al.* 2000: 32).

Afterlife

Relatively little documentary evidence survives of the castle between the 1380s and the end of the Middle Ages, and the occupation history and date of its eventual abandonment is uncertain. Treads on the stairs in the castle are heavily worn, and there are possible modifications and rebuilds, particularly in the west range of buildings, though none of these suggest a major rebuilding campaign. The castle passed to the Lewknor family upon the end of the Dallingridge line in the 1470s, when Phillipa Dallingridge married Sir Thomas Lewknor

(Mate 1998: 136); after this point, if not before, lords were largely non-resident. It is possible that the castle was definitively abandoned and much of the walls facing the internal courtyard were quarried for building elsewhere, starting in the mid-17th century or even before (Johnson *et al.* 2000); the earliest graffiti inside the castle seems to date from the later 17th century onwards.

The landscape of Bodiam was the subject of extensive work by John 'Mad Jack' Fuller following his purchase of the castle in 1829 (Holland 2011). Fuller's work at Bodiam was part of his wider construction of landscapes, follies and monuments in and around his Brightling estate 12 km to the south-west, such as the 'Sugar Loaf' off the Battle to Heathfield road and the Pyramid in Brightling churchyard. Fuller's accounts remain unpublished, but they may indicate substantial expenditure on the surroundings of the castle in the early 1830s. The precise nature of much of Fuller's work is uncertain; Brittany Holland found it difficult to link his accounts to specific features in the landscape. Much of the present landscape character of Bodiam suggests that it owes some of its character to 19th-century landscaping. However a tree survey by Julia Lewis did not identify planting that could be securely dated to the period of Fuller (Johnson *et al.* 2000, appendix one). Fuller and his successor, George Cubitt (Lord Ashcombe, who purchased the property in 1862), both carried out some restoration work in the castle and its environs.

In the 1860s, Cubitt drained the moat for the first documented time. It is probable that additional undocumented dredging or draining had occurred on a more or less regular basis since the castle's construction in the late 14th century. The site manager until 2016, George Bailey, comments that:

> *Historically the moat has been dredged in the 1920s, and then in the 1970s. That would suggest [that the moat was drained] about every 50 years. However the moat prior to the 1970s was filled with water lilies which decayed to the bottom of the moat. Now they have been removed for aesthetic reasons, the volume of decay falling to the bottom of the moat has been massively depleted and I would assess that the impact would be to increase the time between dredging to at least 100 years.*
>
> (Bailey, pers. comm.)

Draining of the moat for archaeological or renovation work often resulted in spoil heaps that are likely to have been deposited in or around the medieval ponds. The moat was drained again in 1970, and the original bridges and abutments were excavated and re-recorded (Martin

1973). Small-scale work followed in the late 1970s and 80s, including the first geophysical survey of the property. This early survey employed magnetometry and resistivity in the floodplain, and the results were inconclusive.

Lord Curzon's restoration of the castle in 1919-1920, and his associated alterations of the surrounding landscape, is well known, in part from the volume that he wrote and published on the castle (Curzon 1926). Among other activities, Curzon raised the level of the foreshore, attempted unsuccessfully to drain the area of the mill pond to create a cricket pitch, drained and dredged the moat, and recorded the timber footings of the bridges. The work of generations preceding Curzon has been less acknowledged, though in his book Curzon himself made copious reference to the prior work of Cubitt in restoring the castle (Curzon 1926: 82-4). It is worth observing that much of the popularity and plausibility of the interpretation of Bodiam as a landscape designed with aesthetic intent may, in part, be indirectly inspired by Fuller's and Curzon's re-landscaping of the area around the castle, followed by the National Trust's policy of maintaining the area as grassed parkland traversed by gravelled paths offering defined routes for contemporary visitors.

On Curzon's death in 1925, the property passed to the National Trust. The pillbox was constructed to the north-east of the mill pond, just south of the castle, in 1940. It has an aperture for an anti-tank gun commanding a view of Bodiam bridge, a presumed avenue of German attack following an invasion on the coast 20 km to the south. In 2006, the Trust purchased the field to the south of the River Rother, incorporating a portion of the Roman site and bringing the National Trust property at Bodiam to its current size and extent.

Discussion

The following themes emerge from the research of the last 10 years; they serve as a springboard for the rest of the discussion of Bodiam in this book and will be revisited in the chapters which follow.

First, Bodiam must be seen as a multi-phase site with a long-term history. It is a mistake to see it as simply, or only, the personal creation of Dallingridge in the 1380s. The importance of the site stems, in part, from its position at the junction of the Weald and the Rother Valley. The building programmes of the 1380s did not take place in a vacuum; they were directly constrained and influenced by a much older landscape. First, there is the prior location of the manor house which became Court Lodge and, we have suggested here, probably continued to have manorial functions. Second, the tenurial layout of the site suggests that the 1380s programme was heavily constrained; Bodiam was 'fitted into' the interstices of an older landscape. This older landscape has to be understood over the very long term: the complex palaeoenvironmental sequence discussed above highlights how the Weald has changed and developed over the millennia, and the interdependence in terms of human settlement of the ecologies, economies and cultures of the Weald and of the river valley.

The location of Bodiam has been distinctive from later prehistory onwards. It is an important point in terms of communication and transport. Prehistoric zones of movement, and later Roman roads, ran north-south and intersect with the ford, and later a bridge, over the River Rother at this point. The location of Bodiam Castle, then, does face east, along the Rother Valley towards the medieval coastal ports of Rye and Winchelsea; but it also faces west and north, upriver towards Robertsbridge Abbey and Salehurst and west and north towards the heart of the Weald; after all, this is the orientation of the main gatehouse.

It follows that Bodiam should be set in its regional and local context more effectively than many scholars have previously done. If Bodiam should be seen at a series of temporal scales, it should also be seen at a series of spatial scales. Hitherto, Bodiam has been generally discussed at the micro-level (architecture and immediate setting of the castle) and at the national and international scale (defence against French raids; typological comparison with other late medieval English and French castles hundreds of miles away). We suggest that there is an intermediate, regional scale that should be grasped if Bodiam is to be properly understood.

The striking nature of Bodiam as a castle should be understood within the particular and unusual nature of the Wealden landscape in which it sits. Most location maps of Bodiam emphasise its position relative to coastal and urban settlements, most obviously Hastings, Battle, Rye, Winchelsea, and the route of the River Rother. These are all important elements. However, the Wealden landscape is also a highly distinctive form of medieval settlement. As is well known to scholars of medieval landscape, the Weald is not an area of open fields and nucleated villages. Rather, it is a patchwork of often ancient woodland, and isolated churches and farmsteads, with its own particular qualities, but also with features in common with 'bocage' or woodland landscape elsewhere in England and across the Channel (Roberts & Wrathmell 2002; Rippon 2008).

This chapter has argued, then, that a contextual approach needs to be taken to the castle and landscape of Bodiam. The extensive investigations since the 1990s have given us a much more complex and nuanced picture of the site than might be inferred from some recent published discussions. Bodiam continues to harbour surprises and provoke new observations. This local context needs to be understood and interpreted before Bodiam can be assimilated into wider arguments. If every generation gets the Bodiam it deserves, then the Bodiam that will be outlined in Chapters Three to Five will be a complex and local landscape that should be understood on its own terms. Chapter Six onwards will set Bodiam alongside equally fascinating and complex sites at Scotney, Knole and Ightham, as well as other moated sites in the region as a whole.

Addendum: Review of Archaeological Investigations

A range of archaeological projects have taken place within the estate owned by the National Trust at Bodiam since the 1980s. Seventeen are reviewed here with the majority being watching briefs on infrastructure works and repairs. The results of the work are reported in unpublished client reports lodged with the National Trust and the county Historic Environment Record at East Sussex County Council and available at ESRO. All of the work reported on here has been carried out by Archaeology South-East, the field unit of University College London.

Set out below in broadly chronological order are the more significant observations that have been made.

Prehistoric and Roman

A watching brief during stabilisation works on the moat bank found a probable Mesolithic core (in Area 5B). It was found in disturbed deposits in the upper sequence, and may have been imported from elsewhere with make-up material (Stevens 1995: 147).

A watching brief in April – May 1998 during installation of a new sewage plant (15 m x 7 m, with a depth of c. 4.5 m) found a 2 m thick deposit of peat (Context 6), comprising branches and bark/twig fragments set within a dark grey to black organic/fibrous clay matrix. The upper surface of the deposit was c. 2 m below ground level. Two C14 samples gave calibrated dates of 2050-1730 BCE (Beta Analytic No. 121615 – 1.8 m OD) and 2500-2195 BCE (Beta Analytic No. 121616 – 0.74 m OD). This Bronze Age peat formation overlay sterile alluvial deposits, and may represent a low-energy deposition phase associated with quantities of organic material such as driftwood and/or the formation of freshwater carr-type environments seen to be forming during the later prehistoric around the coast and in the valleys and embayments of East Sussex. The peat was overlain by alluvial deposits of medieval date, suggesting that the original deposits relating to later Bronze Age and subsequent activity may have been truncated by the construction of the flote or harbour, thought likely to have been constructed at or before the late 14th century (Barber 1998).

Two further observations of the stratigraphy in the area between the Castle Inn and the former mill pond have been made. They include:

A watching brief in September 2003 during the excavation of 26 m of trenching from the sewage plant into the western end of the car park located a 0.1 m thick peaty deposit at a depth of 0.8 m below the modern ground level. This deposit was located to the west of the footpath (i.e. adjacent to the sewage plant) and was interpreted as the same Bronze Age peat deposit examined in 1998. It would appear to thin out as it extends to the east, although its exact relationship with the earlier recorded sample is hampered by the absence of height/depth levels (Worrall 2003).

A watching brief maintained in January – March 2007 during excavations for drain runs in the car park and across the road in the car park of the Castle Inn. Trench 1 adjacent to the sewage plant located pieces of wood/peat within a medieval deposit below 1.7 m in depth, suggesting the presence of the underlying Bronze Age peat deposit. Trench 6, in the Castle Inn car park, exposed the peat layer at a depth of 2.7 m below the ground surface (1.85 m OD). It was 0.3 m thick and graded into a blue-grey silt clay, from which a sample of wood was retrieved at 1.25 m OD for C14 dating (this was subsequently abandoned on specialist advice). This deposit continued to a depth of at least 3.5 m below ground level but was not bottomed (Barber 2007b).

Archaeological and geoarchaeological evaluation was carried out in advance of a proposed new sewage system in the area of the Rose Garden in April 2009. Three evaluation trenches, two geoarchaeological test pits and one borehole were used. The evaluation confirmed the presence of the Bronze Age peat and underlying alluvium. Pollen and plant macro-fossil assessment showed that the change from peat to alluvial deposition appears to relate to changes in vegetation in the valley itself. The most likely hypothesis is that anthropogenic activity led to wide scale deforestation at this time (Priestley-Bell & Pope 2009).

A watching brief during excavations for a drain run adjacent to the sewage plant produced an unabraded but possibly residual piece of Roman imbrex tile from an otherwise undated layer immediately above the peat deposit (Barber 2007b).

Medieval

A watching brief during repair to the moat banks during stabilisation works (May – November 1995) found evidence of a possible late medieval / early post-medieval raising of the moat bank. Two sherds of 15th-century pottery were found in Areas 9 and 10 in a deposit at a depth of 0.72 m below the modern ground surface, overlying the probable original moat bank. In Area 10 the bank deposits were observed to slope up to the stone bridge abutment, suggesting the abutment was constructed prior to the building up of the bank (Stevens 1995: 147).

A watching brief during the installation of a new sewage plant located a silty clay alluvial deposit (Context 4) overlying a prehistoric peat deposit. The lower 0.6 m of this context produced a sherd of 13th-14th-century pottery together with several animal bones, an oyster shell and a tile fragment. A rough alignment of water-rounded cobbles at 3.15 m OD was interpreted as ship's ballast. The deposit was interpreted as representing alluvial silt associated with the former flote, thought to have been created before the late 14th century, truncating earlier deposits (Barber 1998); subsequent plotting of the location suggests it may be within the western part of the mill pond (Drury & Copeman 2016).

A watching brief in November 2002 during the excavation of footing trenches for a bench on the south-eastern corner of the mill pond dam, thought to be of 14th-century date, located a compacted silty clay deposit sloping down to the east at a depth of 0.42-0.5 m below ground level. Although no dating evidence was recovered, this was interpreted as the medieval embankment, and appears to confirm that the mill pond curved round at this point (Johnson 2002).

A watching brief in February 2007 during the removal of an 11.3 m x 5.75 m strip of damaged turf within the interior of the castle revealed several masonry walls. An east-west wall protruding from, and bonded to, the south side of the north wall of the Great Hall was exposed for 8.5 m. It ran alongside the present north wall, but slightly off-set. It was built of massive roughly-faced unmortared sandstone blocks with smaller pieces of sandstones filling the interstices. It was interpreted as either a foundation for the hall wall, or a foundation for beams supporting a first floor over a putative and now-backfilled cellar, such as exist along the eastern range (Barber 2007a).

A watching brief during drainage runs produced a number of medieval deposits confirming the sequence identified in 1998 (Barber 2007b).

Archaeological and geoarchaeological evaluation was carried out in advance of a proposed new sewage system in the area of the Rose Garden in April 2009. Three evaluation trenches, two geoarchaeological test pits and one borehole were used. The evaluation confirmed the presence of an alluvial sequence above Bronze Age peat and the underlying alluvium. Above the peat and within the overlying alluvium, wood was recorded at a depth of c. 1.80 m below the present ground level. A radiocarbon date on the wood produced a calibrated date in the range ADE 550-660. The overlying alluvial deposits produced pottery and ceramic building material with a date range from c. ADE 1275 to 1600. The remains of a structure related to a 19th-century building known to have existed close to the site were recorded (Priestley-Bell & Pope 2009).

In 2005 David and Barbara Martin, for Archaeology South East, carried out a targeted programme of recording and interpretation of the portcullis and gatehouse stonework surrounding it. The portcullis is made of oak with iron fittings. The structural evidence (absence of splicing or scarf joints, its masonry housing) makes it highly likely the portcullis is original. A radiocarbon date of ADE 1280-1410 with a 95.4% certainty was obtained from the wood (Martin & Martin 2005).

Post-medieval

A watching brief during installation of new sewage plant identified four deposits of post-medieval date, up to 1.4 m thick in total. The lowest (the upper part of Context 4) was an alluvial silt containing numerous sherds of late 15th- early 16th-century pottery, some of which represented an almost complete bowl that had been thrown into water. The deposits are likely to relate to the silting up of the medieval flote, which at its northern end was being encroached upon in the 17th century and appears to have been used for rubbish disposal from at least the early 16th century. This was sealed (at a depth of 0.55 m below ground level) by a deposit containing 18th- early 19th-century pottery, which was itself cut by a drain or soakaway of 19th-century date. The upper deposit was a modern hardcore (Barber 1998).

A watching brief during tree and shrub planting around the new sewage plant in March 1999 involved hand excavation of planting holes to a depth of <0.45 m. Several contexts representing current and former garden soils produced 18th-20th-century pottery (Johnson 1999).

Watching brief during removal of worn turf revealed three walls set at right angles, and butted against the medieval wall located in the area of the Great Hall. These walls were made of reused sandstone blocks, lined with smaller sandstone pieces and roof tile. They were interpreted as a fireplace / chimney breast of post-medieval date, possibly associated with an historically attested 18th-century cottage that formerly occupied this area (Barber 2007a).

A watching brief during drainage runs confirming the presence of the early post-medieval water-lain deposits identified in 1998. Later 18th-19th-century deposits relating to earlier phases of the Castle Inn were observed across the road (Barber 2007b).

No period

A watching brief in July 1995 produced no archaeological deposits or features. Area A was the repair of a footpath and installation of a French drain (80 m^2); Area B was a 12 m long pipe trench (0.3 m wide); Area C was a 76 m long pipe trench (0.3 m wide). Excavated depths did not exceed 0.3 m (Priestley-Bell 1995).

A watching brief in November 1996 during groundworks for five benches and a drainage inspection pit. The benches involved 10 footing excavations 0.3 m x 0.5 m and up to 0.49 m deep. Stratigraphy comprised topsoil overlying brickearth. The pit was 0.92 m x 0.75 m and 1.4 m deep, with a concrete slab associated with the drainage pipe found at this level. The overburden was redeposited silty clay. No archaeological deposits or finds were observed (Speed 1996).

A watching brief during the excavation of a 7 m long drainage run linking the World War Two Type 28A pillbox with the existing drainage system. The drain was dug to a maximum depth of 0.6 m, and encountered no archaeological deposits or finds, being dug largely thorough redeposited clay derived from drainage works in 1992 (James 2001).

A watching brief in October 2004 during the excavation of a 30 m long drainage trench from the foot of the southern moat embankment towards the modern drainage ditch produced no archaeological features or finds. The trench was dug to a depth of 0.95 m, largely through made ground (Riccoboni 2004).

List of Unpublished Reports, 1994-2010

These references to the grey literature will be found in the general bibliography, but for convenience, they are also set out below. Many are available at East Sussex Record Office (ESRO) in the series R/R 36; the full records numbers are given below. PDFs can also be obtained via the East Sussex Historic Environment Record https://new.eastsussex.gov.uk/environment/archaeology/her (accessed 19th April 2016).

Barber, L., 1998. *An Archaeological Watching Brief at Bodiam Castle, East Sussex (The New Sewage Treatment Plant).* Unpublished Archaeology South-East report 858.

Barber, L., 2007a. *An Archaeological Watching Brief at Bodiam Castle, Robertsbridge, East Sussex: The Drainage Scheme.* Unpublished Archaeology South-East report 2776. ESRO R/R/36/14811.

Barber, L., 2007b. *An Archaeological Watching Brief at Bodiam Castle, Robertsbridge, East Sussex: The Moat Banks and Great Hall.* Unpublished Archaeology South-East report 2819.

Fallon, D., 2008. *An Archaeological Excavation at Bodiam Castle, Robertsbridge, East Sussex.* Unpublished Archaeology South-East report 2008022. ESRO R/R/36/14810.

Gardiner, M. and Barber, L., 1994. *A Catalogue of Finds from Bodiam Castle, East Sussex.* Unpublished South Eastern Archaeological Services report 1993/8.

Honess, D., 2009. *New Pumping Station, Bodiam Castle, East Sussex: Geophysical Survey Report.* Unpublished Archaeology South-East report 2009005. ESRO R/R/36/14451.

James, R., 2001. *Bodiam Castle, East Sussex: Summary Report of a Watching Brief during Drainage Works.* Unpublished Archaeology South-East report 1437.

James, R. and Whittick, C., 2008. *Archaeological and Historic Landscape Survey: Land South of Bodiam Castle, East Sussex.* Unpublished Archaeology South-East report 2007201. ESRO R/R/36/14405 and R/R/24/5/4.

Johnson, C., 1999. *An Archaeological Watching Brief at Bodiam Castle, East Sussex (Tree and Shrub Planting).* Unpublished Archaeology South-East report 1062.

Johnson, C., 2002. *An Archaeological Watching Brief at Bodiam Castle, Bodiam, East Sussex.* Unpublished Archaeology South-East report 1627.

Johnson, C., Martin, D. and Whittick, C., 2000. *Archaeological & Historic Landscape Survey: Bodiam Castle, East Sussex.* Unpublished Archaeology South-East report P7 (2 vols.). ESRO R/R/36/14944, R/R/36/14944B and R/R/24/5/2.

Martin, D. and Martin, B., 2005. *An Archaeological Record and Overview of the Portcullis at Bodiam Castle, Bodiam, East Sussex.* Unpublished Archaeology South-East report 1992. ESRO R/R/36/14206.

Pope, M., 2009. *A Geoarchaeological Watching Brief at the Rose Garden, Bodiam, Robertsbridge, East Sussex.* Unpublished Archaeology South-East report 2008254.

Priestley-Bell, G., 1995. *An Archaeological Watching Brief at Bodiam Castle, Bodiam, East Sussex.* Unpublished South Eastern Archaeological Services report 310.

Priestley-Bell, G. and Pope, M., 2009. *An Archaeological and Geo-Archaeological Evaluation at the 'Rose Garden', Bodiam Castle, East Sussex.* Unpublished Archaeology South-East report 2009095. ESRO R/R/36/14598; also available at http://www.ucl.ac.uk/archaeologyse/resources/report-library/pdf-library-map-all (accessed 17th June 2015) and at http://archaeologydataservice.ac.uk/archives/view/greylit/query.cfm?REDSQUIDARCHIVES_825336_D811A97B-39BE-4EE8-901F3E1D8D2B3FC7 (accessed 19th June 2016).

Riccoboni, P., 2004. *Bodiam Castle Drainage Work (Ph 2).* Unpublished Archaeology South-East report 1935. ESRO R/R/36/14064.

Speed, L., 1996. *An Archaeological Watching Brief at Bodiam Castle, Bodiam, East Sussex.* Unpublished Archaeology South-East report 494. ESRO R/R/36/14131.

Statton, M., 2009. *An Archaeological Assessment of Bodiam Castle, Rother, East Sussex.* Unpublished Archaeology South-East report 2009055.

Stevens, S., 1995. *Bodiam Castle Moat Bank Protection Scheme.* Unpublished South Eastern Archaeological Services report 147.

Worrall, S., 2003. *An Archaeological Watching Brief during Drainage Works at Bodiam Castle, East Sussex.* Unpublished Archaeology South-East report. 1752. ESRO R/R/36/13954 and R/R/24/5/1.

3

BODIAM CASTLE: A NEW SURVEY OF THE INTERIOR

Catriona Cooper, Penny Copeland, Matthew Johnson[1]

Abstract. This chapter discusses the form and interpretation of the internal layout of Bodiam Castle, East Sussex, England. It first reviews previous work before presenting new plans based on a detailed total station survey of the castle interior. The interpretation of the internal form of the castle is reassessed in the light of this new plan. We draw attention to the evidence for changes of mind and other inconsistencies behind what at first sight is a very regular layout. We go on to discuss the implications of Bodiam for wider interpretation of later medieval domestic spaces.

Introduction

Bodiam Castle is one of the most famous and extensively discussed medieval buildings in Europe (Clark 1884: 239-47; Sands 1903; Thompson 1912: 322-7; Simpson 1931; Hohler 1966; Turner 1986; Coulson 1992; Goodall 1998b and Johnson 2002: 19-33, are a very few salient references in a vast literature). The nature and form of its external defences, and the nature of the landscape features around it, have been the topic of seemingly endless debate (Taylor *et al.* 1990; Johnson 2002; Liddiard & Williamson 2008; see also Whittick 1993). A striking omission from much of this discussion, however, has been the interior of the castle. Many scholars have concentrated on the landscape setting of the castle, and the impression conveyed by its external façades. Ironically, Bodiam has been treated rather as traditional architectural historians might approach a Classical building, in which an appreciation of the form and composition of the external façades has taken precedence over an understanding of the internal spaces. One of the purposes of this chapter is very simple: to remind scholars that whatever the debates over the landscape setting of Bodiam and the wider interpretation of the castle's function, there is an interesting and complex domestic building here to be explored (Fig. 3.1), whatever one's view of its external walls and towers.

This chapter will first review previous interpretations of the interior of Bodiam, and evaluate issues in understanding it arising from later modifications and restoration activity. It will then present a new survey of the interior and discuss its implications. We highlight irregularities and evidence for changes of mind in the construction of a building that appears highly regular and symmetrical at first sight, and go on to discuss a number of interpretive issues that the building raises.

The introduction to this volume stressed the importance of lived experience in understanding the late medieval buildings discussed in this monograph. In our discussion of Bodiam, below, we suggest that an understanding of this and other late medieval buildings based exclusively on the plan view, and on stylistic and typological comparison with other buildings, is not the whole story. Discussions of the evolution of different plan forms need to be complemented by a more holistic, human understanding of space. Catriona Cooper will discuss these issues more fully with reference to her work on lived experience and digital technologies in Chapter Nine.

---

[1] Catriona Cooper and Penny Copeland undertook the survey reported on here, together with James Miles. Cooper, Copeland and Johnson wrote and revised the text of the chapter together.

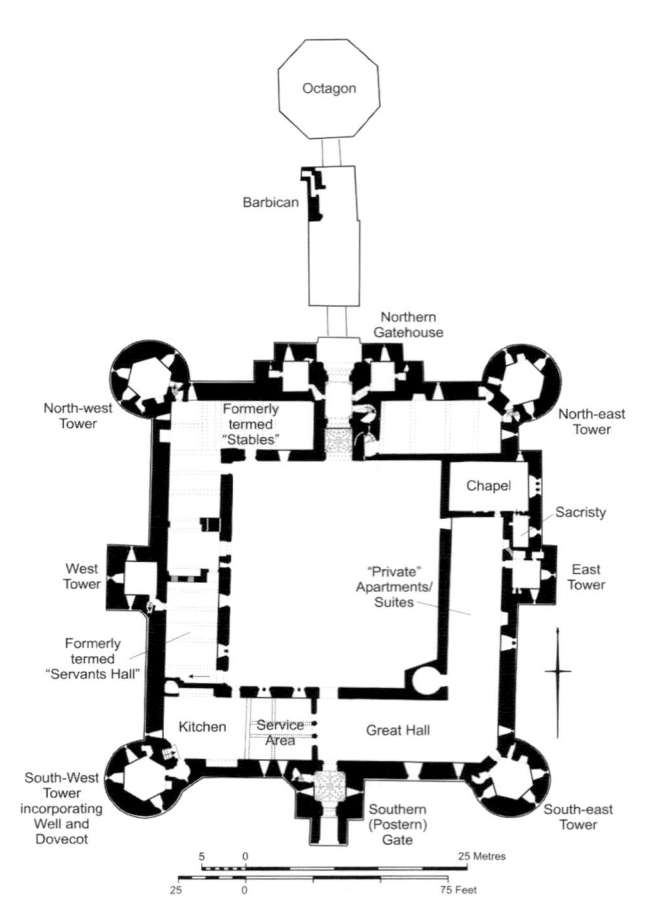

Fig. 3.1: Simplified plan of Bodiam Castle with key elements designated.

Previous Interpretations

Though the interior of Bodiam has been generally less well discussed relative to the amount of ink spilt discussing its exterior, it is interesting that Bodiam has been the vehicle for two of the most famous examples of social interpretation in earlier generations. In the 1930s, Douglas Simpson discussed Bodiam as an example of his theory of 'bastard feudalism'. Simpson believed that late medieval castles were often garrisoned by paid mercenaries, and that the lord and household were almost as distrustful of their own unruly and potentially dangerous mercenaries as they were afraid of external attack. He interpreted the internal layout of late medieval castles, then, as one of division and segregation between the lord's family and household and what he saw as secondary and independent accommodation for mercenaries. At Bodiam, Simpson noted the (apparently) blank wall between kitchen and north range and saw it as just such an example of segregation, with the 'mercenaries' blocked from penetration into the kitchen-hall-upper suite (Simpson 1931; 1946). Though his views on bastard feudalism and segregation in buildings are now completely out of favour, Simpson deserves credit for developing an early social interpretation of late medieval buildings based on an appreciation of the importance of spatial organisation.

In the 1960s, Patrick Faulkner also used Bodiam as a case study in a wider argument. In a seminal article, Faulkner used an early form of access diagram to illustrate the evolution of domestic planning in larger medieval buildings between the 12th and the 14th centuries (Faulkner 1963; Johnson 2012b; see Fig. 3.2). Faulkner pointed to the number and importance of lodgings in the later middle ages and talked of the multiple-household arrangement at Bolton, Bodiam and other buildings. We will look at the 'lodgings' at Bodiam more closely below.

Since Faulkner, there has been relatively little discussion of the interior of the castle. David Thackray and Nikolaus Pevsner both made brief comments in the guidebook and guide to Sussex respectively (Nairn & Pevsner 1965: 421; Thackray 1991: 42). John Goodall's comments on the interpretation of Bodiam in *The English Castle* say little about the interior, though they are accompanied by an impressive reconstruction drawing of the upper suite and do draw a key link with Edward III's work at Windsor (Goodall 2011: 314-7 and fig. 237). Charles Coulson assesses the building in terms of its degree of defensibility and makes remarks on its appearance and general aesthetics, but does not engage in detail with its internal layout (1992). Anthony Emery's gazetteer entry on Bodiam in his *Greater Medieval Houses* refers students to wider debates over the castle, again without closely discussing its internal organisation (Emery 2006: 317).

Measured and Ground Penetrating Radar (GPR) Survey

The standing building survey presented here is the result of a total of six weeks' intensive survey of the interior of the castle by Catriona Cooper and Penny Copeland, as well as James Miles, of the University of Southampton, under the direction of Matthew Johnson, latterly of Northwestern University (Fig. 3.3). The team was assisted by various undergraduate students. Work was spread over three seasons in 2010, 2011 and 2012, at the end of which the building had been viewed in different lights, at different times of the day and in both spring and late summer. During the process, a number of different experts on medieval buildings visited and offered their views on our provisional interpretations. At the end of the process Cooper and Copeland had developed a close eye for original medieval fabric versus post-medieval restoration.

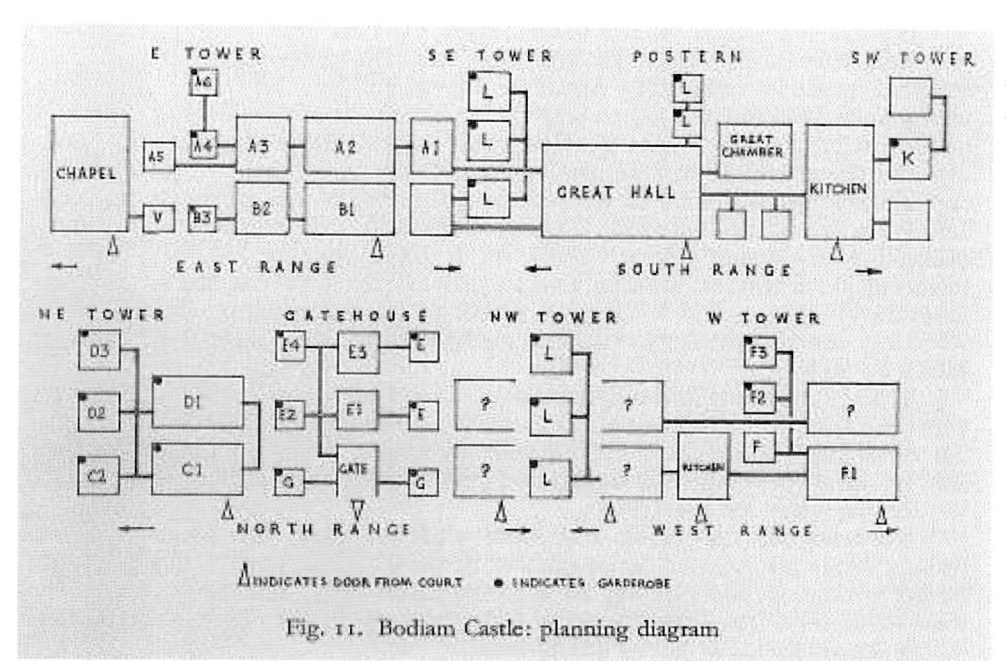

Fig. 3.2: Faulkner's access diagram (after Faulkner 1963, fig. 11).

The equipment used was a Leica reflectorless total station. TheoLt, a programme to download the data straight into AutoCad software, was used, so that the plans and drawings could be visualised instantly on screen as the work progressed. Two teams of three to four students and staff worked simultaneously. The drawings were then manipulated to produce the two-dimensional plans and elevations reproduced here; the final versions were then edited in CorelDraw. The AutoCad data was also used by Cooper to create visualisations in 3DSMax, which we discuss below.

Though perhaps more than 95% of the castle was examined in detail, it was not possible to gain access to all areas due to health and safety considerations (for example in the eastern part of the northern gatehouse). The restrictions on space in many of the small corridors and latrines made it impossible to carry the total station survey through to these areas and in these instances, measured survey was carried out on paper (Figs 3.4-3.8).

A GPR survey was also carried out of all areas of the castle interior where survey was feasible. Initial survey was carried out in 2010, directed by Kris Strutt. The team returned in 2016 to resurvey the area, and the results of this latter survey are presented in Figs 3.9 and 3.10, and are discussed below. A more detailed account and interpretation of the survey results is on file with Historic England.

In its latter stages, the survey and interpretation of the castle was helped considerably by the input of Paul Drury and his team, who undertook their own survey of the building including elevations of the principal façades as part of their research for the 2016 Conservation Management Plan at Bodiam (Drury & Copeman 2016). We thank Paul and his team for

Fig. 3.3: Students from Southampton and Northwestern Universities at work. Photo by Matthew Johnson.

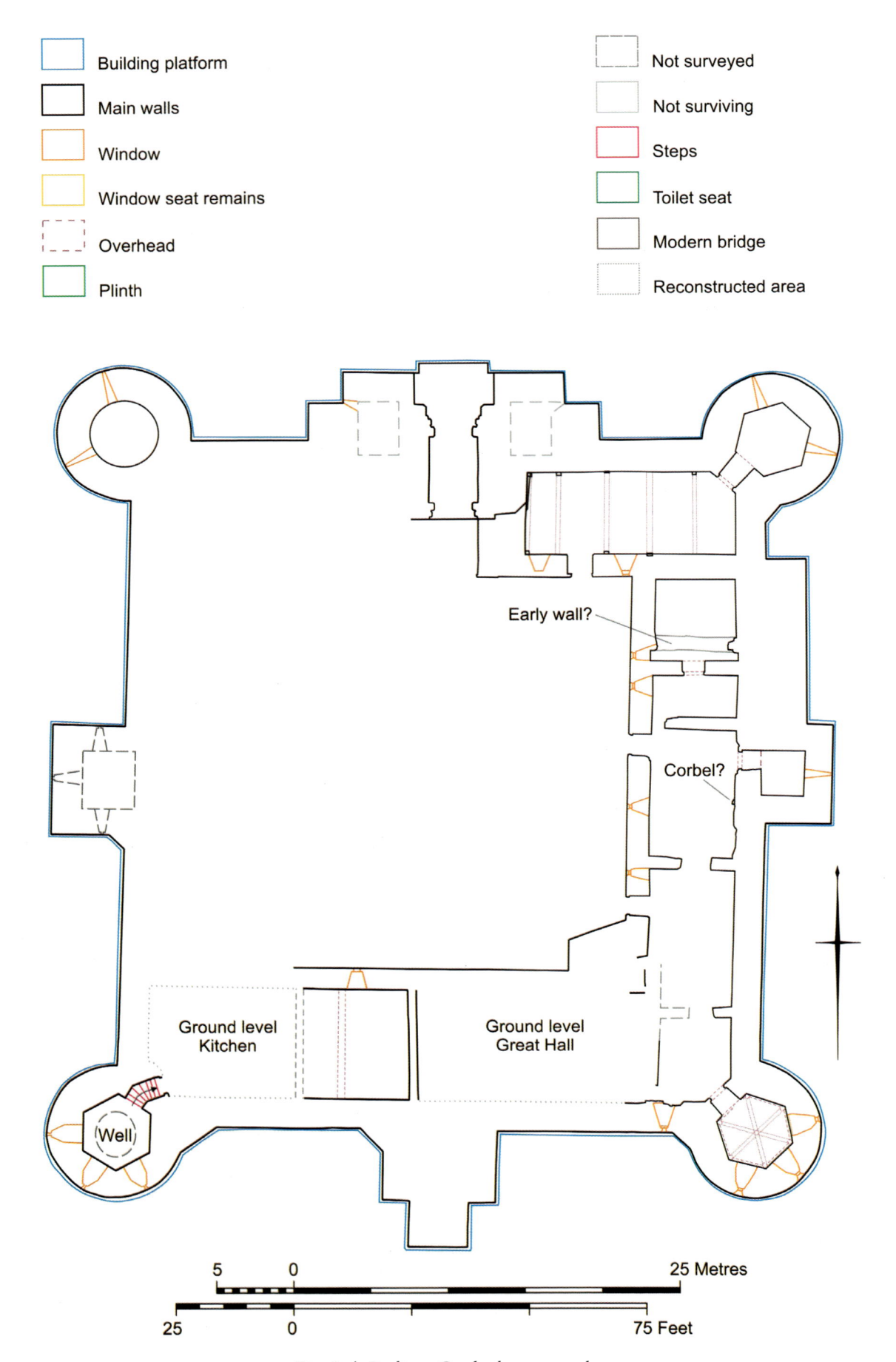

Fig. 3.4: Bodiam Castle, basement plan.

BODIAM CASTLE: A NEW SURVEY OF THE INTERIOR

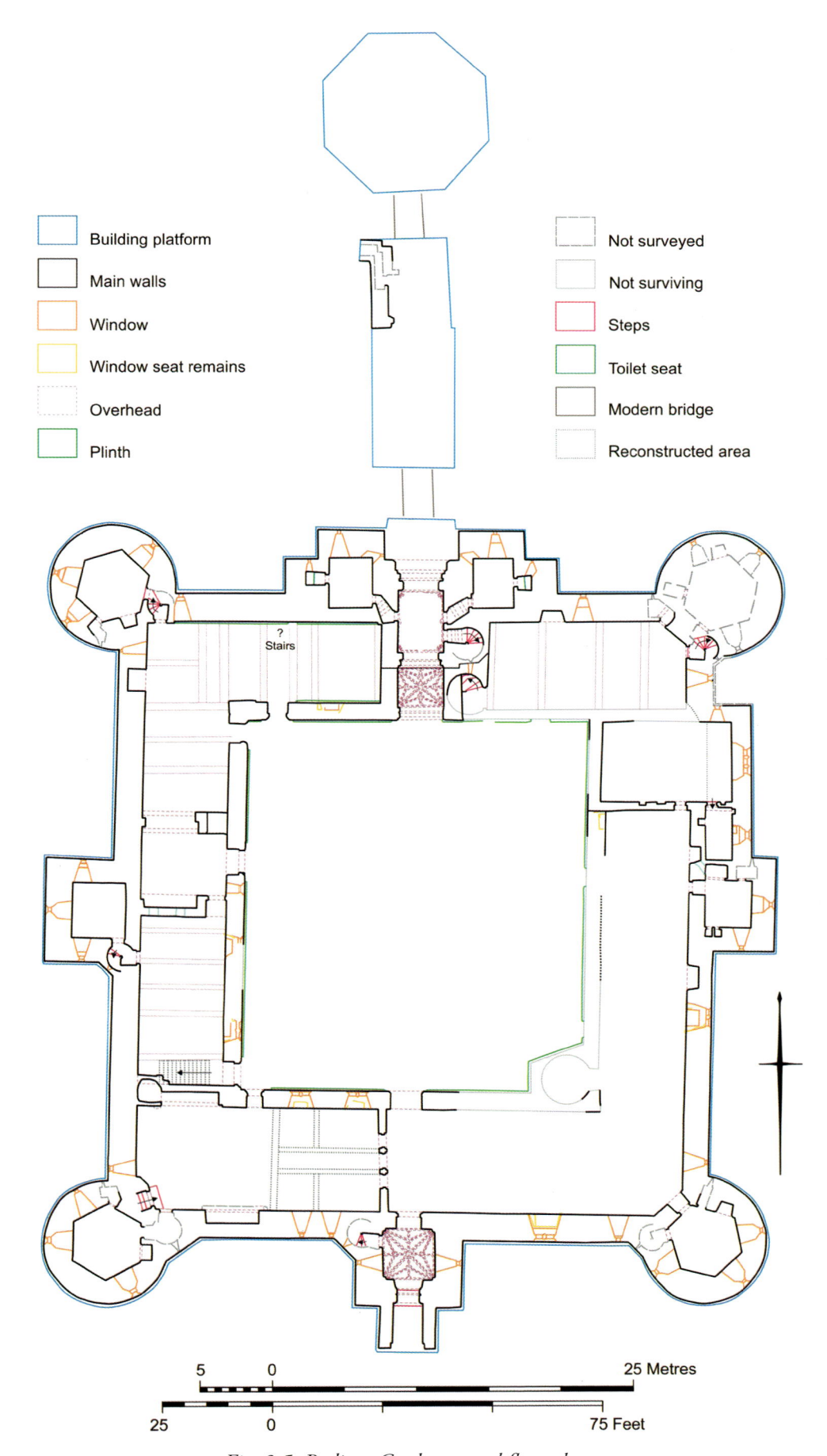

Fig. 3.5: Bodiam Castle, ground floor plan.

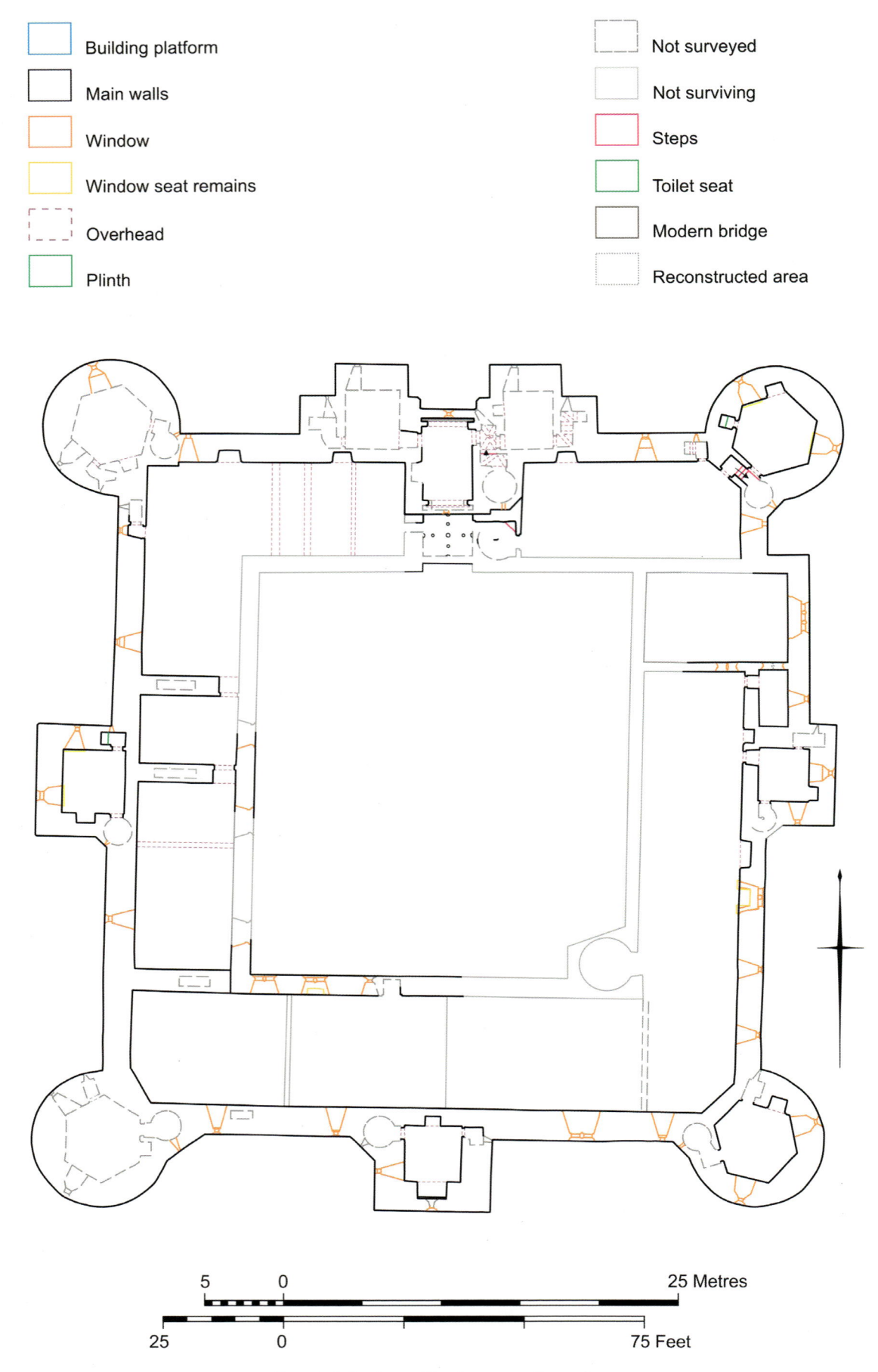

Fig. 3.6: Bodiam Castle, upper floor plan.

BODIAM CASTLE: A NEW SURVEY OF THE INTERIOR

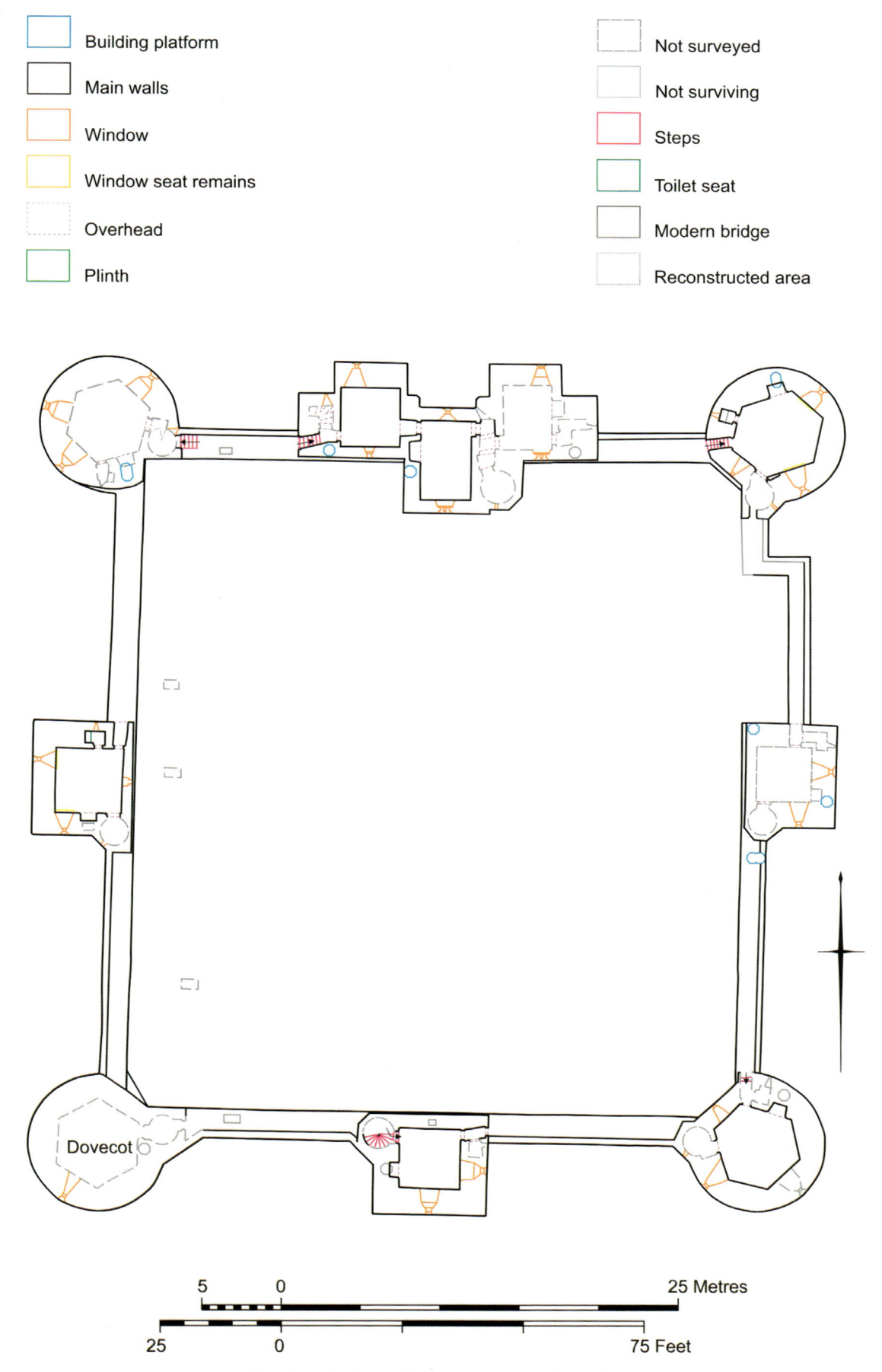

- Building platform
- Main walls
- Window
- Window seat remains
- Overhead
- Plinth
- Not surveyed
- Not surviving
- Steps
- Toilet seat
- Modern bridge
- Reconstructed area

Fig. 3.7: Bodiam Castle, upper chambers plan.

Fig. 3.8: Elevation of east curtain wall, as seen from the courtyard looking east.

their collegiate attitude in sharing their work and in comparing notes on different aspects of the building.

In what follows we describe the castle closely. The reader may find it helpful to consult with Fig. 3.1, a simplified plan of the castle with key elements designated. To be clear about terminology: all the main ranges have at least two floors which we designate ground floor and upper floor, following the British system. There are basements underneath the ground floor on the eastern and southern sides of the buildings (see Fig. 3.4). The towers all have a chamber above the upper floor of the main ranges.

Post-Medieval Use and Restoration

As is characteristic of so many medieval ruins, the fabric of Bodiam was altered in the course of 'restoration' in the 19th to 20th centuries, and these alterations need to be mentally peeled away before an assessment of the medieval fabric can begin. Eighteenth-century watercolours on display at the castle today show the castle in decay, with a small cottage built up against the ruined south range and vegetable gardens in the courtyard (see Chapter Five). Close inspection of the watercolours indicates that this cottage did not simply occupy the space of the former hall; it extended forward into the courtyard, and its rooms possibly extended back into the postern tower. Evidence for this cottage was found in excavations in this area (Barber 2007a); it is visible in joist holes surviving in the masonry above the northern cross-passage door, and also a blocked hole indicating a fireplace in the postern tower that has been opened and reblocked. Pollen evidence from cores taken in the inner courtyard confirms the watercolours' impression of tilled gardens adjoining this cottage (Scaife 2013; see also Chapter Five). There is also evidence in many of the tower rooms of inserted floors to provide more space (Fig. 3.11). It could be related to agricultural storage but when and why this was done is not clear.

It is known that John 'Mad Jack' Fuller bought the castle to save it from destruction in 1829, and that Fuller spent considerable sums on the estate as a whole (Curzon 1926: 48; Thackray 1991: 26-7; Holland 2011). The nature and extent of Fuller's work on the fabric of the castle itself, however, is quite unclear.

George Cubitt also engaged in restoration work following his purchase of the castle in 1864 but the best known of these restorations is Lord Curzon's work in the years before 1921. Curzon also makes reference in his publication to the earlier work of Cubitt. According to Curzon (1926: 83-4), Cubitt emptied the moat to recover fallen stones and restored them to their (presumed) correct location on the battlements. He also strengthened the foundations of the castle with sandstone and concrete. Cubitt did extensive repairs to the south-west and postern towers, including roofing the postern tower so that views could be taken in from its battlements, and commissioned measured drawings by Tavernor Perry (Curzon 1926: 18, 84), which are of a high quality for their time (Fig. 3.12).

Curzon's work included draining the moat, dredging the outer areas, recording the foundation timbers for the bridges, and doing more work in lifting fallen stones from the moat and strengthening the foundations; his concrete 'apron' or render to the plinth is visible when the level of the moat is low (Fig. 3.13). Curzon also discovered and emptied the well in the south-west tower,

BODIAM CASTLE: A NEW SURVEY OF THE INTERIOR

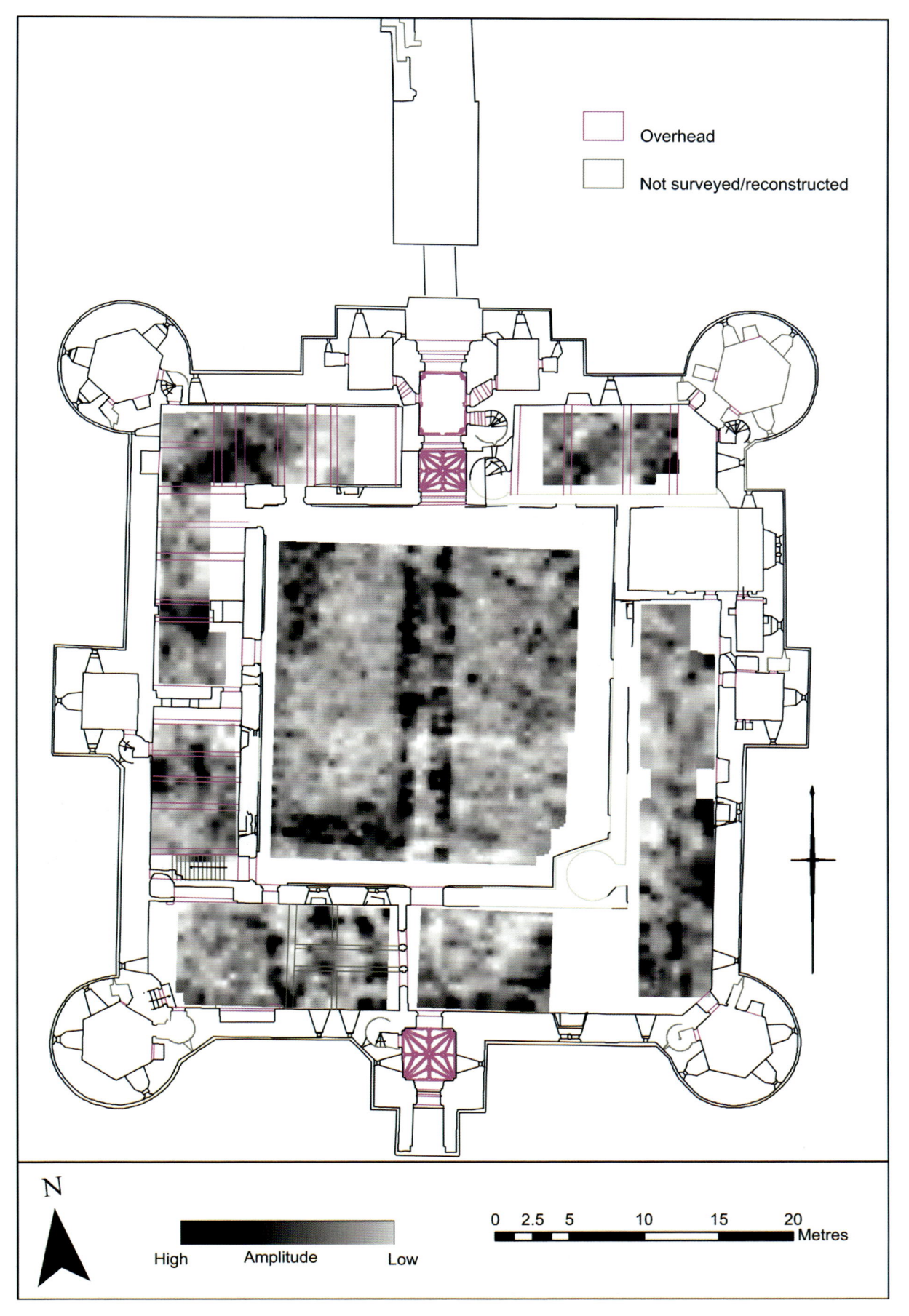

Fig. 3.9: Bodiam Castle, GPR results.

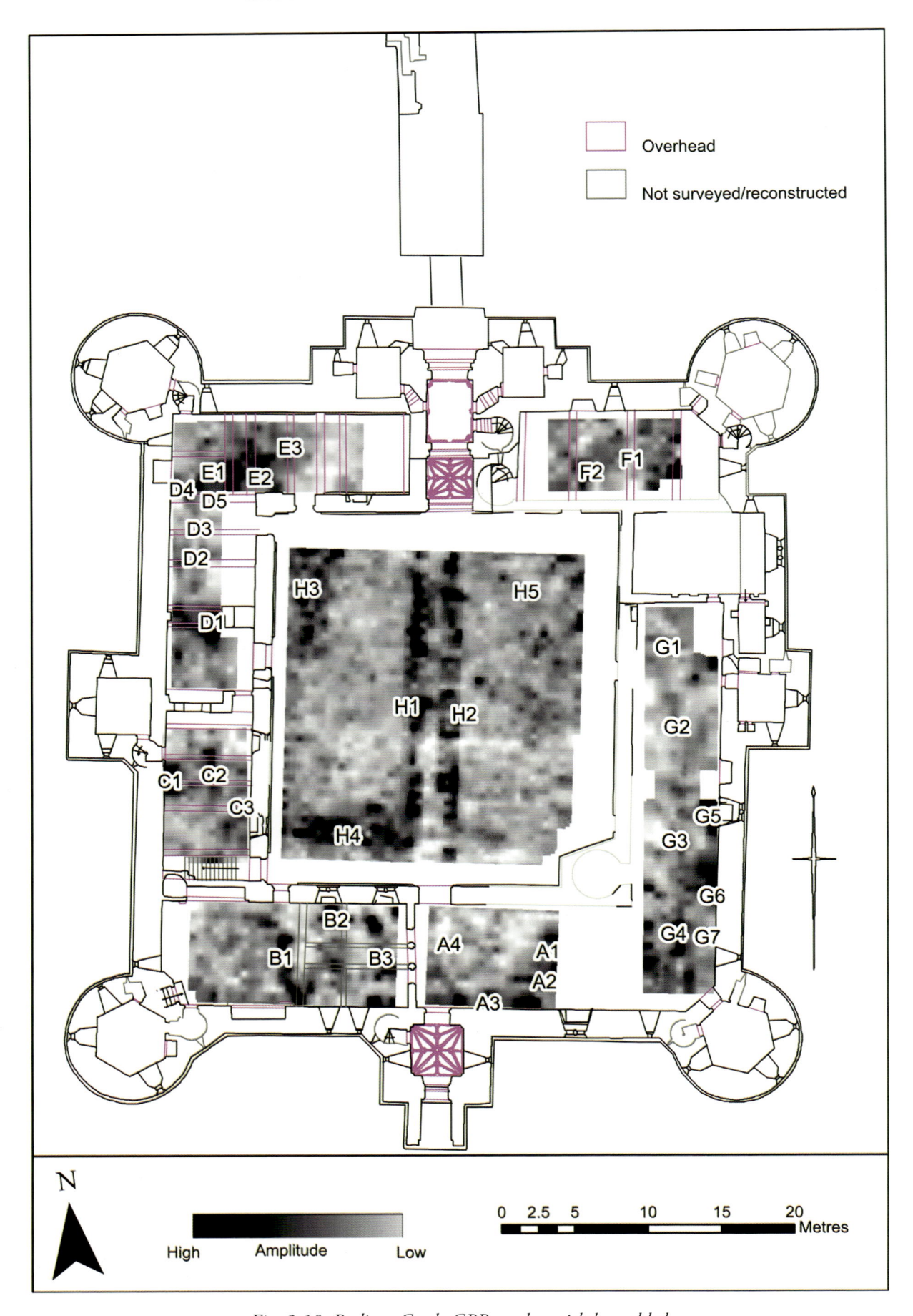

Fig. 3.10: Bodiam Castle GPR results, with key added.

Fig. 3.11: Evidence for inserted floors, western ground floor room of gatehouse. Photo by Penny Copeland.

Fig. 3.13: Curzon's render to the plinth or 'apron'. Photo by Penny Copeland.

strengthening the wall of the tower which in places only survived to a thickness of one stone. He cleared out fallen debris and trees from the interior of the castle, clearing the basements in the process. The courtyard was laid to lawns at this time. The central north-south pathway would have been relaid, but Lambert's 1780s drawing suggests it was done so along an earlier line; the GPR results show the feature running to a great depth, perhaps indicating that it is of some antiquity (Fig. 3.10, H1 & H2).

It is not always easy to distinguish Curzon and Cubitt's work from the original medieval fabric, particularly as original stone was reused and subsequent repointing has concealed changes in mortar. Although the outer walls stand nearly or completely to their full height, the ruinous state of the internal walls hampers interpretation. Much of the battlements are missing, and where they appear complete, they may well be reconstructions following the salvage of stones from the moat during Cubitt's and Curzon's dredging.

Close observation of the fabric has led us to conclude that there are a number of areas which are most likely to be the work of Fuller, Cubitt and Curzon. The most obvious area is the supporting of the inner cell of the northern gatehouse on the east side (Fig. 3.14). The buttressing wall thickening was built over a spiral staircase and probably uses stone from the first floor of the gatehouse. Obvious restoration was also observed in the large fireplaces in the west range where the openings or chimney walls have been supported by stone voussoirs. In the wall above the window of the great hall very large blocks can be observed which appear out of place. On

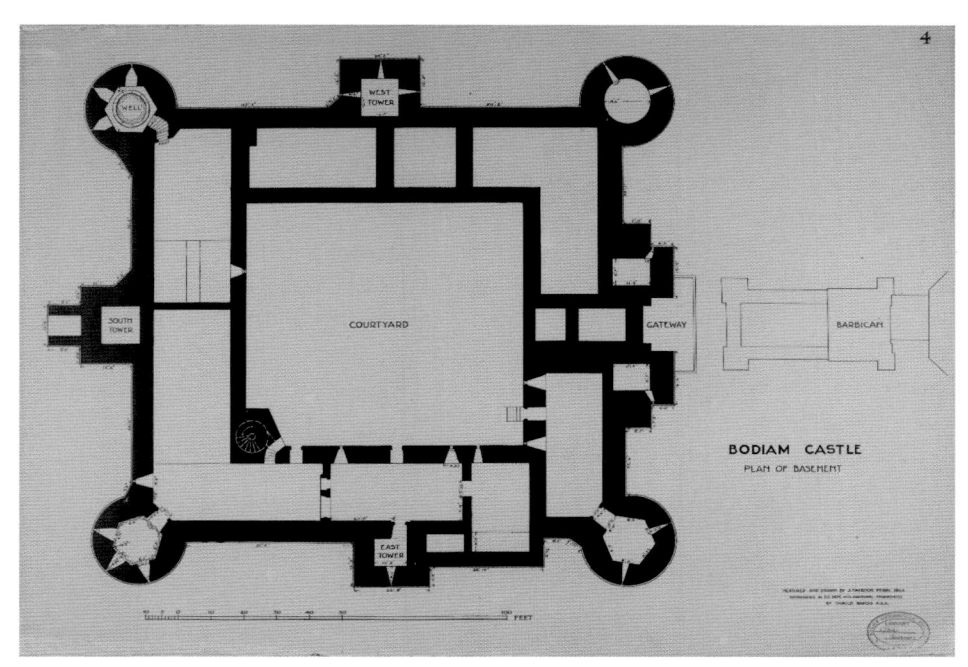

Fig. 3.12: One of Tavernor Perry's drawings, commissioned by Lord Curzon in the 1920s.

Fig. 3.14: Buttress against gatehouse, built up against stair to reach chamber. Photo by Penny Copeland.

the same elevation, the wall above the pantry and buttery around one of the windows appears to have been rebuilt using slightly irregular, less prepared, smaller stones. It is also clear that part of the courtyard wall of the east range has been substantially rebuilt, and this may account for discrepancies in the basement plan of this area between Tavernor Perry in 1864 and the present location of one of the windows. Finally, it seems likely that Fuller is responsible for the roofing over of the postern gatehouse vaulting. There is surviving evidence in the first floor room of lead flashing being pinned to the wall, close to floor level and sloping towards the portcullis grating. This entailed cutting the usual groove in the wall, including through a chamfer stop. The location of the iron pegs also suggests it may have happened when the fireplace was blocked on the inside.

The castle has been in the National Trust's custodianship since Curzon's death in 1925 and much of the work carried out to make the castle accessible and safe for visitors is clearly identifiable, for example the new stairs installed in the chapel since our work commenced in 2010, and the concrete roofs on the towers, dated 1962. Other work is not so obvious or so easily dateable. However, sufficient fabric exists to indicate the nature of much of the late 14th-century interior. First, the nature of interior spaces is indicated by the presence of fenestration and other piercing of the largely surviving external walls. To clarify, external walls are pierced by, for example, the window lighting the upper end of the hall, windows with window seats for the private apartments and other spaces, doorways into towers and so on. Second, interpretation is helped by the abandonment of Bodiam as a dwelling in the 17th century, and the consequent absence of later structural changes during the life of the castle as a residence that might have obscured or destroyed original detail.

Bodiam 1400-1650

As just noted, there are relatively few changes to the internal fabric of Bodiam that can be dated between the initial build of the 1380s and the abandonment of the building in the 17th century. There is relatively little information on the history and occupation of the castle after the 1380s. The castle passed to the Lewknors in the later 15th century, where the ownership was split among the family until the 1630s when it was united under the Earls of Thanet (Johnson *et al.* 2000: 36). It was probably finally abandoned in the 17th century having quickly changed hands during the Civil War; there is no secure date for this abandonment, but it is perhaps revealing that much of the most visible post-abandonment graffiti in the castle dates to the later 17th century (Cooper 2010). The partial dismantling of the castle interior has been attributed to Nathaniel Powell around 1645, who was building his own house at Ewhurst Place (Johnson *et al.* 2000: 34-9); however, that house is principally built of brick, and it is perhaps more likely that stone went to the early 17th-century rebuilding of Court Lodge (see Chapter Four). The GPR results indicate areas of possible demolition debris in the courtyard (Fig. 3.10, H2, H4 and possibly H5, though this last may alternatively indicate a drain). There is heavy wear on most of the treads of staircases in the castle, and numerous examples of knife sharpening wear on fireplaces, but it is unclear precisely how much of a period of use this wear might indicate.

There appears to be a complex arrangement of fireplaces in the partition walls of the west range; the GPR survey also indicated a series of anomalies in this area that are difficult to explain (Fig. 3.10, C1-C3, with D1 a possible hearth and D2-D5). It has been assumed in the past that this whole area in the western range of the castle is best interpreted in terms of a sequence of changes that were 15th or 16th century in date (for example Goodall 2001). The southern fireplace may have been reduced in size and then shifted in orientation, so that the opening faced north rather than south. It is noteworthy that knife sharpening had

Fig. 3.15: Southern cross wall of western range showing relieving arch and flue or stoke holes. A further retaining arch is visible on the northern side. Note knife sharpening effect on doorway. Photo by Penny Copeland.

taken place on the door jamb in that room; such marks are more commonly found on or next to fireplaces (see Fig. 3.15). The GPR results (Fig. 3.10, D1) appear to show that the northern fireplace had a backing wall to the south suggesting the hearth opened to the north, presumably the earliest arrangement. There is also a door immediately to the east of this fireplace that has been blocked. The date of this blocking is uncertain but there is no indication of a door on Cubitt's plan so it must have been early. However, Paul Drury believes that although the fabric in this area dates from a late period of primary construction, it is not a much later phase, noting that the hearths are integral with the cross walls.

Having discussed later alterations and restoration activity, we can now turn to the surviving remains of the building as it was first constructed in the 1380s.

Building Irregularities

Over the last two decades, the use of advanced survey techniques on high-status medieval buildings, combined with close and informed observation of medieval fabric, has produced new understandings. In particular, evidence has been found of unexpected changes of mind, conflict between builder and client, and other irregularities and anomalies (for example Dixon & Marshall 1993a; 1993b; Impey 2008). Bodiam is no exception. At first sight, it appears to be a single-phase structure of remarkably regular plan with an overall impression of symmetry. However, when one starts to look at the details, a series of anomalies reveal a more complex picture – a picture of builders and owners changing their mind, of different work patterns, of mistakes and changes in alignment – a picture that raises issues in its turn of landscapes of work and lived experience.

We will first list the most significant of these irregularities, working round the castle from the gatehouse in a clockwise fashion, before discussing their interpretation.

Northern gatehouse

It is well known that the rear of the gatehouse incorporates changes of mind, apparently towards the close of the building campaign. The rear, southern, chamber of the gatehouse has a straight joint visible on the east and west sides to indicate that it has been added to the main structure at the front (Fig. 3.16). As a result, the chamber over the rear section is not connected to other chambers in the gatehouse, but is accessed independently from a separate staircase (Fig. 3.14). It is possible that this separate southern staircase gave access to the upper floor of the north-east range, and also, via the room above the southern gatehouse chamber, to the north-west range as well.

Less well known is the leafy boss (Fig. 3.17). This is the centrepiece of the vault in the narrow corridor linking the gatehouse stair to the first floor chamber over the gate passage and also to the chamber in its east tower; it was first pointed out to us by David and Barbara Martin. This boss is the only surviving piece of figurative sculpture in the whole building; Coulson has noted that the building as a whole is remarkably plain (1993: 76-7). There is an oral tradition that the boss has been moved to this location from the now-ruined barbican, where such a boss is visible in a watercolour of 1784 by S.H. Grimm. However the extant boss is carved as a single piece with four radiating ribs and looks particularly well built in to the surrounding stonework. The Grimm drawing shows the barbican boss with six radiating ribs which, if it is accurate, must rule out its identification with the extant boss. It is possible that there were further carved bosses in

Fig. 3.16: West side of gatehouse showing the straight joint between the original and the southern sections. Photo by Matthew Johnson.

Fig. 3.17: Leafy boss in the first floor corridor of the gatehouse. Photos by Penny Copeland.

Fig. 3.18: Plinth to the east of the gatehouse showing a slight misalignment reused to support a beam. Photo by Penny Copeland.

Fig. 3.19: Window in north-east range of unusual design. Photo by Penny Copeland.

the castle but apart from the south-eastern tower basement, there are no other surviving vaulted ceilings of a similar type, and although similar locations could have been used their vaulting generally consists of a series of substantial single ribs. The extant vaults in the north-western and southern gatehouses do not have bosses of a similar type. The boss appears to have been lime washed or some other application at some point but apart from the heraldry on the gates, which was presumably painted, there is no evidence anywhere in the castle for decorative paint, though there is pecking for plaster on many surfaces.

A further anomaly exists at basement level to the east of the gatehouse. What appears to be a small plinth protrudes from the northern half of the gatehouse, on a slightly different alignment from the wall above. A further small plinth protrudes at a lower level on the southern half of the gatehouse (Fig. 3.18). Both these plinths would be concealed on the western side if they exist, as there are no basements on this side. Neither of these plinths has corresponding features on other walls.

The small turret housing the newel staircase at the southern side of the gatehouse has a change in diameter close to the top of the tower rooms, reducing in size marginally at this point. This turret is anomalous in the design of the gatehouse as it is the only part with a string course. The south-east tower also has a definite change in the shape of its corresponding staircase turret where the diameter of the turret just below the string course increases noticeably.

having to be slightly recessed to allow the door to open. The recess is capped by a shouldered arch at a matching height to that of the adjacent window, making the recess a decorative feature while supporting the wall above (Fig. 3.21). This is strongly suggestive of a change of mind, perhaps for access to the stairwell.

Eastern range

The interpretation of the eastern range, particularly in the area of the chapel, the eastern tower and the adjacent areas, is particularly complex. There are a number of reasons for this. First, Paul Drury and his team have discovered that an earlier stone structure consisting of two rectangular cells is embedded in the lower levels of the east range, its north wall within what is now the chapel, its south wall running a little south of the western tower and its east and west walls embedded in the later castle walls (Drury & Copeman 2016, fig. 14). It is unclear how much earlier this structure is, and whether it relates to an earlier phase of occupation on the site; but it is probable that it dates to no more than a few years before the castle proper.

Second, there are indications of changes of mind during the early stages of castle construction. The external chapel and sacristy wall is on a slightly different alignment

Fig. 3.20: Straight joint in external wall to east of gatehouse. Photo by Penny Copeland.

North-east side of castle

The curtain wall east of the gatehouse has fireplaces and windows consistent with lodgings over two storeys. However, there is one window that is anomalous (Fig. 3.19). Its apex is too high for the ceiling of the lower floor, and is also of a unique design within the building. A further window in the south side of the north-eastern range has the top of the window apparently above or very close to the floor level above. Unrelated to the window, there has been a possible subsequent insertion of a cross wall dividing up this range, indicated by a low amplitude trench in the GPR (Fig. 3.10, F1) running from north to south, lining up with a corbel and roof timber notch.

On the exterior wall between the gatehouse and the north-eastern tower there is a straight joint in the masonry (Fig. 3.20). This is probably no more than the result of masons working in different teams or in different building seasons but there may have been some ancient structural failure here as a crack seems to have been filled between seasons. There are stones above the crack which appear to be original but do not display signs of cracking.

In the topmost floor of the north-eastern tower, the location of the door onto the spiral staircase, close to the door onto the walkways, has resulted in the wall

Fig. 3.21: Recess with lintel in wall of chamber floor of north-east tower. Photo by Penny Copeland.

to the rest of the east curtain wall, extending into the moat from the line of the curtain wall. The line of the main curtain wall appears to continue as the line of an internal wall through the basement of the chapel and the ground floor of the sacristy. This internal wall however is thinner than the other curtain walls of the castle, so the extension of the sacristy and chapel into the moat cannot be a later addition. A stub of a wall remains in the chapel basement which is too close to another wall to define a corridor or second room but which on Drury's analysis formed the north wall of the earlier structure (Fig. 3.22), removed when the south wall of the chapel basement was built. Curzon states clearly that foundations of this wall, over two feet thick, were found

> *running parallel to the south wall of the nave and leaving a space or passage of about two feet between them. The wall appears to have been cut off where it abutted on to the retaining wall of the sanctuary and the west wall of the chapel*
>
> (Curzon 1926: 103)

Interpretation of this area is hampered by Curzon's extensive restoration here.

The two doors on the south side of the chapel, giving access to the private apartments and the sacristy respectively, are on different levels (Fig. 3.22); the stairs up to the sacristy have been restored, probably by Curzon. A difference in level between the altar space and the rest of the chapel is to be expected, but the sacristy is on a third, higher level again. This means that the door leading into the sacristy is higher than the door leading into the apartments. It is an unusual arrangement, with the areas below the sacristy and the chancel altar of the chapel being the only 'dead' spaces in the castle, with no access and no apparent purpose.

Fig. 3.22: Differences in floor levels in the chapel. Photo by Penny Copeland.

Fig. 3.23: Straight joint and rebuilt walls in basement level of east tower, also showing cupboards where stair access would normally be. Photo by Penny Copeland.

It is tempting to think that this dead space is due to the change in design once the new chapel arrangement had been proposed and the builders just trying to catch up.

The east tower is slightly north of where it should be to be precisely symmetrical with the west tower (see Figs 3.4-3.7). The interior of this tower shows many irregularities in construction (Fig. 3.23). At basement level, both inside and in the rooms outside the tower, the walls appear to have been reconstructed or thickened at a later date, so that the door to the tower is recessed. Entering the tower, the thicker, rougher wall continues around clockwise until it meets a straight joint in the south-west corner of the tower. Although this straight joint continues up to ground floor level, there has been some obvious rebuilding of the lower part of the west wall so interpretation is difficult. In the corner of the room above the basement is a pair of cupboards built into the thickness of the wall, with rebates for doors. The equivalent position on both the floors above is the doorway to a spiral staircase leading upwards. The lack of access to the stair at this point prohibits movement from ground to upper floor within these apartments. The cupboard is considerably shallower than the staircase suggesting a void or particularly thick wall behind it.

On the north side of the east tower at ground floor level there is now a doorway into a latrine. On closer

Fig. 3.24: Fireplace in main range that connects through to east tower recess. Photo by Penny Copeland.

inspection, the doorway replaces an earlier, now blocked, opening where the relieving arch survives in the same position to the window on the opposite wall. The position of the blocked window is such that it would have opened onto the thickness of the sacristy wall to its north. This is further evidence that the chapel is a later amendment. Externally, matters are further confused by the perfect course matching on the exterior stone between the tower and the chapel extension but the coursing is mismatched between the chapel and the east wall of the original build. Mismatched coursing is not unusual on the exterior face of the castle however, and should be considered the norm, and only the very lowest courses of the external castle walls are regularly bonded in at internal corners.

The fireplace heating the lower, inner room to the private apartments has an arch composed of tiles on its inner, southern face that now opens into the tower. From the apartment side, it looks like a bread oven framed with voussoir tiles (Fig. 3.24), but from the tower, it opens into a recess with a segmented arch above it; this segmented arch is of a similar form to relieving arches elsewhere in the castle. The purpose of this space remains uncertain but the connection is deliberate, and the recess has no flue so it is dependent on the connected fireplace for fuel such as charcoal.

Along the central part of the east range, it is noticeable that the wall surfaces are extremely poorly preserved, with no recognisable surface surviving. This is unusual within the castle and, together with a corbel, has suggested that there was stone vaulting here which has been robbed out. However, the floor level of the ground floor is easy to see and there is little height for such vaulting above the windows. It is possible therefore that some of the facing has been removed or sold off and the remainder of the damage is weathering.

To the north of the south-east tower the room east of the great hall is narrower than the rooms to the north - a clear change somewhere around the access to the spiral stair in the corner of the courtyard. There is no clear reason for this change in alignment, though it may be related to the width being defined by the masonry cross wall of the south range (that is, the wall behind the high end of the hall). It does suggest that the room dividing walls were not thought out at the same time as the external walls.

Above the basement level, there is almost no surviving evidence for room divisions in the upper floors of the east range, the only clues being the arrangement of the windows and doors. In other areas of the castle, there are mortices for beams or slots for roof supports but neither of these are clear here. The possible presence of a drain, indicated in the GPR results (Fig. 3.10, G2-G4) should also be noted here.

Southern (postern) gatehouse

In the upper floor chamber over the gatehouse, a pair of mortices in the southern wall, about 1.5 m above the present floor, might be made out. Copeland and Cooper interpret these as possible mortices for a drawbridge chain. Johnson is not persuaded that these mortices exist; it is certainly the case that if these really are mortices that were subsequently plugged, the plugging was done very neatly. Readers can make up their own minds (Fig. 3.25). There are also two mortices lower down in this wall, just above the present floor. These have been plugged with lead and stone, possibly at the same time the vaulting below was protected with a roof, an action we attributed above to Fuller.

Fig. 3.25: Possible sites of mortices for drawbridge chain. Photo by Penny Copeland.

Fig. 3.26: Window to basement of service range excavated by Curzon, also showing the substantial mortices for wall partitions. Photo by Penny Copeland.

Fig. 3.27: Kitchen layout showing the unusual ledge at upper floor level for a possible partition of the well and staircase areas. Note the difference in height and width between the staircase door and the well door. Photo by Penny Copeland.

The service range and south-west tower

The northern wall of the service range (Fig. 3.26) features a small window which should give light onto a basement which Curzon is known to have excavated, and for which there is some evidence in the GPR results (Fig. 3.10, B1-B3). The height of the window would have overlapped with the floor level to either side if the floor in this area was not also raised over the basement. The height of the steps through the three doors in the cross-passage and large mortices in the walls suggest that the whole of the service end was raised over a basement, although the floor level in the kitchen itself appears to have been similar to the present day level.

There are a number of chamfer anomalies on the service and western range. For example, the door opening from the kitchen into the courtyard has a chamfer that is wider than the opening. The overlap is now visible on the west side but has been cunningly concealed to the east by small shaped stones. The southern, external face of the wall of the kitchen fireplace between the postern and the south-west tower has a straight joint visible and an irregular joint created by mismatched coursing. Like others in the building, this is probably no more than evidence for different masons' work or building seasons. The joints do not continue to the full height of the wall. The northern wall of the kitchen has a full height vertical straight joint meeting the corner of the internal courtyard wall. The corbelling of the fireplace suggests that it is part of the original design, so the joint is probably no more than an indication of the method of building.

The entrance to the chamber containing the well in the south-west tower protrudes slightly from the line of the wall above (Fig. 3.27). The first angle is almost 90 degrees from the south wall; it is then angled northwest to meet the west external wall. The wall above for the first floor has a single angle between the south and west walls, but the angle neither runs parallel to the tower or to either of the walls below. The change in angle of the first floor creates a ledge; however it is not clear what the ledge is for. The possibility that this supported a floor runs counter to the indication of the full height window and the assumption that the kitchen was two storeys high. There may have been a partition at this point with joists for a mezzanine resting on the ledge. A further detail of this area is the raised step into the staircase doorway next to the well. We can imagine the kitchen being mopped regularly and this raised step would have kept the water and grease out of the area. This might also explain the raised floor level in the pantry/buttery area.

Fig. 3.28: Double latrine and window at northern end of western range with inconsistent chamfers. Photo by Penny Copeland.

Western range

Another anomaly occurs in the window on the ground floor next to the double latrine towards the north end of the western range (Fig. 3.28). The chamfer above this window is of a standard type, stopping at a straight edge down. However, on the south side of the window, the outer edge of the jamb opening has been chamfered starting from the stone below the lintel. The north side is not chamfered. The double latrine, which is the only one in the castle, has a continuous chamfered opening on both sides and the top of the arch.

North-west tower

The north-west tower has an odd plan externally. Where the other towers have diagonal walls on the courtyard face, here there is an internal right angle, as if a 'bite' has been taken out of the plan. Just below parapet level on the east side of the tower above the wall-walk door, there is what appears to be a single corbel with no apparent function. The string course common to all towers without gates ends here just short of the corbel (Fig. 3.29). It is possible that the stones here were some of those replaced by Curzon, but there is no other indication of restoration at this point. A notch has been carved above this corbel, possibly to divert rainwater from its top, similar to treatment of chimneys against walls in other areas.

There is a straight joint between the north-west tower and the adjacent curtain wall, when observed internally, with the tower apparently built up against the wall. This may be another result of different masons' activities, particularly when it is considered in conjunction with the small but unique rebate with slight overhang/notch found where the northern elevation meets the north-western tower (Fig. 3.30).

Fig. 3.29: Change from corbel to string course on the north-west tower. Photo by Penny Copeland.

Fig. 3.30: Possible straight joint between north-west tower and north wall. Photo by Penny Copeland.

The Building Process

Many of these irregularities have no obvious or convincing explanation, but the following general comments can be offered. As seems to have been common practice with comparable buildings, the circuit of the outer curtain wall was largely built before the inner walls. It is most likely that building started around the northern gatehouse area and moved east and then south. Around the chapel/eastern tower area, before construction of the walls got beyond 2 m or so above ground level, the archaeological evidence suggests that there may have been a change of mind over the plan. If so, this change of mind was rapidly resolved and the building of the outer curtain wall continued, with some irregularities, around the south-west corner of the castle. At this point, that is with the outer walls built around to the south-west tower, the position of the upper chambers, hall, kitchen and latrines of the castle had all been thought out, as they were defined by the piercing of the hall and other windows, chimney flues and latrine chutes even if the inner walls were not yet in place. After this point in the building process the planning of the building becomes less integrated. The west curtain wall, and north wall west of the gatehouse, have few piercings and it is possible that the function of the western range had not been fully determined at this point. Work then continued with construction of the inner walls. The problem with the inner walls and the need for an inner gatehouse became apparent very early. The completeness of the northern gatehouse before the inner gatehouse was added is apparent from the slit windows in the staircase on the first floor that were later concealed.

The change of mind over the chapel area was not the only design alteration during the building of the castle. There is evidence from the exterior of the castle that its design was changed either in the latter stages of the building campaign or immediately afterwards. Excavations by David Martin during draining and dredging of the moat in 1970 indicated that the stone causeway between the barbican and the main gate were inserted after the initial construction of a timber bridge. Martin noted 'evidence for a complete reorganisation of the main entrance layout soon after its initial construction', possibly due to problems with the functioning of the original bridge and drawbridge arrangements (1973: 17).

We can possibly attribute the change in style between the gatehouses with substantial machicolations and the towers with string courses but without machicolations to a change in design also. At neighbouring Scotney, built in the 1370s, the surviving corner tower is notable for its machicolated summit. We know that the north gatehouse at Bodiam was built early in the construction sequence and it seems possible that the unusual corbel on the north-west tower may be the point at which the design of the tower summits changed (Fig. 3.29).

The change in work between seasons is clearly visible in the stone work of the southern part of the east curtain wall (Fig. 3.31). The south-east tower has been completed up to the top of the ground floor window and the wall to the north is staggered downwards to a lower level. The top few courses are completed in smaller stones. When the next building season arrived, larger stones were used and had to be cut to shape over those in place. No attempt was made to continue a course.

The lack of surviving building accounts means that dating of the building campaign is not certain; the licence to crenellate of 1385 has no necessary relationship to the beginning, end or duration of building works. Whittick's assessment is that it probably marks the end of a campaign possibly stretching back to the late 1370s; Dallingridge was selling manors elsewhere in the country in the years before this, possibly to finance the building works (Johnson *et al.* 2000: 31). Drury on the other hand views it as likely that building started

Fig. 3.31: Southern section of the east curtain wall showing different building seasons. Photo by Penny Copeland.

later than this and continued into the early 1390s. The length of the building campaign can be estimated at five to ten years. The stylistic uniformity of the building is evidence for its rapid completion, and our general impression of the form and size of the pig joints suggest this also.

It is worth noting broadly that little attention has been paid to the economics of the castle-building process at Bodiam, as opposed to the supposedly defensive or display elements of the final product. The lack of building accounts also means that any assessment of the cost of the castle must be an estimate. At the contemporary Cooling Castle, accounts for almost £600 survive and the whole building at Cooling may have cost over double this (Goodall 2011: 314). Bodiam castle is built of Wealden sandstone of generally good but occasionally variable quality (Fig. 3.20). The source is not certain but may well be from a quarry site some hundreds of metres to the north of the castle, where the sandstone ridge is close to the surface. Batches of highly variable quality were used; it would seem that a single quarry or outcrop produced batches of variable stone. There are twelve mason's marks described by Curzon (1926: 112) and we have observed at least another two.

Understanding the Bodiam Layout

In its broader outlines, elements of the Bodiam plan are quite standard for a later 14th-century building. The plan is centred around a ground floor hall with 'private' suites of rooms coming out from its upper end and a service range beyond the cross-passage, with triple doors leading to buttery, pantry and kitchen (for comparable examples see Wood 1965, and for the development of this plan see Gardiner 2000 and Johnson 2010b: 68-77). Other elements of the plan –

gatehouse, chapel, lodgings – are also to be found in most houses of similar date and social standing. There are however several elements of the Bodiam layout that are worth commenting on.

'Regularity' and integrated nature of the plan

As noted above, there are irregularities and apparent changes of mind in different elements of the castle. Nevertheless, the final result is a tightly integrated building, particularly on the east and south ranges of the castle. The plan is oriented to the cardinal points with a 1.2 degree of accuracy and the rectangle of the castle walls is almost perfect (Figs 3.4 & 3.5). Other later 14th-century buildings in south-east England are not so tightly integrated. The main domestic elements at Scotney lie in a solar-service range that runs across the middle of a roughly rhomboid enclosure with four corner towers, one of which survives. At Cooling the two courtyards cover a much larger area than at Bodiam; what remains of the curtain wall of the inner courtyard has few fenestrations and domestic buildings seem to have been built up against them. At Westenhanger the plan of the inner courtyard bears a superficial resemblance to Bodiam. Circular corner towers alternate with rectangular interval towers. However, the late medieval layout of Westenhanger is the result of piecemeal accretion rather than a single building campaign (Martin & Martin 2001).

In addition to the tightly integrated nature of the plan, the building is remarkably stylistically consistent. There is a range of different window and arch types including four-centred and segmented forms. Somebody standing in the inner courtyard at Bodiam would have been surrounded by ranges of doors and windows that would have been remarkably uniform. The most notable parallel here is Edward III's building in the upper court at Windsor, dating to the 1360s (Goodall 2011: 289). This building has a uniform and even monotonous series of very tall windows whose design and tracery are in the Perpendicular style. Goodall comments 'the regular proportions of the two-storey range enclosing the inner court are ultimately derived from the upper ward at Windsor'. The royal castle of Windsor is clearly a very different social level to Bodiam but the stylistic similarities are apparent. John Harvey has suggested that the design of Bodiam bears the influence of the architect/mason Henry Yevele. Yevele, like most master masons of his time, worked on a wide range of building projects from royal to gentry level and spanning both religious and domestic architecture (Harvey 1954: 358-66; Goodall 2011: 310-17).

On the other hand the uniformity of plan and architectural detail is less apparent on the west side of the building than on the east. The suite of private apartments of the hall clearly had a very regular design; the pattern of these designs is repeated in some elements on the west side. However, the west side is clearly not as regular, or at least is laid out to slightly different principles. The subsequent alterations on the west side make interpretation problematic here. In any case the inner walls are so ruinous as to make further comment difficult.

The closest parallels to the tightly integrated plan of Bodiam lie a little further afield: the later 14th-century castles of north-east England, particularly Wressle, Sheriff Hutton and Bolton. These castles were all of rectangular or subrectangular plan, they feature a multiplicity of lodgings, and the domestic ranges are integral to the external walls rather than simply being built up against them. Though their towers are rectangular or square rather than circular, they contain lodgings in a manner similar to Bodiam. Of these, Wressle and Sheriff Hutton were residences of the great Percy earls of Northumberland, but Bolton was built by Lord Scrope who was of a broadly comparable social standard to Dallingridge. Despite its bleak and imposing external appearance, and its lack of a moat and prominent gatehouse, the 'footprint' of Bolton is quite modest and of a comparable size to Bodiam.

The western range

The functions of the rooms in the west range of the castle remain uncertain. It was here that Douglas Simpson located accommodation for mercenaries, and following this line of thought, the southern room next to the kitchen has sometimes been misleadingly designated the 'servants' hall'. Though highly ruinous, enough remains of the inner walls to suggest that the fenestration and detailing of this part of the castle was conducted to the same integrated scheme as the rest, and with the same high standards of masonry and detailing. However, there are few windows piercing the western and north curtain walls, and the stairs on this side of the building are wooden flights rather than stone spirals. One possibility is that that the intended function of this area may have been unclear to the builders as they constructed the outer circuit. (An alternative possibility is that windows were excluded from this area as being the area adjacent to high ground and therefore considered most vulnerable to attack, or more broadly that given that the west curtain wall faced higher ground and the north-west approach, this façade was intended to have a more severe appearance). This is, of course, the one area of the interior of the castle where there may have been substantial post-1380s changes.

It is perfectly possible that the service rooms with large fireplaces had a range of uses. The fireplaces are so large as to suggest a kitchen but this may be extended to a brewery, oast, laundry or light industrial use for example; magnetic anomalies found during geophysical work indicate that either iron or ceramic production took place in the area between the western edge of the castle moat and the eastern edge of the village tenements though the date of this activity is not clear (see Chapter Four for further discussion). The GPR results indicate a series of features in this area, including a possible drain, and deep hearth (Fig. 3.10, D3 and D1 respectively).

The north range west of the gatehouse has been identified as stables, and the position is at first sight a logical one. However the doorways appear to be too narrow for this purpose, and the plinths for a suspended floor argue against this, although GPR anomalies indicate possible subsurface drains both here and on the other side of the gatehouse (Fig. 3.10, E1-E3 & F2). Indications in the GPR results of foundations of a cross wall between 'stables' and western service range should also be noted here (D4 & D5). There is also evidence for a large window with a window seat (Fig. 3.32) – an unusual feature for a stable. If the stables are indeed not within the central court, they must be elsewhere, and we suggest below that they may have been sited on the ridge to the north as part of a detached 'base court'.

Lack of a base court

Bodiam is unusual in, apparently, lacking a base or lower court. Contemporary structures in south-east England such as Cooling, Scotney, and Westenhanger all have a base court; even the local moated site at Iden, licenced to crenellate in 1318, has a second or base court outside the inner moated enclosure. Amberley, Scotney, Cooling and Farleigh Hungerford all have two courts, created in all three cases by the laying-out of a roughly quadrangular curtain wall and ranges of buildings around an earlier hall-service-chamber block, thus creating courtyards on both the front and back sides of the block. The little-studied Halnaker House appears to have a similar arrangement with a court to the south of the hall and a second area to the north (Emery 2006: 299, 342 and fig. 77). Further afield, Bolton in north Yorkshire lacks a base court but the other great later 14th-century castles of the north-east (for example Wressle and Sheriff Hutton) do not. Warkworth has two 'courts' in the sense of possessing both the very large and complex donjon on the motte and the hall-service-chamber block in the courtyard. Chris Currie, in specific reference to the late 14th-century Dartington Hall (2004), has argued that the use of base courts was not so widespread in the middle ages, but Emery (2007) is in fundamental disagreement. It might be considered puzzling then that Bodiam is of a single court plan.

One possible solution to this issue lies in the earthworks at the top of the hill. Named the 'Gun Garden', and interpreted as a viewing platform by the Royal Commission survey (Taylor *et al.* 1990), these earthworks probably mark the site of the earlier manor, as discussed in Chapters Two and Four. Documentary references indicate that the manorial court continued at this location into the 15th century (Johnson *et al.* 2000: 32). It is very possible, then, that this hilltop site served the functions that at other castles were carried out in the base court. They are admittedly quite a distance of c. 250 m from the castle. A possible alternative that has been mooted is that ancillary buildings including stables lay to the immediate north of the castle, underneath what was until 2015 the ticket office, but there is no archaeological evidence supporting such a suggestion.

If in fact the 'castle' of Bodiam is split between these two sites, then we might think of the inner courtyard, splendidly isolated within its moat and set apart from the rest of the landscape, in rather different terms: as a larger version of a gloriette as at Leeds and the northern French castle of Hesdin, or as an isolated courtyard-keep.

The northern gatehouse

We commented above on the changes of mind involved in the layout of the northern gatehouse. In its original conception, the northern gatehouse consisted of a single chamber whose vaults were ribbed and provided with 'murder holes'. This single chamber had a staircase

Fig. 3.32: Window seat and plinth in northern range often interpreted as stables. Photo by Penny Copeland.

Fig. 3.33: Suites at the upper end of the hall, viewed from the summit of the southern gatehouse; see also Fig. 3.7. Photo by Matthew Johnson.

turret to its east and a pair of projecting towers flanking the doorway. The external walls are well provided with gunports suitable for smaller hand guns. In these respects, the original conception of the gatehouse was very similar to the Westgate, part of the city walls of Canterbury, first documented in 1380 and completed by 1385; the gatehouse of Saltwood in Kent, built in the last two decades of the 14th century; and further afield, the gatehouse of Caldicot in Monmouthshire, another 1380s building (Goodall 2011: 309, 336). Both the Westgate and Saltwood are also associated with Henry Yevele (Harvey 1954: 358-66). Both the Westgate and Saltwood have slim towers that are circular rather than rectangular but otherwise the similarities are striking. Internally, above the ground floor, the northern gatehouse at Bodiam is divided into lodgings, a feature it shares with Saltwood and the southern gatehouse. Parts of the wooden portcullis for the northern gatehouse survive within its original groove and housing and have been radiocarbon dated to the later 14th century, suggesting that they are original (Martin & Martin 2005).

Suites above the hall

At the upper end of the hall, running up the east range, are two suites, each indicated by fenestration and other features and divided up by now-vanished timber partitions (Figs 3.7 & 3.33). Both consisted of an unheated outer room, an inner chamber with fireplace and window seat, and a further inner chamber with fireplace and window seat facing onto the courtyard. Both inner chambers have doors to rooms in the east tower, which do not intercommunicate. This is the only tower where these two levels do not have a connecting stair. The lower suite has a door into the chapel, while the upper suite has a northern window and door into a smaller chamber that looks down into the chapel. The two suites are linked with each other and with the hall solely through the now-destroyed spiral staircase at the junction of the two ranges.

The double nature is unusual for this date, and not easily explained. Pevsner, Goodall and Thackray all note this arrangement without proposing a convincing explanation. It is possible that Dallingridge and his wife Elizabeth Wardedieu had separate suites. The upper suite has a private chamber looking down into the chapel, a feature that Gilchrist (1999) has identified as characteristic of spaces for elite women. Gilchrist also observes that such women's spaces were often relatively inaccessible, and it is striking that the upper floors of the west tower confirm what Gilchrist would expect, although there is a wall-walk here linking the north and north-east towers. Enhanced provision for Wardedieu might also reflect her status in the area – the manor of Bodiam was originally that of her family, and only passed to Dallingridge on her father's death. However the upper suite also has the larger and more ornamented fireplace. A final possibility is that the lower suite was intended for a steward or other chief officer of the Dallingridge household.

However, the similar nature of these two suites may be overemphasised. Their plans are indeed very similar, but when considered as three-dimensional spaces, they might be considered as different. The lower suite had a relatively low ceiling and less lighting. The upper suite is more secluded in terms of access, had different access arrangements, at its northern end looked down into the chapel rather than having direct access to it. It does not have access to the south-east tower, as the lower suite does at its southern end. It was also probably open to the roof, suggesting a different, much airier impression to its internal spaces. It is important, then, to consider the lived experience of these spaces as much as their formal plan, a subject that Cooper will return to in Chapter Nine.

Great Hall and service area

The hall may have been heated by a central hearth; there are indications of anomalies in the GPR results which may relate to such a feature (A1 & A2 on Fig. 3.10). There may alternatively have been a fireplace embedded in the cross wall between the hall and chamber to its east. The presence or absence of an open hearth carries implications for the possible roof structure. The rest of the courtyard ranges had shallow-pitched roofs, but a steeply pitched roof, plus a louvre, would have been necessary over the hall to disperse the smoke. If, however, there was a fireplace over the hearth, the hall roof could also have had a shallow pitch. The appearance of the four ranges of the courtyard would be more uniform if that were the case. The hall may have had a screens passage rather than a cross-passage; at the lower end of the hall, a linear feature of low amplitude can be picked out (A4), which may indicate the presence of a wooden screen here. The GPR results in this area must however be treated with caution as remains of the later cottage in this area may have affected them.

The stone partition at the lower end of the hall, west of the cross-passage, has three openings which is a standard arrangement in halls of this time. The partition does not appear to extend up to the upper floor so it is assumed that a wooden partition would be in place. It has been assumed that this is a straightforward pantry/buttery arrangement with a central corridor between the two rooms linking cross-passage and kitchen, an arrangement that is characteristic of late medieval service areas. However, the pairs of windows on both sides suggest that each side was not a single pantry or buttery but rather subdivided into two rooms. The mortices in the stonework for a large cross beam between the windows would provide support for a partition. The subdivision could not continue on the first floor where a window is located, although the mortices do confirm the partitioning of the kitchen from the space over the pantry/buttery. In the courtyard wall of the upper floor room, there are two interesting features: a narrow window, at a lower level to the adjacent, larger, window to the west, and next to this window evidence for a small door in the style of latrine doors, and slightly overlapping the stone wall below, providing evidence that the wooden dividing wall or partition was narrow, or perhaps jettied out over the cross-passage (Fig. 3.34). The small door suggests either a 'pot' cupboard or a cupboard linked to the use of the hall, which raises the question in turn of how the upper floor was reached.

It seems possible that the narrow window could relate to a stair to access the gallery and the upper room or rooms above the service rooms. It therefore seems likely that such a stair might also serve the basement, which may therefore have served as a wine cellar for the hall. The GPR results (Fig. 3.10, B1-B3) may indicate evidence for this cellar.

The towers

No two towers are exactly alike. The north-east, east, south-east and south-west towers follow a common pattern of separate external access to the basement

Fig. 3.34: View down only narrow window jamb to west, and rebated door jamb to right. The door jamb sits slightly over the triple door wall at the end of the Great Hall. Photo by Penny Copeland.

and to the floor above. The south-east tower has a vaulted basement (Fig. 3.35). The vault is now largely destroyed but enough remains to indicate that it was finely constructed in a manner similar to the gatehouse vaults. The function of this room is not certain but its location at the lower end of the private apartments and just off from the Great Hall suggests it may have been a strongroom similar to rooms found at Penshurst, Ightham and Great Chalfield. The south-west tower has a well in the basement and a dovecote in its upper storey; this tower was heavily restored by Cubitt and later Curzon (Fig. 3.36). Large parts of the dovecote have been entirely rebuilt but enough remains to demonstrate that it was an original feature of the 1380s.

The west and north-west towers and the east and west rooms of the main gatehouse are entered at ground floor level and have a room below that level that has

Fig. 3.35: Vaulted basement room of the south-east tower. Photo by Penny Copeland.

Fig. 3.36: Interior of south-west tower, with two lodgings and a dovecote above, partially restored. Photo by Penny Copeland.

no stair access but does have at least one small window. These rooms are accessed by trapdoor. One of them may have functioned as a prison. The north-west tower cellar or basement is a completely circular room with two windows. It is commonly referred to as the Oubliette and it certainly has no evidence for access at present, but that was also the case during inspection of the cellar of the west room of the main gatehouse. These rooms have been accessed in the 20th century to construct the floors.

Each tower has a small turret rising from the roof housing the spiral staircase for access to the roofs. However, there is no clear pattern to their alignment; they are positioned differently on each tower. Three of the corner towers have angled walls to the courtyard side, except for the north-west tower which as noted above has a 'bite' taken out of it. The corner towers may have had conical roofs: a slate shaped for a conical roof was recovered from the moat in 1970 (Martin *et al.* 2011: 336). It is interesting that the crenellated design is repeated on the turrets despite there being no access to their roofs, and therefore having no practical purpose, but it serves as a repeated design motif on the chimneys and the fireplace of one of the great chambers (Fig. 3.37).

Lodgings

A series of rooms all have a window, a fireplace, and a latrine reached through a separate door or corridor. They are quite uniform in appearance, and while at other castles such as Bolton such rooms are paired or multiple in nature, we term them 'lodgings' following Faulkner's insight. Lodgings can be found in the north range east and west of the gatehouse, and all the towers (for example Fig. 3.35). The various rooms above the northern gatehouse can also be interpreted as lodgings, though they are not so self-contained, for example that containing the portcullis mechanism. Depending on how one counts, there are between 22 and 26 lodgings in the castle.

The wall-walks

The majority of wall-walks are accessed from only one adjacent tower. There are doors allowing access via the wall-walk from one tower to the next in only two cases, between the northern gatehouse and the north-west tower, and between the north-east and east towers. This latter case is interesting, because as noted elsewhere this tower has a distinctive arrangement where its upper storeys do not intercommunicate. The other exception is the wall-walk between the west and the south-west tower which has no access from the towers. There is the faint scar, and mortices with a gap for a trimmer, for a wooden stair rising from ground to upper floor level against the north side of the north wall of the kitchen; however this may be coincidental as evidence that the stair continued to the roof is lacking (Fig. 3.38). Slots on the towers for the leaded gutters of the roofs suggest that the roof structure rested directly on top of the wall-walk, and probably had lead gutter runs. In some places, fragments of lead are still visible in the slots with the use of binoculars. The curtain walls are about 1.84 m (6 ft) thick but it would be necessary to allow 38 cm (c. 16 inches) for the battlement screen. It is also necessary to allow for the rafters and lead roofs to rest upon the wall-walk. In addition, there are a number of chimney flues that rise up to form chimneys directly on the parapet each of the curtain walls (Fig. 3.33). All of these elements place restrictions on the space available on the wall-walks, and the chimneys blocked the wall-walks completely.

Fig. 3.37: Stair turret and chimney of the north-west tower. Photo by Penny Copeland.

Fig. 3.38: Floor joists with gap for trimmer and faint scar in surviving plaster for staircase from ground floor against the external northern wall of the kitchen. Note the rebuilt oven below. Photo by Penny Copeland.

The significance of these observations on wall-walk access is not clear, though it is a feature of some importance to 'defence versus status' enthusiasts. It might well have been perfectly possible to complete the whole circuit of the castle walls (with the exception of the main gatehouse) by walking on the roof, which would have had a very shallow pitch and for which the creasings for the lead cover are visible, rather than on the top of the masonry wall.

Profiles and mouldings

The shape of the fireplaces within the castle does suggest some organisation by status. There are three fireplaces with segmented arched heads (as opposed to shallow four-centred arches). Two of these are in the main rooms of the apartments and one of those is the only decorated fireplace in the castle. The third fireplace with segmented arched head is located in an apartment directly to the east of the gatehouse. A further obscurity with this fireplace is that it is the only fireplace in the building with a rounded profile. The associated window of this apartment is the window with the bar across to support the floor above. Both this window and the window in the apartment above are arranged to suggest a window seat.

Conclusion

The survey of Bodiam has produced a series of new insights into this complex and fascinating structure. First, we have identified irregularities and changes of mind underlying an apparently regular and even symmetrical structure. Second, we have made a series of observations that reinterpret Bodiam in terms of its size, accommodation, and position within a traditional narrative of late medieval buildings. Third, we have made a series of comments on the interpretation of the castle, comments that link Bodiam into a discussion of its importance within late medieval buildings generally.

The overall direction of this discussion has been to understand Bodiam in terms not just of its formal layout, but also in terms of the nature and subjective experience of the spaces within the castle walls. Ultimately a full understanding of Bodiam is not possible without first considering its wider landscape context, and moving on to a more serious and sustained commentary on the nature of lived experience within this space. These are the subjects of Chapters Four and Nine respectively.

4

BODIAM AS A LANDSCAPE OF WORK: TOPOGRAPHICAL AND GEOPHYSICAL SURVEY

Dominic Barker, Kathryn A Catlin, Matthew Johnson, Timothy Sly, Kristian Strutt[1]

Abstract. This chapter reports on a new, comprehensive geophysical and topographic survey of the Bodiam landscape. Features evident in the geophysical results emphasise that the landscape of Bodiam is much more than either military or recreational; rather, it was also a landscape of work, home to countless individuals who lived and laboured in this small part of the Rother Valley over the last two millennia and more. The landscape of Bodiam should be understood as a continuously occupied, multi-period site, a landscape of labour, movement, travel, commerce, and industry. The geophysical survey results allow us to consider the specific kinds of activities that took place across the landscape, and how built landscape features like the Roman road, the approaches to the castle, the mill pond, and the village earthworks shaped the experience of moving through and working with the land from the Roman occupation to today's National Trust property and park.

Introduction[1]

Previous chapters described how Bodiam gained its reputation as one of the most discussed and recognisable medieval castles in Europe. A large part of that recognition stems from the castle's distinctive position in the landscape. The castle and its moat lie to the north of and just above the River Rother and its floodplain (Fig. 4.1). The ground slopes up to the north and west of the castle, and the castle and moat are sited within a dip in the terrain. It is now well established that the landscape around Bodiam is the result of intense modification through human activity. Perhaps most obviously, depressions in the land around the castle include earthen banks holding back the moat, a mill pond, and a series of water features. Chapter Two established that the castle and its watery setting were inserted into a landscape that had already been managed or cultivated for millennia, and had hosted a ford and later a bridge, harbour, and associated settlement. Today's castle and its landscape are parts of the same whole, for one would not exist in the shape it does without the active presence of the other.

Chapters One and Two also outlined the important role of the landscape in the 'Battle for Bodiam' (Goodall 1998b), a debate over the castle's function and purpose, with wider resonance for the study of medieval archaeology and history. As we have seen, this debate is often presented in binary, either-or terms: either the castle is primarily military, a defence against the French, or primarily symbolic and to do with status, an old soldier's dream house. The materiality of the

---

1   The fieldwork reported on in this chapter was undertaken by approximately 90 students over three field seasons, 80 from Southampton and 10 from Northwestern, under the supervision of Kristian Strutt, Timothy Sly and Dominic Barker. Kristian Strutt prepared the more detailed report on which this chapter is partly based, available at http://sites.northwestern.edu/medieval-buildings/. Kathryn Catlin took part in the fieldwork and prepared drafts of this chapter, which were revised and edited by Strutt, Sly, Barker and Johnson. Thanks also to James Cole, David Underhill, and numerous undergraduates for significant assistance with fieldwork.

LIVED EXPERIENCE IN THE LATER MIDDLE AGES

Fig. 4.1: Bodiam Castle in its landscape; photo facing south from the Gun Garden. The National Trust facilities can be seen in front of the castle; the floodplain and railway track behind. The village of Ewhurst Green is on the horizon, at the summit of the slope. Photo by Matthew Johnson.

landscape is an important factor in these arguments: does it provide an adequate view of the river and surrounding countryside for advance warning should the French invade? Is it instead a contrived, ornamental landscape designed to impress high-status visitors as well as manorial tenants?

This chapter will suggest a third view: that whatever else it was, the immediate landscape of Bodiam should be also viewed as a landscape of work. This orientation to the landscape helps us to understand the castle not simply as an elite site, but as it was experienced every day by the people who moved through and around it, people of all ages, social classes and identities. The landscape was shaped and used by a variety of individuals and groups, including a landscape setting that inherited important elements from previous centuries. The landscape of the 1380s was composed with reference to practices and

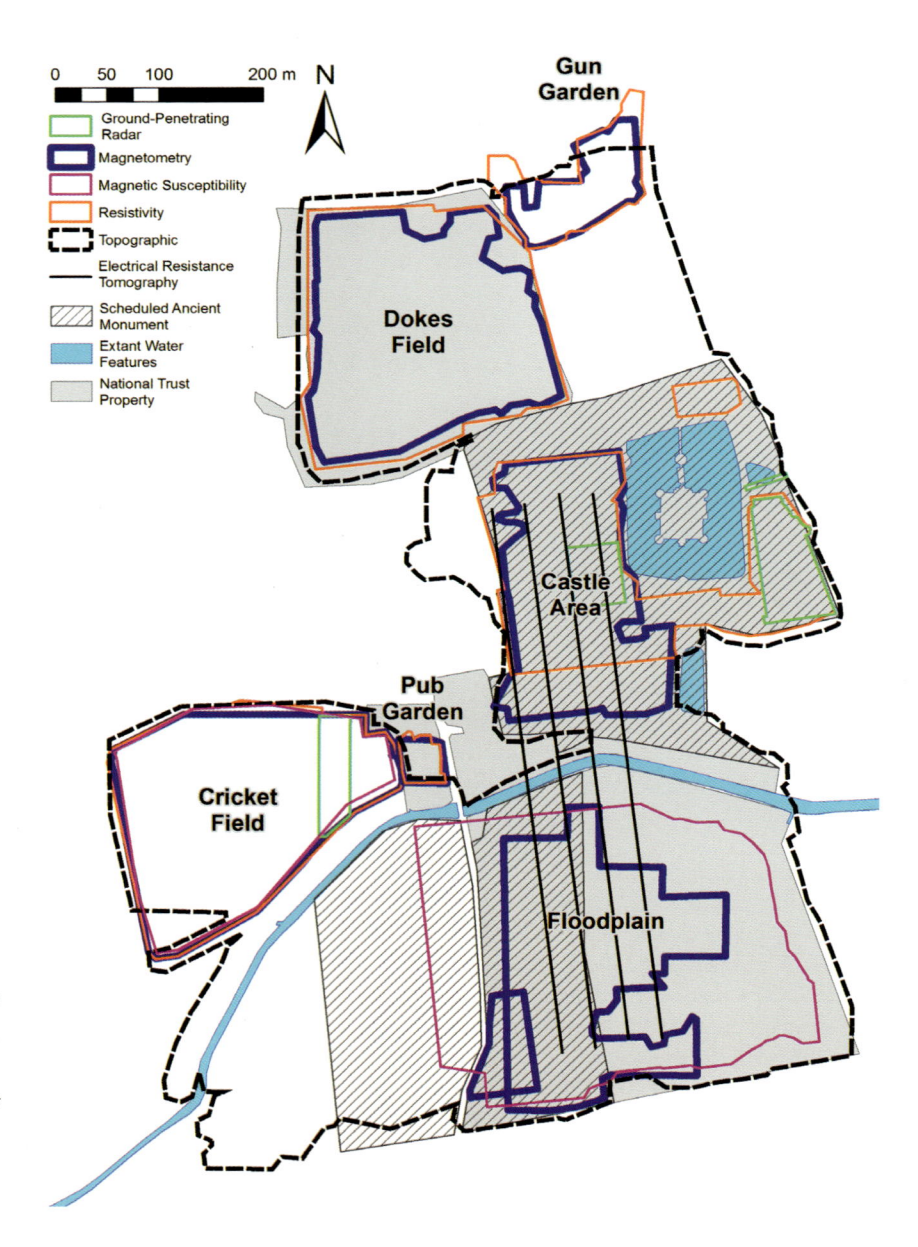

Fig. 4.2: Map of the Bodiam landscape, showing survey areas, the National Trust property, and the Scheduled Ancient Monument boundaries.

52

institutions that had practical, quotidian and economic roles – the mill and mill pond, the dovecote, the older manorial site, the harbour or flote, the north-south route way and its crossing of the River Rother. It is shaped, and was shaped, by the everyday practices of the inhabitants of the village and wider landscape over the long term, as well as by the conscious intentions of Dallingridge and his immediate household in the 1380s and later landowners.

Despite the landscape's recognised importance to the way people understood and experienced Bodiam in the past, no complete geophysical or topographic survey had been carried out until the current project. The most extensive survey to date was performed in 1988 by the Royal Commission on the Historical Monuments of England (RCHME, now part of Historic England), and resulted in a hachured plan and interpretation of the complex earthworks surrounding the castle. This interpretation claimed to establish

> *without doubt that the majority of the extensive earthworks around the castle are the remains of elaborate gardens and water features all intended to enhance the visual appearance of the building*

(Taylor *et al.* 1990: 155; see Figs 1.2 & 2.6, this volume)

Our detailed geophysical and topographic survey builds upon this work, and reveals details of the landscape that may be obscured or unnoticed in the course of a walking survey. These details speak to the everyday labour performed by women and men of different classes and occupational groups over the course of centuries.

The fieldwork was carried out in the Bodiam landscape by researchers from the University of Southampton and Northwestern University, in partnership with the National Trust, between 2010 and 2012 (Fig. 4.2; Table 4.A). We collected centimetre-accuracy Geographic Positioning System (GPS) data to generate a topographic map of the entire area owned and managed by the National Trust as well as several surrounding properties, including a portion of Court Lodge (the 'Gun Garden' or 'Viewing Platform'), the cricket field to the south-west of Bodiam village, the property behind the Old Rectory, and the floodplain south of the River Rother. Dokes Field, the cricket pitch, and the floodplain are new additions to areas surveyed that were not a part of the RCHME work. The magnetometry and earth resistance surveys provide new data to describe the buried archaeological landscape of Bodiam, which would not otherwise be revealed without intensive excavation.

Bodiam Today

The area now owned and managed by the National Trust consists of 27.84 hectares (68.05 acres) to the north and south of the River Rother near Robertsbridge, East Sussex, an area that has been exploited and inhabited by humans from at least the Bronze Age (c. 2500 BCE) to the present day (Fig. 4.3).

Today, a visitor to the castle driving north from Hastings crosses the River Rother at Bodiam bridge. The present bridge was constructed in 1797, but a bridge was first constructed here prior to 1230 (James & Whittick 2008: 23). The visitor turns right into the car park across the lane from the Castle Inn. The visitor facilities and car park sit atop the site of the medieval wharf or flote, on the north bank of the Rother. After parking, the visitor heads to the east, walks along the southern edge of a wide, deep depression, now the overflow car park (sometimes known as the 'tilt-yard', after Curzon's designation, but in actuality the medieval mill pond), and a World War II pillbox immediately above and to the north of it. The visitor then turns sharply north, past the ticket office and then approaches the castle and moat from the south.

The castle is at a low point in the terrain. A series of broad, deep depressions known as the 'cascade', formerly one or more ponds, runs downhill towards the north-west corner of the moat, and another pond lies east of the moat. To the north, a sloping vineyard rises behind the National Trust offices to Court Lodge on the summit of the ridge, gaining 30 m in elevation over a horizontal distance of 300 m (Figs 4.4 & 4.5). The Court Lodge property (under private ownership) contains the earthwork often called the Gun Garden, the edge of which is accessible via a public footpath from the north-east corner of the Trust property. To the west of the vineyard is the rolling expanse of Dokes Field, also spelled variously as Doke's, Dokes', Doakes Field or Doakes Meadow. Bodiam parish church lies 250 m north of Dokes, and another 500 m north-west of the church is a medieval moated site which has sometimes been incorrectly identified as the earlier manor site, though excavations by David Martin in 1970 showed that the site dates to no earlier than the 13th century (Martin 1990).

After strolling around the grounds and the slopes north of the castle, the visitor might return south to the car park by way of the road, passing through Bodiam village. Houses line the road to the east, and to the west a modern village green lies just north of Castle Inn, now encircled by homes of recent construction. To the west

Table 4.A: Summary of geophysical survey techniques. See Appendix Two for more details of the techniques.

Technique	Details	Dim.	Instrument	Depth BGS	Locations	Grid Size	Interval Spacing	Transect Spacing	Direction
Topography	Uses GPS signals and/or laser ranging to create a precise 3D map of the land surface	3D	GPS Rover + base station Leica TC 307 Total Station	0 m	Entire landscape	N/A	5 m	5 m	N/A
Magnetometry (Gradiometry)	measures changes in the earth's magnetic field and is best at detecting metallic, burnt, or disturbed features	2D	dual sensor Bartington Instruments 602-1 fluxgate gradiometer	Up to 0.5 m	See Fig. 4.2	30 m	0.25 m	0.5 m	bi-directional
Earth resistance	passes an electrical current through the ground and compares the earth resistance to a background reading	2D	Geoscan Research RM-15 50-cm twin probe	0.5 to 0.75 m	See Fig. 4.2	30 m	0.5 m	0.5 m	bi-directional
GPR	detect changes in the density of buried material based on the time it takes for a microwave pulse to be reflected back to the instrument	3D	500 MHz Sensors & Software Noggin Plus 200 MHz GSSI	up to 2 m up to 4 m	Castle & vicinity Cricket field	N/A N/A	0.05 m 10 m	0.5 m 10 m	uni-directional bi-directional
Magnetic Susceptibility	measures magnetic flux density at point locations (similar to a metal detector)	2D	Bartington Instruments MS-2	up to 0.06 m	Floodplain & cricket field	N/A	10 m	10 m	N/A
ERT	measures earth resistance along a transect	2D vertical	Allied Associates Tigre 64-probe	up to 20 m	west of castle to floodplain across Rother	550 m linear	2 m	variable	N/A

Fig. 4.3: Features in the Bodiam landscape. Photos by Matthew Johnson (bridge), Kat Catlin (others).

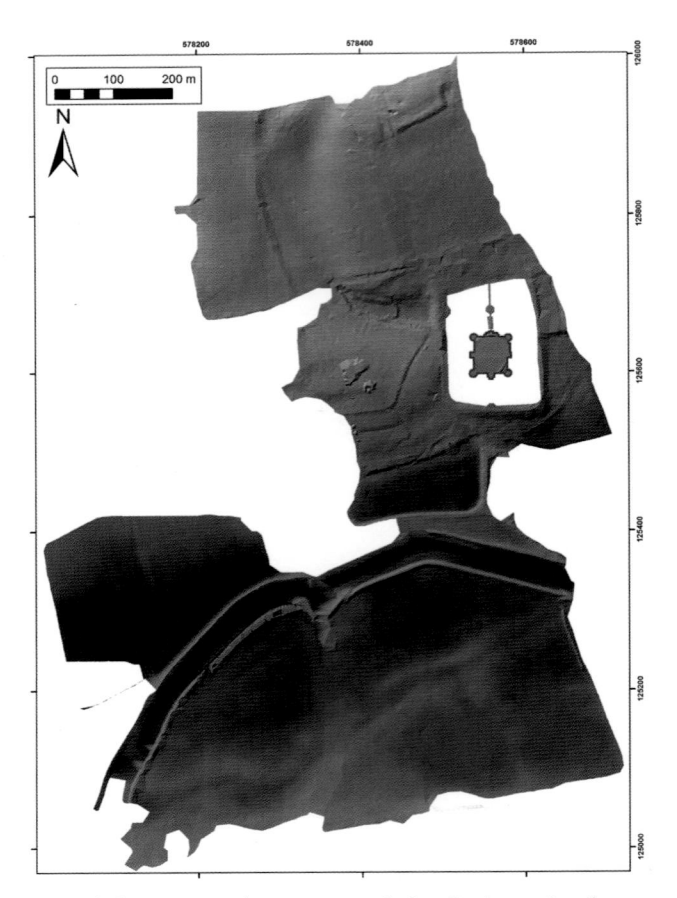

Fig. 4.4: Topographic survey of the Bodiam landscape (hillshaded Triangulated Irregular Network (TIN)).

of the Inn lies a flat, grassy floodplain that serves as a park and cricket ground for the community. From Bodiam bridge, the view opens up to the south and east. Two fields in the floodplain are separated by the road south of the River Rother. The western field is often used as a hay meadow. The field to the east is now owned by the National Trust, and within it lie archaeological remains of Romano-British origin which were partly excavated in the late 1950s (anonymous 1959-60; Lemmon & Darrell Hill 1966; Johnson *et al.* 2000: 26-7). The Kent & East Sussex Railway follows the southern edge of the floodplain; beyond the tracks, the Weald rises once more amid rolling fields and woods to the south, with the church and settlement of Ewhurst Green strung out along the ridge, and far away to the east the flat plains of Romney Marsh roll away towards the sea.

Bodiam is located in an ecological boundary zone, between the High Weald to the north and west, and the floodplain of the River Rother leading to Romney Marsh and east. The underlying geology is for the most part sandy-silty soils, with some Wadhurst Clay and Ashdown sandstone bedrock emerging at higher elevations (see Fig. 12.1, this volume). The floodplains and lower areas near the river are primarily alluvial deposits, with some inclusions of buried Bronze Age peat (Burrin & Scaife 1988; Waller *et al.* 1988; Johnson *et al.* 2000; see also Chapters Two & Five, this volume).

Fieldwork at Bodiam, 2010-2012

In 2010, the University of Southampton began work at Bodiam in partnership with the National Trust. Matthew Johnson's move to the United States in 2011 brought Northwestern University onto the team, forming a transatlantic collaborative project between the three institutions. Survey seasons in the spring of 2010 and 2011, and the summer of 2012, have revealed the layered and complex buried history of the Bodiam landscape. The full survey of the landscape, largely carried out by undergraduate students from Southampton and Northwestern, has significantly added to our knowledge about the many and varied human activities in which the landscape has participated over the last two millennia.

Survey techniques included topographic survey, magnetometry (gradiometer survey), magnetic susceptibility, earth resistance, electrical resistivity tomography (ERT), and Ground Penetrating Radar (GPR) (Fig. 4.2; Table 4.A). The geophysical survey covered 17 hectares, including the floodplain to the south of the River Rother, Trust-owned property to all sides of the moat, the Gun Garden, Dokes Field, and the modern cricket field. The topographic survey covered these areas as well as the vineyard between the Trust office and the Gun Garden, a portion of the rear lot of the Old Rectory, the car park, and the cultivated field south of the Rother (Fig. 4.4). In the cricket field (outside the scheduled area), the survey was followed up with limited augering. The project also included a full building survey of the standing castle, including three-dimensional modelling of the building and some GPR and coring inside the structure (see Chapters Three & Five). The topographic and geophysical data were processed in Geoplot, GPR Slice, and Res2DInv, and imported into ArcGIS for analysis. For more information about the geophysical techniques, refer to Appendix Two.

For each survey, we have presented images here both with and without interpretive overlay. Interpretations are visualised as dashed lines and ovals; the same features are marked on all plots to facilitate comparison between the results of various geophysical techniques. The digitised plots are also presented, along with a more detailed and technical discussion of the results, in a different, more complex format, in the longer 'grey literature' report that accompanies this chapter (Barker *et al.* 2012, available at http://sites.northwestern.edu/medieval-buildings/).

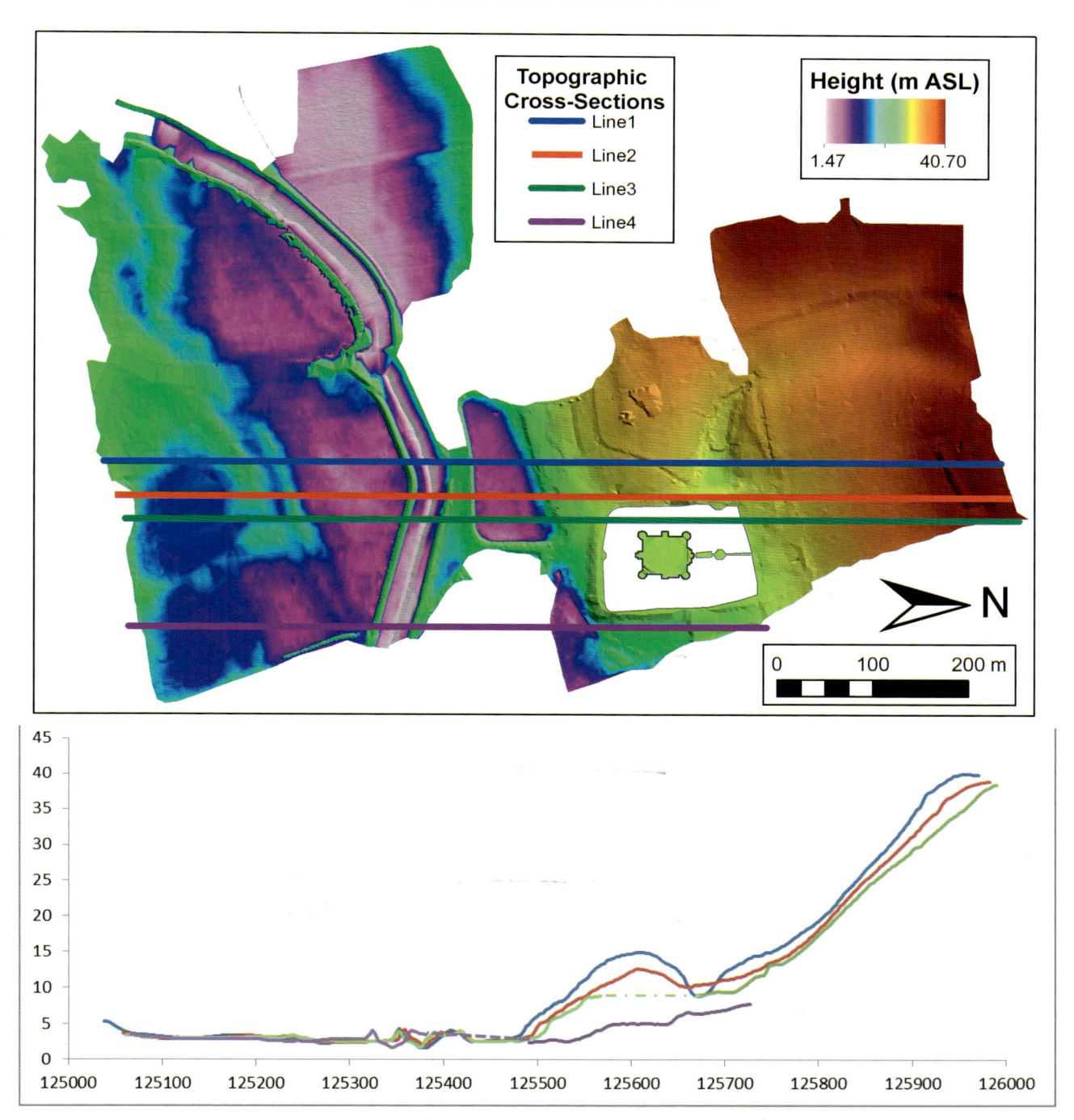

Fig. 4.5: A. Topography (TIN) of the Bodiam landscape. B. Exaggerated vertical profile of the Bodiam landscape. Scale in metres.

In magnetometry results, darker areas have a positive magnetic gradient; lighter areas have a negative gradient. Dipoles, or point locations showing both strong positive and negative readings, usually indicate buried ferric (iron) material. In earth resistance results, darker areas have higher electrical resistance while lighter areas are of lower resistance. Parallel linear anomalies of high and low resistance tend to indicate bank and ditch features. Magnetometry and resistivity earth resistance surveys can detect buried features up to about 50 cm below the surface, or in some cases up to 1 m. In GPR results, darker areas correspond to reflectors (materials denser than their surroundings, such as wall foundations or roads). The depth of GPR slices is provided in the figure captions.

The following descriptions are organised roughly by time period. However, geophysical anomalies cannot be dated with certainty in the absence of accompanying excavation data. In some cases the data from historical sources, previous excavation work, landscape survey, and geophysical survey point to multiple possible interpretations for the date of a single feature. Some anomalies are therefore discussed in multiple sections

Fig. 4.6: *Floodplain of the River Rother. a) Topographic (TIN), showing locations of ERT transects and probable palaeochannel. b) LiDAR data with palaeochannel outlined (© Environment Agency). c) Magnetometry survey; palaeochannel emphasised in dark black. The boxes on Figs 4.6a and 4.6b correspond to the outline of Fig. 4.6c. d) Results of ERT survey. Areas of high resistance corresponding to the probable palaeochannel are circled.*

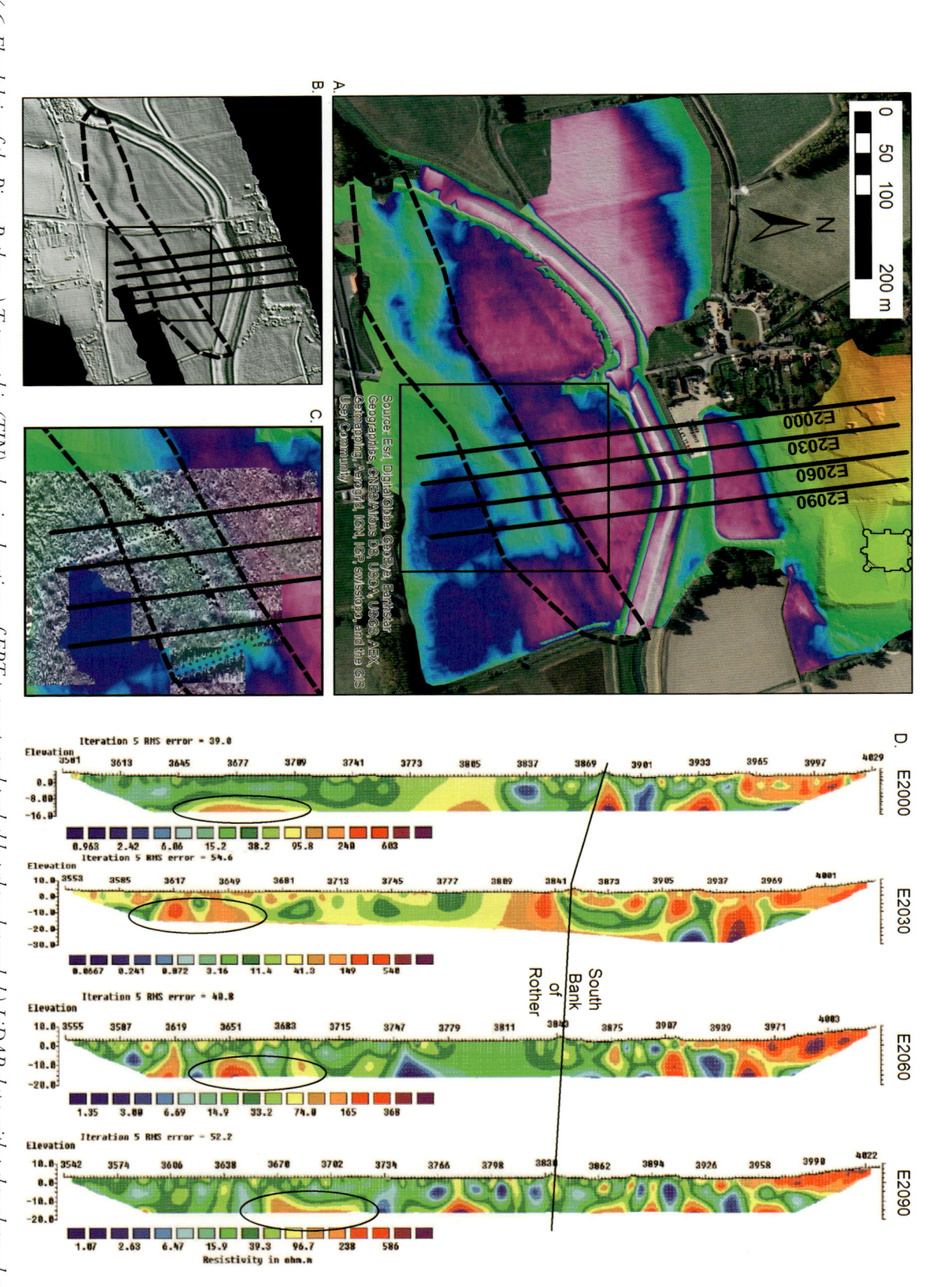

58

(as with certain features in Dokes Field), or discussed in terms of multiple periods within a given section (as with the Gun Garden).

The Prehistoric Landscape

The river and floodplain of the Rother is a dynamic estuarine environment, leading from the high weald through Romney Marsh and out to the sea near the port at Rye (see Fig. 2.1, this volume). The wetlands ecosystem to the south of Bodiam Castle has always been changing, as it continues to do today. Stratigraphic and botanical analysis of pollen cores in the vicinity of the castle suggests that from the middle Holocene through to the Bronze Age, a stable landscape of woodland and peat bogs dominated the valley. Late in the Bronze Age, environmental and climatic changes pushed the landscape in the direction of alluvial instability. Up to 10 m of alluvial deposits accumulated in the river valleys over about two thousand years as significant amounts of soil were transported down the river from the surrounding hills. The modern, more stable estuarine environment developed atop these thick layers of prehistoric peat and alluvium, a combination that encourages the emergence of freshwater springs where the water table is high. Springs within low basins tend to lead to the development of ponds, which may have made this location especially attractive for the establishment of a settlement, and later a moated castle (see Chapter Five, this volume).

The River Rother

The path of the Rother has meandered across the floodplain for thousands of years. The topographic survey of the floodplain directly south of the castle shows evidence of a palaeochannel in the form of a slight hollow flanked by slightly raised banks, stretching south-west to north-east across the field (Fig. 4.6). The channel corresponds to a linear magnetic anomaly in the gradiometer survey, and is also visible in the publicly available LiDAR data produced by the Environment Agency (Fig. 4.6b). The palaeochannel is virtually invisible to the naked eye, and is probably comprised of the silt and sand of a former riverbed; the relict peat bog to either side of the ancient channel has since deflated and sunk, leaving the former channel and its banks now higher than the surrounding ground surface (Casper Johnson, pers. comm.). The results of our ERT survey are consistent with this interpretation of the river's dynamic movements: several high resistance anomalies, suggesting sandy riverine deposits, are apparent approximately 200-250 m to the south of the current riverbed, corresponding to the linear feature visible in the topographic data (Fig. 4.6d). Though we cannot ascertain the temporal sequence of the river's meandering from the geophysical data, knowledge of the river's approximate previous locations help to contextualise the location and type of activities that took place on and around the river during the prehistoric and Roman periods. This provides a more secure context for the Roman settlement that was located on the floodplain, and also helps us envision a dynamic estuarine context for the later medieval and modern periods.

Bronze Age peat

The iron-rich peat bogs that dotted the early landscape of Bodiam may have served as a source of iron ore for prehistoric, Roman, and later populations. Gradiometer survey in the cricket field revealed numerous positive and dipolar anomalies that resembled the signature of archaeological kiln features. However, augering at several positive anomalies corresponding to points of low resistance showed that they were caused by deeply buried (approximately 2 m below ground surface) iron-rich peat dating to the Bronze Age or earlier, consistent with geomorphological investigations and core sampling (Fig. 4.7; Burrin & Scaife 1988; see also Chapter Five, this volume). Dipolar or positive magnetic anomalies seen elsewhere in the Bodiam floodplain may likewise indicate buried peat rather than archaeological kilns, hearths or other human-created features.

The Roman Landscape

A Roman settlement was located in the floodplain along the south bank of the ancient channel of the River Rother, partially within the area of our survey (Fig. 4.3). Field walking and excavations through the 20th century have uncovered pottery scatter and building debris, as well as some evidence for ironworking and the possible presence of a port serving the *Classis Britannica* fleet (anonymous 1959-60; Puckle 1960; Lemmon & Darrell Hill 1966; Johnson *et al.* 2000: 26-7; Thackray & Bailey 2007: 6; Drury & Copeman 2016: 27-32).

Magnetometry survey along the Rother floodplain south of the castle provided evidence that is consistent with the location of the Roman settlement (Fig. 4.8; see also Kellala 2013). The location of magnetic anomalies interpreted as kilns roughly corresponds to find spots of Roman material collected over the course of the 20th century (Lemmon & Darrell Hill 1966) although, again, dipolar anomalies may also be associated with the buried natural iron-rich peat formations common in the area. The proximity of the site to the East Sussex

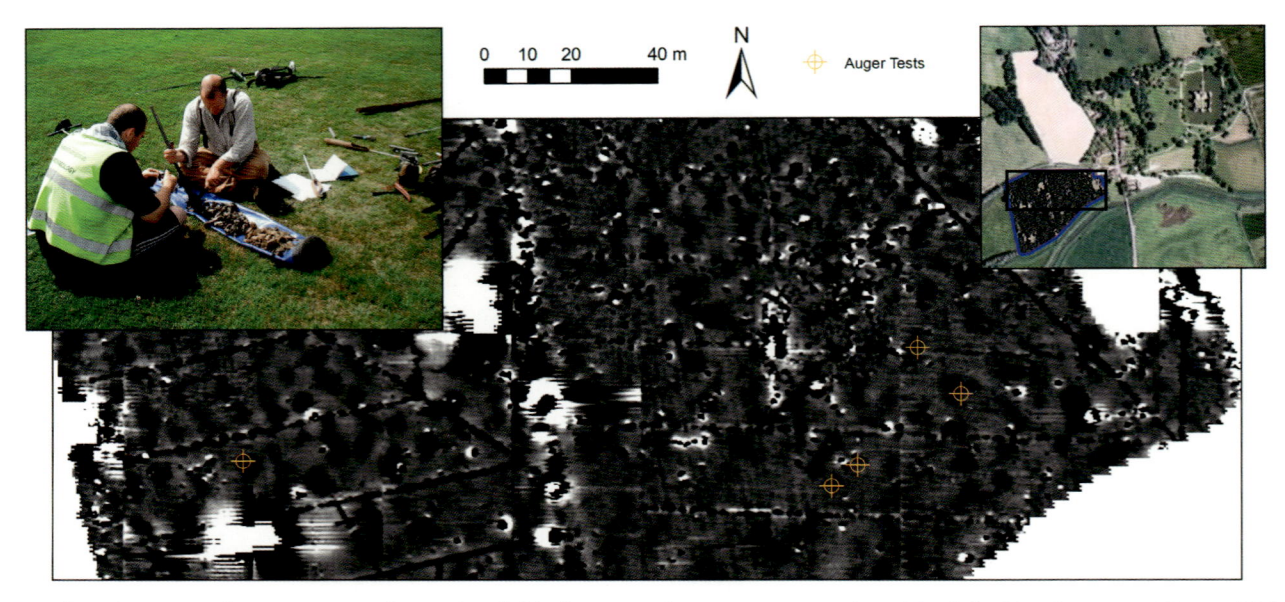

Fig. 4.7: Location of auger tests in the cricket field, shown with magnetometry data. Top left: Kris Strutt and James Miles examine a core. See also Fig. 4.13 below.

Railway further complicates the interpretation of magnetic anomalies in the survey results, such as the branching magnetic anomalies in the south-west corner of the site. These probably represent ferrous runoff from iron infrastructure of some sort – but whether these reflect Roman era iron processing or the modern operation of the railway is not possible to determine from the geophysical evidence. Earth resistance survey was not conducted in this part of the floodplain due to the extremely wet conditions.

The Roman road

The road that currently serves Bodiam village and castle also dates to the Roman period. North of the village, the Roman road originally cut through Dokes Field; some time during the early medieval period, it appears to have been diverted to its present track, skirting what may at the time have been a green (Drury & Copeman 2016, 41).

Geophysical survey in Dokes Field indicates the location of the Roman road, following the contour of the field in a north-south direction (Fig. 4.9). The location of this road is consistent with prior geophysical survey of the area performed in 2010 by the Hastings Area Archaeological Research Group (Cornwell *et al.* 2010). The road enters the field at the highest point along its northern boundary. As it continues south, the road does not simply consist of a single track, as it might appear in a walking survey. The road instead appears to split into two routes about 100 m after it enters the field. The western branch continues south and is aligned towards the road through Bodiam village. The second, fainter branch of the road heads to the south-east. Although fainter in the geophysics, it is this eastern fork of the road that is prominent in the topographic survey (Fig. 4.4).

The date of this eastern branch is not certain. If it is Roman, and continued through the modern National Trust property on the same alignment, it would pass through the back lot of the Old Rectory (not far from the location where pre-Roman or Roman cinerary urns were found in 1902) (Whistler 1940; Johnson *et al.* 2000: 113) towards the modern car park and general area of the harbour. However, no evidence of such an alternate pathway is visible in the geophysical results to the west or south-west of the castle, though admittedly any such evidence may have been obscured by more recent activity. It is therefore possible that the eastern branch of the road could also be of more recent date, and below we will discuss the possibility that it is part of the approach to the castle laid out in the 1380s.

In the south-west corner of Dokes Field one can make out three sides of a subrectangular feature (Figs 4.9a & 4.9b). We discuss this feature below in the context of the 'funnel' feature it appears to underlie, but we should note at this point that it may well be late prehistoric/early Roman in date, particularly given its proximity to the cinerary urns noted above.

The Medieval Landscape: Before the Castle

Bodiam Castle was constructed in the 1380s within an already complex medieval landscape. There was a manor at Bodiam by 1086, as noted in the Domesday Book. The moated site approximately 1 km to the north

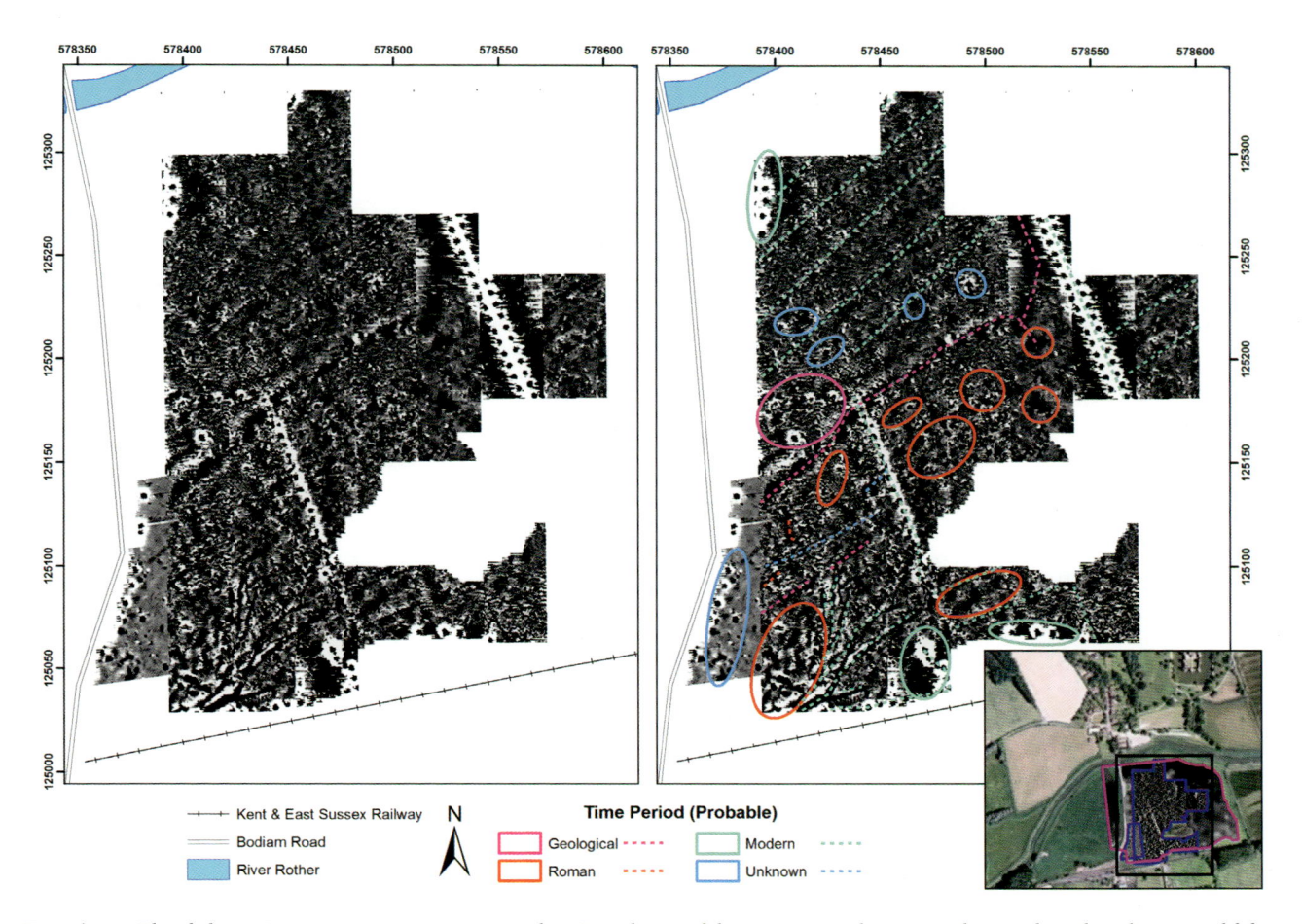

Fig. 4.8a: Floodplain: Magnetometry survey results. Dipolar and linear anomalies near the road and railway could be related to either modern or ancient industry. Other modern features are likely field drains or utilities. The probably relict channel of the River Rother is marked in pink (see Fig. 4.6).

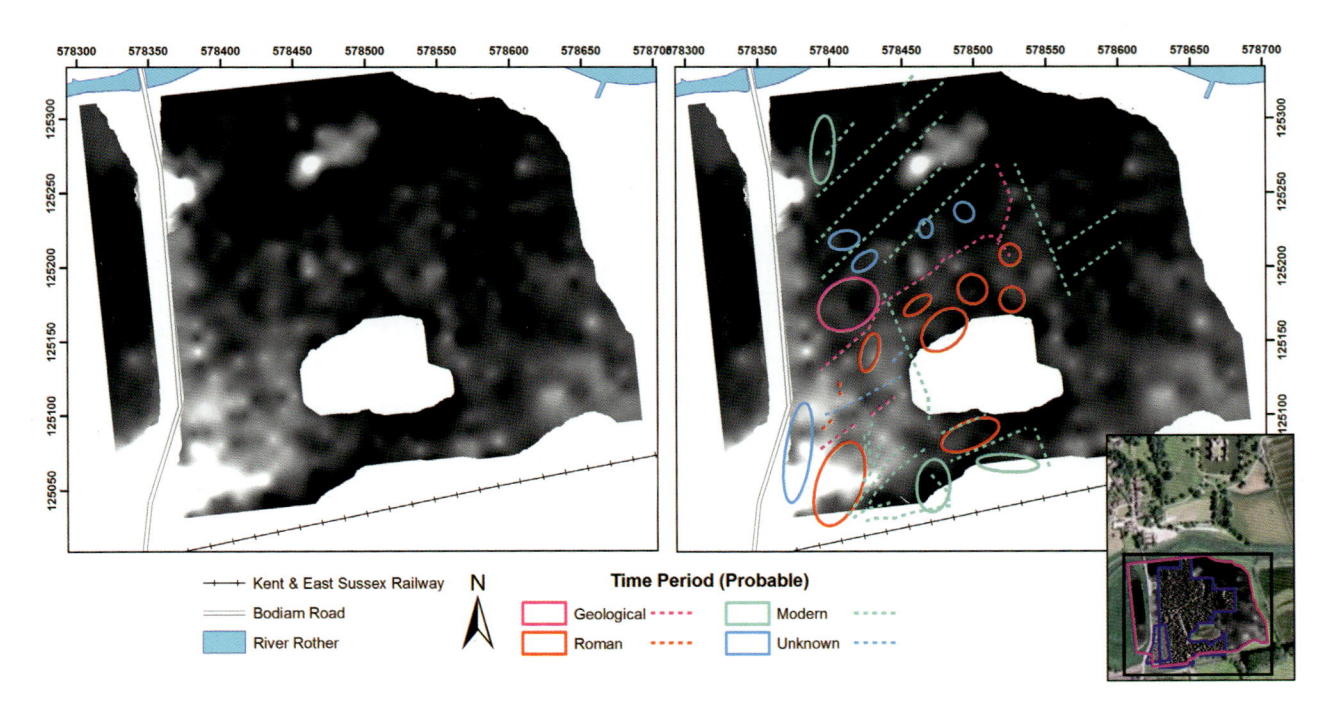

Fig. 4.8b: Floodplain: Magnetic susceptibility survey results. The ancient riverbed is faintly visible along with evidence of industrial activity beside the road.

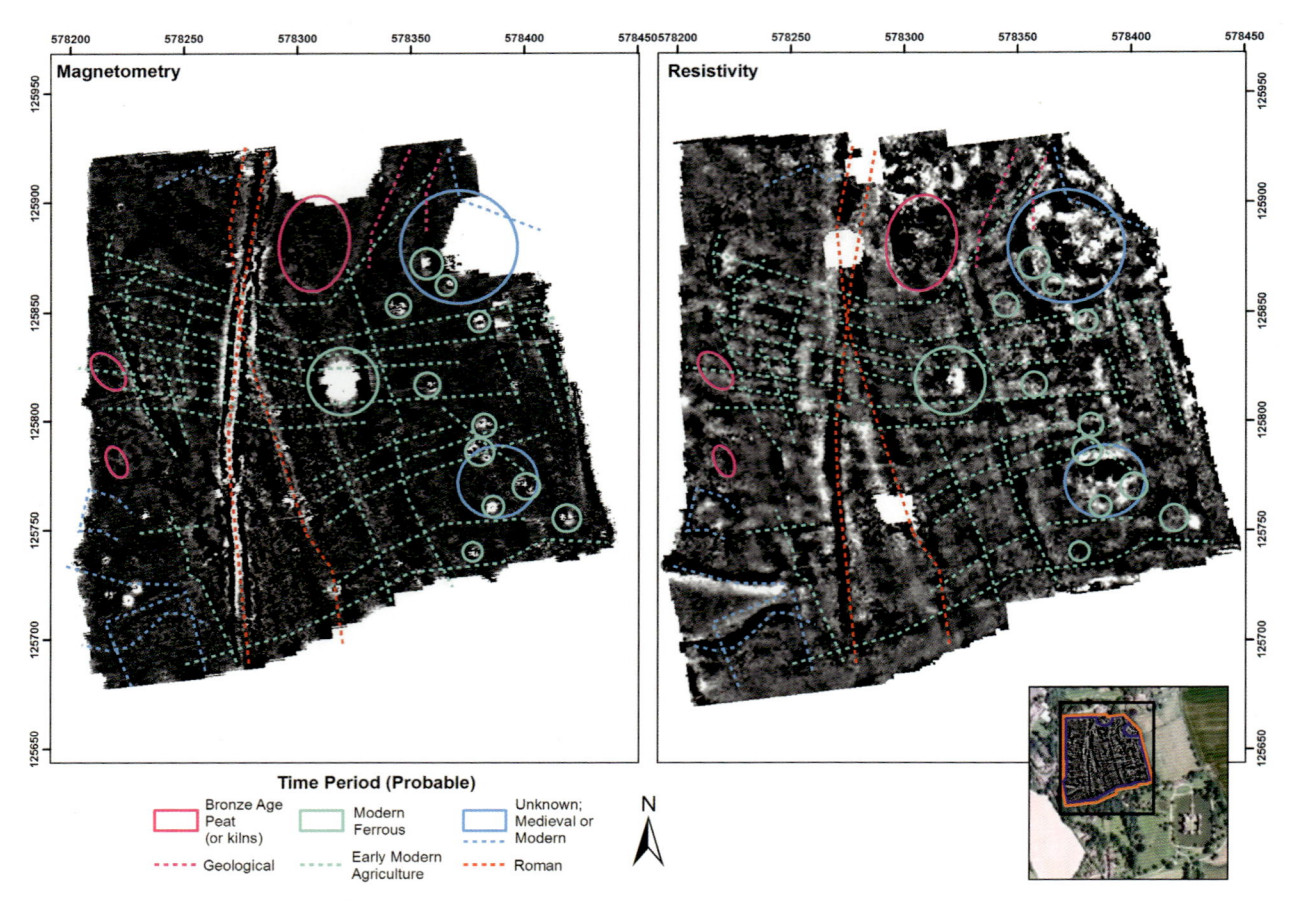

Fig. 4.9a: Dokes Field: Interpreted magnetometry and earth resistance survey results.

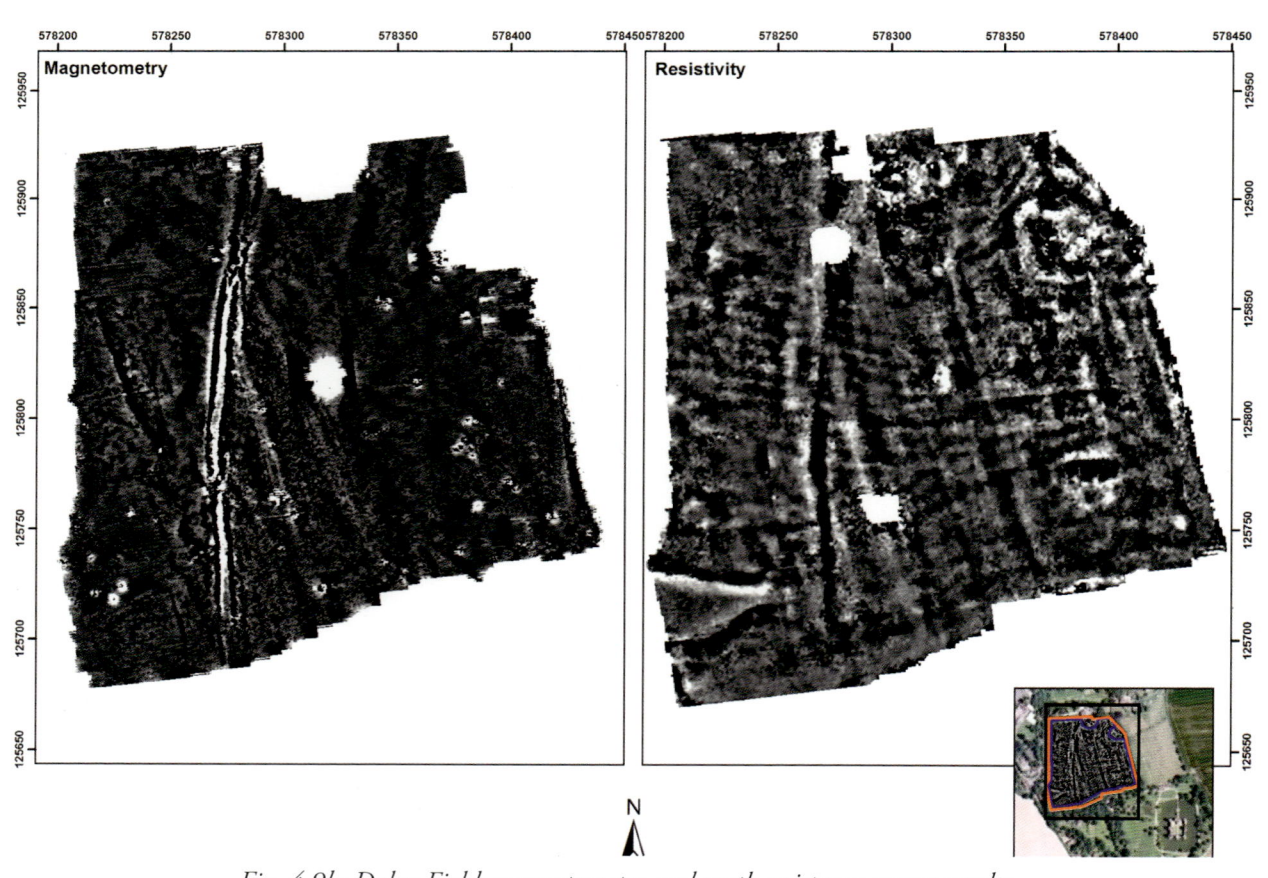

Fig. 4.9b: Dokes Field: magnetometry and earth resistance survey results.

of the castle (Fig. 4.3) has sometimes been suggested as the site of the manorial hall, but it dates to no earlier than the late 13th century (Darrell Hill 1960-61; Martin 1990: 97-8; Johnson *et al.* 2000: 30-3). The hall was more probably located at Ewhurst (Drury & Copeman 2016: 38). The de Bodiam family held lands at Bodiam from c. 1166, later passing through marriages to the Sywell and Wardedieu families. Bodiam village may have been founded before the castle's construction (Johnson *et al.* 2000), and the site of Bodiam church, located along the road connecting the village to both Court Lodge and the moated site, also pre-dates the castle. There is also some evidence for a medieval farmstead on the other side of the River Rother (Thackray & Bailey 2007: 13).

The 'Gun Garden'/'Viewing Platform'

The most discussed and controversial aspect of the Bodiam landscape may be the Gun Garden, also known since the RCHME work as the Viewing Platform. The Gun Garden is located on the Court Lodge property at the top of a steep rise about 300 m north of the castle, and has been variously interpreted as the location of a manor house prior to the castle's construction, the location of stables and ancillary buildings during the castle's use, a feature intended for observation of the castle landscape (hence, Viewing Platform), or the site of military emplacements associated with the English Civil War (hence, Gun Garden, despite a lack of evidence for fighting in the vicinity of Bodiam during the conflict: Curzon 1926: 77). A 1730 map shows an orchard and landscape garden in this space, which was probably constructed in the late 17th century by Samuel Hyland, to whom Court Lodge was sold in 1645. It is therefore likely that the present form of the Gun Garden, including surface features, geophysical anomalies, and possibly even its name, may be due in large part to 17th-century landscaping (Drury & Copeman 2016: 130-5).

The geophysical survey results for this area were difficult to interpret, and did not reveal any conclusive evidence of structures in this area (Fig. 4.10), although the edge of the platform is prominent in the topographic survey (Fig. 4.4). More detailed geophysical survey and excavation may yet reveal additional information about the history of the platform's use. Our results do suggest that the sand and soils of the Gun Garden have been considerably disturbed, subject both to landscape alterations by property owners and to high levels of erosion. There is some suggestion of possible drains (areas of low resistance) running north-south through the eastern end of the area. Modern electrical lines or piping and other recent metallic debris obscure any evidence of other archaeological features in the magnetometer results. The survey of adjacent areas of Dokes Field suggests that the platform may have at some point in the past extended through the current wooded area into Dokes (the circular anomaly here could also be associated with trees, perhaps coppicing: Fig. 4.9).

A portion of the Gun Garden was excavated in 1961. This excavation has repeatedly been cited as archaeological evidence for the suggestion that a former manor house of Bodiam was located on the hilltop (e.g. Taylor *et al.* 1990: 157; Johnson *et al.* 2000: 30, 33). A three-page report of excavations at Court Lodge and the moated site to the north was published in the *Battle and District Historical Society Transactions* in their 1960-61 issue. The report is concise, contains no maps or drawings of the site, and describes the excavation as

> *a main trench driven through the ditch and embankment of the earthwork as far as a circular depressed area in the middle, and four small subsidiary trenches running north and south across the southern edge of the embankment.*

The excavation exposed 'the foundation stones of a narrow roughly-made wall' in all of the trenches, along with several floors and some tiles, charcoal, ash, and other evidence of a structure, dated by the excavators to the late 13th or 14th century. A hearth was located 'in the most westerly of the subsidiary trenches' (Darrell Hill 1960-61: 22-3). This collection of walls and artefacts could easily be associated with a stable, barn or other industrial or agricultural outbuilding.

The geophysical results contain some ambiguous evidence that is in line with the reported excavation findings. Little evidence of wall features is evident in the geophysical results, though there is a very slight suggestion of a magnetic rectilinear feature along the eastern boundary of the property. Its small size suggests a shed or byre of unknown date. If a manor house was located close to the modern structures of the Court Lodge farm, the platform could certainly have served a purpose with respect to the operations of the manor. Archaeological trenches are usually easily visible in geophysical results, but in this case, locating the trenches from the 1960 excavation proved difficult. The earth resistance data includes at least one low resistance anomaly consistent with a possible excavation trench, located to the east of the possible drainage features, but it is difficult to reconcile this location with the description of four to five trenches given in the report.

LIVED EXPERIENCE IN THE LATER MIDDLE AGES

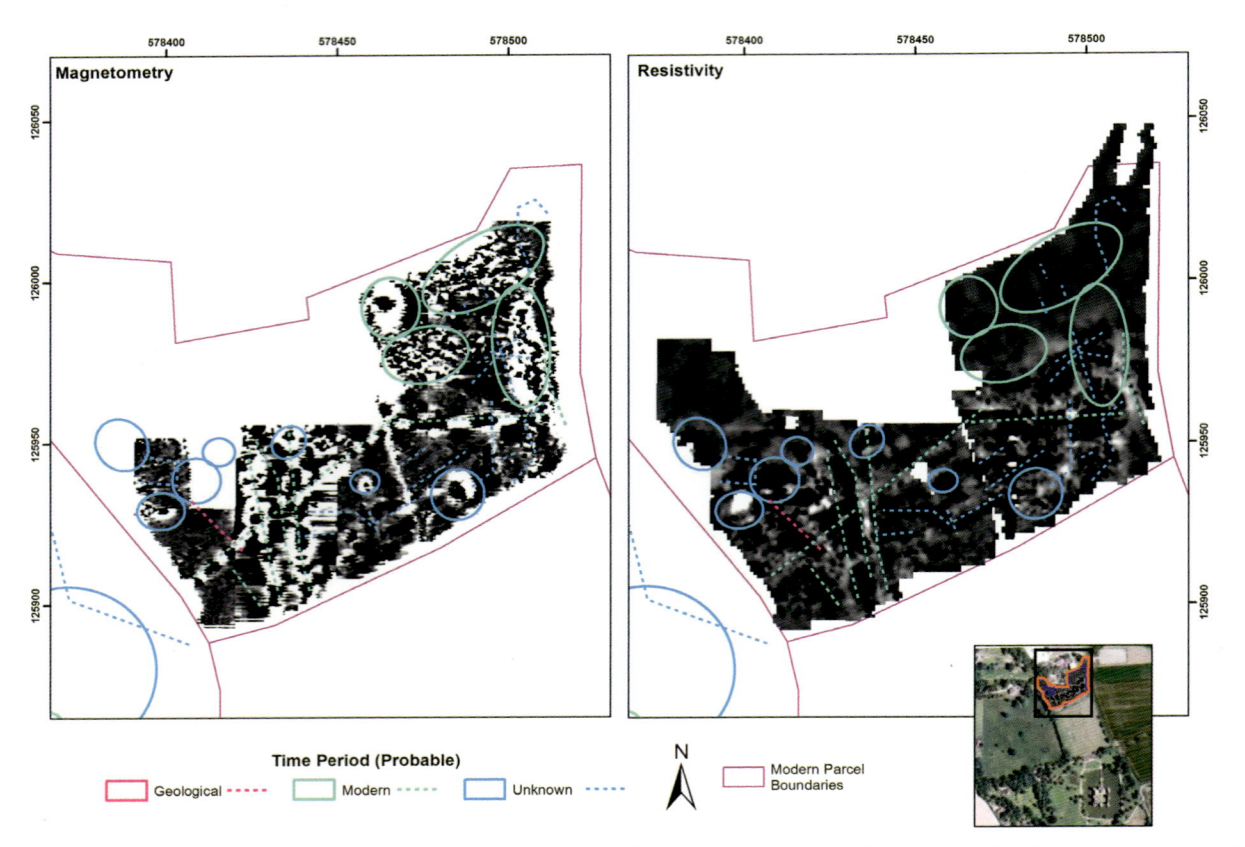

Fig. 4.10a: Gun Garden: Interpreted magnetometry and earth resistance survey results. Linear dipole magnetic anomalies are likely modern pipes or utilities. No clear evidence of medieval or other earlier structures is visible amidst modern disturbance. Some linear low resistance anomalies may be drains, or could suggest the location of 1960s excavation trenches.

Fig. 4.10b: Gun Garden: magnetometry and earth resistance survey results.

In summary, the geophysical results are inconclusive with respect to the possibility of a structure on the southern edge of the Gun Garden. Such a structure may never have existed; it might be located beneath the modern structures to the north of our survey area; the evidence might have eroded away or been destroyed as part of 17th-century modifications to the site; or a more detailed survey and excavation of the site may yet lead to additional insights. There may have been some kind of structure atop this rise during the medieval period and prior to the castle's construction, as the 1960s excavation findings did include structural features. However, there remains no clear archaeological evidence of a manor house in the area covered by the survey and excavations.

Bodiam village

The dwellings of Bodiam village, along the east side of the road, at one time had rear boundaries that extended significantly into what is now the National Trust property (Johnson *et al.* 2000). The rear boundaries of these plots are very clear in the magnetometry and earth resistance survey results to the west and south-west of the castle (Fig. 4.11), and correspond to property boundaries shown on a 1671 estate map (Drury & Copeman 2016: 119). The topographic survey also shows clear landscape features corresponding to these geophysical signatures (Fig. 4.4). Several of these features are apparent when walking over the grounds, and many were also recorded in hachure form during the 1988 RCHME survey (Taylor *et al.* 1990, Fig. 1.2, this volume).

A linear feature running south-west from the lower end of the cascade is most prominent, and corresponds to a topographic rise in the now grassy lawn to the west of the castle, possibly connecting at its north end to a similar linear feature that runs just south of the cascade. The feature runs south-west for approximately 90 m before turning abruptly to the west at its southern end, continuing to the edge of the National Trust property. The linear anomaly is consistent with the presence of a bank and ditch feature (a line of higher readings next to a line of lower readings in the geophysical results), though it could also indicate the development of a lynchet or earthen terrace over centuries of ploughing. While the topographic signature of this feature is only about 5 m across, the geophysical signature consistent with bank, ditch, and remobilised spoil is up to 20 m across, which suggests that the original feature may have been up to a metre in height. This feature probably marks the boundary associated with the edge of a field shown on maps from the 17th through 19th centuries (Johnson *et al.* 2000; Drury & Copeman 2016, fig. 38). The feature itself and the property division it represents are probably much older, contemporary with the oldest plots to the south. Large, roughly circular resistance anomalies within this enclosure are associated with the root systems of 19th and 20th-century tree groves.

To the south of this most prominent bank and ditch feature, several additional linear anomalies are evident in the geophysics. One such feature heads south-east from the south-east corner of the rectory tenement, connecting it to the modern path from the car park to the castle. Four linear features run just south of west from this feature to the west edge of the National Trust property, corresponding very closely to the boundaries of the tenement properties lining the road (Fuggles, Castle View, May Cottage, and Knollys; Johnson *et al.* 2000; Drury & Copeman 2016).

While the modern landscape does show a series of slight breaks in slope, the geophysics suggest that these earthworks, especially the linear feature to the north, were much more prominent in earlier centuries, very probably during the medieval period prior to the castle's construction. The most southerly properties may have been truncated during the creation of the mill pond. Both earth resistance and magnetic anomalies within the rear plots suggest the presence of outbuildings, household industry, or further property divisions, perhaps in association with or predating the construction of the castle. These plots may be the location of possible pottery kilns at Bodiam. Myres (1935: 226), in his analysis of pottery from Bodiam, suggested there may have been pottery kilns on site, though he did not propose a precise location, nor did he observe any component of the ceramic assemblage that could be described as a waster associated with production (Gardiner *et al.* 1994).

The bridge and wharf

Bodiam bridge is referred to in the documents as existing before 1230, although the current bridge has the date 1797 inscribed on its fabric. The modern road that crosses the River Rother at the bridge runs along the same line as both the medieval and Roman roads (see above), the bridge probably having replaced an earlier ford or ferry.

The Rother had moved to a more northerly course by the late 14th century, the older channel now referred to as a ditch (see Fig. 4.6 above). During the 16th century, there were two bridges at Bodiam, probably one over the present Rother and the second over the

LIVED EXPERIENCE IN THE LATER MIDDLE AGES

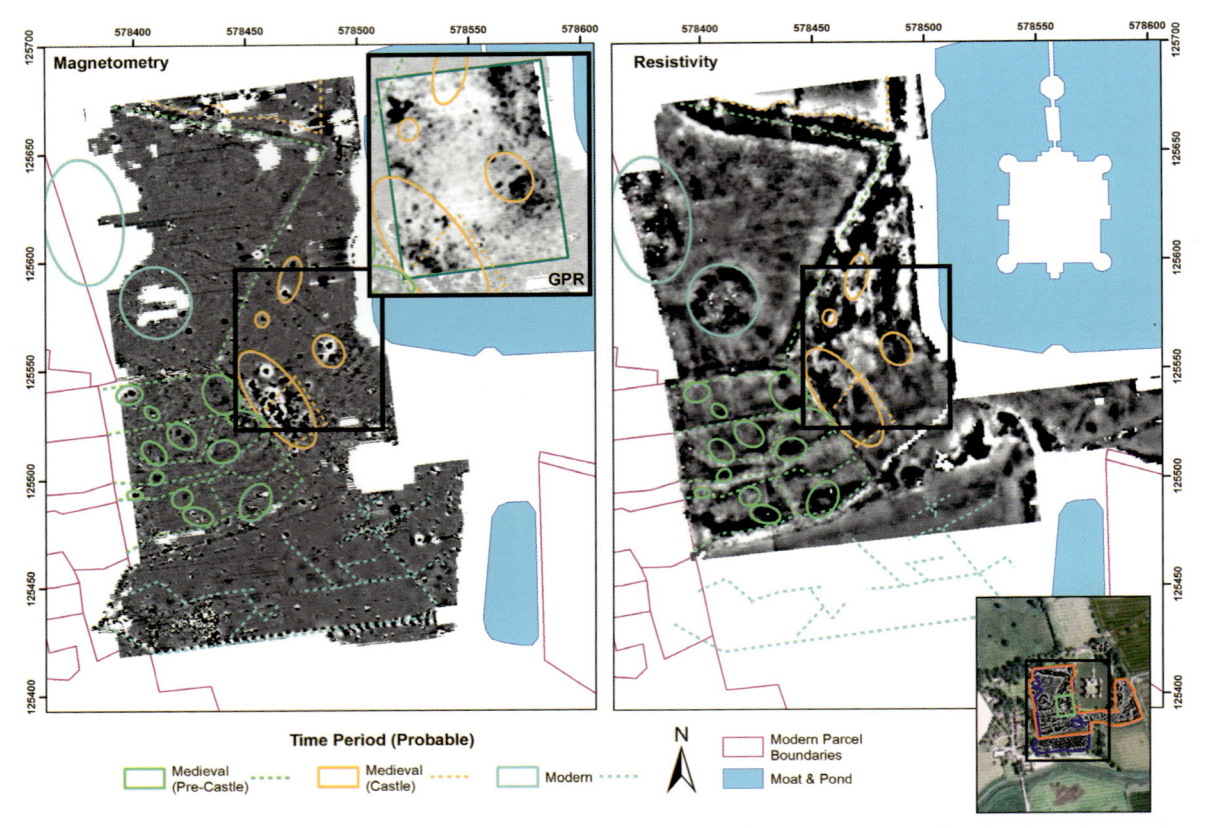

Fig. 4.11a: Castle West: Interpreted magnetometry, earth resistance, and GPR survey results. Modern linear magnetic anomalies are Curzon's drains and probable modern drain or pipe. Note that tenement boundaries visible in the geophysics correspond to extensions of existing property lines. The GPR slice shown is approximately 30-40 cm below ground surface.

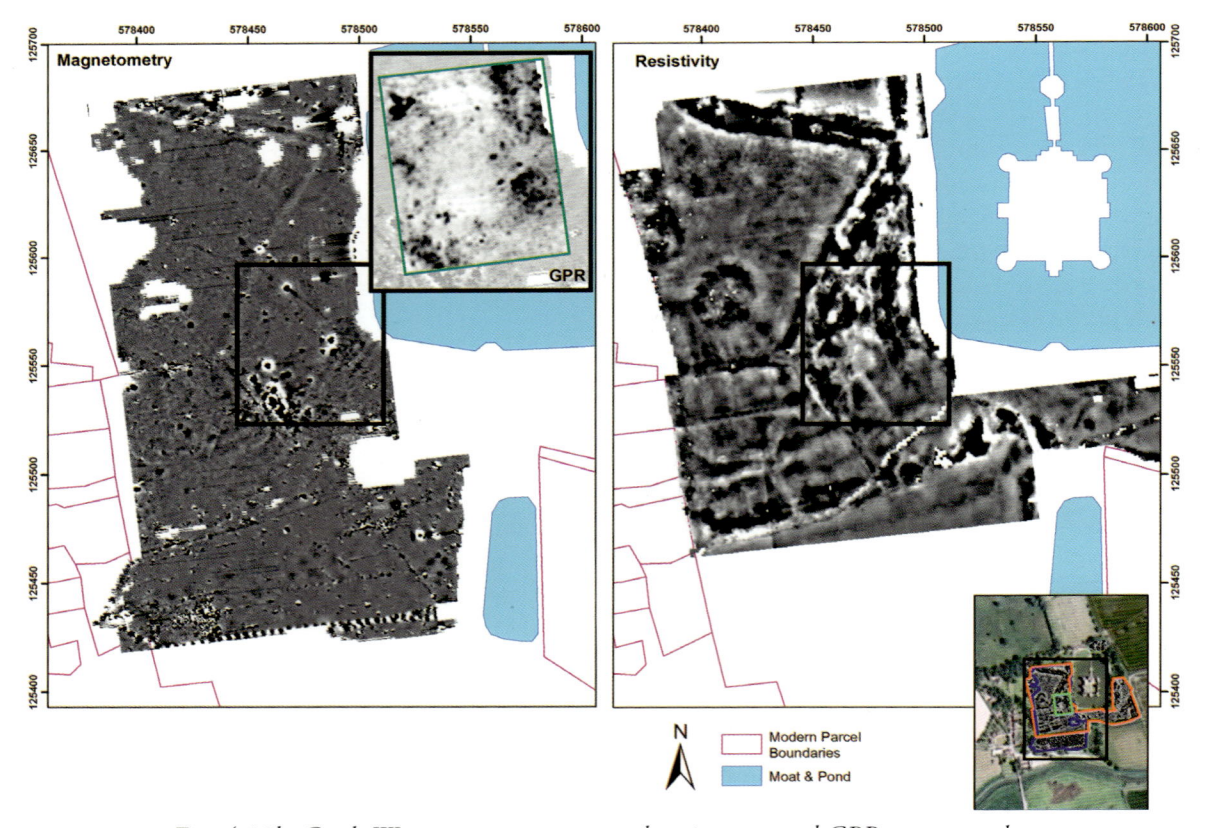

Fig. 4.11b: Castle West: magnetometry, earth resistance, and GPR survey results.

earlier channel (Drury & Copeman 2016: 44-6). To the east and west of Bodiam the river still follows its earlier course, which suggests the river was purposefully diverted to the north in this area. The date and reason for the river's shift are unknown, but the Rother most likely held a course similar to its present one by the time the medieval village and wharf were established.

The wharf would have been a key element in the busy medieval landscape of Bodiam. The wharf may have been active before the mid-12th century, when a boat landing is first mentioned in documentary sources (Drury & Copeman 2016: 43). Previous excavations, in particular work at the west end of the mill pond, suggest that the remains of the wharf lie beneath the area of the modern visitor facilities and 'rose garden', perhaps extending into the car park (Pope et al. 2011: 41-2). As this area is under continuous use as a car park, we were unable to clear the area as needed for geophysical survey during our field seasons and therefore could not make any progress in identifying the form of a harbour or wharf at this location. Place-name evidence (Flote Marsh, Flote Field) and a sunken rectangular area south of the original river course suggest another possible location for a dock (lower right of Fig. 4.4), though as Drury & Copeman note, an alternate meaning of *flote* is a low-lying, permanently flooded marsh (2016: 46), which certainly describes this space.

Fields around the village, manor, wharf, and road were actively farmed and cultivated by the village inhabitants; the pollen evidence is indicative of both pastoral and arable agriculture in the Bodiam area throughout the medieval period (see Chapter Five, this volume). It was into this active, working, day-to-day landscape of agriculture, commerce, industry, travel, and social life that Sir Edward Dallingridge decided to place his new castle at Bodiam in the last decades of the 14th century.

The Castle Landscape

After his marriage to Elizabeth Wardedieu in 1363, Sir Edward Dallingridge was in possession of the property at Bodiam by 1378. He obtained a licence to crenellate the manor at Bodiam in 1385. Previously, in 1383, Dallingridge had received a grant to hold a market and fair at Bodiam, and in 1386 he obtained a licence to divert the River Rother for a mill. The entire castle landscape, including numerous outbuildings and water features, appears to have been constructed within the space of ten years or less – a massive undertaking of construction, and a significant alteration to the village landscape, in a very short period of time (Whittick 1993; Johnson et al. 2000: 29-34).

West of the castle

Strong dipolar magnetic anomalies cluster in a line just to the castle side of the village earthworks described above (Fig. 4.11). A faint rectangular feature in the earth resistance survey roughly circumscribes this cluster of anomalies, suggesting that the practices occurring in this area were spatially separated from the surrounding areas by earthen walls or some other structure. The position of the magnetic anomalies, against the boundaries of the plots and not appearing to cross them at any point, suggests that the earthworks were in place when the ferrous material was deposited here. It is therefore likely that the source of these dipolar anomalies post-dates the plots of Bodiam village, and pre-dates the restructuring of the landscape that resulted in the demolition of these rear lots (possibly c. 1671 (Johnson et al. 2000: 40-1)). Without excavating, we cannot declare with certainty that these anomalies were associated with the construction of Bodiam Castle; however, they are consistent with the expected signature of a builder's yard that would have hosted the kinds of industrial works necessary to support such a massive engineering project (including the possibility of kilns, fires, metalworking, and perhaps spoil or slag heaps). Their clustering and alignment, apparently respecting the boundaries of the house plots, makes an industrial explanation more likely than an intrusion of iron-rich natural peat. The geophysics therefore suggests that Bodiam village (or at least the boundary defining the block of plots to the rear of the houses) pre-dates Dallingridge's construction of Bodiam Castle (consistent with Johnson et al. 2000: 6).

Discrete dipolar anomalies between this faint rectangular feature and the castle moat suggest the possible presence of kilns in this area as well. A small (50 m x 60 m) GPR survey was performed to further investigate the area, and results showed reflective anomalies corresponding to several of the magnetic dipoles at approximately 30-40 cm below ground surface. However, geological cores from the mill pond and around the moat contained significant deposits of iron-rich peat which can appear as dipolar anomalies (similar to our observations in the cricket field, see above and Chapter Five, this volume; also Scaife 2013). It may be of interest to note that both the north-western approach to the castle discussed below, and also the southern approach suggested by the RCHME survey (from the south, turning east to circle the moat counter-clockwise (Taylor et al. 1990; Everson 1996 and Fig. 2.6, this volume)) avoids this possible industrial landscape, suggesting that such activities may have been strategically located out of sight of the castle's more elite visitors and inhabitants, during or after the phase of active construction. Excavation may help to determine what kind of activities were taking place in this area.

To the north of the possible industrial area lies the 'cascade'. This consists of a series of depressions in the hillside, leading from the current access road south of Dokes Field to the north-western corner of the moat (Figs 4.3, 4.4 & 4.11). These depressions have been interpreted as former water features, perhaps one or more fishponds, which fell in succession down to the moat and were a key element of the watery landscape of Bodiam. This area was difficult to survey due to dense vegetation and extremely dry soils. Furthermore, when the moat was drained prior to 1970, spoil from the clearance was often piled in or around these depressions. There are some suggestions of features of interest in the survey results, particularly the magnetometry, but no clear conclusions can be drawn given the difficult conditions.

The 'tilt-yard'/mill pond, leat and possible mill site

In 1386 Dallingridge obtained a licence to divert the course of the River Rother to power a mill at Bodiam, and earthworks suggest the former position of the mill pond in the area misidentified by Curzon as 'the tiltyard' (Curzon 1926). At this time, the Rother may have run directly against the southern edge of the mill pond, a little to the north of its present course. Some time later, probably by 1410, the river was again diverted slightly to the south to its present course, perhaps to stop the mill pond embankment from being undermined or to create space for the harbour or dock (Drury & Copeman 2016: 114-7).

Magnetometry survey of the mill pond did not reveal any anomalies that are likely to correspond to a medieval date (Fig. 4.11). However, pollen analysis of a core from the pond indicates the presence of wetland fringe vegetation (including willows, water plantain, and sedges) concurrent with alluvial deposits, consistent with a pond environment (see Chapter Five, this volume).

Chris Whittick (1993) has suggested that the mill leat (artificially constructed stream) referenced in the 1386 licence was diverted from the Rother far upstream near Salehurst, and brought to the mill pond by way of a route that would have, in part, followed the current trackway north of Castle Inn and the cricket field (Fig. 4.12). If the actual location of the leat was slightly south of the current track, evidence of its path should have appeared in the geophysics of the cricket field. However, the survey results did not contain any clear suggestion of the line of a mill leat through the cricket field (Fig. 4.13). The leat may more likely have run along the ditch to the north of the present lane, a possibility that merits further investigation.

To the south-east of the castle, resistivity and GPR surveys showed evidence of a highly resistive, dense, subrectangular anomaly of about 20 m x 25 m, at the south-eastern corner of the National Trust property (Fig. 4.14). The southern and eastern edges of this feature extend outwards to the north and west along the property boundaries, about 70 m in each direction. Given the position of the mill pond a little to the west, it is tempting to suggest that this anomaly could be the location of a mill foundation and the walls of an associated mill yard. If this were the case, then it would have been possibly served by a leat that would have run from the north-east corner of the mill pond along the approximate route of the modern east/west ditch. Further geophysical signatures in this area are obscured by the modern pathway that runs north-east to south-west, and upcast associated with the construction of the moat and its earthwork bank.

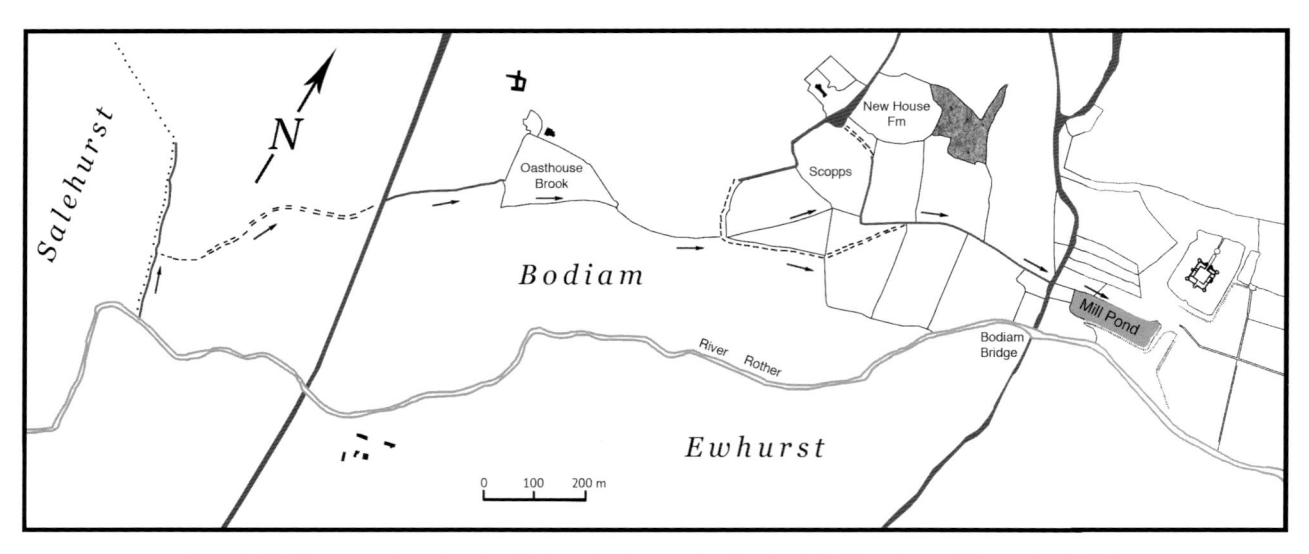

Fig. 4.12: Suggested path of mill leat (redrawn by Kayley McPhee from Whittick 1993).

BODIAM AS A LANDSCAPE OF WORK

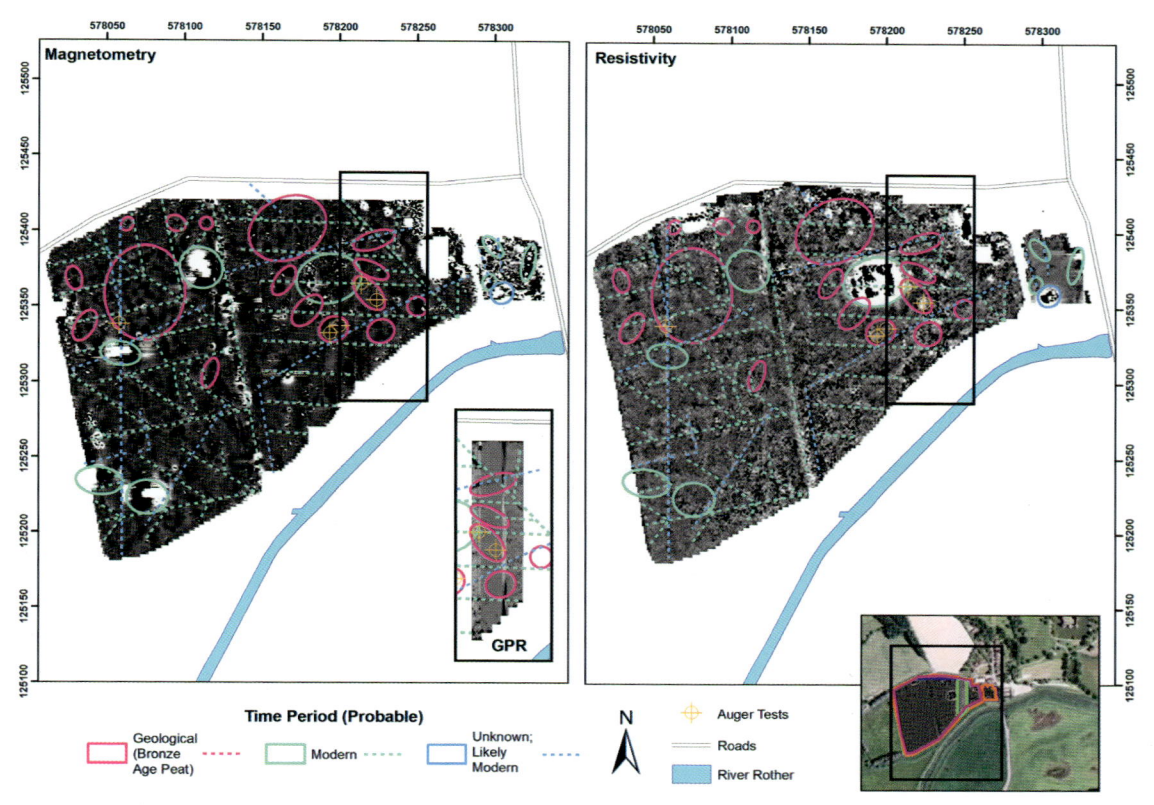

Fig. 4.13a: Cricket Field: Interpreted magnetometry, earth resistance, and GPR survey results. Large dipolar anomalies suggest large modern metallic deposits, while small dipoles could be modern debris, ancient peat, or any metallic deposit of intermediate age. Positive magnetic anomalies are likely Bronze Age peat deposits. The large resistance anomaly is the modern, maintained cricket pitch. Linear magnetic anomalies are almost certainly post-medieval or early modern drains; linear resistive anomalies are less certain. No evidence of a leat was observed.

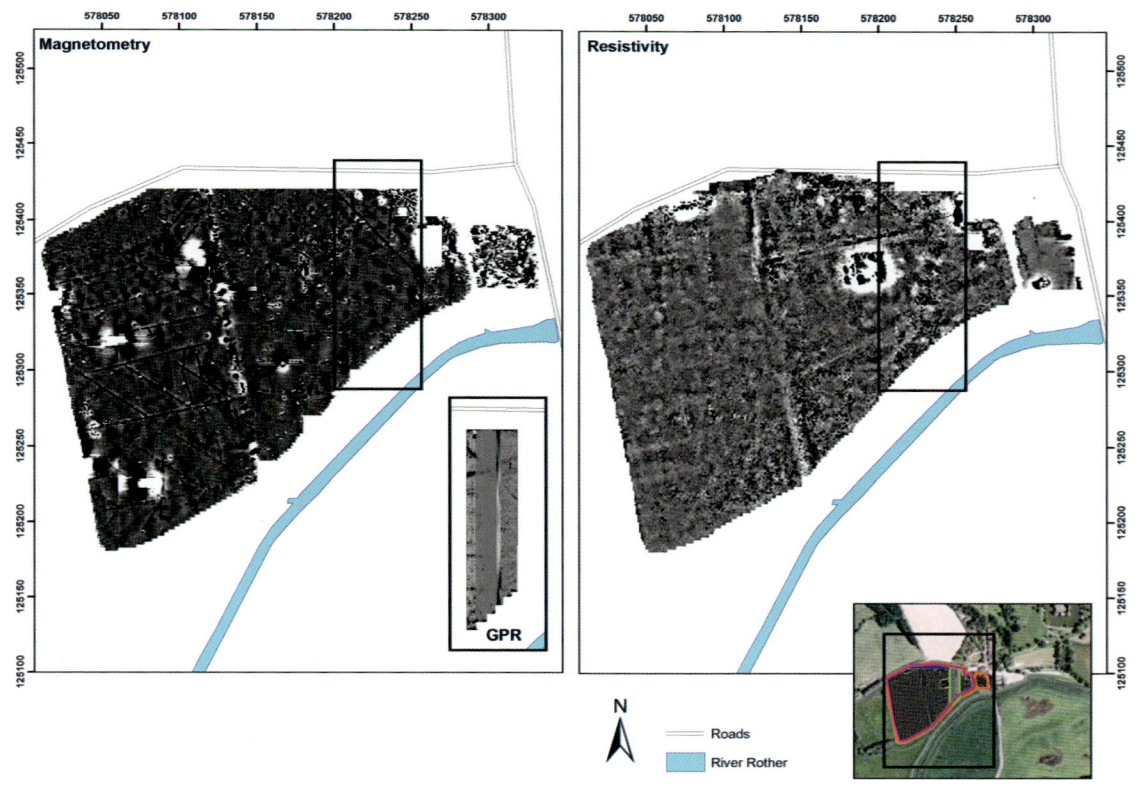

Fig. 4.13b: Cricket Field: magnetometry, earth resistance, and GPR survey results.

LIVED EXPERIENCE IN THE LATER MIDDLE AGES

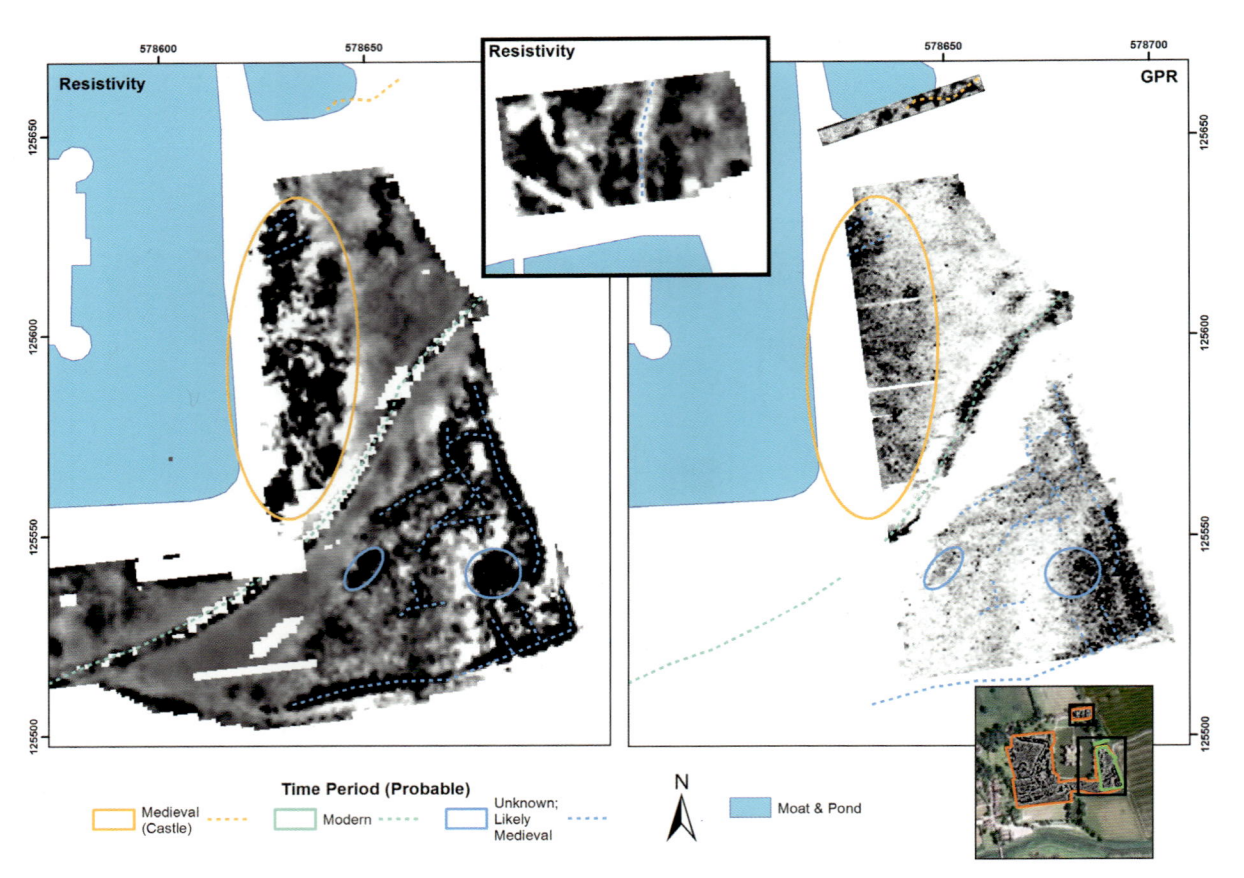

Fig. 4.14a: Castle East: Interpreted earth resistance and GPR survey results. The GPR slices shown are approximately 30-40 cm below ground surface.

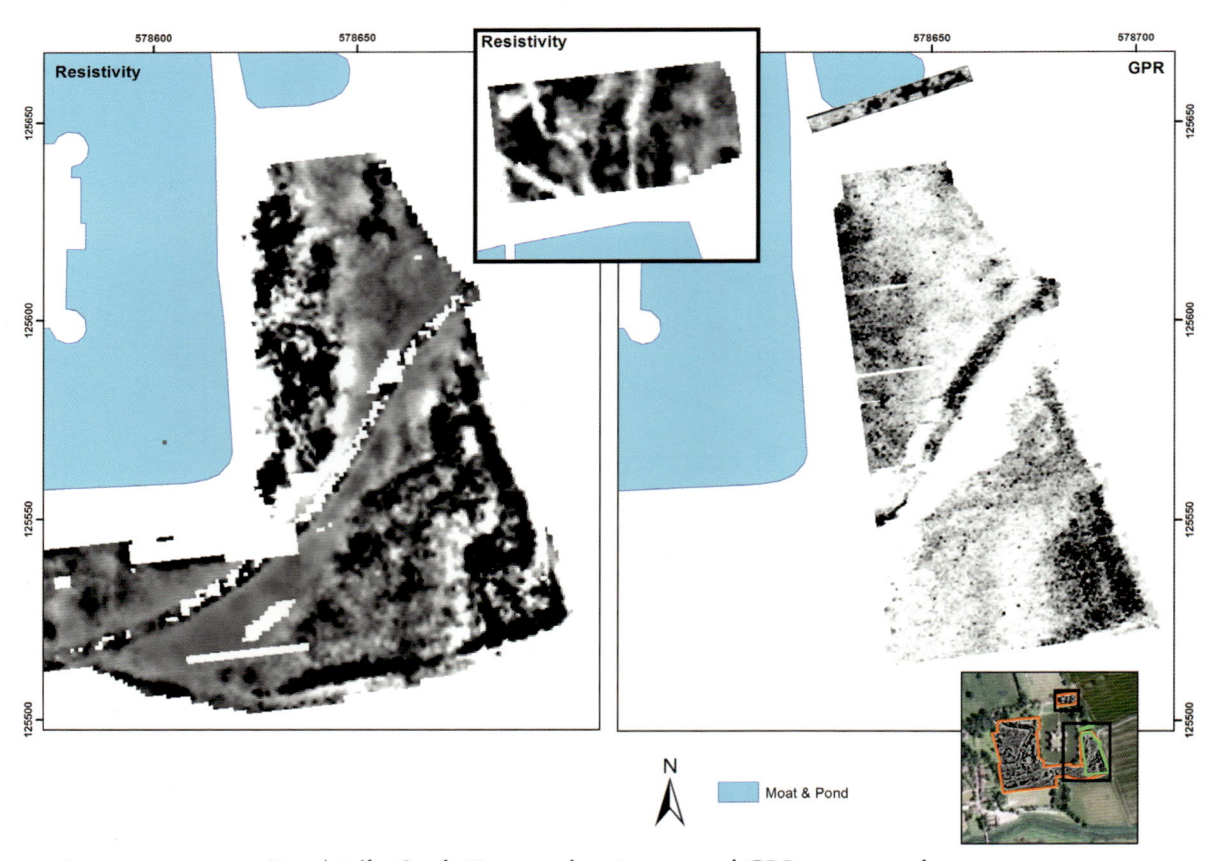

Fig. 4.14b: Castle East: earth resistance and GPR survey results.

The suggestion that this subrectangular anomaly may have been the mill site differs from the general assumption that the mill site was immediately east of the mill pond, at the north end of the dam. There is evidence for this assumption in the form of a ditch that runs north-south from that point before curving to the south-east to join up with the River Rother (visible on Figs 1.2, 2.2 and 4.12). This ditch could be the remnant of the medieval tail race. This ditch is visible today and in earlier maps, such as the 1840 Tithe Map (Drury & Copeman 2016: 114-5 and fig. 51). However, this ditch, and the assumed mill site it connects to, lie either outside or just on the edge of the National Trust property, and much of this area was heavily altered by the activities of Curzon and others, so the area is very difficult to interpret.

Stratigraphic and pollen data from coring in the area south-east of the castle suggested the presence of thick, high-quality pasture land, built up over the last millennium. This suggests an alternative possibility for the subrectangular anomaly, namely that it could be evidence of a cattle pen or yard rather than a mill (see Chapter Five, this volume). Some caution is warranted, as the proximity of the linear anomalies to the drainage ditches at the edge of the property suggests that there is likely some upcast from the excavation of the ditches, which could produce a comparable geophysical signature. Additional work is needed to test for buried structures in this area.

A small-scale GPR survey was carried out just to the north of this area along the pond bank in 2010 in advance of works to mitigate an apparent water leak on the grounds (Fig. 4.14). The survey showed denser materials lower down the bank to the east, perhaps stone or masonry, and a less dense subsurface matrix to the west, perhaps clay or silt. These observations are probably related to the construction of the retaining dam south of the fishpond and perhaps also to maintenance operations along the moat bank.

Castle approaches

Second only to the debate over the significance of the Gun Garden, the most contested aspect of the Bodiam landscape is perhaps the path taken by the original approach to the castle as envisioned by Dallingridge. When the RCHME reported on their comprehensive earthworks survey in 1990, they contended that the watery landscape of the castle was intended to guide visitors to the castle through an ornamental landscape, to 'experience views whose components continually change' (Taylor *et al.* 1990: 155). In their words,

the main approach to the castle from the W. would have been along the S. side of The Tiltyard pond [mill pond], giving distant views of the castle across water, thence along the causeway between ponds where only the upper part of the castle was visible, and crossing between further areas of water over a bridge. At this point the climb to the moat dam must have had, indeed still has, a dramatic effect, as the whole castle seems to rise up out of its moat. The visitor, if not using the postern gate, was then directed E. along the moat dam, then N. along the moat and the one or perhaps two ponds to the E. and finally back W. on the northern edge of the moat. At the NW. corner of the moat the approach road turned again between the moat and the two ponds to the W. and finally crossed the moat in two stages to reach the main gate of the castle

(Taylor *et al.* 1990: 155-7)

Issues with this proposed southern route were raised in Chapter Two. Whether this southern route was the intended, or indeed the only, approach to the castle during the medieval period remains an open question. Most contemporary castles had two or more approaches to several gates (see e.g. Johnson 2002). Indeed, there are numerous other routes to Bodiam Castle, including the south entrance through the postern gate, a northern route that may have come from the old Roman road south of Dokes Field along the cascade and a modern approach from the north along the public right-of-way leading down from Court Lodge (Johnson 2002b: 29; Thackray & Bailey 2007: 4). Whether the majority of earthworks were intended purely for aesthetic appreciation is also an open question; some of the works to the south may have been necessary for the operation of the mill, for example. The RCHME's description of a contrived, ornamental approach from the south should be regarded as one possible experience among several, very much oriented to the imagined perspective of an elite visitor, rather than to the everyday experiences of those who lived and worked in and around the castle, village, mill and wharf.

The approach to the castle from the north-west is of most interest in relation to the results of the geophysical survey. It has been generally presumed by modern staff, visitors, and neighbours of the property that the northern approach makes more practical sense if one wishes to quickly arrive at the castle. Indeed, the National Trust staff entrance to the property currently takes this approximate path, turning down a gravel road just south of Dokes Field into a small car park at the top of the cascade and continuing on foot to the Trust offices at the base of the hill north of the castle.

However, the general view of scholars, from Lord Curzon to Johnson *et al.* to Drury & Copeman (2016: 119), is that the north-western approach ran immediately south of the cascade. The RCHME noted possible routes defined by terraces both immediately north and immediately south of the cascade, but the northern terrace may be the result of modern damage and dumping (Johnson *et al.* 2000, vol 2, 46). This southern approach also links up neatly with the geophysical signature of the eastern branch of the Roman road noted above. It would suggest an approach to the castle descending what is now Dokes Field, with gradually unfolding views of the northern façade; then turning to the left and east to run along the cascade, before a further turn left and north atop the dam between cascade and moat, then immediately right and east across the moat itself. Such an approach would be less circuitous, but just as carefully 'composed' with respect to views and water features, as the RCHME's hypothesised approach from the south. It would also share striking parallels with the hypothesised south-western approach to nearby Scotney, possibly laid out in the 1370s (see Chapter Six, this volume).

The results of our survey are inconclusive, and leave open the possibility of an approach to the castle that ran somewhere north of the cascade rather than to its immediate south. The linear anomaly just to the south of the cascade that would mark such a route is apparent in the topographic, magnetometry, and earth resistance results, but its form generally appears more consistent with a bank and ditch feature (similar to the other anomalies associated with the tenement boundaries) than a pathway. The magnetometry and earth resistance surveys only included a portion of the southern edge of the cascade and did not cover the area between the cascade and Dokes Field, so we do not have geophysical data for a potential path north of the cascade. However, to the north of the cascade there is a level area that could have served as a road, and then of course the modern entrance lane runs between the cascade and Dokes Field, linking up with the diverted road to the west. This 'coach road' was established some time prior to 1671, though its earliest date of use is not known (Drury & Copeman 2016: 131). Different members of our team have different views of the more probable route, south or north of the cascade; we have presented the evidence, and leave readers to make up their own minds.

The south-west corner of Dokes Field shows evidence of an unusual feature, or perhaps two unusual features, in the magnetometry and earth resistance data. The resistance feature appears in the form of two linear anomalies in a funnel shape, appearing to constrain movement into (or out of) the field at this location. The northernmost anomaly clearly shows parallel lines of high and low resistance, characteristic of bank and ditch construction as seen elsewhere on the site. The southern edge of the 'funnel' consists of a high resistance linear feature. The gradiometer data, in contrast, shows only a hint of this funnel-shaped feature – noticeable only when compared to the resistance survey. The second unusual feature does appear very clearly in the gradiometer data in the same area of the south-west corner of Dokes Field, as three sides of a subrectangular feature measuring approximately 40 m x 40 m. This feature does not correspond to the resistance anomaly; in fact, the rectilinear magnetic anomaly appears crosscut by the southern line of the funnel shape. The features are therefore unlikely to be related or contemporary. The order of construction is unknown, though a hint of a subrectangular feature in the earth resistance results, crosscut and overpowered by the funnel feature, suggests that the rectilinear feature may be significantly older. It is possible that, as noted above, it is prehistoric/early Roman in date.

It is tempting to interpret the funnel feature as part of the arrangements for a north-western approach to the castle, one that would have connected to the modern access road just at the top of the cascade near the south gate into Dokes Field. The feature does not crosscut the Roman road; in fact, it seems to end before it reaches the Roman road, which suggest that the road was still in use or at least extant when the funnel feature was put in place. One intriguing possibility is the similarity this shape bears to descriptions of 'deer-leaps', structures that encouraged escaped game to return to the confines of a medieval deer park (Fletcher 2001; Blandford 2012: 13). Many other medieval and later manors in Kent and East Sussex had their own associated deer park, including Scotney, Knole and possibly Ightham (Chapters Six, Seven & Eight). A park is historically known at Bodiam from the late 14th and 15th centuries, but it was most probably located farther to the west and south of our survey area, on the edge of the parish to the north of Robertsbridge Abbey (Drury & Copeman 2016: 122-3). It is also possible that the feature corresponds to an access point into the field during more recent centuries, perhaps associated with 19th-century hop cultivation, use of the field as pasture, or Fuller's unknown landscape modifications (see below). The subrectangular structure is equally obscure in its origin and function. Nevertheless, the geophysical results serve as a necessary reminder that the castle was visited and used by many people coming from all directions and all social classes.

Another resistance linear anomaly is present in the small area to the north-east of the castle, appearing to lead from the moat to the public right-of-way that climbs the hill towards the Gun Garden from the north-east corner of the Trust property (Fig. 4.14). A line of low resistance runs next to it, suggesting a path beside a ditch that drained runoff from the hills into the moat. It is not possible to date this feature from the geophysical results, but it again reminds us that there are numerous approaches to the castle even today, depending on one's purpose as a visitor, employee, hiker, festival-goer, or archaeologist. The right-of-way may post-date the 1730 field boundary along which it runs, making this north-eastern approach to the castle landscape nearly as old and well-travelled as those that have been remade, confirmed, and reinforced by vehicular traffic, asphalt, and gravel.

Post-Medieval Landscape

Between the 15th and 19th centuries, Bodiam changed hands numerous times. The historical record contains little information directly related to the changing physical landscape around Bodiam, though it is during this period that the interior of the castle was significantly dismantled, largely by the Tuftons and Powells during the 17th century. Late in the 18th century, Bodiam once again become an important port, with wharves constructed on both banks of the river and at least one nearby coal yard (Johnson *et al.* 2000: 41). Scattered throughout the site are numerous dipolar magnetic anomalies that may be associated with this early modern industry. The dipoles may also correspond to more recent industrial activities associated with road traffic, the railway, modern construction and renovation of the castle and its landscape, or the presence of visitors on holiday over the last two centuries, and some probably signify intrusions of iron-rich natural peat deposits.

Dokes Field

John 'Mad Jack' Fuller purchased the Bodiam property in 1829 and proceeded to carry out landscape alterations in line with his vision for a picturesque garden, a continuation of his programme of follies and other features on his Brightling estate nearby. Fuller's unpublished accounts show that he paid for significant landscape work, including ditches, stonework, paths, and levelling, but there are few references in the accounts that can be related to specific topographic features, and little to indicate where precisely such work took place, if the recorded work even occurred at Bodiam at all rather than one of his numerous other properties (Holland 2011: 16; Drury & Copeman 2016: 141). Brittany Holland uses cartographic evidence to suggest that alterations to the coach road (the present north-western approach to the castle, see above) may have been the focus of some of Fuller's attentions. It is possible, therefore, that the funnel-shaped, resistance feature in the south-west corner of Dokes (described above; Fig. 4.9) may be related to Fuller's alterations of this road. If this were the case, however, Fuller's road would be expected to obscure traces of the Roman road at the point where the two cross paths, and it does no such thing; rather, the funnel feature appears to end just before it would cross the Roman road. It is possible to imagine Fuller creating a massive entrance without a road, in the spirit of his famous follies, or perhaps in reference to the deer-leaps of a bygone age. Furthermore, any road here may have been used lightly enough during Fuller's tenure that it never became substantial enough to obscure older, buried features.

The earth resistance survey of Dokes Field shows a series of lines, about 10 m apart, stretching east-west and running perpendicular to the slope of the field (Fig. 4.9). The lines occur in at least two groups at a slight angle to one another and they crosscut the Roman road, indicating that they are of a date after the road had fallen into disuse and become obscured in the landscape. Although these linear features superficially resemble the traces of medieval ridge and furrow agriculture, this is highly unlikely to be the case; ridge and furrow is almost unheard of in south-east England (Roberts & Wrathmell 2002; Rippon 2008) and to encounter it in the Bodiam landscape would be highly unlikely. Ridge and furrow would also be expected to run up and down the slope rather than across it. The features are also not visible on the topographical survey or in the gradiometry results, as would be expected of ridge and furrow, which is usually apparent as positive magnetic anomalies (e.g. Linford & Martin 2008; Johnston *et al.* 2009; Archaeological Services Durham University 2010; Bunn 2010; Watkeys 2011). More plausibly, this pattern of linear resistance anomalies may correspond to 19th-century hop cultivation which is much more common in the region (Gardiner 1994: 16; Martin & Martin 2006: 150), although hop ditches are often more closely spaced than those we observe in Dokes Field. A second alternative is that of a vineyard. Future archaeobotanical analysis or excavation may help to interpret these features as ridge and furrow, hop terracing, a vineyard, or something else.

The cricket field

Linear features in the magnetometry and earth resistance results for the cricket field, including the prominent dip that runs north-south through the field in the topographic data, are consistent with late or post-medieval drainage ditches (Fig. 4.13). The high resistance rectilinear feature corresponds to the modern cricket pitch, which is regularly trodden, compressed, played upon, and maintained by the current inhabitants of Bodiam and neighbouring villages.

The 'tilt-yard' (mill pond)

As part of Curzon's comprehensive landscape work at Bodiam in the 1920s, he drained what he called the 'tilt-yard', to 'provide an excellent cricket ground or recreation ground for the village' (Curzon 1926: 101) – a move reminiscent of similar initiatives instigated by British imperial administrators during Curzon's time as colonial Viceroy of India. Although 'the result was a disastrous failure' as 'there was not sufficient fall to carry away the surface water', Curzon tells us that in the process he 'constructed a big drain down the centre and herring-boned the remainder with broad drains about 30ft. apart' (Curzon 1926: 101). The herringbone pattern of linear features visible in the magnetometry results is entirely consistent with these drainage activities as Curzon described them (Fig. 4.11).

The pillbox

The pillbox dates to 1940. As noted in Chapter Two, it has an opening for an anti-tank gun which commands a view of the bridge; an unconfirmed tradition states that the parapet of the bridge was taken down during the war, and rebuilt afterward, so as to give the gunner a clear field of fire. It is one of a series of pillboxes along the South East Command: Corps (Rother) Stop Line from Uckfield to Romney Marsh, part of a system of 'stop lines' across southern England that were intended to halt the feared German advance and render it vulnerable to air attack (Foot 2006; see also Defence of Britain archive, http://archaeologydataservice.ac.uk/archives/view/dob/ai_q.cfm, accessed 25th May 2016).

Conclusion

The results of the 2010-2012 topographical and geophysical survey at Bodiam Castle suggest some avenues for future work, particularly certain areas of the landscape that would benefit from a more detailed geophysical survey at a higher resolution. These include the Gun Garden, the features in the south-western corner of Dokes Field, and the possible location of the medieval mill in the south-eastern corner of the National Trust property. Additional LiDAR survey would be of great help in interpreting the landscape palimpsest. In addition, test excavations should be carried out to verify the geophysical interpretations provided here.

To many visitors today, researchers and holiday-makers alike, Bodiam appears as a designed landscape park, intended for pleasure, relaxation, and beauty. But of course, Bodiam *is* a landscape park – it was made that way over the last two centuries by Fuller, Cubitt, Curzon, and the National Trust. These overlapping layers of aesthetic construction and development as a public monument and amenity make it a difficult and fascinating challenge to see through to the early village landscapes, to the medieval worlds of Dallingridge, his successors, and the everyday people who lived and worked in the shadow of the castle. The trees, for example, were mostly planted in the 19th and 20th centuries, with only a few very old oaks and other species likely dating to the 18th century (Johnson *et al.* 2000; Appendix One, this volume). The only suggestions of medieval foliage and greenery come from analysis of archaeological pollen samples, which can provide a list of species but only broad hints as to their spatial arrangement (Chapter Five, this volume). The landscape, ever changing, obscures its own past. Geophysical survey offers only a glimpse at a few buried remnants of action, centuries past, dimly reflected on the screen.

We will never know for certain why Dallingridge chose to build his castle where and how he did – whether he intended to defend the ramparts against the French, to relax in a country estate, to display his status as a knight of the realm, or some combination of these and other reasons. But we can say that during his tenure, and the centuries that stretch before and after the castle's construction, Bodiam and its environs were an active, dynamic landscape of labour, of movement, travel, and commerce, for generations of men and women who lived in the village or passed through it on their way to London, Rye, or across the continent to Rome. Geophysical and topographic survey of the full landscape shows traces of these everyday activities through which past peoples engaged with the land and with each other, revealing a landscape that cannot fit comfortably into categories like *warfare* or *luxury* – the landscape of Bodiam is, and has always been, complex, messy, contradictory, and ultimately human.

5

THE ENVIRONMENT OF BODIAM: LAND, VEGETATION, AND HUMAN IMPACTS

Kathryn A Catlin, Penny Copeland, Matthew Johnson, Rob Scaife[1]

Abstract. This chapter reports on pollen and stratigraphic analysis of multiple soil cores extracted from the landscape in and around Bodiam Castle. Over the last six thousand years, the Bodiam landscape has shifted from wet alder carr fen woodland to seasonal floodplain. The critical changes occurred during the Bronze Age, when deforestation by local communities to create fields for arable agriculture led to significant erosion and alluvial sedimentation. As a result, the river channel deepened and widened, the wetland expanded, springs developed, and the river Rother began to regularly flood its banks. These alterations set the stage for the development of the Roman and medieval harbours, and later, for the excavation of the moat and watery landscape in which Bodiam Castle is set. The landscape and ecology of Bodiam's position between the floodplain and the Weald has been critical to understanding its place through millennia of interaction between human life and agricultural practices.

Introduction

Bodiam Castle is situated on the boundary between the Rother floodplain and the Weald (Chapter Two, this volume, Figs 2.1 & 2.3). This critical location, at the convergence between two environmental zones, has had significant effects on both the environmental and social histories of the landscape. Over the last five millennia, changes in climate, movement of the river, and human activities have led to multiple transformations between riverine, woodland, wetland, and grassland ecosystems. Each new environmental development represented a change in the way people related to the landscape, including different agricultural methods, transportation and commercial infrastructure, and the range of possible choices available for construction and landscape alteration.

In this chapter, we set out to identify and describe the geological, hydrological, and vegetation history of the immediate environs of the castle. This dynamic environmental context sets the stage for the daily lives and practices of the people who lived and worked here, both defining the range of possible productive activity and comprising the materiality through which inhabitants and visitors have understood their relationship to the land and society. When did people begin to actively farm at Bodiam, and what crops were they growing? Where were the medieval ponds located, and what is their earlier history? What sort of managed woodlands have grown near Bodiam since Roman times and earlier? How might the moat construction have taken advantage of existing landscape features? The environmental context of the Bodiam landscape during the medieval period may suggest why the inhabitants found this an ideal location for a village and castle. Finally, how does all of this accumulated environmental history affect the way the landscape was understood during the later Middle Ages, and the ways in which the Bodiam landscape is experienced and modified today?

[1] The pollen analysis was conducted by Rob Scaife. A longer and more detailed report on the results of the Bodiam coring and pollen analysis was written by Rob Scaife and Penny Copeland (Scaife & Copeland 2015, available at http://sites.northwestern.edu/medieval-buildings/). Kathryn Catlin prepared this more concise chapter, with further edits by Matthew Johnson.

Fig. 5.1: Coring locations relative to the Bodiam grounds. Note the linear resistive anomalies near cores C1 and C2 (the possible mill yard or cattle yard), and the linear magnetic anomalies in the overflow car park/mill pond near core B (likely Curzon's 1920s drainage works).

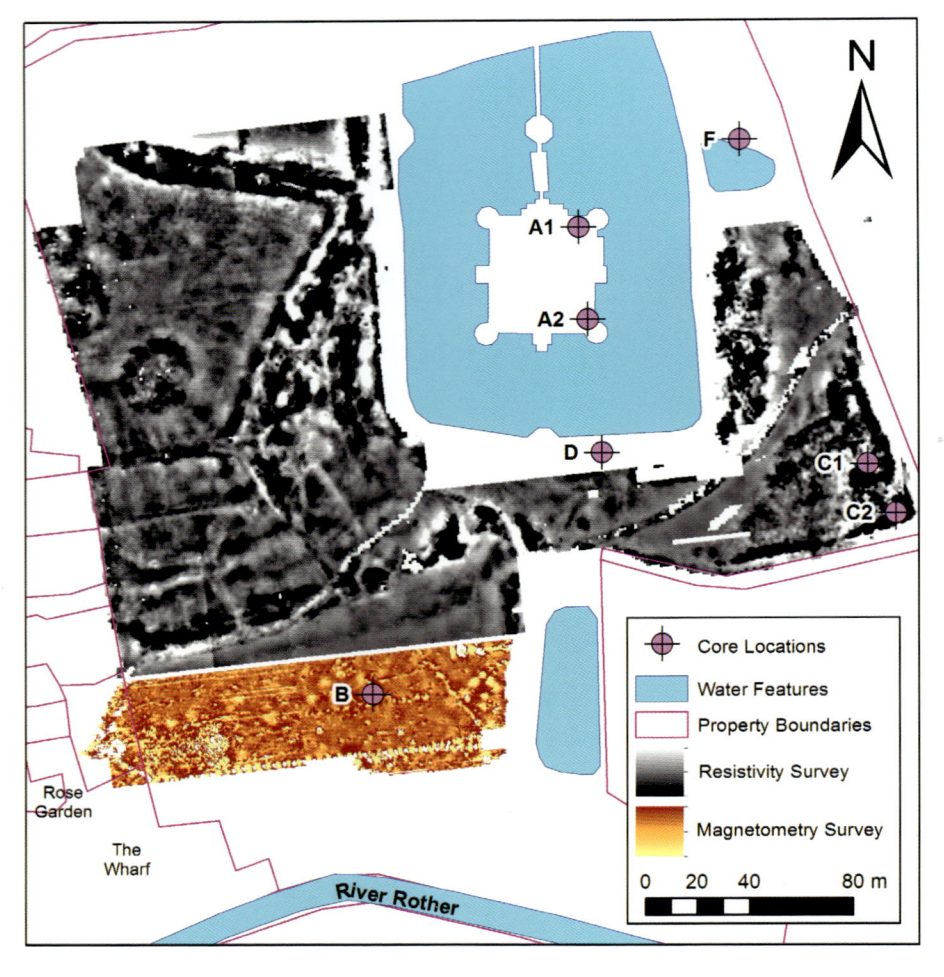

To address these and other questions, we employed soil coring to collect a series of seven sediment profiles around the castle landscape. The project was funded by the Arts and Humanities Research Council as part of the Parnassus Project, a multi-disciplinary study of the effects of climate on historic buildings (www.ucl.ac.uk/parnassus, accessed 25th April 2015). The profiles were brought to the laboratories at the University of Southampton and subjected to stratigraphic, palynological (pollen), and radiocarbon analysis by Rob Scaife. Two cores inside the castle (A1 & A2) span the occupation and abandonment horizons and the underlying, pre-castle, sediment. Five profiles outside of the castle include samples taken from sediment underlying the moat bank (D), a nearby pond (F), the overflow car park (B), and the site of a possible structure to the east of the castle (C1 & C2) (Fig. 5.1). These data have been combined with the results of other pollen studies to describe a vegetation and environmental history of the castle and its landscape, as it relates to human use and occupation of the site.

Sediment profiles are described in tables and represented in diagrams; the key to stratigraphic diagrams can be found in Fig. 5.2. For a detailed account of methods of sediment profile collection and analysis, refer to Appendix Three. The detailed technical report on the work has been lodged with English Heritage (Scaife & Copeland 2015).

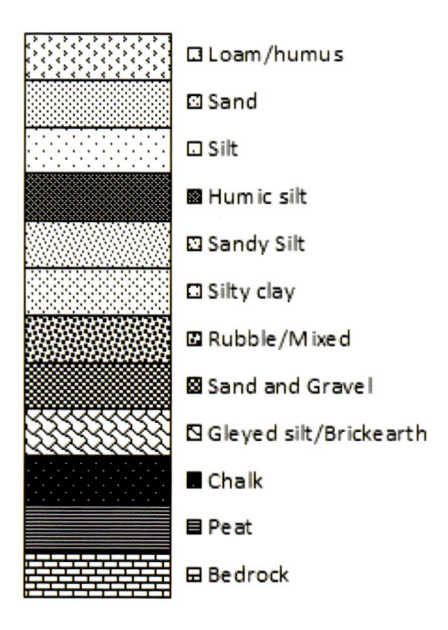

Fig. 5.2: Key to stratigraphic diagrams.

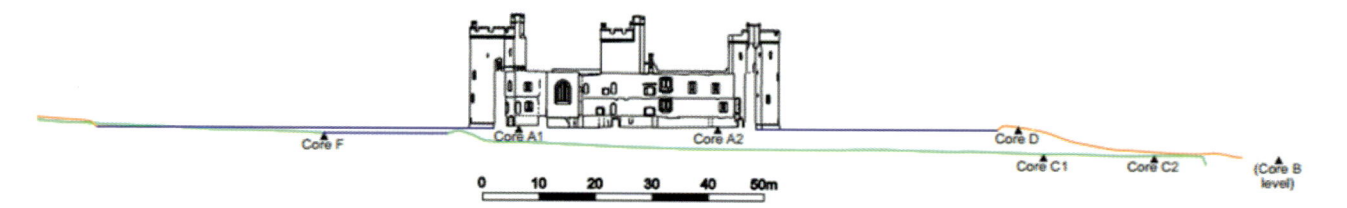

Fig. 5.3: Relative heights of the cores, facing east. Blue lines=Moat and pond; Green lines=Land east of the moat; Red lines=North and south moat banks. The creation of an artificial raised floor beneath the castle is suggested by comparison to the lower ground directly east (green).

Inside the Castle: Profiles A1 and A2

On 8th May 2013, researchers from the University of Southampton were on site at Bodiam in the early morning hours to complete coring inside the castle before it opened for visitors. With the help of National Trust staff, drains and connecting pipes were avoided, and recently-laid gravel was brushed aside to begin coring at a stable ground surface.

We planned to sample sediments from the eastern side of the castle to investigate the origins of the castle platform. Was the castle constructed on an existing ground surface, or had sediment been brought in to create the castle foundation? The 'half-basement' level along the eastern range of the castle was chosen to test this question, because underneath a basement any built-up ground to create a platform should be shallow enough that a core could completely penetrate it, reaching into the presumed *in situ* soil beneath. We were also looking for any evidence of habitation prior to the castle's construction, to understand the long-term human use of the Bodiam landscape and to address whether existing hydrology might have contributed to the choice of this particular spot for the construction of the castle and moat. Two cores were collected in this area, one in the northern range and one in the eastern range, just north of the door to the south-eastern tower (Figs 5.1 & 5.3).

Profile A1: Pollen analysis

Sample A1 was located in the eastern corner of the northern range. The sediment was a fine, inorganic marl, likely from a freshwater, spring-fed (lacustrine) basin. The core was not retained for stratigraphic analysis, though some evidence of floor preparation was observed prior to discarding the sediment (see below, Profile A2). Two spot samples for pollen analysis were collected at depths of 130 cm and 160 cm, most likely predating the castle and of post-Roman date, both of which showed evidence of woodlands, wetlands, and agriculture in varying proportions (Table 5.A).

The upper sample (130 cm) includes a single but important occurrence of walnut (*Juglans regia*)[2]. Walnut was a Roman introduction to Europe as a whole, and in England it has been increasingly recovered from Romano-British and later sites (Scaife 2000; 2004). Walnut is therefore a useful biostratigraphic marker of Roman or post-Roman presence, and dates the sediment at 130 cm to a Roman or later period. The lower sediment, at 160 cm, is less easily dated, but may predate a Roman presence in the area.

Oak (*Quercus*) and hazel (*Corylus avellana* type) are the dominant tree taxa from both samples. The landscape of Bodiam probably supported substantial oak and hazel on local well-drained soils throughout the pre- and post-Roman periods. This woodland is likely to have been managed for timber and coppice (Rackham 1986; 1990).

Trees and shrubs from the upper sample also include small numbers of birch (*Betula*) and beech (*Fagus sylvatica*). The relatively small amount of birch in the sample suggests that birch trees may not have been present in the immediate vicinity, because birch trees produce a large amount of pollen that can move significant distances with the wind. Beech, in contrast, is poorly represented in pollen assemblages unless the sample site is close to the tree canopy (Andersen 1970; 1973); therefore, beech was probably growing locally but not immediately on the site during the later, post-Roman period.

The higher pollen numbers of alder (*Alnus glutinosa*) in the upper sample suggest that there was an area of wetlands, possibly near a spring, on or very close to the site during the later post-Roman period. High values of both polypody fern (*Polypodium vulgare*) and wood fern (monolete *Dryopteris*) spores present in

---

[2] Scientific names are included in parentheses following the first use. Thereafter, common names are employed for ease of reading. See Appendix Two for a chart of common and scientific names of encountered flora.

Table 5.A: Pollen count data from Profile A1 (north-eastern corner, castle interior). This core was not retained for stratigraphic analysis; only two spot samples were collected for pollen analysis.

Depth	1.30 m	1.60 m
Trees & Shrubs		
Betula (birch)	16	1
Quercus (oak)	56	45
Fagus sylvatica (beech)	2	1
Juglans regia (walnut)	1	-
Corylus avellana type (hazel)	62	72
Erica (heather)		1
Herbs		
Poaceae (Grass family)	74	100
Cereal type	10	39
Large Poaceae (non-cereal)	1	-
Secale cereal (rye)	-	9
Ranunculaceae (Buttercup family)	-	1
Ranunculus type (buttercup)	1	-
Sinapis type (mustard)	-	1
Caryophyllaceae (Carnation family)		
Dianthus type (carnation genus)	-	11
Cerastium type (chickweed)	1	1
Chenopodiaceae (Goosefoot family)	-	1
Lysimachia (loosestrife)	-	11
Plantago lanceolata (ribwort plantain)	4	1
Succisa type	1	-
Asteraceae (Daisy family)	-	-
Bidens type (beggarticks)	-	4
Anthemis type (chamomile)	9	-
Artemisia (wormwood genus)	-	1
Centaurea nigra type (knapweed)	-	9
Centaurea scabiosa type (greater knapweed)	-	5
Lactucoideae (dandelion & lettuce subfamily)	11	21
Unidentified	-	2
Wetland		
Alnus glutinosa (alder)	155	67
Typha angustifolia type (cattail)	3	1
Cyperaceae (Sedge family)	5	11
Sphagnum (peat moss)	-	1
Ferns		
Pteridium aquilinum (bracken fern)	43	143
Dryopteris type (wood fern)	47	102
Polypodium vulgare (polypody fern)	5	47

the lower sample may be associated with this nearby alder woodland. High counts of bracken (*Pteridium aquilinum*) suggest local waste ground on the acid sandy soils that are typical of the region.

In addition to woodlands, both well drained and wet, there is also strong evidence for arable agriculture. Cereal pollen numbers are especially high in the lower (earlier) sample from 160 cm. The herbaceous diversity is also greater in this older sample. Grass (*Poaceae*) pollen with dandelion type (*Lactucoideae*) are evidence of grassland, possibly pasture, at this time. It is probable that a mixed agricultural economy with areas of woodland management existed during roughly the pre-Roman period. The upper sample appears to show some reduction in arable and an expansion of woodland in the post-Roman period, with increased hazel, possibly indicating the secession of arable ground into woodland.

Profile A2

Profile A2 was obtained in the eastern range, just north of the door to the south-eastern tower (Figs 5.1 & 5.3). Here, we observed a well-defined occupation horizon, consisting of dark, humic, charcoal-rich sediment overlying what appeared to be a chalk floor (Table 5.B). This possible anthropogenic horizon had also been observed in Profile A1, albeit less clearly.

The meter-deep stratigraphic sequence from Profile A2 begins with a dark humic occupation horizon, including sand and silt with some charcoal fragments from 0-43 cm, possibly preparation for the grass surface laid down by Curzon in the 1920s. This overlies a well-defined anthropogenic horizon of distinct chalky rubble above puddle chalk and pebbles (43-47 cm). Beneath this layer, gleyed and oxidised alluvial silts (brickearth) extend from 47 cm to the end of the core at 99 cm.

The chalk horizon in sample A2 is a chalk rubble layer. The architectural evidence suggests that this is floor preparation. A flagstone floor above the chalk is a strong possibility, although there are no surviving original ground floor surfaces in the castle for comparison. The height of the top of the core is approximately the same as the top of the chamfer stops on the east tower door frame, about 43 cm above the chalk horizon. If we assume that the distance between the chamfer stops and the floor was the same as on all other stories, the floor should be about 30-35 cm (depending on weathering) below the chamfer stops (and modern ground surface). The chalk horizon is instead 43 cm below the surface, or about 10 cm deeper than expected for a floor surface (Fig. 5.4). The chalky rubble horizon probably

THE ENVIRONMENT OF BODIAM

Table 5.B: Stratigraphy of Profile A2.

Depth cm	Stratigraphy
0 - 13	Contemporary surface. Sand and sharp gravel.
13 - 24	Silt, fine and medium texture, grey-brown. Grey (10YR 4/2)[1] becoming greyer at base. Some buff coloured inclusions. Sharp boundary at base.
24 - 32	Sand, pale yellow, fine texture (10YR 8/8).
32 - 43	Probable occupation layer: charcoal inclusions and some mixed humic fill. Silt, fine and medium texture, dark grey (10YR 2/1 to 2/2). Pebble at base (43 mm diameter).
43 - 43.5	Chalky rubble layer. Likely preparation for a (now removed) stone floor.
43.5 - 47	Disturbed gritty layer. Sand, silt, chalk mottling, and small stones (to 10 mm diameter).
47 - 51	Brickearth. Pale at top becoming darker in lower context.
51 - 78	Silt, grey (10YR 5/8) to pale brown. Mottled, possibly gleyed, with oxidised rootlet channels. Calcareous inclusions at 72-73 cm.
76 - 77	Iron staining.
77 - 99	Silt, slightly finer, darker grey (10YR 5/6) than above. May be less gleyed.

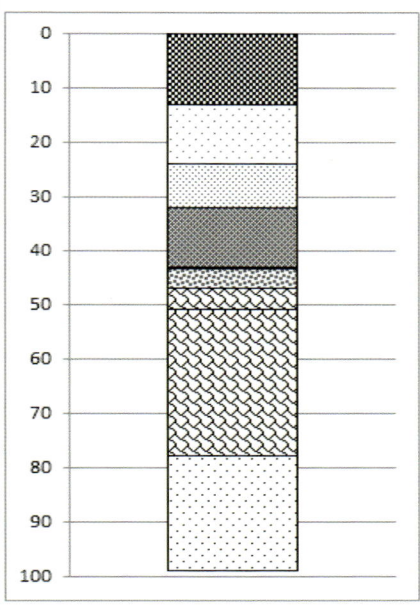

[1] Munsell soil colour description. Used throughout.

represents packing underneath a finished, durable floor surface. Ten centimetres of cobbles or flagstones atop the chalk would have raised the castle floor above the water level of the moat, which is currently only about 3 cm higher than the chalk horizon.

These findings are consistent with Lord Curzon's observation of a 'floor' in the south-west corner tower under the water level (Curzon 1926: 134). Curzon suggested that the level of the moat had changed. However, given the evidence from the level of thresholds and doorframe chamfers, a large change in the moat level is unlikely. Rather, the floor Curzon observed was most likely originally underlay for a substantial layer of stone slabs or cobbles c. 10 cm or more thick, raising the functional floor above the moat level. Such a floor would have been substantial enough to be worth money when stripped out in the 17th century, when many parts of the castle were torn down and repurposed (Johnson *et al.* 2000: 38).

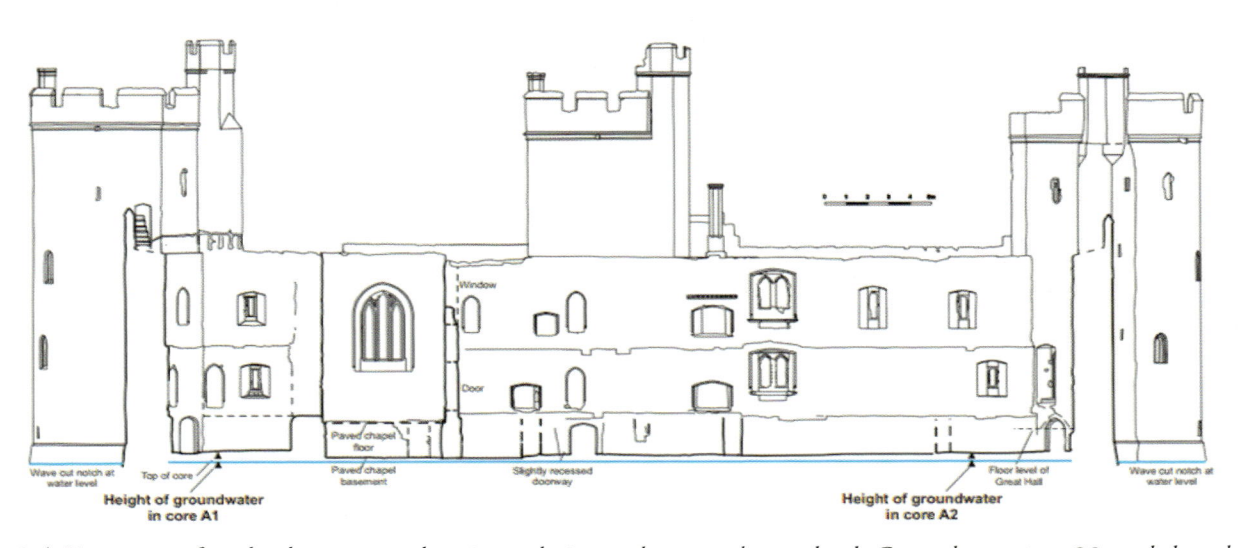

Fig. 5.4: East range of castle, showing core locations relative to the groundwater level. Groundwater is c. 20 cm below the basement floor level. (The slight difference between the water level of the moat and groundwater below the castle is likely due to the fact that the interior and exterior surveys took place months apart, and water levels can fluctuate throughout the year.)

Ground Penetrating Radar (GPR) carried out inside the castle in February of 2016 shows a few reflectors in the south-east corner at a depth of approximately 40-90 cm (Chapter Three, Fig. 3.8, this volume). These may correspond to the chalky rubble observed in core A2. Reflectors at approximately 40-80 cm in the north-east corner may also correspond to similar structures observed in core A1.

Profile A2 pollen analysis

Pollen was analysed at alternate 2 cm intervals through the anthropogenic/occupation horizon, between 32-45 cm (Fig. 5.5). The pollen spectra obtained are generally similar throughout the profile, but there are some minor differences above and below 38 cm. This difference may signify an occupation horizon, but could also represent the phase of castle abandonment that began c. 1643 and continued through the early 19th century. The lower part of this deposit, from 39-43 cm, contains pre-Quaternary fossilised pollen, which suggests that the silt above the chalk is a secondary deposit that was moved inside the castle from elsewhere, possibly from flooding, or perhaps as an intentional living surface. A flooding event could easily have followed the removal of thick flagstones, corresponding to site abandonment. This silt tails off in a more humic upper horizon above 37 cm, possibly a sign of early post-medieval occupation or related to more recent landscape work to maintain the modern grass surface.

The pollen and spores deposited within the castle include pollen that primarily came from plants growing in the immediate vicinity of the castle walls, as well as pollen derived from secondary sources such as domestic waste. Tree and shrub pollen come largely from wind-pollinated taxa, which generally produce more pollen, and will have travelled from outside the castle. These taxa include primarily oak, hazel, and alder, as well as smaller amounts of birch, pine (*Pinus*), and occasional elm (*Ulmus*) and hornbeam (*Carpinus betulus*). Lime[3] (*Tilia cordata*) and spindle (*Euonymous*) are present, and because these taxa are usually less well represented in pollen assemblages, they are likely to have grown within the castle grounds.

The high levels of grass pollen and cereals are typical of anthropogenic deposits. Grassland and pasture taxa also include ribwort plantain (*Plantago lanceolata*), dandelion, and knapweeds (*Centaurea* spp.). This grassland pollen may derive from pastures exterior to the castle, but it could also come from secondary sources such as floor covering, thatch, or domestic waste. Cereals are most likely to come from secondary sources such as crop processing and resultant debris, waste food and faecal material, or straw used as floor covering. Small numbers of sedges (*Cyperaceae*), reed mace/cattails (*Typha angustifolia*), bur-reed (*Sparganium*), and occasional other wetland types, may be of similar secondary origin or could have grown in the moat.

Ivy (*Hedera helix*) and polypody fern spores were also common in the pollen assemblage, suggesting that these may have been growing along the inner walls of the castle after abandonment, consistent with 18th-century watercolours of the castle interior (Fig. 5.6).

The Mill Pond/'Tiltyard': Profile B

A profile was obtained from the overflow car park (Fig. 5.1), which was not in use for parking the day of the fieldwork. Lord Curzon (1926) called this area the 'tiltyard', but it was almost certainly a mill pond during the medieval period. The core was placed not far from the location of a harbour, marked as 'the wharf' in Fig. 5.1, dating from the medieval period and earlier (Priestley-Bell & Pope 2009). We intended to use this core, first, to assess the origin and development of the mill pond as it related to the castle and second, to address silting of the former harbour area and the economic relationship between the castle and the river. Thanks to recent geophysical work also performed by the University of Southampton (Chapter Four, this volume), we were able to avoid coring through drainage channels and overburden left from work performed by Curzon in the 1920s.

Peat appears at 96 cm below the current surface and continues beyond 1 m (the depth of the core) (Table 5.C). The peat is capped by a transitional layer of humic clay-silt, below brown-grey, gleyed, silty brickearth sediment that continues to the modern surface. A radiocarbon date of cal. 2455-2200 BCE (calibrated *Beta*-382481; measured as 3840+/-30BP) has been obtained from an alder twig at 98-96 cm, within the top of the peat. The stratigraphy therefore shows a progressive transition from a stable peat-forming habitat during the late Neolithic, through wetter fen conditions, and finally to alluvial sedimentation. This is consistent with peat previously observed in this area at 2-4 m depth (Barber 1998).

Pollen analysis

Pollen analysis was performed at 0.05 m intervals on the lower, wetter, and more humic sediments from 60-100 cm, consisting of detrital peat below humic, laminated silt. The gleyed sediments above 60 cm

---

[3]   Tilia cordata is known as linden in some parts of the world. We follow UK standard taxonomy and refer to tilia as lime.

THE ENVIRONMENT OF BODIAM

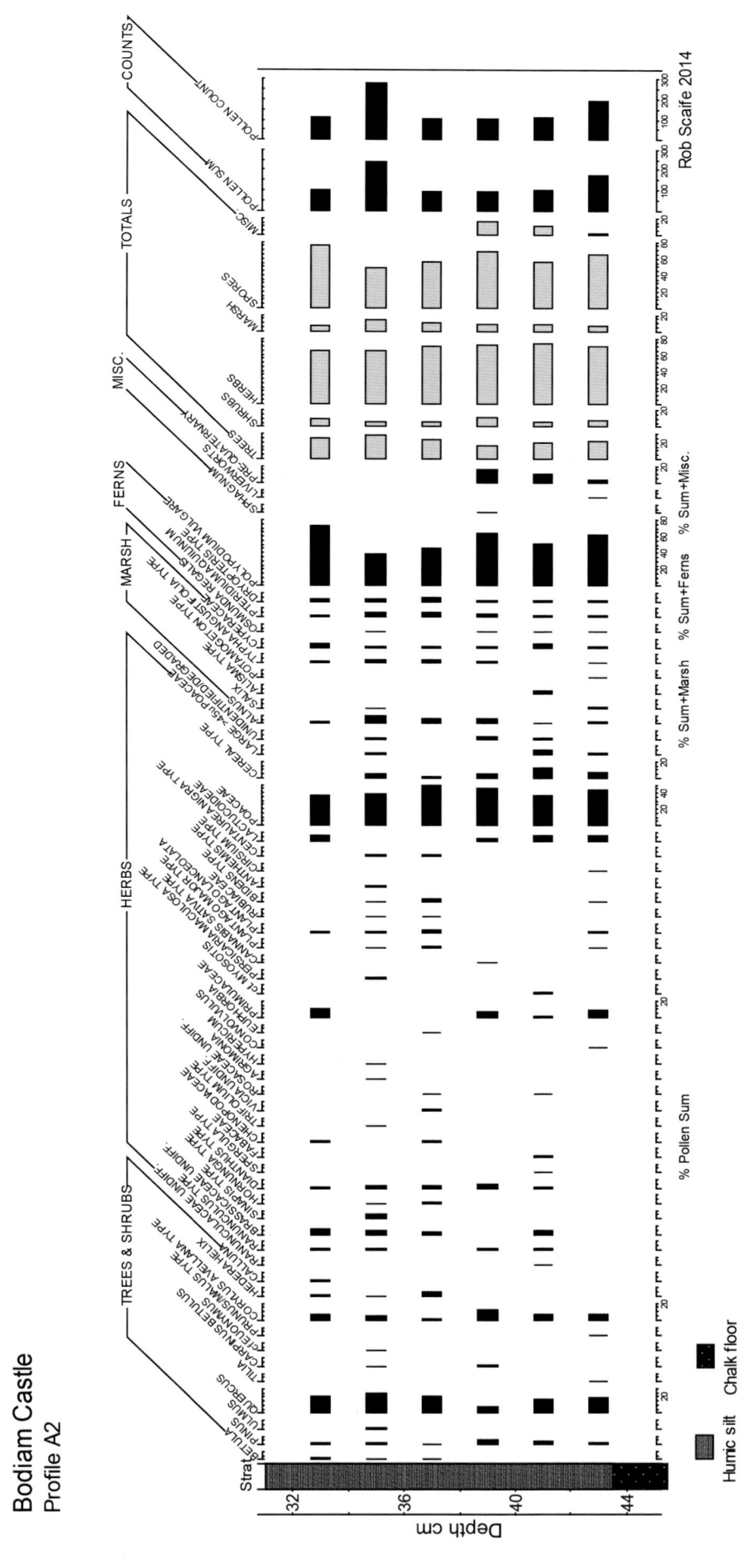

Fig. 5.5: Pollen diagram from Profile A2.

Fig. 5.6: 'A colored view of the interior of the east side of Bodiham Castle; drawn by S.H. Grimm, in 1784'. Note the ivy and ferns growing along the castle walls. © The British Library Board, Add.5670 f10 (no.18).

were deemed too oxidised to produce reliable pollen counts. The pollen profile is homogeneous with few changes in the pollen spectra over time (Fig. 5.7).

The column contained a diverse range of tree and shrub pollen throughout the sequence. Oak and hazel were the most common, with some lime, pine, birch, ash (*Fraxinus*), beech, holly (*Ilex*), viburnum (*Viburnum*), buckthorn (*Rhamnus cathartica*), willow (*Salix*), and alder buckthorn (*Frangula alnus*). Smaller amounts of herbs and ferns, including grasses, cereals, and weeds also appear throughout – including, interestingly, a single instance of hemp (*Cannabis sativa*) pollen just above the peat transition. These generally consistent proportions suggest that the local terrestrial, dryland area changed little in woody and herbaceous character over the time period investigated, and included some degree of arable cultivation at a distance from the sample site.

In contrast, on-site wetland taxa experienced a shift in proportions over time. Similar to the north-eastern pond (Profile F), Profile B contained very high values of alder (99%) at the base, decreasing to 40% by the top of the sampled section. Meanwhile, sedge, water plantain (*Alisma plantago-aquatica*), iris (*Iris*), cattails, and wetland fern taxa become increasingly prominent, suggesting a shift from a wet, boggy depression dominated by alder woodland into open water.

This evidence is entirely consistent with the presence of a mill pond, though not conclusive. There is no evidence of water lilies or other aquaphiles here. However, mill ponds are periodically cleared and constantly in motion when in use, which reduces the potential for pollen preservation. The shallow depth of the peat, along with data from the topographic survey (Chapter Four, this volume), suggests that the mill pond during the medieval period was probably relatively shallow. A mill under these circumstances would necessarily have employed an undershot wheel.

The radiocarbon date places the transition from alder fen carr peat to alluvial sediment in the middle of third millennium BCE, similar to dates obtained from peat elsewhere in the Bodiam landscape (Priestley-Bell & Pope 2009). The change appears to have been gradual, although some kind of destabilising event (possibly intensified land use) occurred in the late Neolithic or early Bronze Age. This event changed a stable peat-forming habitat to one dominated by soil erosion, transport, and deposition, possibly a floodplain.

Cattle or Mill Yard? Profiles C1 and C2

Two core profiles were obtained from this grassy area just to the south-east of the castle. As discussed in the previous chapter, geophysical survey suggested that a structure once stood in this corner of the property. Our initial suggestion was that this was a possible mill site given its relationship to existing ponds and ditches, but other evidence places the mill to the south-west of the castle (Chapter Four). We placed cores along linear anomalies evident in the geophysical results that had been identified as possible building foundations, next to or over water channels (Fig. 5.1). We were looking for low-lying silts beneath demolition debris. We were also on the alert for deep deposits that might represent a wheel pit, or any stratigraphic evidence for flowing fresh water, cereal cultivation, or waterlogged wood, any of which would suggest the operation of a

Table 5.C: Stratigraphy of Profile B.

Depth cm	Stratigraphy
0 - 3	Contemporary soil.
3 - 24	Fine-medium gleyed grey-brown silt (brickearth) (10YR 5/5 to 5/6). Some clay content.
24 - 46	Silt, grey (10YR 6/2). Gley with iron staining. Oxidised plant rootlets (especially 40-45 cm).
46 - 61	Clay and fine silt (10YR 6/2). Pale and diffuse mottling (10YR 6/8); greyer and wetter downwards. Oxidised rootlets.
61 - 69	Transitional context between humic silt (below) and brickearth (above). Pale brown to grey clay-silt with occasional charcoal specks.
69 - 88.5	Organic/humic silt, fibrous, coarsely laminated (10YR 3/1 to 4/1).
88.5 - 96	Humic silt with small plant inclusions, e.g. stems. Wood at 96-98 cm.
96 - 99	Dark grey-black peat (10YR 2/1 to 10YR 2/2).
99 - 102	Laminated, humic silt at base.

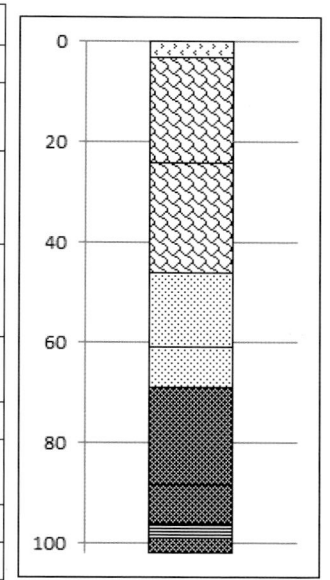

mill. However, instead, the cores suggest that the area has a long history of use as pasture with little sign of disturbance; the area as a whole may well have been a water meadow at some point. The shift to pasture likely occurred well before the medieval period, and it is more probable that the resistivity results are showing a cattle yard or byre complex. The anomalies could also reflect more recent upcast from moat excavations or clearing of drainage ditches. Excavation would be needed to confirm either interpretation.

Stratigraphically, the two profiles are very similar, as expected given their proximity. The 1 m profiles both had silty peat at their base, extending below the end of the core, overlaid by a transition from alluvial grey silt up to the modern soil horizon, including a thick layer of mature pasture soil (Tables 5.D & 5.E).

Pollen analysis

Because both profiles are stratigraphically similar, only one was examined for pollen and spores (C1; Fig. 5.8). Analysis again concentrated on the better-preserved peat and the transition into overlying alluvium (88-105 cm below the surface). The environment and vegetation significantly changed at around 99 cm depth, from an earlier alder carr woodland with peat accumulation, to an open herb fen, including a possible intermediate stage of wet fen with sedges.

The lower part of the profile (within the peat), from c. 99-104 cm, is dominated by trees and shrubs, particularly alder pollen (80%), significant proportions of oak (40%) and hazel (48%), and some few examples of lime and ash. Like other profiles, this suggests terrestrial oak and hazel woodland in the nearby vicinity, with wetter alder woodland directly on site. Some few grasses (3%) and a single grain of cereal pollen appear at this depth, along with multiple taxa of fern spores. Some wetland taxa are present at this level, including sedges such as cattails and water plantains.

The higher zone, silty soils from c. 88-99 cm, is defined by a reduction in the proportion of trees and shrubs, and a corresponding increase in herbs and wetland taxa. This opening of the pollen catchment may be due to woodland clearance, which may also be responsible for the change from a stable peat-forming regime to a more dynamic riverine environment. Sedges and ferns are present at higher proportions at the base of this section of the profile, declining higher in the section (88 cm). The proportion of grass pollen rises to 78% at the later time, with other herbs including ribwort plantain and small numbers of cereals. This increase suggests pastoral and arable agriculture in the near vicinity, perhaps on site, though it could also be the result of fluvial or aerial transport from more distant sources, or autochthonous, non-cultivated grassland. The high proportion of grass pollen together with the well-developed soil observed in the stratigraphic profile suggest that the earlier wetland was succeeded by very good pasture land, of a sort that generally takes hundreds of years to accumulate.

The Moat Bank: Profile D

Core D, located in the southern bank of the moat (Fig. 5.1), was obtained mid-morning while the castle grounds had few visitors. The core was placed just off the

LIVED EXPERIENCE IN THE LATER MIDDLE AGES

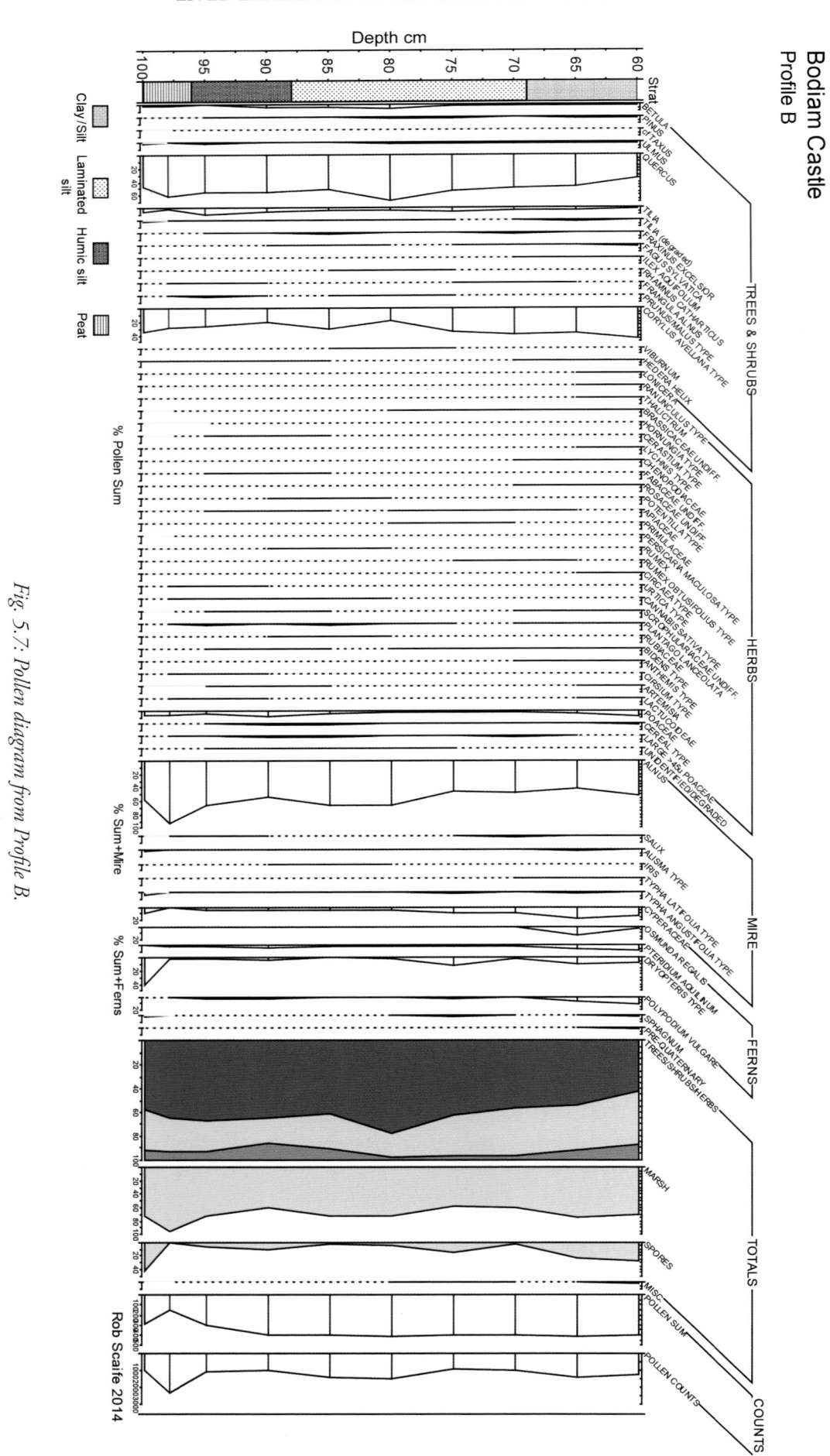

Fig. 5.7: Pollen diagram from Profile B.

Table 5.D: Stratigraphy of Profile C1.

Depth cm	Stratigraphy
0 - 3	Contemporary surface.
3 - 35	Thick, humic pasture soil. Fine sandy silt (10YR 5/6). Crumbly texture.
35 - 44	Finer and more compacted silty sub-soil. Pale grey band of medium silt c. 46-47 cm.
44 - 96	Gleyed brickearth (fine silt and clay), pale grey/buff brown (10YR 6/4). Iron mottling with oxidised rootlets. Silty clay towards base (homogeneous pale grey) (10YR 6/2 or 6/3).
96 - 01	Silt, darker grey with pale brown mottling. Wood fragment at 99 cm (probable modern root).
101 - 104	Humic silty peat, dark grey (10YR 4/2).

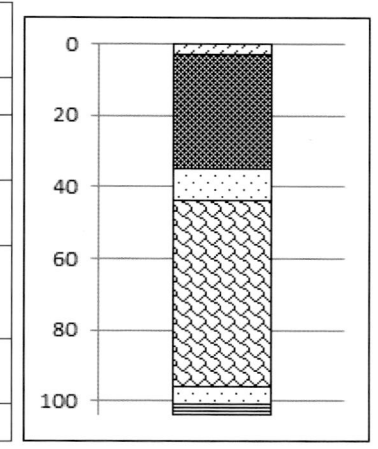

edge of the gravelled path on a grass surface (Fig. 5.9). We planned to assess whether excavated soil from the moat had been redeposited to create the bank, possibly manifesting as a clear division between a paleo soil and a layer of dumped fill. Lacking such a divide, we might have been able to suggest that earlier buildings were present on the site prior to the castle construction.

This profile is the deepest we obtained at Bodiam, with sediments to bedrock at 320 cm (Table 5.F). We tentatively identified a land surface at 88 to 93 cm below the modern surface. This is higher than expected for a natural land surface, which might be expected to slope gently towards the river at this point. The ground to the south of the moat therefore tentatively appears to have been sculpted to create a higher bank than was necessary, perhaps by layering dredged clay from the moat atop an existing scarp, or by cutting away soil to the south of the bank. This might also have had the effect of enlarging the mill pond.

The upper sediment consists largely of gleyed silt (brickearth) with sand lenses, possibly material built up during later additions to the moat bank. Below the possible land surface is a series of coarse-textured, silty marls, overlying lower, non-oxidised, grey silt, atop the bedrock.

These results are consistent with the moat bank section that was exposed next to the postern gate bridge abutment during alterations to the bank in 1995 (Stevens 1999), not far from our Profile D. This earlier work also showed a possible sloping surface at c. 1 m below the present ground surface, interpreted as the original 14th-century moat bank, with heightening of the bank tentatively dated via ceramic sherds to the 15th century. In contrast, sections of the north and west moat banks have shown no evidence of artificial construction (Barber 2007b). The moat appears to have been cut into the slope of the valley on the north and west, and artificially banked to the south and east, to create a level basin (see Fig. 5.3).

Table 5.E: Stratigraphy of Profile C2.

Depth cm	Stratigraphy
0 - 2	Contemporary surface.
2 - 5	Brown, well-sorted sub-soil. Probable worm action.
5 - 43	Thick, humic, sandy, mature pasture soil. Well-developed crumb structure. Many monocotyledonous roots.
43 - 84	Gleyed silty clay, pale grey and pale brown. Oxidised iron stains, possible roots. Some magnesium staining (esp. 84-86 cm).
84 - 101	Mottled silt, pale brown (10YR 3/3) and pale grey (10YR 6/1). Oxidised root stains. Sharp transition at base.
101 - 103	Humic silty peat. Black oxidised detrital with wood fragment.

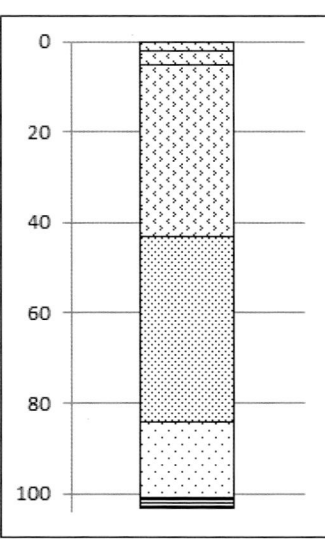

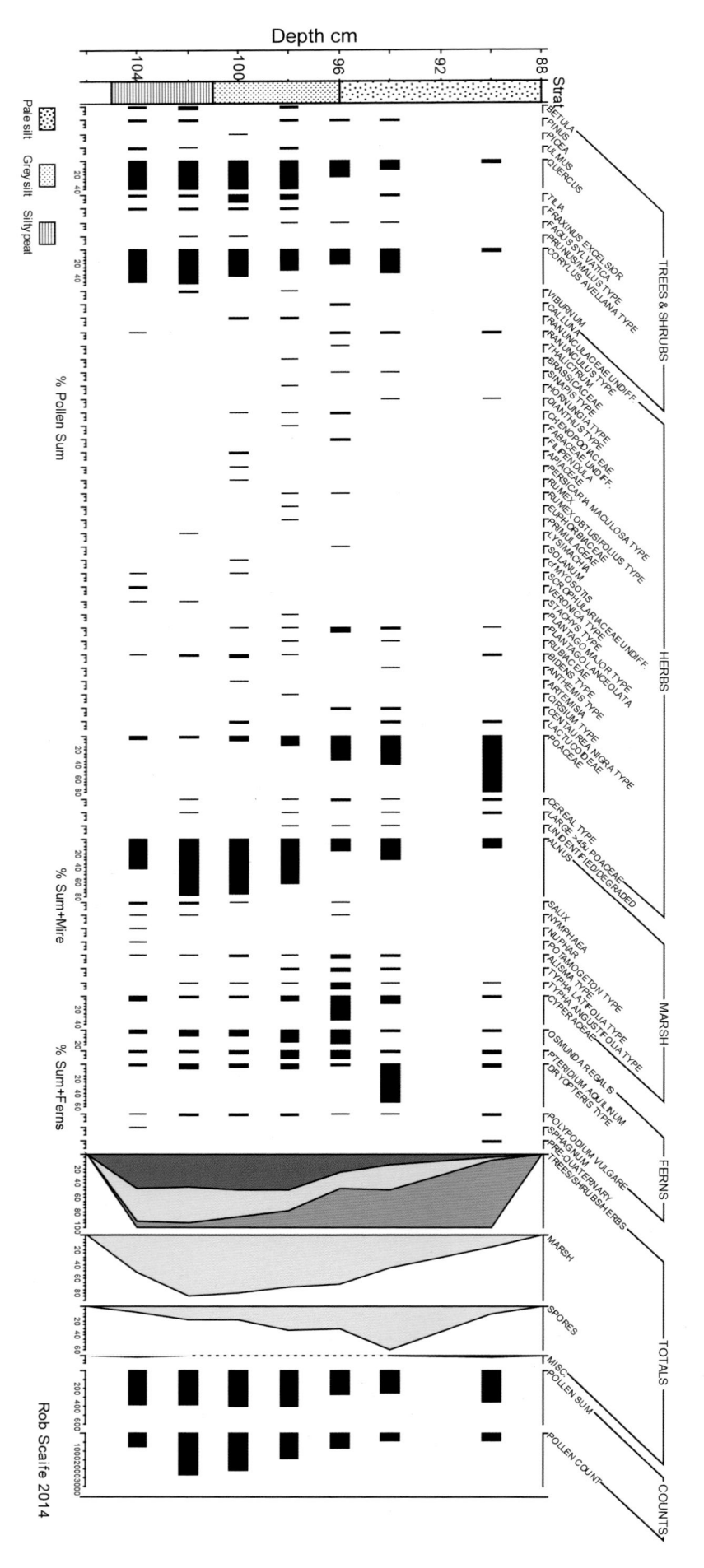

Fig. 5.8: Pollen diagram for Profile C1.

THE ENVIRONMENT OF BODIAM

Pollen analysis

Pollen could only be recovered from the lower, waterlogged, grey silty sediments, c. 2.86-3.20 m below the surface (Fig. 5.10). The oxidised and gleyed character of higher sediments resulted in very poor pollen preservation.

The lower zone, from c. 300-320 cm, suggests a watery habitat, perhaps a marginal aquatic fringe to a local alluvial or spring-fed wetland, with both alder fen carr and hazel woodland nearby. The assemblage is dominated by diverse woodland taxa, probably originating at a slight remove from the sample site. These include high values of hazel and alder, with some oak, birch, holly, and lime, and occasional pine, maple (*Acer*), and elm as well as ivy, viburnum, and willow. Herbs, especially grasses, are present in small numbers, with some ribwort plantain, chickweed (*Caryophyllaceaea cerastium*) and related species, and assorted flowering herbs (*Asteraceae*). There is also a small amount of sedges, including cattails, and some ferns, especially royal fern (*Osmunda regalis*) near the base of the section.

In the higher zone, from c. 286-300 cm, local conditions became wetter, and the fringing woodland declined or moved farther away from the sample site, likely giving way to pasture. Grasses are dominant, along with some cereals, ribwort plantain, hemp, and other pastoral and arable herbs. Woodland taxa include significantly lower amounts of hazel and alder pollen than in the lower zone, but oak increases near the top of the section. Sedges, cattails, and ferns are also reduced, though there is a single example of water-lily pollen (*Nymphaea alba*).

Fig. 5.9: James Miles, Dominic Barker, and Victoria Stevenson coring on the south bank of the moat (Core D in progress). Photo by Penny Copeland.

The East Pond: Profile F

Core F was obtained on the northern edge of the present small pond, located to the east of the moat (Fig. 5.1). While the castle was in use, the pond might have held fish, or served as a headwater pond for the mill, constrained movement around the castle, or most likely some combination of all three. This area has also been used several times as a dumping area for residue when the moat was dredged over the course of the 20th century (Johnson *et al.* 2000).

Though the area is currently vegetated wetland, we hoped that analysis of the underlying silt and pollen would suggest when and how the pond was constructed and used. The profile demonstrates that the pond existed during the whole history of the castle, and was almost certainly wetland before it became a pond.

This site had a 2 m thick, continuous sequence of largely humic mineral sediment and some peat (Table 5.G; Fig. 5.11). The very thick, undisturbed sediments under a layer of compacted leaves at c. 60 cm suggest that the area has been a pond for a considerable time. Above c. 60 cm, the stratigraphy consists of sand, gravel, and other dumped material. A radiocarbon measurement from a wood twig at 118 cm provided a date of 130+/-BP. This date can be calibrated to either 1670-1780, or to 1800-1950 (the calibration curve has two peaks at this point). The former date, close to the abandonment of the castle, is much more likely given the stratigraphic location of the sample. The 50-60 cm of structured sediments between this twig and the fill material suggests that the pond was undisturbed for many years after the castle's abandonment, before it began to see use as a dumping ground in conjunction with the landscape work of the 19th and 20th centuries.

Pollen analysis

Pollen analysis was only performed in the more structured sediments below 60 cm. There is a distinct division between the pollen assemblages above and below c. 1.70 m (Figs 5.11 & 5.12). The stratigraphy is very similar on either side of this divide, so it is probable that this small pond remained similar in form and structure over time, despite changes to the fringing vegetation. In the earlier phase, alder was dominant on the site, with some hazel and oak and few grasses, algae, and ferns. This habitat later changed to an open pond with fen herb type vegetation, including willow, with higher amounts of oak and diverse grasses and cereals, and lower numbers of wetland taxa and alder.

Table 5.F: Stratigraphy of Profile D.

Depth cm	Stratigraphy
0 - 4	Gravel below contemporary turf.
4 - 36	Bank material. Fine, friable, sandy silt.
36 - 88	Bank material. Brickearth; gleyed orange/yellow/brown silt (10YR 5/6). Iron staining. Oxidised plant roots.
88 - 93	Possible old land surface. Greyer silt. Limestone fragments up to 20 mm in diameter.
93 - 108	Sandy silt, orange/grey/brown (10YR 5/6). Fine sand inclusions. Gleying and charcoal specks, c. 103 cm.
108 - 129	Fine pale yellow sand (10YR 7/6).
129 - 161	Fine pale brown/yellow sand. Fine silt clasts give an almost brechiated texture.
161 - 174	Greyer sandy silt, brechiated texture.
174 - 203	Pale brown/yellow sandy silt (10YR 7/8 to 7/6). Paly grey clasts/intrusions c. 188 cm.
203 - 210	Orange silty sand.
210 - 274	Pale white/yellow to orange/brown calcareous sand/marl. Coarse, brechiated texture. No visible organic content.
274 - 285	Greyer silt.
285 - 286	Specks of magnesium (possibly charcoal).
286 - 315	Medium grey homogeneous silt (10YR 4/1 to 5/1). Magnesium (or charcoal) specks.
315 - 400	Bedrock. Mottled pale grey very stiff, brechiated silt. Some clay and calcareous inclusions.

The pollen evidence suggests that this area changed from a muddy depression in the ground with ephemeral standing water, to a proper pond later in the investigated time period. Dense alder woodland may have used the available water within the damp basin, leaving little for the use of other taxa or to accumulate in a permanent body of water. After the alder declined, possibly through woodland clearance by humans, the basin became wetter and marginal aquatic plants arrived, including water plantain, sedges, and marsh marigold (*Caltha palustris*). Standing water at this later time is evidenced by the cysts (dormant spores) of the algae *Pediastrum*.

The decline of the alder woodland opened the pollen catchment, allowing windborne pollen from the surrounding dry land to fall into the newly formed pond. Lower amounts of oak and herb flora during the earlier pollen assemblage are probably due to the masking effect of the alder rather than a true absence of the taxa in the area (Tauber 1965; 1967). Oak and hornbeam appear to have been consistently present in the local and near regional landscape throughout the time-span represented by the sediment. This may be evidence of regional managed woodland during later periods, maintained for construction materials or as a hunting park.

There is considerable evidence for arable activity throughout the later pollen assemblage zone, as expected for the late medieval and early modern periods. Small numbers of either hemp or hop (*Humulus lupulus*) pollen are present between 100-120 cm, around the time of the dated twig (118 cm, mid-17th century). These could be due to native local growth, or to cultivation for either fibre or brewing; the taxa have similar pollen morphology and cannot be distinguished. Hemp was also seen in the pollen spectra from the car park (B) and moat bank (D), see above.

At the top of the profile, the change to silt and possible dumped fill material also shows interesting changes

THE ENVIRONMENT OF BODIAM

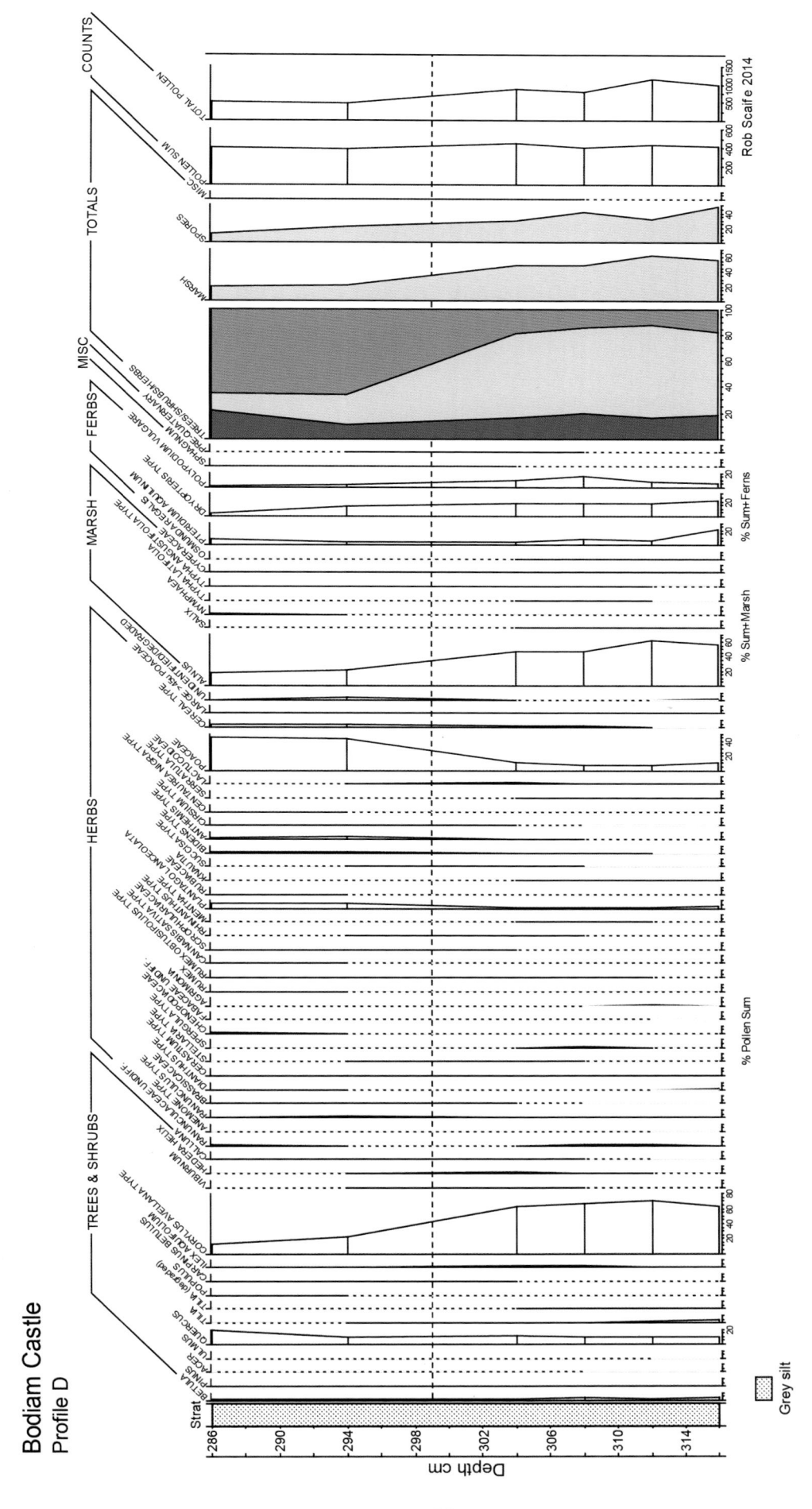

Fig. 5.10: Pollen profile of section D.

in the pollen. New taxa are probably associated with trees planted on the castle grounds by its more recent owners, including pine, spruce (*Picea*), lime, beech and holly. This expansion of pine and spruce may also provide a useful date marker for c. 1700-1750, as exotics (including reintroduced pine) were often planted in parks and gardens during this time.

Discussion

The landscape of Bodiam has a complex history and pattern of wetland activity and sediment types, spanning the late prehistoric to the post-medieval period. In general, the results provided here are consistent with previous work, which has shown the valley bottom near Bodiam to consist of layers of peat interspersed with alluvial sediments (see Chapter Two, this volume). Borehole work has suggested a V-shaped profile for the Rother valley near Bodiam, with more than 10 m of alluvial silt atop bedrock, upon which peat deposits have been deposited to a depth of up to 6 m deep in places (Fig. 2.4, this volume; Burrin & Scaife 1984; Burrin 1988). Previous pollen analysis of sediments from Robertsbridge also showed a similar pollen spectrum to those observed here at Bodiam (Chapter Two, this volume).

Until around the 3rd millennium BCE (the early Bronze Age), peat fens accrued in a stable environment of alder carr woodland, which had developed atop earlier alluvial sediments (Barber 1998; Priestley-Bell & Pope 2009). The environment then transitioned to one dominated by grey alluvial sediment (now gleyed, that is water-saturated and depleted of oxygen). The evidence presented here does not support a sudden, catastrophic change; rather, the pollen data supports a slow, continuous transition of increasing wetness, from alder woodland through wet fen and finally to alluvial floodplain (Priestley-Bell & Pope 2009).

Although there are documentary references to 'salt water' at Bodiam in the later Middle Ages (Chapter Two, this volume), there is no evidence of saltwater vegetation, salt marshes, or any other indication from the pollen assemblages that the sea ever extended inland to Bodiam, excepting perhaps occasional catastrophic flooding events that left little to no botanical trace.

Arable agriculture was present in the vicinity of Bodiam continuously from the Bronze Age through the present. This long-term evidence of arable might surprise the casual observer, as the prevailing image of the Weald is of heavy reliance on pastoral agriculture. These results remind us of two important facts. First, that most areas of preindustrial England featured a combination of arable and pastoral agriculture, even if there was a relative emphasis on one or the other that became more marked through time as market relations and regional specialisation deepened (Johnson 1996, chapter 2). Second, although some parts of the Wealden claylands may have been poorly drained and difficult to work, the Weald also provided fertile land that could be used for arable cultivation.

Prehistoric

On well-drained soils, lime woodland was dominant in the region during the middle Holocene (c. 8000-1000 BCE, or the late Mesolithic, Neolithic, and early to middle Bronze Ages), in association with oak, elm, hazel, and other deciduous flora. Lime began to decline in many places during the late Neolithic (c. 2000 BCE) (Scaife 1980; 2000; 2004; Greig 1992; Waller 1993; 1994a; 1994b), perhaps due to either climatic changes or changes in human use of the landscape, such as increased agriculture (Godwin 1956; 1975; Turner 1962). A reduction in lime pollen such as we observed at Bodiam may in part have been due to expanding wetlands, as fen growth pushed well-drained land and associated flora away from the sample site (Waller 1994b). The decline of the lime woodland and expansion of alder carr wetland have been radiocarbon dated to the early Bronze Age at Bodiam (2050-1730 BCE and 2500-2518 BCE (Barber 1998); 2455 BCE (this study)), and both could have been consequences of human activity, including woodland clearance.

Climatic elements that could have influenced a shift towards wetter conditions include post-glacial sea level increase, which could have pushed freshwater streams back, leading to waterlogging upstream and the development of ponds. Though these effects have been documented elsewhere in England (Long 1992; Long

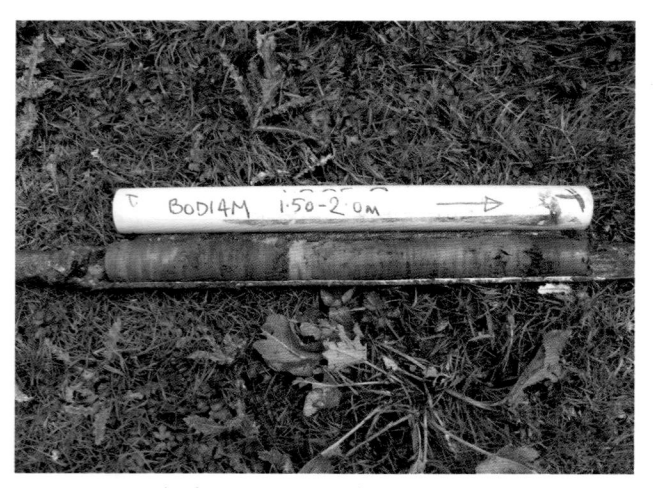

Fig. 5.11: The lowest 50 cm of Core F, in the east pond.

Table 5.G: Stratigraphy of Profile F.

Depth cm	Stratigraphy
0 - 19	Grey-brown peat. Plant remains (monocotyledons).
19 - 40	Grey silt (10YR 5/1). Gleyed (10YR 6/4). Occasional pebbles. Small twig at 35 cm.
40 - 68	Grey silt (10YR 5/1) becoming paler (10YR 4/1 to 6/2). Flint gravel rounded, subangular pebbles (up to 20 mm diameter). Compacted leaf fragments at 60 cm.
68 - 76	Black peat (10YR 2/1 to 2/2).
76 - 82	Brown-grey humic silt (10YR 4/2).
82 - 86	Peat with wood fragments.
86 - 111	Grey silt (10YR 4/2). Pebbles (up to 25 mm diameter) lower down.
111 - 114	Dark, humic peat.
114 - 170	Pale grey silt (10YR 5/1), oxidising to pale brown (10YR 5/4). Possibly freshwater environment. Magnesium mottling in places. Stone at 160 cm.
170 - 200	Brown, increasingly humic silt (10YR 3/2). Lenses of fine pale grey silt. No visible organic content.

& Innes 1993; Long & Scaife 1995; Waller *et al.* 1988; Sidell *et al.* 2000; Wilkinson *et al.* 2000), the changes at Bodiam seem to have occurred significantly later than the glacial retreat and corresponding sea level rise (c. 10000 BCE). Human impact, especially clearance of lime for agricultural expansion during the Bronze Age (c. 2500-700 BCE), would have caused a reduction in local evapotranspiration, leading to a higher water table and increased surface runoff. The overall result would have been a wetter local environment, changing the on-site mire from alder carr to wet herb fen, as observed in the pollen data.

Late Prehistoric and Early Roman

From the Neolithic through the middle Bronze Age, woodland and peat bogs dominated the deeper valleys and steeper hillsides. This period of stability came to an end in the middle Bronze Age (c. 1500-1000 BCE) when the landscape changed to grassland floodplain with seasonal alluvial sedimentation from the overflowing riverbank (Burrin 1981). The change was due to a combination of deforestation, sea level changes, and climatic shifts, but the primary cause appears to have been increased woodland clearance by humans, which destabilised local soils until significant erosion thresholds were crossed, a cusp event that precipitated the shift from a stable peat environment to an alluvial floodplain (Burrin 1988).

Woodland clearance, along with arable and pastoral agriculture, encouraged sediment deposition onto the valley floodplain and subsequent alluviation downstream. Woodland clearance causes a decrease in evaporative transpiration (or the amount of water that evaporates from leaves, stems, and flowers) and more surface runoff after rain. These changes in the local water cycle can raise the water table, leading to the development of springs, which appears to have occurred at Bodiam. More spring-fed streams further increased surface runoff, which led to higher rates of sediment and alluvium deposition into the river. River valleys in the area, including the Rother, contain up to 10 m or more of alluvium starting in the middle Bronze Age. This build-up was derived from erosion off of adjacent slopes, as well as sediment transported downstream along the river.

As dramatically larger volumes of sediment reached the river valleys, the valleys became shallower and hillsides less steep. Soils formerly attaching woodland to hillsides and mountaintops had entered the alluvial system, eroding the hills while increasing the depth of valley sediments, the width of floodplains, and the volume of sediment washed out to sea. Similar slow, progressive human-induced colluviation has been inferred along multiple Sussex rivers for the Neolithic and Bronze Ages (c. 4000-700 BCE) (Scaife & Burrin 1983; 1985; 1987; 1992; Burrin & Scaife 1984). This period of instability,

LIVED EXPERIENCE IN THE LATER MIDDLE AGES

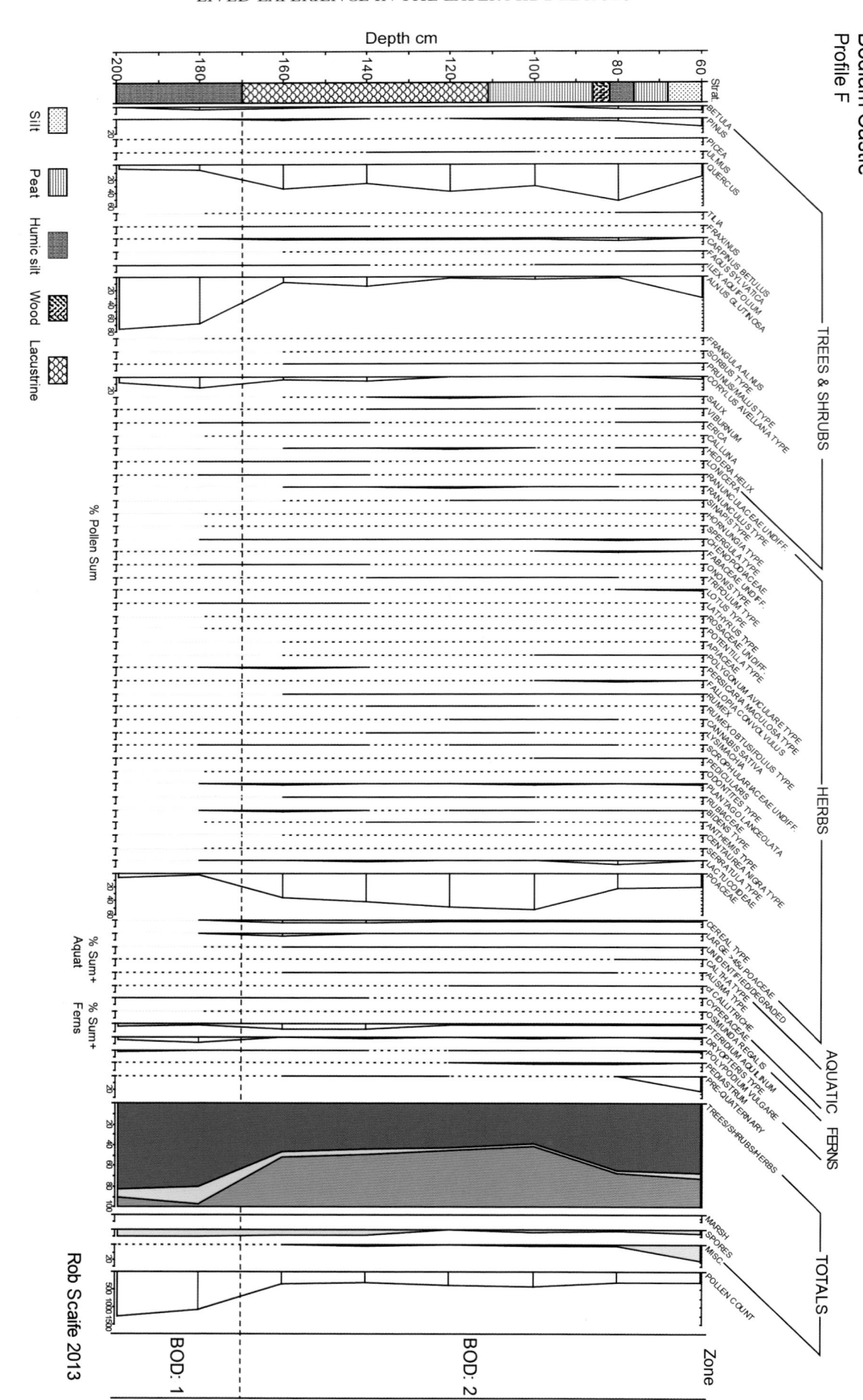

Fig. 5.12: Pollen diagram from Profile F.

characterised by sediment deposition in the Sussex valleys, likely lasted for about 1500 years, resulting in a new but very different environment into the Roman period.

Roman and early medieval

In general, stable wet alluvial conditions appear to have continued through to the medieval period, with mixed woodland, open grassland, and arable mixed agriculture at not too great a distance from the site. The transition of alder carr wetlands (dominated by trees and shrubs) to more open herb fen (dominated by grasses) widened the pollen catchment, allowing pollen from the more distant landscape to accumulate at the sample sites due to both fluvial and airborne transport. This opening of the landscape and increased erosion may also correspond to the infilling of river meanders, creating a wider, deeper channel that facilitated river traffic to and from the harbour at Bodiam throughout the medieval period. A shift from a wooded landscape to open grasslands was also observed in the vicinity of the medieval harbour during work in the Rose Garden (Priestley-Bell & Pope 2009) (see Chapter Two, this volume).

After the decline of lime pollen, oak and hazel (probably managed) became the dominant woodland on well-drained soils, with some birch, pine, and hornbeam. These taxa produce pollen that can travel significant distances on the wind, and so the mixed woodland may have been located at some remove from the site. However, less common taxa like ash, beech, holly, and some remaining lime do not travel such distances (Andersen 1970; 1973), and were therefore likely growing in close proximity to the site, despite the wet conditions. Furthermore, there are some indications (especially in Profile A) that earlier cultivated fields may have been successioning into woodland during this time.

Late medieval and post-medieval

Bodiam Castle was constructed in the 1380s, most probably in a low-lying, already wet place, either within or just adjacent to the Rother floodplain and close to woodlands and mixed arable agricultural land. The fine-grained, low-energy, freshwater sediments in the castle profiles (A1 & A2) suggest that the castle and moat might have been deliberately placed atop a freshwater spring, making full use of the watercourses and natural springs to feed the newly constructed moat. It may be worth considering how this change in local hydrology would have affected the villagers, who may have used nearby springs to supply household water and irrigation.

We found no evidence that the castle was built atop a much older manorial site, nor that a raised platform was constructed purposely for the castle foundation. Rather, the moat appears to have been excavated around the castle site, with some additional building up and levelling off of the floor within the castle. Excavated sediment from the moat was dumped close by, to build up the moat bank, and in low-lying wet areas such as nearby ponds. Proximity to water and aquatic resources would have been important to the castle inhabitants: for domestic use, to fill the moat and fishponds, to run the watermill, and to transport goods up and down the Rother via the flote or harbour (James & Whittick 2008).

The present study also did not provide evidence for or against the presence of a harbour as attested by documentary sources. Dallingridge may have diverted the course of the river from an original course slightly farther north (encroaching the present car park and touching the south-west corner of the mill pond), with the old course serving temporarily as mill runoff or as a small harbour (Whittick pers. comm.; Drury & Copeman 2016). However, Core B would not have intercepted either river course, so the present study cannot address this possibility.

Sediments within the castle, especially Profile A2, suggest that some of the original castle floors may have been flagstones atop a padding of chalk. After the castle was abandoned, probably in the middle of the 17th century, the flagstones were removed and humic, silty soils accumulated atop the chalk. Very small quantities of tree pollen suggest that trees were never common within the castle itself; limited amounts of pollen would have blown across the moat, while small amounts of cereals and herbs are likely the result of food processing, domestic waste, sweepings, and floor coverings during the active habitation of the castle. On the other hand, significant quantities of non-cereal grasses, ferns, and ivy pollen suggest these were growing within the castle and along the walls of the castle, probably after abandonment, consistent with eyewitness reports and artwork from the post-medieval to early modern periods (Fig. 5.6).

Woodlands, both wet alder carr and dryland oak and hazel, remained an important element of the landscape of Bodiam through the medieval and post-medieval periods. Better drained soils may have hosted enclosed parklands, actively managed and likely coppiced, that included pine, spruce, hornbeam, lime, beech, and holly. These taxa may have been introductions to the managed landscape surrounding the castle. Hornbeam, lime, beech, and holly are usually poorly represented in pollen profiles unless the trees were in close proximity to the sample site. Historical records suggest that pine and spruce in particular may have been introduced during the first half of the 18th century, when they become a popular feature of elite gardens (Evelyn 1664).

Though pollen profiles cannot distinguish between nearby fields and secondary sources such as processing activity or domestic waste, it is clear that cereals including rye (*Secale cereal*), hemp or hops, and grazing livestock were important elements of village and castle economy. The presence of grassland, both pasture and cereal, reiterates the significance of a mixed arable agricultural economy to the Bodiam landscape throughout its history, especially during the medieval period.

Conclusion

Through most of the Neolithic and into the early Bronze Age, the landscape near what would become Bodiam Castle and Village was a waterlogged, swampy woodland in the floodplain of the Rother, with alder trees forming the canopy above soggy peat growth. In slightly higher areas, where the land was drier and better drained (likely in the direction of the Weald), grew deciduous woodlands of lime, oak, elm, and hazel. The wetland expanded during the early Bronze Age, encroaching into previously drier areas, with alder trees replacing lime.

Though some of these early changes may have been due to woodland clearance for agriculture, the major effects of agricultural activity manifested during the middle Bronze Age. Soil erosion from surrounding areas increased, and the Bodiam landscape became a seasonal alluvial floodplain, clogged with sediment during much of the year and hosting wet grasses and herbs when the soils were sufficiently stable.

By the Roman period and into the early medieval period, this increased erosion and water runoff had created a deeper, wider river channel, facilitating maritime trade. The landscape near what would become the castle was still primarily wet for much of the year, likely fed by springs, with some woodlands and arable agricultural fields at not too great a distance. This low, wet place, between the floodplain with its harbour and the dry agricultural fields, presented an ideal location to dig a moat by the late 14th century. From the late medieval period to the present, managed watery features and active landscaping practices have kept the Bodiam landscape largely dry and dominated by woodland, grassland, and cereal production, though low-lying areas (such as the overflow car park/medieval mill pond) are still prone to flooding in severe weather.

Through analysis of pollen and the stratigraphic record of the site at point locations, we were able to investigate the evolving relationship between the Bodiam landscape and the people who lived in the area over the last six thousand years, from the Neolithic to the present. Most critically, early arable agriculture during the Bronze Age caused a shift from swampy alder wetlands to an eroding floodplain with high sediment flux. These changes created a landscape that supported the creation of a harbour, and later, a self-sustaining moat and a series of ponds that in part helped to drain the surrounding land. Bodiam's position, between the Weald and the marsh, made it not just an ideal location for trade and commerce between the two regions, but also continued a long history of negotiations between people and their landscape, as the push and pull between wetland, floodplain, and woodland both shaped and was managed by the human occupation of this dynamic landscape at the convergence of ecological zones.

6

SCOTNEY: ARCHAEOLOGICAL SURVEY AND MAP ANALYSIS

Eric D. Johnson, Matthew Johnson, Timothy Sly[1]

Abstract. This chapter focuses on the landscape of Scotney. Scotney is a late medieval castle close to Bodiam and built in the later 14th century. It also has a complex landscape, with water features, much of which survives within a 19th-century picturesque landscape park. The area of parkland south and west of the castle was surveyed by the Southampton/Northwestern team. This chapter reports on this work, and places the survey results in the context of wider evidence for the Scotney landscape in the later medieval period.

Introduction

Scotney Castle is situated in the middle of the Weald, on the border between Kent and Sussex in southeast England (Fig. 6.1). It is about 18 km north-west of Bodiam. Though not as well known as Bodiam, Scotney shares close parallels, both in terms of the building and the surrounding landscape, and is also owned and managed by the National Trust. It is a late medieval castle, surrounded by a landscape with complex water features, including a moat in the form of a small artificial lake. Its builders and owners were the Ashburnhams, a gentry family closely associated with Dallingridge (Saul 1986).

The modern visitor to Scotney approaches the site from the south-west, along a curving private road about 1 km from the public highway. The road runs on higher ground through wooded areas before affording views down to a valley to its right. The valley is now parkland, with wide grassy slopes and occasional trees, surrounded by wooded areas on the higher ground. The ruins of Scotney Castle are hardly visible behind dense tree growth at the bottom of this valley. The modern car park is next to the, much later, 19th-century Scotney New Castle, which stands on higher ground looking down on the older castle. The overall first impression for the visitor is thus of a 19th-century 'picturesque' landscape, laid out with parkland and carriage drives (Fig. 6.2). The modern approach to the site, and the features of the later picturesque landscape as a whole, have to be 'thought away' by the modern visitor before an understanding of the medieval site and landscape can begin.

The standing fabric of Scotney Castle has been the subject of a thorough analysis and interpretation, published in *Archaeologia Cantiana* (Martin *et al.* 2008; 2011; 2012). The castle is moated, and the inner court rises directly from the water, without a berm, as at Bodiam (Fig. 6.3). The water surrounding the castle is fed by streams from the south and south-west, and held back by an artificial dam to the west. This body of water has three islands within it, two of which have definite structural evidence from the Middle Ages. The middle island appears to have functioned as an outer court, with stables and other buildings. It was approached via a bridge from the north-west, as it is

---

[1] Timothy Sly directed the survey work for the field seasons of 2011 and 2012. Eric Johnson collated the 'grey literature', worked on relating map and survey evidence, and prepared the first draft of this chapter. Subsequent drafts were then revised by Eric Johnson, Timothy Sly and Matthew Johnson.

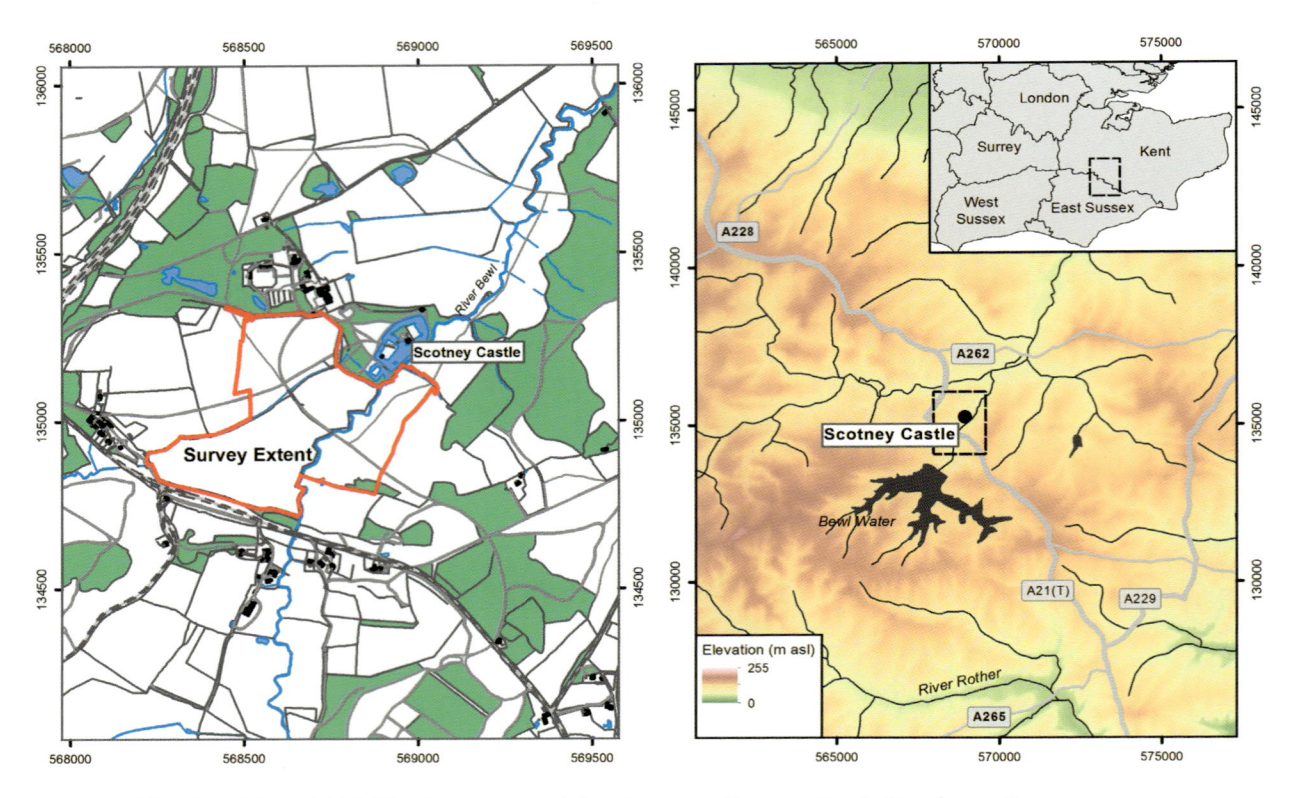

Fig. 6.1: 2011-2012 Northwestern and Southampton Scotney Castle Landscape Survey extent.

today. The inner court, on the island to the north-east, was approached via the outer court; it was rhomboidal in form, with a circular tower at each of the four main corners. The present structure is much more ruinous than Bodiam, with only one machicolated tower surviving to battlement level and the others largely destroyed; internally, the associated domestic buildings were much rebuilt in the post-medieval period. The medieval domestic arrangements, rather than being laid out around the sides of the courtyard as at Bodiam, instead formed a central block running from one side of the rhomboid to the other, with the hall in the centre and services to the south-east. This block was partially demolished in a wholesale rebuilding of the hall block dating to the 1630s, a rebuilding that was apparently never finished.

In the spring of 2011 and the summer of 2012, teams from the University of Southampton and Northwestern University carried out an archaeological survey of the landscape surrounding Scotney Castle, with Timothy Sly of Southampton as the primary director and supervisor of the work. The total area surveyed in 2011 and 2012 comprised the fields directly south-west of the castle, stretching to the boundary with the A21 bypass and up the slopes of the valley to the north-west and east (Fig. 6.1). The fieldwork at Scotney had three main goals. First, we wanted to gather data for the analysis of the wider medieval landscape surrounding Scotney Castle. Second, we wanted to provide data for the purposes of conservation management at the site and enhancement of the visitor experience, and third, it enabled us to train students in topographical and geophysical survey methods.

This chapter synthesises the data from the 2011 and 2012 surveys, historical documents and maps, and past literature (mostly unpublished) on the medieval landscape of Scotney Castle. The results of the survey contribute to a more detailed understanding of Scotney Castle and its landscape in the medieval period.

Fig. 6.2: General appearance of Scotney Park today, looking north from the valley bottom. Photo by Matthew Johnson.

Fig. 6.3: The inner court of Scotney Castle and moat, from the south-west. Photo by Matthew Johnson.

Much of the medieval landscape at Scotney remains conjectural, and there are many possible avenues for future research. However, we were able to establish that the Scotney landscape was every bit as complex as that at Bodiam in the later Middle Ages.

The Scotney estate is currently owned and maintained by the National Trust. The medieval moated site, often referred to as 'The Old Castle', lies along the confluence of the Sweetbourne and the River Bewl, in a valley south of the River Teise, about 1.5 km south-east of Lamberhurst. As noted above, much of the surrounding landscape was converted to a picturesque park in the 19th century by Edward Hussey III. As a result, most of the current vistas and pathways through the park have been arranged according to 19th-century aesthetic choices. The extensive 19th-century landscape alterations at Scotney present challenges in understanding and interpreting its medieval landscape. Confusingly, the designation 'Scotney Castle' sometimes refers to the neo-Tudor country house, also known as the 'New House', built by Edward Hussey from 1837-1844, located up the valley slope, north-west of the medieval site.

The data from the topographic survey provided evidence for medieval ponds and a possible mill site along the Sweetbourne, a sunken approach running parallel with the Sweetbourne down the hill to the castle, and a meadow which may have been flooded at various points in the past, just south-west of the moated site (Figs 6.4-6.6). One 60 x 60 m resistivity survey, targeted at earthworks south-west of the castle, confirmed the continuation of the sunken pathway from the south-west towards the castle (Fig. 6.4). A second 60 x 60 m resistivity survey was targeted over a number of large, possibly worked, stones within a copse along the southern slope of the valley, largely for the purposes of archaeological instruction in geophysics. The results of this survey were, unfortunately, inconclusive (Figs 6.6 & 6.7).

Scholars have recently described the 'designed' qualities of 14th-century elite landscapes as 'vehicles for contemporary elites to showcase their wealth and sophistication' (Creighton 2009: 1) or as active and complex stage settings for social action (Johnson 2002). As discussed in Chapters One and Two, surveys of other sites in the region, such as Bodiam Castle, have suggested that later 14th-century landscapes were organised around specific paths of movement and views of the castle along the approach (Taylor *et al.* 1990; Everson 1996). This may have been the case at Scotney Castle as well, considering the owners of Scotney and Bodiam, Roger Ashburnham and Edward Dallingridge, were contemporaries and associates. However, in order to understand the medieval landscape at Scotney, the highly ornamental 19th-century picturesque landscape must first be carefully unraveled from the medieval — both in the field and in the conceptual interpretation of the data.

Evidence for Medieval Landscape Features at Scotney Castle

Past surveys of Scotney Castle and the surrounding landscape have been carried out primarily for the purposes of conservation management (Bannister 2001; ACTA 2007; Hancock 2008; Martin *et al.* 2008; 2011; 2012; National Trust 2009). These 'grey

Fig. 6.4: Sunken approach to the castle, as viewed from the north-east looking up towards the higher ground. Photo by Matthew Johnson.

literature' reports are unpublished, but they provide a wealth of information on the archaeological and historical context of Scotney Castle and its surrounding environment. There is evidence of a complex medieval landscape at Scotney, which may have included a mill and associated ponds, a park, a moat with three islands, three possible approaches to the castle, and a possible floodplain south-west of the moat. The evidence for each of these features and the 2011-2012 survey's contribution to the evidence is summarised below.

Scotney stands in a boundary location. The current extent of the Scotney estate, now owned and managed by the National Trust, actually comprised three separate manorial holdings from the medieval period and into the 18th century: Scotney (alias Curtehope, Courthope), Chingley, and Marden. The manor of Scotney consisted of the land west of the River Bewl to Lamberhurst, while Chingley and Marden lay to the east of the Bewl, with the manorial boundary between the two running south-east through Kilndown Common (Fig. 6.8; Bannister 2001: 17). The River Bewl has been an important political boundary, dating from 1077 to the present. Described in a land charter of AD 1077, it was the early medieval boundary between the dioceses of Rochester and Chichester, the former boundary between Kent and Sussex (1077-1894), and the parish boundary of Lamberhurst and Goudhurst (1077-present) (Sawyer 1968: 1564).

Scoteni phase (13th century): Mill and ponds

The historical record suggests three possible phases of medieval landscape alteration at Scotney Castle. The first phase is associated with the Scoteni family in the late 13th century. Sir Peter de Scotney inherited and occupied the manor of Curtehope in 1285, and in 1295 he held half a knight's fee as lord of Curtehope (Redwood & Wilson 1958: 117; Witney 1976). This knight's fee is later described as comprising 80 acres of land and a mill (Du Boulay 1966: 372).

There is no definitive archaeological evidence for occupation at the current location of the moated site before the mid-14th century, but it is possible that the system of embankments and earthworks running along the Sweetbourne may be associated with the 13th-century mill (Bannister 2001: 37). William Clout's set of maps depicting the Scotney estate in 1757, copies of which are held at the National Trust archives at Scotney, identifies three fields along the Sweetbourne as 'Upper Pond', 'Lower Pond', and 'Mill Garden'. The course of the Sweetbourne also appears to have been artificially straightened, indicating possible human intervention and water management at the site. If the earthworks were in fact associated with ponds, the areas named Upper and Lower Ponds do not appear as water features on any historical maps, suggesting they were out of use by the 17th century (Bannister 2001: 38). While the River Bewl could also be a candidate for the location of the mill, it forms a boundary between three medieval manors, two counties and two parishes. Consequently, it may have been more difficult to negotiate the rights to use the Bewl to power a mill, instead of the Sweetbourne (Bannister 2001: 37). There are other known mills along the River Teise in Lamberhurst which de Scoteni could have owned, and to which the document is referring, but it seems

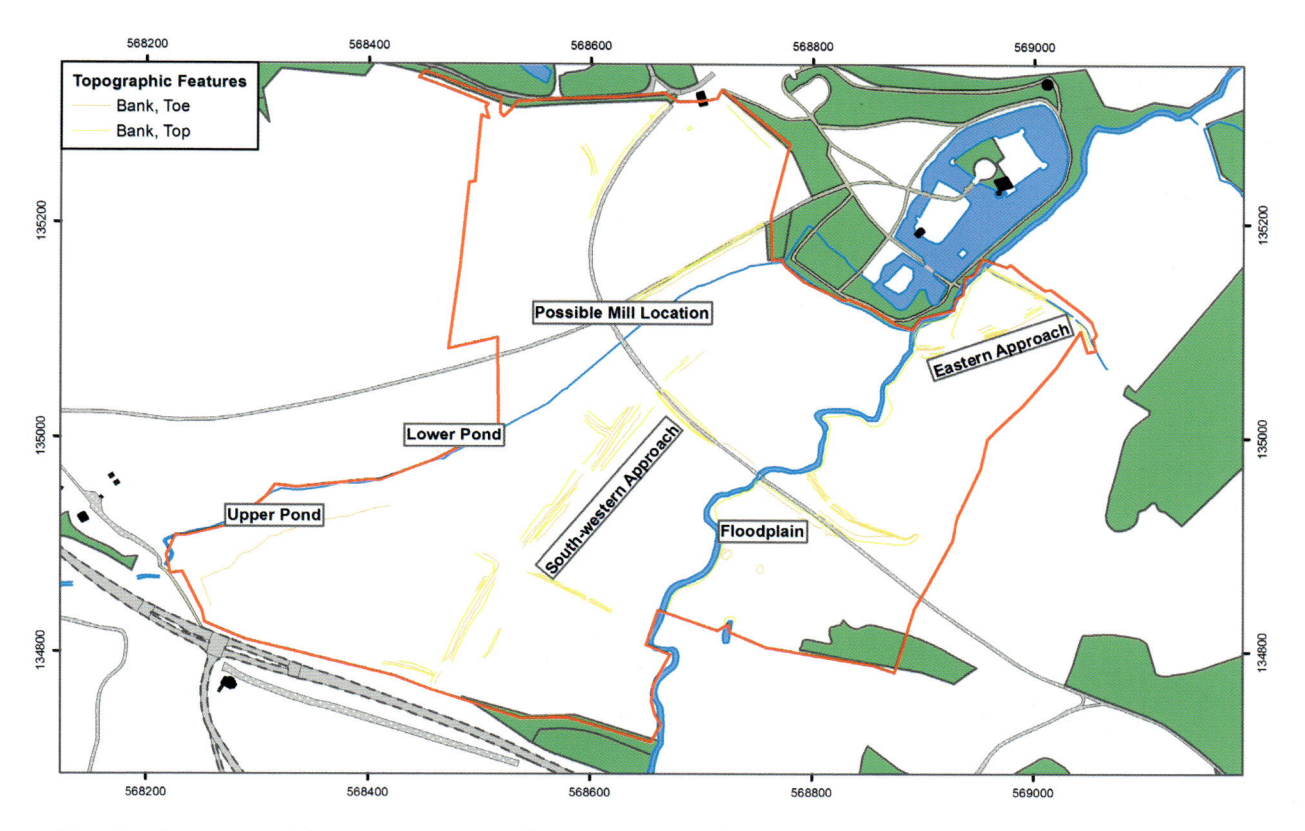

SCOTNEY: ARCHAEOLOGICAL SURVEY AND MAP ANALYSIS

Fig. 6.5: Summary of the 2011-2012 Northwestern and Southampton Scotney Castle Landscape Survey results.

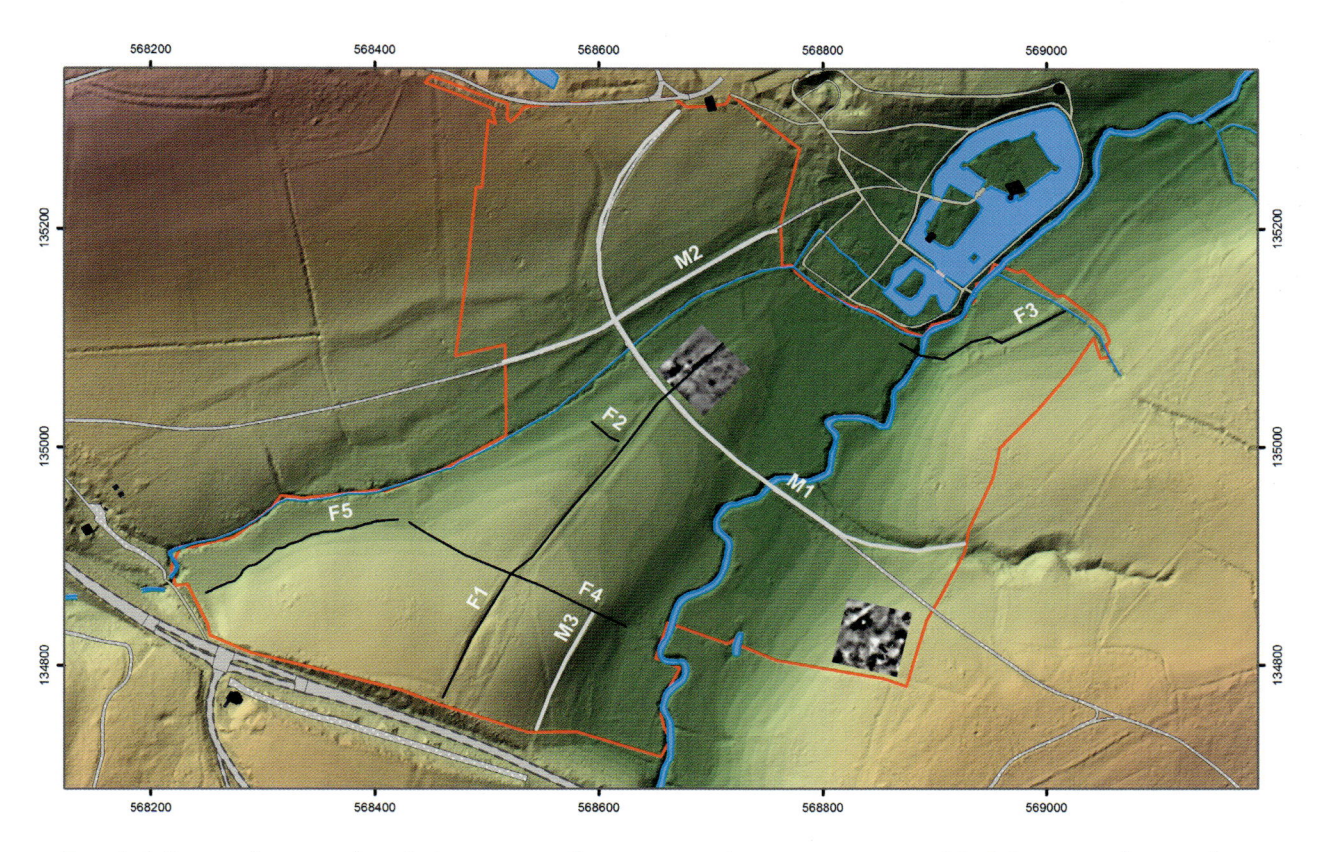

Fig. 6.6: Linear features identified in topographic survey and resistivity surveys; M1-M3 are modern pathways constructed in the 18th and 19th century.

as if a miller, called Helyas, controlled the mills in Lamberhurst at the time, as he granted 20s from mills in Lamberhurst to Leeds Priory in 1285 (CKS U47/32 Q1; Bannister 2001: 37).

The 2012 topographic survey confirmed the presence of possible pond bays, generally aligning with the location and shape of the Upper Pond and Lower Pond fields denoted on the 1757 map (Figs 6.9 & 6.10). Just south of where the Sweetbourne enters the estate the sharp base of the hill forms a linear topographic feature (F5), which aligns with the boundary in the 1757 map surrounding Upper Pond field (Fig. 6.9). The linear sunken feature running north-west (F2), perpendicular to the Sweetbourne and just south of the modern trackway, probably represents the field boundary identified in the 1757 map between Lower Pond and Mill Garden fields. At the point where the Sweetbourne enters the Scotney estate, just outside of the 2012 survey extent, there are significant earthworks, which may represent the artificial pond-bay boundary of the Upper Pond. There is no evidence for the dating of the ponds, and so they may have been constructed or modified any period before the 17th century. However, if the mill mentioned in the historical documents existed at this location in the late 13th century, then it would follow that there was least one pond associated with it.

Grovehurst phase (1300-1358): Park

The second phase of medieval landscape alteration at Scotney can be attributed to the Grovehurst family in the early 14th century. According to Nicola Bannister's research, derived from charters in Lambeth Palace Library (2001), in 1310 John de Grovehurst was granted the right of free warren in Scotney (Charter Rolls) and in 1312 he was granted permission to build a private chapel at his manor at Scotney. John de Grovehurst probably resided at a manor house on the Scotney estate by this time. Therefore, it is possible that an early phase of the current moated complex and medieval house dates to the early 14th century. However, there is no surviving fabric from such an early phase (Martin *et al.* 2008: 10). Besides the mention of Grovehurst's right of free warren in 1310, Henry Allen's 1619 map depicts 'Scotney Parke' and the fields bounded by the road through Lamberhurst and the River Teise (CKS U1776 P1). When oriented correctly, the outer boundary of the park depicted in the 1619 map broadly corresponds to parts of the current boundary of the National Trust estate today, north-west of the castle, along Collier's Wood and north-west to Claypits Wood. The 'interior' of the park is depicted as north-west of this boundary, outside of the current estate, towards Lamberhurst (Fig. 6.8). There are earthwork features on the ground, roughly tracing the park boundary depicted in the 1619 map, and Nicola Bannister has described these earthworks as the medieval park pale implied by John de Grovehurst's right of free warren in 1310 (Bannister 2001: 29).

Although this area was outside the scope of the 2011-2012 topographic survey, a preliminary walking survey was carried out to investigate the area. Without a more comprehensive topographical survey, there is currently not enough evidence to determine whether the system of banks and ditches is definitively a medieval park pale, or simply a substantial field boundary of any date.

Ashburnham phase (1358-1418)

Scotney passed to the Ashburnham family after Isabel, the widow of John de Grovehurst, married John de Ashburnham. John's son, Roger, Conservator of the Peace in Kent and Sussex, together with John Etchingham and Edward Dallingridge, from 1376-1380, inherited Scotney in 1358 (Martin *et al.* 2008). Roger Ashburnham can be associated with a third postulated phase of medieval landscape alteration. Although there is no licence to crenellate for Scotney, it is assumed Roger de Ashburnham constructed curtain walls, a tower, and a gatehouse at the site. The date of this construction has been given as c. 1378 (Bannister 2001: 20; ACTA 2007: 27; Martin *et al.* 2008: 10; National Trust 2009: 22), giving the site at least the appearance of a castle or fortified manor house.

The rationale given by scholars for such a specific date of construction is based entirely on comparative stylistic, architectural evidence and because of the French attacks on Winchelsea, Rye and Hastings in 1377. It has been suggested that the fear of a French

Fig. 6.7: Geophysical survey in the valley bottom, 2010. Photo by Matthew Johnson.

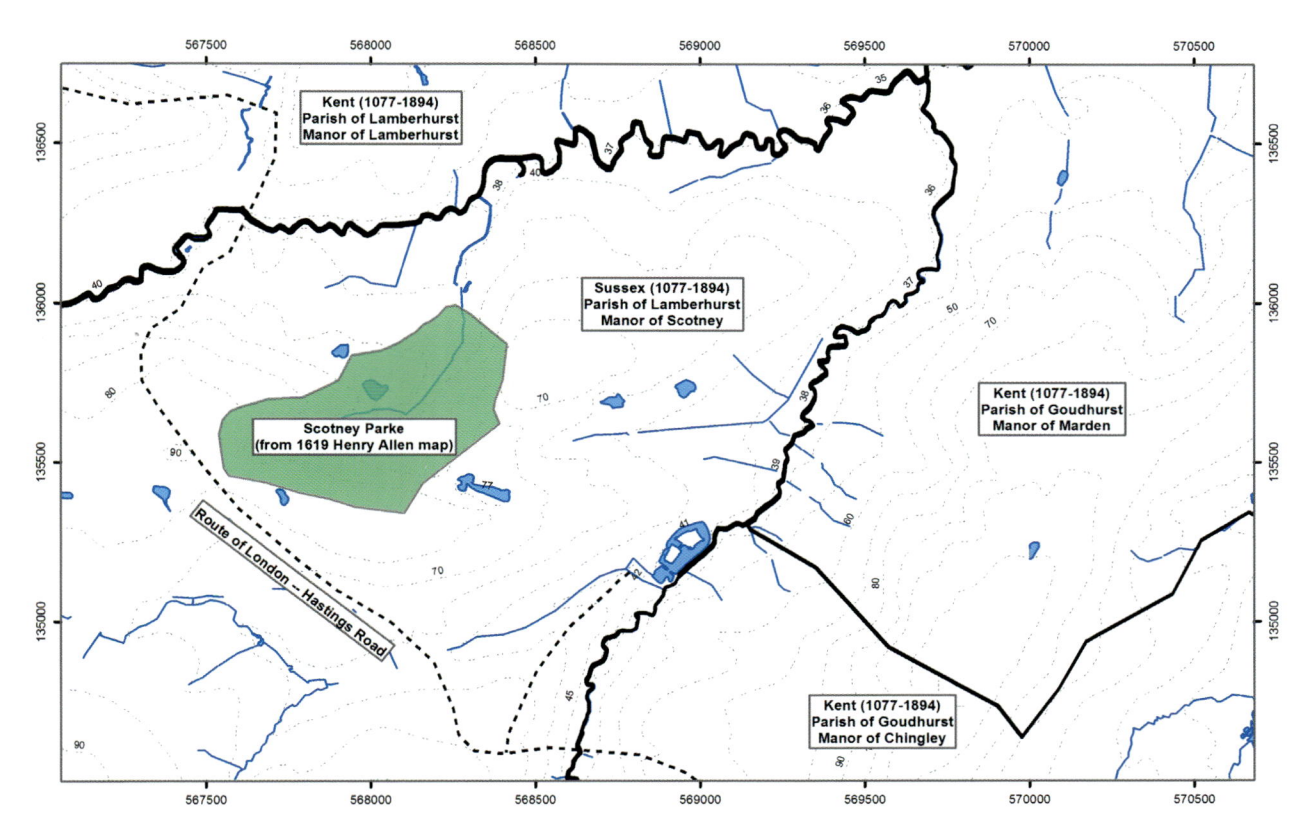

Fig. 6.8: Medieval administrative boundaries at Scotney, after Bannister (2001).

invasion would have provided the necessary motivation for building a castle without a licence (National Trust 2009: 22). However, the location of Scotney is much further inland than Bodiam, and is much further away from navigable water routes; it is therefore possible to be skeptical of a primarily defensive intent. However, the stylistic and other features of the castle make a date in the 1370s a reasonable assumption.

As David Martin and colleagues carefully point out, in an archaeological interpretive survey of Scotney Castle, 'it is not known whether the fortifications were placed around an existing house or whether a new site was chosen for the moated house' (Martin *et al.* 2008: 10). Given that there is no berm at Scotney, and the water of the moat abuts the Ashburnham Tower on the inner island, it is likely that the moat was at least modified or drained, if not constructed, at some point during Roger de Ashburnham's occupation of the site (1358-1392).

Features of unknown date: medieval approaches, moat, and meadow

The Clout map of 1757 shows three approaches to Scotney Castle, likely used by the Darell family during the post-medieval period, but possibly earlier — one from Kilndown, one from Lamberhurst, and one from Bewl Bridge Farm (Bannister 2001: 34). The earthworks running down the hill from the south-west and parallel to the Sweetbourne have been interpreted as a possible principal approach to the medieval castle (National Trust 2009: 24; Goulding and Clubb 2010: 6-7), although there is little concrete evidence for this claim. These approaches were altered or went into disuse in the mid-19th century, when Edward Hussey III transformed the landscape into a picturesque park and gardens (Bannister 2001: 30) (CKS U1776 F1/4-6). For instance, the 1870 Ordnance Survey Map, in contrast to the 1757 Clout map, depicts no pathway running north-east through the fields between the Sweetbourne and Bewl, south-west of the castle. Instead, the south-western half of the pathway is depicted as a simple field boundary, which was identified in the topographical survey (Fig. 6.6, F4).

The 2011-2012 topographic survey confirmed the presence of a slightly sunken linear earthwork feature running roughly parallel with the Sweetbourne and continuing towards the castle (Figs 6.4 & 6.5, F1). When georeferenced with the 1757 Clout map, this topographic feature conforms to the area marked 'Lane' on the map and the field boundary in the 1870 Ordnance Survey Map. The resistivity survey straddling this earthwork feature, just north-east of the modern trackway, revealed a linear patch of high resistance, which may indicate compacted soil associated with the Lane depicted in the 1757 map (Fig. 6.6). The 2011-2012 survey also identified earthworks just east of the Bewl and south of the castle (Fig. 6.6, F3). These earthworks align with the Lane depicted in another 1757 Clout map of the area, east of the Bewl, running down the valley slope through Kilndown wood (Fig. 6.9).

Unfortunately, the date of construction for the moat remains unconfirmed. Considering that the general moat-building chronology in England is 1200-1325 (Aberg 1978), it is possible a moat existed at the site during the Scoteni or Grovehurst phases of occupation, although the Grovehurst phase seems the more likely of the two. John de Grovehurst was granted right of free warren in 1310 and granted permission to build a chapel in 1312, two features often associated with elite moated sites in the area. For example, the nearby moated site known as The Mote, near Iden, with a licence to crenellate in 1318, and a permission to build a chapel in 1320, was presumably constructed within the same decade as Grovehurst's initial occupation of Scotney (Gardiner & Whittick 2011).

It is also possible, however, that the moat was constructed during the Ashburnham phase of construction. Nearby Bodiam Castle has a licence to crenellate dating to 1385, and assuming the moat was dug around the same time as the castle was constructed, this is within a decade of the presumed Ashburnham phase of construction. It is also possible that the moat had multiple phases of construction, perhaps starting with a single island and then other islands were added over time with different owners, although there is no concrete evidence for this claim. As is usual with topographical surveys, the 2011-2012 survey of Scotney produced no direct evidence for the date of construction, or alteration, of the moat.

An unpublished report on the Scotney estate suggests the large flat area just south of the gardens, at the confluence of the moat and the River Bewl, may have been seasonally flooded as another piece of a 'designed landscape', but the report gives no evidence for this claim (ACTA 2007: 28). The 2011-2012 survey confirmed the general topography of this meadow and, indeed, the flat area stretching south of the moat and straddling the River Bewl appears to be a floodplain (Fig. 6.6). It is possible that before the Bewl reservoir dam was constructed in 1975 the whole area surrounding the River Bewl was either seasonally, or permanently, flooded at various points in the past.

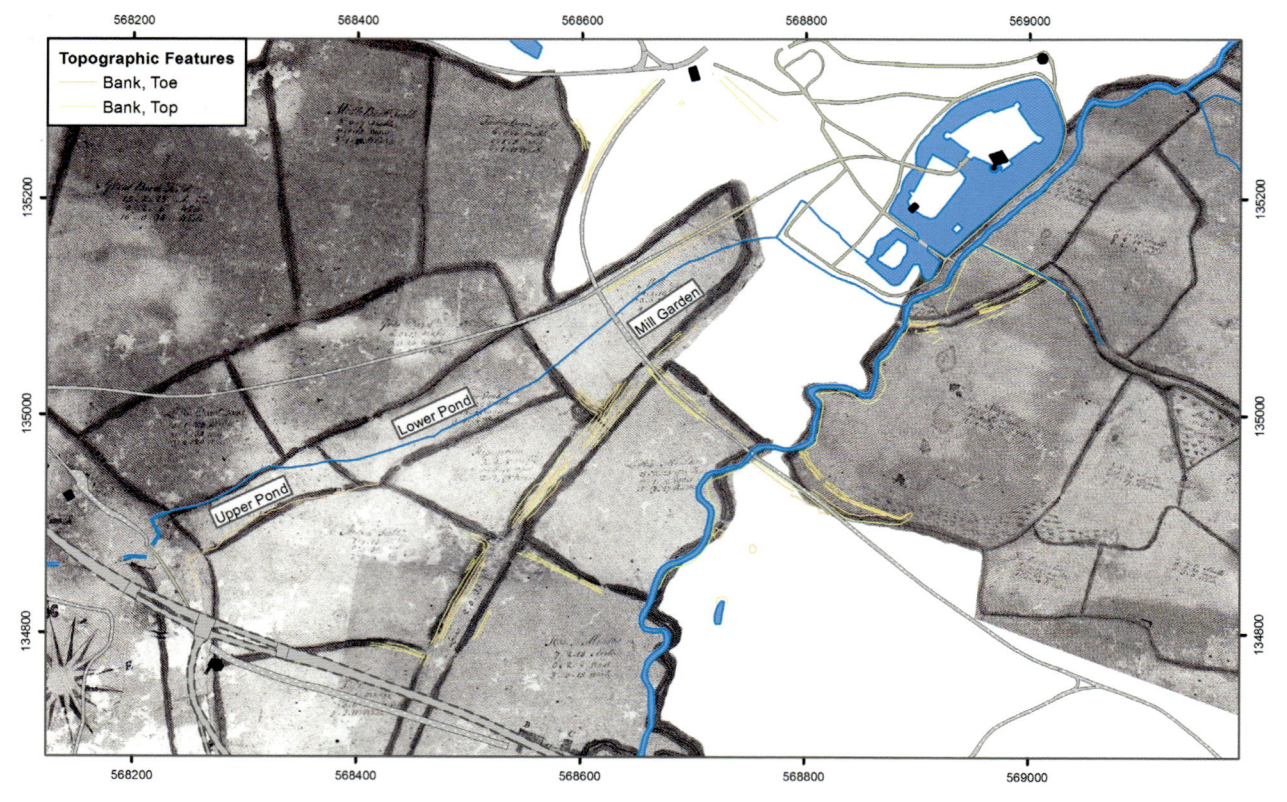

Fig. 6.9: 1757 William Clout map (south-west of castle) georeferenced and overlaid with topographic features identified in the 2011-2012 survey of Scotney Castle.

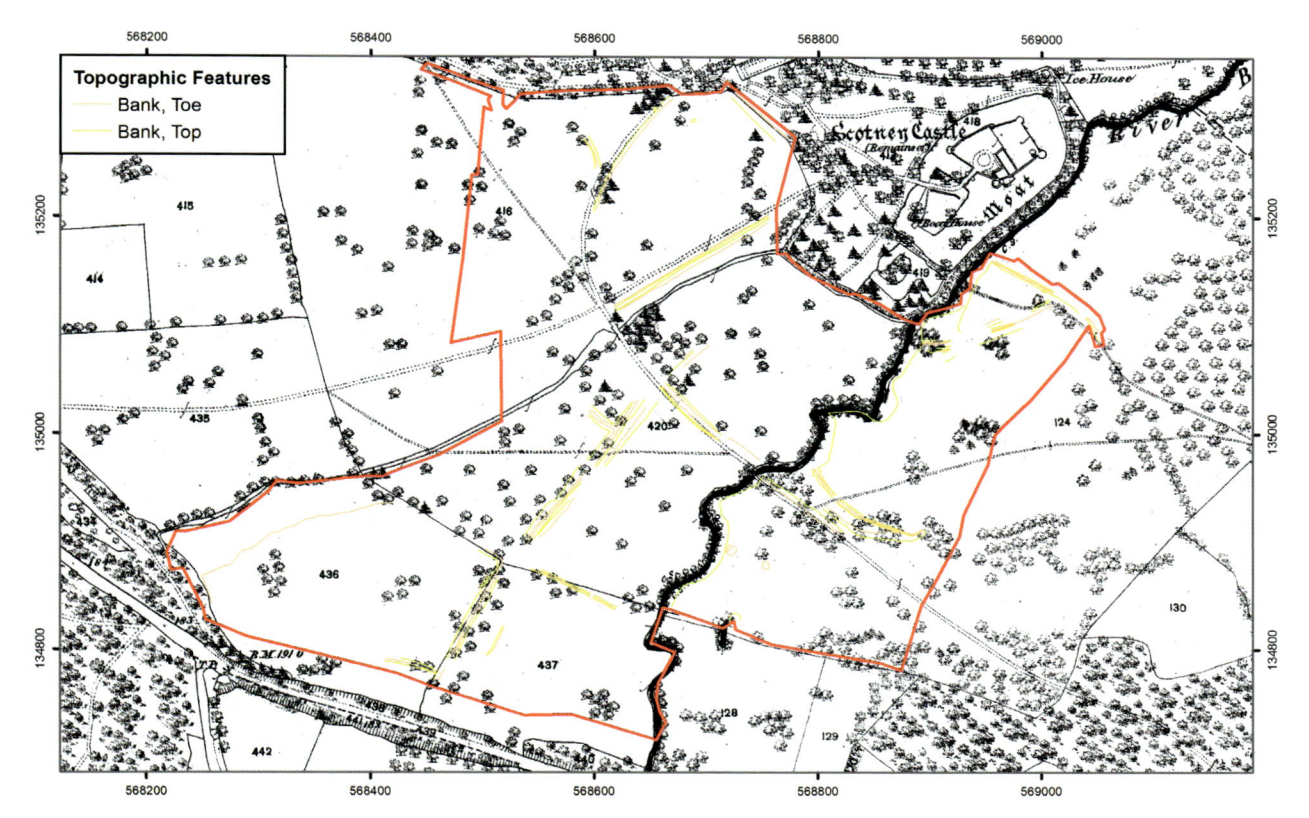

Fig. 6.10: 1870 Ordnance Survey map (south-west of castle) georeferenced and overlaid with topographic features identified in the 2011-2012 survey of Scotney Castle.

A Designed Landscape?

Based on the available evidence, Scotney Castle as it appeared in the later Middle Ages probably had a much more elaborate watery medieval landscape than is apparent today. If the mill, mill ponds, park, moat, and possible floodplain were all in existence, along with the south-west approach, during the Ashburnham phase of construction, this would be compelling evidence for the landscape being experienced as an impressively 'designed', elite medieval site — much like its neighbour Bodiam Castle (Taylor *et al.* 1990; Everson 1996). In accordance with emergent perspectives on medieval castles and their 'designed landscapes' in the past decade (Johnson 2002; Creighton 2009), this possible landscape affords specific vistas of the castle and surrounding moat, while travelling on a route surrounded on either side by mill ponds and a flooded meadow. The visitor would then pass by the mill and turn at a 90 degree angle to enter the central moat island, probably the outer court (Martin *et al.* 2008: 11), and then turn again to enter the inner court under the gatehouse.

However, the argument for a complex designed landscape, which was intended to impress, requires, in part, that this set of water features be visible from the principal approach to Scotney. It is clear from Edward Hasted's experience of the site in the late 18th century that visibility of the castle was not a priority, at least for the Darells, the post-medieval owners of the estate:

> *About half a mile below Bewle bridge near the east bank of the stream, is the mansion of Scotney, situated in a deep vale, and so surrounded with woods, as to give it a most gloomy and recluse appearance.*
>
> (Hasted 1798: 297)

The views provided by the current picturesque landscape are tightly controlled and radically different than they would have been before the late 18th and 19th century. While much of the surrounding woodland would probably have been managed and coppiced, especially on the slopes of the valley (Bannister 2001: 24), it is still unknown whether the fields south-west of the estate were covered in woodland, or not, during the medieval period. The 1757 map names the fields on either side of the south-western approach as 'Quarry Field', 'Stream Field' and 'Hop Garden', suggesting that these areas were not heavily wooded, at least in the post-medieval period. More archaeological investigation is required to reconstruct the density of woodland in the medieval period along this approach.

Bodiam, Scotney and Etchingham

Scotney has parallels with Bodiam, in terms of its social context, its architecture, and its landscape. These parallels are quite striking, though they are not as straightforward as they appear at first sight, and they need to be set out with care.

Scotney's builder, Roger Ashburnham, was closely associated with Sir Edward Dallingridge. Dallingridge, Ashburnham, and Sir William de Etchingham were three local gentry named together as Conservators of the Peace in Kent and Sussex between 1376 and 1380. Sir William de Etchingham, whose family was at least as important as the Ashburnhams and had indeed been the most important family within the Rape of Hastings, had houses at the settlement at Etchingham (about 9 km west of Bodiam and 14 km south of Scotney, from which he took his name and where he also rebuilt the church) and at Udimore. Both houses have been completely destroyed, though some earthworks survive east of the church at Etchingham, and documentary information indicates this was a place of some status and importance, with a long history stretching back to before the 13th century (Vivian 1953). Ashburnham, however, was not a knight; he also did not obtain a licence to crenellate for Scotney. It is tempting to link these two observations: if Charles Coulson and others are right in seeing licences to crenellate in largely honorific terms (Coulson 1993; Davis 2007), then Ashburnham's apparent lack of concern for a title may be linked to his apparent lack of concern about a licence.

Etchingham, Scotney and Bodiam are all moated sites. They are also larger examples of the class of moated sites that is so frequently found in the Weald, and will be discussed further in Chapter Ten. Etchingham sits in a flat and level location, while Scotney and Bodiam sit in a dip in the landscape, with higher ground on at least two sides. This location has, in all cases, been utilised to construct and maintain water features. Both Bodiam and Scotney sit close to the boundary between the counties of Kent and Sussex. Bodiam is in the middle of its manor, whereas the Scotney site sits on the margins of several different manorial estates.

Scotney shares design parallels with Bodiam. The 'footprint' of Scotney's inner court and that of Bodiam are roughly similar in size. Scotney is surrounded by a moat and other complex water features; it has four circular towers linked by curtain walls. It has been suggested that Henry Yevele had a hand in both designs, though the evidence is stylistic and based on inference (Harvey 1954). However, it also has important differences. The towers are much more squat than at Bodiam. The surviving Ashburnham Tower has machicolations; what those machicolations supported is unclear: a full-height parapet and crenellations or smaller battlements. Scotney is approached via an outer court. Its domestic buildings are not in line around four ranges, but are arranged across the centre of the site. The surrounding curtain wall is much thinner and also much lower than at Bodiam. Though building accounts do not survive for either site, Bodiam clearly represents a much larger input of labour and resources. Etchingham was a somewhat larger and more important place than Scotney, and as is common in the later Middle Ages, had a substantial church associated with it. Taken as a whole, a comparison of Etchingham, Bodiam and Scotney adds support to Coulson's assertion that the complex landscape and architecture of Bodiam is an example of a common phenomenon in the later Middle Ages, rather than an unusual or exceptional piece of architecture (Coulson 1992: 75, 89).

Conclusion

The 2011-2012 archaeological survey of Scotney Castle has provided evidence for medieval ponds, a possible mill, a south-west approach to the castle, and a possible floodplain south-west of the moat. If these features were all in use at the time of the Ashburnham phase of construction, the landscape at Scotney Castle can be seen as a close parallel to that of nearby Bodiam Castle. This is a feasible claim, considering their owners were contemporaries, both being appointed as Conservators of the Peace in Kent and Sussex, along with William de Etchingham, from 1376-1380. Indeed, while Ashburnham may have been responsible for the fortification of the manor house, it is problematic to attribute the elite landscape at Scotney to Ashburnham alone; the historical record suggests that, like Bodiam, Scotney accumulated a palimpsest of landscape features over time, with various owners contributing to what we can identify today. Regardless of the 'designed' characteristics of the Scotney landscape, this survey has also contributed to our understanding of how an elite manorial residence used the surrounding environment to organise and manage the flow of water, materials, and people in and out of the estate.

More evidence is required to flesh out our understanding of the Scotney landscape. First, the topographical survey could be expanded to cover the entire area surrounding the castle. Beyond this area, the field boundaries associated with a possible park pale need further attention. This should be done in conjunction with LiDAR data, and a detailed examination of the

1619 map by Henry Allen (CKS U1776 P1) and a walking survey of the fields north-west of the Scotney estate, following the boundary of the supposed park. Second, the geophysical survey could be expanded in two locations. The current 60 x 60 m resistivity area, close to the Sweetbourne, should be extended north-east to determine if the sunken trackway continues to the edge of the modern garden boundary. A geophysical survey could also be carried out on the north side of the Sweetbourne, along the boundary of the field denoted 'Mill Garden' on the 1757 Clout map, in order to locate the foundations of the mill referred to in the 1295 document (Fig. 6.9). Finally, further environmental archaeological methods may be able to reconstruct parts of the medieval landscape at Scotney. Systematic coring of the pond areas and floodplain north and south of the hollow way could confirm possible periods in which these areas were covered with water. Extensive pollen sampling may be able to reconstruct past density of woodland, relative to the present day.

7

KNOLE: SPORT, LABOUR, AND SOCIAL CONTEST

Dominic Barker, Ryan Lash, Kristian Strutt[1]

Abstract. This chapter presents the results of the topographic and geophysical survey undertaken at Knole, Kent, in August 2013. Drawing upon a variety of primary and secondary sources, these results are situated within the context of the long-term history of the Knole landscape and its deer park. A former archiepiscopal property, and still an active deer park and private residence, Knole may appear distinctive among the other National Trust properties surveyed in this volume. However, deer parks were once also crucial elements of the landscapes attached to Bodiam, Ightham, and Scotney. Knole's particular history and landscape demonstrate the changing role of deer parks as scenes of sport, labour, and the negotiation of social hierarchy from the late medieval period onwards.

Introduction

To a contemporary visitor, Knole House and its surrounding landscape look very different from the other National Trust properties in this book (Figs 7.1 & 7.2). The vast house is now laid out around seven main courtyards, dwarfing the plans of Bodiam, Ightham and Scotney (Fig. 7.3). Walled gardens adjacent to the house enclose an area even larger than the house itself. Though Bodiam and Scotney, and possibly Ightham, were once associated with nearby deer parks, only Knole still maintains an active park – indeed the largest surviving medieval deer park in England. Set hard by the bustling market town of Sevenoaks, Knole is also the only property in the survey that still functions in part as a private residence. The Sackville Estate owns most of the deer park and shares stewardship of the house with the National Trust (Fig. 7.4).

However distinctive it may appear today, Knole, like Bodiam, Ightham and Scotney, was a manorial property in the late medieval period. Indeed, construction of a manorial residence appears to have been underway when William Fiennes sold the property to Thomas Bourchier, Archbishop of Canterbury in 1456. Writers usually credit Bourchier with the consolidation of earlier works into a habitable residence and the foundation of the deer park. Bourchier's successors acquired Knole along with their archiepiscopal title until Henry VIII obliged Archbishop Cranmer to cede him the property in 1537. Knole remained a royal property, intermittently leased out to aristocratic residents, until Thomas Sackville (after many years of divided lease) acquired complete ownership of the property in 1604. Little of the exterior fabric of the building has been altered since Thomas's renovations in the first decade of the 17th century, and the Sackville name has been associated with Knole ever since.

Scholars have failed to reach a consensus on the chronology of development for particular aspects of the house, walled gardens, and surrounding deer park (for

---

1 The fieldwork report presented in this chapter was directed and supervised by Kristian Strutt and Dominic Barker and was conducted by 12-15 students from Northwestern University and the University of Southampton in summer 2013. The final survey results were written-up by Dominic Barker, Ryan Lash and Kristian Strutt. Ryan Lash collated and synthesised the 'grey literature', and developed the wider arguments on deer parks and hunting presented here. The chapter was edited and revised by Kristian Strutt and Matthew Johnson.

Fig. 7.1: The west frontage of Knole House dominated by the four turrets of the gatehouse tower of Green Court. Early etchings and geophysical results indicate that this area was once more elaborately designed with bowling greens and pathways. Photo by Ryan Lash.

recent accounts see Dixon 2008; Gregory 2010; Town 2010; Newman 2012: 337-49). Indeed, the divided stewardship of the property has meant that archaeological assessments commissioned by the Trust or the Sackville Estate have tended to focus research and discussion on only one or another of these three aspects of Knole. This chapter contextualises recent research alongside Knole's existing 'grey literature' and recent discussions of medieval deer parks. It is intended as a starting point for better integrating analyses of the house, park, and gardens.

As with the other sites in our study, the primary goal of the geophysical survey at Knole was to identify remains of late medieval activity at the property and to understand these in terms of lived experience and political ecology. The team applied a number of different techniques including topographic survey, magnetometry, earth resistance, and Ground Penetrating Radar (GPR). Largely, though not entirely, confined to the western area of the house and its two westernmost courtyards, that is the areas under the

Fig. 7.2: This view of Knole House and the surrounding garden wall from the north illustrates how much more expansive this property is from the others surveyed in this book. Photo by Matthew Johnson.

LIVED EXPERIENCE IN THE LATER MIDDLE AGES

stewardship of the National Trust, our survey identified a number of features that merit further investigation. Most interestingly, GPR survey within the western outer court (Green Court) suggests the presence of sub-surface remains that may predate the construction of the courtyard. Additional investigation of this area, including open area excavation, could shed light on the ongoing debate concerning the origins of Green Court (Bridgman 1817: 149-50; Colvin 1963-82: 218; Faulkner 1970: 145-6; Gregory 2010: 76-8).

In addition to the geophysical and topographic surveys, the team conducted an informal survey of the deer park more broadly, guided in part by an earthwork survey commissioned by the Trustees of the Knole Park Estate in 2008 (Wright 2008). Identifying, dating, and even recognising earthworks within the deer park are difficult endeavours. However, juxtaposing survey results

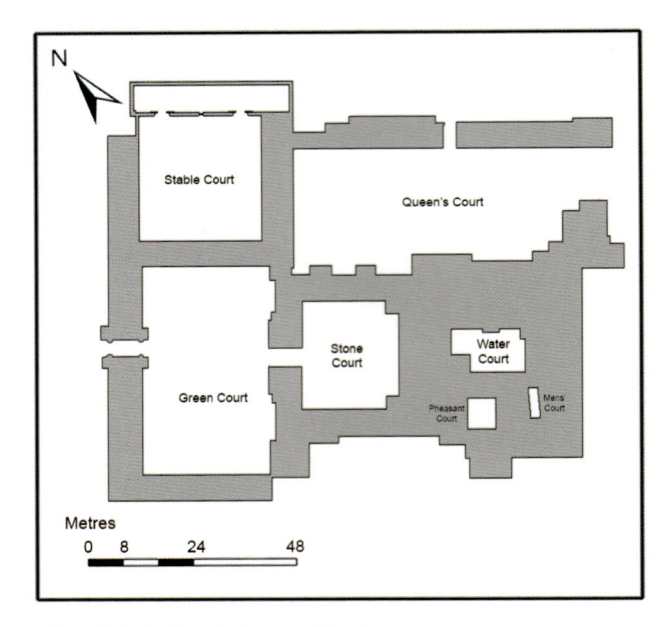

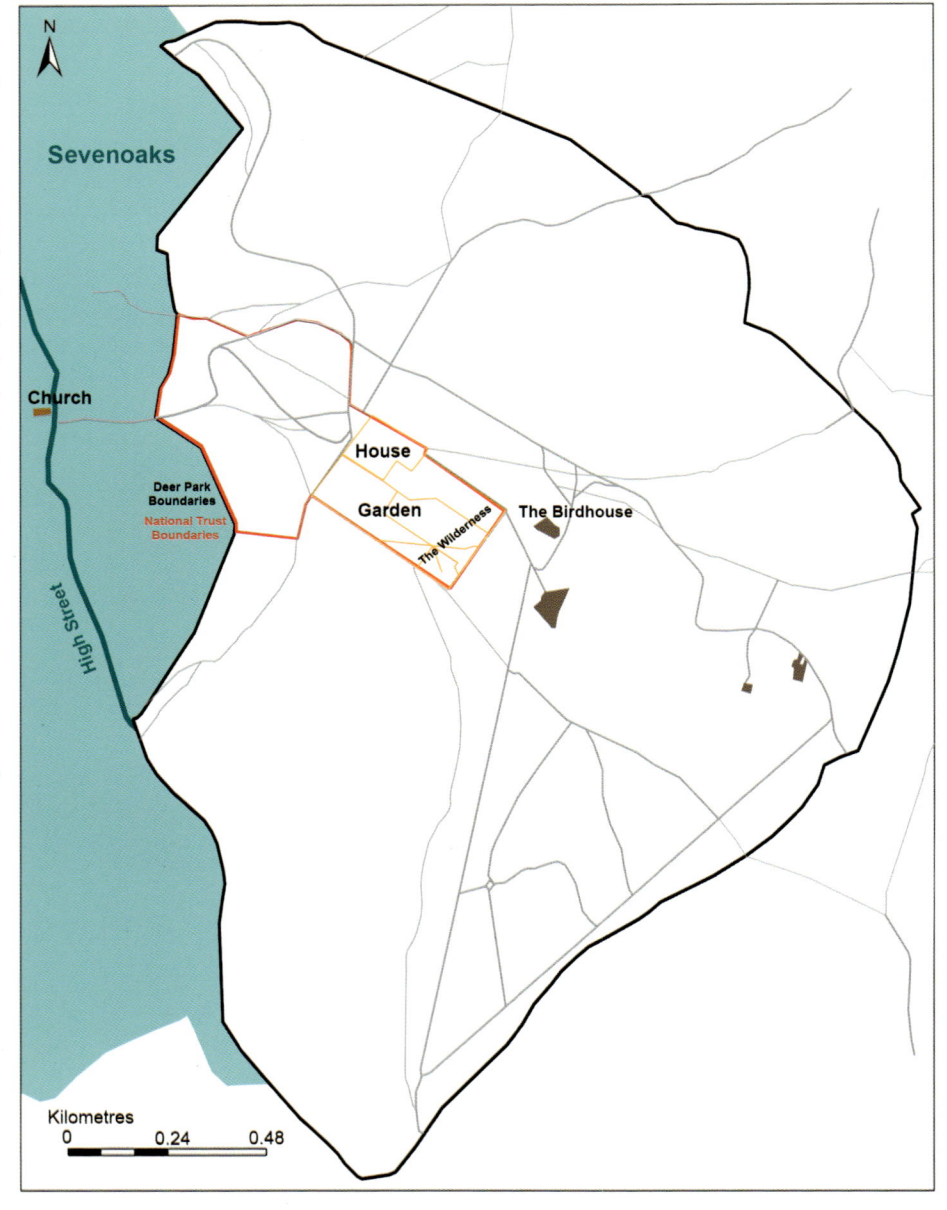

Fig. 7.3: (Above) A simplified plan view showing the main courtyards of Knole House. Scholars have offered various interpretations of the structure's phasing with the date of Green Court as the major point of debate. GPR survey in 2013 identified a buried rectilinear feature within the courtyard. Future excavation of this feature could help to resolve the chronology of Green Court's construction. Drawing by Kayley McPhee.

Fig. 7.4: (Right) Plan of Knole landscape indicating the areas under the stewardship of the National Trust and the Sackville Estate. The park's 930 acres were acquired incrementally over many centuries with final acquisitions in 1825-1826. Drawing by Kayley McPhee.

108

alongside archival records, other contemporary hunting grounds, and contextual evidence for the many different practices and resonances of medieval hunting, allows us to discuss a topic relevant to all of the residences in our survey: the lived experience of late medieval parks as places of sport, labour, and social contest. Knole Park was periodically the scene of elaborate staged hunts, of the mundane work of agriculture and industry, and of riotous protests by common people opposed to the claims of elite privilege. Knole's deer park, like other landscapes in this study, emerges not just as a stage setting for elite performance, but also as a place of work and social disobedience that implicated people from different class backgrounds across many centuries.

Knole: History and Context

The Knole landscape's deep historical and political ecological context

The complex underlying geology of south-east England has had significant repercussions for patterns of human settlement over the millennia. Set between the chalk downs to the north and the Wealden clay lands to the south, the Knole estate is located along the Lower Greensand ridge, whose bedrock formed some 100-125 million years ago. While not particularly productive for arable cultivation, the greensand ridge supports heath and woodland that was particularly appropriate for a medieval deer park. From a broader perspective, Knole's position along the greensand ridge places it at the junction of different landscapes that have afforded different forms of settlement, subsistence, and political relations.

Just north of the greensand ridge, the Darent Valley has been seen as an important channel of movement and settlement within Kent since prehistory (Everitt 1977). From its formation in Westerham, the Darent River runs east towards Sevenoaks and then north through a gap in the North Downs before flowing into the Thames. In contrast to the greensands of Knole, the Darent Valley is characterised by the more fertile Gault Clay. The appeal of this landscape for settlement is apparent in the density of archaeological remains within the valley. Just 6 km north of Knole along the Darent valley sits Otford. In proximity to Otford's town centre are a Bronze Age bowl barrow and multiple Roman sites from the early centuries CE, including a villa and a cremation cemetery at Frogfarm (Pearce 1930; Ward 1990). Additionally, the 7th to 8th-century inhumation cemetery at Polhill is thought to have served an Anglo-Saxon community dwelling at Otford (Philip 2002: 33). By the 9th century, Otford was the centre of an estate owned by the see of Canterbury. Today it houses the ruins of an archiepiscopal palace commissioned by Archbishop William Warham in the first quarter of the 15th century.

Regardless of the density of archaeology in the Darent Valley, early settlers were certainly not avoiding the greensand ridge. The earliest evidence of human activity within the park comes from a series of Mesolithic (8,500-4,000 BCE) flint finds (Wright 2008: 2). Later prehistoric settlement remains are apparent further afield. A Bronze Age bowl barrow sits on the crest of a prominent sandy ridge at Millpond Wood, some 1.3 km north of Knole Park. Excavation showed that this barrow had been constructed over an earlier Mesolithic flint working site (Abbott 1896). Alastair Oswald has recently suggested that a similar site may lie within Knole Park. The low mound surmounting Echo Mount, now surrounded by a clump of trees, may represent a much-eroded Bronze Age barrow (Alastair Oswald, pers. comm.). The setting – what appears as a high-point in the landscape today – as well as the recent recovery of flint flakes in this area, supports this hypothesis (Fig. 7.5).

Compared to the Darent Valley, there is a dearth of archaeological evidence for Roman and Anglo-Saxon settlement activity at Knole and Sevenoaks. However, a combination of place-name and documentary evidence suggests that early medieval people used the greensands for woodland resources and rough grazing

Fig. 7.5: Neolithic or Bronze Age worked flint uncovered at Echo Mount in 2015. Similar pieces have been found over the last few years, while the Sevenoaks Museum holds a bag of flints reportedly collected from Echo Mount in the early 20th century. These likely also represent surface finds, as the area does not seem to have ever been excavated. Photo by Nathalie Cohen.

(Everitt 1977; 1986). The north-south running hollow ways that traverse the greensand ridge and lead into the Weald were constructed in this period to facilitate the seasonal movement of stock. One such droveway is still visible near Sevenoaks at Kettleswell (Killingray 2010: 40). In Alan Everitt's interpretation (1977; 1986), early medieval settlers eventually transformed seasonal encampments on the greensand ridge and the Weald into permanent settlements dependent on estate centres located on the fertile river valleys and foothills to the north. By the later medieval period, this process created a distinctive pattern of settlement and political relations. This landscape was characterised by relatively isolated small farms, whose tenants enjoyed greater independence from elites – or at least less onerous feudal obligations. This settlement history was a probable factor in the particular perceived unruliness of Kentish husbandmen and yeomen in the later medieval period (see below and Chapter Twelve).

The origins of Sevenoaks and Knole may well belong in the early medieval context of this north to south movement of people, animals, goods, and legal authority between estate centres along the North Downs, settlements in the Weald, and ports along the south coast (Knocker 1926). Whatever the case, the landscape of Knole developed into a major stage for the production and contestation of political authority in subsequent centuries.

The development of Knole Manor, c. 1200–1456

Du Boulay (1974) and Gregory (2010) offer the most detailed accounts of the early history of the Knole estate leading up to its possession by the Archbishop of Canterbury, Thomas Bourchier, in 1456. The earliest references to the estate at Knole and the adjacent town of Sevenoaks date to the 13th century. Sevenoaks was certified as a market town as early as 1200. It was at this time a portion of the manor of Otford. In 1297, a number of tenants from Sevenoaks owed pannage (swine grazing) rents to the Archbishop of Canterbury (Du Boulay 1974: 2). Tenants appear to be mostly smallholders, engaged in various crafts and woodland management rather than arable agriculture. During the 13th and 14th centuries, three local families accumulated rent-paying estates in the vicinity of Sevenoaks – the de Knoles, the Grovehursts, and the Ashburnhams. As their surname suggests, the de Knole's property was concentrated to the south-east of Sevenoaks in the area of present day Knole Park. The head of this family in the late 13th century, Robert de Knole, was bailiff to the Archbishop of Canterbury's Liberty from 1292-1295 (Du Boulay 1974: 5).

During the 14th century, Knole was acquired by and incorporated into the estates of the Grovehursts and then the Ashburnhams. The accumulated property is first referred to as the 'Manor of Knole' when it was inherited by Roger Ashburnham in 1364 (Du Boulay 1974: 6). Roger is unlikely to have had his primary residence at Knole, as he simultaneously owned the Scotney estate where the remains of his manor house still stand. The next two owners are also unlikely to have resided at Knole. Thomas Langley, the Bishop of Durham, purchased the manor in 1419 and it fell to his son-in-law Ralph Leigh after his death. The principal properties of both men were far from Knole (Gregory 2010: 12-3).

At some stage between 1444 and 1450, Knole was purchased by James Fiennes, the Lord Say and Sele. Fiennes had begun work and may nearly have completed building a manor house when he was killed during the Jack Cade rebellion of 1450. Within the existing house at Knole there is no evidence of architectural fabric predating the mid-15th century. Hence, it is unclear whether there was any large-scale manorial residence at Knole prior to Fiennes's work. Gregory offers the intriguing suggestion that the ruins of a house predating Fiennes's work may lie elsewhere at Knole Park. To the east of the house, on a hill that forms the highest point of the park, is set an octagonal cottage and a series of low, ruinous walls. The former, called the 'Birdhouse', is a neo-Gothic structure probably built in the mid-18th century. The latter was described by Vita Sackville-West as a sham ruin fabricated around 1761 (Fig. 7.6; Sackville-West 1922: 26). Knole's late 18th-century residences may well have created the folly from existing stone remains. The main gate arch is certainly no earlier than the 16th century. There is a possibility that other portions of the ruin – of flint construction with rubble core and freestone dressing – may represent medieval architecture, perhaps *spolia* from Otford if not an early manorial residence at Knole. Extending geophysical survey to this area in the future could identify the original form of the ruins or any activity predating the Birdhouse.

Archiepiscopal and royal residence: 1456-1604

Over the last decade, building surveys and archaeological assessments accompanying renovations and construction at Knole have afforded opportunities to examine the building sequence at Knole (Munby 2007; Bartlett 2007; Dixon 2008; Peyre 2010). Synthesising this work, Gregory suggests that James Fiennes had nearly completed a manor house at Knole when the estate was bought from his son by the Archbishop Thomas Bourchier in 1456 (2010: 20-1, 27). Though isolating this building within the existing

Fig. 7.6: Detail of the folly ruins near the Birdhouse. Some of the architectural fabric may have been salvaged from earlier ruins in this location or from Otford. Photo by Matthew Johnson.

fabric of Knole House is difficult, it is likely that this building was centred on what is now known as Water Court (Fig. 7.2; Gregory 2010: 29-38).

Scholars have debated Bourchier's contribution to the house, park, and gardens visible at Knole today. Most agree that Stone Court and the Chapel belong to his tenure (Colvin 1963-82; Faulkner 1970; Emery 2006; Munby 2007). Of Bourchier's successors, the majority of building work is credited to John Morton (1486-1500) or William Warham (1503-32) (Kilburne 1659: 244; Hasted 1798; Bridgman 1817: 149-50; Gregory 2010: 3-7). This work included the construction of the ranges enclosing Pheasant Court and the remodelling of the east range around the Leicester Gallery, the Spangle Bedroom, and the Kitchen. The origins of Green Court remain obscure. Most accounts attribute Green Court either to Bourchier's archiepiscopal successors or to Henry VIII (Colvin 1963-82; Faulkner 1970; Emery 2006; Munby 2007). Building accounts and limited archaeological investigation offer an alternative possibility. Annual account records from the 1470s indicate an emphasis on the purchase of bricks. Though few bricks are visible in ranges of Green Court, their fabric does include brick. More importantly, small excavations in Green Court have uncovered rubble layers of brick and mortar below the courtyard's south range (Martinez-Jausoro 2009; Peyre 2010: 6). Potentially, the internal ranges of Green Court were originally constructed in this brick, but later rebuilt during renovations in the 17th century (Gregory 2010: 82-3). Geophysical survey within Green Court in 2013 identified a linear anomaly running at an angle to the courtyard walls (see Fig. 7.17 below). Additional exploration of this feature could shed light on the chronology of Green Court.

Bourchier is also often credited with the foundation of an orchard and lavender garden, though the source of this claim is unknown (O'Halloran & Woudstra 2012: 35). The first reference to the paling of the park comes from 1468, and so Bourchier was probably responsible for the foundation of the deer park at Knole. The extent of the park at this time is unknown, but it expanded incrementally in subsequent centuries. (A larger consideration of the use, labour demands, and social dynamics of the deer park is pursued below,).

The deer park is perhaps what attracted Henry VIII to the property. The king visited Archbishop Warham at Knole many times between 1504 and 1514 (Taylor 2003: 165). In 1537, Henry pressured Warham's successor, Thomas Cranmer, to cede him the property. The extent of Henry's contribution to Knole is debated. However, expense records indicate that one Sir Richard Longe was paid 'for making the King's garden at Knole' (O'Halloran & Woudstra 2012: 35). It is unclear how this garden related to the existing gardens at Knole. The estate remained a royal property, leased out to a series of tenants until the early 17th century. The final royal tenant, John Lennard, built a 12 ft ragstone wall to protect four springs within the garden that supplied the house. This work defined the existing boundaries of the garden, and the ragstone wall still encloses much of the garden today (Rardin 2006: 7; O'Halloran & Woudstra 2012: 35).

Under the Sackvilles: 1603-Present

In 1603, Thomas Sackville, Lord Treasurer and cousin to Elizabeth I, used the powers of his office to sell the freehold of Knole to himself. Between 1605 and 1608, Sackville undertook major renovations that gave Knole House the form it largely retains today. Sackville oversaw the rebuilding or remodelling of aspects of Stone Court, Water Court, Stable Court, and Green Court (Munby 2007; Town 2010). At this time, the south range of Green Court was demolished and rebuilt further south. This range was renovated again in the mid-18th century as the Orangery. A parch-mark visible within Green Court running parallel to the Orangery likely marks the original foundation of the south range.

With the exception of a brief occupation by Parliamentary forces during the English Civil War, Knole House has remained in the Sackville family for more than 400 years. Though the house saw few major changes after Thomas Sackville's work, the Sackville family continued to modify the park landscape in subsequent centuries, not least by the incorporation of additional land. In the early 18th century, the Earls of Sackville became the Dukes of Dorset. The earliest etchings of Knole from the late 17th and early 18th century offer a glimpse of the landscape immediately surrounding the house at this time. The Knyff and Kip engraving, produced in 1698 but not published until 1709, shows the garden at its full extent and a rectangular enclosure lined with trees outside the house's western front (Fig. 7.7). A later engraving published in 1716, shows the addition of an oval-shaped bowling green within the garden and a series of tree-lined pathways radiating from the western front of the house. One of these pathways is the Duchess Walk in today's landscape (Fig. 7.8). Other familiar aspects of the modern park landscape – including Chestnut Walk, Broad Walk, and the octagonal Birdhouse – were constructed during the occupation of Lionel Sackville (1706-65), the first Sackville Duke of Dorset (Rardin 2006: 3-4). Lionel's son, Charles Sackville, removed thousands of trees when he became the second Duke of Dorset in 1765. He began a replanting project in 1768 that was continued by his nephew, John Sackville, as the third Duke of Dorset. Many trees in the park date to this period (Rardin 2006: 4).

With final acquisitions in 1825-6, the park reached its current area of around 930 acres. This brought to a close a long history of acquiring parcels of land, including commons, in the vicinity of the park. Villagers of Sevenoaks nevertheless maintained certain rights of access to the park. The most important of these was the use of the bridle path that bisected the park from Fawke Common in the east to the border with Sevenoaks in

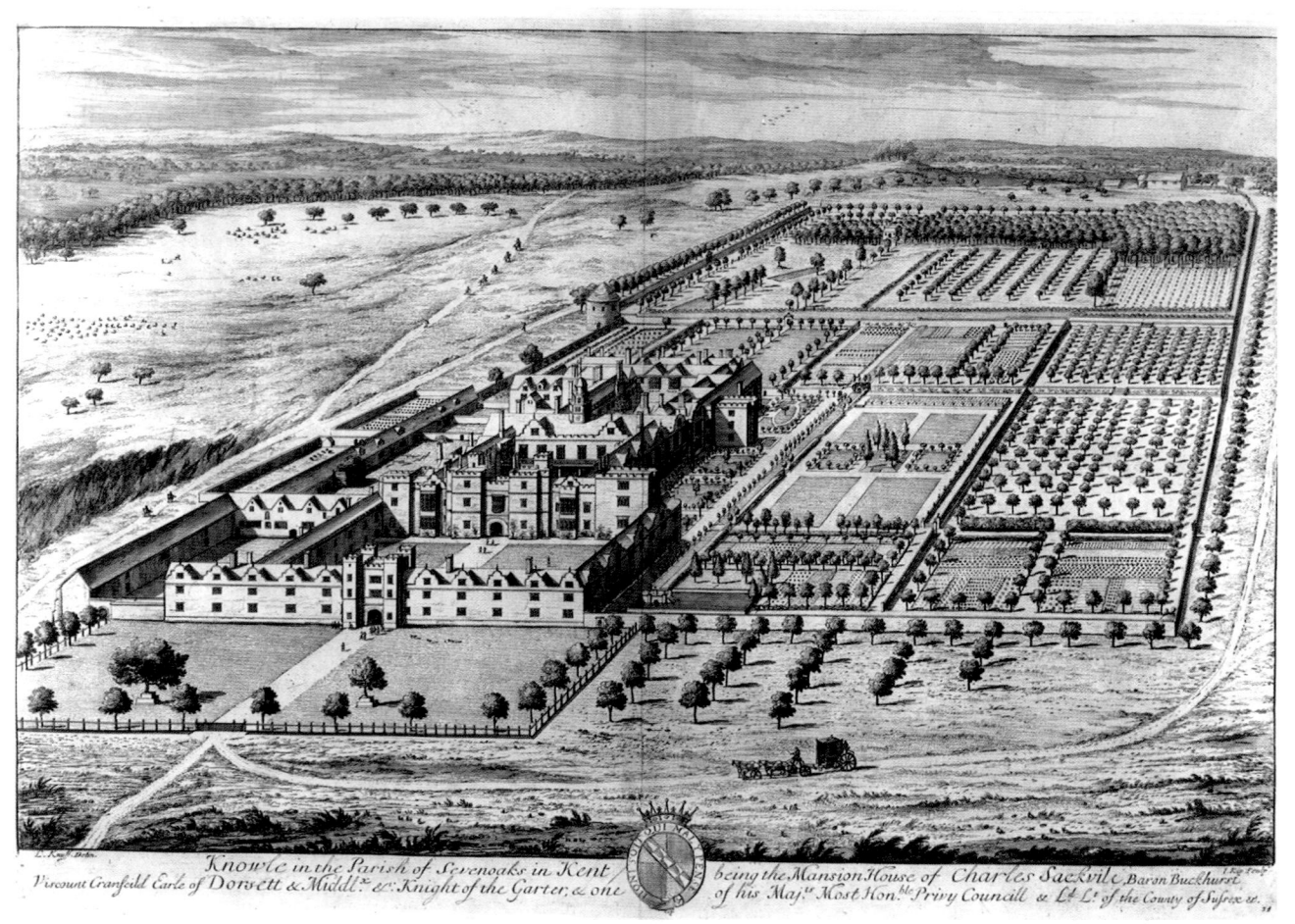

Fig. 7.7: The extent of the house and gardens at Knole has changed little since Leonard Knyff and Jan Kip produced this engraving in 1698. However, note the large rectangular enclosure surrounding a flat green along the west front of the house. Some indication of a feature following the line of this enclosure was revealed in the 2013 earth resistance survey.

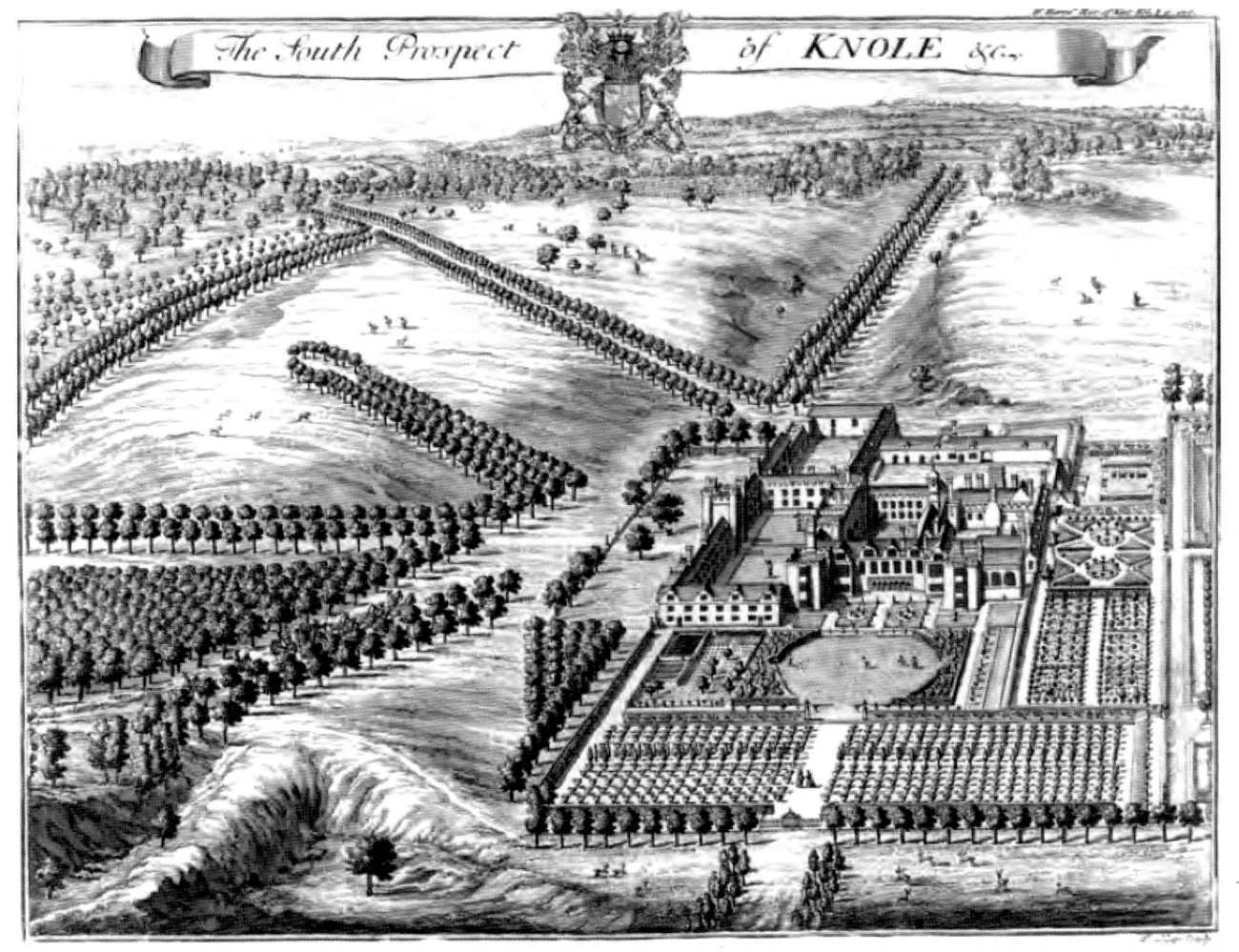

Fig. 7.8: John Harris and Jan Kip produced this engraving for John Harris's History of Kent, published in 1716. Note the tree-lined avenues extending radially from the west front of the house, including one that surmounts Echo Mount.

the west. Frustrated with the influx of day-trippers to Knole Park made possible by the new railway line to London, Mortimer Sackville-West closed public access to the house in 1879 and obstructed the bridle path in 1883. Protesting this affront to traditional rights of access, townspeople from Sevenoaks and villagers from surrounding settlements, stormed the park in 1884, destroyed barriers and dragged their ruins before the door of Knole House. Access to the bridle path was eventually renegotiated, and limited public access to the house was restored under Mortimer's successor, Lionel Sackville-West.

Modifications to Knole Park continued in the 20th century. A golf course inserted in the north-east area of the park in 1923 required major modifications of the landscape, including the clearance of trees and the removal or damaging of earlier landscape features (Wright 2008). The use of the southern portion of the park as a rifle range from at least 1870 and for other military exercises during World War One and Two may have caused additional disturbances. Portions of the house and the western area of the park came under National Trust stewardship in 1946. Major recent transformations of the park include the insertion of the car park and the great storm of 1987, in which around 70% of the park's trees were destroyed (Sclater 1989). Other notable events of the 20th century include the featuring of the park landscape in The Beatles' music videos for 'Penny Lane' and 'Strawberry Fields Forever', both filmed in 1967.

The 2013 Topographic and Geophysical Survey

Background and methods

The project undertook a survey campaign at Knole with the aim of identifying features that would help to reconstruct the lived experience of the late medieval landscape. A team of students and staff from the University of Southampton and Northwestern University conducted the survey work at Knole between 3rd August and 22nd August 2013 (Fig. 7.9). The area surveyed lay largely within the stewardship of

Fig. 7.9: Conducting survey in the park meant interacting closely with inquisitive locals and day-trippers. Photo by Matthew Johnson.

the Trust, though we thank Lord Sackville for granting permission for us to also survey strips along the north-eastern side of the house and the south-western side of the garden enclosure.

The geology and the presence of brick and masonry within the large survey area at Knole Park meant that earth resistance and magnetometry were the most expedient techniques to apply. GPR was also used on a limited basis to target specific areas of interest or to further explore anomalies apparent in the magnetometer survey results.

For the geophysical survey, grids of 30 m x 30 m were set out across the entire survey area using a Leica GS15 GPS with SmartNet. This instrument was also used to conduct topographic survey, with spot elevation measurements taken at 1 m intervals or at 0.2 m elevation variation, along traverses at 2.5 m separation. The magnetometer survey was carried out using a Bartington Instruments 601-2 dual sensor fluxgate gradiometer (Fig. 7.10). Readings were taken at 0.25 m intervals along 0.5 m traverses, with traverses of data collected in zig-zag mode. Earth resistance was carried out using a Geoscan Research RM15 resistance meter, with measurements taken at 1 m intervals along traverses spaced 1 m apart (Fig. 7.11).

The magnetometer and earth resistance survey data were imported into and processed using Geoplot 3.0 software. The processing of magnetometer data was necessary to remove any effects produced by changes in the earth's magnetic field during the course of survey, and to minimise any interference in the magnetometer data from surface scatters of modern ferrous material

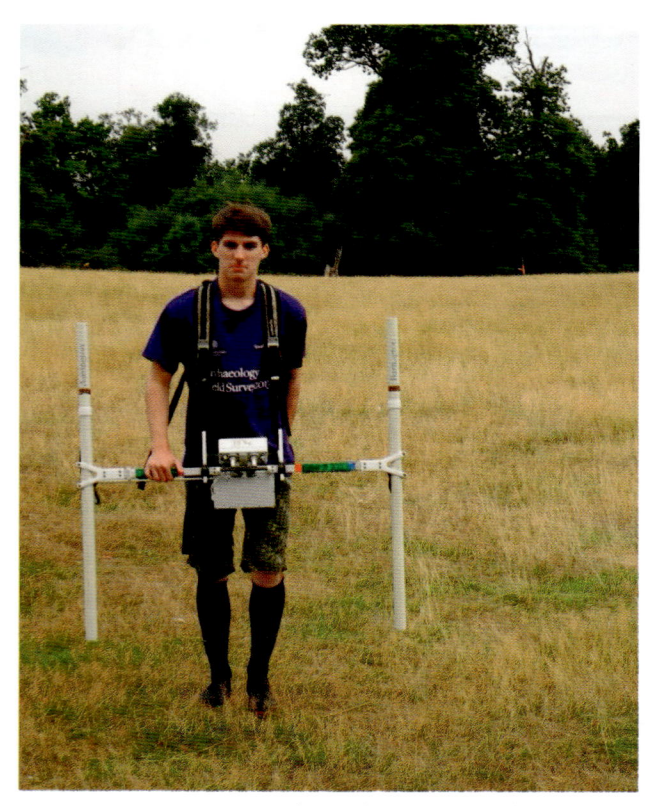

Fig. 7.10: University of Southampton student Patrick Thewlis wearing the non-magnetic clothing required for magnetometry survey. Photo by Peter Tolly.

Fig. 7.11: Team members conducting earth resistance survey. Photo by Dominic Barker.

and ceramics. Data were de-spiked to remove any large peaks or 'spikes' from the data produced by material on the surface of the field. A mean traverse function was then applied to average out any changes in the data produced by the 'drift' in the earth's magnetic field. Filters were subsequently applied to smooth out any high frequency, small disturbances in the data. Finally 0.5 m values were interpolated from the existing readings to improve the spatial resolution of the results across the traverse lines.

The earth resistance data also required processing to remove any high resistance spikes in the data, to edgematch the grids, and to remove any effects in the data from broad geological variations in the subsoil. As such, the data were de-spiked, and the grids were edgematched to ensure uniformity of background measurements across the survey area. Additionally, High Pass and Low Pass filters were applied to the dataset.

The GPR survey was conducted using a Sensors and Software instrument with Smart Cart (Fig. 7.12). A 500 MHz antenna was used, with traverses collected at 0.5 m intervals in zig-zag fashion. The GPR data were processed using GPR Slice, with background and bandpass filter functions being used on the datasets. The processed radargrams were then collated and sliced in the software to provide a series of horizontal datasets showing the changes in amplitude at increasing depth.

The following sections detail the results of our survey, organised according to the location of features identified within the survey area. Where possible, we use published and unpublished archaeological research to interpret geophysical or topographic anomalies.

The elevated area north-west of the house

The elevated ground to the north-west of the house is now one of the most conspicuous highpoints within the park. Whether this 'knoll' represents the estate's namesake is only speculation. However, it certainly is a crucial component of the lived experience of the landscape today. When approaching the estate along the modern drive, the house is obscured from view before appearing, as if from nowhere, as one proceeds around the curve of the knoll.

The 2013 survey aimed to shed additional light on peoples' use and experience of this area in the past. Two major anomalies are apparent in the data warrant discussion. The first is a linear feature immediately to the west of Echo Mount, extending on a rough north-south alignment. Visible to the naked eye as a low ridge, this same feature is apparent in the magnetometry as a positive linear anomaly, some 120 m in length and tapering at its northern and southern ends from a width of 15 m (Figs 7.14 & 7.15). The resistance survey also detected this feature as a strip of low resistance (Fig. 7.18). Following identification of the feature with magnetometry and resistance survey, a trial GPR grid was placed in this area to target the linear feature. The results indicate the presence of a broad feature some 15 m across, which then widens out at increased depth. This seems to suggest that the anomaly is a break in the geology of the area (Fig. 7.16).

Alastair Oswald (pers. comm.) has suggested that this ridge is related to one of a series of relict agricultural lynchets and hollowed trackways to the north of the car park. The 2008 survey by Wessex Archaeology (Wright 2008: 73) also identified a series of linear earthworks in the area north of Echo Mount. Interestingly, there is a reference of 1612 to 'paling about the mount', but it is unclear precisely to what and where this refers (Taylor 2003: 179). The 2013 geophysical survey suggests that the low ridge identified by Oswald is not a humanly

Fig. 7.12: Team members operate the GPR equipment. Photo by Matthew Johnson.

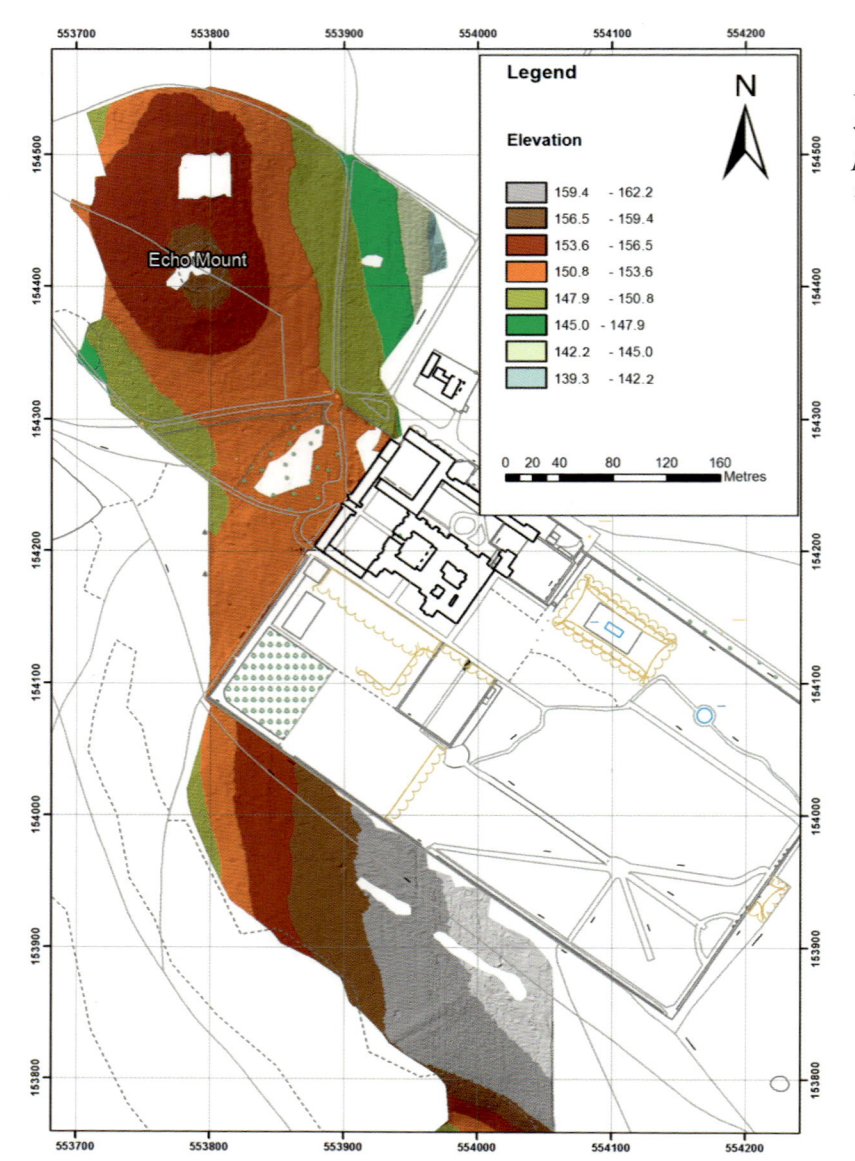

Fig. 7.13: Results of the topographic survey at Knole. Despite Echo Mount's prominence, it is not the highest point in the landscape.

constructed feature, but rather reflects an anomaly in the underlying geology. If there were lynchets or palings here, their remains were not detected by geophysical survey.

The second feature apparent in the geophysical survey of this area suggests the former presence of a rectangular enclosure near the clump of trees north of Echo Mount. The magnetometry readings identified a rectilinear positive anomaly here measuring 25 m x 25 m (Fig. 7.15). This response may relate to earth or stonework here associated with a standing or viewing platform. A letter written by John Lennard, the leasee of Knole, to Lord Burghley in 1587 references a bill issued for the repair of a 'stanyng'. It is uncertain where this standing was and what its intended function was. Lady Anne Clifford, wife to Richard Sackville, mentions the 'standing in the garden' multiple times in her diary. Notably, each reference includes the qualifier 'in the garden', suggesting that other standings may also once have been present at Knole (Taylor 2003: 167-9). Timber standings associated with hunting grounds, such as the remodelled example in Epping Forest, are thought to have been used to advantage spectators or archers during the coursing or hunting of deer. A multi-storied standing by this clump of trees may have provided an impressive vista, but not advantageous views of any areas particularly suited to coursing or driving deer (see below).

An early depiction of Knole suggests that this elevated area was formerly an important component of a planned park landscape at Knole. The Harris and Kip engraving of the south prospect of Knole, published in 1716, shows a number of tree-lined pathways extending out from the western front of the house. One path leads up to the top of the elevated area to a circular area enclosed by trees (Fig. 7.8). This circular clump of trees appears to correspond with a small mound surmounting Echo Mount, though alternatively, it may correspond to the position of the rectilinear anomaly slightly further north. Whatever the case, the spot likely provided a better vista towards Sevenoaks than towards the house itself.

Despite its conspicuousness within the park, the mound atop Echo Mount itself yielded no significant anomalies in the geophysical survey results. As mentioned above, recent flint finds from Echo Mount suggest that the low mound there may represent an eroded prehistoric monument. As the ground was too dry in August 2013 for our equipment to measure earth resistance on Echo Mount, only magnetometry was undertaken in this area. The results yielded no evidence in support of any manner of substantial archaeological remains on the mound atop Echo Mount.

Topographic survey revealed a somewhat surprising observation concerning the relative elevation of Echo Mount and the Knole gardens. Today, Echo Mount appears as a prominent highpoint in the park landscape. However, as seen in the topographic model (Fig. 7.13), the highest elevation of Echo Mount is actually 2-3 m lower than the area along the southern side of the garden wall. The high ground around Echo Mount is still conspicuous in terms of the pitch of elevation change over a small area. Nevertheless, it may not have offered the best vantage point in a prehistoric or even early medieval landscape prior to the construction of the house and garden walls.

The western front of Knole House

Earth resistance survey along the western front of the house revealed a series of linear features of low resistance (Fig. 7.18). One long thin feature runs north-east to south-west at approximately 50 m from and parallel to the western wall of the house. This feature intersects with a wider (c. 10 m) linear feature of high resistance whose alignment corresponds with that of the entrance

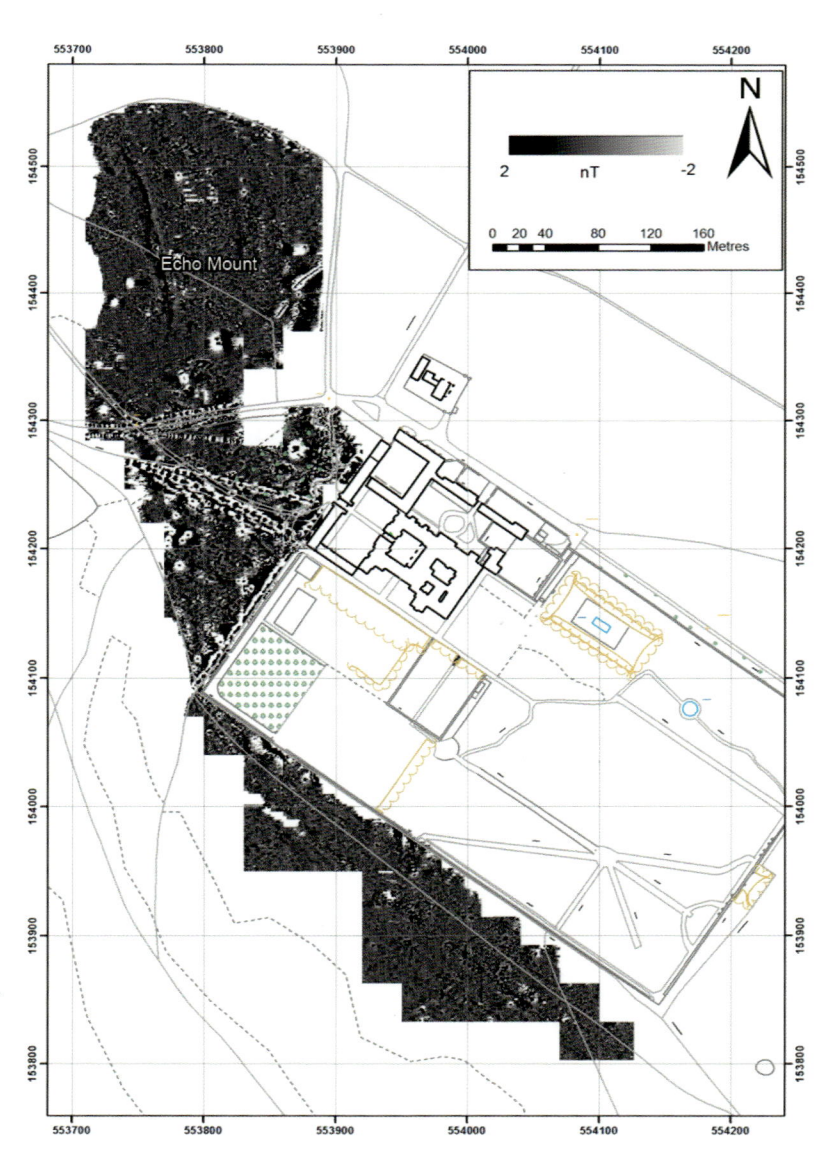

Fig. 7.14: Results of the magnetometry survey. The long linear features extending from the western front of the house represent utility pipes.

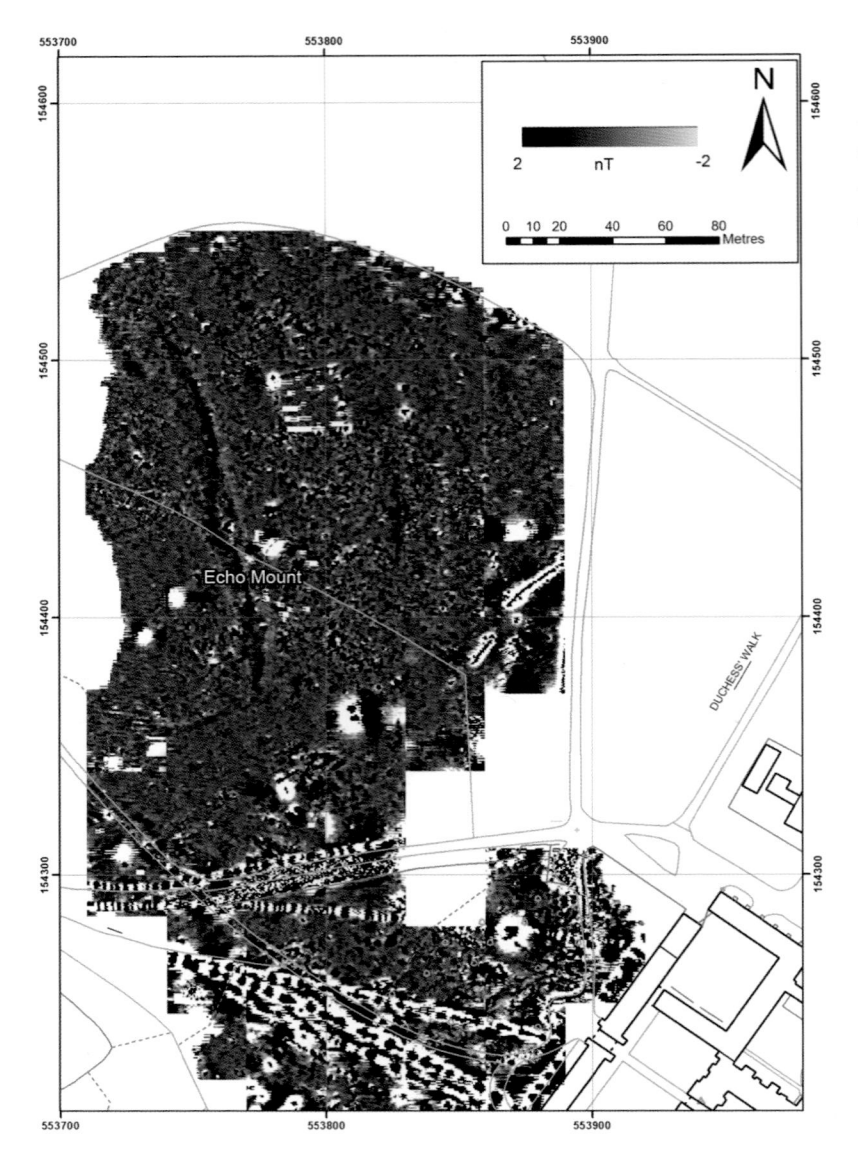

Fig. 7.15: Detailed view of the magnetometry around Echo Mount. Note the long north-south ridge and the rectilinear feature.

way to Green Court. These features appear to correspond with the enclosure and pathway visible on the earliest engravings of Knole House from the late 17th and early 18th century. Though it corresponds spatially, it is unlikely that the tree-lined fence shown in the engravings accounts on its own for the linear low resistance anomaly. Perhaps a ditch was dug around this area, either as part of a 'ha-ha', or merely to introduce soil to create a level surface for bowling greens that are mentioned here in an early 17th-century text (Ravilious 2016: 48).

GPR survey also provided evidence for a structure undocumented in early texts or depictions of the house. As seen in the GPR results, the line of the entrance to the house is visible with high amplitude responses on either side some 50 m from the western front of the house (Fig. 7.17). These responses may relate to the buried remains of some gateway arch or other structure here. Excavation could shed additional light on this hypothesis.

A number of other linear and curvilinear low resistance anomalies were detected to the south-west of the former front enclosure. These features likely represent the trenches excavated for utility pipes detected in this area with the magnetometry survey. Finally, earth resistance survey identified a number of discrete low resistance anomalies that appear to correspond with positive magnetic anomalies in the magnetometry. These may represent pits dug around the park, but their purpose remains enigmatic.

Along the southern garden wall

In addition to the line of the modern pathway along the southern garden wall magnetometry revealed a series of linear positive anomalies cutting across the ridge from south-west to north-east (Fig. 7.14). Topographic survey noted a ditch in this area running on a similar south-west/north-east alignment (Fig. 7.13). These results may relate to tillage in this area, either predating or associated with the deer park.

Fig. 7.16: Results of the GPR survey.

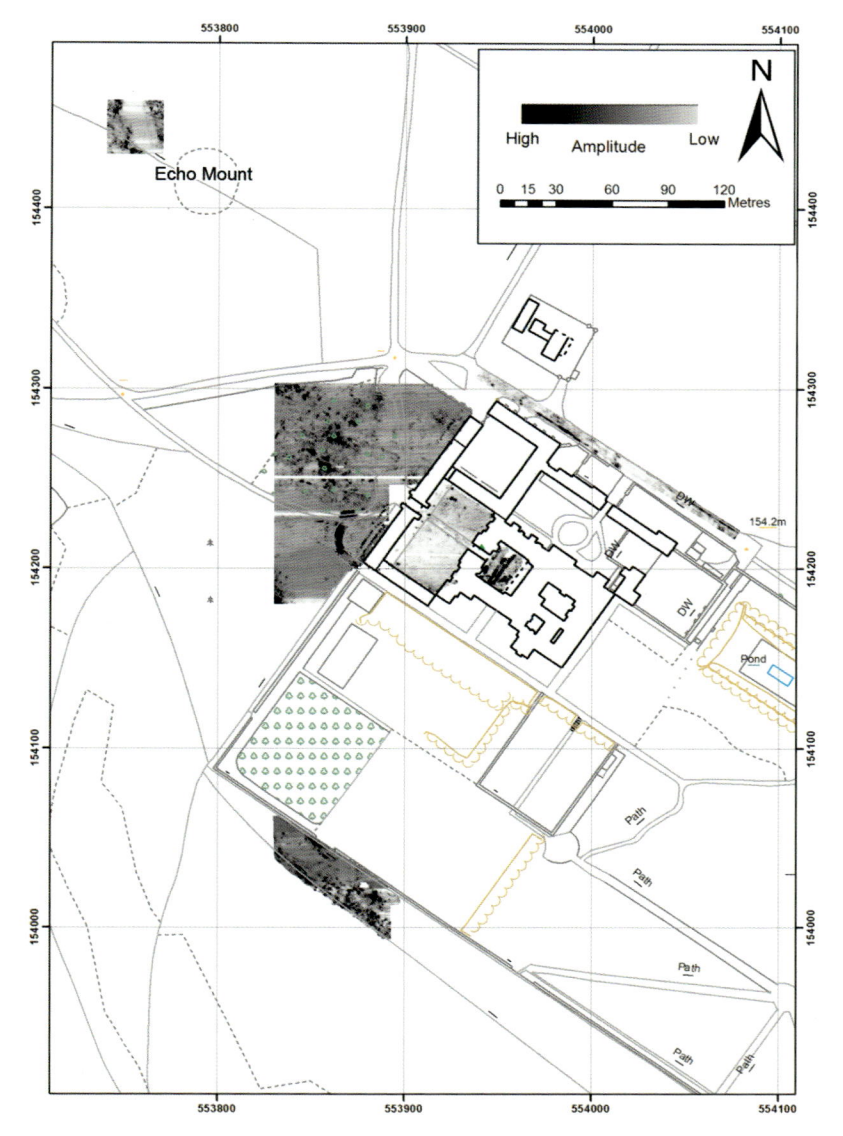

Stone Court and Green Court

GPR survey was also undertaken within the areas enclosed by Stone Court and Green Court (Fig. 7.17). Two linear high amplitude anomalies run south-west/north-east across the centre of Stone Court. These likely represent two brick built cisterns previously identified by archaeological assessments within Stone Court (Miller Tritton & Partners 2003; Osiris Marine Services Ltd 2005; Henderson 2007: 4-5). Other high amplitude readings within the court may represent other drainage features underlying Stone Court.

In Green Court, high amplitude responses appear to relate to a rectilinear feature underlying the grass to the north of the pathway dividing the courtyard. Notably, the alignment of this feature runs at a tangent to the alignment of the courtyard wall; nor does it correspond to the alignment of a metal utility pipe identified by the earth resistance survey undertaken in 2007 (Bartlett 2007). This probable rectilinear feature may be interpreted in the light of excavation results previously undertaken in Green Court (Henderson 2007). An archaeological watching brief was commissioned during the removal, repair, and replacement of the flagstone pathway leading through Green Court. Only the area covered by the flagstone path was excavated, but excavators identified an alignment of four ragstone blocks set within a cut feature underlying the northern edge of the pathway, some 8-10 m from the external entrance to Green Court (Henderson 2007: 6). Given the correspondence in position, it is possible that the excavated ragstone feature represents the edge of the rectilinear feature identified in the GPR.

The presence of architectural remains underlying Green Court potentially has significant implications for understanding the chronology of the house. As discussed above, the date of construction of Green Court remains a sticking point in debates concerning the development of Knole. Further investigation of this feature, ideally with open area excavation, could shed light on the matter: any secure dating evidence from the purported architectural feature would provide a *terminus post quem* for Green Court, and thereby suggest which resident of the estate commissioned its construction.

Summary of the 2013 survey

Our survey campaign raises a series of questions and avenues for future investigation. Geophysical analysis and previous landscape surveys suggest that three areas in particular would reward additional investigation, particularly excavation. The first is the elevated area around Echo Mount. GPR or trial excavation may shed light on the possibility of a Bronze Age monument here. Geophysical results could not define the identity of earthworks observed here by other researchers. Nevertheless, the conspicuousness of this elevated area appears to have appealed to people as a vantage point or focus of activity in different centuries.

The second area is along the main entrance path to the house, about 50 m west of Green Court. High amplitude responses in the GPR suggest buried stone remains here, possibly a gateway arch. Identification and dating of this feature would inform understandings of how one of the approaches to Knole House was framed in the past. The route of formalised approaches in the late medieval or early modern period was likely very different than the route taken by most visitors today.

The third area is within Green Court. Opening up a wider area of excavation in this courtyard would identify the linear feature apparent in the GPR survey and define its relationship to the flagstone feature excavated in 2007. Results could clarify when Green Court was constructed and determine what structures previously lay in this area.

Fig. 7.17: Detailed view of the GPR survey results from the west front of the house and within Green Court and Stone Court. The faint rectilinear feature within Green Court probably corresponds with a ragstone feature encountered during maintenance work in 2007.

Fig. 7.18: Results of the resistance survey. Note the linear feature of low resistance that runs parallel to the west front of the house. The line of this feature, perhaps the remnants of an in-filled ditch, corresponds with the fence enclosing a flat green depicted on early engravings of Knole.

Pursuing these three areas of research would enrich current understandings of Knole's landscape. At present, the work of documentary historians and archaeological surveys and investigations commissioned by the trustees of the Knole estate allow for a more detailed consideration of how the lived-experience of Knole Park fostered certain political and ideological dynamics. The last section of this chapter takes up this task. Though the focus remains on Knole, consideration of hunting, park-making, and poaching as means of social contest are relevant to the deer parks at other properties in the survey.

Sport, Labour, and Social Contest in Knole Park

Compared to the amount of detailed scholarship concerned with the development and chronology of Knole House, scholars have devoted relatively little attention to the deer park at Knole (Taylor 2003). There are both practical and theoretical reasons for these circumstances. The National Trust's stewardship of the house means that maintenance and construction work within the house are accompanied by archaeological assessments. When cross-checked with surviving building records and early depictions of the house, these assessments can provide great insight into the history of the house (Dixon 2008; Gregory 2010; Town 2010). The wider landscape is a different matter. Much of the park lies outside the stewardship of the Trust, and so archaeological assessments associated with construction works have been far fewer. However, an earthwork survey commissioned by the Trustees of the Knole Estate in 2008 identified over 300 elements of earthwork features throughout the park (Wright 2008). Stratigraphic relationships and cross-checking with archival records and early depictions of the landscape are again an important means of dating.

Unfortunately, earthworks are often very difficult to identify given levels of vegetation or unless seen under certain light conditions.

These logistical factors aside, scholars' concerns to identify building works at Knole with one of the elite men who owned the house results from two dominant perspectives common to historical disciplines. The first is a simple and valid historical concern to establish a detailed chronology of development – who commissioned what and when? The second is an equally valid assumption of a link between large-scale building works and the status of medieval elites. It is the contention of this volume that such concerns are entirely valid but can be complemented by an analysis of the wider context. In our view, focusing more attention on the lived experience of the deer park as a place of sport and labour reveals how social difference and identity was created and contested by both everyday and extraordinary actions of people from various class backgrounds.

Hunting the Park

Hunting was one of the most pervasive cultural practices of the Middle Ages. The chase – whether physical or imagined – acted as a metaphor for sentiments ranging from the salacious to the spiritual (Cummins 1988). For the elite, hunting was a leisure pastime, a preparation for combat, an opportunity for networking, and a performance of social privilege (Mileson 2007). More often than not, elite hunting took place on land especially set aside for that purpose, whether forests, chases, warrens, or parks (Bond 1994). Access to hunting in these landscapes was, in theory, highly restricted. For commoners, elite hunting grounds could represent a means of employment or an affront to traditional land-use rights. Effacing elite privilege by trespassing and poaching within a park could be a means of food acquisition as well as a form of social disobedience. To understand the late medieval deer park at Knole, one must confront this multifariousness. One must imagine how the park's symbolic resonances, hunting events, maintenance demands, and landscape setting structured the thoughts and actions of both nobles and commoners. Juxtaposing Knole's landscape alongside comparative sites, contemporary hunting methods, documentary sources, and artwork aids this imagining.

Medieval parks were areas of carefully managed animal and plant resources. The boundaries of parks were often delimited by an internal ditch and embankment topped with oaken staves, or in some cases, a thick hornbeam hedge. Parks functioned primarily as hunting grounds for deer, especially fallow deer, but also included other quarries, such as rabbits, pheasants, herons, peafowl, partridges, swans, and freshwater fish (Sykes 2007: 50). The extent to which these animals were hunted for aristocratic leisure rather than unceremoniously culled by servants to supply lordly feasts is a matter of some debate (Rackman 1986: 125; Mileson 2009). Larger forests were likely better suited to the elaborate ceremony of the *chasse par force de chiens* (chase with use of dogs). Gaston Phébus Count de Foix, author of the 14th-century hunting manual *Livre de Chasse*, considered this multi-staged rite the noblest form of hunting. The quarry of this hunt was the male red deer, or hart. Mounted hunters aided by dogs singled out the strongest looking hart, running him to exhaustion over many miles. Once the hart was brought to bay, the lord would dismount to kill the animal. An elaborate butchering or 'breaking' ritual followed, in which the feudal hierarchy was symbolically reaffirmed as the lord apportioned different cuts of the meat to his retainers, the church, the dogs, and even the poor (Judkins 2013).

Though less elaborate, the bow-and-stable method was more effective at killing deer *en masse*. In this method, dogs and hunters would drive deer – principally fallow deer, but also roe and red deer – towards a pre-positioned group of archers. The archers would then fire upon those animals in season. Greyhounds positioned with the archers would run down those animals not immediately killed. Notably, the 14th-century poem Sir Gawain and the Green Knight depicts the bow-and-stable method underway within a park surrounding a castle. Smaller, enclosed park landscapes, were better suited to the bow-and-stable method, though *par force* hunts, or hybrid forms, were likely possible in larger parks (Cummins 2002: 43-52; Sykes 2007: 50-1; Mileson 2009: 30-3). The advantage of parks was the ability to modify the landscape to facilitate one or the other form of hunting. The bow-and-stable method was particularly contingent on the landscape. Topography and tree cover aided hunters in channeling deer towards hidden archers.

Later forms of sport relied to an even greater extent on specifically designed landscapes. In 'paddock coursing', a single deer was chased or 'coursed' down an enclosed trackway by a number of greyhounds. Onlookers made wagers on the outcome – which of the hounds would catch the deer, or might it outrun them all? Cartographic evidence illustrates the landscape settings constructed for such practices. A map of Windsor Little Park produced in 1607 shows a deer course enclosed with a hedge and fit with a greyhound in hot pursuit of a fallow deer (Mileson 2009: 174).

Formalised paddock coursing was especially popular in the 17th and 18th centuries. Yet, some limited textual and landscape evidence suggests that coursing or analogous practices developed in the late medieval period (Taylor 2003).

At Knole there is no unambiguous evidence of landscape modification to aid any of these forms of sport. However, there are a series of dry river valleys with steep sloping sides that run through the park. With hedges, fences, or close coordination between dogs and hunters, these valleys could have aided the channeling of deer along predetermined routes. Additionally, the top of the slopes would have afforded advantageous views over the action unfolding in the valleys below. Paddock coursing was designed entirely for spectating, but other forms of sport might also include spectators. As mentioned above, there is documentary evidence for a standing at Knole, but it is unclear where this structure was located and whether it had anything to do with hunting. The fallow deer that roam the park today are reportedly of the same stock introduced in the 15th century (Fig. 7.19). The tendency of this breed to maintain a herd structure when flushed made them particularly susceptible to bow-and-stable hunting (Recarte *et al.* 1998; Sykes 2007: 51). The inclusion of 'redeere pie hott' on a banquet menu from Knole in 1636 is the first hint that red deer may also have been hunted in the park (Taylor 2003: 166).

The kinds of hunting activities undertaken at Knole would have been crucial to the park's role in constituting the status and identities of its elite residences. Different hunting techniques and quarries were endowed with different gendered status associations in the Middle Ages. The *par force* hunt for the male red deer was the masculine hunt *par excellence*. At the opposite end of the spectrum, according to Gaston Phébus, trapping was

> *properly the delight of a fat man or an old man or a priest or a man who doesn't want to work, and it is a good hunt for them, but not for a man who wants to hunt by mastery and true venery*
> (Judkins 2013: 77)

Perhaps tellingly, Edward of Norwich, when adapting Phébus's work for the English royal court in the early 15th century, totally omitted the section on trapping. Yet, elite men were not the only people to hunt. The 15th-century *Debate between the Heralds* indicates that hunting deer in parks with long bows was a pleasure enjoyed by noble ladies in England (Cummins 1988: 7). Thus, hunting was not exclusive to one group of people, but its conduct and context had important implications for the performance of gender.

As (at least ideally) sedentary and celibate men, male clergy held ambiguous positions within medieval conceptions of gender difference (Gilchrist 2012: 98) Canon Law officially restricted clergy from hunting, because the use of weapons and mode of exercise were considered military in nature (Miller 2010: 209). Nevertheless, many bishops and monastic establishments kept deer parks. Actual participation in hunting likely varied widely among clergy, and perhaps especially between monastic and episcopal elites. In some cases, ecclesiastically owned parks may have functioned primarily to meet demands of hospitality. Elected in 1182, Abbot Samson of Bury St Edmunds neither hunted nor ate meat, but retained many parks and huntsmen and hounds. Important guests would hunt for entertainment, while *'the abbot would sit with his monks in a woodland clearing to watch the hounds giving chase'* (Greenway & Sayers 1989: 26). In other cases, great churchmen were avid hunters. The Boldon Book of 1183 records the various obligations that tenants owed to facilitate the Bishop of Durham's enthusiasm for the chase. High-ranking ecclesiastics often came from elite families. Thomas Bourchier's lineage was royal – he was a grandson of Edward III. It is not unlikely that churchmen of Bourchier's background shared aristocratic enthusiasm for hunting as a leisure activity and perhaps also as a performance of elite masculinity (Roberts 1988; Miller 2010).

Despite official disapproval for clerical hunting, the pursuit of game could also have spiritual connotations. Due to their superlative fertility and subterranean dwellings, rabbits evoked the resurrection of Christ from his tomb (Stocker & Stocker 1996). Hence, the

Fig. 7.19: A group of fallow deer rest in the August sun, 2014. Because fallow deer herd together when startled, they would have been particularly susceptible to the bow-and-stable method of hunting. Photo by Ryan Lash.

artificial mounds – warrens – used to breed and trap rabbits could have indexed theological concepts within the landscape of medieval parks, including Knole. A few mounds visible today amid the wooded area south of the main entrance to Knole may represent former rabbit warrens (Fig. 7.20). Even deer hunting might have evoked spiritual meanings. The image of the white hart was associated with Christ, and its pursuit could evoke the spiritual pursuit of Christ's example of purity (Cummins 1988; Fletcher 2001: 78). It is difficult to know how Thomas Bourchier and his archiepiscopal successors negotiated the tensions and potential harmonies between deer hunting and a spiritual life. Did Bourchier establish a park to entertain secular guests, to stock his tables, or to give chase himself?

There are no definite answers to these questions. Hunting was certainly taking place at Knole. Under Archbishop Morton, a building known as 'the Dranes' was renewed as a private slaughter-house for the park even though there was no shortage of butchers in Sevenoaks (DuBoulay 1976: 10; Taylor 2003: 164). Whether the Dranes was kept stocked by paid hunters, aristocratic guests, or the archbishops is another matter. However, a wall painting from Canterbury Cathedral, dated around 1480, suggests that an Archbishop of Canterbury could at least recognise the symbolic potency of the hunt. Set along the north aisle of the cathedral, the wall painting depicts a series of scenes from the life of St Eustace. Depicted prominently and nearest eye-level is the scene in which Eustace, a pagan, is converted while hunting when he beholds an

Fig. 7.20: One of four possible rabbit warrens located in the wooded area across the long valley south-west of the house. Photo by Ryan Lash.

image of the crucified Christ between the antlers of a stag (Fig. 7.21). It is not impossible that Bourchier was involved with the commissioning of this painting. Bourchier died in 1486 and his tomb is set a little further down the north aisle of the cathedral. In any case, the presence of the painting in the late 15th century suggests that men of the highest clerical status could imagine a harmony between the pursuit of game and the pursuit of grace.

Making and breaking the Park

Regardless of Bourchier and his successors' predilections for the chase, hunting would always have represented a

Fig. 7.21: The conversion of St Eustace from a wall painting along the north aisle of the choir of Canterbury Cathedral. The scene is the most distinctive episode in Eustace's biography and is featured most prominently in the wall painting. The late 15th-century date of the painting makes it a close contemporary with Bourchier and his archiepiscopal successors.

small portion of the activity undertaken in the park. Parklands served a variety of economic functions. They provided important supplies of timber, and a park owner might grant rights or collect fees for local tenants to collect fallen branches or graze pigs (pannage). A document from Maidstone Archive indicates that swine were kept in the park in the early 16th century (Strutt & Parker 1989). According to Vita Sackville-West's account, during the 17th century, cattle grazed the park in the summer months and the sale of rabbits constituted one-fifth of the park's income (Sackville-West 1922: 91). Though some of the lynchets observed by Alastair Oswald may date to prehistory, documentary sources indicate that some portions of the park were intermittently used for arable agriculture (Sackville-West 1922: 25; Taylor 2003: 169). As mentioned above, carefully managing woodland and open fields facilitated different methods of hunting such that the pursuit of sport and economic productivity were not necessarily in conflict.

Parks could also be the scene and supplier of resources for manufacture. John Lennard leased a portion of the Knole estate in 1570 for the purpose of glass manufacture. The actual glassworks may have been located south-west of the park at Hubbard's Hill, but the park no doubt was a crucial source of sand and timber for the furnaces (Eve 2014). A number of quarries throughout the park likely represent the large-scale gathering of sand for the glassworks, and later, for brick manufacture in the 18th century (Wright 2008: 18).

Thus, even if parks were created principally as exclusive spaces for elites to pursue game, they fulfilled many other functions that relied on the labour of people from many different class backgrounds. The park pale perhaps best represents this tension between social exclusion and entanglement. Pales were among the most vital material components of parks – they delimited the extent of exclusive space and prevented game from escaping. They also required a great deal of intermittent maintenance as embankments and staves decayed or as a park's boundaries fluctuated. At Knole, there is both documentary and archaeological evidence for the maintenance and replacement of the pale.

In one of the earliest recorded palings in 1468, money was paid for the production and transportation of 1000 palings from the nearby farm of Breton to Knole (Taylor 2003: 154). Each addition of land to the park required a new paling campaign. By 1561, much land had been added to the park and presumably paled, as a survey by the Earl of Leicester recorded the park extent in this year at 446 acres (Taylor 2003: 154). The pale would have been extended again when St Julian's, Rumshott, and Fawke Commons were purchased in 1724. Wessex Archaeology's 2008 earthwork survey identified eleven landscape features that potentially represent the remnants of embankments for former park pales (Wright 2008). One of the most prominent examples cuts across the golf course north of the house (Fig. 7.22). Another possible pale remnant is a low rounded ridge that runs east to west across the long north-south river valley west of the house. Based on the number of references to paling in the documentary record, Taylor concludes that the park pale was *'continually and conscientiously repaired from its first enclosing'* (2003: 154).

The constant rhythm of decay, maintenance, and rebuilding of the pale is no small matter. At Knole Park, as everywhere, social relations were tied to material qualities and temporal flows implicit in the landscape. From a deep historical perspective, the ecology and geology of south-east England afforded a certain process of settlement expansion throughout the medieval period. This in turn afforded certain patterns of settlement, agriculture, and feudal relations (see above Part II and Chapter Twelve). Built elements within the landscape emerge over shorter time scales, but can still influence generations or centuries of human interactions. Consider the key role played by the durability of stone architecture and its rhythms of maintenance in each of the buildings surveyed in this book. Amassing the labour to heap great amounts of stone together makes a durable product from what are often temporary and contingent power relations. The construction of an elite residence literally 'materialised' the power relationships between elite residents, workers, and people in the surrounding landscape. Without relationships of coercion,

Fig. 7.22: This rounded embankment, now part of a fairway in the golf course, may represent a former park pale. Photo by Matthew Johnson.

monetary exchange, and feudal obligation, elites could not organise the labour to build their residences in the first instance. However, the material product of this labour could work to perpetuate ideologies of aristocratic authority and maintain relations of inequality. The layout and (in)accessibility of buildings can organise movements and interactions according to differences of status, age, and gender. Meanwhile, the sheer scale of elite residences, evoke the authority that built them and threaten the mobilisation of that authority against challengers. In fact, the maintenance demands of elite buildings forced their residents either to mobilise their network of social privilege or allow their building to decay. Park pales can be seen in the same way. The tendency of oaken palisades to decay, embankments to slip, and ditches to silt up established a tempo to social life. At Knole Park periodic decay challenged park owners to remobilise their authority. The park pale, as a material boundary, simultaneously required the labour of commoners while excluding their access to game in the park. Moments of repair or extension were potential turning points where the social privilege that premised the park might be either reproduced or put to challenge.

Indeed, breaking into parks to poach animals or simply cause destruction was a method used by both elites and commoners to contest lordly authority. When the king's uncle John of Gaunt gained land in Sussex in the late 14th century, resentful local gentry, including Bodiam's Edward Dallingridge, mounted a campaign of violence and intimidation against Gaunt's officials and estates. In 1377, Gaunt's chase at Ashdown Forest was illegally hunted (Walker 1983: 88). In what appears to be an instance of deliberate trespass that turned to violence, Dallingridge was prosecuted in 1384 for attacking the ranger of Ashdown and killing a sub-forester, Nicholas Mouse (Walker 1983: 88).

Park-breaking was not confined to the quibbling of secular elites. Breaking into and vandalising episcopal hunting grounds is well documented in feuds between bishops and secular elites. The religious vows and duties of bishops may have made them particularly susceptible to park-breaking as a symbol of emasculated authority (Miller 2010). For commoners, poaching was more often a dangerous economic opportunity or a challenge to elite privileges rather than a desperate means of food procurement. Elites particularly feared poaching as a challenge to social hierarchy in the wake of the Peasants' Revolt of 1381. Fearing that poaching offered opportunities for conspiratorial assembly, legislation passed by Richard II in 1390, placed new restrictions on hunting. Previously, restrictions on hunting were based on territory. Certain hunting grounds – forests, parks, warrens, etc. – were reserved for elite privilege, but commoners could hunt elsewhere. The new legislation issued restrictions based on class. It forbade lay persons with lands or tenements worth less than 40 shillings a year (or priests with incomes less than 10 pounds a year) from even owning animals or equipment for taking 'gentlemen's game' (Harvey 2004: 174; Mileson 2009: 145).

Half a century later, Kent and Sussex were rife with poaching during the lead up to the Jack Cade Rebellion. For example, in 1448, a group of Sussex poachers led by a dyer from Salehurst took three bucks and six doe from Bodiam park (Harvey 2004: 180). Poaching may even have offered an opportunity for organisation among discontents. Harvey's survey of the textual accounts of contemporary legal proceedings shows that poaching gangs were composed of people from different parishes in multiple counties (2004: 178). Furthermore, not only were poachers largely from the same yeomanry class that led the rebellion, some men who sought pardoning for their part in the uprising had previously been convicted as poachers (Harvey 2004: 176-7).

The creation of the park at Knole has to be seen in the context of the fallout of the Jack Cade uprising. Sevenoaks was the scene of one of the earliest skirmishes between the rebels and royal forces. Six years after the revolt, Bourchier acquired Knole from William Fiennes, whose father James had been executed by the Jack Cade rebels for his apparent corruption as Lord Treasurer and representative of Kent in parliament. The first known paling of the park in 1468 was followed in 1486 by new legislation reaffirming old restrictions on the owning of hunting equipment. This legal reaffirmation reflected growing fear of social disorder, especially in Kent, Surrey, and Sussex (Harvey 2004: 182). In the early years of Bourchier's ownership, he appointed many very powerful servants as trustees to buy up property in the vicinity of Knole to add to the park. Du Boulay compares this acquisition campaign to the pressure later applied by Henry VIII to acquire Knole from Archbishop Cranmer. In his words, *'what could be done by obscure men like William Quyntyn, John Walder, John Brydde or William Merden who possessed acres in or about Knole Park which the archbishop wanted?'* (Du Boulay 1974: 8).

If the making of the park was expedited by political pressure, it also would have required renegotiation of traditional land-use rights for nearby tenants. Indeed, this would have been required each time new properties, especially commons, were added to the park. Thus, while every new impaling reiterated the

Fig. 7.23: Several national newspapers covered the events at Knole Park in June 1884. These illustrations come from The Penny Pictorial News and Family Story Paper 28th June 1884.

privilege of the great household of Knole, breaking the park and poaching offered an opportunity to challenge or at least display discontent with that privilege. There are, in fact, intermittent references to illicit hunting in Knole Park (Taylor 2003: 165-6). For example, in 1539 *'several local men who went muffleyd to Knole about 8pm and hunted deer with dogs and bows: a number were killed including a grey one'* (Phillips 1923: 395). This incident took place soon after Henry VIII confiscated the estate, but it is unclear whether this timing reflects any particular political motivation on the part of the poachers or merely a coincidence of preservation.

Later incidences of park-breaking were clearly inspired by more pointed political grievances. Mortimer Sackville-West restricted access to the bridle path in 1883 by closing Fawke Common Gate and erecting a wooden post at the town entrance that excluded horses from entering. This pathway was essential for local tradespeople to bring their goods into town via horse-drawn carts (Killingray 1994: 67). After multiple attempts at destruction, Mortimer had the posts at the town entrance reinforced in wrought iron. On 18th June 1884, frustrated townspeople and neighboring villagers tore down these new posts and the Fawke Common Gate and placed their ruins before the main door to Knole House (Fig. 7.23). Protests continued the following night in a carnival-like atmosphere, with people riding symbolically back and forth along the bridle way and men dressed as women pushing prams across the park (Killingray 1994: 70-1). Though the political circumstances were very different, one cannot help but see a similarity between the character of these protests and the group of poachers who broke into Penshurst in 1450 with charcoaled faces and false beards, carried off 82 deer, and called themselves servants of the Queen of the Fairies (Harvey 2004: 176).

The actions undertaken by townspeople of Sevenoaks during the Knole 'disturbances' of 1884 highlight how the park's material enclosing features were barriers that attempted to impose elite privilege while presenting a material medium through which that privilege could be challenged. Like elite buildings, deer parks were stage settings for the performance of social difference, whether to do with class, spiritual status, or gender (Johnson 2002). But crucially, these stages were constructed and could be contested by many different hands across time.

Conclusion

Today Knole is carefully managed by the National Trust and the Sackville estate and the vast majority of the grounds are open to the public. As this chapter has attempted to show, Knole Park, like other elite landscapes in this book, was deeply implicated in the negotiation of status, gender identity, and political and economic relationships between elites and commoners. Late medieval deer parks, like manorial residences, were both products and producers of political inequality and ideologies of elite privilege. Their environmental attributes, spatial dynamics and maintenance demands influenced the lived experience of elites and commons alike by structuring the character and rhythms of social interactions.

Survey work in 2013 points towards new avenues of exploration for deciphering the history of building works within Green Court and along the western front of Knole. In addition to excavation in these areas, LiDAR survey would provide a valuable means of identifying and displaying earthworks within the park. At the time of writing, volunteer groups are working with Alastair Oswald to conduct a pedestrian survey of the park. This not only offers a means of identifying and reappraising sites, it also offers a way for community members to participate in the maintenance and exploration of the park. It is hoped that more opportunities for community collaboration become possible in the future. The National Trust does valuable work when maintaining and augmenting public access to heritage sites. Strategies of heritage maintenance do well to heed the rhyme first raised in ridicule of the enclosure movement in the 17th century, and later recited by James German to a meeting of townspeople on the first night of the Knole protests in 1884:

> The law imprisons man or woman
> Who steal the goose from off the common
> But leaves the greater felon loose
> Who steals the Common from the goose

8

IGHTHAM MOTE: TOPOGRAPHICAL ANALYSIS OF THE LANDSCAPE

Matthew Johnson, Timothy Sly, Carrie Willis[1]

Abstract. This chapter reports on survey at Ightham Mote in 2013 and 2014, and puts the survey results in the context of a wider analysis of the Ightham landscape. Ightham is another late medieval building surrounded by water features, whose setting might be seen as a 'designed landscape'. Here, we outline and evaluate the evidence for the landscape as it developed through time. As with the other buildings and landscapes discussed in this volume, rather than argue for either an exclusively utilitarian or exclusively aesthetic view, we provide an alternative framework with which to explore the way that barriers and constraints on movement in physical space reflect boundaries in social space. Rather than labelling a landscape aesthetic or practical, we can identify the practices and experiences implicated in landscapes, and their active role in social relations.

Ightham Mote is the fourth late medieval building and landscape to be discussed in this volume (Fig. 8.1; for location see Fig. 1.1). Like the others, Ightham is a National Trust property. The buildings consist of an inner and outer court, whose 'footprint' and external appearance was probably substantially complete by the end of the Middle Ages. The standing structure is a patchwork of different building phases from the early 14th century to the present day. Most recently, the building went through a comprehensive conservation programme costing over ten million pounds, and involving the controlled disassembly and reconstruction of large parts of the house. The information revealed by this process enabled others to put together a very detailed outline of the development of the house from the 14th century to the present (Leach n.d., a-f).

Fig. 8.1: The inner court of Ightham Mote, from the south-west.

The buildings at Ightham sit within a very distinctive landscape. The house is placed at the bottom of a narrow valley running north-south. The inner court is moated, and there is a series of artificial ponds to both the north and south of the inner court. The present form of these water features is the result of post-medieval landscaping, and there is no direct physical

---

[1] The topographical and geophysical survey work reported on in this chapter was carried out under the direction of Timothy Sly. The 'grey literature' and contextual information on Ightham was collated by Matthew Johnson, Ryan Lash and Carrie Willis. The first draft of this chapter was written by Carrie Willis, with additions and revisions by Matthew Johnson and Timothy Sly.

LIVED EXPERIENCE IN THE LATER MIDDLE AGES

evidence for their medieval form. However, most if not all of these water features probably existed in some form in the later Middle Ages.

The Southampton/Northwestern team worked at Ightham in the summers of 2013 and 2014. We wanted to reconstruct and understand the form of the landscape at Ightham as it might have appeared in the later Middle Ages. To this end, in 2013, Timothy Sly and a team of Southampton and Northwestern students did a complete topographical survey of the valley area (LiDAR data not being available for the site), while Ryan Lash and Matthew Johnson collated and digitised the relevant archival and 'grey literature'. In 2014, we returned to do a geophysical survey of the orchard. During and after the 2014 field season, Carrie Willis worked up the data into the geospatial models that are

Fig. 8.3: Contour map of the area surveyed at Ightham Mote. The eastern and western ridges are higher than the centre of the valley, and descend in height from north to south. Note that the highest point in this surveyed area is the northern extent of the western ridge, shown in red. Rendered by Carrie Willis.

presented below, and put together the first draft of this chapter as her Senior Thesis at Northwestern.

Ightham Mote's landscape offers an opportunity to investigate some of the ideas of 'lived experience' first raised in the Introduction. Specifically, it offers insights into embodied daily practice and the constraint and control of movement throughout the environment. The Ightham landscape inspires questions that throw into perspective the traditional conception of designed landscapes in the medieval context (Liddiard & Williamson 2008, Creighton 2009). How does the landscape at Ightham help us to understand what it

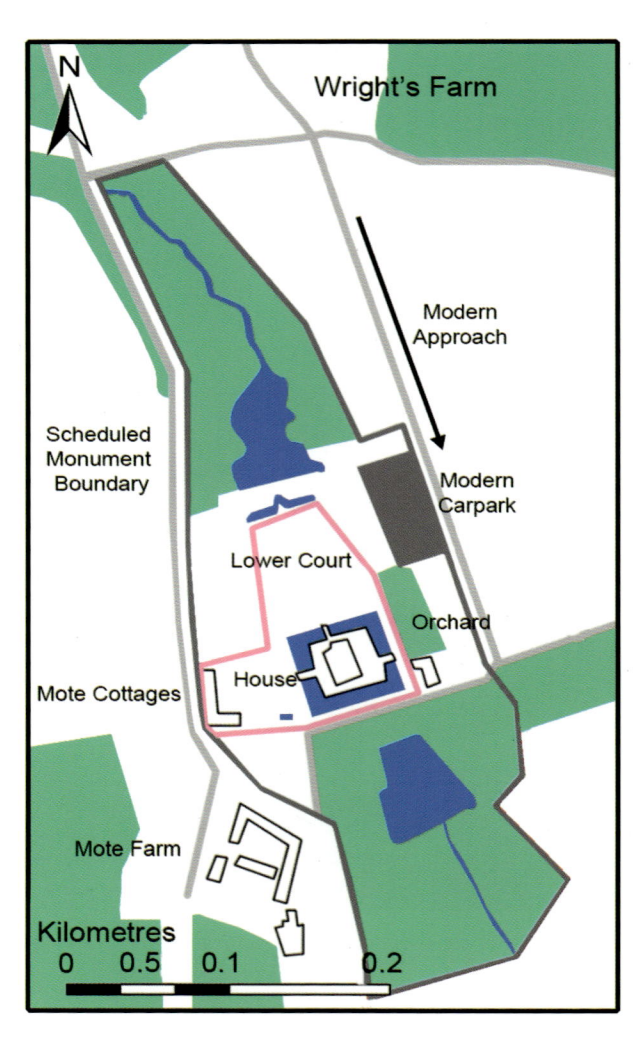

Fig. 8.2: A simplified diagram of Ightham Mote as it exists today, with key features indicated. The northern pond, fed by the Mote Stream, appears at the north, with the house in the middle of the diagram, and the south pond and farm courtyard complex to the south-west and south-east respectively. Diagram by Kayley McPhee.

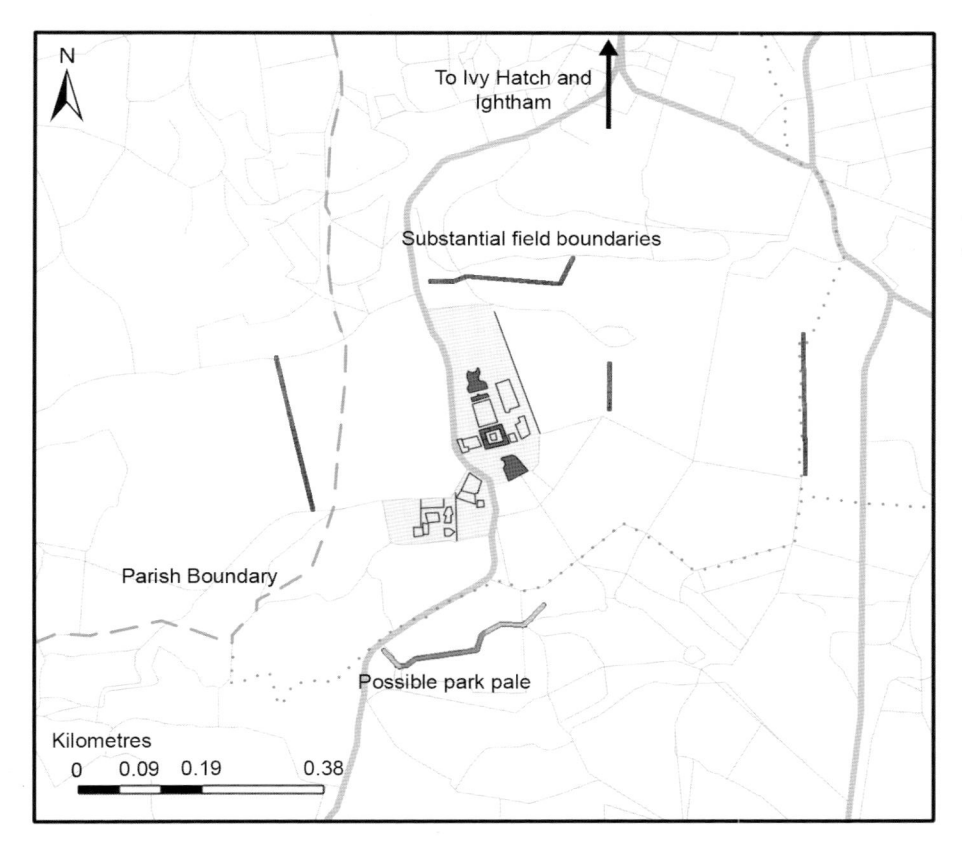

Fig. 8.4: The wider landscape of Ightham Mote, with the location of possible sections of park pale and other substantial field boundaries indicated. The dotted and dashed lines indicate the parish boundary; the dashed line is also the district boundary. Drawing by Kayley McPhee.

means for a landscape to be 'designed'? Likewise, how does the landscape at Ightham enter into the discourse of landscapes as places of work, pleasure grounds, or reflections of social status?

The concluding discussion in this chapter will investigate the ways in which the landscape at Ightham Mote reflects and reinforces ideas of practice and lived experience. Through the analysis of three-dimensional models of the topography, we examine the way the features of the landscape, both natural and modified, constrain and express movement throughout space, and how this movement both reflects, reinforces and renegotiates ideas of status and social identity.

Ightham Mote: Description and History

Ightham Mote is a moated manor house owned and managed by the National Trust. The site is located 8 km east of the town of Sevenoaks in Kent, and 7 km east of the Knole Estate and deer park discussed in the previous chapter. The house is located within a north-south oriented valley, which decreases in elevation from north to south (Figs 8.2 & 8.3). The estate currently includes the two-storey house, its outer courtyard and stables, an orchard, gardens, farm complex, and surrounding fields and woodland (see Figs 8.3 & 8.4). The water features that exist today include one large and two small ponds towards the north of the house and one large pond towards the southern extent. The inner court of the house is oriented with its main entrance facing west, facing directly towards the outer court.

The estate is composed of 208.42 hectares (515 acres), including 149.74 hectares (370 acres) of farmland and 58.68 hectares (145 acres) of woodland. The site is located at the junction between the Upper and Lower Greensand on the edge of the Weald. Geologically, it is built on a combination of loam, sand, and mudstone, phasing into the Wealden clay towards the southern extent of the property. The property contains multiple springheads feeding into a stream which runs through the property on a north-south axis.

Human occupation in the vicinity of Ightham has been dated to as early as the Mesolithic period. At Oldbury, a site to the north of Ightham Mote, occupation scatters have been dated to 100 BCE (Thompson 1986). Nicola Bannister (1999: 21) and Peter Rumley (2007) suggested that a previous settlement may have existed at the site of Ightham Mote before the manor house was built. However, archaeological excavations undertaken during renovations of the house in 2003 did not indicate any pre-existing structures below the site of the house (Leach n.d., a&b). In the 8th to 12th centuries, when many English villages were created and much of the agricultural

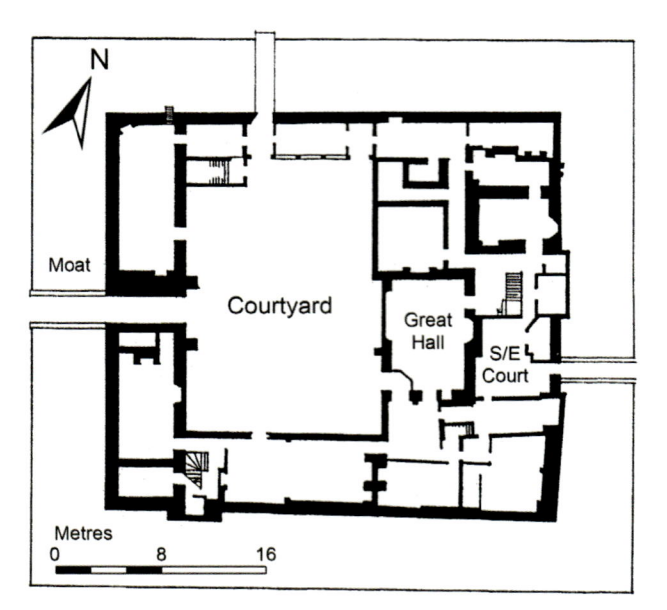

Fig. 8.5: Ground plan of the inner court as it exists today. The bridge at the left centre of the image, crossing the moat, lines up with the opening of the outer courtyard, allowing for a processional approach. The bridge at the right, just below the centre of the image, would have allowed for a rear approach to the house. Drawing by Kayley McPhee, after Nicolson 2005 [1998], inside front cover.

The very earliest standing fabric probably dates to the 1320s. The outer court was added towards the end of the 15th century. While the footprint and external walls of the inner court are mostly medieval, the room interiors have been adapted and transformed over the centuries in a continuous, generation-by-generation process that has left the built structure of Ightham as a patchwork of different phases and periods from the 14th to 20th centuries (Figs 8.1, 8.5 & 8.6).

The experience of the modern visitor to Ightham Mote is quite distinctive. Most visitors arrive from the north, along some kilometres of narrow, winding country lanes flanked by hedgerows, small fields and woodland. The road forks north of the house, and the eastern branch leads down through woodland to the visitor car park, partly housed within the walls of a former orchard. From here, two routes lead steeply down, either a path through the modern ticket office or a road winding round to the south. The overall impression is of a small-scale, occluded landscape, without sweeping views (though these may be obtained by a short walk east or west, leading to commanding views over the Weald). Ightham Mote affords a strong subjective impression of a tucked away, forgotten place, unlike other grand country houses.

However, this modern visitor experience has to be 'thought away' before an understanding of the earlier landscape can be attempted. The modern visitor's approach to the property, culminating in parking within and to the north of enclosed garden walls, may well not have been the approach of most medieval visitors (below we argue for the possibility that this was a high-status, perhaps exclusive, route of approach to the house, with most traffic approaching the lower court via a western route). Much of the woodland, orchard and garden walls are products of the last two centuries. Beyond this, it is difficult to make definitive statements

landscape reorganised, Wealden Kent was less affected by this process than, for example, the Midlands or North of England. The Wealden landscape exhibited continuity and piecemeal change rather than large-scale transformation during these centuries (Cantor 1982; Everitt 1986; see also Chapter Twelve, this volume).

It is not possible to associate a name with the initial building of the present structure of Ightham Mote, as documentary records from the very earliest phases of the house do not exist or have not been located. An entry in the Assize Rolls for Kent from 1371 lists Ightham Mote as belonging to Sir Thomas Couen (variously spelt Coven, Couen or Cawne). Additional documentary evidence lists Couen as a resident from 1360 to 1374 (Minihan 2015). Prior to this, there is some evidence that the estate was owned by a widow, Isolde Inge, in the 1340s.

The best published account of the structural history of the house itself can be found in Anthony Emery's gazetteer of later medieval houses (Emery 2006: 257-64). In its earliest phases, the house consisted of a kitchen-service-hall-solar block in one range; successive generations extended this into a courtyard house, with the addition of the second courtyard in the later 15th century. Tree-ring dating performed on roof timbers in the solar, hall, and chapel of the house dates these areas to 1340, 1344 and 1347 respectively (Leach n.d., a).

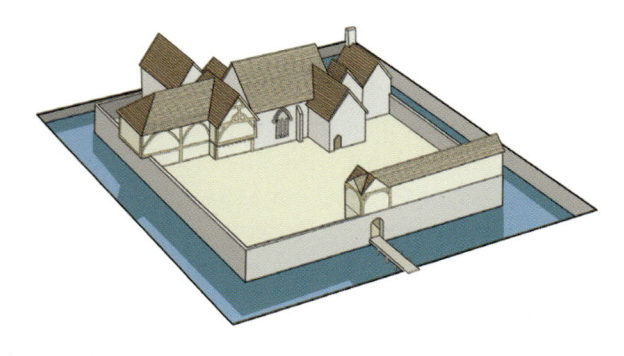

Fig. 8.6: Reconstruction of the inner court in the 14th century. This reconstruction shows the house without the outer court, which was added towards the end of the 15th century. Drawing by Kayley McPhee, after Nicolson 2005 [1998]: 6.

about which features of the modern landscape may have existed when Ightham Mote was first created. The stables at Ightham Mote are dated to the 19th century, while the farm complex dates from the post-medieval period. The surrounding copses of trees immediately adjacent to the valley on either side are primarily composed of mature trees planted between the 16th and 19th centuries, with some old growth scattered throughout (Bannister 1999; Rumley 2007). Historic maps only reach as far back as the late 17th century. The wooded areas that appear in these maps had not been natural forest for some millennia; in common with virtually all woodland in the lowland British Isles, they would have been humanly managed to a greater or lesser extent from prehistory onwards (Rackham 1990).

If the existing field and forest boundaries can be extrapolated further back into the past, we can use 17th through 19th-century Tithe maps, Ordnance Survey maps, and other documentary evidence to approximate landholdings in the first few years after Ightham Mote

Fig. 8.8: Water features north of the house as they exist today, with valley sides and woods beyond, viewed from the gatehouse tower. Photo by Matthew Johnson.

was erected. It is clear from the Ordnance Survey and Tithe maps and other documentary evidence that by the 18th century, Ightham Mote's holdings included the house, farm, gardens, orchard, southern meadow, a significant expanse of fields to the east and west, and tracts of Scathes Wood and Martin's Wood. The earliest map known of Ightham Mote and its surrounding land, a 1692 estate map by Abraham Walter, confirms these landholdings in the 17th century, though the whereabouts of this map is currently unknown.

The wider landscape context of the house is well known from estate maps dating to the 17th to 19th centuries, but is less clear for the later Middle Ages. The general pattern with later medieval houses of this status would lead one to look for the possibility of surrounding water features, and possibly a wider landscape setting such as a deer park. The evidence for a deer park is fragmentary at best; that for water features circumstantial but very likely (Figs 8.7-8.9).

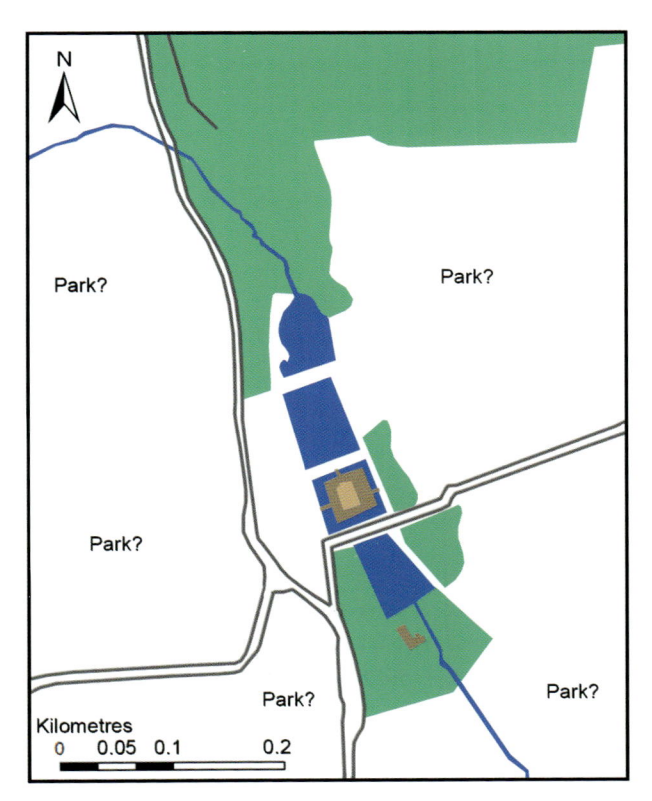

Fig. 8.7: Possible layout of landscape and water features around the house in the 14th century, before the addition of the outer court. The area between the house and the north pond would have been used as a middle pond for the storage of fish bred in the north pond. The south pond may have functioned as a mill pond, drawing water away from the house via the Moat Stream. The possibility of a park beyond is discussed in the text. Diagram by Kayley McPhee, after Rumley 2007: 42.

Fig. 8.9: Dam, of post-medieval form but possibly of medieval origin, between the two ponds north of the house, looking east. Photo by Matthew Johnson.

Seven hundred metres south of the house, towards and just below the summit of a slope, there is a section of an earthwork now used as a modern field boundary (Fig. 8.10). It is possible this earthwork represents part of a park pale. It has a ditch on the 'inner' side, and faces up the slope. Elsewhere, however, it is very difficult to trace a hypothetical deer park. There are substantial field boundaries north, east and west of the house, but none have the appearance of a park pale, and nor can they be easily joined up to form the classic oval shape of a deer park. The boundary on the shoulder of the rise to the west is quite massive. However, it has no trace of an accompanying ditch. The boundary to the east is wide but of little height, and the trees upon it are of no great antiquity. The existence of a deer park at Ightham must therefore remain unproven one way or the other; the lack of intensive survey, excavation, and coring done on the earthworks surrounding Ightham Mote limits our ability to make claims about park boundaries based on these features.

Documentary sources indicate that there was a watermill at Ightham, and the ease with which the valley could be dammed to create a mill pond is quite apparent. However, the date of its foundation remains uncertain and while the ideal location for a mill somewhere in the vicinity of the dam for the south pond is clear, its precise site is a matter of debate. The belief that a mill existed at Ightham Mote stems from a church record from the parish church of Shipbourne, which details that 'John sonne of Samuel Lyn, the miller of Mote in Ightham' was baptized on 16th November 1583 (Bannister 1999: 21; Rumley 2007). Despite the documentary record of the existence of a mill at Ightham Mote, and the general plausibility of the presence of a watermill at a site of this kind, no archaeological or geophysical evidence exists to validate its existence. Likewise, no other documentary evidence, including building permits or maps, list the mill or its location on the property.

North of the house itself, there are a series of banks retaining bodies of water. The modern form of these banks is the result of the post-medieval landscaping of the area, and there is no direct evidence that these banks existed in the Middle Ages. However, given the form of the valley, and the position of the house, it is unlikely that a medieval owner would have forsaken the opportunity to create a series of fishponds or other water features. Ightham Mote may have had four bodies of water in the Middle Ages, each fed in turn by the Mote Stream that originates to the north in the Upper Greensand and runs down the length of the valley on a north-south axis (Rumley 2007; see Figs 8.7-8.9). The last bank would have stopped the Mote Stream at its southern extent, creating what is now known as the south pond. In 2003, N. Griffin and colleagues undertook geophysical survey in the north lawn to determine whether this area was in fact a lake in the past. The results of this geophysical survey were inconclusive (Griffin 2003; Rumley 2007). Additional auguring or coring in this area may prove beneficial in identifying whether this lawn may have constituted a 'middle pond' in the early or middle medieval period. If these bodies of water existed in anything like their present form in the Middle Ages, one would expect them, in parallel with similar features elsewhere (Creighton 2009), to have practical as well as visual purposes: the north pond and middle pond would have been used to breed and store fish, respectively; the moat would have been used for the discharge of refuse from the kitchens and garderobes; and the south pond would have functioned as a mill pond. It is likely that the whole valley was set up as an hydraulic system: as water flowed from the moat into the south pond, the watermill would employ the water flow, discharging it into the Moat Stream at the southern extent, away from the house, flowing southwards towards the Low Weald.

Fig. 8.10: An earthwork ditch, now used as a modern field boundary, 700 m south of the house (see Fig. 8.3). This earthwork may be the possible remnants of a park pale; it also marks the parish boundary. Photo by Matthew Johnson.

Fieldwork at Ightham Mote

An intensive programme of restoration and conservation has taken place at Ightham Mote since its acquisition by the National Trust in 1984. Since then, multiple geophysical, topographical, and building survey methods have been applied at Ightham Mote (see Leach n.d., a-f; Bannister 1999; Rumley 2002; 2006; 2007; Griffin 2003; Leach & Rumley n.d.). The systematic taking-apart and reconstruction of the house was accompanied by detailed record-keeping; a series

IGHTHAM MOTE: TOPOGRAPHICAL ANALYSIS OF THE LANDSCAPE

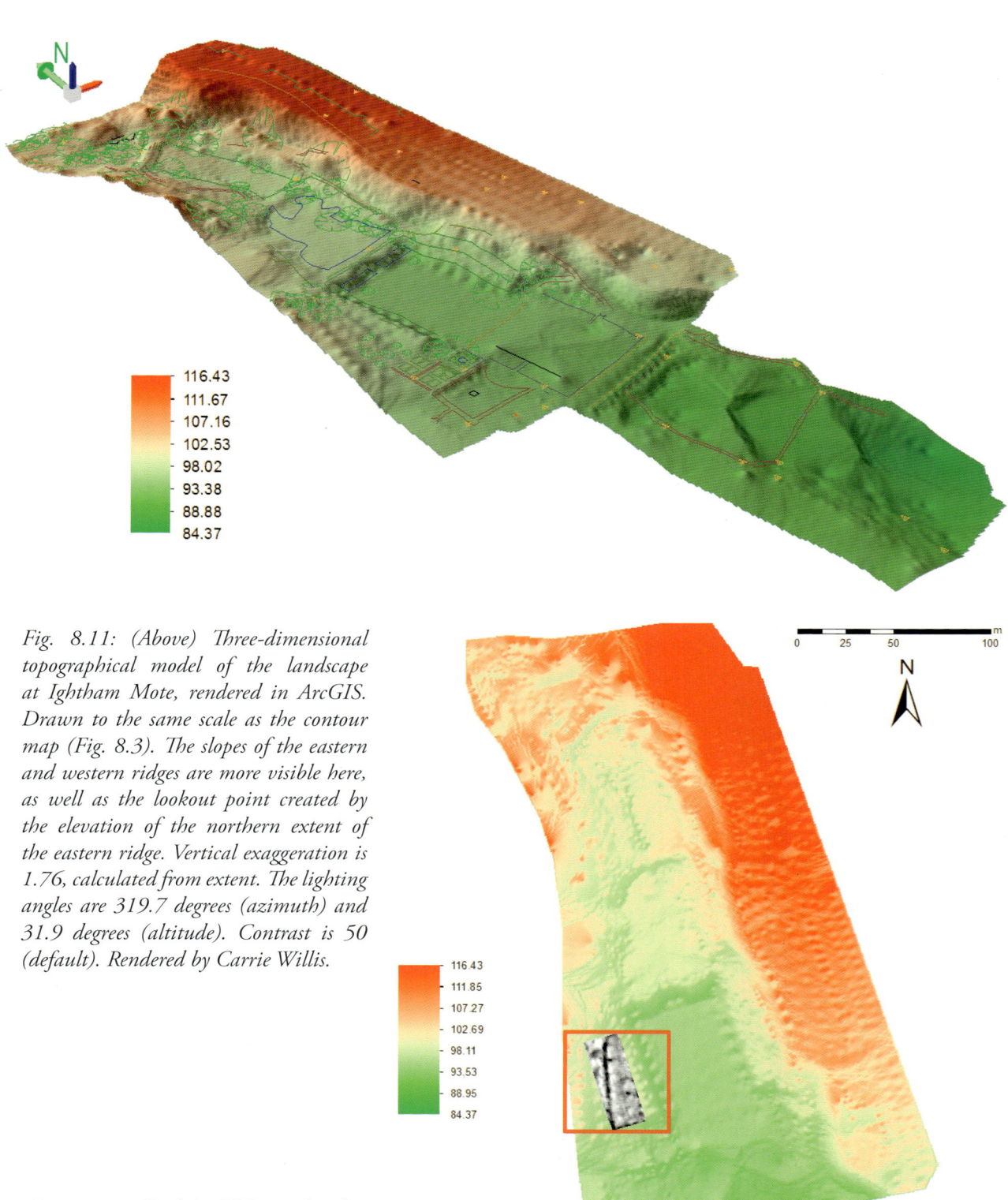

Fig. 8.11: (Above) Three-dimensional topographical model of the landscape at Ightham Mote, rendered in ArcGIS. Drawn to the same scale as the contour map (Fig. 8.3). The slopes of the eastern and western ridges are more visible here, as well as the lookout point created by the elevation of the northern extent of the eastern ridge. Vertical exaggeration is 1.76, calculated from extent. The lighting angles are 319.7 degrees (azimuth) and 31.9 degrees (altitude). Contrast is 50 (default). Rendered by Carrie Willis.

Fig. 8.12: (Right) GPR results from survey in the orchard at Ightham Mote. The thick black line at a north-south axis indicates that the material here is more densely packed than the surrounding white areas; we believe that this indicates a densely-packed or even-paved path cutting through the orchard on a north-south axis. Rendered by Carrie Willis.

135

Fig. 8.13: View north-west from the gatehouse tower towards the orchard, with modern reconstructed gardens in the foreground and the valley sides beyond. Photo by Matthew Johnson.

of unpublished volumes of recording and analysis were produced by Peter Leach (Leach n.d., a-f) before his untimely death. At the same time, a variety of traditional craftsmen were employed in the reconstruction work; the lively interactions between members of the conservation and restoration programme, and their different viewpoints on the work, were recorded in a special episode of the Channel 4 TV documentary series *Time Team*. An account of this work, and the insights it provided on the development of the house and on medieval buildings generally, remains unpublished, but is of great significance, not simply in telling us about the history of the building, but also in terms of method – a very rare opportunity to take down a medieval house and build it up again.

The most recent round of fieldwork on the immediate landscape around Ightham Mote was conducted between 2012 and 2014 as an international collaborative effort between the National Trust, the University of Southampton, and Northwestern University.

Fieldwork by Northwestern and Southampton Universities at Ightham Mote commenced in 2013. A team of six Northwestern undergraduates and six Southampton undergraduates conducted topographic and geophysical survey at Knole, and topographic survey at Ightham. Rotating teams of three undergraduates under the direction of Timothy Sly used a total station to plot and code over 500 three-dimensional points. The work progressed at a much faster rate than anticipated, and the bulk of fieldwork at both Ightham and Knole was completed in the 2013 season. At Ightham, this work consisted of a detailed topographical (contour) analysis of the area of the property owned by the National Trust.

The 2014 season was initially planned as a second and final season for the work at Ightham and Knole. However, the success of the 2013 field season left little additional survey to be done, particularly at Knole, and thus the 2014 field season was used for more analytic work. The 2014 team was much smaller, composed of two Northwestern undergraduates, two Northwestern graduate students, and one Southampton graduate student. The team was tasked with completing additional geophysical survey at Ightham, preparing geospatial renderings of the Ightham and Bodiam landscapes, and compiling copies of the grey literature for previous seasons at Bodiam, Ightham, and Knole. The team created three-dimensional topographic renderings of the Ightham Mote landscape, which are presented in this chapter.

Figs 8.3, 8.11 & 8.12 are different views of the results: a three-dimensional model of the immediate valley landscape of Ightham Mote. The model shows the narrow valley in which the house is located. This valley runs from the elevated Upper Greensand ridge at the north all the way through to the rolling clay hills of the south, where the land is considerably lower. The house is located at the southern end of the valley, where the valley widens out. One can see the higher ridges at the north and east of the valley. Mote Stream, which feeds the ponds at Ightham Mote, begins somewhere over the top of this northern greensand ridge, and follows the slope to the south to fill the northern ponds, then the moat, then the southern pond.

Geophysical Survey of the Orchard, 2014

The plan set for the 2014 field season was to conduct Ground Penetrating Radar (GPR) in the orchard, outer courtyard, and an area near the south pond. Time permitting, our team were in discussion with the National Trust to potentially use GPR in the Great Hall. The area near the south pond proved too difficult to work with. The area was being treated for an invasive strain of weed, and the team was not able to remove weeds from the area as this would have hastened further spread of the species. This would have made it impossible to use the GPR unit, and thus the decision was made to abandon that area and go on with the rest of the survey as planned. Survey commenced with the orchard area, and a significant amount of this area was surveyed. Logistical difficulties, however, meant that further plans to survey the outer courtyard and other areas could not be carried out.

The results of the GPR survey in the orchard contain the clear signature of a path cutting running across it. The results show a well-delineated linear anomaly crossing the survey area on a north-south axis, curving to the east at its northern extent (see Figs 8.12 & 8.13 for a general view of the area). The darkness of the line in Fig. 8.12, at the 5-8 ns level, indicates that the material which composes the anomaly is dense. The GPR results of this area at a shallower depth shows the line, particularly at the northern extent where it curves east, in a much lighter shade. This indicates that the material here is much looser. We suggest that these findings represent a well-packed or even-paved path cutting through the orchard, overlain by looser soil.

Images and maps of Ightham Mote from the 1800s indicate a curved footpath cutting through the garden. In 2015, gardeners at Ightham Mote removed the top layer of soil from this area and exposed a linear row of stones or paving slabs. We suggest that this finding corroborates the existence of a path in this area of the orchard. However, further investigation into the soil composition of this area is necessary to confirm whether the anomaly represents a formally constructed path or one created by consistent use.

Topographic Analysis: Possible Routes of Approach

The topography of the site, as revealed both through the 2013 topographical survey and the map evidence of the surrounding area, gives some indication of the different possible routes of approach to Ightham Mote. Analysis of these different routes offers an initial understanding of different possible experiences of the place in the Middle Ages. This may have been very different from the modern experience, conditioned as it is by large areas of more recent woodland and vegetation.

The contour survey clearly depicts the very steep slope of the western and eastern ridges that form the valley. These slopes would be difficult and costly – in terms of energy – to scale, and potentially hazardous for carts or other vehicles. It is unlikely that travellers to and from Ightham Mote would have used paths that went straight up and down these ridges. It is more likely, based on the topography of the landscape, that travellers would

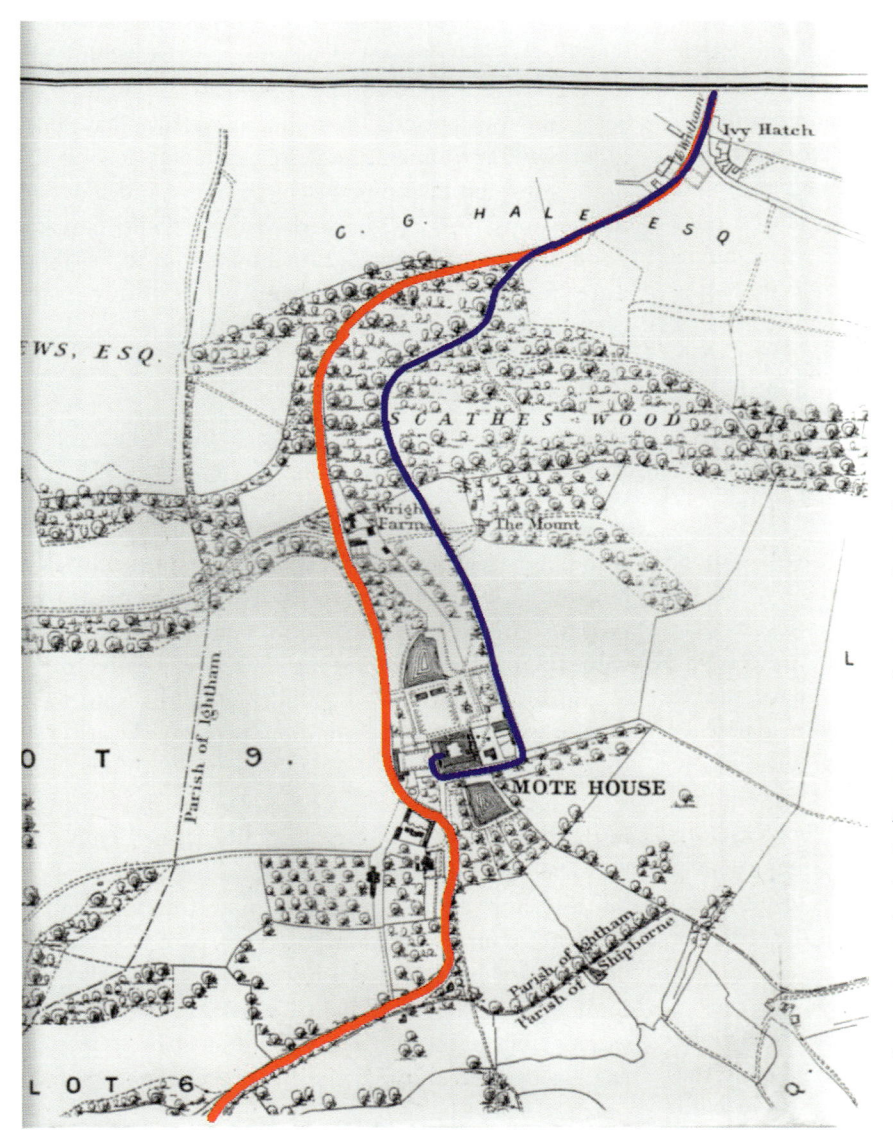

Fig. 8.14: The route of approach to Ightham Mote from the eastern side of the valley (blue line) and western side of the valley (red line), superimposed on the 1889 Sale Particulars map. The red line indicates the public path, serving traffic through the area, while the blue line represents a more private path, serving traffic to the house. Routes of approach to Ightham Mote from the eastern and western sides of the valley. The western route served general traffic through the area, while the eastern route may have been a more exclusive approach, serving traffic to the house. Drawing by Carrie Willis.

have walked down the gentle descent of the eastern or western ridges to approach the property from the north, or up the gradual incline from the south.

19th-century Ordnance Survey, estate, and Sale Particulars maps, can be used to indicate former routes that may have been used to reach the property. From the Sale Particulars map, one can see two routeways lead directly to Ightham Mote (see Fig. 8.14). Both run south from the hamlet of Ivy Hatch; one runs along the eastern ridge and the other runs along the slope of the eastern side.

Approach via the western side of the valley

The 19th-century Sale Particulars map indicates that a north-south route runs south from Ightham village and divides to the south-east and south-west (see Fig. 8.14). The western branch of this main road continues south-west, through the hamlet of Ivy Hatch, and cuts through Scathes Wood to the north of Ightham Mote, almost on the outskirts of the wood. The road then continues south along the western side of the valley which houses Ightham Mote. The road extends south, past Ightham Mote, past Budd's Green, and continues south towards Hildenborough. Topographically, the energy cost of using this road is minimal; the land decreases at varying degrees of steepness as one goes south. The road is a route that connects up a range of places across the landscape; although it passes Ightham Mote, and indeed may have been diverted to accommodate the new outer court in the later 15th century, it is not intended as a route specifically for travellers to Ightham Mote. It serves major foot and horse traffic from wider areas of the region, with Ightham Mote as only one stop along its path.

A visitor travelling south on the major road would first come through the outskirts of Scathes Wood to cross fields and a minor wooded area (see Fig. 8.14). The age of Scathes Wood is not known for certain, so the visual effect of this approach may have varied over time. An earlier map by Andrews *et al.* dated to 1769 does not appear to show the wood, although it does appear to show the major (western) and minor (eastern) roads that cut through it. The woods appear in the subsequent 1801 Ordnance Survey map, which suggests that the shape of the wood as it appears on later maps through to the present time was the result of 18th-century landscape modifications.

The traveller would then proceed south along a slight incline and through a smaller copse of trees before the property was revealed to their left. Because the land decreases in elevation from north to south, the visitor would have a clear view of the property, slightly from above, viewing it from across the area now occupied by the north pond and lawn, and probably the site of water features in the Middle Ages. The visitor would continue south with the house at their left, along the side of the west front of the outer court, and would then either turn into the outer court through the western gate, or continue around to the south-west corner of the south pond. From this position, the visitor would turn sharply left and head north, viewing the house's southern aspect, with the north lawn and pond providing a backdrop, to come to the entrance between the inner and outer courts. Alternatively, such a visitor would continue on the road as it veered to the south-west towards Nuttree Green and the intersection with what is now Hildenborough Road.

A visitor travelling north-east on the major road, from Nuttree Green and the Low Weald, would also first see the house framed by water features; the land increases in elevation when coming from the south, so the individual would come north through a copse of trees and initially see the tower, roofs and upper parts of the house from across the south pond. The mill may well also have been highly visible from this angle of approach, to one side of the south pond and between the house and the road. As the house was approached, visitors would have the pond on their right and see the house with its northern water features in the background before turning right into the western courtyard.

Approach from the eastern ridge

To return to the northern side, a route now forks from the major road where it meets the northern extent of Scathes Wood, cutting through an area of woodland (see Fig. 8.14). This is the approach taken by contemporary visitors to the Trust property. It then moves south through the wood, curves slightly to the west, then comes south along the eastern valley ridge. It continues south until parallel with the south-east corner of the house, and then turns westward at a sharp right angle.

It then moves west along a tightly defined causeway between the south pond and the southern aspect of the house, before turning north, through the perimeter of the outer court, to terminate at the space between the outer court and main entrance. Topographically, this route of approach would also be a convenient one; the eastern ridge of the property, though steep on its western face, is a gentle and manageable descent moving from north to south.

The approach from the western side of the valley covers additional ground by running along the northern and western outskirts of Scathes Wood, and is also the main routeway running north-south between Ivy Hatch and Nuttree Green. The minor road affords more direct access from the north, cutting through Scathes Wood on a direct path to the more gentle eastern face of the valley at Ightham Mote. The major road does provide access to Ightham Mote, but the minor road appears to be less heavily trafficked, more private, and with more direct access to Ightham Mote.

The Scathes Wood route is listed in a 19th-century map as a 'carriage drive'. It may have been created in the 1600s by the Selby family (Rumley 2007: 58), and it may have been either created or modified at some other date in the post-medieval period. However, it may well be earlier. It may be that rather than the trees being planted to create the carriage drive, the trees were planted to accentuate an existing routeway, and that this routeway was the most common route of access from the northern villages to Ightham Mote.

A visitor travelling south on this route would be in the woods for slightly longer, emerging at the north-east corner of the property (see Fig. 8.14). Upon exiting the woods, a visitor would emerge at the top of an elevated area of the eastern ridge. The north-east point of the property is much higher than the surrounding land; from this point, the visitor would have been able to see the entire property, including the south pond, from this vantage point. As the visitor descended the slope to the south, a full view of the eastern face of the house would be visible. At the base of the slope, the visitor would turn sharply to the west, and either enter the house across the bridge and through the small eastern entrance, or proceed with the south pond to the left and the house to the right. Another right turn would deliver them almost immediately into the space between the outer and inner courts. The minor road appears to join up with the major road at the south-west corner of the south pond. Therefore, a southerly approach is not possible from the minor road.

Both roads lead through Scathes Wood, the minor road more deeply through the wood and the major road on its outskirts. From the point where they fork, the minor road is a shorter distance and time to Ightham Mote. While the northerly approach from the major road would have gradually revealed first the north pond, then the middle pond or north lawn, then the house, the high elevation of the northern aspect of the eastern ridge would have made the entire property visible upon exiting Scathes Wood. This would have had the effect of emerging from the limited visual range of the enclosed wood to be immediately met with an impressive view of the landscape in its entirety. While the major road leads past the outer court to the south-west corner of the south pond and back up, the placement of the main entrance away from the eastern ridge would have forced the traveller using the minor road to come across the southern face of the house, lengthening the travel time.

Fig. 8.15: The outer court, probably added in the 1470s, as seen looking west from the summit of the gate tower. The ground rises beyond the road to the edge of the parish and a substantial field boundary beyond, indicated in Fig. 8.4. Photo by Matthew Johnson.

The two routes of approach appear to be complementary: the western route is that of an everyday route, along with the main traffic through the valley on the way north to Ivy Hatch and south to Nuttree and the Low Weald, and leading to the lower court and the service activities housed therein, while the eastern route is more specialised and possibly restricted to household staff and/or visitors.

Discussion

To summarise the evidence that we have for the later medieval landscape at Ightham Mote:

- The house itself, and the moat surrounding the inner court, date back to at least the 1320s.
- The outer court was added in the later 15th century.
- There is no direct evidence for a series of ponds or water features north and south of the house, but the existence of most or all of these is probable given the context and parallels with other late medieval sites.
- Similarly, there is no physical evidence for medieval gardens, but one would expect a house like Ightham to have one or more gardens after the medieval pattern, that is small enclosed spaces.

- There is documentary reference to a mill; the pond to the south probably served as the mill pond.
- The approach along the western side of the valley is part of a route likely to be early medieval in origin, but was probably diverted to run around the new outer court in the later 15th century.
- The approach along the eastern side of the valley may well also have existed in the Middle Ages.
- Both approaches would have afforded impressive views of the house in its landscape setting that are now not possible due to tree planting and other post-medieval modifications to the site.
- There is at least one fragment of what appears to be a park pale to the south of the house.

To these observations, we add a further speculative point:

- The addition of the outer court in the later 15th century, under the Hautes, was a major transformation in the scale of the house (Fig. 8.15); it is possible that insofar as there was ever a designed landscape at Ightham Mote, it may have been created or enlarged at this point.

How best to interpret these observations? It is very tempting to note the likely existence of a series of water features, combined with approach routes that probably afforded views over the valley and the house therein, and the possibility of a deer park beyond, and conclude that Ightham Mote is an example of a designed landscape. This was the view taken in the 2007 archaeological assessment of the garden, in which Peter Rumley joined together the field boundaries outlined in Fig. 8.4 to postulate the presence of a deer park (Rumley 2007: 51). This view was sharply rebutted by the landscape archaeologist Chris Taylor in an appendix to the Garden Conservation Plan of 2008 (Ford & Rutherford 2009: 120). Taylor pointed to the lack of physical evidence at Ightham for medieval gardens, and that the field boundaries marked in Fig. 8.4 could not be plausibly joined up to create the oval form characteristic of medieval parks. However, as we have seen with Bodiam and Scotney in earlier chapters, the underlying problem here is the use and definition of the term 'designed landscape'. This has a series of issues, both in terms of the concept, and in terms of the evidence that might be marshalled in support of it.

Despite its extreme popularity in landscape archaeology, the phrase designed landscape has some problematic conceptual baggage associated with it. Primarily, it is a difficult term to define within the medieval context. As Creighton (2009) explains, the phrase designed landscape was not originally created to describe features of medieval landscape archaeology. The phrase is typically used to describe post-medieval parks and gardens surrounding large country homes, beginning in the Tudor period and popularised in the 19th century (Johnson 2002; Liddiard & Williamson 2008; Creighton 2009). Using the term designed landscape in the medieval context indexes 19th-century ideas of the role and experience of landscape, which may not match medieval perceptions and understandings of the landscape (Smith 2003). Furthermore, as Creighton (2009) mentions, the boundaries of the designed landscape are hazy at best; where does the designed portion of the landscape end and the 'natural' part begin? Are designed and natural landscapes mutually exclusive (Edgeworth 2011)? Furthermore, how complex does a landscape have to be in order to be considered designed (Creighton 2009)? Can vernacular, peasant landscapes also be designed?

The word 'design' also implies a governing scheme or concept in which there is an *a priori* blueprint or template and construction takes place, for the most part, in one phase. At Ightham, the different elements of the landscape strongly suggest a piecemeal evolution. The wider structure of the landscape – the north-south routeways, the overall dispersed nature of the settlement -- was of some antiquity by the 1300s, and the house was fitted into it. The origins of the house itself are unclear, and the form of the immediate landscape in its initial phases must remain uncertain. As stated above, it is very possible that the addition of the outer court in the 1470s was not simply a major addition to the house, but marked a transformation in the surrounding landscape as well; it is probable that the line of the road was diverted at this juncture, and it may be that the series of northern ponds were added or formalised at this quite late stage.

It is easier to say what Ightham Mote was not. The popular image of the house is one of a modest retreat, never built or rebuilt in the grand manner, and tucked away in a forgotten, isolated valley. The post-medieval history and current appearance of Ightham lends additional force to this perception, and it is a vision which animates much of the popular presentation and understanding of the site. However, to a late medieval visitor, particularly after the construction of the outer court, Ightham may well have appeared as quite a grand place. The view down into the valley, coming after an extended journey to an isolated location, would have revealed an extensive suite of buildings, arranged around two major courtyards and with a gatehouse tower at its centre, its walls and gate tower reflected in the waters of the moat and probably framed on either side by outer gardens and extensive water features.

If the landscape was designed, what was it designed to do? One could argue that the landscape at Ightham Mote was designed to be viewed and enjoyed, and to provide a 'theatrical route of approach' (Creighton 2009: 86) which controlled movement and revealed the house and its surroundings in stages. The hypothesised routes of approach certainly do this, though they achieve this effect through the use of the pre-existing lie of the land. The stage-by-stage revealing of different elements of the landscape is a result of the landscape's natural topography.

The landscape at Ightham is a perfect illustration of the use of the natural topography of the landscape to create a setting for a house. Rather than the *landscape* being designed, the *house* was designed – or rather, carefully placed and oriented – to enhance and make use of the landscape's natural features. The house's main gate and outer court are oriented away from the approach from the east, towards the north-south route to the west. This directs visitors or inhabitants using the eastern approach to come around the house in a sharp turn in order to enter, prolonging the amount of time viewing the house, and exposing different sides of the house and aspects of the landscape to the viewer. The north-south decline in elevation and natural spring allow for a cascading effect of water features throughout the landscape. The placement of a pond at either extreme of the landscape with the house between ensures that the house is seen across a lake from either a northerly or southerly approach, while the cascading effect of the water also ensures that waste deposited into the moat is flushed out and deposited in the south pond.

The existence of two approaches, one for general traffic and one for accessing Ightham Mote directly, has implications for different power dynamics within the landscape. Ightham Mote is isolated, at the southern end of the parish of Ightham and the border with the parish of Shipbourne. Furthermore, it has its own chapel, which means that those who lived at Ightham Mote may not have needed to regularly leave the property to attend the church at the far north of the parish of Ightham. Those who worked in the house and in its immediate landscape would have lived in the house as servants and domestic workers, while those who worked in the more distant outfields and demesne lands would likely have only approached as far as the fields. Thus, the only individuals who would regularly travel to and from Ightham Mote would be the owners on occasional travel, those invited directly, and those who walked or rode past the property on their way down the main road.

It is not known whether the eastern route was created especially for the house, whether it already existed in the landscape, or indeed if it was a post-medieval addition. In the first two cases, it is very possible that by the later Middle Ages, the minor road was used more or less exclusively to access Ightham Mote. The gentle slope of the eastern ridge, procession between the south pond and house, and termination between the inner and outer court, as opposed to meeting the major road, seem to support this interpretation. If it is the case that the eastern approach was used as a more social, restricted access to Ightham Mote, then it holds that use of the road would be limited to the household, its guests, and household staff.

The presence of a separate route of approach of some length, over 1000 m from the northern fork to the house – either formally or through frequent use – intended primarily for members of the household of Ightham Mote, reflects a social segregation in the landscape. This ideological and social separation is expressed through the use of physical separation. However, as Adam T Smith explains in *The Political Landscape*, 'space not only expresses but also argues' (Smith 2003: 61). Smith claims that when practices are limited to certain spaces – for example, limiting the driving of automobiles to the road – these practices legitimise the spaces, give them power to limit behaviours and practices. However, the limitation of practices to particular spaces also reinforces the social and political institutions that the creation of these spaces directly benefit. The designation of a road for 'procession' or 'approach' and a road for simply 'passing by' designates the landscape as set apart, not an element of the daily back and forth through the landscape, of people of a variety of social classes and identities, but rather for a privileged class. Those lower-class individuals accessing the landscape by either approach, whether invited or not, would have been aware of this distinction as they entered the property. This creates a very tangible social space around the immediate landscape of Ightham Mote.

If the experience of space is the framework of human knowledge of the world (Hillier & Hanson 1989), then the existence of two roads which spatially and socially segregate two separate groups shapes our understanding of the social relationships between those who use the main road and those who use the private drive. This distinction reinforces the ideology of social differentiation by distributing it across the landscape. Spatially constrained activities – processing on the minor road, versus passing by on the major road – are assigned to particular social identities: those with a certain level of material wealth and those without it, respectively. Through the repeated daily practice of taking the public highway, with the understanding that a more exclusive or processional approach exists, individuals with less access to material wealth are made aware of their exclusion from this social space. While passersby may not have felt subjugated or excluded by the fact that they were taking the public road, or even been aware of it, their taking it would have contributed to a system in which different social positions enjoyed different levels of power. This embodied experience, understanding of social position, and understanding of the world, contribute to the maintenance of the existing relational, hierarchical social structure which defines social classes in the first place.

This is not to say that individuals are enslaved by their spatial constraints; deer parks, considered almost universally to be 'elite' spaces (Cantor 1982; Johnson 2002; Creighton 2009; Creighton & Barry 2012), were commonly broken into by individuals of lower social status, particularly when food was scarce and deer within the lord or earl's private deer park were plenty (see also Chapter Seven). Likewise, non-elite individuals likely would have taken the minor road to come to Ightham Mote for temporary work, by invitation, or potentially to steal food or simply to trespass. However, by entering into what is understood as private space, delineated by the major and minor roads or the simultaneously physical and social boundaries of the park pale, trespassers are aware that their behaviour challenges the power of the landowner. They are not acting outside of the relational social hierarchy in place, but simply challenging it. The spatial segregation of social identities, as illustrated at Ightham Mote, contributes to a hierarchical structure of social relations. This hierarchy, reflected in physical space, reinforces the knowledge that those with less material wealth are socially distinct from and excluded by those with more material wealth.

Conclusion

Our survey and analysis of the Ightham landscape has led to several general conclusions about its form, and whether it can be considered a formal or designed landscape.

First, the present appearance of the landscape at Ightham Mote is probably misleading. The landscape was not designed in that it was tailor made for the house; rather, the house was positioned to fit the lie of the land as it existed and the landscape was modified rather than created.

Second, the 'expression of social status' at Ightham Mote is anything but intangible. The reinforcement of social status is an undoubtedly physical phenomenon in the landscape. Modifications to the landscape reflected and prompted embodied patterns of movement. In this way, the landscape acted upon the bodies of those who moved through it, reinforcing existing social hierarchies and power structures that defined social life in the medieval world.

Finally, the concept of designed landscapes is simultaneously redundant and paradoxical: redundant in that all landscapes that have been modified by human activity, intentional or not, are in some capacity designed and paradoxical in that no landscape can be completely designed in its entirety. Rather than focusing our efforts on identifying *designed* landscapes in the archaeological record, we should search for *modified* landscapes.

Our goal should not be to find out 'for what purpose was this landscape designed', but rather 'how do modifications in the landscape constrain and facilitate human work, movement, and other practices?' Topographical analysis of movement through the landscape, as evidenced at Ightham Mote, has the ability to address more complex questions about the way landscape reflects, reinforces, challenges, and embodies differential power dynamics through experience of the landscape and daily practices inside, around, and within it.

9

LIVED EXPERIENCE AT BODIAM AND IGHTHAM

Catriona Cooper[1]

Abstract. This chapter explores the theme of 'lived experience' at Bodiam and Ightham, through the lens of digital techniques and a phenomenological approach. It is based on my PhD thesis *The exploration of lived experience in medieval buildings through the use of digital technology* (2015). Phenomenology has initiated a number of discussions concerning how we can think about human experience in the past based on bodily experience in the world. However, it has been rarely applied to medieval studies despite a much richer dataset compared to earlier archaeological periods. In this chapter I present two case studies that demonstrate alternative and complementary techniques to explore the notion and implementation of a digital lived experience of late medieval buildings. My first case study based at Bodiam Castle uses digital visualisation techniques to explore the lived experience of the private apartments. I propose a mixed media approach for the presentation of visualisations. In my second case study I present an assessment of a series of auralisations of Ightham Mote. I demonstrate that digital techniques that work across senses can provide a robust mechanism for exploring the concept of lived experience, and for exploring the lived experience of specific medieval buildings.

Introduction

Successive chapters in this book have introduced the idea of lived experience and explored different dimensions of this concept in relation to the sites and landscapes of Bodiam, Scotney, Knole and Ightham. The aim of this chapter focuses on two case studies at Bodiam and Ightham, exploring how digital technologies can add further depth to this discussion.

From the publication and following critique of Tilley's (1994) *Phenomenology of Landscape* the study of prehistory has focused on exploring everyday life and experience in the past. Medievalists have traditionally held back from the lived experience/phenomenological way of thinking, instead accessing the study of the day-to-day through historical sources and traditional remains (see Woolgar 2006). However, the medieval dataset is rich in remains and resources which would be well suited to an exploration of this type, an area of research led by Gilchrist (2012).

The use of digital images and computer graphics to visualise scenes is not something new to the study of the past. Digital images in this context have been biased towards aesthetic appraisal, although analytical approaches have also been championed to a fairly limited degree. However, the process of digital creation of these scenes can be used as a method for looking at the experience of life in the past. Multisensory perspectives and experiences of the past only exist, to date, in a limited sense (Tilley 1994; 2004; 2008; Gillings 2005; Hamilton *et al.* 2006) and again they focus overwhelmingly on prehistoric settings (Johnson

---

[1] This chapter was written by Catriona Cooper, based on her PhD research, which was supervised by Matthew Johnson, Graeme Earl, Alison Gascoigne, Caroline Thackray and Nathalie Cohen.

2012a). I will take the process a step further; apply the same methodology to the study of the acoustical properties of a space.

In this chapter I present two case studies showing how different methodologies (visualisation and auralisation) can further our understanding of medieval life in a 14th-century secular building.

Phenomenology and the Medieval Past

Lived experience has been discussed in prehistory through a phenomenological approach. Phenomenology emerged as a theoretical approach to address issues of subjectivity and meaning in landscape studies (Hodder 1987; Tilley 1990; Hodder *et al.* 1995; Hodder & Hutson 2003; Johnson 2012a). Research (for example Ingold 1993; Gosden 1994; Tilley 1994; Bender 1998; Cummings 2002; Cosgrove 2006) has explored the subjective understanding of landscape, or rather the understanding of landscape based on bodily experience, and in doing so has moved away from the Cartesian (thinking about space in a geometric; x, y, z coordinate system) or 'objective' way of thinking about space, which when carefully analysed is not really objective at all (Cosgrove 2006; Cosgrove & Daniels 1988, Rose 1993; Massey 1994; Johnson 2011). Lived experience provides a way to think about life focusing on the elements which make people understand the world around them on a multisensory level: how people move, their activities, everyday paths and places and memory. Documentary and physical evidence are not enough, because the living in the past goes beyond these remains, it is a subjective experience of each individual memory: both personal and inherited are important (Johnson 2012a; Hamilakis 2014).

The phenomenological approach has been critiqued at length due, according to its critics, to the lack of empirical, or objective, evaluation often associated with its reflections. This critique has been particularly sharp where it has been applied to prehistory (Gosden 1994; Bender 1998; Pollard & Gillings 1998; Tilley 2004; Brück 2005; Ingold 2005; Fleming 2006; A.M. Jones 2007).

The subject of living in the Middle Ages, approached in a phenomenological way, has to a great extent been avoided by archaeologists, despite the richer dataset and the many books entitled 'Daily/Everyday Life' in the literature. Medieval archaeologists have tended to focus on the abundant material culture and documentary evidence without addressing, at least in any considerable depth, questions on the experience of living (exceptions include Giles 2007; Gies & Gies 2010; Gilchrist 2012 and Johnson 2012b). Historians, although appearing to approach questions of the experience of living, rarely engage with phenomenology in a direct way. An exception is Stephen Murray, who states that [we need to be] 'reconciling our experiential responses with the task of dealing with buildings as entities that can go beyond the written document in providing vital access to the past'. (Murray 2008: 383). Murray's ideas have rarely been applied to medieval sites or buildings. Murray's work also highlights the link between phenomenology and lived experience.

The phenomenological approach has been described as the interrogation of lived experience (Johnson 2012a). It is however just one in several ways to approach the experience of living in the past. By taking the approaches suggested in phenomenology we can begin to move towards lived experience by taking these ideas and supporting them with the quantity and quality of data available from the medieval period.

What is a Medieval Building?

Buildings are the product of human construction and inhabitation (Hillier & Hanson 1989; Parker Pearson & Richards 1994; Steane 2001). Buildings define the spaces (rooms) they create. This is a social process, in that the building is created (like any artefact), according to some previously conceived plan by the builder according to socially conceived ideas about the use of space. Therefore, I suggest that there is a connection between the realm of the social and the organisation of space which can be seen through the study of buildings. Buildings both mediate the space they create as well as being designed according to social concepts about how domestic, ecclesiastical or working space should be ordered (Fig. 9.1).

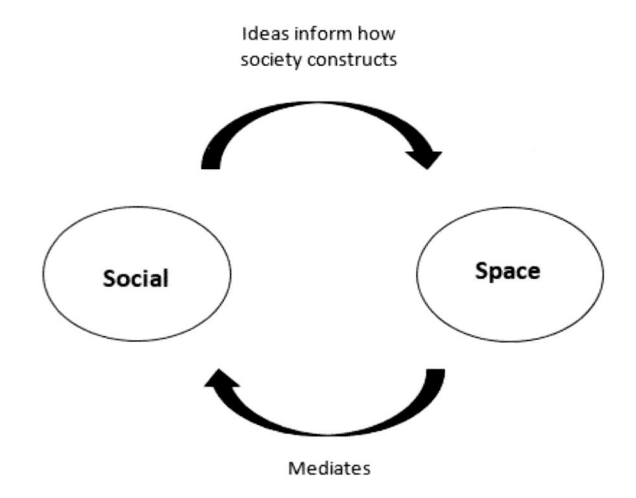

Fig. 9.1: This diagram shows how social ideas are linked to space.

Fig. 9.2: The eastern elevation of Bodiam Castle, taken from the west. Photo by Penny Copeland.

There is an underlying assumption in much of the literature that houses built between the late 14th and early 15th century straddle the gap between the austere castle keeps of the medieval period and the comforts of Tudor palaces and gentry houses (Tipping 1921; Curzon 1926: 10-11; Brown 1970: 144; Platt 1982: 118). For those subscribing to this assumption, buildings of this period are presented as 'transitional' in evolutionary terms. They form an interim phase between two groups of buildings. In so doing, an understanding of these changes and the reasons for them is bypassed (Johnson 2002: 133-4). I suggest that we should move away from considering them in this way and instead think about buildings as agents which stage social interactions and how the use of space defines this. Focusing on the individual elements of buildings allows us to explore the social context within which these buildings were constructed, and to explore builders' intentions in their creations instead of focusing on their position in a timeline (Olsen 2003: 100). We can therefore present a holistic picture of how they were lived in.

Although the subject of living in buildings in the medieval period is not one that has been neglected (Wood 1965; Woolgar 1999; Emery 1996; 2006; Airs & Barnwell 2011) there are remarkably few texts discussing late medieval secular buildings beyond collections which foreground architectural interest or act as gazetteers (Turner & Parker 1859; Nairn & Pevsner 1965; Pearson 1994; Emery 2006a; Woolgar 2006 and Brears 2010 are exceptions). Where social life has been addressed, there has been a particular focus on the study of castles (Hohler 1966; Fairclough 1992; Dixon & Lott 1993; Mathieu 1999; Creighton 2005; Liddiard 2005a). Also underrepresented from the literature is work on buildings of the middling classes and gentry society. Neglecting this category of building (secular dwelling) during this period means our understanding of the built environment is lacking. The general structure of these buildings has been discussed in detail by first Faulkner (1975) in reference to castles and then by Johnson with a focus on the vernacular (Johnson 2002; 2010). The classic plan develops from early medieval buildings (pre 1200 CE) centring on the hall, with an extension at one end containing a buttery and pantry (services) and passage through to an external kitchen (Wood 1965: 247; Gardiner 2000). This develops to also include a withdrawing chamber, private apartments and chapel; a pattern which is seen across both castles and other secular dwellings.

Space is traditionally explored in plan view, using floor plans. In the earlier chapters of this book we followed this convention by presenting a series of plans of Bodiam Castle to disseminate our research about the building. Elevations were also presented, but these still do not give an impression of how the space exists in three dimensions. By contrast, much phenomenological work has discussed how spaces are experienced in terms of moving through them in the present. However, movement through space can be overlooked and it is even more likely that internal furnishings will not be considered. For example, modern understandings of medieval French cathedrals are of large open spaces, when in fact the buildings in the middle ages would have been divided by screens and encumbered by liturgical furniture and tombs (Murray 2008: 390).

To approach questions focused on living in these buildings I have chosen to explore the social interpretations of Bodiam (a castle) and Ightham (a moated manor house) alongside the physical buildings of Bodiam Castle (Figs 9.2 & 3.1) and Ightham Mote (Figs 8.1, 8.5 & 8.6), their furnishings, fittings and three dimensional construction.

Bodiam Castle

As discussed in Chapter Three most of the literature relating to Bodiam explores the exterior and overall appearance of the building (Grose 1791; Turner & Parker 1859; Blaauw 1861; Savery 1868; Timbs & Gunn 1872; Clark 1884; Mackenzie 1896; Sands 1903; Thompson 1912; Tipping 1921; Braun 1936; Toy 1953; O'Neil 1960; Brown 1970; Harvey 1978; Kenyon 1981; Platt 1982; 2007; Hohler 1966; Turner 1986; Stocker 1992; Saul 1995; Johnson *et al.* 2000; Morris 2003; Creighton 2005; Liddiard 2005a; Creighton & Liddiard 2008). In what follows, I will examine the interior of the building alongside research on medieval interiors and landscape. Visualisation is the perfect tool for this, allowing a range of different datasets to be observed together. The recording of the building (discussed in Chapter Three), detailed research into the furnishings, fittings and decorations of domestic rooms, and an understanding of the use of the rooms, and how this can be interpreted visually, can all be presented in one image. The undertaking of this research is just as important as the final image, or images, as the very nature of this creation process can allow for multiple views of a space to be produced. The images themselves are a stage in an interpretation of the evidence about medieval life. Researching how to create these images requires rigorous questioning and critiquing of a huge range of evidence for each stage of the creation process. Therefore, the final images seen here are not the final product; they can be continually updated and adapted based on new research and further critique.

The digital media approach has, until recently, been mostly concerned with the visualisation of the past through a variety of media. This has mostly been described as 'Reconstruction' and is mostly made up of standalone images, websites, animations or virtual realities. It has met with much criticism from wider areas of the discipline, being understood as expensive, technically demanding and of little interpretive value (see discussion in Goodrick & Earl 2004). The technology was driven by a 'this would be cool' (Kantner 2000) mind set and an experimental approach. The results of this approach have meant that in most cases the focus is on the aesthetics of the models. Further, the models have been produced with the intention of displaying results of data collection rather than as a method for interpretation (Gillings 2005). Exceptions include analysis projects such as those discussed by Wittur (2013).

This situation led to the assumption that display was the only use for computer-generated images in archaeology. Therefore, the critique of these images has been towards the display of 'results', rather than being part of a process of reflection and revision. Technologically produced visualisations fall into a void between technological products and subjective renderings of archaeological material. They engage elements of both practices but frequently fail in embracing the advantages of both. For example, they do not engage with the ability to change and develop the renderings following presentation of the final image (Bateman 2000).

When produced as a method for displaying results, images of this kind are often incorrectly perceived as being 'self-explanatory and less theory-laden' (Moser 1992: 832). Instead the images need to be approached with the same critical eye that is applied to other areas of archaeological illustration. The process of engaging with images is the beginning; they need to be critiqued, explored and further developed before being presented. They also need to be engaged with in a state beyond the final presentation of results: they can be used to develop an interpretation and as a method for recording.

Presenting multiple interpretations has been a popular suggestion by digital specialists (Fawcett *et al.* 2008; Koerner & Russell 2010: 327; Lozny 2011: vii). Through this method multiple interpretations of the past can be presented though a series of images detailing the development of the simulation. However, this ideal has yet to be fully realised. I believe that this technique can be applied as more than a mechanism for interpretation and engagement but also as a method for exploring space. These images can be used as a method for fostering discussion about the use of space allowing the subjective nature of the creation process to be questioned at every step, encouraging further engagement with the building from the public. The intention is to explore how to engage with the building and respond to it through the use of visualisation to try and understand its lived experience. Instead of presenting a series of images in creation, or completed images, I bring together the final images produced through the 3D model alongside elements of the research which created it (furniture, manuscripts, art).

Presenting multiple images in this way is a phenomenon which has been developed in social media over the last few years. The most popular examples of this can be found on the internet service and company Pinterest. It allows users to create and catalogue collections of visual bookmarks. Catalogues are chosen by the user and the visual bookmarks can be added via upload, searching the internet, other people's boards or through other media content (Pinterest 2014).

I have isolated a small but complicated area of the building to envision, the eastern elevation, focusing on the 'private apartments' (Fig. 9.2; see also Chapter Three, Figs 3.1, 3.7 & 3.33). In my visualisation, the apartments are not only furnished appropriately, they are decorated according to the period and populated in the same manner. The modelling process allows us to consider how the building fulfils the 'spatial grammar of expectation' (Johnson 2002: 20) that govern the layout of late medieval buildings but equally how Bodiam differs from the expected norms associated with such buildings. In essence, it explores how the spaces are both individual and part of a conforming dataset by looking at the building as an artefact of medieval society. The project itself is also concerned with the concept of an interpretative methodology. Creating visualisations is the method for interpretation of the site. A narrative is produced from the observation of the archaeological record through to how the 'real' of the simulated past is perceived. Through the recording of the entire process of creation, an understanding is achieved of how the uncertainty and assumption inherent in the simulation process is important: it can therefore be highlighted and it can be critiqued. Choices made during the recording of Bodiam: research into decoration of medieval chambers, furniture and social uses of space, are all included as part of the creation process. Making these decisions informs the creation of the final image; therefore the decision-making process is embedded in the appearance of the final image and is an important part of the interpretation.

One recent study (Frankland 2012) has suggested that visualisations are not considered as compelling to the public as their creators like to think. It is understood that the final image is an interpretation and viewers are interested in the creation process. 'Mood boards' bring together multiple media to present a single concept or idea. I present the final CGI images which intend to show a particular concept or theme alongside the images that went into creating it (furniture and fittings, illustrations from medieval manuscripts and paintings from the 14th century). In doing so, the images allow the viewer to consider the sources of the visualisation and question them. By being capable of producing a number of images the same space can be considered in a number of ways and further allow the viewer to think about the experience of living in that space.

All of the decisions concerning materials, structure and furnishings inform our understanding of the space, and the parts of my work that are discarded are as important as those used. These issues with uncertainty and subjectivity are unavoidable when using digital technologies: I propose them as a method for engagement and not as an overarching issue.

The models were based on the survey data discussed in Chapter Three. This was done by importing the survey into 3DS MAX, a modelling and rendering software, and using the survey as a guide. The survey methodology informed much of the visualisation process. Putting together the spaces was more complex than just examining the survey data, which only really considers one wall of the suites (see eastern elevation drawing). Decisions concerning the layout of windows, walls and room partitions had to be considered, as well as the nature of the roofing and flooring. Evidence for building materials was drawn from Kathryn Catlin's report on the finds found in Appendix One, in combination with careful examination of the standing remains and comparisons with other contemporary buildings.

Decorations, furnishings and fittings were a different challenge. As Kathryn Catlin's report (Appendix One) suggests, there are remarkably few finds relating directly to Bodiam; although these can inform types of ceramic found within the building they are otherwise limiting. As discussed in Chapter Three, this has led scholars to question whether Bodiam was inhabited for any length of time. The documentary sources are equally as fragmentary, focusing on building construction with no written wills or other ordinances. As such, evidence had to be drawn more generally from other documentary sources such as the Will of Thomas Couen and James Peckham concerning Ightham Mote. More generally, other wills of the period (http://name.umdl.umich.edu/EEWills, accessed 26th April 2016), illustrated manuscripts, and paintings (such as Fig. 9.3) were helpful at visualising and sourcing appropriate items. Extant furnishings, although limited, were possible to find (Fig. 9.4) and recent physical reconstructions (Fig. 9.5) could be used to further envision spaces. Unfortunately, there is not the space here to discuss each decision and each item modelled but as one example I will review some of the evidence for the construction of the bed.

Jude Jones (2007) undertook research into sleeping and the construction of gender between 1350-1750, for which she created a catalogue of beds between those dates. She discussed the presence of two types of bed: the four poster (such as the Great Bed of Ware) and the hung bed. The four poster bed, although first appearing in 1242, did not become popular until the 15th century (Eames 1977: 75). The relative lack of medieval examples has been attributed to the peripatetic nature of medieval elite life. The hung bed provides an elegant

Fig. 9.3: The Arnolfini Portrait by Jan van Eyck (© Copyright The National Gallery, London 2016). Another hung bed can be seen in the background.

bed that can be constructed and taken down easily and taken to the next house, whereas the four poster is not so easily transported (Hunt 1965: 22).

The bed was not totally devoted to nocturnal use. By lifting and tying back the curtains, the bed could be used as part of a living room (Ash 1965: 33). There are no surviving examples of these beds remaining from the late 14th century (Eames, 1977: 75). However, the bed hangings appear frequently in documents from the end of the 13th century onwards. The textiles were very valuable and appear as part of inventories such as that of John Chelmyswk, Esq of Shropshire (Furnivall 1882) and John Rogerysson of London (Furnivall 1882), and the more popular examples of the Inventory of the Duke of Burgundy from 1404. They are also found in wills, such as The Will of Richard Earl of Arundel in 1392, and the wills of James Peckham and Thomas Couen (of Ightham Mote) which also feature bed hangings. These examples support the argument that beds of this type were not just of the upper classes but also the middling and gentry classes (Eames, 1977: 78-83). There is a quotation from Chaucer's *Book of the Duchess* that reveals how highly valued textiles were in this period:

> *I will give him a feather bed of down of pure white doves, arrayed with gold and finely covered in fine black satin from abroad, and many pillows, and every pillowcase of linen from Reynes, to sleep softly he will not need to toss and turn so often. And I will give him everything that belongs to a bedchamber, and all his rooms I will have painted with pure gold and arrayed with many matching tapestries.*

(Chaucer, Book of the Duchess: EChaucer 2011: 269)

These pieces of evidence discuss the existence of the textiles but do not help much with our understanding of how they appeared. The best resource we have for this is iconography. Paintings by Van der Weyden (1400-1464: Fig. 9.6), van Eyck (1390-1441: Fig. 9.3) and other illuminations such as Fig. 9.7 show hung beds as part of their images.

Fig. 9.4: Medieval chest, Chester Cathedral.

Fig. 9.5: Dover Castle, reconstructed interior. Particularly of interest is the hung bed. For more information on the creation of the furnishings at Dover Castle see Blog Post 'The Making of the Great Tower at Dover Castle' via my blog http://catrionacooper.wordpress.com.

While no beds remain from this period a number of replicas have been produced. The reconstructed Bayleaf at the Weald and Downland Museum, The Medieval Merchant's House in Southampton, and Dover Castle (Fig. 9.5) are just three examples of them. As replicas their construction can be carefully examined to see how they are hung from the ceiling, taken apart and put together, particularly at the Medieval Merchant's house in Southampton.

3DS max allows lighting systems to be built in. These allow sunlight and daylight to be added to a scene according to location. Location is set based on latitude, longitude and direction (north can be set). Implementing this type of lighting system allows a scene to be lit from the correct angles, and allows movement over time, meaning that they are physically plausible and allow accurate rendering of daylight scenes. I also added lighting from a fire and from candles (that change position and number in the later visualisations), and these effects are also considered here.

I undertook a basic lighting assessment allowing me to see how the lighting conditions changed over the course of the day. In the first instance I used a plain, non-reflective, material to observe how light responded with the geometry, before adding materials and textures appropriate to the space. A few of the images were reproduced to show the changing conditions (Fig. 9.8). From this, I chose to light my spaces later in the day as I

Fig. 9.6: The Annunciation by Rogier van der Weyden. This image is one of the representations of a hung bed from the 14th-15th century (Musee Du Louvre 2014).

LIVED EXPERIENCE IN THE LATER MIDDLE AGES

Fig. 9.7: Detail of a miniature of the birth of Alexander the Great, at the beginning of Book Five, from the Miroir Historial (translated by Jean de Vignay from Vincent of Beauvais's Speculum Historiale), Netherlands (Bruges), 1479-1480 (British Library, MS Royal).

felt the play of light in the room was more engaging. Fig. 9.9 is an example of one of the final images. I found it particularly frustrating and theoretically difficult to select a lighting condition as my choices were largely aesthetic. Also, once the scene was close to completion, with appropriate decorations and surface textures applied, the scenes appeared particularly dark when printed. It was hard to resist using photographic correction software to increase the brightness and contrast to make the image more aesthetically pleasing and easier to see. However, this added to our understanding of the lived experience of the visualisation. The images were dark because they were produced using physically accurate lighting techniques, (Figs 9.10 and 9.11 have been included in this printed book to demonstrate the darkness of the images).

From the creation of the model, a series of concepts or themes were selected as the subjects for the mood boards (Figs 9.12 & 9.13). Some of these themes are connected with the use of Bodiam Castle specifically (Business and Status) while others use visuals to try to invoke an idea of the multisensory experience of the past (touch, scent, reverberation). I then selected ten images to represent each concept. These images were a mixture of renders, photographs of the site, photographs of period furniture, photographs of reconstructed domestic interiors and images from medieval manuscripts. Many of these sources were used as references when creating the model.

Some of the mood boards were easier to create than others. Reading (Fig. 9.12) for example drew on a range of images from manuscripts showing people reading, as well as the addition of books and documents that could easily suggest the theme; the more abstract or ephemeral concepts were harder to construct. Sound (Fig. 9.13) had to incorporate images that suggested sound. Chris Woolgar's discussion of the senses in medieval England (2006) was particularly useful in thinking about sound as a sense of the mouth while I could also consider presenting things that created sound.

Lived experience is complex. It brings together so many elements of personal understanding of a space. As a result, it is theoretically and practically difficult to assess whether I have been successful, and what the criteria for 'success' should be. As a research methodology, I felt the creation of the digital model allowed me to bring together a whole range of different resources and material evidence for the use of that space at Bodiam

Fig. 9.8: Lighting assessment of the modelled private apartments of Bodiam Castle. The top left image is for lighting conditions of 21st June at 6 a.m. with the bottom right being 21st June 6 p.m.

Fig. 9.9: An example of the modelled space.

Castle in the first instance. Through this I achieved a better understanding of how the space could have been used during the medieval period, and I could question the accepted understanding of its experience. I have also brought together a whole range of different pieces of evidence for the furnishings of late medieval domestic spaces of the gentry.

However, we no longer need to focus on only visualising the past. When creating the mood boards I struggled to find images that presented sound (and for that matter smell, touch and taste). Understanding experience goes beyond visual engagement and is multisensory. Therefore the second case study at Ightham Mote looks at using auralisation as a methodology for understanding the experience of a space.

Ightham Mote

> *general characteristic of contemporary society is our fascination, indeed obsession, with the visual*
> (Moser 2001: 266)

This chapter so far has been primarily concerned with the visual and the visual simulation of the past. To move beyond this visual focus to the study of the past, my work at Ightham Mote has explored acoustical methods. As discussed in Chapter Eight Ightham Mote is a late medieval building which has been latterly developed. I explored how the Great Hall has been understood. The Great Hall here is of a middling size but has a very high ceiling (Figs 9.14 & 9.15). Of particular interest to this study are a number of carved minstrel figures at

Fig. 9.10: Internal space which appears dark when printed without adjustments for lighting.

Fig. 9.11: The same image lighted for printing.

LIVED EXPERIENCE IN THE LATER MIDDLE AGES

the base of the beams (Fig. 9.16) who appear to be part of a play, suggesting this as a possible use for the space. More generally there is an abundance of literature referring to Great Halls during this period (James *et al.* 1984; Thompson 1995; Johnson 2012b), and these discussions tend to focus on the appearance and use of the space. Much of our understanding has to do with the different functions of the space: a lord giving judgement, assemblies, mealtimes, music, poetry and conversation. However, how the space sounds and its acoustic properties have rarely been considered.

The visual focus of research is unsurprising. It is estimated that 60% of human mental processing power is devoted to visual processing (Hermon & Fabian 2000); consequently, humans are programmed to experience the world in a primarily visual way (Ray 2008). However, it is not the only way. The first applications of Geographical Information Systems (GIS) were critiqued as being 'primarily visual and distanced', far removed from the way past communities would have engaged with the landscape and environment (Thomas & Jorge 2008: 1). Although visual analysis of the past is the most accessible today, our understanding of the world is based on all of the senses in combination not just one in isolation (Chalmers & Zanyi 2010). This is not the only reason it is a focus in the wider field of archaeology – there is a huge amount of visually engaging material left behind, whereas smells, sounds and tastes have arguably gone (Dawson *et al.* 2007).

Fig. 9.12: Reading mood board.

In the creation of visualisations, without explicit consideration of the other senses, we are creating a past that is 'silent, odourless and intangible' (Mlekuz 2004). We can use visual analysis to explore the other senses, thereby presenting a multisensory past. There has also been a move to try and embrace the study of the senses in archaeology, both as a method for simulating past experiences as well as to explore how the senses were

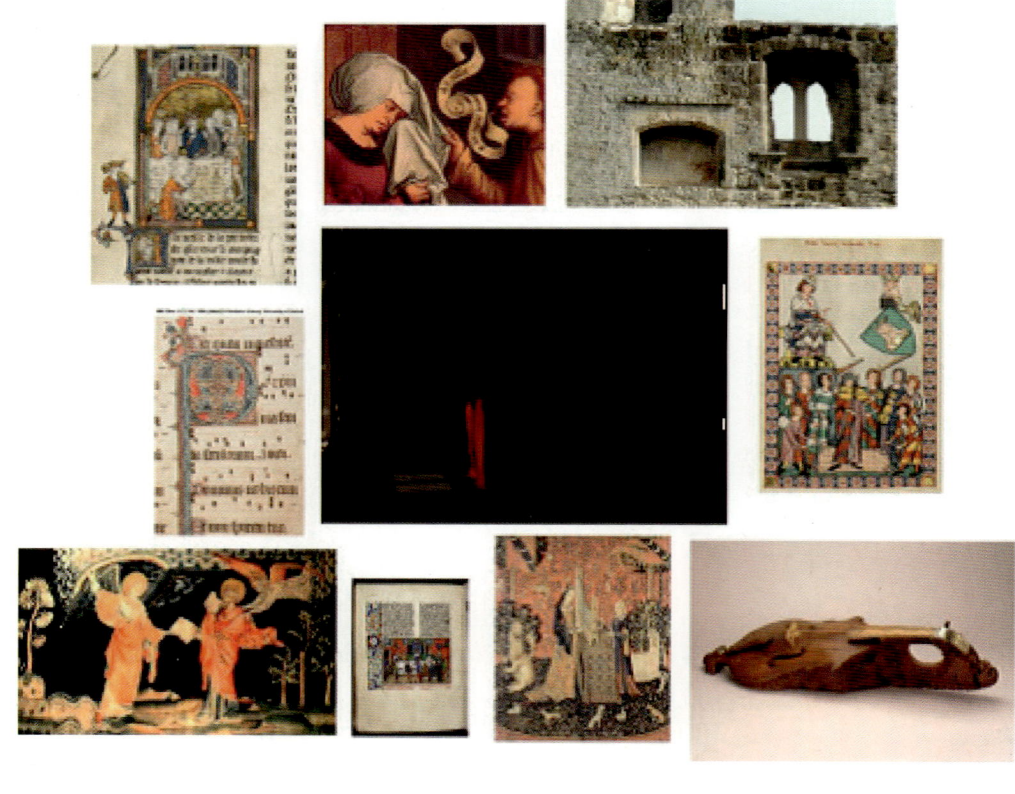

Fig. 9.13: Sound mood board.

Fig. 9.14: The Great Hall at Ightham Mote from the courtyard.

perceived in the past. When simulating the past through senses other than visual, they are often portrayed with accompanying images, as without the visual they lack the authenticity required to make them believable (Thomas & Jorge 2008). Technological approaches should be complemented by a more human experience of place. When discussing societies whose sensory map is different to our own this becomes particularly relevant.

Fig. 9.15: The Great Hall at Ightham Mote looking towards the upper end of the Hall.

Fig. 9.16: Minstrel carved into the beam ends.

Devereux and Jahn stated that the reason sound has been overlooked in archaeology is 'it is instinctively felt that sound is too immediate and ephemeral to have significance for archaeological investigation' (1996: 665). Unlike the visual or tangible remains of the past, sound does not leave a mark. It has to be studied indirectly through re-creation of soundfields, the soundmakers, or experiences. Since their statement, the study of archaeology has moved towards trying to explore the experience of the past through phenomenological discourse, critiquing its overly visual methods (Hamilakis 2002; Weiss 2008: 15). Through these studies, focusing on the ephemeral or intangible, such as work undertaken by Daisy Abbott of the Glasgow School of Art (discussed in Hamilakis 2011), aspects of the past have become more important to archaeological investigation. These include papers discussing oral histories, echoes, and weather, which also have no method for quantitative enquiry but engage with the lived experience of the past.

I have created a series of auralisations of the Great Hall at Ightham Mote as it stands today to explore its acoustical characteristics and, by inference, the lived experience of the space. I have also modelled the Great Hall as it would have stood in the late medieval period and created auralisations in that space. In undertaking this, the same issues associated with creating visualisations are still present and become more complicated by using software that is still developing. Therefore, the modelled space of the Great Hall as it stands today has been calibrated using a series of measurements taken in the space: making the technique most appropriate for a space like Ightham which is not ruined. Then, as the development of the space has been traced so carefully, it is possible to take apart and rebuild the same space adjusting for wooden panelling, changes in windows and changes in furnishings. We use a program called CATT-Acoustic to produce these models and as a means to generate numerical values that can also give visual descriptions of these results. Finally, and most importantly for this project, they can present results by auralisation (Vigran 2008: 144).

Auralisation is the technique of making audible the acoustical parameters of a specific environment (Kleiner *et al.* 1993). Vigran (2008: 144), when discussing the technique in reference to room design, describes it more succinctly as suggesting the technique '...implies that one may listen to music or speech 'played' in a room at the design stage'. That is, just as architects can model buildings before their construction, acousticians can model the acoustical properties of a space allowing people to listen to their soundfield. Like visualisation this is based on numerical data collected via survey of the specific environment, either acoustically or visually (which will lead to a prediction of the responses). When applied to archaeological environments this gives us the opportunity to interpret soundfields of past environments. We know we cannot record the response of a space as it stood in the past so we are, therefore, already having to consider how we predict (accurately) the environment we will be working with.

Modelling and recording the acoustical properties of spaces requires information about the physical space (size and shape) and the properties of the building materials. These both affect how sound is reflected and absorbed and therefore dictate the experience of sound within a space. For the standing remains at Bodiam, the space was surveyed using the same methodology we discussed in Chapter Three, with a second survey recording the nature of furnishings and fittings within the space such as tapestries and wooden panelling, plastered walls, and other features. To begin to understand the experience of the space, impulse responses of the space were measured and recorded (with the support of the Institute of Sound and Vibration at the University of Southampton (ISVR); see Fig. 9.17). Impulse Response is in essence the sound pressure recorded at a point in a room following the excitation of the room by a source (ISO 2008). This can be used as a method for obtaining the decay curves (results of the Room Impulse Response, or RIR) needed to calculate a series of measures that can be used to discuss the experience of the space according to numerical values.

I will focus specifically on reverberation time. This value is very useful when determining the reverberation of a space in response to standing noise volume (Vigran 2008: 106). It has also been used as a measure to suggest whether a space is suitable for different types of music,

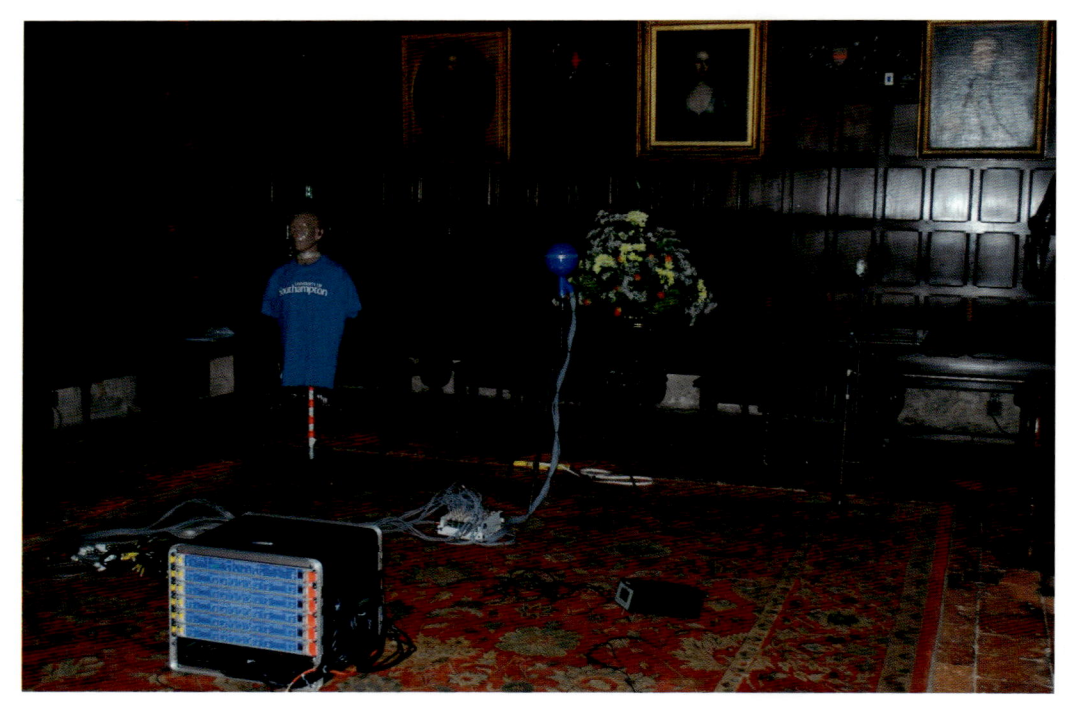

Fig. 9.17: Undertaking the acoustical survey at Ightham Mote.

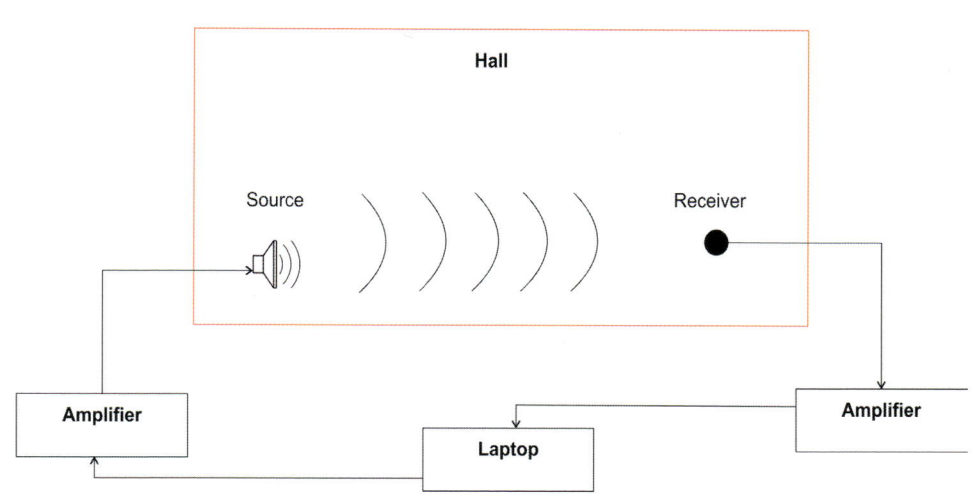

Fig. 9.18: Equipment setup for recording acoustical properties.

and public or private speaking (Barron 2009: 30). Music written to be played by an organ, for example, sounds best with a long reverberation time as the polyphonic nature of the instrument allows notes to overlap and for pieces written for it to embrace this feature, for example, Bach's *Toccata* and *Fugue in D minor* (MovieMongerHZ 2010). In contrast, early classical music tends to be homophonic with compositions being lighter and clearer without overlapping; a shorter reverberation time is required for this to be clear, but not so short as to sound dry. An example of this is the iconic *Eine kleine Nachtmusik* (Mozart 2011).

Broadly, the methodology for creating auralisations involves estimating the RIR, making the convolution with anechoic audio material, and reproducing the result through a sound reproduction system. This means using a piece of software to model the space (shape, surface properties, position of source and receiver), this can be used to calculate the specified measurements. To create the auralisation one needs a sound file of an anechoic recording (something recorded in a room that does not reverberate) which one will convolute (where the sound signal is adapted to sound like the room that has been modelled) to represent the designated sound and speaker combination (Vigran 2008: 144; Kuttruff 2009: 101).

The basic set up for recording the acoustics of a space can be seen in Fig. 9.18. The laptop sends out a signal noise which is passed through an amplifier to the source which excites the room; the receiver records the response to the source which is sent back through an amplifier to the laptop. By recording the range of frequencies we can look at how noises of different pitch are affected by the space. Frequency is proportional to wavelength which has a significant affect in small spaces.

To help establish the nature of the models that were being compared we recorded myself reading a sentence about Ightham: 'This is the great hall at Ightham Mote near Sevenoaks in Kent. It is one of the oldest areas of the building dating from the 14th century.' This was undertaken in the anechoic chamber in the ISVR at the University of Southampton, and allowed us to not only use it during modelling but also for auralising the recorded characteristics from the survey.

The model is created by defining planes and surface properties of the space. The geometry is taken from the basic building survey discussed above; surface properties of each plane are defined according to their material. This contains information about the scattering and absorption properties of the fabric (see Fig. 9.19: Model of Ightham Mote, each colour represents a different surface property). Information about the physical properties of the materials has been taken from a number of references (Vorländer 2007; Dalenbäck 2011). These can be later adjusted as the model is calibrated using the results taken from the measured recordings of the space.

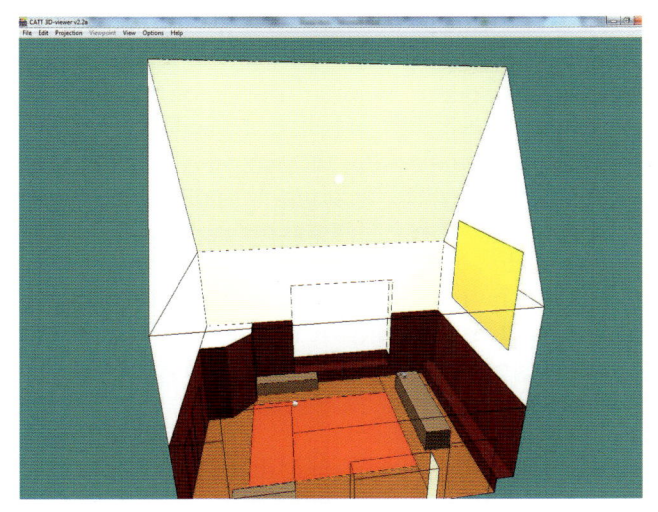

Fig. 9.19: Model of Ightham Mote. Each colour represents a different surface property.

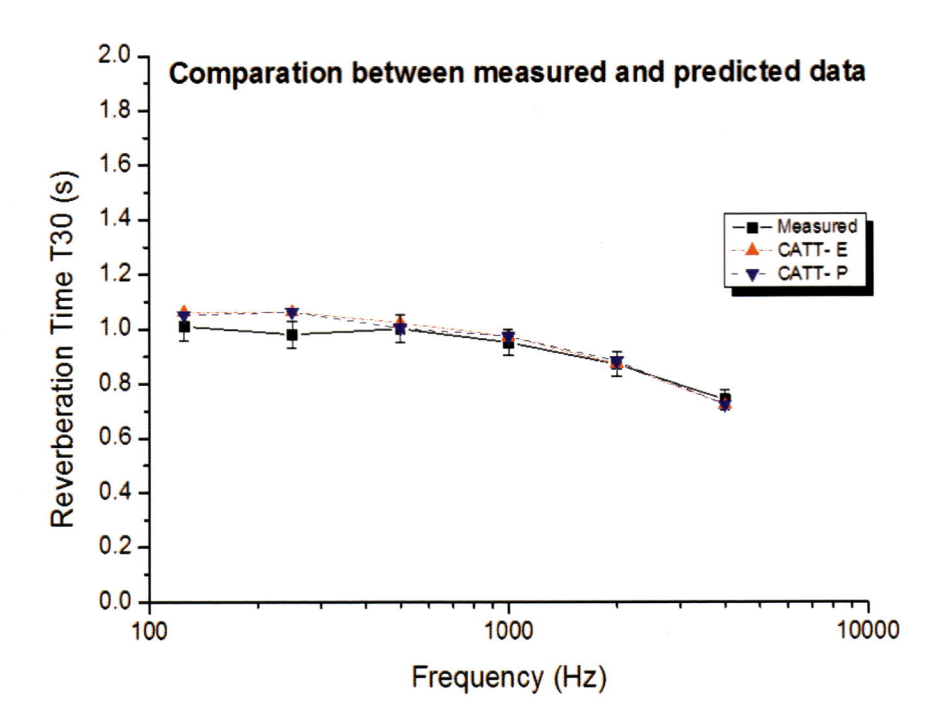

Fig. 9.20: This graph shows the differences between the modelled and simulated Great Halls.

The graph (Fig. 9.20) shows that the final model and measured responses to the Hall were nearly the same, allowing us to assume that we could correctly refurnish the space as it would have stood in the late medieval period.

The numerical results of the modelling show that the reverberation of the space remained fairly consistent despite the changes in furnishing and fittings; this is likely to be a result of the height of the ceiling. The reverberation time was short for such a large space (around one second), suggesting that it is a perfect space for drama and the spoken word (Barron 2009: 452) but not really for music (Barron 2009: 30). This is on the proviso that the measurements were recorded when the space was empty; when full, we can take away 0.2 seconds which would make it even less suitable for music (AV INFO, 1995). The results of this case study lend some support to Woolgar's discussion, based on the documentary evidence, of halls as generally quiet places (Woolgar 2006) allowing the acoustical properties to encourage a ritualised decorum not polluted by excess sound. Ightham Great Hall was perhaps more suited to formal readings and public speeches rather than music. It was perhaps more suited to formal, ritualised dining, akin to an Oxbridge college hall, than the raucous music and boisterous laughter and shouting often associated with the medieval hall.

It was particularly interesting that the reverberation time was constant across the board. This means that the experience of sound was the same for those seated at the lowest and highest ends of the hall. Because of this, we can assume that the lord did not have any better experience of any of the performances and, therefore, there was no class restriction of the experience of being in the hall. Some forms of church architecture limit sound from reaching the ends of the church building meaning that the experience of the service was different across the classes. These results may have been affected by the size and regularity of the space. It would be interesting to undertake the same analysis in a much larger hall like that at Penshurst.

The print format of this publication does not allow me to share the resulting auralisations with the reader but they can be accessed via the project website at http://sites.northwestern.edu/medieval-buildings/. To assess the results of the auralisations I ran a basic listening test, getting people to listen, compare and contrast the models of the old and new hall. Modelling the old hall and comparing the subjective experience to the new hall suggests that the experience of reverberation was less in the new hall. It was also slightly easier to understand speech in the new hall. This highlighted that in this case it was still not a space in which to listen to music, at least according to my suggestion for the furnishings within the space. However, these are only preliminary investigations.

To summarise: these models allow us to consider the aural experience of Ightham Mote as a space where speeches can be given easily, but music would fall short. The research therefore suggests that Ightham Mote Great Hall may have been an intimate and calm space, particularly well suited for private conversation rather than entertainment. This interpretation appears at odds with the room decorations; the carved minstrels give the impression of a much less formal space. In this way it is easy to highlight how a great hall can have multiple uses, without it necessarily being particularly well suited to any environment. The experience of sound in the space suggests that while the hall was a place with a variety of functions and activities, it was not the best suited space for music, and the size of the hall not the most well suited for dancing.

Conclusion

The chapter shows how digital techniques can be used to explore lived experience in late medieval buildings. I have presented work at Bodiam and Ightham that implements two different techniques to investigate living within late medieval buildings. This shows the advantages of two separate methodologies for exploring lived experience in late medieval buildings. It provides new ways to think about the experience of a building beyond a written narrative.

It is important to add a caution that these methodologies, taken independently, do not allow us to access the totality of lived experience of a medieval building. Both case studies in fact isolate a single sense when in fact experience is multisensory. To take these first steps further the next stage would be to combine both visualisation and auralisation techniques to explore a range of spaces. By consuming both visual and aural outputs at the same time a more multisensory engagement could be achieved. Undertaking the studies across a range of buildings will allow us to discuss in more depth the commonality and differences in buildings of the period.

10

MOATED SITES IN THE WEALDEN LANDSCAPE

Eric D. Johnson[1]

Abstract. This chapter looks at the general class of moated sites, of which Bodiam, Scotney and Ightham can be considered particularly large and complex examples, in the context of the Wealden landscape of south-east England as a whole. A general discussion of the literature on moated sites is followed by a discussion of 'what do moats do?' in terms of lived experience.

One of the most striking common features of the sites examined in this volume is the way that the flow of water was altered and manipulated in their surrounding landscapes for various purposes. Bodiam, Scotney and Ightham can all be classified as 'moated sites'. Ditches were dug around the main dwelling and filled with water at each site, suggesting that this use of water, for whatever purpose, was an important element of elite identity in the region. (The well drained site of Knole is not suitable for a moat). This common use of water raises a further question, however: how best to understand these sites in the context of the hundreds of other moated sites in the region? If we designate them as 'elite', linking their archaeological signature to the legal or social status of their owners, what does that imply for sites with similar signatures but whose owners may have had different statuses?

In what follows, I examine the broader geographic scope of moated sites in the surrounding region of the Weald. By putting sites like Bodiam, Scotney and Ightham in a wider landscape context through the lens of moated sites, it is clear that they are particular examples of a much wider phenomenon stretching across space, time and social status. Moats, of course, are not the only similarity between the landscapes of the above sites and others in the region, but moats are one of the most common and readily identifiable features found at many different types of sites during the Middle Ages. In addition, thanks to the efforts of previous surveys such as those conducted by the Moated Sites Research Group (MSRG) the presence and location of medieval moated sites in the Weald is relatively well-documented and can be correlated with other spatial variables using Geographical Information Systems (GIS) software.

This chapter contributes in two ways to our understanding of the medieval landscape. First, a comprehensive survey of moated sites in the Weald has not yet been conducted. Examining the similarities and differences between conditions in the Weald and other regions can shed light on the moat-building phenomenon more broadly as well as help us understand individual sites like Bodiam, Scotney and Ightham in a new light. Second, the following analysis seeks to advance our theoretical and interpretive approach to regional analyses of moated sites. Previous studies have contributed greatly to our understanding of 'why moats exist'. This question is usually framed in terms of environmental factors and the functional utility of moated sites (Emery 1962; Taylor 1972; Le Patourel 1973; Aberg 1978; Le Patourel & Roberts 1978; Aberg & Brown 1981; Barry 1981; Verhaeghe 1981; Wilson 1985; Martin, D. 1989; Martin 1990; Jones 1999; Fradley 2005; Platt 2010a). I draw heavily on this body

---

[1] The research that forms the basis of this chapter was conducted by Eric Johnson and written up for his Senior Thesis as an undergraduate at Northwestern University. The chapter was edited and revisions suggested by Matthew Johnson, incorporating comments by David Martin.

of research in order to understand 'why moats exist' in the Weald, but I also seek to understand the effect that moated sites have on the social landscape after they were dug. In short, I also ask 'what do moats do?' when taken collectively as a regional phenomenon (see also Johnson 2015). My discussion is divided into two parts centring on these two questions.

In studying south-eastern England as a unit of analysis, this study recognises that a region is in danger of being

> *inadequately conceptualized in the sense that both its temporal relations (connections with the past and future) and spatial relations (connections with other areas at the same scale and at larger and smaller scales) are unspecified*
>
> (Marquardt & Crumley 1987: 9)

While the moated sites in this survey can be studied at the regional scale *in toto* with certain variables, this approach is also multiscalar and multitemporal, shifting from the household to the parish and back to the region while embracing the past and future of moated sites. The data discussed consist of 257 identified moated sites from the counties of Kent, Sussex and Surrey gathered from the National Heritage List, English Heritage Archive and from the East Sussex HER held by East Sussex County Council. It should be noted that this is not a complete list of moated sites in south-eastern England; many sites are yet unidentified and undocumented in databases and still others have been lost to the archaeological record. However, it can serve as a general outline for moat-building trends.

I will first briefly outline the history of moated-site studies, highlighting the strengths and limitations of previous approaches. Then, I will present and compare the distribution of moated sites to various environmental, historical and social factors to describe the Weald as a set of affordances related to moat construction in order to understand basic reasons 'why moats exist'. Then, to describe 'what moats do' at the scale of individual experience and meaning, moated case studies are briefly examined as active features of the landscape. In addition to Bodiam and Scotney, I include other pertinent case studies from the immediate area such as The Mote near Iden, Glottenham in Mountfield, and Share Farm in Horsmonden. I discuss

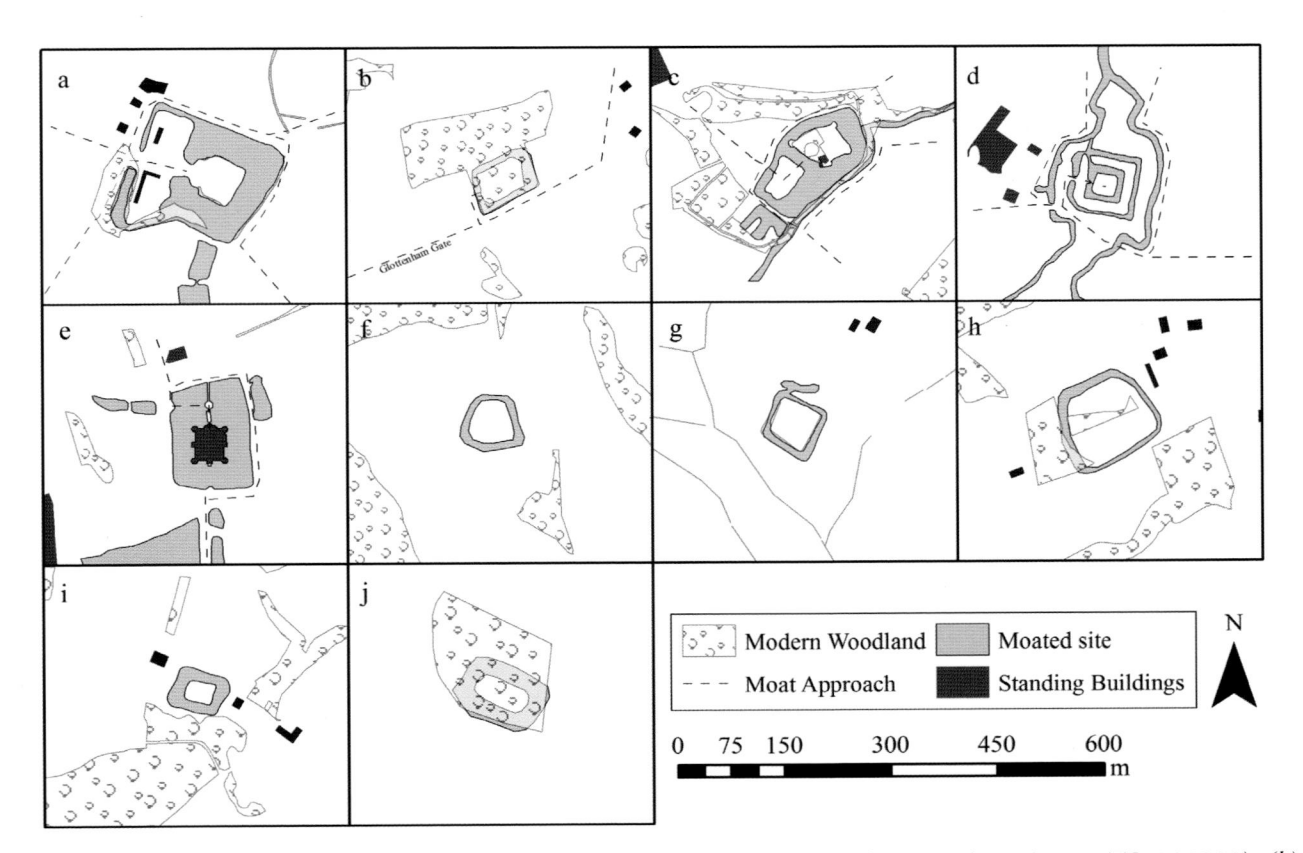

Fig. 10.1: Selection of individual moated sites in south-eastern England. (a) The Mote (East Sussex, TQ 900239), (b) Glottenham (East Sussex, TQ 726221), (c) Scotney (Kent, TQ 689352), (d) Share Farm (Kent, TQ 715392), (e) Bodiam (East Sussex, TQ 785256), (f) Bodiam Homestead (East Sussex, TQ 784264), (g) Lowden (Kent, TQ 854294), (h) Palstre Court (Kent, TQ 882283), (i) Furnace Farm (Kent, TQ 738348), (j) Old Conghurst (Kent, TQ 763280).

Fig. 10.2: Part of the ditch surrounding the moated site at Bodiam (East Sussex, TQ 784264). Photo by Eric Johnson.

specific case studies detailing how the spatial structure of moats actively constitutes authority at the intersection of experienced, perceived and imagined space, an analysis derived from my previous work on the topic (Johnson 2015). In conclusion, my analysis returns to the regional scale to describe how moats result from and may have contributed to a wider distillation of power and authority in the political landscape of the Weald.

History of Moated Sites Research

Moated sites are a well-known archaeological feature of the medieval world (Figs 10.1 & 10.2). In one of the earliest studies in Yorkshire, Jean Le Patourel (1973: 1) defines moated sites as 'islands surrounded by ditches which in antiquity were generally, though not invariably, filled with water'. This definition remains consistent to the present, despite the wide variation in size, shape and character of moated sites (Creighton & Barry 2012). Research in the 1970s and 1980s led to an initial flourishing of documentation, classification and detailed regional studies of moats (Aberg 1978; Aberg & Brown 1981). Since the efforts of the Moated Sites Research Group (later merging with the Deserted Medieval Village Research Group under the new title Medieval Settlement Research Group (MSRG)), the number of moats identified in England has risen to roughly 5,500 and counting (Creighton & Barry 2012: 64). Although the most famous are visible at the high-status castles of the elite, the vast majority of moats are associated with smaller manorial centres or wealthy freeholding peasants. The term 'homestead moat' has been given to the sites that fall under a lower-status category (Taylor 1972; Le Patourel 1973; Aberg 1978; Le Patourel & Roberts 1978; Taylor 1984; Platt 2010a; Creighton & Barry 2012). However, the use of the term 'homestead moat' is ambiguous. It often does not differentiate between what may be a peasant's dwelling place, a lesser manorial centre or even an ecclesiastical centre. While more complex moats often correlate to higher-status sites, only a close examination of a site's context will confirm its feudal association. Some higher-status manorial centres, for example, have simple, shallow moats, and many of course do not have moats at all.

Fewer than 700 moats have been excavated to some extent in England, a sampling which hovers around 12% (Gerrard 2003). Creating an accurate chronology can be problematic (Platt 2010a). Evidence for dating can come in the form of documentary references such as licences to crenellate or dateable finds in archaeological excavations. Licences to crenellate are medieval documents granting permission from the king or higher authority to the holder to fortify their property, but fortifications may have occurred at any point before or after the dated document and therefore provide only speculative evidence for the date of moat construction (see Coulson 1993 and 1994; also Davis 2007). Licences to crenellate are also not found at sites of a lower social status, skewing the data along class lines. Despite these issues, it is generally assumed that the greatest concentration of moat-building took place from 1200-1325 (Le Patourel 1973; Aberg 1978; Taylor 1984; Creighton 2009; Creighton & Barry 2012).

Creighton and Barry (2012: 65) accurately summarise the present state of literature on moated sites, showing how an explanation of the moat-building phenomenon has usually involved balancing perceived functional incentives (drainage; provision of fishponds and water supply; serious military defence/security against lawlessness) with social motivations (emulation of social superiors; status of moat possession; symbolic division from lower social orders). These explanations largely result from past regional econometric studies (Taylor 1972; Le Patourel 1973; Aberg 1978; Aberg & Brown 1981). In accounts of moats as 'one index of capital accumulation and reinvestment in ostentation and security' (Le Patourel & Roberts 1978: 48), or describing 'subsoil' as 'the decisive factor' in moat-building (Le Patourel 1973), econometric studies, as critiqued by Kosiba and Bauer (2013: 3), 'generally describe humans as rational actors who optimize their livelihood by maximizing socioeconomic gains and minimizing socioeconomic costs'.

If we are to advance our understanding of moated sites at a regional scale, these kinds of econometric approaches to regional analysis should be refined but not be jettisoned. It is important to explain the environmental factors that go into building a moated site or their potential functional or social utility. However, two issues arise if our analysis ends here. First, we run the risk of falling into environmentally or functionally deterministic interpretations. Second, as Ian Hodder (1982: 207) explains, 'material culture does not reflect, it transforms the relationships in other non-material spheres'. We must seek to understand the ways in which moated sites transformed the political landscape in tandem with their production.

The Production of Moated Sites: from 'Cause and Effect' to 'Affordances and Relational Spaces'

In order to explain 'why moats exist' in the Wealden landscape without devolving into environmentally or functionally deterministic explanations, we can consider the Weald as a web of affordances bound up with specific environmental, historical and social contexts. The theoretical concept of affordances has been expanded and redefined (and muddied) along different ecological and anthropological lines (Gibson 1986; Ingold 1992; Llobera 1996; Gillings 2012; Hodder 2012). Clarifying (and perhaps simplifying) our understanding of affordances holds great interpretive advantages.

As I define it here, three factors distinguish an affordance from an environmental constraint or some cost reducing/gain optimising factor. The first benefit of the term affordance is apparent in its semantic realm. *Afford*, as synonymous with 'capable of yielding or providing', comfortably avoids determinism: what something 'allows for the possibility of' does not 'determine the existence of'. Second, as defined by various anthropologists, an affordance is not limited to the objective material world. Ingold (1992: 46), for instance, advocates for affordances 'as directly perceived by an agent in the context of practical action'. Summarising Gibson (1986), Gillings (2012: 604) notes that 'in the direct model of perception, the environment is laden with meaning that animals (like us) extract during the course of our sensory engagement with it'. The Weald, as perceived and experienced by a range of different people, does not consist of physical material reducible to attributes such as geology or elevation. Put another way, the Weald is a *place* as well as a material backdrop: 'personal and cultural identity is bound up with a place', and thus an analysis of landscape 'is one exploring the creation of self-identity through place' (Tilley 1994: 15). A third distinguishing factor of affordances is that they are fundamentally relational; in fact, some consider an affordance itself to be the act of encountering an object rather than the object itself (Gillings 2012). In this light, while affordances provide a specific (and subjective) context favorable to a particular action such as moat construction, these contextual (and subjective) meanings can be negotiated in turn through this interaction. The transformative, recursive property of the landscape then brings my analysis to a second question: 'what do moats *do*?'.

Adam T. Smith (2003: 32), drawing from Lefebvre (1974), argues that landscapes are

> *encompassing not only specific places and monuments but also the stretches between them: physical, aesthetic, and representational…they are rooted in specific perspectives that advance particular ways of seeing, of living, and of understanding.*

As representations of specific worldviews and social orders, landscapes are cumulative of the spaces produced by individuals holding particular ideologies. Relational spaces define boundaries, arranging subjects, objects and spaces *in relation* to other objects (humans, animals, other structures, materials, etc.) and spaces (inside/outside, safe/hostile, civilised/natural, sacred/profane, warm/cold, etc.) in the physical world. The world of these relations is also anything but static; boundaries engender specific patterns of movement through space by delimiting how (or whether) bodies (both human and material) can ultimately travel from point A to B. When relational spaces are experienced and perceived, political ideologies are then internalised as they are embodied, reifying the social order they display (Hillier & Hanson 1989). However, just as 'ideology *per se* might well be said to consist primarily in a discourse upon social space' (Lefebvre 1974: 44), the cumulative production of new relational spaces can also actively resist, redefine or fragment prevailing political structures depending on the understandings of the producers and others' experience of relational spaces.

Why Do Moats Exist?

Environmental context

The Weald in south-eastern England can be described as an environmental region distinct in topography, geology and vegetation from its neighbours. While on the whole elevation is relatively low (max of 250 m above sea level), the terrain is marked by rapid changes in elevation, creating a constantly changing, hilly terrain. Topographic variability increases as one distinguishes between the Low Weald to the west, south and north wrapping around the High Weald (see Fig. 10.3). The Weald is also a wooded region and would have been even more densely forested at the start of the 13th century (Brandon 1969). By

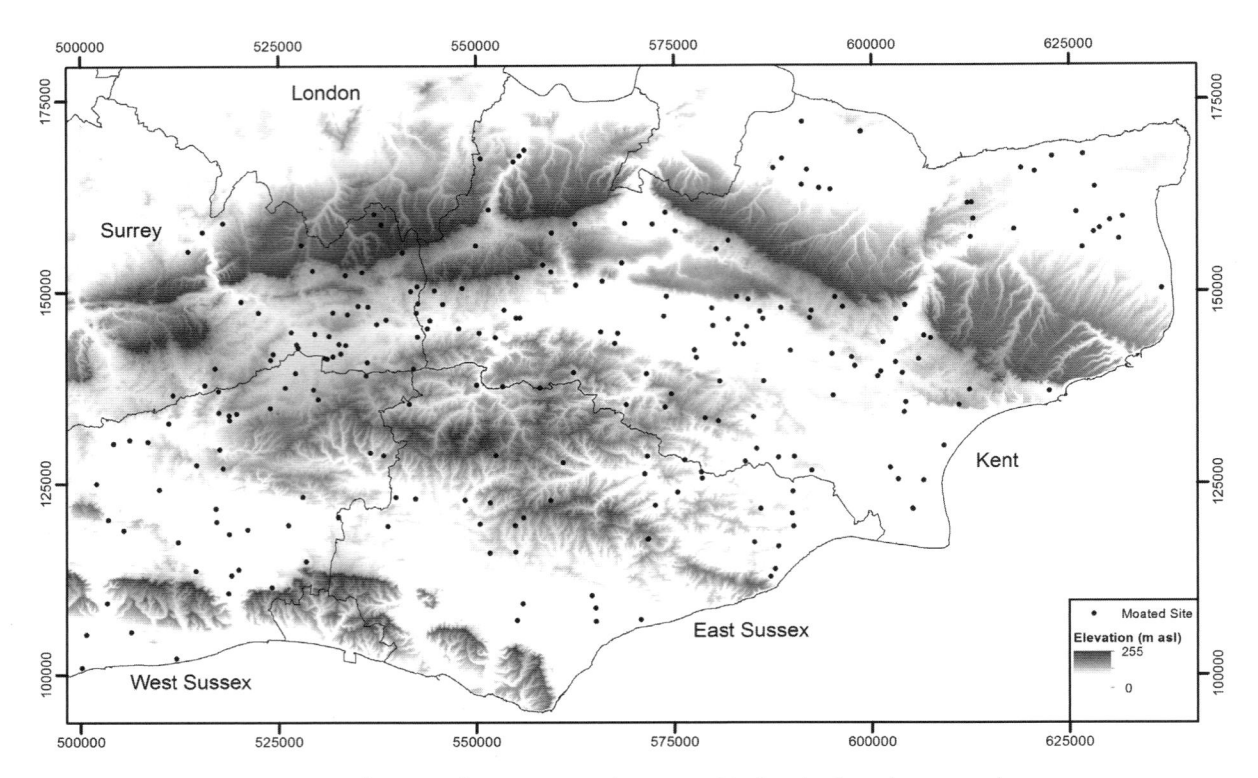

Fig. 10.3: Distribution of moats in south-eastern England, plotted against elevation.

minimising visibility and facilitating a greater degree of visual privacy, these two environmental factors combine to provide the phenomenological context of moat construction; vegetation and topography obstruct wide views normally provided by hilltops. Even today, after medieval clearances and modern agriculture have deforested a percentage of the medieval woodland, many moated sites cannot be seen until they are immediately encountered. The environment makes control over sightlines, seclusion and privacy possible, echoing notions of separateness embodied in the spatial structure of moated sites.

Past regional studies have noted the correlation between moated sites and lowland areas (Taylor 1972; Le Patourel 1973). This correlation holds true in the Weald (Fig.10.3). Approximately 70% of identified moated sites in south-eastern England lie less than 50 m above sea level, and 90% of identified moated sites are less than 88 m above sea level. Lowland areas facilitate the catchment of water flowing from higher elevations; in most cases, moats were fed by natural waterways in the landscape (unless a site was fed by a hilltop spring, as is the case at Glottenham in East Sussex (Martin, D. 1989)).

Geology is another environmental factor related to moat construction (Fig.10.4). Ninety percent of the moated sites in south-eastern England are seated in clay deposits, while only 10% are found in the chalk lands to the north and south of the Weald. When compared to the total area of clay (60%) and chalk (40%) in the survey, this reveals an association between moated sites and clay geology. Clay is more impermeable to water than other soil types. Therefore, a clay bed for a moat retains water more effectively than chalk, allowing for greater control in constructing watery landscapes.

Social context

As has been implied thus far, the social status of an individual is another context which affords moat construction. The time, effort and labour required to dig moat ditches and manage the flow of water could have only been undertaken by those who had a degree of agency, authority and economic means. Understanding this social context first requires an abbreviated outline of medieval feudalism in relation to moated sites. The largest and most ostentatious moated sites in the Weald are found surrounding the castles and houses of the gentry such as Bodiam, Scotney, Glottenham, The Mote and others. For instance, Edward Dallingridge and Roger Ashburnham, owners of Bodiam and Scotney, were Keepers of the Peace in Sussex in the 1380s, along with William de Etchingham, builder of an important but now destroyed moated house at Etchingham and a relation of Robert de Etchingham, builder of Glottenham (Saul 1986 1-7; Martin *et al.* 2008).

Many moated sites, to judge from their size and general appearance, are found further down on the social scale, and fall into the national category of 'homestead moats'. In other parts of the country, for example Edward Martin's work in Suffolk, these sites would be immediately interpreted as the dwelling places of wealthy freeholding peasants. In the manorial system, a freeholding peasant was distinct from dependent or villein peasants by the labour or monetary debt owed to a manorial centre. A greater degree of agency, authority and accumulation was therefore afforded to the freeholding class, providing the social context for moat construction at the lower end of the social spectrum. Given that in some areas of England actual wealth disparities within the peasant class may not have aligned with freeholding or villein distinctions, Platt (2010: 125-6) suggests that even some wealthy dependent tenants may have dug ditches around their homesteads.

It is important to note that the situation in the Sussex Weald does not appear to correspond to this broader national picture. Unpublished documentary work by Chris Whittick and David and Barbara Martin has established in a very large number of instances that these smaller, less significant moated sites are in fact manorial or sub-manorial centres, however humble their appearance or similarity to homestead moats elsewhere in the country. It may well be the case that the moats found on the Kent side of the border follow a similar pattern.

The authority of an elite and his household was in part constituted by his military role within the feudal ideology. We can observe this process firsthand in medieval documents. For example, in 1318 Sir Edmund de Pashley, lord of the manor of Leigh in Iden, obtained a licence to crenellate his dwelling place of The Mote (Gardiner & Whittick 2011). Fig.10.5 is an illustration of The Mote in the capital letter of the document. This licence to crenellate flowed from a higher authority to Sir Edmund, granting him permission to construct a castle with crenellations at his dwelling place. A licence to crenellate in part produces the authority of the holder, and this production is conceptually linked to the permission to defend embodied by a moat. Of course, this type of formal permission was not required to construct a moat, but notions of 'defensibility' implied by a moated site still appropriate these meanings (Taylor 1972).

Historical context

Well before the majority of moats were built in England, the Anglo-Saxon Chronicle states that in 1086:

> [The King] *commissioned them to record in writing... 'What, or how much, each man had, who was an occupier of land in England, either in land or in stock, and how much money it were worth'... there was not one single hide, nor a yard of land...not even an ox, nor a cow, nor a swine was there left, that was not set down in his writ.*

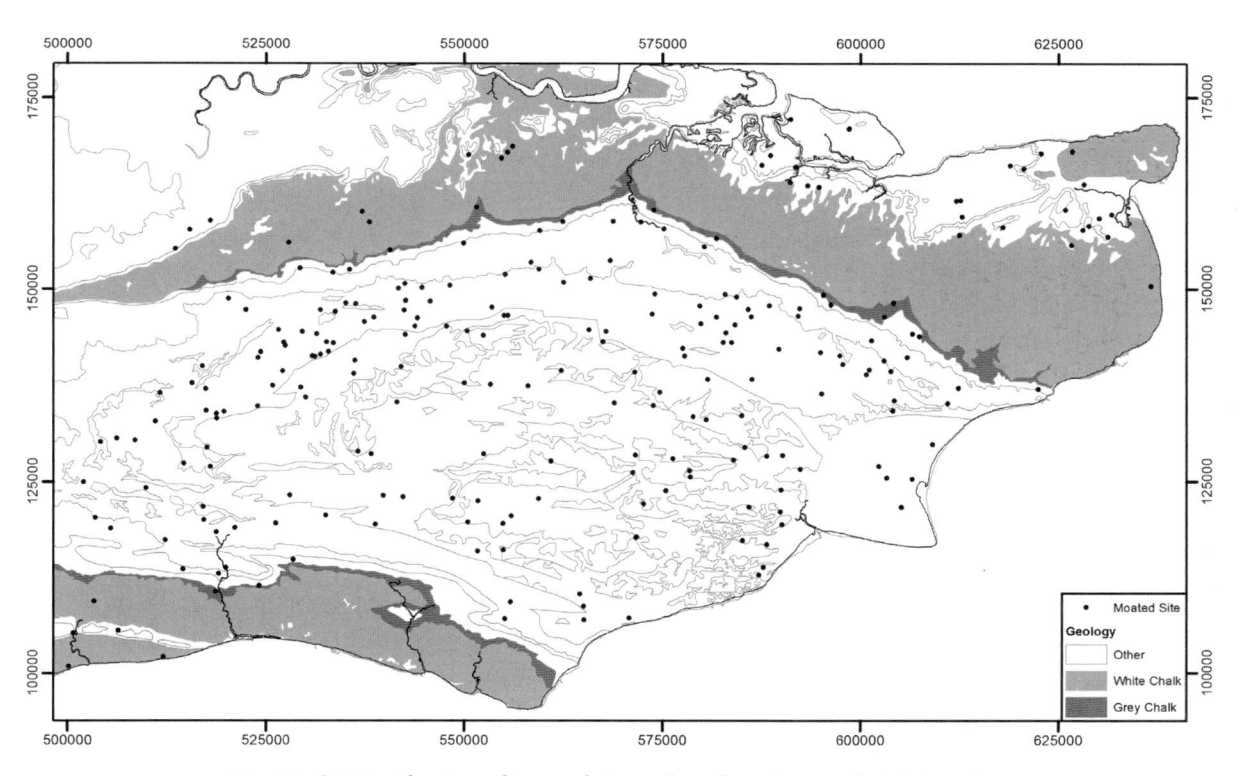

Fig. 10.4: Distribution of moated sites, plotted against underlying geology.

Fig. 10.5: A representation of a moated manor house and park in the initial capital of the licence to crenellate the dwelling place of 'La Mote' granted to Sir Edmund de Pashley in 1318 (ESRO ACC 7001). Source: Gardiner & Whittick 2011, frontispiece.

This record, known as the Domesday Book, defines the territory of the King as a sovereign totality, documenting taxation and population density. As a perceptual space of a burgeoning state, however, it is better described as an attempt to make a population of subjects visible. The places mentioned in Domesday Book are mapped in Fig.10.6. If this map is taken literally, the Weald appears as a relatively uninhabited region in 1086, and this is how previous generations of archaeologists and historians have often interpreted it. Fig.10.6 is a graphic representation of the traditional understanding of the Weald as a place of late colonisation and 'assarting', a symptom of the population rise and economic expansion of the 11th to 13th centuries in Europe (Brandon 2003: 43-52).

When the moated-site distribution is mapped on top of the Domesday record (Fig.10.6), Domesday mentions appear to be inversely correlated with moated-site distributions in the Weald. This apparent contrast has traditionally been interpreted in terms of two historical settlement dynamics in the Weald. First, it has been suggested that, as populations rose in the 12th and 13th centuries, more and more wealthy freeholding peasants began to colonise the less densely populated woodland of the Weald in both East Sussex (Brandon 1969) and Kent (Mate 2010a: 3). Studies have painted a general picture of increasing population densities, new settlements through assarting (the clearance of woodland for arable) and have cited moated sites as a key piece of evidence for this (Roberts 1964; Taylor 1972; Le Patourel 1973; Aberg 1978; Le Patourel & Roberts 1978; Aberg & Brown 1981). Second, as manors (in this view) expanded their jurisdiction after 1086, previous inhabitants of the Weald (those 'invisible' to the Domesday record) were not absorbed into the demesne lands of manors. Instead, these settlements were also treated as freehold (Witney 1990: 22). Thus, the traditional view has been that homestead moats are one index of a strong contingent of Wealden freeholding tenants. This traditional view, combined with the observation that 'The High Weald was largely the preserve of lesser gentlemen' (Fleming 2010: 222), has resulted in a perception by some scholars of a weaker institutional structure of manorialism when compared with other areas of England.

However, this view needs some qualification, at least for the Sussex Weald. Fig.10.6 should not necessarily be seen as an objective record, but rather as a map of gaps in political knowledge (Hauser 2008) in 1086. It does in fact depict a Wealden landscape that is at least partly populated, but not one that is visible to state authority in a straightforward way. Unpublished documentary work by Chris Whittick and David and Barbara Martin has established that the general pattern in the Sussex Weald is one of fragmented manorial holdings. Manors often had their centres outside or on the margins of the Weald, on the coast or in the river valleys. These manors then also had fragmented holdings within the Weald at some distance from their centres. It is not clear whether these outlying holdings were always disclosed to the Domesday commissioners, but when they were, they appeared under the general heading of the 'parent' manor. Consequently they do not appear on Fig.10.6.

David and Barbara Martin point out that in the Rape of Hastings,

> *all 'unclaimed' land was deemed to be demesne of the overlord of Hastings Rape. Where colonisation took place the colonising lord quickly established it as a manor held by him direct of the rape's overlord. Except for pockets of woodland and heath, by the 16th century only residual areas of wasteland remained, but even these were still considered by the overlord to be demesne of the rape and were leased out accordingly, a practice which continued into the 19th century*
>
> (David and Barbara Martin, pers. comm.)

The proliferation of moated sites, in this revised view, is not to do with a class of freeholding peasants but is rather an index of the fragmentation of manorial holdings across the Weald; manors are indeed weaker in the Weald, but this is to do with their fragmented and dispersed nature. It should be stressed that

> *this revision does not mean that the Weald was heavily populated at Domesday: it was not, and it certainly experienced higher levels of colonization in post-Conquest years than did the adjacent coastal areas. But it was not as empty of people as previous scholarship has implied, nor were those who did occupy the area free from manorial control: instead the manorial lords of these people resided at a distance, as did the bulk of the manors tenantry*
> (David and Barbara Martin, pers. comm.)

The broader point remains, then, that the agency to construct a moat is, in part, afforded by the Weald as a landscape which historically was one of greater invisibility from state power and therefore greater political autonomy than other areas in England.

The historical context of moat construction also provides a set of symbolic meanings appropriated by a moat. The owners of moats for instance may also be appropriating a (real or imagined) past military function of watery boundaries. After deconstructing the defensive utility of moated sites Christopher Taylor (1972: 246) suggests that 'their origins may lie in the pre-Conquest ringworks which were probably built for protection around the homes of thegns] at a time when defence was a necessity'. In a critique of Taylor, Colin Platt has recently asserted the necessity of moat's defensive function for moat owners (Platt 2010a). While the debate over the conscious intent of moat owners and defensive utility distances us from how moats were perceived and experienced, we cannot ignore the symbolic importance of defence in medieval life: 'The 'militaristic' conceptions of late fourteenth-century warfare were…intimately bound up with… ideas of masculinity, knighthood, and martial valor, ideas that were historically transient' (Johnson 2002: 30). Notions of defence, conceived symbolically, are therefore inextricable from those of status and gender, and the historically transient martial meanings are embedded in moats, regardless of whether the owner consciously built a moat in reaction to 'endemic lawlessness' (Platt 2010a: 128) or with 'the desire to show off his prosperity' (Taylor 1972: 246).

What Do Moats Do?

I have briefly described some of the environmental, historical and social contexts affording the act of moat construction in an effort to better understand 'why moats exist' in south-eastern England, but the life of

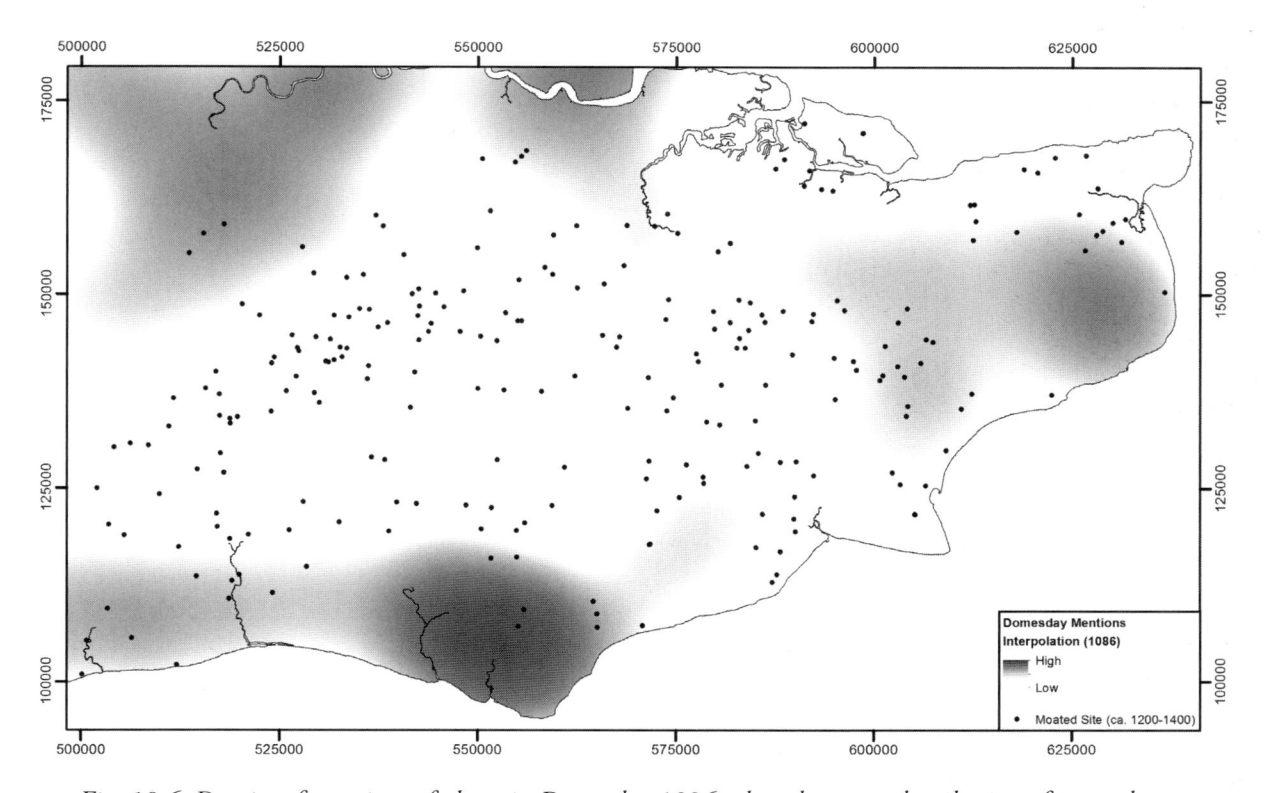

Fig. 10.6: Density of mentions of places in Domesday 1086, plotted against distribution of moated sites.

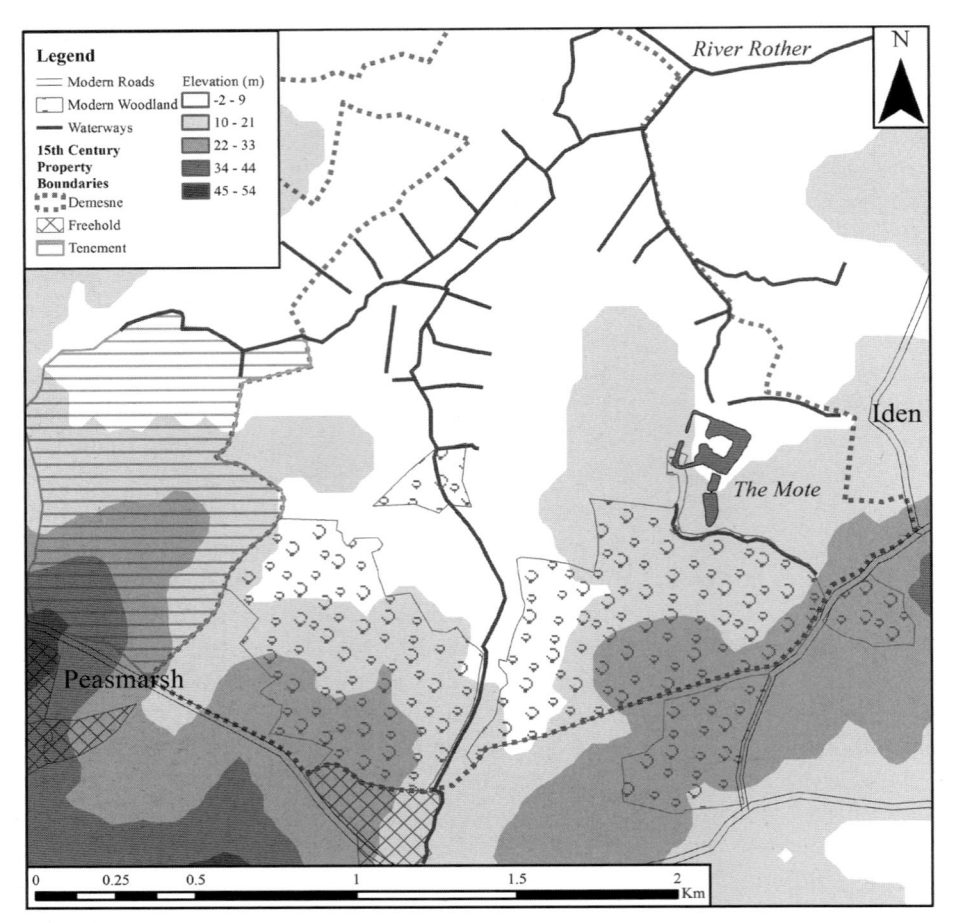

Fig. 10.7: Landscape context of The Mote, near Iden (East Sussex, TQ 900239). Based on work by David and Barbara Martin in Gardiner & Whittick 2011.

Moats as experienced

a moated site does not end at its inception. Therefore, my analysis continues with the question 'what do moats do' as features in the landscape. Even as authority and agency is afforded to individuals in specific contexts, I argue that moats then actively contribute to the agency and authority of those inhabiting their inner islands. The scale of analysis shifts to individual case studies to examine the recursive constitution of power at the 'intersection of space with experience, perception, and imagination' (Smith 2003: 72-3; see also Lefebvre 1991).

Moats as experienced

Examining survey evidence from The Mote near Iden, we can immediately see similarities between its moat and other elite moated sites such as Bodiam and Scotney. Fig.10.7 illustrates the 17th-century field boundaries reconstructed using historical documents from the manorial centre at The Mote (Gardiner & Whittick 2011). These boundaries have likely remained close to their 14th-century counterparts. The Mote, as the place of court hearings and tax collection, was a locus of authority for Iden and Peasmarsh, a place approached and navigated by a range of people of different social classes, both peasants under the jurisdiction of the manorial household as well as other visiting elite households. The demesne fields of the manor for instance may have been worked by dependent peasants indebted to The Mote through labour.

Surviving earthworks at The Mote provide evidence for what the moat does as an experienced space (Johnson 2015). Moats increase the time and effort required to travel to the innermost island. Simultaneously, the placid surface of the water flattens the surrounding topography, maximising the visibility of the vicinity surrounding the island. In its present state, the inner island of The Mote is clearly delineated by a partially water-filled ditch, and a single piece of upstanding masonry marks the possible location of the former gatehouse structure. Two subsidiary moat 'arms' branch to the north-west outlining a second space within their boundaries, presumably the outer court. An outer or lower court (sometimes called a base court) is a common feature of moated sites and could have contained subordinate houses for servants, stables, granaries or barns (Rigold 1968). At Iden, in fact, 'a single timber wall of a barn still survives on the outer enclosure, now incorporated into the modern farm buildings. The wall may date to the 1470s', and a 'lower court' is mentioned in account documents from 1480 (Gardiner & Whittick 2011: xlvii). The Mote would have been approached from either the village of Iden to the east, Peasmarsh to the west, or the River Rother to the north, as suggested by David and Barbara Martin (See Fig.10.7, and see also Gardiner & Whittick 2011: lxxxi).

The boundaries of the spaces produced by a moat are relatively static, but the bodies navigating their spatial layout are in constant motion. The order established by this spatial layout is thus maintained through movement. As to the depth of the inner and outer courts, movement reinforces the spatial and social order with a temporal order: first/posterior/lower court → second/anterior/upper court. At higher-status sites, an itinerant elite's household would process to the inner court on different occasions. The repeated performative act of entering a castle—drawn out by the moat—helped constitute the status of social actors as the landscape was both stage and reality for social practice (Johnson 2002). This is especially clear at Bodiam Castle where the processional route is tightly delineated and visibly unobstructed across the narrow bridge to the small octagonal island and then turning south to cross a second bridge and pass under the castle gate. For those experiencing the greater or lesser mobility defined by the moat and class, this order is internalised as it is embodied and the authority of those within is actively (re)produced.

Moats as perceived and imagined

According to Adam T. Smith, the perceived dimension of landscape

> *is a space of signs, signals, cues, and codes—the analytical dimension of space where we are no longer simply drones moving through space but sensible creatures aware of spatial form and aesthetics*
>
> (Smith 2003: 73)

Here moats become laden with meaning and subjectively interpreted by the range of people navigating their boundaries. It must first be noted that moated meanings varied greatly along gender, class, age and literacy lines (Johnson 2002: 29). Therefore, the following suggestions should not be taken as uniform medieval interpretations of moats, but they do provide a context to help us understand broadly how they may have been perceived and understood as their spatial order was experienced. Moated meanings are rooted in the representational spaces of the medieval world such as texts and imagery.

The medieval world was thought to be made up of four basic elements: earth, air, fire and water. In the body, different balances of these substances led to distinct temperaments. In strictly dichotomous gendered discourse, women were associated with water; they were cold and changeable while men were considered hot and dry. Roberta Gilchrist notes that

> *Under the medieval feudal system…the accumulation of property in land required monogamy and inheritance by primogeniture (inheritance through the eldest male). Female fidelity, and its display through the physical confinement of women, became essential to the perpetuation of successful lineages*
>
> (Gilchrist 1999: 112)

In a patrilineal and patriarchal society, a watery moat may have been a metaphor of sexual seclusion, (explicitly or implicitly) protecting the fidelity of the woman within, thereby cementing the power and authority of the household. It is clear from documents that the medieval elite were concerned with the fidelity of wives, but this was also probably important for freeholding peasants in order to retain their freeholding status.

The image in the capital letter of The Mote's licence to crenellate (Fig.10.5) depicts an idealised manorial complex, complete with hunting grounds for deer and rabbit, a chapel for the pious owner and a curiously interwoven flow of fish in the surrounding moat. It is no surprise that the chapel is the focus of this image; Sir Edmund Pashley had founded the chapel of Leigh in 1304 and transferred it to The Mote in 1320 (Gardiner & Whittick 2011). The interwoven flow of fish in the moat is depicted beneath the chapel centrepiece of the image, reinforcing the religious authority of the site bound up in its moated representation. Power and authority were also associated with production and consumption at a manorial centre. As is clear in the case of carefully regulated medieval deer parks, 'hunting opportunities available to any individual depended…on social rank' (Creighton 2009: 100). The consumption of fish from the moat or associated fishpond was a specifically elite activity.

The social relationships defined by feudal order may have been naturalised by the moat as a feature of the landscape. The water filling these ditches was considered a fundamental element of the medieval world, part of the natural order. Moats appropriate the powerful permanence and barrier qualities of natural waterways for specific social ordering. Much like the elite practice of capturing deer into a deer park with a pale, moats draw the natural world into the cultural. The spatial relationships produced by moats may have been perceived as fundamentally as the medieval conceptions of earth, air, fire and water and as temporally static as rivers that feed them. Indeed, moats' ubiquity in the archaeological record today is a testament to their lasting physical presence. The naturalising attributes of moats are most obvious at the site near Share Farm in Horsmonden, Kent. Classified as a 'double concentric' moat and bounded by a fork in the river, here the river actually *is* another moat in the sense that the experience of moving across the river boundary is essentially the same as the movement across the 'artificial' boundaries of the double concentric moat. The pattern of movement delineated by the river and moats contributes to the naturalisation of the social order.

All this being said, the meanings of moated sites could easily be manipulated for subverting dominant social relationships and furthering individual agendas. For instance, the historical record of The Mote suggests some doubt as to the legitimacy of Margaret de Basing and Edmund de Pashley's marriage in the early 14th century. Upon Edmund's death, both Margaret de Basing and another woman — Joan of the Greyly family — claimed to be his widow. According to Joan, Margaret murdered Edmund and two of her alleged stepchildren in order to legitimise the inheritance of the Pashley estate to her children of a previous marriage. Despite legal cases brought against Margaret, the manor of Mote passed to her sons in 1341 (Saul 1984; 1986: 86). Margaret's occupation of the manor house and its impressive moat may have been one factor reifying Margaret's bounded sexual relationship with Edmund, bolstering her claim to inheritance over Joan despite its possible illegitimacy (Johnson 2015: 248-9).

The Wealden Political Landscape

I have detailed in part 'why moats exist' and the set of affordances producing the agency of an individual to construct a moat, and I have explained 'what moats do' at the household scale to (re)produce the authority of their owners. In conclusion, I return to the regional scale to ask 'what do moats do' as they constitute the wider political landscape. As a spatial and social discourse, the political ideology of feudalism rigidly defines classes such as gentry, yeoman, freeholder, etc. In reality, however, the political economy of medieval England and its associated identities were more fluid, negotiated in part through marital ties, military service, economic accumulation, and so on. Wealden lesser gentlemen, for instance, often 'led lives not very different from the non-gentle yeomen immediately beneath them' (Fleming 2010: 221). In addition to the freeholding squatters already occupying land in the Weald before the 13th century, some tracts of land were 'opened up by individual enterprise and partitioned into freehold and customary farms' in the 13th century (Brandon 1969: 141). The fragmentation of manorial holdings noted above may have contributed to a more permeable notion of social boundaries. According to some historians of the Weald, peasants may have also had a more comfortable degree of economic autonomy relative to other regions in England:

> [in the late 13th century] *a new wave of pioneers entered the forest in larger numbers…On their small farms they planted fruit trees, grew oats and legumes, and kept animals. They also utilized the resources of the woods around them*
> (Mate 2010a: 3)

All of these factors combine to produce a landscape where power and authority was diffused and dispersed across a larger group of people and a relatively 'weaker' institutional structure of manorialism.

I argue that greater concentrations of homestead moats in the Weald – whether owned by freeholding peasants or lesser elite – may be an index of economic and political autonomy diffused to lower classes, as has been more or less argued by others working in different regions (Emery 1962; Le Patourel 1973; Le Patourel & Roberts 1978). As I have shown, the Weald is a specific environmental, historical and social context which affords the agency to construct a moat. However, I also argue that moats, as experienced, perceived and imagined relational spaces transform, and perhaps magnify, afforded authority into normative reality (Johnson 2015). Fig.10.8 illustrates the boundaries of modern parishes (a comparable artefact of medieval parishes) relative to the location of moated sites and topography in the High Weald. Many lower-status sites are situated near the parish boundaries, mirroring Edward Martin's findings in Suffolk (Martin, E. 1989). There is a clear correlation here, though precisely what it means is unclear, as parish boundaries do not equate to manorial boundaries in much of the Weald. It may be that the power of the elite was weaker at the periphery of territorial boundaries, a context (combined with environmental factors such as topography shown in Fig.10.3) affording the act of moat construction. While this political affordance was by no means permanent, moated sites then reified the authority of their owners for the reasons outlined above. Those occupying the inner islands, while perhaps not ideologically defined as members of 'the elite', may have been perceived as having a degree of religious authority, or retaining a monogamous wife and securing a 'free' bloodline, or as having obtained some degree of privilege to defend one's home.

MOATED SITES IN THE WEALDEN LANDSCAPE

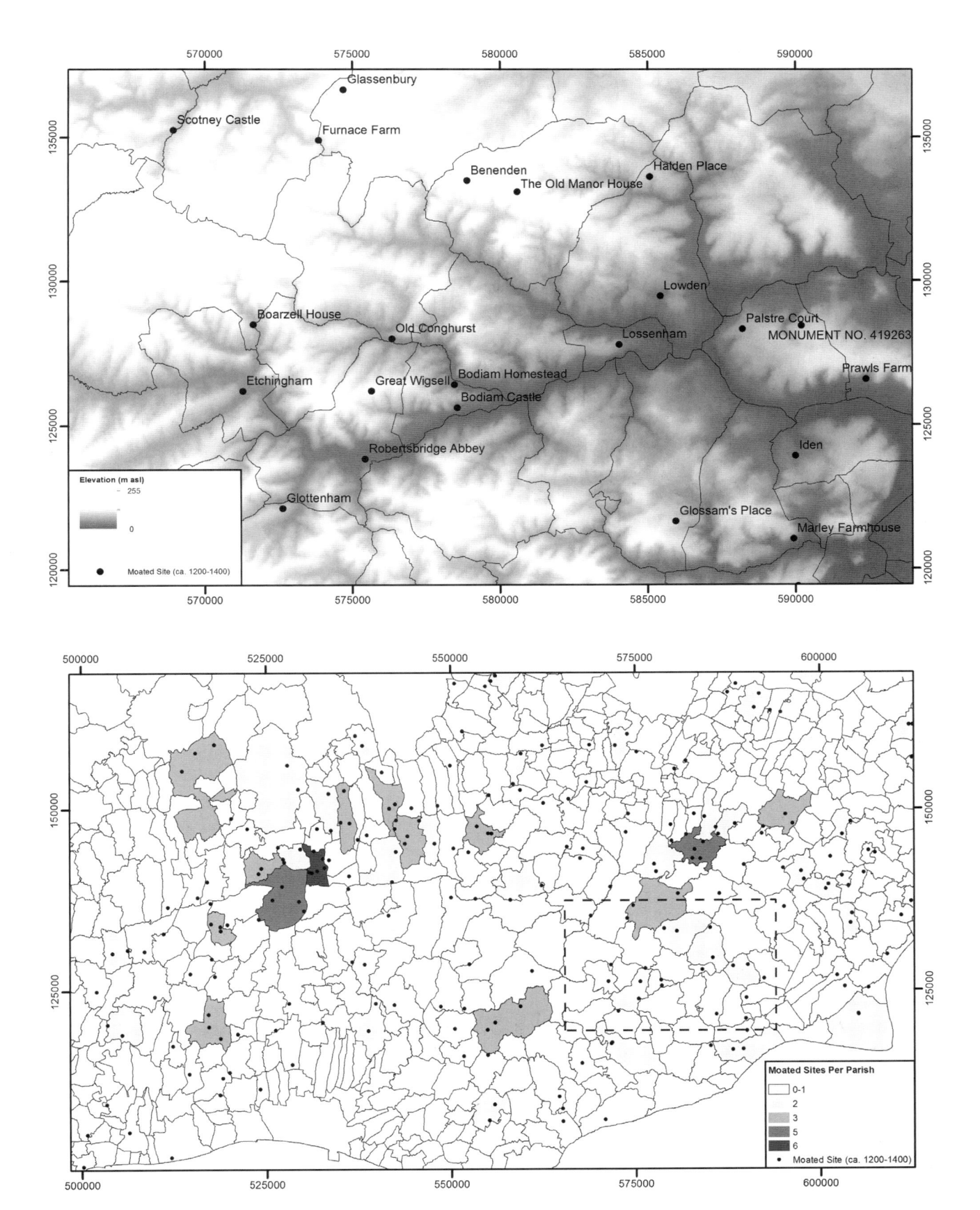

Fig. 10.8: Moated sites in relation to parish boundaries. Above: inset of the Eastern Weald. Below: distribution of moated sites within parish boundaries.

In conclusion, we can compare these parishes to the region as a whole. Fig.10.8 displays the number of moated sites found within each parish. Shaded parishes contain at least one moated site, and darker parishes contain greater concentrations. The exact percentage of non-manorial moated sites in Fig. 10.8 is unknown, but at least some of these moats likely surrounded freeholding peasant's dwellings. The clustering of moated sites of a manorial status indexes the unconsolidated nature of manorial holdings in the Weald. Thus, on both accounts this map suggests the geography of political fragmentation as viewed through the distribution of moated sites. It should be noted that Fig.10.8 does not accurately describe where power was diffuse so much as where moats may have contributed to political diffusion. Nor does this map seek to describe the dynamics of power between parish boundaries, but rather, it reveals possible differential fragmentation *within each parish* as produced by moated sites.

Of course, Fig. 10.8 flattens the dynamic temporality of the Wealden landscape. Hard dating evidence for the vast majority of moated sites is limited; a more accurate picture may not be possible without extensive excavations. Additionally, the Black Death (1348-50), as a major historical event, signaled a radical change in medieval demographics and slices through the tail end of moated-site chronology displayed here. As others have noted (Le Patourel 1973; Taylor 1984; Platt 2010a), the phenomenon of homestead moat-building sharply declines if not disappears after the mid-14th century. Several of the moated sites discussed here, however, date to the later 14th century. They are certainly not unique in their complex use of water to communicate and reify certain social relationships. It is possible that these 14th-century moats draw on the longer social history of moated-site production in the broader landscape as a claim to authority in the eastern Weald after the dramatic decline in population in 1348.

I have shown using GIS methodology how we can reconstruct the Weald as a set of affordances arising from specific environmental, historical and social contexts. In the process, I have avoided conclusive statements about the intention of individuals at the moment of moat construction in terms of either a symbolic fashion statement or a defensive feature. Rather, an analysis of the experienced, perceived, and imagined moat opens up the discussion to how political ideologies were expressed 'on the ground' and how the landscape then shaped people in the past.

11

PUBLICS, VOLUNTEERS AND COMMUNITIES: PUBLIC ENGAGEMENT AT BODIAM, SCOTNEY, KNOLE AND IGHTHAM

Becky Peacock

Abstract. This chapter discusses the public engagement that took place during the course of the project. The diversity of visitor background and experience, the two-way nature of the engagement, and the different experiences of both visitors and volunteer staff at all four sites are discussed.

This chapter discusses the public engagement work carried out as part of the University of Southampton and Northwestern University field survey, 2010-2013. Public engagement was conducted by myself throughout the project, although its practice changed slightly over the seasons. The first season (2010) took place solely at Bodiam Castle over a two-week period. The second season (2011) saw work being split between Bodiam and Scotney over a two-week period. The third season (2012) saw the team return to Bodiam concentrating on the wider landscape surrounding the castle, for example Dokes Field and the cricket field. The last field season (2013) saw a change in sites with teams of Southampton and Northwestern students being split between Knole and Ightham.

Public engagement in the UK heritage sector is a process by which heritage organisations aim to engage the general public in their history. Engagement means 'the power associated with 'being and feeling engaged' which is a whole person experience that envelops the senses' (Fear *et al.* 2002). The common purpose of engagement is to let people know about your work (National Co-ordinating Centre for Public Engagement online, retrieved 8th December 2012). There are two major questions surrounding engagement: what is it to feel engaged and what is it to engage? To be and feel engaged 'is a resonant experience, enabling participants to gain a deeper understanding about themselves, others and their work' (Fear *et al.* 2002: 59). To engage means to involve people in one's work. There are three methods of engaging people. The first is informing; this can take the form of many different actions from communicating engaging presentations to podcasting. Second, consulting, which is any action involving the meeting of outside groups from user groups to online consultation. Lastly, collaborating contains activities ranging from 'communities of practice' to 'participatory research partnerships' (National Co-ordinating Centre for Public Engagement online, retrieved 8th February 2012). The most common forms of engagement within the UK are informing and consulting. However, over the last few years there has been more collaboration.

I have been part of this project from its start in 2010, originally collecting data for my Master's dissertation; *The Role of Bodiam Castle in Popular Memory* (Peacock 2010). The dissertation focused on collecting memories of visitors, staff and volunteers via interviews. The interviews were structured on a questionnaire that covered a set number of criteria. It seemed appropriate to undertake public engagement at the same time as collecting data for my Masters, as I was already interacting with a variety of people around the site. Since early on in my studies I have been interested in how people interact with heritage and what these hidden aspects can add to our understanding of archaeology and heritage. This was a central theme within *The Role of Bodiam Castle in Popular Memory* and other statements collected became the focus for reflection and discussion within the project, adding to our understanding of the sites. At the end of each season, reports on the public engagement were written and a separate review of the public engagement at Bodiam from 2010-2012 was undertaken. The chapter is based on an amalgamation of these reports and sections of the Masters thesis (Peacock 2010). The chapter is also informed by my recent PhD research. The dissertation is entitled *The Future of Museum Communication: Strategies on Engaging Audiences on Archaeology*. It focuses on museum outreach practices in Hampshire, England and has had a marked impact on this chapter (Peacock 2015; available at https://www-lib.soton.ac.uk/uhtbin/cgisirsi/?ps=73TK1tqM8Y/HARTLEY/252980547/123, accessed 6th May 2016).

It has been a number of years since finishing the public engagement role for this project in 2013. Distance and wider knowledge of engagement practices within the heritage industry in the UK have meant that I have a developing understanding of the interactions and relationships occurring within these sites. The reports I made at the time documented the actions undertaken as part of the public engagement and highlighted a few themes around visitor engagement with the sites. However, there was little cross-comparison between sites and many themes were unexplored. A deeper understanding of engagement practices within the heritage industry has meant that the themes picked up in the previous reports are explored and a wider range of examples for these facets can now be included. Overall, this has meant that this summary of public engagement has become more in-depth.

It was important for the project to undertake public engagement as all the sites are 'public', under the stewardship of the National Trust. The Trust is a charity which was founded in 1895 by Octavia Hill, Hardwicke Rawnsley and Robert Hunter (Weideger 1994: 6). It is 'national in name and function, independent of the Government' (Benson *et al.* 1968: 13). It was established to 'promote the permanent preservation of lands and tenements of beauty or historic interest for the benefit of the nation' (Benson *et al.* 1968: 13; Weideger 1994: 8); at a time of industrial revolution the Trust aimed 'to offer natural therapy to the benighted urban poor of Victorian Britain' (Weideger 1994: 9; Reynolds 1998). The National Trust came to be associated with elite culture through its developing 20th-century engagement with the management of 'stately homes' and it has been provocatively stated that it is an 'organisation run by toffs for the middle classes' (Hetherington 2006). However, there has been a conscious effort by the organisation to move away from this perception (arguably always unfair) through various initiatives (see Henley 2010; National Trust 2015; Furness 2013).

The open access to these properties (of different kinds at different sites) afforded a high level of interaction with the general public and therefore it was important for the project to answer any visitor questions that might arise from the team's presence. Public engagement provided the best solution to how questions would be answered and brought the project in line with best practice in archaeological research as a whole, as well as more specifically the principles and policies of the University of Southampton, Northwestern University and the National Trust. Public engagement was from the start seen as an essential aspect of the project, but as it developed, the insights gleaned from this engagement came to inform the changing research aims and priorities of the Southampton/Northwestern team.

The aims and objectives of the public engagement were determined by the author of this chapter and the project director, Matthew Johnson, at the start of the first season (in 2010). It was intended to inform visitors, staff, volunteers and interest groups at these sites about the field survey project and any further research being conducted in relation to these sites. However, public engagement is not a one-way process (Morgan & Welton 1994: 32; Cushman 2012; National Co-ordinating Centre for Public Engagement online, retrieved 8th February 2012); and this process of information transfer was integral to furthering our understanding of the site in its modern and historical context. The memories collected for *The Role of Bodiam Castle in Popular Memory* served to increase our understanding of this site from the perspectives of staff, visitors and volunteers (Peacock 2010).

During my initial interactions with people, I employed a questionnaire to collect the data required for my Masters. I then moved on to using a (deliberately) informal and qualitative method that meant that the process of information transfer was in the form of a conversation. This meant that I found out aspects of people's experiences at the sites that would not be gleaned using more formal and quantitative methods such as questionnaires.

People were at ease as they were less focused on what they thought I wanted from the conversation and therefore, I was able to gather more meaningful information. Employing the technique of conversation meant that both parties involved gained information and mutual benefit. The public engagement being completed by the same person throughout the project has been beneficial as experience from previous years influenced the practice in subsequent seasons.

The public engagement was undertaken solely by myself up until 2013; between 2011 and 2013 there were no additional projects running in conjunction with the public engagement. This meant that the nature of the engagement changed slightly over the years. During 2010 interactions with volunteers, staff and visitors were actively sought to fulfil the data requirement for my Masters dissertation. In subsequent years, interactions with these groups were more complex to organise and not as many people were spoken to. In 2010 a set of interview questions were employed to gather information, and after this was completed conversations progressed onto the wider project. Without the use of interview questions, I engaged people in conversations about the activities of the students situated across the sites. This posed some problems as only people that were interested in the work of the team were open to conversing with me. However, it could be countered that the people whom were interviewed in 2010 were open to being interviewed because they were interested in my work and the project. Therefore, there need not be a discrepancy in the number of people interacted with as part of the public engagement.

I employed the same public engagement technique across all of the sites. All of the team were provided with distinctive project T-shirts each season which made them easy to identify in the landscape. While the rest of the team got on with the survey work I wandered around the landscape. At Bodiam this included walking around the interior of the castle as well as outside in the wider environment. It was important to cover all areas as people engaged with the sites in different ways (as will be discussed below). While wandering around the site, I would engage visitors in conversation around the topics of what the team were doing, any results from previous seasons and what the team were hoping to find. After this had been covered the conversation would progress to include any memories they had about the site, why they visited and any other information they wished to share with me.

It should be noted that in addition to my specific responsibilities, all other members of the team regardless their role were instructed to respond fully to visitor queries whatever they were doing at the time, even at the expense of the pace of the work. Further, Matthew Johnson and others gave public lectures to audiences including Trust volunteers, local amateur groups and the general public in a variety of contexts. Local amateur societies made a collective visit to Bodiam in 2010 to see the work and in particular learn about the geophysical techniques being used (Fig. 11.1). Early methods and experiences iteratively informed practices in later years.

Fig. 11.1: Members of local archaeology societies inspect the GPR equipment at Bodiam, April 2010. Professor David Hinton of the University of Southampton looks on (far right). Photo by Matthew Johnson.

Bodiam 2010-2012

Bodiam Castle has been owned and managed by the National Trust since 1926 (Dixon-Scott 1937: 12; Hinton 1990; Johnson 2002). During 2010, as previously stated, the public engagement was undertaken as part of my Masters research (Peacock 2010). Before 2015, the landscape around the castle was freely accessible, with visitors only needing to pay for parking during opening hours and for access to the interior of the castle. Consequently, visitors were free to move around the very large area managed by the Trust in different ways. Time was therefore split between the castle and its surrounding landscape.

Different types of visitors interacted with the site in a variety of ways. Local or return visitors tended to walk in a circuit around the outside of the property, while first time or long distance visitors would go straight into the castle (Peacock 2010). This was attributed to a number of factors. First, local or return visitors used the wider landscape as prior to 2015 it was free to access (parking was £2.00 if not a National Trust member). This made the site for these visitors in essence a park landscape, an area to walk and spend some time without large financial outlay. In particular, the car park and the landscape before the castle opening at 11:00 a.m. saw a large number of local dog walkers (Fig. 11.2).

This frequent use by locals prior to 2015 means that Bodiam is a notable exception to Lynch's statement that 'many symbolic and historic locations…are rarely visited by its inhabitants' (Lynch 1972: 40). The site's use as a 'park' by locals puts the castle within the definition of Lynch's 'historic location' (Lynch 1972: 40). First time or long distance visitors, on the other hand, go straight to the ticket office which at that time was on the northern side of the moat and thence to the castle, as their trip was specifically made to see the castle and therefore they were comfortable with paying for entry as well as parking. It was also more productive for me to split time around the site as the teams of students were dispersed across the surrounding landscape and the castle.

The stories and memories that were collected gave us a perspective on the values and priorities that visitors brought to the site, and a more layered and multivocal perspective, and in so doing added to our understanding of the site both in the present and in the past. Those stories that added to our understanding of the site in the past related mostly to the pillbox constructed as part of home defence in 1940. As discussed in Chapter Four, the Bodiam pillbox was constructed in World War II to guard the bridge at Bodiam. The pillbox is the focus of an annual World War II event at Bodiam Castle. There were a number of local visitors who stated that they knew the person who was tasked to

Fig. 11.2: Becky Peacock interviews a dog walker at Bodiam, April 2010. Photo by Matthew Johnson.

man the pillbox during World War II. Most people simply stated 'I know the person who manned the pillbox' or 'the person who manned the pillbox lives in my street/village'. This was interesting as everyone seemed to know this person, but over and over again when asked for a name they were unable to provide one. Therefore, it seems that many locals 'know' the person who manned the pillbox during World War II but this is more of a local legend than anyone actually knowing this individual. It appeared that being able to state 'I know the person who was stationed here' gave them a direct link to the past, a human connection; which has been seen to be an important sentiment within museum experiences in general (Bailey 1998: 92; DCMS 2001: 8; Little & Zimmerman 2010). It is a shared, empathetic history that is reiterated and affirmed by these statements.

Another aspect of history that was brought up frequently by visitors and locals was the Roman road and whether we found any remnants of Roman occupation of the area. The most memorable recollection I have about the Roman road revolves around the story of a local. They recounted a night they were making their way back from the pub through the field and they encountered the ghost of a Roman soldier. This piece of information was imparted when we were discussing the presence of a linear feature through one of the fields. I believe this was a way for them to suggest that it had to be the Roman road. The location of the Roman road and anything associated with the Romans was a particular focus for the local amateur societies that visited the site in 2010. It is not clear why these groups were so focused on 'the Romans' but it might be tied in part to issues of local identity.

A number of comments were made about the site in relation to the form and appearance of the castle. This ranged from 'it is a fairy tale castle' to 'it is what you imagine a castle to be'. These comments inform us about the way people view the site and castles in particular. The maintained landscape projects a sense of timelessness to the visitor; even as a ruin it appears to be untouched by time. There is a feeling of romanticism about the site which links to this fairy tale image that visitors have about the building and castles. Romanticism is a 'literary and critical movement' (Beiser 2006: 1) and has qualities of 'fantasy and sentimentality' (Beiser 2006: 12; Johnson 2007). Romanticism therefore has a particular relationship to nostalgia and memory. Another issue is the conflation of the real and imagined when visitors comment that the 'castle is real' (Peacock 2010). This can be linked to the image of the castle as presented in film, particularly those produced by the

Fig. 11.3: Cinderella Castle, Magic Kingdom, Tokyo Disneyland. Photo by Matt Wade, CC-BY-SA-3.0/Matt H. Wade at Wikipedia.

Disney Corporation, where 'Disneyfication' takes place with the trivialisation of structures of the past (Samuel 1994; Goodacre & Baldwin 2002: 20). This imitation can be seen in parks such as Disneyland (Fantasyland) and Legoland (Dragon Knights Castle), where the castle image is placed within the realms of fantasy and imagination (Samuel 1994: 242; Fig. 11.3).

Therefore, a real castle which is not completely ruined could be considered by most people to be within the realms of the imaginary. Many castles, apart from those still lived in, are 'ruins' whereas Bodiam has a largely complete external façade, has undergone limited renovations (by Lord Curzon and the National Trust) and has a wide, surviving moat. It has all the ingredients for the fantasy/imaginary castle that people come into contact with through literature and film. It is the romanticism of the site that places this castle within the world of both the imagined and the real (Beiser 2006: 8-9; Prager 2007).

It was interesting to see the strong connections/feelings to this site held by many people. In many cases the site was integral to visitors' memories of both childhood and family. Memories work on a scale ranging from individual and family, through group and institutional affiliations, to the national and global. Individual memories are personal, 'made not of disastrous events but rather a weaving together of humdrum but revealing details… with major events that are significant' (Connerton 1989; Conway 1990; Engel 1999: 97; Wrigglesworth 2009). Family memories, on the other hand, are created in a collective setting (Halbuachs 1992), and may be shared. In these memories the individuals may remember themselves to be more central to the past event than they really were (Engel 1999: 8). Frequent visitors use Bodiam to create memories with those they visit with, either consciously or unconsciously. Conscious construction of memories is seen when people choose to bring other people to Bodiam during visits, for example family members being brought during a family visit. Unconscious construction of memories happens at times such as a family day out.

These memories are used within identity construction and inform people where they come from (geographically) and the family they belong to. There were many cases of 'local' visitors bringing family members from other countries to the site (Peacock 2010, appendix 1 & appendix 2). During these visits the 'local' family members would recall previous visits to the site for those 'outside' family members. This process of recollection was part of a conscious construction of memory, where the 'local' family members chose this location to bring 'outside' family members as part of a process of inclusion. This site had significance to the 'local' family members and was the setting for many of their family memories. Including the 'outside' family members in these memories, the 'local' members are not just recalling memories but reconstructing them to include the 'new' members of the family. This ongoing process reaffirms the family group and ties between the members whether they were participants in the original remembered events or not.

There were also cases where older family members brought younger members to the site to share in their recollections. In one case a visitor recalled that their mother brought them to the site as a child. She had a number of her own memories of the site as she had been a hop picker in the area (Peacock 2010, appendix 1). These visits would include not only the new construction of memory but the sharing of older memories with younger generations.

Trust staff and volunteers feel a strong sense of ownership over the site. This is seen in a statement made by one member of Trust staff who stated: 'I live on the Marina and people say to me, don't you miss a garden and I say no because look what I have got (Bodiam Castle) it's enough garden!'. In this case Bodiam Castle is a substitute for the lack of garden at home, and this staff member views it as their own. This shows the sense of ownership that volunteers and staff feel towards the site. All these different types of memory show the complex nature of people's relationship to the castle and their sense of ownership over the site.

In 2011, with the completion of my research in the previous year, I decided to utilise a number of activities already organised by the National Trust with an input from the team to increase public engagement. There were information boards displaying information about the Southampton/Northwestern project as well as Trust-organised children's activities revolving around the archaeology of the site (Fig. 11.4). A local archaeological group also displayed some objects that they had found relating to the medieval period. All these activities increased the visitors' awareness of the archaeology of the property and the project. Visual and hands-on aids such as these attract the public's attention, and therefore it seemed more appropriate to concentrate the engagement inside the castle where these were housed. Centring on these activities allowed for easier interaction with families as children were entertained while the parents were able to find out more about our survey work. In the previous year it had been noted how

Fig. 11.4: Charlotte and Davy Allen dig for artefacts at Bodiam; operations directed by Sarah Johnson. Photo by Matthew Johnson.

difficult it was to engage with families. Children became bored quickly as the adults conversed and this ended interactions with families prematurely. Therefore, the activities drew in a group that were otherwise difficult to engage with in normal circumstances.

During all the field work seasons (2010-2012) the public engagement at Bodiam received positive feedback from visitors, staff and volunteers. Many people had some familiarity with the resistivity and magnetometry equipment being used from watching archaeological programmes on TV such as *Time Team*. Therefore, it was useful to work from this basis and explain why these methods were being used. The local amateur societies were also interested in the equipment that the team was employing. The public engagement throughout increased people's knowledge of the practices employed within archaeology. It also highlighted the importance of exploring the wider landscape around an existing historical building to understand what has happened before, during and after a property's construction. It served to highlight that landscapes are palimpsests (Hoskins 1955, Whyte 2009: 8); that they are forever changing and the pristine surroundings now apparent are not how they would have been in the past. The feedback from 2011 was even more positive as there were survey results from the previous year which we had printed out and laminated to show people rather than just discussing the project in the abstract. Viewing these results allowed visitors to see the evidence of previous occupation, other uses of the site and why the project is important to the broadening of our understanding of the property. In 2012 interaction with visitors was more difficult as students were not as visible as they had been previously. Student visibility was not a factor in engagement with staff and volunteers; however it was a factor in visitor engagement.

Scotney 2011

Scotney is an interesting site from the point of view of public engagement as it has two different buildings within the grounds; a 14th-century moated castle and a Victorian country house. The project focused on the surroundings of the 14th-century castle as seen across the surrounding parkland. This presented me with a similar working set up as seen at Bodiam where my time was split around the site in order to maximise public engagement. The level of engagement with visitors however was much lower than at Bodiam. First, at the time, the site was only open Wednesday to Sunday. Second, the very large extent of the surrounding parkland landscape of the site and the consequent very wide dispersal of the students around the landscape also meant that interactions with visitors were limited as visitors were less immediately aware of any work being carried out. Therefore, as noted at Bodiam the visibility of the students affected the level of engagement with visitors. However, at this property it was the interactions with the volunteers that were most informative. When I first arrived at the site I believed the situation to be similar to the one that I had found at Bodiam. This turned out not to be the case. It quickly became clear that there was a more marked segregation between the volunteers who worked in the house and those that worked in the gardens/parkland. This was definitely not the case at Bodiam where everyone worked together whether maintaining the landscape or working in the castle. Through interacting with volunteers around the site it became clear that the house and the garden/parklands were much more distinct both in terms of the teams that worked in them and the way they were viewed.

This distinctiveness came to the fore when I went round the Victorian house with a number of students. I was stopped by a volunteer and asked what the project was about. When I said that we were surveying the 14th-century moated castle and surrounding landscape the volunteer stated 'why would you want to focus on that it isn't very interesting, it is just a ruin, and this house is much more interesting'. I found this perception surprising as I had never had anyone question why we had chosen a site, but then the castle of Bodiam had no other buildings to compete with it. The view articulated here was that the Victorian house was more interesting to people as it was complete, was lived in and they could look at things; whereas the 14th-century castle was 'just a ruin'. This perception that surveying the castle and the parklands would not provide us with any more knowledge on these buildings seemed to be related to perceptions of the importance of furnishing and occupation; the 14th-century castle is unoccupied and largely unfurnished compared to the Victorian house.

It would appear that some volunteers are drawn to Scotney for very different reasons; for some it is the furnished Victorian house, for others it is the landscape and gardens. According to one informant, the different groups of volunteers tended to work in one or other area. In general, those working within the gardens/parklands were more interested in our work and findings than those situated in the house. We had further confirmation of this impression when at the invitation of Trust staff, the project put on a guided tour for the volunteers; only the garden volunteers attended.

In summary, the site of Scotney is different to Bodiam because there are two different types of buildings (one medieval and one more recent). The furnishings and sense of occupation of the Victorian house adds a different level to the visitor experience compared to Bodiam. If the house was not occupied, then this dynamic would not be present.

Knole 2013

Knole is a very large English country house situated within a surviving medieval deer park, located adjacent to the town of Sevenoaks in West Kent (Figs 7.1 & 7.2). Knole occupies an important place in national culture; as the family home of the Sackvilles over more than four centuries, it is associated with figures such as the writer and garden designer Vita Sackville-West and her circle. In particular, Knole is famous as the setting for *Orlando*, a novel written by Virginia Woolf, one of Sackville-West's lovers. As a place, then, Knole has a rather different cultural profile from the other three sites.

Only a small part of the landscape between the entrance and the house itself is managed by the National Trust. The rest is owned/managed by Lord Sackville and there is even a golf course on the site (Fig. 7.4). The house itself is also divided between publicly accessible areas managed by the Trust and the private residence of the Sackvilles. The nature of visitor use is interesting as entrance to the park by walkers was possible at any time and was free. However, this has not always been the case; there is a long history at this site of battles over access (as access was restricted in the past and this did not go down well with the local visitors (as was discussed in Chapter Seven; Fig. 7.23). Cars could enter the property between the hours of 10.00 a.m. and 6.00 p.m.; parking cost £4 per car. The only other charge to visitors was to enter the house, which was not open all the time.

It was noted that visitors used the site in different ways, as previously discussed at Bodiam. Many visitors used the park rather than going into the house and these users were mainly families who brought toys and picnics, spending a proportion of the day within the landscape. This could be the case for a number of reasons. First, Knole is used more as a local 'park' for the people of Sevenoaks rather than as a 'normal' National Trust attraction. (The National Trust has identified this in its planning for the site which aims to address this with different 'kinds' of visits to the property available in the future). Second, for some families, Knole House is viewed by them as a 'typical National Trust' property that requires a certain behaviour within it and therefore they choose to use the surrounding parkland rather than enter the house. It is unclear if either of these factors fully explains the visitor use of the site but each has been documented at other properties. Other visitors went into the property and then spent some time wandering around the park. These visitors could be seen to be long distance and were of a smaller number than those that visited just for the use of the park.

It has been observed in previous seasons that the process of engagement benefited from the visibility of the students, and from high visitor traffic. Knole was no different, at times when the students were not visible to the general public, engagement declined considerably. In some circumstances when the students were in full view of the public many people did not ask about the work, although I often observed that they were clearly intrigued by the activities of the students and would discuss amongst themselves. It is clear that in many cases people are curious about the work but will not actively seek the information they require and feel that they are hindering work if they do. This is where the public engagement came into play as I could interact with these people without them feeling they had interrupted work.

Interactions with volunteers were relatively few as most were located within the house and gardens rather than outside in the landscape. This was partly due to the divided nature of ownership of the site. Only a small proportion of the site is owned by the National Trust with the rest of it still owned by Knole Estates. The volunteers that were spoken to divulged knowledge about the house and its surrounding landscape. This mainly referred to the presence of a bowling green at the front of the property, and to other archaeological work ongoing both in the house and in the surrounding landscape. Other information included a World War II story referencing Knole's location within 'Bomb Alley', a corridor of land between London and the English Channel where German aircraft were liable to jettison bomb loads when under attack. The story was of a bomb being dropped outside the front of the house, smashing the windows and destroying a tree.

When the first results from the fieldwork were available and printed out, perhaps a week after fieldwork had started, interactions with volunteers became more focused. One example of this is when evidence for an original entrance to the house and possible gardens at the front of the property was printed out. This led volunteers to mention that there was a drawing in the house that showed formal gardens outside the property. Another transfer of information occurred when it was mentioned that Ground Penetrating

Radar (GPR) was being used within the Stone Court. This led the volunteer to state that there was a water cistern underneath the court and that there had been a diver sent down into it. Other pieces of information passed on were about the possible evidence of a glass production site on the property. Volunteers during these interactions liked to divulge information that we might not know about the site and, therefore aid in the interpretation of the results. It was their way of being actively involved in the fieldwork without actually being an active participant in the work.

Engagements with visitors had the same two-way transfer of information in some cases. One visitor referred to a supposed article about the Sackville family and the mention of a child stating 'why do people always visit my house?' This story foregrounds the perspective of the Sackville family, rather than the National Trust, its visitors and the site. It is interesting that this is what the visitor chose to pass on about the site and highlights the interest and identification the local population has with the Sackville family. Other people enquired about specifics on the fieldwork, such as availability of the results and specifics on the geophysical methods. Many questions revolved around whether there would be any excavation of the site if the survey brought up any interesting results. We responded that an excavation was not the aim of the project and that these non-intrusive techniques could inform us about the site. It is clear that many see archaeology as coterminous with excavation and many were surprised to find out that we can glean knowledge about a site through other methods. One visitor did enquire about what it was like to work with the National Trust. They related that they had been to many of the Trust's properties and found varying levels of friendliness of the volunteers from site to site (English Heritage 2014; Heritage Lottery Fund 2015). These different modes of engagement with visitors were also seen at Scotney between volunteers in the gardens and the house.

The public engagement at Knole met with varying degrees of success dependent on the visibility of the students during their fieldwork activities. The process of dissemination of information was more diffuse and widespread than at other sites; it could be either from one member of a group to others or from volunteers to visitors. Therefore, knowledge about the project was more widespread than just those that I spoke to directly. At Knole, there was a process of word-of-mouth dissemination which I have seen in other contexts; most notably in outreach projects frequented by families (see Peacock 2015).

Ightham Mote 2013

Ightham Mote is a 14th-century manor house surrounded by a garden (see Chapter Eight). The nature of the site is much more occluded, with visitor routes around the houses being quite narrow and the landscape as a whole being smaller in scale. It therefore presents more logistical problems for the Trust in terms of visitor movements than the wide landscapes of the other three sites. Therefore, visitors have only a few ways to move around the property. All visitors enter through the same entrance and move around the house in the same direction. Visitors can move through the gardens differently as there are a number of paths to take around the landscape. There were a number of talks and guided tours provided around the site for visitors and this showed a more structured information dispersal system. The public engagement was again dependent on the visibility of the students within the property. The project deployed a smaller team than at the other sites, and they were often less visible in the Ightham landscape given the greater number of walls, hedges and other divisions, combined with the greater tree cover, and also when they were engaged in survey work around the mill pond where there is no visitor access. However, the lack of visibility did not hinder interaction with volunteers who had been informed of the students' presence on the site, and were actively interested in the project.

The volunteers were very enthusiastic about the work of the students. Many of them enquired about the project and the techniques that the students were using. A number of the volunteers enquired about whether the techniques were similar to those used on archaeology TV programmes. One volunteer did state that there was little information about what we were doing passed on to them although this does not seem to be generally true of the relationship between staff and volunteers at this site.

Visitor interaction occurred more frequently during the times when students were more visible at the site. Many visitor enquiries related to what the students were doing and the equipment being used. Some visitors related the work to their own experience with archaeology and the archaeology display within the house. Also, as at Knole, a number of people enquired whether there would be any excavation after the survey work had been finished and asked why a survey would be completed if there was to be no excavation. It is apparent people associate excavation with archaeological investigation, but do not believe that non-invasive techniques can tell us as much about the history of the site. In other respects, the interactions at this site were very different from those at the other National Trust properties involved in this project. There was little to no two-way information transfer as visitors, staff and volunteers appeared to be happy with just being informed about the project without any input. This is very different to the other sites where most if not all interactions included two-way information transfer. There are a few possible explanations as to why this occurred at this site but these are mainly based on the difference in the logistical issues and affordances of the management of the properties. Ightham, as stated earlier, controls the movement of visitors both around the landscape and house, as well as into the site. This control of visitors as well as the lack of access into the site without paying full entrance fee may have affected the level of interaction. The atmosphere at this site was less like the atmosphere of a public park as observed at other properties. Visitors may have not been as interested in the work being carried out as they had paid to enter the property and wanted to experience it without any distractions. Also there were guided walks at regular times around the garden and onto the roof which meant the visitors' experience was more organised than at the other properties. The lack of conversational anecdotes imparted by the volunteers is very interesting as within most National Trust properties volunteers have a sense of 'ownership' (English Heritage 2014; Heritage Lottery Fund 2015) and are very free to share information.

The volunteers were actively interested in the work of the students and the team had more contact with the volunteers on a daily basis as they used the staff/volunteer room for breaks. Visitors were interested in the work of the students but not to the same degree as we experienced at other sites. In certain locations in the landscape the work of the students affected the movement of the visitors. This happened most notably when work was carried out in the orchard, causing visitors to walk through areas of the orchard that they would not have done naturally in order to avoid being in the way. Therefore, the work in certain cases did have an impact on the visitor experience of the site. At this site the visitor's movement is more controlled and there is no access to the site without payment. Therefore, there is less variation in how a visitor engages with the site compared to the multiple ways documented at the other properties.

Discussion

Even though each of the sites is different there are a number of themes that have been highlighted by the public engagement. The most notable theme has been the different types of visitors and their differing uses of the sites. This is not surprising as heritage organisations have always had different visitors and they all use the services in different ways (Bailey 1998: 92; DCMS 2001: 8; Little & Zimmerman 2010). However, in the cases of Bodiam (until 2015), Scotney and Knole where there is access to the site by locals for free there is a considerable difference in use to paying visitors. Local visitors use these sites as 'parks', they are a place to walk the dog and go for picnics. Therefore, they do not arrive at the site with the intention of entering the properties but utilise the surrounding landscape. As such the site is a different kind of space for these visitors. The properties are at the centre of a landscape that is habitually used by this group, but its historic character is not foregrounded for them (Lynch 1972: 40). Other visitors pay to enter the properties but will not spend as much time exploring the wider landscape. For them the property itself is important rather than the surrounding environment because of their fleeting engagement with the site. However, this difference in visitor use is only applicable at sites where there is access to the landscape for free or a minimal charge for parking. Ightham has restricted visitor access to the site and this results in only one type of visitor and use. The fact that all visitors have to pay to enter the site means that it cannot be used as a 'park' by locals; therefore it is solely a visitor attraction. The site's control of visitor movement and the structured activities available means that the visitor experience is more controlled compared to the other sites.

A second theme has been the experiences of the volunteers on these sites. Volunteers as with most heritage organisations are an integral part to the maintenance and running of a site. However, it became clear at Scotney that volunteers can develop separate identities based on the area that they are involved in, for example house or garden. The separation between volunteer groups was not documented at any other sites. It could be safe to say that the reason for this separation at Scotney is based on the spatial separation between the house and the gardens/parklands. However, this separation could also be due to a sense of occupation. The house is an occupied site, whereas the central focus to the gardens, the 14th-century castle, is not. At Ightham, though volunteers were friendly and helpful, there was little information input which was different from the other sites where volunteers had been very forthcoming with ideas and information that they thought could aid in the project. It is still unclear why this is the case. The readiness of volunteers to impart their knowledge about these sites is linked to their view of ownership or stewardship over these properties. Volunteers put in a number of person hours at these sites and are proud of the work that they do at them. This instils a level of ownership over the property as it becomes their site (English Heritage 2014; Heritage Lottery Fund 2015). There was relatively little interaction with volunteers at Knole and I attribute this to the nature of ownership over the site. The split ownership means that volunteers' activities focused on the house and courtyard. There was only one team of students surveying in the courtyard with the others surveying the wider landscape (see Figs 7.9 & A2.10). Therefore, my time spent within this area was limited compared to the time I spent within the inside of the other buildings in this project. I did engage with some volunteers but these were not as frequent as at other sites and in set locations, particularly the entrance and courtyard. Each site moulds its visitor experience through layout and structure but it also has the same effect on the volunteers of these sites.

A third theme is the information transfer process witnessed during this public engagement. The information transfer was very much a two-way process. I provided people with information about the project, while, in most cases they divulged something about the site or their relationship to it. The information provided helped us in understanding the site in terms of diverse viewpoints and perspectives, a theme that will be returned to in Chapter Thirteen. However, it also opened our eyes to the hidden world of each site. The memories and stories that only certain groups are privy to added another layer of understanding to the sites. It was not just about the history of each site in the past but the importance of the buildings to the modern population using them. These stories and memories informed us not just about how the site was viewed and used in the present day; but also about the historical narratives that people chose to associate with. All these aspects add another layer to each site that can be utilised in the interpretation and presentation of each of these sites.

Conclusion

Within this chapter I have tried to summarise the main findings from the public engagement. All these sites have produced interesting details about the properties, how visitors use them, the volunteers and staff, and the visitor's memories. The public engagements main aim was to increase visitor, staff, volunteer and interest group knowledge in the project and this central aim was achieved. Engagement was not a one-way process of information transfer and the knowledge that volunteers, staff and visitors imparted about these sites was integral to our understanding of the site both in the past and the present.

In my view the public engagement highlighted throughout all the sites the complex relationships that visitors, locals, staff and volunteers have with them. My understanding of these sites is heavily biased towards Bodiam but this is down to the number of seasons that the team spent at this location.

One critical lesson learned was the importance of time depth to successful public engagement. I tried within the time limitations to understand the other sites in as much depth as I could but this was difficult to do in the space of a single three-week field season. The first step I had to undertake at each site was a qualitative and patient exploration or 'excavation' of hidden meanings, meanings that are important and that vary between select groups; be they volunteers, locals, families or individuals. My role started off as one of public engagement, where I disseminated information and I tried to glean something from my recipients about their relationship to the site. However, my role and identity changed during the process of engagement; I ended up being a chameleon. In order to get people to open up to me about their memories and relationships with the sites I had to become one of the select group. In most cases this had to be done very quickly, I had what could be a 10-minute conversation in which to convince them to trust me with these hidden stories. In recalling these memories people were consciously constructing memories with me. I straddled the world of 'insider' and 'outsider'; able to understand the terms and references but simultaneously deconstructing them. The process is much harder to do when you have to undertake this learning within a period of two to three weeks. At Bodiam although I was there a short space of time each season, I could build on previous knowledge and reflect upon my experiences from the previous year to gain a deeper understanding.

Highlighting the relationship and memories of the staff/volunteers, visitors and locals to the sites not only helps our interpretation of the site. It can highlight areas of the site that have importance to these groups which may not be visually significant, for example the role of the wider landscape as a 'park'. It creates a map of hidden importance that only select people are privy to and people are introduced to through inclusion in the site and memories. The memories of visitors, locals and staff/volunteers can be used as another aspect of interpretation present at sites. At the time of writing, I am exploring the use of memories in relation to the Watercress Line (a heritage steam railway located in Hampshire, UK: www.watercressline.co.uk) to increase visitor experience. Many visitors have expressed a need to have a more human element to the interpretation and memories are a good way to add this to the interpretation materials. It also introduces the visitor into the world of the locals, staff and volunteers, making them part of that group.

I hope that this chapter has demonstrated the importance of public engagement on these projects, and the struggles that can be faced trying to undertake engagement in changing circumstances over a number of sites. There is interesting information that can be gleaned from locals, visitors, staff and volunteers that can be hidden to outsiders. That information, and the different perspectives and world-views that go along with it, adds to our understanding of the site both in the past and at the current time. These insights should not just be confined to assisting the research process, but should also play a wider role and dimension within all aspects of on-site and public interpretation.

12

DISCUSSION: ELITE SITES, POLITICAL LANDSCAPES AND LIVED EXPERIENCE IN THE LATER MIDDLE AGES

Matthew Johnson

Abstract. This concluding discussion draws together themes discussed through the volume, and tries to place them in a larger framework. This larger framework engages with the context of the sites within the Weald and in turn within the British Isles as a whole. It uses the approaches of lived experience to present a fresh understanding of the four sites in human terms, and situates the sites in a broader frame of changing landscapes and environments in south-east England and beyond.

In this concluding discussion, I want to try to draw together some of the strands running through previous chapters, and set them within a larger framework. There are three governing themes to this chapter. First, all four of the sites that are the subject of this volume need to be placed in their landscape and regional context, with reference to their long-term geological and environmental history. Second, we need to tie this wider history in to the agencies and lived experience of each place. In other words, we need to understand each place in human terms. Thirdly, and finally, we will broaden the canvas to make some general comments on cultural process and transformation in south-east England in the later Middle Ages and beyond.

Geology and Landscape

I take as my starting point the underlying geology of south-east England. I invite the reader to look carefully at a map of the geology of Britain, and look at the place of what are now the south-eastern counties of Kent and Sussex within that geology (Fig. 12.1).

The geology of Britain as a whole has a distinctive pattern: the layers of rock that make it up are tilted, in such a way that older and harder rocks are close to the surface in the north and west, while the south and east have a surface geology of younger and softer rocks (Fig. 12.2). Consequently, as any visitor to or inhabitant of Britain will have noted, the physical landscape of the south and east is softer, less rugged and mountainous than the hills and mountain ranges of western and northern England, Wales and Scotland. This distinctive pattern has been hugely significant in many different ways in British and world history. For economic historians, it determined the presence and distribution of raw materials (coal, iron ore) needed for the Industrial Revolution. For intellectual historians, the observation and developing understanding of this geological pattern framed the 19th-century intellectual understanding of geological time and its implications for evolutionary process (Winchester 2001; Weiss 2011). For historical geographers and landscape historians and archaeologists, it was and remains central in the powerful and continuing perception of distinctive and contrasting Highland and Lowland Zones in the 'personality of Britain' (Fox 1938).

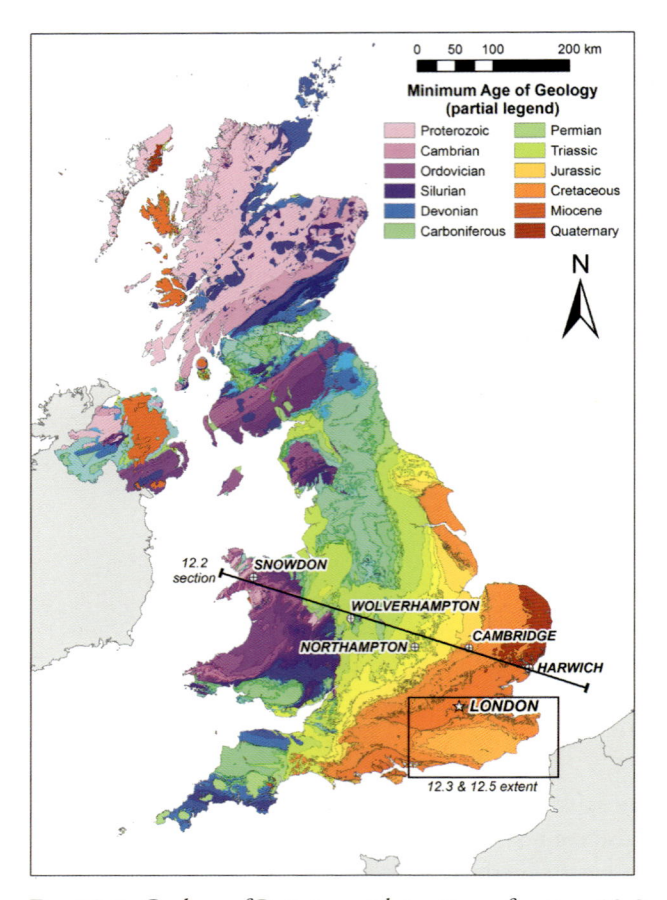

Fig. 12.1: Geology of Britain, with position of section 12.2 indicated. Based upon DiGMap625 layer from BGS, with the permission of the British Geological Survey.

The area south and east of the Thames Valley lies firmly within what the great Cyril Fox called the 'lowland zone'; its geological makeup is distinctive (Figs 12.3 & 12.4; Fox 1938). Millions of years ago, the layers of chalk and sandstone that underlie the area that is now south and east of London formed a dome or 'anticline'. Glacial action shaved off the top of this dome, exposing the tilted geological layers beneath: the topmost layer of chalk, and underlying layers of sandstone and clay.

These layers then eroded differentially, creating the chalk ridges we know today as the North and South Downs, and further bands of sandstone running within those ridges. Within the semicircle formed by these ridges, post-glacial deposits of gravel and particularly clay formed. Today we know these central areas, within the great chalk and sandstone crescent, as the Sussex and Kentish Weald.

Thus, someone who travels from north to south from London to the south coast, across the Sussex and Kentish Weald, moves first backward and then forward in geological time. Crossing first the high chalk ridges of the North Downs, they come down onto a ridge of greensand. Descending this in turn, they come to the claylands of the Low Weald. Rising up then to the sandstones of the High Weald and Ashdown Forest, they drop down again before coming finally to the chalklands of the South Downs and to the famous chalk cliffs of the coast.

The land was affected by glacial action during the Ice Age. The glaciers left gravel deposits in their wake. The land was also cut by the action of rivers, creating river valleys that in some cases, for example the valley of the Rother, were much more pronounced than they are today. We have seen how at Bodiam, there are at least 10 m of alluvial deposit on the floodplain; if we were to form a mental picture of the Rother Valley some thousands of years ago, before these deposits were laid down and with the surrounding hills a little higher before erosion, we would see a landscape that was much sharper, less soft, even rugged. These valleys became flat floodplains and, where they met the sea, extensive areas of tidal estuary and marshland developed.

One of the results of this distinctive set of geological processes is a set of places that exhibit great ecological diversity within a very few kilometres of each other, and which consequently have been of the first importance in the history of science. The naturalist Gilbert White's observations of the natural history of Selborne, in the county of Hampshire close to the Sussex border, were significant in part because of Selborne's position at the western extremity of this geological formation, where chalk, greensand and clayland meet. Charles Darwin's

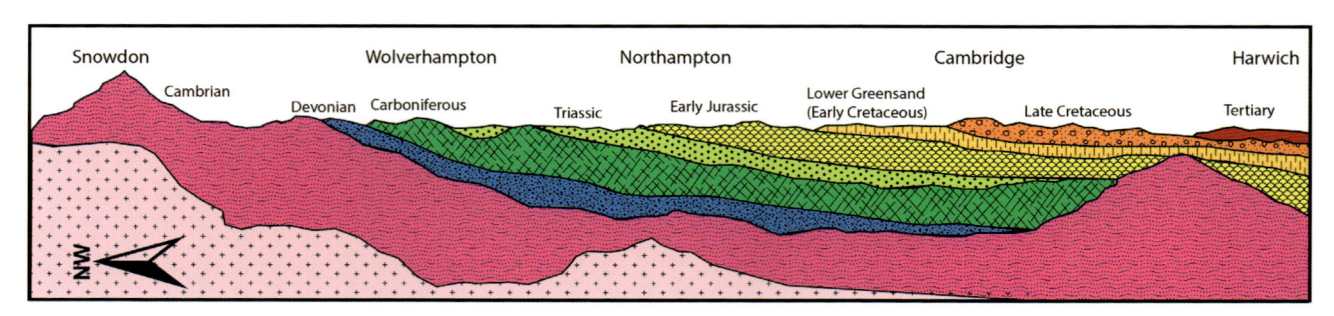

Fig. 12.2: Simplified section through the geology of Britain from Snowdon to Harwich, with vertical scale exaggerated.

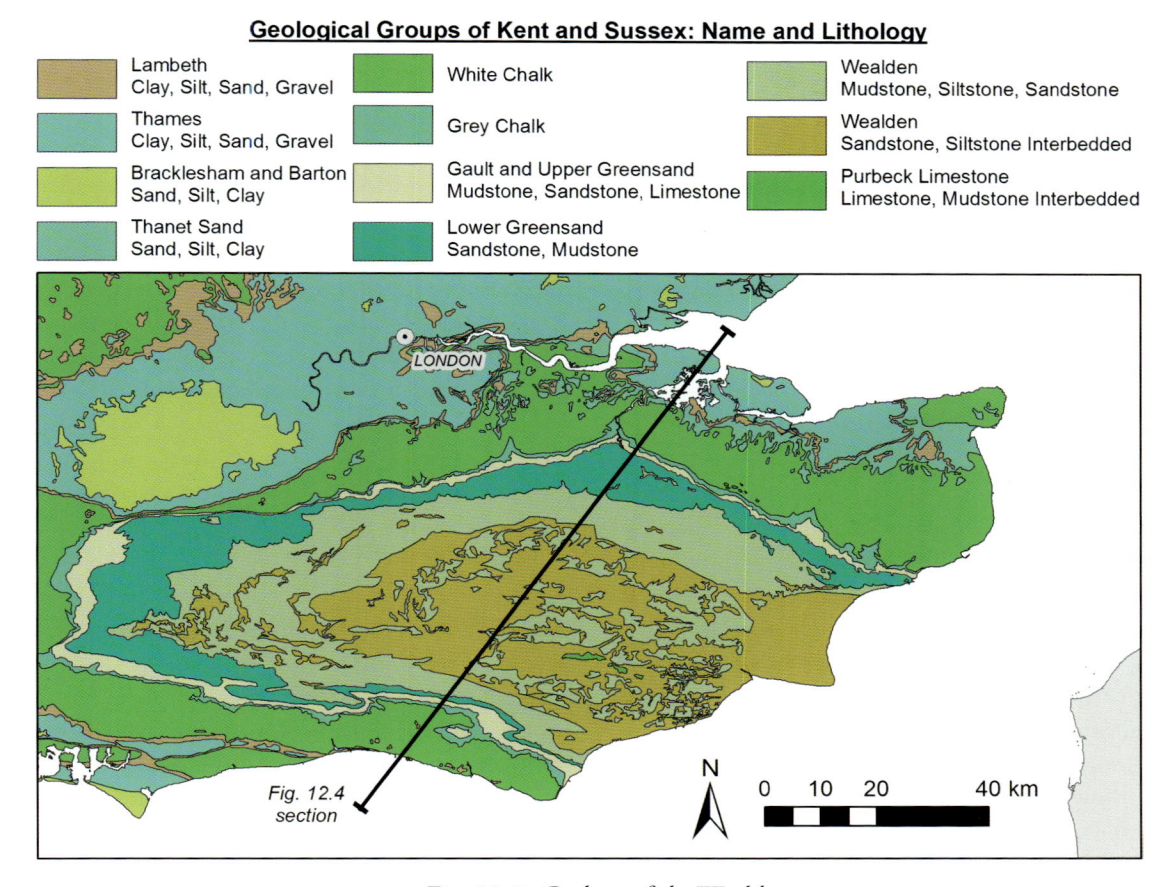

Geological Groups of Kent and Sussex: Name and Lithology

- Lambeth — Clay, Silt, Sand, Gravel
- Thames — Clay, Silt, Sand, Gravel
- Bracklesham and Barton — Sand, Silt, Clay
- Thanet Sand — Sand, Silt, Clay
- White Chalk
- Grey Chalk
- Gault and Upper Greensand — Mudstone, Sandstone, Limestone
- Lower Greensand — Sandstone, Mudstone
- Wealden — Mudstone, Siltstone, Sandstone
- Wealden — Sandstone, Siltstone Interbedded
- Purbeck Limestone — Limestone, Mudstone Interbedded

Fig. 12.3: Geology of the Weald.

home on the North Downs, at Down House 14 km north-west of Knole, meant again that he was able to observe a particularly diverse ecology and landscape on his famous Sunday walks while his family were attending church. Standing on the Downs and looking across the Weald, Darwin observed how the great dome had eroded away and estimated the length of time that it must have taken to do so at hundreds of millions of years (Johnson 2010c; Weiss 2011). More infamous are the post-glacial gravel deposits at Piltdown, 30 km south-east of Scotney, which in all probability afforded Charles Dawson the opportunity to plant his forged remains of early humans (Russell 2004).

Human Landscapes: Second Nature

The physical landscape created by these geological processes afforded different kinds of human landscape in its turn. The historical geographer William Cronon calls such landscapes 'second nature' (Cronon 1991: 56). What Cronon means by this is that these landscapes appear 'natural' to the observer – the field patterns, areas of woodland and forest, roads and communications are external and 'given' to the modern person, whether local or a visitor. At first sight, they are natural, just the way things are, and this 'natural' impression is deepened when the fields, woods, roads and communications are used and experienced on a daily, quotidian basis. However, all these elements were and are in fact products of human agency. Field patterns, areas of woodland, roads and communications may have been laid down hundreds or even thousands of years ago. Human responses may have been determined to a greater or lesser extent by factors such as geology or climate, but they were and are nevertheless products of human agency, of women and men making their own history.

The light soils of the chalk downs afforded open landscapes, relatively easy for prehistoric settlers to clear of woodland and to farm but not as potentially fertile as the heavier claylands. The central sandstone ridge of the High Weald had heathland which became medieval 'forest'. In between, the claylands of the Weald had a variety of soils including heavy claylands that were potentially fertile, but poorly drained. These heavy soils were difficult to work before the advent of mechanised agriculture, and they could also be difficult for travellers to get across, particularly in cold or wet conditions. The famous 17th-century writer of early agricultural and other how-to manuals, Gervase Markham, devoted an entire book to the problems of farming in the Weald (Markham 1625).

In the first half of the 20th century, archaeologists and historians told a distinctive story about how the Wealden landscape developed, as part of a wider story about prehistoric Britain as a whole. In his classic *The Personality of Britain,* Cyril Fox painted a powerful national picture across the British Isles (Fox 1938). As we have seen, Fox divided the British Isles as a whole into a Highland Zone to the north and west, and a Lowland Zone to the south and east. The differences between the two zones were not simply ones of physical geography and climate; they were also related, in Fox's vision, to relative proximity to Continental Europe and the consequent ease of what he called 'penetration' of peoples and ideas.

Within the Lowland Zone, Fox suggested that the chalk ridges were cleared of woodland first by incoming prehistoric settlers, and that these ridges, for example the North Downs or Cambridgeshire south-east of the Fenlands, became important zones of movement and communication between different regions. He noted the existence of ancient trackways running along these ridges. Alongside and below these routeways running along the downlands, Fox assumed that there were large tracts of dense, impenetrable forest, with, he believed, little evidence of human settlement to be found therein. Fox noted the distribution of burial mounds and archaeological features as known to him, which in their concentration upon the ridge, appeared to confirm his picture (Fox 1922, maps 1-5).

In the vision of Fox and his earlier 20th-century contemporaries, the Weald and other areas of lowland below the downs and ridges were seen as a particularly dense mass of impenetrable forest. It was this forest that Anglo-Saxon and medieval settlers penetrated and settled. Early medieval documentary records appeared to confirm this picture. Scholars working with early charters and other texts found few specific references to early settlement inside the Weald.

More recent work has heavily qualified this picture: the distribution of prehistoric and Roman settlement at a national scale has been reassessed (Bradley & Fulford 2008; Bradley 2014). For Cyril Fox and his generation, archaeological sites did appear to concentrate on the chalk downlands, but over fifty years later, we can see that this distribution is more apparent than real: there is plenty of archaeological evidence for early human settlement away from these areas, but it is more difficult to see and to map given variation in terrain and underlying soil.

At the same time, the underlying vision driving Fox's model, with Anglo-Saxon settlers clearing the hitherto untamed forest and making a home, has to modern eyes a decidedly colonial ring to it. It echoes the subjective experiences of settler colonists in different contexts, in North America, Africa and elsewhere. In other words, it seems to say more about the cultural values of earlier 20th-century Britain and British perception of settlement in her colonies around the world than it does about the prehistoric past.

It was certainly a view which held and continues to hold great cultural resonance, from the dark forests in Sir Walter Scott's *Ivanhoe* to JRR Tolkein's *Wild Wood* to WG Hoskins's embrace of this vision in his classic *The Making of the English Landscape* where he wrote, referring to the Anglo-Saxon period, of 'the first men [*sic*] to break into a virgin landscape' (Hoskins 1955: 18; discussed further in Johnson 2007). Sir Arthur

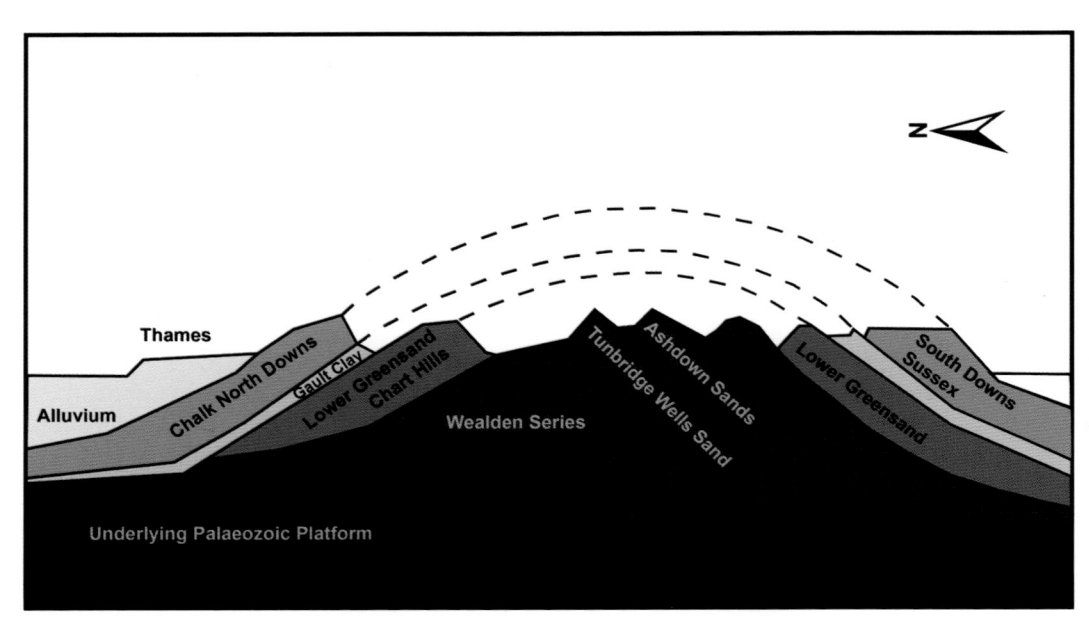

Fig. 12.4: Simplified section through the geology of the Weald, with vertical axis exaggerated.

Conan Doyle made the Weald the dark, forbidding backdrop to several Sherlock Holmes stories, though he gave it an industrial twist:

Alighting from the small wayside station, we drove for some miles through the remains of widespread woods, which were once part of that great forest which for so long held the Saxon invaders at bay – the impenetrable 'weald', for sixty years the bulwark of Britain. Vast sections of it have been cleared, for this is the seat of the first iron-works of the country, and the trees have been felled to smelt the ore…

(Sir Arthur Conan Doyle, *The Adventure of Black Peter*; Conan Doyle 1981 [1904]: 563-4)

The early medieval Weald was seen in this earlier view to be gradually cleared and brought under cultivation in a piecemeal process some centuries after the end of the Roman period, starting with the creation of north-south drove roads from the higher and more open chalklands into the Wealden forest for the pasturing of livestock. Cattle and sheep were moved seasonally, in this view, to summer pastures in Wealden clearances in the woodlands, and then back to the older estate centres based on the downlands and coastal areas to the north and south. This pattern of transhumance meant that as manorial estates defined by these movements became formalised, they had a tendency to be fragmented, combining lands inside and outside the Weald often quite a distance apart. Many Wealden settlements may have originated as summer sheilings or 'dens', linked to these older estate centres (hence the frequency of the –den place-name: Tenterden, Newenden, Iden).

Settlement expansion continued, in this earlier account, with the process known as 'assarting', a term taken from medieval documentary records (Brandon 1969; Witney 1976). This process of 'colonization' (as it is habitually termed by local and landscape historians and archaeologists: cf. Everitt 1986) was deemed to have unfolded in the centuries before 1300. The governing view of medieval colonisation of primordial forest was also derived in part from a scholarly methodology giving priority to documentary evidence, in which the first documented reference to a location such as a farmstead or hamlet was equated with the creation of that farmstead or hamlet. Since many individual farmsteads and settlements in the Weald first appear in tax records of the 11th, 12th and 13th centuries, these first recorded dates were sometimes taken as indicative of 11th-, 12th- and 13th- century colonisation (cf. Brandon & Short 1990: 49-55; Mate 2010a). Much colonisation may well have taken place centuries earlier in the middle Saxon period, before feudal record-keeping, and much of the land colonised had been under cultivation in earlier periods of climatic optimum in the Roman and prehistoric periods.

More recent scholarship has not entirely overturned this picture: clearance of land, and patterns of transhumance, clearly played an important role in the creation of the landscape and in the formation of the second nature of Kent and Sussex. However, the picture has been heavily qualified and reframed. Assarting was an important process in medieval Europe generally; documentary references to assarting or its equivalent are found in the 11th to 13th centuries across England and much of the rest of Europe; and assarting did involve the bringing of uncultivated land under arable cultivation. In this sense, the settlement of the Weald of Kent and Sussex is one small variation on the theme that runs across medieval Europe in the centuries up to c. 1250, of a climatic warm period, of population rise, of greater social complexity with the emergence of 'feudalism' however defined, and of settlement and agricultural intensification (Hatcher & Bailey 2001; Graham-Campbell & Valor 2007).

There was no such thing as an original primeval forest; medieval woodlands were characteristically heavily managed throughout their history, through coppicing, pollarding and other practices, and were also the focus of different kinds of property and use rights, for example pannage (the right to graze pigs or other animals in a wood) or rights to collect firewood (Rackham 1990). These rights were often referred to by people in the Middle Ages as 'customary' and ascribed to tradition, and their emergence into the documentary record does not have a straightforward relationship to their prior existence. In other words, the first documentary reference does not necessarily equate to a date of origin. When the documentary record, then, shows us a more populated landscape in the Weald as the Middle Ages advanced, it is not necessarily indicating expansion of settlers into uncultivated primordial forest, but rather a more complex picture of an evolving property and agricultural regime, in which social practices of settlement and agriculture were being drawn more and more into the net of legal relations which were written down as part of feudal record-keeping. Michael Clanchy (1979) discusses the wider cultural context within which more and more documents were being generated in the centuries before 1300.

Given that documentary traces are very often in the form of tax records, the first documentary reference to a place, then, has more to do with its first inclusion within a system of extraction of rent, rather than first settlement as such. In other words, assarting as it is discussed by documentary and landscape historians can be seen as not simply or only the colonisation of virgin forest or uncleared land, but rather the bringing of this land under an organised feudal regime of the organised extraction of rent. Assarting, then, is about changing and intensifying regimes of property and power as well as agricultural expansion.

The eventual outcome of this process was an earlier 14th-century Wealden landscape that was quite distinctive compared to other areas of England and north-western Europe, in the form both of its physical landscape and the affordances of that landscape, and its social relations. The heavy claylands were suitable for the raising of cattle and sheep; however, arable was also an important element of the economy (as indicated by the pollen evidence discussed in Chapter Four, and also by the presence of a number of substantial barns that survive: Martin & Martin 2006: 36). The legal conditions of many manors, as they had evolved through the process of assarting and through the fragmentation of holdings, gave many tenants considerable independence. This meant that after the demographic contraction of the Black Death, they were able to accumulate land under relatively 'free' conditions of tenure. In other words, rents paid by peasants to the manorial lord were not as onerous as in other areas, and tenants enjoyed relative security of possession; they could not easily be evicted or have their rents arbitrarily raised. These 'yeoman' tenants often lived in isolated locations of individual farmsteads and small hamlets away from churches and village centres, and their houses were surrounded not by open fields or by common land, but rather by enclosed fields and woodlands.

After the Black Death, many hundreds of the post-1348 farmhouses built by these relatively independent, prosperous and secure farmers were substantially built in timber framing and still survive today as occupied 'vernacular' houses and farmsteads (Everitt 1986: 55; Pearson 1994; Martin & Martin 2006); many of these vernacular houses can be observed in the settlements and landscapes around Bodiam, Scotney and Ightham. Their occupants were frequently engaged in market relations; the sheep and cows they kept produced dairy products and wool for sale. Many households in the region were also engaged in industrial production. This industrial production included charcoal burning, the production of pig iron, and glass (Cleere & Crossley 1985). All of these activities used large quantities of wood, which was in good local supply.

However they were created, areas like the Weald continue to be highly distinctive today. First, as Conan Doyle observed, they are areas with much woodland. Second, nucleated villages are relatively rarely found within them or are of more recent origin. Churches are often isolated, and farmsteads are either in isolated locations, cluster in small hamlets, or are strung out along routes that run along ridges (such as the east-west ridge of Ewhurst Green, just south of Bodiam). This dispersed pattern contrasts strongly with the classic nucleated English village (Rippon 2008; Roberts 2008). Third, also absent are the large 18th- or 19th-century fields that replaced the open field systems of the sort seen in the English Midlands and northern France; instead, patchworks of smaller, enclosed 'ancient' fields are the norm. Fourth, travel and communication across this landscape in the Middle Ages was via narrow, winding and often sunken lanes (making waterborne transport, whether along rivers or around the Kent and Sussex coast, all the more important). These routeways either run north-south, with possible origins in early medieval transhumance as drove roads, or east-west, along the tops of the gentle ridges of the High Weald.

Bordering the Weald to the north were the greensand (sandstone) ridges. These ridges were less potentially fertile than the Weald itself, but more open. Many areas of the greensand were particularly suitable for the development of parkland and 'forest'. Medieval forests should not be thought of as natural woodland: rather, they were often composed of heath, pasture and woodland, subject to distinctive forms of medieval 'forest law' (Rackham 1990). Forests and parklands were managed for the grazing and hunting of deer, as well as for the production of other resources such as wood and timber, as discussed at Knole in Chapter Seven. As such, they were a particular and contested focus for class conflict, between lord and peasant over who had rights (to collect firewood, to graze pigs on the acorns from oak trees, to hunt or to poach…).

The areas of tidal estuary, coast and marsh formed another distinctive zone. They were open on the one hand to schemes for draining, and on the other hand, they were especially vulnerable to climate change, weather extremes and changes in sea level and currents. At different points in the Middle Ages, both Pevensey and Romney Marshes (Fig. 2.1) had areas that were drained and turned into farmland through a variety of collective and individual efforts, only for sea walls to be breached and land return to marsh or to the sea itself during the adverse climatic changes of the 14th century that marked the onset of the 'Little Ice Age' (Grove 1988; Mate 2010b). Sea walls required large inputs

DISCUSSION

of labour, which was in short supply after the Black Death. This 'precarious fertility' (Everitt 1986: 60) was exploited by corporate institutions acting as landlords such as Christ Church Canterbury, institutions centred in other parts of the region, who grazed large flocks of sheep on the reclaimed land. The most notable artefacts of these changes are the position of the old ports of Rye and Winchelsea. Both were important ports in the 12th and 13th centuries whose merchants traded via the English Channel with the North Sea and Baltic in one direction and France and the Atlantic in the other. The site of Winchelsea was moved after the older site had to be abandoned; the harbours of both sites silted up after the 14th century and both towns now sit 1 to 3 km inland (Martin & Martin 2004; Long *et al.* 2007).

Elite Sites in the Landscape

If we want to engage with the sites of Bodiam, Scotney, Ightham and Knole, this very distinctive landscape context, a combination of what William Cronon would call first and second natures, is the first fact to be considered. Of the four sites, the location of three is very striking in terms of the junction of different landscapes. Bodiam is at the junction of Weald and marsh; Knole and Ightham are at the junction of Weald and sandstone ridge. Scotney sits in the middle of the Weald, but is itself in an isolated location, and like Bodiam, sits very close to the Sussex/Kent border.

All four sites sit within the interstices of the geography of medieval lordship and administration. Most obviously, the boundary between the counties of Kent and Sussex runs through the middle of the Weald. Settlement in the Sussex Weald tends to be linked to settlement further south on the Sussex coast and downlands; conversely, settlement in the Kentish Weald links northwards to the North Downs and river valleys of northern Kent (Everitt 1986). Subdivisions within the counties make this picture still more complex and fragmented (Fig. 12.5). In the Middle Ages, Sussex was divided into six 'rapes', or feudal lordships. The origins of this division lie before the Norman Conquest, but the lordships were at the very least modified by William the Conqueror after 1066. Now each lordship was set up with a distinctive set of elements: a chief castle and town (Chichester, Arundel, Bramber, Lewes, Pevensey, Hastings), access to the coast and coastal resources, corn-producing villages on the downlands, areas of parkland suitable for hunting, areas of the Weald for grazing and other resources… the political boundaries of the rapes, then, with the partial exception of Hastings, run in a ladder-like form across the grain of the landscape as defined through geological zones, with the boundaries running north-south across the east-west lie of the landscape.

The sites of Bodiam and Scotney Castles arose and developed as places of importance in the later Middle Ages, within the interstices of this system, at a social level below that of the great lordships. Knole and Ightham, in Kent, had a different set of antecedents, but in their origins were also below the very highest level. At Knole in the mid-15th century, James Fiennes was in the process of building a double-courtyard house before his execution, and the great family who came to own Knole, the Sackvilles, started as a more modest Sussex gentry family in the later Middle Ages (Saul 1986). It is part of the popular image and identity of Ightham that its successive owners never aspired to build a house or castle of the first rank. In Chapter Ten, Eric Johnson explored how moated sites in the Weald could be understood as a general phenomenon; part of

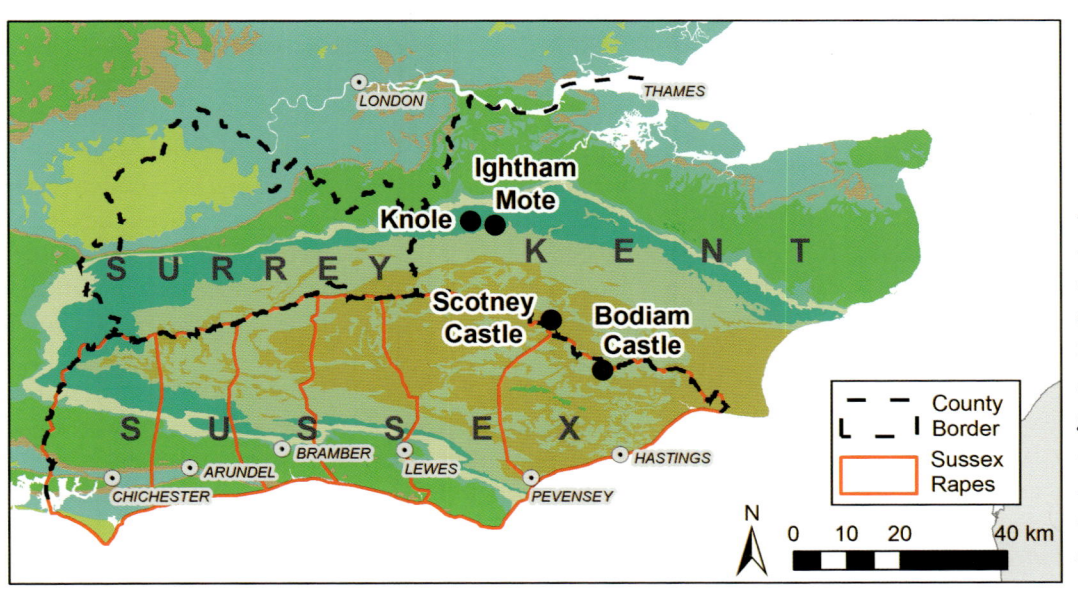

Fig. 12.5: Bodiam, Scotney, Knole and Ightham, mapped against the underlying geology and the boundaries of Kent, Sussex and the rapes of Sussex.

understanding Bodiam, Scotney and Ightham is to see them as examples of this wider class of monuments, albeit particularly large and impressive ones.

So far, this discussion has emphasised the importance of placing all four sites in the context of the long term and of the regional landscape of south-east England. I will now turn to each site in turn to make more particular comments about their position in terms of region, landscape and long-term development.

Weald, Marsh and Greensand

An understanding of Bodiam Castle as a site should start, if not before, then at the outset of the Bronze Age and with the environmental record. The results of coring and excavation (Chapter Five) have shown that this was the point at which peat formation came to an end, and alluvial deposits began to build up in the river valley. It was at this point that the distinctive form and rhythm of the Bodiam landscape was created. Before this moment, the Rother Valley was quite rugged; now it developed as a valley that was from time to time under water or a tidal estuary, alternating with drier and warmer climatic periods when it reverted to river and floodplain. This rhythm at Bodiam between water and land continues. If the River Rother was tidal estuary or marsh up until and beyond the end of the Middle Ages, it was drained in the post-medieval period and used as the fertile plain it is today (Eddison 1985; 1993). However, if climate change continues, it is very possible that the Rother Valley at least up to Bodiam will revert to being tidal or even be permanently under water within a century or so.

The 'Bodiam' place-name, as recorded in the Middle Ages, refers directly to this position between land and water. It connects the Old English personal name Boda with –ham indicating a settlement; the form Bodihamme, which is recorded in 1259, probably indicates 'land hemmed in by water' (Mawer *et al.* 1929-30: 518).

The location of Bodiam, at the head of a tidal estuary in the later Middle Ages, has been seen as a defence against the French. This volume deliberately refuses to take a view on this proposition, as the whole thrust of what we have been trying to do in this project is to get beyond the false, misleading choice of a 'military versus status' opposition. It may be worth noting that there is a more obvious point in the landscape to construct a defence against an invading or raiding force up the estuary, at the end of the peninsula projecting into Romney Marsh, at the site now known as Castle Toll (Fig. 2.1).

Indeed, here, there is a 12th/13th-century motte-and-bailey castle, itself placed within an earthwork identified as the possibly unfinished defences of an Anglo-Saxon burh (Davison 1972). This site was excavated in 1965 and again in 1971 (King 1983: 232).

The riverine location of Bodiam links in one direction with Romney Marsh, the ports of Rye and Winchelsea, and the English Channel beyond. From Rye and Winchelsea, goods including grain, timber and especially fish were transported, not just up and down the Channel, but around the coastline of Kent to London – the impassable nature of the Weald making this a more economical route to the capital. Goods also flowed inwards; wine and fish were imported from a range of French Atlantic ports (Martin & Martin 2004: 8); the fish would be destined especially for Battle and Robertsbridge abbeys.

Romney Marsh was transformed in the period after 1348-9. First, as we have seen, climatic deterioration led to destruction of sea barriers and a return of much of the marsh to its former state. Second, much of the highly fertile land on the marsh, formerly controlled by landowners such as the great institutions of Canterbury Cathedral Priory, was now leased out. Peasant landholders could now accumulate substantial holdings by taking advantage of the post-1348 demographic decline and also this leasing-out (Draper 1998), though much of this engrossing and formation of substantial farms, often seen in a wider context by economic historians as proto-capitalist, did not fully unfold until the late 15th century (Gardiner 1998).

However, the River Rother and its floodplain also links Bodiam in the other direction. Upriver is the Cistercian abbey of Robertsbridge, founded in the 1170s and with eight monks in 1418 (Page 1907: 71-4). Edward Dallingridge, his son John, and his wife Elizabeth Wardedieu, were all buried at Robertsbridge. Part of John Dallingridge's tomb effigy still survives, and is on display at Bodiam Castle; it has been misidentified in the past as Edward's (Fig. 12.6). The Dallingridge family were patrons of Robertsbridge. The patronage of the Dallingridge family flowed up the river, while water flowed both down the Rother and also along the artificial leat that Dallingridge constructed to feed the mill pond.

Where Bodiam sits at the junction of Weald and marsh, Knole and Ightham sit at the junction of Weald and greensand. Both sites should be understood in this context. Knole stands on top of the greensand ridge; its park, the largest surviving medieval deer park in England, overlooks the clayland of the Weald to the south. As

Fig. 12.6: Mutilated tomb effigy of Sir John Dallingridge, on display at Bodiam Castle.

Chapter Seven has shown, the decision by Archbishop Bourchier and before him James Fiennes to develop the site of Knole was tied up with the creation and expansion of a deer park of immense size. The landscape of the greensand ridge, with its light soils and heathland, was particularly appropriate for such a deer park.

The understanding of Knole is also tied up with the complementary nature of the site to the nearby archbishop's palace at Otford. To the casual observer, the proximity of the two archiepiscopal palaces of Otford and Knole is surprising. Otford is a large double-courtyard house, built by Archbishop Warham in the earlier 15th century, only 6 km to the north of Knole (Fig. 12.7). Little remains of Otford Palace above ground save part of a gatehouse, a tower, and fragments of the intervening range, now reused as a row of private houses. Otford is in many respects very similar to the house that Bourchier constructed at Knole. However, its placing in the landscape is very different.

Alden Gregory (2010) suggests that the two houses of Otford and Knole need to be understood in terms of complementary functions. In his view Otford was the administrative and 'public' centre, while Knole was intended to be a 'private' place for the Archbishop's repose. Again, this suggestion has great merit, but it has a geographical and landscape component that lies behind the expression of Archbishop Bourchier's personal preferences. Otford sits astride east-west travel and communication routes, most obviously the Pilgrims Way to Canterbury, and was part of the very earliest phase of post-Roman settlement of the Kentish landscape. By contrast, Knole and the associated small town of Sevenoaks sit in an elevated location astride north-south routes; the unusual place-name Sevenoaks suggests it may have originated in the pre-Conquest period as a meeting-place by seven oak trees, at the intersection of a north-south drove road and an east-west ridgeway (Everitt 1986: 209, 269). Contemporaries commented on this more elevated location and in particular the marshy and less salubrious nature of Otford.

As discussed in Chapter Eight, Ightham sits at the bottom of a small north-south valley, again carved out of the greensand ridge. It is the carving-out of this particularly small and occluded landscape that gave the opportunity to furnish a moat for the house, and at that point or later, create a series of ponds or water features, including the mill pond. A few hundred metres south of the house, the ground falls to the claylands of the Weald. While the house is situated at the bottom of the valley, numerous surrounding points in the immediate landscape offer panoramic views east and south over the Weald (Fig. 12.8). The development of settlement at Ightham up to the early 14th century, including the creation of the original moated site, is not at all clear. However, the house is sited on the main route southwards from Ightham church that leads into the heart of the Weald, very possibly another north-south drove road in origin.

Fig. 12.7: The north-west tower and part of the surviving north range of Otford Palace, Kent. Photo by Matthew Johnson.

Fig. 12.8: View south over the Weald, as seen from the top of the greensand ridge between Knole and Ightham. Photo by Matthew Johnson.

Scotney (Chapter Six) can be seen as the exception within these four sites. It stands well within the boundaries of the Weald, with no clear connection or intersection with other kinds of landscape. Scotney does sit in a boundary location, very close to the Kent/Sussex border and at the intersection of lands belonging to several different manors. The early owners of Scotney are missing from the Sussex Lay Subsidy Returns, which suggests that they may have been living across the border in Kent in the early 14th century. Scotney also has no associated village; the settlement of Lamberhurst is over a kilometre away to the north-east. It is difficult now to mentally reconstruct the medieval context of Scotney, after its 19th-century re-landscaping and the creation of the artificial reservoir of Bewl Water to the south, but the overall impression is of quite an isolated location away from the key nodes and routeways of political power and economic flows.

Scotney's owner in the 1370s, and the builder of the tower and other features on site, was Roger Ashburnham. Ashburnham was not a knight. He, Dallingridge and Etchingham could be seen as three key players in local politics, often named together in documents of the time. Again, Ashburnham's social and political networks certainly reached beyond the Weald into south-east England as a whole: Ashburnham was Commissioner for Walls and Dykes on Romney Marsh (Martin *et al.* 2011: 323), and the place-names Scotney Marsh and Scotney Court Lodge testify to links between Scotney and Romney Marshes (Spencer & Woodland 2002). Knole was owned by Roger Ashburnham in the 1360s, at a time when, prior to the building of Fiennes and Bourchier, it may have looked like Old Soar Manor (Gregory 2010: 11), or like the kitchen-hall-solar block at Ightham before it was extended into a full courtyard.

Agency and Lived Experience

So far, in this discussion, I have moved from the very large-scale in terms of time and space, from geological time and the British Isles as a whole, down to regions, second nature and down to human landscapes and the role of our four sites as nodes in particular kinds of networks. I now want to move in the other direction, upwards from the ordinary experiences of individuals.

All four sites are traditionally explained in terms of the agency of elite men. The term 'agency' refers to the aims and goals of individual social actors, and the practical strategies and actions taken to achieve those aims and goals. The broader terms of this agency are clear. All four sites are witnesses to the biographies of men of the later medieval gentry or knightly classes, seeking to materialise the rise of their position in society. Men like Dallingridge, Ashburnham, and Couen have been variously described by traditional historians as upwardly mobile, new men, ambitious, engaging in conspicuous consumption. They were not quite from the upper aristocracy, but the next rung down. They acquired political power and cultural capital through participation in the practice of war, advantageous marriages, shifting political alliances both local and national, and service to the King; and they framed their identities and self-image around contemporary values of elite masculinity, for example ideas of honour and the defence of honour (Radelescu & Truelove 2005; Neal 2008).

Honour was a concept that brought together ideas of status, of martial valour, of prowess in activities like hunting and jousting. Honour was a concept that articulated a structured set of symbols, which were expressed for example through violence. Defence of honour, of one's family and lineage, one's community and one's position at the head of it, was fundamental to the self-image of these men. Elite buildings, among other things, expressed and materialised a powerful idea of honour and defence of that honour, from landscape setting to heraldry to battlements to location and orientation. As I argued in my book *Behind the Castle Gate*, castles and houses acted as stage settings against which elite identities were played out (Johnson 2002).

We can extend this discussion, and give it a landscape context, by relating it back to region and place, by thinking about the networks created and maintained by these elite men, and the role of the four sites as key nodes in those networks, places that maintained their power and framed their social identities. Most obviously, all four sites are within 80 km of London and the political opportunities afforded by the court. At a deeper level, we have seen how the fragmented landscape of the Weald offered opportunities for aggrandisement below the level of the great feudal lords, and this is what we see at our four sites.

At Ightham, Thomas Couen pursued a strategy of social aggrandisement by working an intersection of national, regional and local scales. His family came from the west Midlands, where he spent his earlier life. Through his participation in the system of raising troops to fight in the French wars, he came to have a house and a network of contacts in London. We will never know the precise reasons for his decision to purchase the manor of Ightham, but it represented a shift of Couen interests from the west Midlands to the Kentish Weald, a region he probably first visited *en route* to the coastal ports and embarkation for French expeditions (Minihan 2015). Greater proximity to London may also have been a factor. The purchase of Ightham seems to have been part of a larger intention to settle in that area, only interrupted by his death; one might have expected someone of his background and stature to go on to rebuild the modest manorial structure at Ightham.

It may well be that the reason Ightham was not rebuilt by Couen as a more impressive structure, another Bodiam or perhaps more realistically another Scotney, is to do with the contingencies of inheritance and life cycle. Members of late medieval elites made decisions to build at key moments, often just after an advantageous marriage, at the conclusion of successful military career, or after a death and ensuing inheritance. Thomas Couen died in 1372, of natural causes, on board a ship at Winchelsea waiting to go to war in France; he was buried in Ightham church, where his fine alabaster effigy still survives below a stained glass window he also commissioned (Fig. 12.9). Ashburnham and Dallingridge, on the other hand, lived to a relatively advanced age by the standards of the time and built or rebuilt at a relatively late stage in their careers and lives.

At Knole, Chapter Seven discussed how Archbishop Bourchier's post-1456 building campaign was prefigured by construction on the site initiated by Sir James Fiennes after his purchase of the site in 1445. Fiennes came from a family with origins in the gentry classes. His main seat was at Hever, in the middle of the Weald, 15 km south-west of Knole (Hever was later to attain popular fame as the seat of the Boleyn family). He represented Kent as a Member of Parliament before promotion to the House of Lords in 1457; he became an important national figure and member of the King's inner circle, and a steward of the archbishop' estates, before being caught and executed by Jack Cade and his fellow rebels in 1450. Fiennes also owned estates in Romney Marsh, allegedly acquired through bullying and intimidation (Nigota 2004; Grummitt 2010: 242-7). His brother Roger built Herstmonceux, a quadrangular moated castle in brick often compared to Bodiam, which sits on the edge of the Weald west of Hastings. Herstmonceux was again located at a junction of landscapes, with a now drained tidal inlet of Pevensey Bay to its south-west, and had a deer park (Martin & Martin 2006: 13). However, like Couen, Fiennes never completed a great house: his building campaign at Knole was brought to an abrupt halt by his death.

Dallingridge's personal biography is well known and has been told and re-told in narrative terms several times; the most complete account has been given most recently by Dan Spencer. His career and biography illustrate the intersection between war and violence, structures of political power and authority, and personal and dynastic wealth through landholding. Dallingridge did military service from 1360 onwards, that is from about age thirteen, in France, and possibly also in Ireland and Italy (Spencer 2014: 84). He went to Scotland as part of Richard II's expedition in 1385; and was appointed captain of Brest 1388-9. His military activities probably ended with the French truce of 1389.

Dallingridge's political and administrative appointments show him working between the local community on the one hand, and national politics on the other. In 1380 he was appointed to oversee defences of New Winchelsea; he was wounded in this year during one of the French attacks. He also served as a commissioner of array in 1377, 1385, 1386 and 1392, and as Member of Parliament in nine of the thirteen parliaments held between 1379 and 1388. He was responsible for enforcing the oaths of the Merciless Parliament in

Fig. 12.9: Tomb and effigy of Thomas Couen, died 1372, Ightham church. Photo by Matthew Johnson.

1388, and led a group of chamber knights in regularly attending the King's Council in 1389-90 and 1392-3 (these are the periods for which we have records; he may have filled this role at other times; Saul 1997: 267-8). He also switched allegiance from Arundel to the King at a critical moment: he may have been active militarily on behalf of the Appellant lord Arundel in 1387 but came over to Richard in 1389. His rise meant that Arundel's influence was reduced in the eastern part of Sussex (Saul 1997: 267-8, 372).

The listing of this string of appointments conceals a complex and changing political strategy. From 1377 onwards, Dallingridge engaged in his campaign against the great magnate and King's uncle Gaunt, leading to prison in 1384. One view of the location of Bodiam has been suggested by John Goodall, following a suggestion by Charles Coulson (Coulson 1992: 105-6; Goodall 2011: 314; see also Walker 1983). Dallingridge's grandfather was from Ashdown Forest, in the High Weald to the west of Bodiam and Dallingridge's earlier career had one focus in the political disputes in the area. Ashdown Forest was a key arena in Dallingridge's political manoeuvrings of the 1370s. It was the location where Dallingridge chose to commit trespass against John of Gaunt, and murder one of his foresters, in a calculated move to confront Gaunt's power in the area. Goodall suggests that the subsequent imprisonment and trial of Dallingridge, and eventual reconciliation with Gaunt, afforded a political settlement in which Dallingridge remained a force in the area but built his seat some distance away from Ashdown Forest, at Bodiam, on the Kent/Sussex border. Goodall writes that 'Bodiam looks suspiciously like the physical product of this reconciliation' (Goodall 2011: 314).

Goodall's suggestion is a good one, but again, I draw attention to the underlying social, cultural and landscape factors at play in this political game. Ashdown Forest is part of the High Weald, an area subject to the forms of forest law discussed above. The move away from Ashdown Forest was also a move into a different kind of local economy and landscape. More generally, we observed above how Bodiam was one of a class of sites that sit within the interstices of the feudal system of Sussex rapes. It is unusual in that, as discussed in Chapter Two, it was a manor that was not divided between spatially disparate holdings; the distinctive form of the manor, and the weekly market and annual fair, marked out the site as a key 'bottleneck'. Comparative anthropology has identified bottlenecks of this kind as key nodes in the negotiation of cultural and economic power (Earle 2011).

At Bodiam, the decision to build seems to be correlated with particular moments in the life cycle. In 1377 his father-in-law died, and his estates, including Bodiam, passed to Dallingridge; in 1380 his own father died, leaving him with a huge increase in wealth. Dallingridge sold various Midlands estates in 1382, possibly to fund his building campaign.

Spencer looks at the famous licence to crenellate in context: licences of this kind were mostly awarded to gentry and lesser peerage. The wording is distinctive, authorising him to

> *strengthen with a wall of stone and lime and crenellate and construct and make into a castle his manor house at Bodyham, near the sea in the county of Sussex, for defence of the adjacent county and resistance to our enemies*
>
> (cited in Spencer 2014: 81)

The wording may be to do with his changing relationship with Arundel: Dallingridge wanted to portray himself as leader and protector of the local community at an historical moment when Arundel was unable to do so.

The heraldry above the north and south gates at Bodiam references Dallingridge's political alliances and networks across the political landscape and can be seen as a self-conscious visual expression of those networks (Figs 12.10 & 12.11). Heraldry, by the later 14th century, was a complex visual system expressing and differentiating between different noble and gentry families; its use was closely tied up with elite values of

Fig.12.10: Heraldry above the south gate, Bodiam Castle. Dallingridge's helm above; below, two shields now blank, and between them the arms of Sir Robert Knollys Dallingridge's war captain in France and owner of Derval. Knollys' arms are couché or tilted (i.e. as carried by a mounted knight).

Fig. 12.11: Heraldry above the north gate, Bodiam Castle. Dallingridge's helm above; below, his arms flanked by those of Wardedieu (the family of his wife Elizabeth) and Radynden (the family of his mother Alice).

honour and identity. Dallingridge was without doubt intensely aware of the importance of heraldic symbols in the maintenance of political identities. He testified in the famous Scrope *versus* Grosvenor case, lasting for five years and involving hundreds of witnesses, fighting over who had the right to display the arms *Azure a Bend Or* (Spencer 2014: 84). For Edward's son John Dallingridge, heraldry was a matter of honour serious enough for him to offer to settle a dispute over coats of arms by combat (Saul, Mackman & Whittick 2011).

Above the north gate, then – facing into the Weald – Dallingridge's own arms and helmet were juxtaposed with those of the Wardedieu family from whom he inherited Bodiam, and the local family Radynden; the southern gate – facing towards the river valley, the port, mill and mill pond – again bore Dallingridge's helmet, above the arms of Knollys, his war captain in France.

Elites and Commoners

So far, this discussion has focused on the agency of elite men. However, buildings and landscapes are the product and outcome of the practices of women, men and children of all social classes and identities. Archaeologists and historians often forget this very simple fact, talking of who owned that manor or who built this building.

Commoners most obviously intrude into the documentary narrative told by historians through the narratives of peasant revolts. Sussex and especially Kent were areas that were particularly politically conscious and prone to revolt in the later Middle Ages. Historians have generally attributed this record of disruption to the presence in this area of classes of commoners, in particular relatively affluent and assertive peasants, craftsmen and tradesmen. After the demographic collapse of 1348-9, these commoners took advantage of the shifting balance between the supply of and demand for land and labour. They became much more affluent and politically assertive, seeking to throw off feudal shackles and assert rights that they claimed as customary.

The most famous of these uprisings is the Peasant's Revolt of 1381, in which peasants from Kent and Essex marched on London. The immediate causes of the revolt were various, and it was eventually suppressed; but the peasants' demands included the abolition of serfdom (the unfree status of some peasants), and the revolt is now celebrated as a key event in popular and radical history. The radical cleric John Ball famously preached to the rebels:

> *When Adam dalf, and Eve span, who was thanne a gentilman? From the beginning all men were created equal by nature, and that servitude had been introduced by the unjust and evil oppression of men, against the will of God, who, if it had pleased Him to create serfs, surely in the beginning of the world would have appointed who should be a serf and who a lord*

> (Thomas Walsingham, *Historia Anglicana*, cited in Dobson 1970: 375)

In 1381, after the Peasant's Revolt, Dallingridge played an active part in its suppression and in later commissions to punish those involved (Spencer 2014: 57). Almost as famous is Jack Cade's rebellion of 1450 (most famously, if quite inaccurately, depicted in Shakespeare's Henry VI, in which Cade is eventually killed by the Kentish yeoman Alexander Iden at the Sussex village of Heathfield: Johnson 2010b: 127-8). The Cade rebellion was directed in part at unpopular advisers to the King, of whom Sir James Fiennes was one; he was seized by Cade's followers following their entry into London, given a brief trial, and summarily beheaded, leaving his house at Knole unfinished. Bodiam and Knole, then, were directly involved in the class antagonism of the later Middle Ages; more broadly, all four sites were centres of elite power and authority.

However, these particularly sharp intrusions of commoners into the affairs of elite political history are only the tip of the iceberg. In the Introduction, and in a number of the following chapters, we talked about the idea of lived experience. The theoretical literature behind this concept is vast, and the related concept of phenomenology and its application to landscape archaeology has been highly controversial (a few points in a vast literature are: Tilley 1994; 2004; 2008; Thomas 1999; 2001; Bradley 2000; Ingold 2000; 2010; Brück 2005; Hamilton *et al.* 2006 and Bender *et al.* 2007; for critical assessment see Fleming 2006; Johnson 2007; 2011 and Barrett & Ko 2009).

In the Introduction, we defined lived experience as being about:

- A focus on the everyday – the ordinary routines of work, how people moved around and acted upon landscapes and buildings on a day-to-day basis.
- A focus on the local context – the immediate and regional landscapes around the different sites.
- Meaning as about the subjective experience of different individuals and groups, both elite and commoner, women and men.
- A focus on practice – how the experience of places is bound up with what people do at those places.
- A focus on the senses: how places were experienced through the body.
- Cultural biography and the long term: how buildings and landscapes change through time, at a series of scales, from the daily, weekly, seasonal, to change over millennia.

It is worth pausing for a moment to review why, in the view of this project, understanding lived experience is so important to the study of late medieval buildings and of archaeology generally (see also Johnson 2007; 2010; 2013). One of the key developments in archaeology in the last generation is that it is necessary to explore questions of mentality and of meaning – 'their' view of 'their' world. The problem is that such a project is very difficult. How do we know what is going on between the ears of the person sitting next to us, let alone someone who has been dead for hundreds of years?

A particular problem is the recovery of meaning for different social groups – different classes, different genders, different ages. What the landscape of Scotney may have 'meant' will vary, according to whether one is talking about Roger Ashburnham, a medieval monk, a peasant woman, a visitor from France, one of Ashburnham's children, a household servant…. Each will have had their own view, a viewpoint conditioned by, among other things, their social position, whether and to what degree they were literate, their different experience of Scotney as a place of leisure, a working landscape, or both, and so on.

A second problem has been that an emphasis on lived experience has often been presented, or interpreted by others, as an alternative to an emphasis on environment and ecology. Those advocating a lived-experience approach have often sharply denounced what they see as an inhuman environmental determinism. Conversely, those stressing the environment have seen lived-experience approaches as unduly subjective and disconnected from the 'real world'. Subjective and objective, ideal and material, culture and environment – these are often presented as either/or oppositions. This binary opposition is misleading and unhelpful, just as the military/status opposition has been shown to be misleading and unhelpful.

A third problem: much of the literature has made the misleading claim that lived experience involves a rejection of evidential criteria, that lived experience approaches represent an unwarranted push beyond what can be directly observed. In fact, it represents a return to elements that are more directly observable, particularly if as archaeologists we play to our strengths and take care to think in material, archaeological terms. We can never see 'status' or 'conspicuous consumption', but we can and do see fields, hedges, fences, and the paths and routeways between them.

I reviewed much of this theoretical literature a few years ago (Johnson 2012b), and went on to discuss its application to medieval buildings (Johnson 2012a). One of my conclusions was that new digital technologies offered exciting ways of exploring lived experience, as Catriona Cooper demonstrated in Chapter Nine. A second conclusion was that ideas of lived experience and a stress on economy and ecology in the landscape were often presented as competing, contradictory ideas, but in fact they are complementary. On the one hand, human experience of the landscape is immediately and undeniably subjective. Medieval peasants did not respond to the graphs of climatic deterioration so lovingly compiled by modern historians of climate; they responded to the weather, and to their subjective perception of the weather. On the other hand, the daily routeways and practices of people of all social classes were not somehow ethereal or ritual; they were predominantly those of work, bound up with the hard practical necessities of making a living, often in conditions of great poverty and hardship.

At all four sites, and in the study of medieval buildings more generally, there are particularly good reasons why we should think about lived experience. First, as I observed in the Introduction, much of the debate about medieval buildings has hitherto been unanswerable, in part because it has focused on issues of intention. What did Dallingridge really intend when he built Bodiam? Arguably, we will never know the answer to this question, because 'intention' is a very difficult thing to observe directly. We will never be able to see what was between Dallingridge's ears; his intentions and priorities are unlikely to have remained the same over a ten-year building campaign; and 'intentions' can be unconscious or semi-conscious in nature.

Second, the building and rebuilding of these sites and landscapes was not carried out by single individuals. Bodiam was not, strictly speaking, built by Dallingridge; Knole was not built by Bourchier; all four buildings and landscapes were constructed by a team of skilled and unskilled workers. Anyone who has participated in a major building project, whether as patron, architect, client, craftsman or unskilled labourer, knows that the final result is not so much the product of a single individual volition, and much more a complex and ongoing negotiation between architect, different specialist builders and clients (a point that is brought out well through the interactions of the different craftsmen recorded by the *Time Team* special on the Ightham Mote restoration: https://www.youtube.com/watch?v=4B9WPT5gyNk, accessed 9th May 2016). Major building projects in medieval and early modern England were even more so (Salzman 1952; Airs 1995). The modern idea of architect was a development of the Renaissance, and individual craftsmen brought their own agency and signature to the building, literally so in the case of the more than twelve masons' marks at Bodiam, and more broadly so in terms of the variation in treatment of stylistic and decorative details at all four sites.

Third, all these buildings and landscapes were built and rebuilt, used and reused through time. The later medieval phases of all four sites were structured and constrained by material elements from the deep past, ranging from the natural topography through the traces of several millennia of human settlement, to the presence of earlier buildings on or near the site. Conversely, all four sites were maintained, extended, reused in different ways from the later 14th century onwards. They have a distinctive cultural biography and derive their character, in part, from the reuse and patina of the ages.

Women, Men and Children

We can start by considering the daily paths and practices of different people at Bodiam. These can be mapped out, as they have been in Fig. 12.12, building on the survey results outlined in Chapter Four. We can start with the mill. The precise location of the mill itself was discussed earlier; there is no documentary reference to the identity of the miller but the normative expectation would be that, like most professions in the Middle Ages, he would be male and would live with his family on the site of the mill (Holt 1988). The mill leat, or artificial stream that fed the mill pond, ran for some kilometres to the west, being diverted from the river on the lands of the Abbey of Robertsbridge a few kilometres upstream of Bodiam. Robertsbridge was reached by boat or barge up the river; water flowed from Robertsbridge to power the mill, while patronage from the Dallingridge household flowed in the other direction, as did their deceased bodies destined for burial at the abbey.

The residents of Bodiam village brought their corn here to be ground into flour for bread, but a proportion of the ground flour would be held back for the lord's use, in accordance with manorial sanction and custom. The mill was one way, in classical feudal theory, of extracting rent in the form of flour from tenants (White 1962). Careful analysis of documentary references to milling indicates a great deal of variation around this norm, and a degree of conflict between peasant and lord (Holt 1988: 36-54). So we can visualise women and men carrying sacks of wheat and flour back and forth along the tightly defined causeways to the south of the castle between mill pond and harbour next to the diverted course of the River Rother, and we need to visualise the castle as it was viewed from the south-east not as it is today, sitting in splendid isolation, but as having a watermill in the foreground, either of stone or more likely of timber-framed construction. It must be remembered that a mill was not just a machine – it was a symbol of manorial lordship, prosperity and harmony (as it is presented for example in the Luttrell Psalter: Camille 1998: 212-3) and of a variety of theological and symbolic meanings (Worthen 2006).

Some of these sacks of corn and flour may then have been loaded on to barges and boats at the wharf. Again, the normative expectation would be that harbour masters and manorial officials at the wharf would be men, but the everyday labour may well have been mixed. The wharf was also the nexus of other flows of goods. Fish were probably transported inland from the coast. Iron working took place to the north and quantities of pig iron were probably carried on horses, mules and carts down this Roman road running north-south before being shipped out to the coastal ports of Rye, Winchelsea and the English Channel (Crossley 1981, fig. 29; Cleere & Crossley 1985).

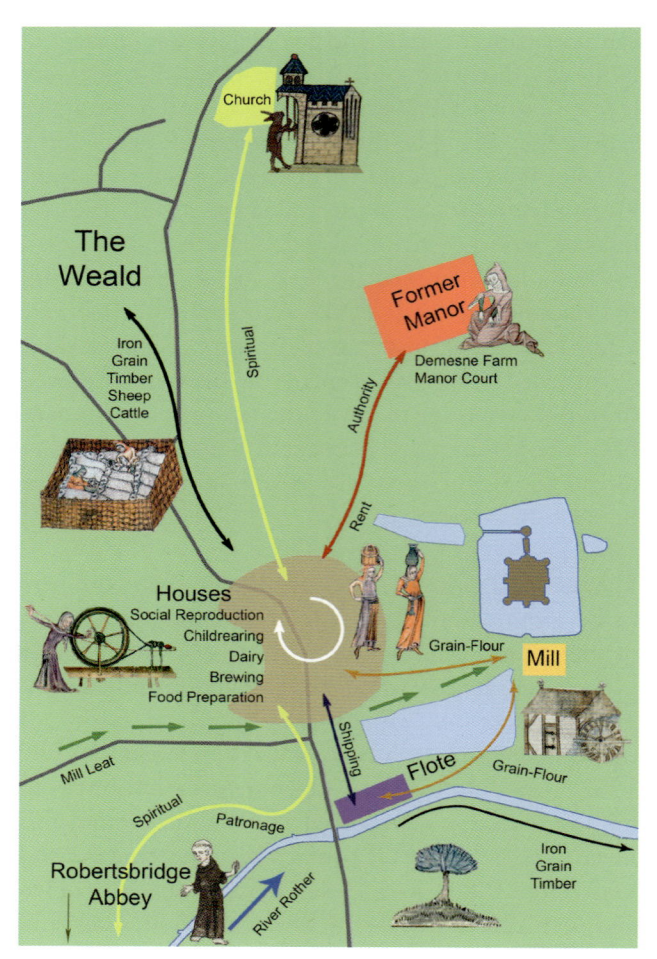

Fig. 12.12: Schematic representation of some of the activities and flows around Bodiam Castle. All images from the Luttrell Psalter (1325-40), © The British Library Board MS42130, apart from the church (Walters Ms. W. 102, Book of Hours, http://creativecommons.org/licenses/by-sa/3.0/legalcode) and monk (MS. Bodl. 264, fol. 22r; The Bodleian Libraries, The University of Oxford).

A third site of work lies at the summit of the slope north of the castle courtyard: the earthworks famously interpreted as a 'viewing platform' overlooking the castle from the north. We have seen that while Dallingridge built the castle, the manorial buildings remained in use as a cluster of farm buildings, and possibly also as stables serving the castle. Most elite buildings of this period have two courts, upper and lower, and here at Bodiam this earlier site had the functions of a lower court, with barn, byre and other buildings. Manorial courts also continued to be held here, at which the officials and the heads of household within the manor would gather to make legal and administrative decisions (Johnson *et al.* 2000: 32).

A fourth site of work was the 'village' itself. As noted in previous chapters, this was more a small row of peasant houses than a typical medieval village. The ladder-like arrangement of property boundaries implied a division into front space and back space – though on this orientation, the houses faced towards the road and turned their backs on the castle. Only one of this row of houses survives from the Middle Ages, the early 16th-century house at the top of the row, a typical house for its time. Its name, 'Ellen Archer's', is likely to be of post-medieval date. These houses acted as nodes that drew in different materials from across the landscape, and then transformed those materials through gendered labour. The Weald was a relatively affluent area in this period, due to the production not just of corn but also dairy products – butter, milk, cheese – also wool and meat from sheep and cattle -- and of course iron. Dairy and industrial products were extracted from the surrounding fields, orchards, and woodlands through the work of women and men, gathered and brought into these households, and there processed. As with the milling and iron production, we have no direct evidence of who participated in such production at Bodiam, but the normative expectation would be that household production of this kind was women's work (Goldberg 1997; Graham 1997). So these houses themselves acted as gendered micro-landscapes, within which women did the cultural work of transforming nature into food and other products for the table and the market.

This discussion has two critical implications for the way we see Bodiam. First, the 'castle' itself appears rather detached from the bulk of this activity. Peasants worked in the fields and in the village, women and men took corn to and from the mill, barges were loaded and unloaded… with the castle itself rather detached, rather like a hole in a doughnut. All of this east-west and north-south activity and movement, the back-and-forth of human bodies, beasts of burden, the carts they were pulling and the goods they were carrying could be monitored from the walls of the castle, but the castle itself, and the elite household inside its walls, could be argued to observe but also to be set apart from this landscape of work.

Rather than seeing Bodiam as a series of facades within a designed, ornamental landscape, I am sketching out for the reader a place where the castle courtyard and towers sat perhaps somewhat in isolation within a busy set of flows of people and goods that moved around their perimeters. The castle is in this sense a set of resources to be drawn upon – the numerous lodgings were probably never fully occupied.

The second implication is that when we start to think about the place in terms of lived experience, it is not at all clear what the term 'the castle' might refer to at Bodiam. The term is generally used to refer to the courtyard, towers and gatehouses, but we have seen that the curtain walls and what they contain may be best seen as an inner court, with stables and other ancillary buildings elsewhere, perhaps up with the manor court on the hill. What is generally termed 'the castle' might be better seen as a kind of large 'gloriette', detached and set off from everyday activities by its moat and elaborate and circuitous entrance arrangements.

We can make very similar observations about later medieval Scotney. We can trace daily paths and practices at Scotney with less confidence, given the very extensive 19th-century re-landscaping and the more ruinous nature of the castle itself. Scotney is also a more difficult and complex landscape to understand given the lack of an adjacent village or settlement; the village of Lamberhurst is a kilometre away. Chapter Seven showed how there are nevertheless traces of water features and the site of a mill in the river valley, and it established the boundaries of a deer park on the ground above and to the west of the castle; and the outer court at Scotney has a collection of farm and other ancillary buildings.

The common denominator at all these sites is that by refocusing comments away from specific institutions often designated through documentary references (manor, demesne, mill), and thinking instead about movements, flows and work practices between these sites, we bring human beings more closely into focus. We see the landscape in dynamic terms, or as what the anthropologist Tim Ingold would call 'taskscapes', rather than simply or only as a series of static institutions (Ingold 2000; Edgeworth 2011). It is also a view of the landscape which resonates strongly with, for example, the idealised image of the medieval estate presented in the Luttrell Psalter, made some decades earlier (Camille 1998).

Designed Landscapes?

Seeing landscapes in terms of lived experience in this way makes a significant contribution to the ongoing debate over the presence and nature of 'designed landscapes' in the late medieval countryside.

If buildings are actually produced through a complex process of collaboration and agency, the same is also true of landscapes. What this means is that, in a sense, all medieval landscapes are designed. Village layouts, field systems, routeways, fishponds and other hydraulic features, are all created, maintained and inhabited through conscious human agency and practice. There is no *a priori* distinction to be drawn between vernacular, working landscapes on the one hand, and polite, 'aesthetic' landscapes on the other. Indeed, one could go further and suggest that modern conceptual divisions of this kind are an historic creation, in part of the Renaissance, in part of the 18th century (Johnson 2007), and as such cannot be meaningfully applied to medieval conceptions of landscape.

In this sense, all four sites sit at the centre of a designed landscape – a designed landscape that is also a working landscape. However, a consideration of lived experience suggests that there were important and subtle differences in the ways landscapes were experienced and understood at different places. Most obviously, the experience of the deer park at Knole was bound up with its association with the world of the Church, as argued in Chapter Seven. The landscape at Ightham, discussed in Chapter Eight, has a complex series of water features, but these may well have been created in a piecemeal fashion, in line with the development by alteration and accretion of the house itself.

Afterlife

The first part of this chapter engaged with the long-term and the way the landscape was structured in terms of geological time and in prehistory – it is equally important to consider the life of all four sites after the later Middle Ages. These are all sites that continued to be inhabited through time, right up to their present role and identity as National Trust properties. As a general theme, long-term cultural biography is an important element of the overall heading of lived experience. In other words, if we are interested in people's embodied understandings of and practices around places, we also need to think about how these understandings and practices changed generation by generation, as different people brought different ideas into dialogue with a place. The process, over the decades and centuries, produced new meanings for any given place – manor house to castle, castle to Renaissance palace, house to Romantic ruin, palace to tourist attraction.

Lived experience also implies maintenance. If places now have well-preserved medieval remains, it is, in part, because they were carefully maintained that way in the centuries after the Middle Ages. At Scotney, Ightham and Bodiam, the water features, left to themselves, would have partially or totally silted up over time. Maintenance of this kind is itself a meaningful action, implying a sense of memory and continuity and, of course, necessitating substantial financial and labour input. Again, at Knole, the medieval deer park survives and continues to be maintained, albeit in a heavily modified form.

Ightham is a place with a strong image of continuity: guidebooks and popular accounts see this as a place where little happened. This perception is linked to its isolated location and lack of ambitious owners, a place that each generation has rebuilt and reformed, without the site undergoing a radical transformation. The discussion in Chapter Seven implies that this is not the whole story at Ightham. First, the medieval landscape should not necessarily be seen in terms of the isolated and secluded setting that we see today, with its dominant tree cover. The 3D topographical reconstruction showed us that different approach routes, both along the east side and the west side of the valley, may well have commanded important views at critical points in the landscape, Second, the house was significantly expanded towards the end of the 15th century when it acquired an outer courtyard; the main approach to the house was altered by these new buildings and there is the possibility that this major transformation was accompanied by changes in the surrounding watery landscape.

Scotney was transformed from a castle/fortified house in the 1630s by the wholesale rebuilding of the central range into a Classically-proportioned building (Martin *et al.* 2011; 2012). This building was never finished, leaving Scotney for some centuries as a collection of fragments. With the laying-out of the 'picturesque' landscape of Scotney, and the building of the New House, the old castle became an element of that landscape. The modern visitor to Scotney descends from the New House into this secluded area, tucked away and partially hidden by trees, and accompanied now by a Henry Moore statue on the adjacent island.

Bodiam appears, at first sight, to be a classic single-phase site. However, we saw in Chapter Three how the building itself may well have been occupied into the earlier 17th century, and went through several significant phases of restoration. The castle is covered with thousands of graffiti. The graffiti are important markers of identity in their own right; they include a member of the Shelley family, and a Canadian soldier from the first world war (Cooper 2010).

The successive restorations and alterations of all four sites from the 18th century onwards tie all four sites in to a much wider set of colonial and national relations. Bodiam was restored in the 1830s and again in the 1920s. In 1829, it was saved from destruction and purchased by John 'Mad Jack' Fuller. Some of Fuller's accounts survive; they indicate that he made a substantial financial input into the restoration of the castle and the re-landscaping of its setting, though the specifics of the work that he financed are difficult to trace with certainty on the ground (Holland 2011). Fuller owned the nearby estate at Brightling, where he built a series of follies. The Fuller family's wealth came from a combination of interests in gun manufacture and in plantations in Jamaica (Crossley & Saville 1991); Fuller owned 44 slaves at the St Catherine and 209 slaves at the St Thomas-in-the-Vale estates (https://www.ucl.ac.uk/lbs/search/, accessed 11th June 2015). Fuller was Member of Parliament for Sussex and spoke in the House of Commons against the abolition of slavery, making the claim that many slaves in the Caribbean lived in better conditions that 'were equal, nay superior, to the condition of the labouring poor of this country' (http://www.oxforddnb.com/view/article/39364?docPos=4, accessed 11th August 2015). Fuller was known as an 'eccentric' and continues to attract a cult following, with a local Morris dancing team named after him.

The restoration of Bodiam by Lord Curzon can also be argued to tie into global and colonial themes. Curzon was Viceroy of India between 1899 and 1906. At the end of his tenure, Curzon returned to British politics as a Conservative and Unionist; the restoration work at Bodiam in the 1920s unfolded while he was a key player in national politics, a senior figure in the Tory party and the House of Lords. Curzon restored a series of 'national monuments', including Walmer, Bodiam, Tattershall, Kedleston and Montacute House; the latter four he bequeathed to the National Trust.

At this time of his viceroyship, British colonial administration in India expressed itself culturally through 'ornamentalism', including architectural references to castles and other medieval monuments (Cannadine 2001). Curzon passed an Ancient Monuments Bill providing for the restoration of the Taj Mahal and other monuments, and creating the post of Director-General of Archaeology, subsequently and famously occupied by Sir Mortimer Wheeler. David Cannadine argues that British imperial administrators saw their colonial subjects not as exotic or 'other', but rather in the same terms as the British lower classes. There is certainly a hint of paternalistic imperialism in Curzon's comments on his attempted drainage of the 'tiltyard' (actually mill pond) and his desire to bring the civilising game of cricket to the Bodiam villagers:

> *The Tilt Yard gave a good deal more trouble… Cherishing the innocent belief that this piece of ground, if drained and levelled and turfed, would provide an excellent cricket ground or recreation ground for the village, I set about its reclamation.*

DISCUSSION

The result was a disastrous failure... my praiseworthy desires for the recreation of my fellow-parishioners at Bodiam have proved altogether abortive...
(Curzon 1926: 100-1)

Scotney and Ightham were also heavily re-landscaped in the 19th century. In all three cases, re-landscaping along 'picturesque' principles involved the creation of expanses of grassland, areas of woodland, the careful setting of the building at the centres of views, and the layout of pathways and carriage drives designed to show off the site and landscape sequentially and to best effect. The landscapes created appear natural, but are in fact the product of human artifice. Given that this is the case, it is not surprising that scholars visiting these sites – Bodiam in particular -- have been immediately attracted to ideas of carefully manipulated views and contrived settings.

Knole is the exception here; its landscape does not have the appearance of being transformed in the 19th century. Such a statement does need to be heavily qualified: there are a number of buildings, paths and routeways that have been laid out, much of the estate now has a substantial estate wall, and the inner area of the gardens has been subject to continual transformation over the centuries. Knole's relative lack of transformation in terms of both its landscape and the building itself after the early 17th century is, of course, part of the identity of the place, most famously celebrated in Virginia Woolf's *Orlando: A Biography* (Woolf 1928), routinely cited as a feminist and modernist classic, in which the eponymous hero(ine) is seemingly blessed with immortality but who changes from a man to a woman part way through the book. Knole is Orlando's country seat and is the central and defining place in the novel; at times, the 'biography' in the title seems to refer as much to the place as to Orlando him/herself.

Bodiam, Scotney, Knole and Ightham should be thought about in terms of their key and distinctive location in the landscape; their nature as landscapes of work and of movement of a diversity of social classes and identities; and their change and persistence over the long term, and at a series of scales. The survey results from all four sites, when combined with the 'grey literature' and our understanding of the wider landscape, paint a compelling picture of these elite sites in terms of their lived experience. It only remains in the Conclusion to make some comments about the wider theoretical parameters within which this understanding should be set.

13

CONCLUSION

Matthew Johnson

Abstract. This chapter presents some concluding thoughts on the main themes addressed in this volume, and intellectual background and context of the project. The main themes of the volume are reviewed and their implications for the study of buildings and landscape enumerated, with particular attention to the way a diversity of viewpoints informed the research process. Finally, I make some suggestions for future thought and research.

The programme of research reported on in this volume had the initial aim of conducting archaeological survey at four high-status later medieval buildings and landscapes in south-east England, all owned and managed by the National Trust. As it has developed, the intellectual themes of the project have broadened and deepened. Themes we have explored in this volume have been gathered together under the umbrella term 'lived experience', and include the following:

First, the landscapes of work, of practice, and of everyday activity and life (Robin 2013; Overholtzer & Robin 2015). We have moved beyond the discussion of individual intentions of elite owners and builders, to focus on how landscapes were implicated in the activities and patterns of cultural life of people of different social classes and identities. We see these landscapes as being 'vernacular' as well as 'polite', that is, as created and coming into being through the everyday actions of different groups of people as much as through the conscious design of elite individuals. In the process, our work has come to engage with some of the issues of definition behind the term 'designed landscapes' (Liddiard & Williamson 2008; Creighton 2009). Collaborative discussion of our findings, over the years of the project, has led us to stress how landscapes should not be seen as either aesthetic or functional, either designed or everyday, just as castles should not be seen as either defensive or symbolic.

Second, the long-term history of these places: their antecedents and other properties of the landscape that structured how they were experienced and modified, stretching back to the geological history of the Weald and adjacent areas. We see these places as having certain enduring characteristics, particular forms of first and second nature. These characteristics afforded and enableed particular kinds of livelihoods, political structures and social strategies to develop and persist.

Third, the landscape settings of all four sites, their local and regional geography and sets of affordances. We suggest that the Weald and adjacent areas should be seen not just as different kinds of region, but also bound together by this difference and the complementarities of that difference, between Weald and marsh, greensand and chalk downs. Wider understanding of places within a regional context and pattern enables us to understand them comparatively. In other words, it helps us grasp their similarities and differences one to another, and move beyond telling particular just-so stories about particular places to draw comparisons on a wider canvas, with later medieval buildings and landscapes across Britain and Europe, and with elite sites across the world.

As outlined in Chapter Twelve what links these three themes together is an understanding of scale. We have come to see scale is an important means of linking different insights together. Our analysis has run from the very small scale (the minute actions of washing one's hands in the Bodiam chapel piscina, different details of the building process) through the immediate landscape and regional setting of each building, to its place within a national and international setting. Chapter Twelve set the landscape of south-east England within an understanding of the British Isles as a whole.

As outlined in the Introduction, the project began its intellectual life around 2008-2009 in more narrow terms, as part of a desire to move the scholarly understanding of Bodiam Castle forward, beyond the rather stale and tired debates over defence versus status. In this sense, the project started as an exploration of some of the ideas outlined in *Behind the Castle Gate* (Johnson 2002). As the study developed, and moved beyond Bodiam to encompass the sites and landscapes of Scotney, Knole and Ightham, our engagement with the evidence increasingly addressed propositions and ideas posited in *Ideas of Landscape* (Johnson 2007), most specifically the later chapters of that book where I argue for the application of ideas of practice, lived experience and a comparative approach to the landscape archaeology and history of medieval and historic England. One intellectual thread of this project, then, has been to revisit the theoretical perspectives outlined in that earlier work and to feed forward lessons learned into a fully fledged and large-scale programme of empirical research.

However, to present the work in this way is to underplay the degree to which the project as it developed has been a collaborative and team effort. It has evolved mainly through the fieldwork, research activities and collaborations, and formal and informal conversations between scholars of different ages, backgrounds and institutional affiliations. It is therefore appropriate to end this book with a few thoughts about the ways in which our collaborative working practices impacted on the intellectual vision underpinning the original project work plan and suggest some implications for archaeological theory and interpretation as a whole.

The first observation I offer is that the progress and intellectual development of our project from 2009 onwards can be understood as an exercise in pragmatism. I do not mean here the popular or colloquial use of the term 'pragmatism'; rather, I am referring to the philosophical framework developed by Charles Sanders Pierce, John Dewey and others in North America. Pragmatism as a philosophy holds that the first principle in evaluating an argument is to ask about its practical consequences. In its modern form, as applied to programmes of research, pragmatism tends to foreground the importance of a diversity of approaches and knowledge claims, to be suspicious of grand claims of an absolute Truth, and to advocate collaborative and engaged approaches in which different stakeholders contribute to the process (Baert 2005; Preucel & Mrozowski 2010).

The project can be seen as an exercise in pragmatism in various ways. First, an important element in the development of the project was the diversity of stakeholders, and the importance of listening to and reflecting on the views and opinions of a variety of voices. In Chapter Two, for example, the work of local archaeologists and historians from a diversity of backgrounds and orientations was central in forging a new understanding of Bodiam by drawing on the 'grey literature' before 2010. In Chapter Eleven, Becky Peacock discussed how public engagement was built into the project from the start, and how amateur and other groups played a role, including local societies and National Trust staff and volunteers. These views were critical to a developing engagement with place and region as it was and is understood within a local context.

Referencing grey literature and talking to the authors of that literature has informed both the interpretation and understanding of our results. For those readers unfamiliar with this term, examples of the grey literature can be found posted on our project website at http://sites.northwestern.edu/medieval-buildings/. The grey literature consists of studies produced in the context of conservation management plans, reports on small-scale excavations in advance of development work, 'watching briefs' in which archaeologists observe the digging of features like sewer and building trenches. Such reports are characteristically commissioned by the 'client', in the case of the material dealt with in this volume the National Trust, on a contractual or freelance basis.

This grey literature was not simply or only an objective recording of evidence; it told a complex and intimate story of different individuals' very deep and often passionate engagement with the buildings and landscapes that were the subject of the reports. Reports were often researched and written by local scholars, who had a stake in the results that was far more than simply professional or contractual obligation. Consequently, the grey literature often went far beyond its brief and presented a great deal of high-quality research and scholarly insight. With it came a personal narrative of enquiry and debate.

The quality of the grey literature, and the compelling nature of the story it had to tell, is perhaps most evocatively illustrated by an example from Ightham. Restoration work that led to Ightham being dubbed the 'ten million pound house' generated a series of volumes lovingly prepared by Peter Leach (Leach n.d., a-f) before his untimely death. These volumes presented an incredibly detailed, minute enquiry into every nook and cranny of the old house that was a labour of love. Grey literature produced a few years later showed that analysis of the garden and surrounding landscape was the subject of a lively debate between Peter Rumley and the great landscape archaeologist Christopher Taylor, with the latter pouring a large bucket of cold water on arguments for a 'designed landscape' and deer park at Ightham (Ford & Rutherford 2009, appendix 10). Reading through the grey literature in the archives at Ightham, being witness to the passions and enthusiasms of different engaged scholars, in an attic high up in the warren of rooms that comprise the building, was one of the most memorable experiences of the whole project.

In this and other ways, our project also illustrated the argument made by many archaeologists that survey and recording methods are not neutral techniques that deliver sets of objective data; each is bound up with a particular way of seeing, engaging with and 'understanding' the landscape (Gillings & Pollard 1998; Bowden 2000; Lucas 2012). One of the most rewarding aspects of the project from my perspective was the opportunity to bring together students, professionals and academics from across Britain and North America. As such, the project was a case study in the ways in which archaeologists from different educational backgrounds and archaeological traditions interpret survey techniques and methods used by different researchers who come to these places. These particular ways of seeing are partly subjective, partly culturally framed – either way the interplay between them is particularly productive of new insights.

One such insight occurred, for example, around the production and viewing of the hachured plan (the paradigmatic example being Fig. 1.2), and the different topographical and geophysical surveys that have formed the core of this volume. The hachured plan mode is characteristic of much of British landscape archaeology's way of seeing. Researchers look at and engage with a landscape analytically before making a judgement about where the hachures begin and end, and making a judgement, however preliminary, about the overall interpretation of the site. Consequently, this way of seeing and mapping is capable of very nuanced and subtle judgements about what is in the landscape, but it arguably puts the 'interpretation' first and the recording second. Further, the interpretation tends to consist of identification of features whose morphology is recognisable and capable of being placed in a typology (this must be a lynchet, that must be a terrace, this is a tenement boundary, etc.; discussed further in Johnson 2007: 93-5).

Some of my North American collaborators were quite sceptical of the very slight humps and bumps that some archaeologists from outside the team working in the British tradition claimed to be seeing, and that are quintessentially expressed in Fig. 1.2. Conversely, outside observers of our work sometimes expressed the view that while our results were invaluable at a larger scale, some of the very subtle breaks in slope that others were interested in might not be picked up through the necessarily coarse resolution of large-scale topographic survey. These differences in perspective, stemming in part from different national training, have a very direct influence on what people 'see' in the landscape, and even on 'what everybody knows' about it. Others have explored this observation as it applied to different national traditions in excavation techniques (Edgeworth 2006; Leighton 2015).

New views of castles and other elite sites have sometimes been termed 'revisionist' (Platt 2007). My experience of working with an international team led me to reflect more fully on the term 'revisionism', and to conclude that the term as applied to castle studies is misleading. Revisionism is a term often used in documentary history, and generally applied to the development of different views or interpretations of specific historical episodes (for example on the battle of Agincourt by Anne Curry: Curry 2005, or the English Civil War by John Morrill and others: Morrill 1984). As such, revisionism is a term that denotes a changing or sharply opposing historical view, but within an accepted framing or paradigm of historical explanation. In other words, apparent controversies nevertheless reflect an underlying consensus on method, on what constitutes legitimate evidence or accepted modes of argument.

Our view of medieval buildings and landscapes, for better or worse, is much more than revisionist. The four buildings and landscapes that we have studied offer an understanding of the complexity, subtlety, and difference of the past. Their fascination for us derives not just from their aesthetic properties, or their offer of an intellectual puzzle, but from the capacity of these places to challenge accepted understandings and to prompt new ways of thinking, from the long-term histories behind a castle landscape to the aural qualities of a medieval hall to the question of 'what do moated sites do?'.

One of the main goals of this project was to develop an evidence-based understanding of medieval sites and their contexts in terms that might bring different elements of current landscape approaches together in a sustained and rigorous way. In the opening chapter I identified political economy and ecology as a method to work through, an intellectual complement to lived experience. Political ecology is a set of approaches which thinks about how the landscape is the product of both human and natural processes, and seeks to question how both are defined in respect to each other. It sees nature not as some pre-existing 'given' to which human respond, but rather as humanly constructed in its turn. As befits its title, political ecology gives particular prominence to issues of power and inequality, and the relationship of environmental and landscape change to different political processes. Like 'lived experience', political ecology can be a fuzzy concept, set of ideas or even seen as a particular kind of argument (Robbins 2012: xii). Political ecology has been defined by Robbins as:

> ... not a method nor theory, nor even a single perspective. Rather... political ecology is an urgent kind of argument or text... that examines winners and losers, is narrated using dialectics, begins and/or ends in a contradiction, and surveys both the status of nature and stories about the status of nature
> (2012: vii)

Other writers in this tradition highlight the importance of bringing together different scales of analysis, both through time and across space.

In this volume, while we have been attentive to different kinds of building, landscape and environmental evidence, and to the need to tie those strands of evidence together, a full and complete account of the interaction and implications of each approach is still a work in progress. Indeed, viewed retrospectively, this volume has barely begun to scratch the surface of what a political ecology of south-east England in the later Middle Ages might look like. By focusing on 'elite sites', for example, our volume could be argued to examine only the 'winners'. By definition, issues of the diversity of social classes and of social contestation are refracted through the legacy managed for us by the National Trust at all four places – it is a challenge for us, as archaeologists and heritage managers, to see beyond this. Whilst we start the process of sampling the landscape and environment and revisiting the multiple relationships between humans and nature over time, our study cannot really be called 'dialectical' in the full philosophical sense of that term, and the 'status of nature' was not interrogated in any sustained theoretical fashion. One might console oneself with the thought that others have yet to bring all these strands together.

The constituent elements are all there: the comparative archaeology of political landscape is a well-developed field (Ashmore & Knapp 1999; Smith 2003). Studies of landscape and settlement in medieval England represent a huge empirical achievement (Roberts & Wrathmell 2002; Rippon 2008; Roberts 2008). There has been close attention to changes in the environment, and a vigorous debate over 'social versus environmental' explanations of medieval rural settlement (Williamson 2004; Jones & Page 2006; Williamson et al. 2013). Interpretations of medieval buildings have moved away from the aesthetic value judgments of traditional art-historical models and towards a fuller grasp of their place within medieval society and culture (Johnson 2010b). The political ecology of modern capitalist societies and colonial contexts is well developed (Robbins 2012).

A sustained theoretical project of this kind is an exciting prospect, but it is for the future. The fieldwork we have completed and reported on here will inform and sustain such a project. The next step requires a sustained intellectual endeavour to generate a theoretically informed understanding of medieval buildings, an understanding fully integrated into changing landscapes of human practice and experience, environmental change, and political inequality.

If Bodiam, Scotney, Knole and Ightham have taught us anything, it is that there is so much more to learn.

APPENDIX 1

SUMMARY AND GUIDE TO ARCHAEOLOGICAL FINDS FROM BODIAM CASTLE

Kathryn A. Catlin

Excavations at Bodiam

The finds from Bodiam have been collected under various circumstances, formal and informal, over the 20th and 21st centuries. Excavations, survey, and collecting can be divided roughly into two phases: excavations that occurred prior to 1994, when the Scheduled Ancient Monument boundary was extended to include the landscape setting and grounds (Johnson *et al.* 2000, appendix four), and those that have occurred in the years since, most of which comprise watching briefs, mitigation activities, and geophysical survey. The total artefact collection also includes miscellaneous, largely unprovenanced finds made by individuals over the last three centuries, including tenants and property owners of the Bodiam estate.

The finds and their current locations are summarised in Table A1.A. For additional information about where the finds are currently held, the interested reader is referred to an earlier version of this chapter that was submitted to the National Trust in 2015 in the form of an unpublished report (Catlin 2015).

18th- and 19th-century collection

It is probable that numerous artefacts were collected prior to Curzon's excavations. No specific record of such early finds is known aside from, first, the cannon or field piece that has come to be known as the 'Bodiam Bombard' and second an oak dug-out canoe that was found in the river Rother near Bodiam Bridge in 1836 (Drury & Copeman 2016: 25).

Curzon's 1926 report on his excavation and survey work at Bodiam includes reference to a 'stone-throwing mortar' that was found in the moat prior to 1824, while the Websters held the land (1723-1829) (Curzon 1926: 95). Nineteenth-century references to this object are somewhat scattered and contradictory, but it was certainly at Bodiam prior to an 1825 publication, and resided in the Great Hall at Battle Abbey by the 1840s (Smith & Brown 1989). In 1862 it was purchased by the Woolwich Rotunda Museum (now the Royal Artillery Museum), where it is currently on display (Fig. A1.1).

The gun, which has been referred to either as the 'Bodiam Bombard' or the 'Bodiam Mortar', was constructed of both wrought and cast iron, a combination which may reflect early experimentation with casting: a 'missing link' between wrought and cast iron (Smith & Brown 1989: 16). It is likely that the mortar was constructed in Sussex, perhaps as late as the 16th century, though there is some disagreement as to the date and the provenance; some scholars have suggested that it could have been made on the Continent, and perhaps as early as c. 1350 (Smith & Brown 1989; Les Smith, pers. comm. 2015; Dan Spencer, pers. comm. 2015). A battle at Bodiam makes a compelling story, and indeed, the castle was briefly the site of action in 1483, during the Wars of the Roses. Though it could have been present at the siege, examination of the mortar has suggested it was most probably never fired (Smith & Brown 1989).

A canoe found in the river Rother in 1836 was likely associated with the underlying Bronze Age peat deposits. It disintegrated almost as soon as it was removed. The

APPENDIX 1

Table A1.A: Excavations, finds, and archived locations as of 2015.

Date	Excavator	Finds	Dates	Location	Citation
18th-19th century	Websters?	Bombard, possibly other finds	c. 15th century	Firepower Royal Artillery Museum	Curzon 1926: 95; Smith & Brown 1989
1836	Fuller?	Bronze Age canoe from the river Rother	Bronze Age	No longer extant	Drury & Copeman 2016: 25, 157
1902	unknown	Pre-Roman cinerary urns (1 survives)	50 BCE-ACE 50	Bodiam Castle	Johnson et al. 2000: 26; Whistler 1940
1919-1920	Curzon & Weir	Building materials; metals (iron, lead, pewter, copper, coins); leather; stone tracery; glass; coins; assorted pottery; faunals; tobacco pipes; cannon balls	13th-20th century	Bodiam Castle	Curzon 1926; Gardiner et al. 1994; Myres 1935
1959-1960	Wingrove Payne	Roman finds	Roman	Battle Museum (probable)	Anonymous 1959-60; Cornwell et al. 2010; Priestley-Bell & Pope 2009: 4
1959-1960	Lemmon & Darrell Hill	Roman finds	Roman	Battle Museum (probable)	Lemmon & Darrell Hill 1966
1960	Puckle & Oliver	Roman road	Roman	Hastings Museum (probable)	Puckle 1960; Walling pers. comm. 2013
1961-1966?	Darrell Hill	Unknown finds from Gun Garden	unknown	Battle Museum (probable)	Darrell Hill 1960-61; Johnson 2002: 26; Taylor et al. 1990: 157
1970	David Martin	Building materials; metals (keys, nails, copper, pewter, iron); stone (tracery, whetstone); assorted pottery; faunals; tobacco pipes; wood	13th-19th century	Bodiam Castle	Gardiner et al. 1994; Martin 1973
1970s	Gwen Jones	Roman and medieval pottery	unknown	unknown	James & Whittick 2008
1990	David Martin	Finds from the moated homestead site	13th-14th century	Hastings Museum (probable)	Martin 1990; Walling pers. comm. 2013
1995	Archaeology South-East (ASE)	Pottery; tile; flint; coin	Mesolithic-20th century	unknown	Barber 2007b; Stevens 1995; 1999
1998	ASE	Assorted pottery; building materials (tile, brick); iron; glass; faunals; ballast flint	13th-19th century	Bodiam Castle	Barber 1998
2005	ASE	Portcullis sample	1280-1410	Bodiam Castle	Martin & Martin 2005; Thackray & Bailey 2007
2007	ASE	Roman tiles; assorted pottery; building materials; tile; glass	14th-20th century	unknown; initially stored at ASE Ditchling	Barber 2007a; b
2009	ASE	Assorted pottery; tiles; faunals; leather and timber (6th century)	13th-20th century	unknown; ASE Portslade?	Priestley-Bell & Pope 2009
2009	ASE	Assorted pottery; building materials (tile, brick)	16th-19th century	unknown; ASE Portslade?	Grant et al. 2009
2010	Hastings Area Archaeological Research Group (HAARG)	Roman iron; Mesolithic flint; tile; ceramic	Mesolithic-14th century	East Sussex County Archaeology Office	Cornwell et al. 2010

207

Fig. A1.1: Bodiam mortar, on a modern carriage at the Royal Artillery Museum. Image courtesy of the Royal Artillery Historical Trust. Photo by L. Smith 2015.

remains were on display at the castle for several years but no trace now remains (Drury & Copeman 2016: 25, 157).

Early 20th century

Several cremation burials were found behind the Old Rectory in 1902, dated to between 50 BCE and CE 50 or possibly a little later (Whistler 1940; Johnson *et al.* 2000: 26; Thackray & Bailey 2007: 5-6; Cornwell *et al.* 2010: 3-4). Only one urn survives; it is part of the permanent Bodiam collection.

Lord Curzon's excavations during 1919/1920 led to some of the most varied finds from the site, including several coins; keys, spurs, and other metal objects; assorted pottery; shoes; and numerous other finds dating from the medieval period and later (Fig. A1.2; Curzon 1926: 157-9; Myres 1935).

1960s-1980s

Several archaeological investigations occurred in the Bodiam landscape between 1959 and 1966. Numerous Romano-British finds were collected from the vicinity of the Roman road, mostly on the floodplain to the south of the castle at Frerens Meade (the field acquired by the Trust in 2006, sometimes known as The Saltings) (Fig. A1.3; anonymous 1959-60; Puckle 1960; Lemmon & Darrell Hill 1966). Additional excavations were carried out south of Court Lodge, exposing finds of Roman, medieval, and later origin (Darrell Hill 1960-61; Lemmon 1960-61; Taylor *et al.* 1990: 157; M.H. Johnson 2002: 26). The moated site north of the castle was partially excavated in 1964 and 1970 (Martin 1990: 89).

In 1970, the National Trust contracted with South Eastern Archaeological Services (now Archaeology South-East) to drain the moat and conduct an excavation of the bridge and abutments under David Martin's direction (Martin 1973). The project led to detailed publications on the construction of the moat and bridges as well as some finds. Later in the 1970s, Gwen Jones carried out some field walking at Freren Meade and collected a small amount of Romano-British and medieval pottery (James & Whittick 2008: 4).

Several survey projects through the 1980s did not result in any recorded artefact finds (Taylor *et al.* 1990; James & Whittick 2008: 4; Holland 2011: 6).

1990s and 2000s

The last 25 years have seen a series of watching briefs, mitigation projects, survey reports, and geophysical prospection within the property at Bodiam. Most of

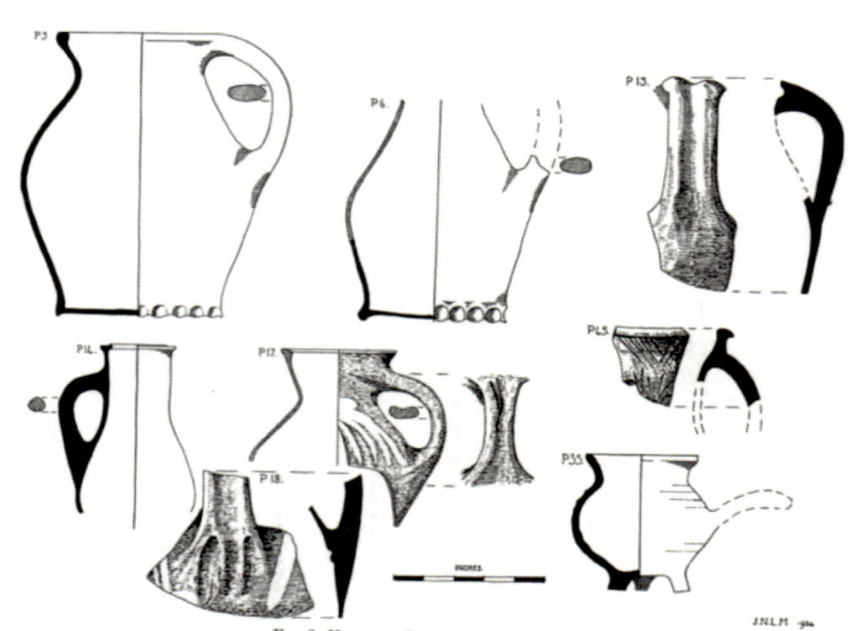

Fig. A1.2: Selection of pottery finds from Curzon's excavations. Reproduced from Myres (1935: 224).

Fig. A1.3: Selection of Roman-period finds, now held at the Battle Museum. Image courtesy of Battle Museum,. Photo by Kathryn Catlin.

these have been undertaken by Archaeology South-East (ASE), with the exception of a recent geophysical survey carried out by the University of Southampton/Northwestern University (this volume). Watching briefs in 1995 (Priestley-Bell), 1996 (Speed), 1999 (Johnson), 2002 (C. Johnson), and 2003 (Johnson) do not appear to have resulted in any finds.

In 1995, ASE sectioned part of the moat bank in order to describe its stratigraphy prior to alterations to the bank and visitor pathways (Stevens 1999). Limited finds dated from the Mesolithic (one flint core) to the 20th century (one 1936 penny).

A 1998 (Barber) watching brief on the installation of a new sewage treatment plant near the car park resulted in a relatively large collection of finds, mostly from the 18th and 19th centuries, but some tile, earthenware, and other artefacts most probably date to the late 15th or 16th century. A single pottery sherd dates to the late 13th century.

A 2007 (Barber 2007a) watching brief on drainage works recovered some Roman tiles, 14th-15th-century pottery and some 17th-century debris (Priestley-Bell & Pope 2009).

A further 2007 watching brief (Barber 2007b) followed the collapse of a portion of the moat bank and the loss of several trees during a storm. At the same time, the interior of the hall of the castle was partially excavated in advance of laying a new gravel surface to support visitor traffic. Small amounts of pottery, tile, glass, and other finds from the 17th-20th centuries were recovered.

In 2009 ASE carried out an evaluation of the Rose Garden (the two lots to the north of the modern tea room) prior to additional drainage and sewage works. Finds ranged from the 6th to the 20th century, including timbers and leather dated to the 6th century, and assorted pottery and tiles (Priestley-Bell & Pope 2009: 17).

A second watching brief in 2009 related to the extension of the car park (Grant *et al.* 2009) resulted in a small box of finds, mostly from the 16th-19th centuries.

Some surface finds were collected during an independent geophysical survey of the Roman road through Dokes Field in 2010 by the Hastings Area Archaeological Research Group (Cornwell *et al.* 2010). These included Roman iron, a Mesolithic flint, and some 14th-century ceramics.

Find Locations

The majority of finds are in storage or on display at Bodiam Castle. These include the majority of Curzon's finds, finds from the 1970 moat excavation, assorted individual finds from the property and wider landscape, and finds from the 1998 sewage project. Also at the castle are a collection of Roman finds, the pre-Roman urn discovered in 1902, and a large collection of tiles. The castle's collection may also include finds from earlier excavations that have been merged with those of Lord Curzon, as well as finds from recent Archaeology South-East projects that have been remitted to the National Trust. Records stored at the castle include a finds catalogue compiled by Gardiner and Barber in 1994 and four boxes of accession cards and photos, documenting both finds and paper archival records as of c. 1989.

Battle Museum of Local History holds numerous Romano-British finds from the 1960s excavations at Bodiam.

Hastings Museum and Art Gallery holds a box of finds from the Bodiam Moated Homestead site (Martin 1990), as well as some finds from excavations in the 1960s, from the Roman road and/or medieval features (e.g. anonymous 1959-60; Lemmon 1960-61; Lemmon & Darrell Hill 1966; Puckle 1960; Walling pers. comm. 12th August 2013). It may also hold at least one of Fuller's fundraising medallions (Bailey pers. comm. 7th August 2013).

The Royal Artillery Museum houses the mortar that was found in the moat at Bodiam during the early 18th century.

Collections from several excavations and watching briefs between 1990 and 2010 may be held at the ASE archives or at a local museum (e.g. Grant *et al.* 2009: 8).

The Finds in Context

Each individual component of the finds collection is small. This is typical of sites like Bodiam, where excavation and artefact collection have largely occurred on an as-needed basis. Taken together, the assemblage comprises an invaluable resource for developing a narrative of the lives, occupations, and priorities of those who lived in and around Bodiam over the past two millennia. The finds provide a potential glimpse into the minutiae of day-to-day, ordinary encounters with objects, and can therefore serve as a fundamentally material way to address the long-term rhythms and cycles of work across the landscape of Bodiam.

The scope of the project reported in this volume did not include an in-depth analysis of the finds. However, several possible future projects might incorporate the finds into an integrated analysis of Bodiam's history and landscape. The finds have the potential to expand and enrich what is known about the history of Bodiam and its landscape, including the importance of the river Rother to the Roman period settlement and trade, the economics and practicalities of daily life on a medieval English manor, and the recent history of the site's excavation and its use as a popular destination for tourism, recreation, and education.

Together with published environmental and landscape reconstructions of the Rother Valley and the Bodiam property (this volume; Burrin & Scaife 1988; Waller *et al.* 1988; Pope *et al.* 2009; Priestley-Bell & Pope 2009; Barker *et al.* 2012), the finds enrich the existing narrative of environmental and social change to build a more complete picture of the combined social and environmental landscapes of Bodiam. The finds include a variety of items from around the world, marking medieval Bodiam as a site of international commerce. The pottery and tiles may hold particular potential, if they can be sourced stylistically, chemically, or by thin-section analysis. Were the tiles imported from a significant distance? Or were they perhaps produced on site during the construction of the castle? Excavation to the south-west of the castle might suggest whether there is any connection between the tiles and the magnetic dipolar anomalies seen in the geophysics (this volume; Barker *et al.* 2012). Finds from excavations in the Roman harbour and the medieval flote could show how trade and consumer behaviour changed over time, likewise shedding light on the changing connections between Bodiam and the rest of the world. The post-medieval finds may suggest the extent of Bodiam's involvement with the Atlantic trade, and can bring to light the experiences of those who worked upon and enjoyed the picturesque landscape in the 19th and early 20th centuries before the National Trust's stewardship began.

Examinations of individual faunal assemblages have so far concluded that each collection is too small to be of interest (e.g. Priestley-Bell & Pope 2009: 21). If the collections were taken together, an examination of the combined faunal assemblage might show illuminating instances of butchery marks or presence of certain species at a particular time even if minimum counts or statistical analyses are not feasible. If available, a comparison with the finds collections of another estate of similar size and date, such as Scotney or Iden, would help to contextualise Bodiam's place within the social world of medieval East Sussex and Kent.

The excavation, distribution, and organisation of the finds over the last hundred years adds a modern component to the biographies of the objects in the collection. The history of the collections tells an interesting story about the changes in archaeological and curatorial practice over the course of the 20th century, both in terms of scientific methodologies and the kinds of artefacts and other evidence that have been deemed sufficiently interesting and informative to keep, store, and display, as well as the research priorities of the various supporting institutions. Numerous individuals who have worked with the Bodiam material, including for example Curzon and J.N.L. Myres, are significant figures in the development of medieval archaeology over the course of the 20th century.

The existing finds hold significant potential for the development of a multi-faceted research project that would explore medieval economies and practices, changes in the perception of the landscape over time, and the changing nature of archaeological and curatorial practices in the 20th century. Additional finds that might result from future excavation would add to the research potential of the collection, whether necessary watching briefs or more extensive archaeological investigation (see Drury & Copeman 2016).

APPENDIX 2

A LAYPERSON'S ACCOUNT OF SURVEY TECHNIQUES

Kathryn A. Catlin, Kristian Strutt[1]

A number of different survey techniques can be applied by archaeologists to record the signatures of surface and sub-surface archaeological structures, remains, and features. The survey work reported on in this volume included both topographic and geophysical survey tied to high accuracy Global Positioning System measurements. Geophysics included magnetometry, earth resistance, and Ground Penetrating Radar techniques, all explained below. These techniques were variously carried out at all four primary research sites, and the results are described in Chapters Three and Four (Bodiam), Six (Scotney), Seven (Knole), and Eight (Ightham Mote).

The different techniques described below each have their strengths and weaknesses. Each is particularly suitable for picking up certain kinds of features. Consequently, archaeologists often prefer to use a range of different methods in combination.

Magnetometer survey is generally chosen as a relatively time-saving and efficient survey technique (Gaffney *et al.* 1991: 6), suitable for detecting kilns, hearths, ovens and ditches. Magnetometry can also detect walls, especially when ceramic material (tiles, bricks) has been used in construction. In areas of modern disturbance, the technique is limited by distribution of modern ferrous (iron-rich) material. Earth resistance survey (sometimes termed resistivity survey), while more time consuming, is generally successful at locating walls, ditches, paved areas, and banks. The application of resistivity tomography allows such features to be recorded at various depths along a linear transect. In addition Ground Penetrating Radar (GPR) is useful for surveying material where sufficient change in the 'permittivity' (resistance to an electric field) of different features provides contrast, including walls, banks, ditches, pits and other types of archaeological feature.

In this work, we also undertook close contour topographic survey over areas of prospection, to record any important archaeological features that are apparent in the present land surface, and also to provide vital information on variations in the ground surface to aid analysis of the geophysical prospection results.

Survey work is generally carried out by archaeologists as part of an integrated survey strategy, designed to affiliate all the results of the geophysical survey techniques to the same grid system. Surveys are normally based on an arbitrary grid coordinate system, tied into a national system or to a series of hard points on the ground corresponding to points on a map. A set of 30 m grids are then set out in which to carry out the magnetometry, earth resistance, and other survey techniques such as fieldwalking and geochemical sampling. The topographic and geophysical data were processed in the

---

[1] The text in this appendix is adapted from the standard text used in reports of Archaeological Prospection Services of Southampton (APSS, directed by Kristian Strutt; see http://www.southampton.ac.uk/archaeology/research/groups/archaeological_prospection_service_southampton.page and the survey blogs at https://generic.wordpress.soton.ac.uk/archaeology/archaeological-prospection-services-of-southampton-apss/). Kathryn A Catlin did most of the revisions and further text, with further edits by Matthew Johnson and Kristian Strutt.

APPENDIX 2

Fig. A2.1: Kristian Strutt engaged in topographic survey using RTK GPS at Bodiam Castle in 2010. Photo by Timothy Sly.

software packages Geoplot, GPR Slice, and Res2DInv, and imported into the Geographical Information Systems software ArcGIS for analysis. For technical details of the processing, see Barker *et al.* (2012).

Topographic Survey

The modern surface topography – humps and bumps on the ground surface, often more or less visible in different light conditions and from different heights and angles -- contains important information on the conditions and nature of an archaeological site or landscape, and can suggest the presence and location of structures or other features buried beneath the soil (Bowden 1999). The changes in topography can also have a great influence on interpretation of anomalies and features observed in a geophysical survey. Therefore it is often vital as a first step to produce a detailed and complete topographic survey as part of the field survey of any given site. This generally entails the recording of elevations across a grid of certain resolution, for instance 5 or 10 m intervals, but also the recording of points on known breaks of slope, to emphasis archaeological features in the landscape.

To record the survey points, we used a Real Time Kinetic (RTK) Global Positioning System (GPS) with a rover and base station (Fig. A2.1) as well as a Leica TC 307 total station (Fig. A2.2). Readings were taken every 5 m, and also on the breaks of slope of important topographical features. Computer software (ArcGIS) was then used to produce Digital Elevation Models (DEMs) of the results.

Earth Resistance (Resistivity) Survey

Earth resistance survey is based on the ability of sub-surface materials to conduct an electrical current passed through them. All materials will conduct electricity to a greater or lesser extent. Differences in the structural and chemical make-up of soils mean that there are varying degrees of ground resistance to an electrical current (Scollar 1990; Clark 1996: 27). Resistance meters pass an electrical current through the ground, and compare the resistivity at point locations in the grid with that of a distant background reading between two potential probes to measure variations in resistance over a survey area (Figs A2.3 & A2.4). Resistance is measured in ohms (Ω), whereas resistivity, the resistance in a given volume of earth, is measured in ohm-metres (Ω m). Electrical profiling usually employs two current and two potential probes (Gaffney *et al.* 1991: 2). We used a Geoscan Research RM15 Resistance Meter in twin electrode probe formation. This array represents the most popular configuration used in British archaeology, usually undertaken with a 0.5 m separation between mobile probes (Gaffney *et al.* 1991; Clark 1996).

Features picked up in this manner can be close to the ground surface. A twin probe array of 0.5 m spacing will rarely recognise features below a depth of 0.75 m (Gaffney *et al.* 1991). More substantial features may

Fig. A2.2: Peter Harris, Ceri Bridgeford, and Patrick Thewlis conduct topographic survey using a Leica TotalStation at Ightham Mote in 2013. Photo by Timothy Sly.

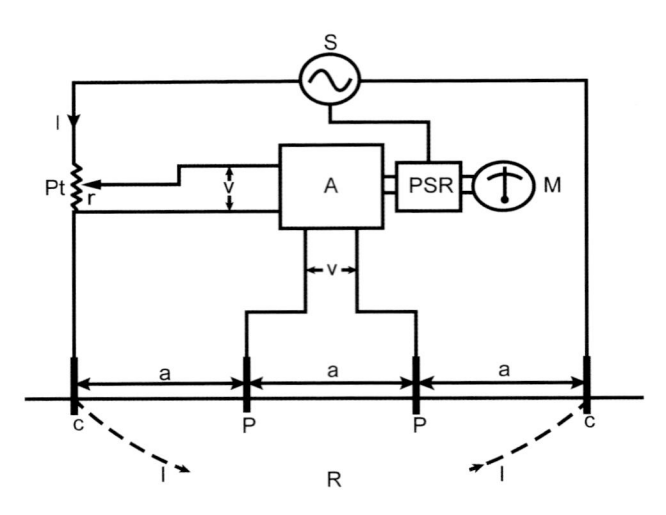

Fig. A2.3: The basic four probe circuit of a resistance meter (after Clark 1996: 27). Current (I) is produced at the AC source (S), passes through the potentiometer (Pt) and is introduced to the ground at electrodes C. The potential gradient is sampled between electrodes P, and the voltage (V) between them is applied to the amplifier (A) and displayed on the meter (M) along with the resistance (R). The phase-sensitive rectifier (PSR) reduces interference between the internal power sources and the signal being measured.

Fig. A2.4: Dominic Barker supervises earth resistance survey at Bodiam Castle in 2010. Photo by Timothy Sly.

register up to a depth of 1 m. The earth resistance survey in this volume was done to a resolution of 1 or 0.1 Ω, with readings every metre or half metre. For this project, data were collected bi-directionally in 30 m grids at 0.5 m intervals with a transect spacing of 0.5 m.

In general, higher resistance features are interpreted as structures which have a limited moisture content, for example walls, mounds, voids, rubble filled pits, and paved or cobbled areas. Lower resistance anomalies usually represent buried ditches, foundation trenches, pits and gullies. A number of factors may affect interpretation of twin probe survey results, including the nature and depth of structures, soil type, terrain, and localised climatic conditions. Changes in the moisture content of the soil, as well as variations in temperature, can affect the form of anomalies present in earth resistance survey results. Non-archaeological features are also detected by resistance meters, which can complicate the interpretation of results.

Electrical Resistivity Tomography

Electrical Resistivity Tomography (ERT) measures the resistivity of the soil matrix and buried materials. It works in a similar manner to the RM15 Resistance Meter discussed above, except that it employs multiple probes. Readings are recorded along a single transect in successively deeper traverses, enabling the device to sense features that are much more deeply buried. The result is a profile view of soil resistivity at multiple depths along a single transect (Figs A2.5 & A2.6). The ERT survey at Bodiam employed an Allied Associates Tigre 64-probe system, with probes spaced at either 1, 2, or 3 m intervals depending on the particular context of the transect. This allowed us to measure resistivity to nearly 20 m below the ground surface along a linear distance of approximately 550 m.

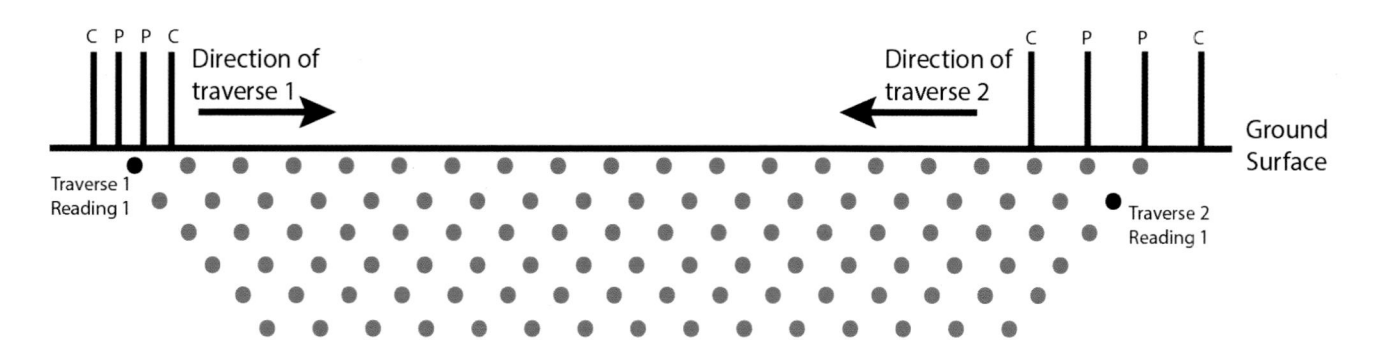

Fig. A2.5: Diagram of an Electrical Resistivity Tomography (ERT) survey. As in Fig. A2.3, the current is introduced to the ground at electrodes C and the voltage potential is measured at electrodes P. See also Fig. 4.6, this volume.

APPENDIX 2

Fig. A2.6: ERT survey in progress at Bodiam in 2010. Photo by Matthew Johnson.

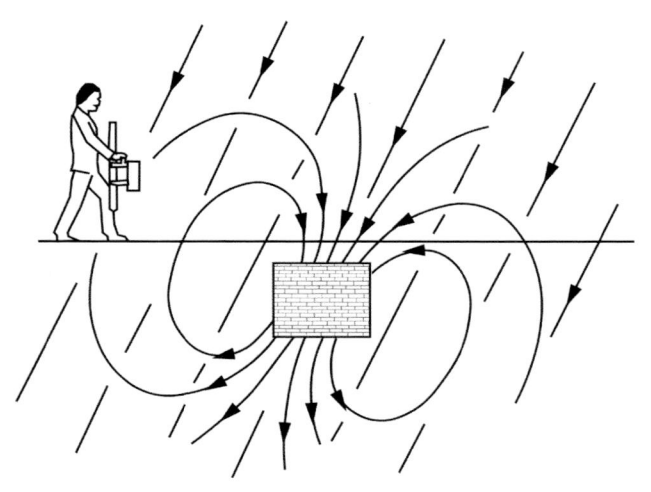

Fig. A2.7: The effect of the earth's magnetic field (straight lines) and the local magnetic field generated by buried material (curved lines), measured during magnetometer survey (after Clark 1996, fig. 50).

Magnetic Survey

Magnetic prospection of soils is based on the measurement of differences in magnitudes of the earth's magnetic field at points over a specific area. The iron content of a soil provides the principal basis for its magnetic properties. The presence of magnetite, maghemite and haematite iron oxides all affect the magnetic properties of soils. The overall strength of the earth's magnetic field is around 48,000 nanoTeslas (nT). Variations in the earth's magnetic field which are associated with archaeological features are relatively weak in comparison, but they can be detected using specific instruments (Gaffney *et al.* 1991; Fig. A2.7).

The work reported on in this volume used a dual sensor Bartington Instruments 601-2 fluxgate gradiometer (Fig. A2.8). The instrument measures changes in the Earth's magnetic field by comparing the strength of the magnetic field induced in two highly permeable nickel iron alloy cores held at a vertical separation of 0.5 m. The nickel iron cores are magnetised by the earth's magnetic field, together with an alternating field applied via a primary winding (Scollar 1990: 456). Due to the fluxgate's directional method of functioning, a single fluxgate cannot be utilised on its own, as it cannot be held at a constant angle to the earth's magnetic field. Gradiometers therefore have two fluxgates positioned vertically to one another on a rigid staff. This reduces the effects of instrument orientation on readings. Fluxgate gradiometers are sensitive to 0.5 nT or below depending on the instrument. They can rarely detect features which are located deeper than 1 m below the surface of the ground.

Magnetometry is best at detecting metallic objects, as well as non-metallic features that have been exposed to high enough temperatures that molecular bonds begin to relax, allowing the magnetic moment of any ferrous content to realign to magnetic North. This includes bricks and other burnt features such as hearths and

Fig. A2.8: Eric Johnson and Meya Kellala conduct magnetometer survey in Dokes Field at Bodiam Castle in 2012. Photo by Kathryn A Catlin.

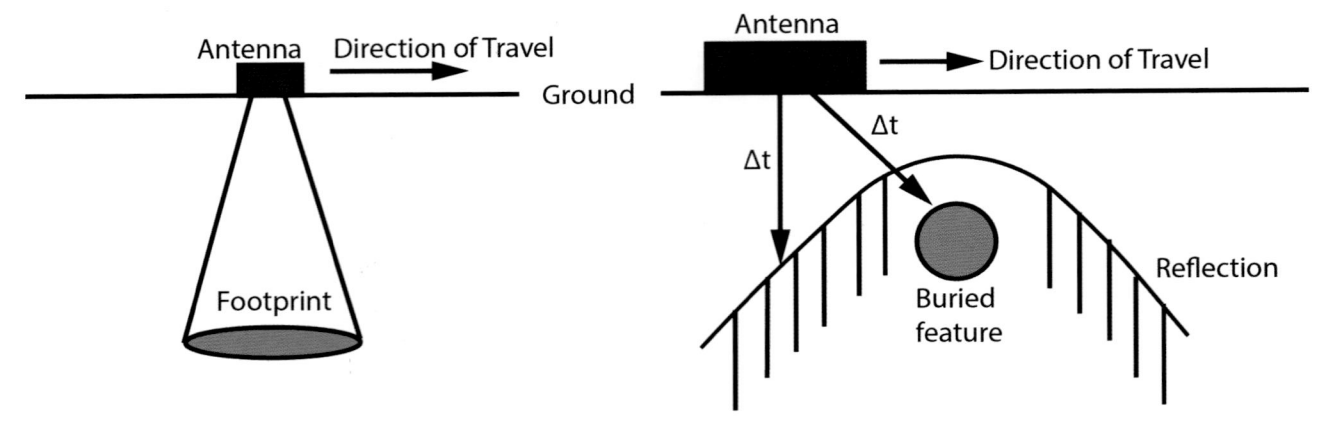

Fig. A2.9: Diagram showing the footprint of a GPR antenna as the radar wave propagates through the ground, and the reflection caused by a circular or oval body located below the surface of the ground as the antenna passes over it.

kilns. Gradiometers also detect the enhanced magnetic susceptibility of anthrosols (topsoils that have gained ferrous material via proximity to human habitation). Buried pits and ditches, where topsoil has infilled a trench dug into less magnetically susceptible subsoil, are therefore also readily detectable by magnetometry techniques under the proper conditions (Aspinall *et al.* 2008). Results are extremely dependent on the geology of the particular area, and whether the archaeological remains are derived from the same materials. Because gradiometers detect magnetic fields, they are particularly sensitive to iron and other metals in the survey area. It can be difficult to distinguish between archaeological materials, modern disturbances or refuse, and naturally occurring iron-rich deposits, such as the peat encountered during our Bodiam survey. Magnetometry data was collected bi-directionally in 30 m grids at 0.25 m intervals with a transect spacing of 0.5 m.

Magnetic Susceptibility Survey

Magnetic susceptibility surveys ('mag sus') were carried out with a Bartington Instruments MS-2 on a 10 m grid. Magnetic susceptibility meters create an alternating magnetic field at a point location and measure the resulting flux density, similar to a metal detector. Susceptibility surveys were intended to supplement the gradiometer data and train students in the technique.

Ground Penetrating Radar Survey

Ground Penetrating Radar (GPR) survey is based on the use of electromagnetic waves propagated through the soil to detect changes in density and composition, including the presence of buried objects. Interfaces between buried materials of different density and dielectric permittivity cause a portion

Fig. A2.10: Katie Fuller and Helena Glover conduct GPR survey in the Green Court at Knole in 2013 using a 500 MHz Sensors and Software Noggin Plus. Photo by Matthew Johnson.

Fig. A2.11: Ivan Yeh, Emily Pierce-Goldberg and Chen Xiaowen conduct GPR survey in 2012 at the Bodiam cricket field using a 200 MHz GSSI instrument. Photo by Kathryn A Catlin.

of the energy to reflect. Energy that reflects off of deeper buried reflectors will take more time to return to the instrument. The time between the generation of the radar wave at the antenna and the return of its reflection to the receiver is measured in nanoseconds (ns) and once the signal velocity is calculated this can be translated into depth (Fig. A2.9). GPR is therefore able to produce a three-dimensional model of buried objects and features of differing density from the soil matrix. Rocks, walls, pits, pathways, and buried solid objects are good targets for GPR prospection.

Lower frequency antennas have higher energy and can penetrate deeper into the ground, depending on soil conditions. A 500 MHz sensor can penetrate up to a few metres, depending on the soil conditions, while a 200 MHz sensor is better at detecting deeper materials and bedrock formations. GPR surveys primarily employed a 500 MHz Sensors & Software Noggin Plus with a SmartCart frame and console, along 0.5 m uni-directional transects (Fig. A2.10). The 2012 GPR survey on the Bodiam cricket field used a 200 MHz GSSI sensor, bi-directionally with 0.5 m transects (Fig. A2.11).

APPENDIX 3

FURTHER DETAILS OF ENVIRONMENTAL METHODS

Kathryn A. Catlin, Penny Copeland, Rob Scaife[1]

Chapter Five discusses the long-term environmental history at Bodiam, and Chapter Twelve discusses environment, ecology and human habitation more generally. The evidence discussed in Chapter Five came from a series of soil cores taken around the Bodiam landscape.

Once extracted and in the laboratory, cores can be analysed in various ways. They can be examined visually to look for particular kinds of sediment of other material. Different materials such as humic peat can be observed, or the traces of made-up ground or old land surfaces can be apparent. Any organic material such as peat or charcoal can be used for radiocarbon dating. Pollen can be extracted from the core by chemical treatment of soil samples, and the different species, types and proportions of pollen suggest what plant species were growing in the locality. Different species, of course, thrive in different conditions, so this information in turn can be used to infer different local conditions (wet, dry) or different climatic regimes (warm, cold).

Several sediment cores were extracted from the grounds at Bodiam Castle for stratigraphic and palynological analysis to reconstruct the changing environmental context of the Bodiam landscape through the Holocene. The results of the analysis are described in Chapter Five. On 8th May 2013, seven profiles were extracted by a University of Southampton team consisting of Dominic Barker, Penny Copeland and James Miles,

along with Victoria Stephenson of University College London. The cores were located within the castle (A1 & A2), in the fill of an adjacent pond (F), sediment underlying the moat bank (D), the car park (B) and the east yard (C1 & C2; see Fig. 5.1). Coring samples were obtained from A1, A2, B, C1, C2, and D using a Cobra two-stroke pneumatic power corer with 1 m tubes; the diameter of the core tapers from 8 to 40 mm, decreasing with depth. All Cobra samples except A1 employed a plastic sleeve to transport the section to the wet laboratory at the Department of Archaeology, University of Southampton for further description and analysis. The pond sample, site F, was obtained using a 0.5 m diameter Russian/Jowsey peat corer due to the very wet nature of the soils (Fig. 5.11), and these samples were chill stored in half sectioned plastic drain pipes prior to sediment description and sampling in the laboratory.

Two radiocarbon samples were dated by Beta Analytic Inc. We planned to investigate a further location (E) corresponding to the Roman road through Dokes Field, but due to time constraints, were unable to do so.

Sediment Analysis

A range of sediment types was recovered, including humic peat and sediment with clear potential for pollen analysis, palaeoenvironmental reconstruction, and radiocarbon dating. Made ground and old land surfaces were also observed, the latter also sampled for pollen analysis to provide a picture of the vegetation and possible land use on and very near the site. The

---

[1] This appendix was prepared by Kathryn A Catlin, from original text by Rob Scaife and Penny Copeland.

characteristics of these profiles are detailed in Tables 5.B-5.G, including colour descriptions as standard Munsell in natural light.

Pollen Analysis

Standard pollen extraction techniques were used on sub-samples of 2 ml volume (Moore & Webb 1978; Moore *et al.* 1991). A sum of 400-500 pollen grains, including dry land taxa plus extant marginal and aquatic taxa, fern spores and miscellaneous palynomorphs, were identified and counted for each sample level. Chemical preparation procedures were carried out in the Palaeoecology Laboratory of the School of Geography, University of Southampton and identification and counting was carried out using an Olympus biological microscope fitted with Leitz optics. Standard pollen diagrams (see Chapter Five) were constructed using Tilia and Tilia Graph.

Pollen percentages were calculated for the sum and sub-groups as follows:

Sum	=	% total dry land pollen (tdlp)
Marsh/aquatic herbs	=	% tdlp + sum of marsh/aquatics
Ferns	=	% tdlp + sum of ferns
Misc	=	% tdlp + sum of misc. taxa (Sphagnum moss, pre-Quaternary palynomorphs and other micro-fossils).

Alnus has been excluded from the pollen sum because of its high pollen productivity (and consequent abundance) and growth on or near the site, which tends to distort the percentage representation of other taxa within the pollen sum (Janssen 1969). Consequently, the percentages of alder have been incorporated within the fen/marsh group of which it is botanically a part. Because *Salix* may be associated with this fen carr taxon/habitat, it was also included in this calculation. Taxonomy, in general, follows that of Moore & Webb (1978) modified according to Bennett *et al.* (1994) for pollen types and Stace (1992) for plant descriptions.

Scientific and Common Names of Observed Taxa

Acer	Maple
Alisma plantago-aquatica	Water plantains
Alnus glutinosa	Alder
Asteraceae	Daisy (aster) family
A. Bidens	Beggarticks
A. Anthemis	Chamomile
A. Artemisia	Wormwood genus
Betula	Birch
Caltha palustris	Marsh marigold
Cannabis sativa	Hemp
Carpinus betulus	Hornbeam
Caryophyllaceae	Carnation family
C. cerastium	Chickweed
C. dianthus	Carnation genus
Centaurea	Knapweeds
Chenopodiaceae	Goosefoot family
Corylus avellana	Hazel
Cyperaceae	Sedges
Dryopteris	Wood fern
Erica	Heather/heath
Euonymous	Spindle
Fagus sylvatica	Beech
Frangula alnus	Alder buckthorn
Fraxinus	Ash
Hedera helix	Ivy
Ilex	Holly
Iris	Iris
Juglans regia	Walnut
Lactucoideae	Dandelion subfamily
Lysimachia	Loosestrife
Nymphaea alba	White water lily
Osmunda regalis	Royal fern
Pediastrum	Algae
Picea	Spruce
Pinus	Pine
Poaceae	Grasses
Polypodium vulgare	Polypody fern
Plantago lanceolata	Ribwort plantain
Pteridium aquilinum	Eagle fern (bracken)
Quercus	Oak
Ranunculaceae	Buttercup family
Rhamnus cathartica	Buckthorn
Secale cereal	Rye
Salix	Willow
Sinapus	Mustard
Sparganium	Bur-reed
Sphagnum	Peat moss
Succisa	Succisa
Tilia cordata	Lime (linden)
Typha angustifolia	Cattail/reed mace
Ulmus	Elm
Viburnum	Viburnum

Glossary

We have included here a variety of scientific, theoretical and technical specialist terms; a number of acronyms; and a few cases where an English term may not be familiar or have a different meaning to a North American audience, or vice versa. For specialist terms relating to topographical and geophysical survey, a layperson's account is given in Appendix Two.

Affordance: a relation between an object or environment and an organism that enhances the opportunity to perform an action, but does not directly determine it. For example, a doorknob affords twisting; heavy clay soil affords the construction of moats

Alluvium: a deposit made up of materials left by the action of flowing water

Anaerobic: lacking in oxygen

Anthropogenic: caused by human activity

Arable: of farming that involved ploughing, tilling, raising of crops

Archiepiscopal: belonging to the Archbishop

Ashlar: stone that is faced and squared

Assarting: the clearing of trees and bushes from land, in order to cultivate it

BCE: before the Common Era (also referred to as BC, Before Christ)

Berm: the strip of ground between the bottom of the curtain wall and the moat or ditch

BP: before present (often defined as 1950 CE)

Brickearth: a term used to describe superficial windblown deposits in southern England

Bronze Age: a period of prehistory characterised by the use of bronze implements, c. 2500 to 800 BCE

Buttery: a service room used for storing ale, beer and other liquour

Carr: waterlogged wooded terrain

CE: the Common Era (also referred to as AD, Anno Domini)

Cell: unit of a house or other building, often corresponding to bay and room divisions

Chamber: a room, though sometimes used to designate its upper floor counterpart: thus the 'hall chamber' can be the room over the hall

Chamfer: the planing away of the corner of the profile of arch, door, window or other recess. A 'chamfer-stop' is the carved end to a chamfer

Coppice: a tree is coppiced when its trunk is cut off near the base, so that young shoots grow quickly from the stump that remains

Corn: in British-English usage, wheat and oats

Cottage: though often used today to refer to smaller vernacular houses indiscriminately, the more precise term refers to the dwellings of those holding little or no land, usually labourers, often built and owned by the landlord from the 18th century onwards

Crenellation: battlement of merlons and embrasures. See also licence to crenellate

Cross-passage: the area between two opposed doors at the lower end of a medieval hall. Where the area is separated by a screen, it is called a 'screens passage'

Crown-post: a post resting on a tie supporting a collar purlin and collar, and often braced to these

Cupboard: either a table upon which items were placed, or similar to a sideboard

Dais: raised platform at the upper end of a hall

Demesne: part of the lord's estate; in the classical feudal model, a 'demesne farm' was worked using the labour services of peasants given as a form of rent, though this practice had largely died out in England by the later 14th century

Dendrochronology: dating by use of tree rings

Detrital: composed of loose fragments or grains that have been broken or worn away from rock

Dipole: a term used in magnetic survey to refer to a point location showing both strong positive and negative readings, usually indicating buried ferric (iron) material

Embrasure: opening

Empiricism: Popularly, the belief that the data will 'speak for themselves' without the need for intervening theories. In its more sophisticated form, as developed in 17th-century philosophy, empiricism rests on a conceptual division between 'things' or 'the real world' on the one hand, 'words' or 'concepts' on the other, and the prioritisation of the former

Episcopal: belonging to a Bishop

Evapotranspiration: the process by which water is transferred from the land to the atmosphere by evaporation from the soil and other surfaces and by transpiration from plants

Fen: a low, marshy area of land, liable to floods

Feudal: in this volume, used loosely of medieval society, in which ties of lordship and ownership of land were central to political power

Gentry: members of the elite though below the aristocracy, typically leaders of the local community

Gley: a sticky waterlogged soil lacking in oxygen

Global Positioning System (GPS): a satellite-based navigation system that uses triangulation of radio signals between four or more satellites and a user's GPS device to calculate the precise location of the device anywhere on Earth with a clear view of the sky. The most accurate GPS devices can determine position to within a centimetre

Gloriette: a term used in the context of medieval castles to refer to a building surrounded by water, set apart from the adjacent courtyard and landscape (as at Leeds in Kent, or Hesdin in France)

Grey literature: a colloquial term referring to reports, generally on small-scale excavations, survey, or other archaeological and historical research, for example in connection with conservation management plans, that has been 'written up' and archived but not fully published in the conventional sense. Grey literature is often commissioned by a public body such as the National Trust to a specific brief, and researched and written by freelance individuals or professional organisations such as Archaeology South-East (https://www.ucl.ac.uk/archaeologyse). In the UK, 'grey literature' is very often archived and freely available to download at the Archaeology Data Service (http://archaeologydataservice.ac.uk/). Increasingly, PhDs are also available to download in electronic form from university libraries

Ha-ha: a ditch with bank or fence constructed in such a way as to give an illusion of unfenced, open country; popular in the 18th/19th centuries

Holocene: the period from the end of the last Ice Age, c. 10,000 years BP

Horizon: a specialist term referring to a distinctive soil layer

Humus: the organic component of soil

Hydrology: the scientific study of water, particularly its flow in relation to land

Ideology: a set of overt or implicit beliefs or views of the world. According to Marxists, ideology serves to legitimate or mask the 'real' state of social relations

Indigenous: of a people inhabiting a region with which they have the earliest known historical connection, often alongside later immigrants; a term whose definition is much debated, and therefore often used with a capital I

Iron Age: in Britain, roughly c. 800 BCE to the start of the Roman period

Lacustrine: spring-fed

Laminated: created by pressing together thin layers of material

Leat: an artificial water channel

Licence to crenellate: a medieval document giving royal permission to fortify a place, which some have argued, at Bodiam and other sites, is largely honorific in nature

LiDAR: derived from Light Detection and Ranging. A survey technology that measures distance with a laser light, often from a drone or aircraft

Lime: In North American usage, linden

Lintel: a horizontal timber or stone over a door, fireplace or other opening

Livery: forms of dress or of badges, signifying allegiance to a feudal lord

Lynchets: earthen terraces in a hillside, often the remains of past cultivation

Machicolations: the projecting parapet of a battlement, enabling defenders to drop missiles or water on those below

Manor: the district over which a lord had domain (the manor house being the lord's residence, from which domain was exercised; see also demesne)

Maps:
Ordnance Survey (OS): maps prepared by the national mapping agency for Great Britain; first edition OS maps generally date to the 1800s
Tithe: maps prepared in the wake of the Tithe Commutation Act of 1836, for the purpose of replacing tithes with an allocation of land to the Church

Marl: rock or soil consisting of clay or lime

Merlon: the upright part of a battlemented parapet, between two openings or embrasures

Mesolithic: the Middle Stone Age, in Britain roughly c. 10,000 to c. 6,000 BP

Methodology: the techniques and methods used to collect and interpret archaeological data

Mortice: socket in a wall or piece of timber

Moulding: the carved profile of a timber or masonry feature

Mullion: an upright dividing a window into lights

Murder-hole: opening in the vaulted ceiling of a gate passageway, to use against attackers passing below, though can also be decorative

NanoTesla (nT): unit of measure of the strength of a magnetic field. A standard refrigerator magnet produces a field of about 0.005 Tesla, or 5 million nT. Variations in the earth's magnetic field due to archaeological features often measure only fractions of a nanoTesla

Neolithic: the New Stone Age, in Britain c. 4000 to c. 2500 BCE

Newel: of a circular staircase that winds round a central pillar or 'newel post'

Oast: a drying kiln, for example for hops, malt or tobacco

Oriel window: a projecting window, often found at the upper end of a hall

Over: on the floor above

Oxidised: combined chemically with oxygen

Pale: boundary, for example of a park

Palynology: the study of pollen grains

Parapet: a wall, usually battlemented in castles, protecting the wall-walk and any roof behind

Particularise: to explain or understand something in terms of its peculiar qualities

Pastoral: of farming centred on the raising of cattle and sheep

Peat: partially decayed vegetable matter, characteristic of bogs and other anaerobic and acidic environments

Peer: great lord or baron

Peripatetic: moving periodically from place to place (a term often used in the context of great medieval households)

Permittivity: the measure of resistance that is encountered when forming an electric field in a medium

Phenomenology: the study of human experience and consciousness in everyday life

Pig joint: a straight joint for a limited length, usually indicating a break in building and/or the work of two masons meeting

Polite: of architecture that is large in scale and national or international in scope and influence (contra vernacular)

Pollard: as with coppicing, the cutting-off of a tree trunk to encourage the growth of shoots from the stump, but pollarding is done at a sufficient height to stop animals grazing on the shoots

Post: any vertical timber forming part of the main frame

Postern: rear or secondary gate

Practice: A term closely linked to agency, associated with Bourdieu rather than Giddens, referring to everyday actions and their relationship to structure

Pragmatism: A philosophy originally developed by Charles Peirce and others proposing that the meaning of an idea or a proposition lies in its observable practical consequences

Puddled: lined, as with clay or chalk in the base and sides of a hole

Quaternary: most recent geological era, from 2.6 million years BP, subdivided into Pleistocene and Holocene

Quoin: dressed stone at the angle of a building

Radiocarbon dating (C14 dating): scientific means of determining the age of an organic object, based on analysis of the ratios of carbon-12 atoms to carbon-14 atoms

Range: a series of rooms in line in a building. Thus a rectangular building arranged around a courtyard has four ranges

Reify: to convert something abstract into a concrete thing; thus a moat could be argued to 'reify' social status

Rendering: covering, for example of plaster and/or of lime

Sacristy: a room in a church where a priest prepares for a service, and where vestments and other things used in worship are kept

Sheiling: a pasture used for the grazing of cattle in summer

Sill: the lower member of a window frame, or the rail at the foot of the frame

Silt: fine sand or clay carried by water and deposited in fine layers

Soffit: the underside of a lintel or arch

Solar: private chamber, usually at upper end of a hall

Spore: a tiny organism or single cell that is able to grow and is resistant to adverse environments

Stratigraphy: the analysis of the order and position of layers of archaeological remains

String course: a horizontal line of projecting ashlar

Taxonomy: the branch of science concerned with classification, especially of plants and animals

Tenement: a piece of land held by an owner

Tenure: form of landholding, of various forms and degrees of security (for example freehold and copyhold tenure)

Terminus post quem (TPQ): refers to a date on or after a given point: thus an archaeological layer with a single coin dating to 1400 CE has a TPQ of that date – the layer could have been deposited at that date, or any date subsequently

Thegn: Member of the Anglo-Saxon elite, below the level of Earl

Tie-beam or tie: the horizontal timber of a truss at wall-plate level connecting the tops of the posts

Toft: the farmyard around the medieval peasant house, often defined by a bank and ditch

Triangulated Irregular Network (TIN): A representation of a surface as a network of irregularly distributed, non-overlapping triangles. Generated from topographic data

Undershot: of a mill wheel, turned by water flowing under it

Vernacular: of regional, local traditions of art, architecture, and culture, for example ordinary farmhouses

Voussoir: a wedge-shaped stone used in building an arch

Water table: the level below which soil or rock is saturated with water

Weald: an area of Sussex and Kent characterised by heavy clay soil, areas of woodland, and dispersed settlement

Wealden: of a particular type of open-hall house with both upper and lower ends jettied to the front. The wall-plate over the jetties continues over the front of the unjettied hall, creating an overhang. 'Wealdens' are found in (but not confined to) the Weald of Kent and Sussex

Yeomen: a socially middling class of tenant farmers of reasonable security and wealth

Bibliography

Where 'grey literature' is referenced, we have appended information on how to retrieve it wherever possible, for example via the East Sussex Record Office (ESRO), the relevant URL at the Archaeology Data Service (http://archaeologydataservice.ac.uk/), our own project website (http://sites.northwestern.edu/medieval-buildings/) or the relevant National Trust archive.

Abbott, W.J.L., 1896. Notes on a remarkable barrow at Sevenoaks. *Journal of the Royal Anthropological Institute of Great Britain and Ireland* 25, 130-7.

Aberg, F.A., 1978. *Medieval Moated Sites.* CBA Research Report 17. York, Council for British Archaeology. Available at http://archaeologydataservice.ac.uk/archives/view/cba_rr/rr17.cfm.

Aberg, F.A. and Brown, A.E., 1981. *Medieval Moated Sites in North-West Europe.* BAR International Series 121. Oxford, British Archaeological Reports.

Acta Heritage and Environmental Consultants, 2007. *Scotney Garden and Estate Conservation Management Plan.* Unpublished report, National Trust archives, Scotney.

Airs, M., 1995. *The Tudor and Jacobean Country House: A Building History.* Stroud, Sutton.

Airs, M. and Barnwell, P.S. (eds), 2011. *The Medieval Great House.* Oxford, Oxbow.

Andersen, S.T., 1970. The relative pollen productivity and pollen representation of north European trees and correction factors for tree pollen spectra. *Danmarks Geologiske Undersogelse* R.II(96), 1-99.

Andersen, S.T., 1973. The differential pollen productivity of trees and its significance for the interpretation of a pollen diagram from a forested region. In H.J.B. Birks and R.G. West (eds), *Quaternary Plant Ecology.* Oxford, Blackwell, 109-15.

Anonymous, 1959-60. The Roman road at Bodiam. *Battle and District Historical Society Transactions,* 32-4.

Archaeological Services Durham University, 2010. *Towthorpe Manor Farm, Driffield, East Riding of Yorkshire: Geophysical Survey.* ASDU Report 2500. Unpublished report, Archaeological Services Durham University.

Ash, D., 1965. Gothic. In H. Hayward (ed.), *World Furniture: An Illustrated History.* London, Paul Hamlyn, 25-35.

Ashmore, W. and Knapp, B. (eds), 1999. *Archaeologies of Landscape: Contemporary Perspectives.* Oxford, Blackwell.

Aspinall, A., Gaffney, C. and Schmidt, A., 2008. *Magnetometry for Archaeologists.* Lanham, AltaMira Press.

Austin, D., 1984. The castle and the landscape: annual lecture to the Society for Landscape Studies, May 1984. *Landscape History* 6(1), 69-81.

Austin, D., 1990. The "proper study" of medieval archaeology. In D. Austin and L. Alcock (eds), *From the Baltic to the Black Sea: Studies in Medieval Archaeology.* London, Unwin Hyman, 9-42.

Austin, D., 2007. *Acts of Perception: A Study of Barnard Castle in Teesdale.* AASN Research Report 6. Architectural and Archaeological Society of Northumberland.

AV INFO, 1995. *Reverberation Time. AV Info: Non-profit Informational Website.* Online resource, available at http://www.bnoack.com/index.html?http&&&www.bnoack.com/acoustic/RT_meetingrooms.html.

Baert, P., 2005. *Philosophy of the Social Sciences: Towards Pragmatism.* Cambridge, Polity.

Bailey, D.W., 1998. Bulgarian archaeology: ideology, socio-politics and the exotic. In L. Meskell (ed.), *Archaeology Under Fire in the Eastern Mediterranean and the Middle East.* London, Routledge, 87-110.

Bannister, N.R., 1999. Ightham *Mote Estate vol. 1. Kent and East Sussex: The National Trust.* Unpublished report, on file in National Trust archives, Ightham.

Bannister, N.R., 2001. *Scotney Castle Estate Historic & Archaeological Landscape Survey*. Unpublished report, on file in National Trust archives, Scotney.

Barber, L., 1998. *An Archaeological Watching Brief at Bodiam Castle, East Sussex (The New Sewage Treatment Plant). Ditchling, East Sussex*. Archaeology South-East. Report 858. Unpublished report, Archaeology South-East.

Barber, L., 2007a. *An Archaeological Watching Brief at Bodiam Castle, Robertsbridge, East Sussex: The Drainage Scheme*. Unpublished report, Archaeology South-East. ESRO R/R/36/14811.

Barber, L., 2007b. *An Archaeological Watching Brief at Bodiam Castle, Robertsbridge, East Sussex: The Moat Banks and Great Hall*. ASE Report 2819. Unpublished report, Archaeology South-East.

Barker, D., Copeland, P., Sly, T. and Strutt, K., 2012. *Report on the Geophysical Survey at Bodiam Castle, East Sussex, August 2012*. Unpublished report, University of Southampton, available at http://sites.northwestern.edu/medieval-buildings/.

Barrett, J. and Ko, I., 2009. A phenomenology of landscape: a crisis in British landscape archaeology? *Journal of Social Archaeology* 9(3), 275-94.

Barron, M., 2009. *Auditorium Acoustics and Architectural Design*, Second edition. Oxford, Spon Press.

Barry, T.B., 1981. The shifting frontier: medieval moated sites in Counties Cork and Limerick. In F.A. Aberg and A.E. Brown (eds), *Medieval Moated Sites in North-West Europe*. BAR International Series 121. Oxford, British Archaeological Reports 71-85.

Bartlett, A., 2007. *Knole, Kent: Report on Archaeogeophysical Survey 2007*. Unpublished report, National Trust archives, Knole.

Bateman, J., 2000. Immediate realities: an anthropology of computer visualisation in archaeology. *Internet Archaeology* 8. Available: http://intarch.ac.uk/journal/issue8/index.html.

Beiser, F.C., 2006. *The Romantic Imperative: The Concept of Early German Romanticism*. Cambridge, Harvard University Press.

Bender, B., 1998. *Stonehenge: Making Space*. Oxford, Berg.

Bender, B., Hamilton, S. and Tilley, C., 2007. *Stone Worlds: Narrative and Reflexivity in Landscape Archaeology*. Walnut Creek, Left Coast Press.

Bennett, K.D., Whittington, G. and Edwards, K.J., 1994. Recent plant nomenclatural changes and pollen morphology in the British Isles. *Quaternary Newsletter* 73, 1-6.

Benson, S.H., Clark, L.J., Gibson, R.P.T. and Hayter, S.W., 1968. *The Benson Report on the National Trust: Report by the Council's Advisory Committee on the Trust's constitution, organisation and responsibilities*. London, National Trust.

Blaauw, W.H., 1861. Royal licenses to fortify towns and houses in Sussex. *Sussex Archaeological Collections* 13, 114.

Blandford, V., 2012. *Tracing the pale of the Ashdown Forest deer park*. Unpublished report, Chris Butler Archaeological Services.

Bond, J., 1994. Forests, chases, warrens and parks in medieval Wessex. In M. Aston and C. Lewis (eds), *The Medieval Landscape of Wessex*. Oxford, Oxbow, 115-8.

Bowden, M., 1999. *Unravelling the Landscape: An Inquisitive Approach to Archaeology*. Stroud, Tempus.

Bowden, M., 2000. Virtual Avebury revisited. *Archaeological Dialogues* 7(1), 84-8.

Bradley, R., 2000. *An Archaeology of Natural Places*. London, Routledge.

Bradley, R., 2014. *The Prehistoric Settlement of Britain*. London, Routledge.

Bradley, R. and Fulford, M.G., 2008. The chronology of co-axial field systems. In P. Rainbird (ed.), *Monuments in the Landscape*. Stroud, Tempus, 114-22.

Brandon, P., 1969. Medieval clearances in the East Sussex Weald. *Transactions of the Institute of British Geographers* 48, 135-53.

Brandon, P., 2003. *The Kent and Sussex Weald*. Oving, Phillimore and Company.

Brandon, P. and Short, B., 1990. *The South East from AD 1000*. London, Routledge.

Braun, H., 1936. *The English Castle*. Alcester, Woods Press.

Brears, P., 2010. Wressle Castle: functions, fixtures and furnishings for Henry Percy, 'The Magnificent' fifth Earl of Northumberland, 1498-1527. *Archaeological Journal* 167, 55-114.

Bridgman, J., 1817. *An Historical and Topographical Sketch of Knole in Kent; with a Brief Genealogy of the Sackville Family*. London, Lindsell.

Brown, R.A., 1970. *English Castles*. London, Chancellor Press.

Brück, J., 2005. Experiencing the past? The development of phenomenological archaeology in British prehistory. *Archaeological Dialogues* 12(1), 47-72.

Bunn, D., 2010. *Geophysical Survey: Land at Manor Farm, Holdfast Worcestershire*. Saxilby, Lincoln, Cotswold Archaeology.

Burrin, P.J., 1981. Loess in the Weald. *Proceedings of the Geologists' Association* 92, 87-92.

Burrin, P.J. and Scaife, R.G., 1984. Aspects of Holocene valley sedimentation and floodplain development in southern England. *Proceedings of the Geologists' Association* 95, 81-96.

Burrin, P.J. and Scaife, R.G., 1988. The Holocene floodplain and alluvial fill deposits of the Rother Valley and their bearing on the evolution of Romney Marsh. In J. Eddison and C. Green (eds), *Romney Marsh: Evolution, Occupation, Reclamation* Oxford, Oxford University Committee for Archaeology, 31-52.

Camille, M., 1998. *Mirror in Parchment*. London, Reaktion.

Cannadine, D., 2001. *Ornamentalism: How the British Saw Their Empire*. London, Penguin.

Cantor, L.M., 1982. Castles, fortified houses, moated homesteads and monastic settlements. In L.M. Cantor (ed.), *The English Medieval Landscape*. London, Croom Helm, 126-53.

Catlin, K.A., 2015. *Report on the nature and disposition of archaeological finds from Bodiam Castle, East Sussex*. Unpublished report, Northwestern University, available at http://sites.northwestern.edu/medieval-buildings/.

Chalmers, A. and Zanyi, E., 2010. Multi-sensory virtual environments for investigating the past. *Virtual Archaeology Review* 1:1, 13-16.

Clanchy, M., 1979. *From Memory to Written Record: England 1066-1307*. London, Arnold.

Clark, A., 1996. *Seeing Beneath the Soil: Prospecting Methods in Archaeology*. Second edition. London, Batsford.

Clark, G.T., 1884. *Medieval Military Architecture in England*. London, Wyman.

Cleere, H. and Crossley, D., 1985. *The Iron Industry of the Weald*. Leicester, Leicester University Press.

Colvin, H. 1963-82. *The History of the King's Works*. Six volumes. London, Her Majesty's Stationery Office.

Connerton, P., 1989. *How Societies Remember*. Cambridge, Cambridge University Press.

Conan Doyle, A., 1981 [1904]. The Return of Sherlock Holmes. In *The Penguin Complete Sherlock Holmes*. London, Penguin, 483-667.

Conway, M., 1990. *Autobiographical Memory: An Introduction*. Maidenhead, Open University.

Cooper, C., 2010. The use of polynomial texture mapping in the recording and study of historical graffiti found at Bodiam castle and Portchester Castle. Available: http://sites.northwestern.edu/medieval-buildings/files/2013/04/CooperMA_Graffiti.pdf.

Cooper, C., 2015. *The Exploration of Lived Experience in Medieval Buildings through the Use of Digital Technologies*. Unpublished PhD thesis, University of Southampton, Available: http://eprints.soton.ac.uk/377916/1.hasCoversheetVersion/CooperCatrionaThesis.pdf.

Cornwell, K., Cornwell, L. and Padgham, D., 2010. Roman road at Bodiam - revised alignment. *Hastings Area Archaeological Research Group Journal, New Series* 29, 1-9.

Cosgrove, D., 1984. *Social Formation and Symbolic Landscape*. London, Croom Helm.

Cosgrove, D., 2006. Modernity, community and the landscape idea. *Journal of Medieval History* 11(1), 49-66.

Cosgrove, D. and Daniels, S. (eds), 1988. *The Iconography of Landscape: Essays on the Symbolic Representation, Design and Use of Past Environments*. Cambridge, Cambridge University Press.

Coulson, C., 1992. Some analysis of the castle of Bodiam, East Sussex. In C. Harper-Bill and R. Harvey (eds), *Medieval Knighthood IV: Papers from the Fifth Strawberry Hill Conference, 1992*. Woodbridge, Boydell, 51-108.

Coulson, C., 1993. Specimens of freedom to crenellate by licence. *Fortress* 18, 3-15.

Coulson, C., 1994. Freedom to crenellate by licence: an historiographical revision. *Nottingham Medieval Studies* 38, 86-137.

Coulson, C., 1996. Cultural realities and reappraisals in English castle-study. *Journal of Medieval History* 22, 171-208.

Creighton, O.H., 2009. *Designs Upon the Land: Elite Landscapes of the Middle Ages*. Woodbridge, Boydell.

Creighton, O.H. and Barry, T., 2012. Seigneurial and elite sites in the medieval landscape. In N. Christie and P. Stamper (eds), *Medieval Rural Settlement: Britain and Ireland, AD 600-1600*. Oxford, Oxbow, 63-80.

Creighton, O.H. and Liddiard, R., 2008. Fighting yesterday's battle? Beyond war or status in castle studies. *Medieval Archaeology* 52, 161-9.

Creighton, O.H., 2005. *Castles and Landscapes: Power, Community and Fortification in Medieval England*. London, Continuum.

Cronon, W., 1991. *Nature's Metropolis: Chicago and the Great West*. New York, Norton.

Crossley, D.W., 1981. Medieval iron smelting. In Crossley (ed.), *Medieval Industry*. CBA Research Report 20. London, Council for British Archaeology. 29-41.

Crossley, D.W. and Saville, R.V. (eds), 1991. *The Fuller Letters: Guns, Slaves and Finance 1728-1755*. Sussex Records Society 76.

Cummings, V., 2002. Experiencing texture and transformation in the British Neolithic. *Oxford Journal of Archaeology* 21(3), 249-61.

Cummins, J.G., 1988. *The Hound and the Hawk: The Art of Medieval Hunting*. New York, St Martin's Press.

Cummins, J.G., 2002. Veneurs s'en vont en Paradis, medieval hunting and the "natural" landscape. In J. Howe and M. Wolfe (eds), *Inventing Medieval Landscapes: Sense of Place in Western Europe*. Gainesville, University Press of Florida, 33-56.

Currie, C.K. and Rushton, N.S., 2004. Dartington Hall and the development of the double-courtyard design. *Archaeological Journal* 161(1), 189-210.

Curry, A., 2005. *Agincourt: A New History*. Stroud, Tempus.

Curzon, N., Marquis of Kedleston, 1926. *Bodiam Castle, Sussex: A Historical & Descriptive Survey*. London, Jonathan Cape.

Cushman, D., 2012. Final thoughts on national-scale cultural resource legislation. In M. Rockman and J. Flatman (eds), *Archaeology in Society: Its Relevance in the Modern World*. New York, Springer, 54-6.

Dalenbäck, B.-I., 2011. CATT-Acoustic v9.0. Online resource, available: http://www.catt.se/.

Darrell Hill, J., 1960-61. The earthwork known as the Gun Garden & finds & fieldwork. *Battle and District Historical Society Transactions* 10, 222-4.

Davis, P., 2007. English licences to crenellate: 1199-1567. *The Castle Studies Group Journal* 20, 226-45.

Davison, B., 1972. The Burghal Hidage fort of Eorpeburnan: a suggested identification. *Medieval Archaeology* 16, 123-7.

Dawson, P., Levy, R., Gardner, D. and Walls, M., 2007. Simulating the behaviour of light inside Arctic dwellings: implications for assessing the role of vision in task performance. *World Archaeology* 39(1), 17-35.

DCMS, 2001. *The Historic Environment: A Force for Our Future*. London, Department for Culture, Media and Sport.

Devereux, P. and Jahn, R.G., 1996. Preliminary investigations and cognitive considerations of the acoustical resonances of selected archaeological sites. *Antiquity* 70, 665-6.

Dixon, P., 2008. *Knole: A Report on the Works of 2007-8*. Unpublished report, National Trust archives, Knole.

Dixon, P. and Lott, B., 1993. The courtyard and the tower: Contexts and symbols in the development of late medieval great houses. *Journal of British Archaeological Association* 146(1), 93-101.

Dixon, P. and Marshall, P., 1993a. The great tower at Hedingham castle: a reassessment. *Fortress* 18, 16-23.

Dixon, P. and Marshall, P., 1993b. The great tower in the twelfth century: the case of Norham castle. *Archaeological Journal* 150, 410-32.

Dixon-Scott, J., 1937. *England Under Trust: The Principal Properties Held by the National Trust in England and Wales*. London, Alexander Madehose.

Dobson, R.B., 1970. *The Peasants Revolt of 1381*. Bath, Pitman.

Draper, G., 1998. The farmers of Canterbury Cathedral Priory and All Souls College on Romney Marsh c.1443-1545. In J. Eddison, M. Gardiner and A. Long (eds), *Romney Marsh: Environmental Change and Human Occupation in a Coastal Lowland*. Oxford, Oxford University Committee for Archaeology 109-28.

Drury, P., 1982. Aspects of the origin and development of Colchester Castle. *Archaeological Journal* 139, 302-419.

Drury, P. and Copeman, M., 2016. *Bodiam Castle, Robertsbridge, East Sussex: Conservation Management Plan for the National Trust*. Unpublished report, Drury McPherson Partnership for the National Trust.

Du Boulay, F.R.H., 1966. *The Lordship of Canterbury: An Essay on Medieval Society*. London, Nelson.

Du Boulay, F.R.H., 1974. The assembling of an estate: Knole in Sevenoaks, c.1275 to c.1525. *Archaeologia Cantiana* 89, 1-10.

Eames, P., 1977. *Medieval Furniture in England, France, and the Netherlands from the Twelfth to the Fifteenth Century.* Leeds, Maney.

Earle, T.K., 2011. Chiefs, chieftaincies, chiefdoms and chiefly confederacies: power in the evolution of political systems. *Social Evolution and History* 10(1), 27-54.

EChaucer, 2011. *The Book of the Duchess. eChaucer: Chaucer in the Twenty-First Century.* Online resouce, available: http://machias.edu/faculty/necastro/chaucer/translation/bd/bd.html.

Eddison, J., 1985. Developments in the lower Rother valleys up to 1600. *Archaeologia Cantiana* 102, 95-110.

Eddison, J., 1993. Attempts to clear the Rother Channel, 1613-1624. In J. Eddison (ed.), *Romney Marsh: The Debateable Ground.* Oxford, Oxbow, 148-63.

Edgeworth, M. (ed.), 2006. *Ethnographies of Archaeological Practice: Cultural Encounters, Material Transformations.* New York, AltaMira Press.

Edgeworth, M., 2011. *Fluid Pasts: Archaeology of Flow.* London, Duckworth.

Emery, A., 1996. *Greater Medieval Houses of England and Wales 1300-1500: Volume 1.* Cambridge, Cambridge University Press.

Emery, A., 2006. *Greater Medieval Houses of England and Wales 1300-1500: Volume 3, Southern England.* Cambridge, Cambridge University Press.

Emery, A., 2007. Dartington Hall: A mirror of the nobility in late medieval Devon. *Archaeological Journal* 164:1, 227-48.

Emery, E. V., 1962. Moated settlements in England. *Geography* 47, 378-88.

Engel, S., 1999. *Context is Everything: The Nature of Memory.* New York, Freeman.

English Heritage, 2014. *Heritage Counts.* London, Park.

Eve, D. 2014. Reinterpreting the site of Knole Glassworks, Kent. *Post-Medieval Archaeology* 32: 1, 139-42.

Evelyn, J., 1664. *Sylva, or A Discourse of Forest-Trees and the Propagation of Timber.* London, Martyn & Allestry.

Everitt, A., 1977. River and wold: Reflections on the historical origins of regions and pays. *Journal of Historical Geography* 3(1), 1-19.

Everitt, A., 1986. *Continuity and Colonization: The Evolution of Kentish Settlement.* Leicester, Leicester University Press.

Everson, P., 1996. Bodiam Castle, East Sussex: A 14th-Century designed landscape. In D.M. Evans, D. Thackray and P.O. Salway (eds), *The Remains of Distant Times: Archaeology and the National Trust.* Woodbridge, Boydell, 66-72.

Fairclough, G., 1992. Meaningful constructions: Spatial and functional analysis of medieval buildings. *Antiquity* 66(251), 348-66.

Fallon, D., 2008. *An Archaeological Excavation at Bodiam Castle, Robertsbridge, East Sussex.* Unpublished report, Archaeology South-East, available at ESRO R/R/36/14810.

Faulkner, P.A., 1963. Castle planning in the fourteenth century. *Archaeological Journal* 120, 215-35.

Faulkner, P.A., 1970. Some medieval archiepiscopal palaces. *Archaeological Journal* 127:1, 130-46.

Faulkner, P.A., 1975. Domestic planning from the twelfth to the fourteenth centuries. In J.T. Smith, P.A. Faulkner and A. Emery (eds), *Medieval Domestic Architecture.* Leeds, The Royal Archaeological Institute, 84-117.

Fawcett, C., Habu, J. and Matsunaga, J.M., 2008. Introduction: evaluating multiple narratives: beyond nationalist, colonialist, imperialist archaeologies. In J. Habu, C. Fawcett and J.M. Matsunaga (eds), *Evaluating Multiple Narratives: Beyond Nationalist, Colonialist, Imperialist Archaeologies.* New York, Springer, 1-11.

Fear, F., Bawden, R., Rosaen, C. and Foster-Fishman, P., 2002. A model of engaged learning: Frames of reference and scholarly underpinnings. *The Journal of Higher Education Outreach and Engagement* 7, 55-68.

Fleming, A., 2006. Post-processual landscape archaeology: a critique. *Cambridge Archaeological Journal* 16(3), 267.

Fleming, P., 2010. The landed elite, 1300-1500. In S. Sweetinburgh (ed.), *Later Medieval Kent 1220-1540.* Woodbridge, Boydell, 209-33.

Fletcher, T. J., 2001. Farmed deer: new domestic animals defined by controlled breeding. *Reproduction, Fertility and Development* 13:8, 511-6.

Ford, A. and Rutherford, D., 2009. *Ightham Mote, Kent: Garden Conservation Plan.* Two volumes. Unpublished report, National Trust, on file in Ightham archives.

Foot, W., 2006. *The Battlefields That Nearly Were: Defended England 1940.* Stroud, Tempus.

Fox, C., 1922. *Archaeology of the Cambridge Region*. Cambridge, Cambridge University Press.

Fox, C., 1938. *The Personality of Britain: Its Influence on Inhabitant and Invader in Prehistoric and Historic Times*. Cardiff, National Museum of Wales.

Fradley, M., 2005. Warrenhall and other moated sites in north-east Shropshire. *Medieval Settlement Research Group Annual Report* 20, 17-18.

Frankland, T., 2012. A CG artist's impression: depicting virtual reconstructions using non-photorealistic rendering. In A. Chrysanthi, P.M. Flores and C. Papadopoulos (eds), *Thinking Beyond the Tool: Archaeological Computing & the Interpretive Process*. BAR International Series 2344. Oxford, Archaeopress, 24-39.

Furness, H., 2013. Visitors to treat National Trust houses 'as their own', *The Telegraph Online*, available: http://www.telegraph.co.uk/ [accessed 4th August 2015].

Furnivall, F.J. (ed.), 1882. *Fifty Earliest English Wills in the Court of Probate, London: A.D. 1387-1439: With a Priest's of 1454: Copied and Edited from the Original Registers in Somerset House, Church of England Province of Canterbury Prerogative Court*. London, Early English Text Society, Trübner & Co.

Gaffney, C., Gater, J. and Ovendon, S., 1991. *The Use of Geophysical Survey Techniques in Archaeological Evaluations*. IFA Report Technical Paper No. 9. London, Institute of Field Archaeologists.

Gardiner, M., 1994. *A review of the 'Secrets of the Norman Invasion' submitted by Mr N. Austin to the Highways Agency*. Report 1994/249. Unpublished report, South Eastern Archaeological Services.

Gardiner, M., 1998. Settlement change on Denge and Walland Marshes, 1400-1550. In J. Eddison, M. Gardiner and A. Long (eds), *Romney Marsh: Environmental Change and Human Occupation in a Coastal Lowland*, 129-45.

Gardiner, M., 2000. Vernacular buildings and the development of the later medieval domestic plan in England. *Medieval Archaeology* 44, 159-80.

Gardiner, M. and Barber, L., 1994. *A Catalogue of Finds from Bodiam Castle, East Sussex*. Unpublished South Eastern Archaeological Services report 1993/8.

Gardiner, M., Barber, L., Rudling, D., Martin, D. and Stevens, S., 1994. *A Catalogue of Finds from Bodiam Castle, East Sussex*. ASE Project Report 1993/8. Unpublished report, South Eastern Archaeological Services.

Gardiner, M. and Whittick, C., 2011. *Accounts and Records of the Manor of Mote in Iden*, SRS monograph vol. 92. Lewes, Sussex Record Society.

Gerrard, C.M., 2003. *Medieval Archaeology: Understanding Traditions and Contemporary Approaches*. London, Routledge.

Gibson, J.J., 1986. *The Ecological Approach to Visual Perception*. London, Earlbaum.

Gies, F. and Gies, J., 2010. *Life in a Medieval Village*. New York, Harper Collins Publishers.

Gilchrist, R., 1999. *Gender and Archaeology: Contesting the Past*. London, Routledge.

Gilchrist, R., 2012. *Medieval Life: Archaeology and the Life Course*. Woodbridge, Boydell Press.

Giles, K., 2007. Seeing and believing: visuality and space in pre-modern England. *World Archaeology* 39(1), 105-21.

Gillings, M., 2005. The real, the virtually real, and the hyperreal: the role of VR in archaeology. In S. Smiles and S. Moser (eds), *Envisioning the Past: Archaeology and the Image*. Oxford, Blackwell, 223-39.

Gillings, M., 2012. Landscape phenomenology, GIS and the role of affordance. *Journal of Archaeological Method and Theory* 19(4), 601-11.

Gillings, M. and Pollard, J., 1998. Romancing the stones: towards a virtual and elemental Avebury. *Archaeological Dialogues* 5:2, 143-64.

Godwin, H., 1956. *The History of the British Flora*, Cambridge, Cambridge University Press.

Godwin, H., 1975. History of the natural forests of Britain: establishment, dominance and destruction. *Philosophical Transactions of the Royal Society B* 271, 47-67.

Goldberg, P.J.P., (ed), 1997. *Women in Medieval English Society*. Stroud, Sutton.

Goodacre, B. and Baldwin, G., 2002. *Living the Past: Reconstruction, Recreation, Re-Enactment and Education at Museums and Historical Sites*. London, Middlesex University Press.

Goodall, J., 1998a. When an Englishman's castle was his house. *Country Life*, April 9, 48-70.

Goodall, J., 1998b. The battle for Bodiam Castle. *Country Life*, April 16, 58-63.

Goodall, J., 2001. *Bodiam Castle, East Sussex*. London, National Trust.

Goodall, J., 2011. *The English Castle*. New Haven, Yale University Press.

Goodrick, G. and Earl, G.P., 2004. A manufactured past : virtual reality in archaeology. *Internet Archaeology* 15. Available: http://intarch.ac.uk/journal/issue15/index.html.

Gosden, C., 1994. *Social Being and Time*. Oxford, Blackwell.

Goulding, R. and Clubb, J., 2010. Castle in the garden. An architectural history of Scotney Castle. *National Trust Historic Houses & Collections*, 4-11.

Graham, H., 1997. 'A woman's work...': labour and gender in the late medieval countryside. In P.J.P. Goldberg (ed.), *Women in Medieval English Society*. Stroud, Sutton 126-48.

Graham-Campbell, J. and Valor, M. (eds), 2007. *Archaeology of Medieval Europe: Eighth to Twelfth Centuries AD*. Aarhus University Press.

Grant, K., Raemen, E. and Porteus, S., 2009. *An Archaeological Watching Brief, (Car Park Extension), at Bodiam Castle, Robertsbridge*. ASE Report 2009198/4065. Unpublished report, Archaeology South-East.

Greenway, D. and Sayers, J. (eds), 1989. *Jocelin of Brakelond: Chronicle of the Abbey of Bury St Edmunds*. Oxford, Oxford University Press.

Gregory, A., 2010 *Knole: An Architectural and Social History of the Archbishop of Canterbury's House, 1456-1538*. Unpublished PhD thesis, University of Sussex, available at http://sro.sussex.ac.uk/6896/.

Greig, J.R.A., 1992. The deforestation of London. *Review of Palaeobotany and Palynology* 73, 71-86.

Griffin, N., 2003. *An Archaeological Geophysical Survey, Ightham Mote*. Unpublished report, National Trust, on file at Ightham archives.

Grose, F., 1791. *The Antiquities of England and Wales*. London, S. Hooper.

Grove, J., 1988. *The Little Ice Age*. London, Methuen.

Grummit, D., 2010. Kent and national politics, 1399-1461. In S. Sweetinburgh (ed.), *Later Medieval Kent 1220-1540*. Woodbridge, Boydell, 235-50.

Halbuachs, M., 1972. *On Collective Memory*. University of Chicago Press: London.

Hamilakis, Y., 2002. Introduction: experience and corporeality. In Y. Hamilakis, M. Pluciennik and S. Tarlow (eds), *Thinking Through the Body: Archaeologies of Corporeality*. New York, Kluwer Academic/Plenum Publishers, 1-21.

Hamilakis, Y., 2011. Archaeologies of the senses. T. Insoll (ed.), *The Oxford Handbook of the Archaeology of Ritual and Religion*. Oxford, Oxford University Press, 208-25.

Hamilakis, Y., 2014. *Archaeology and the Senses: Human Experience, Memory, and Affect*. Cambridge, Cambridge University Press.

Hamilton, S., Whitehouse, R., Brown, K., Combes, P., Herring, E. and Thomas, M.S., 2006. Phenomenology in practice: Towards a methodology for a 'subjective' approach. *European Journal of Archaeology* 9(1), 31-71.

Hancock, A., 2008. *Geophysical Survey: Old Scotney Castle, Lamberhurst, Kent*. Unpublished report, Archaeological Services & Consultancy Ltd, on file in National Trust archives, Scotney. Available: http://archaeologydataservice.ac.uk/archives/view/greylit/details.cfm?id=29207.

Harvey, I., 2004. Poaching and sedition in fifteenth-century England. In R. Evans (ed.), *Lordship and Learning: Studies in Memory of Trevor Aston*. Woodbridge, Boydell, 169-82.

Harvey, J., 1954. *English Medieval Architects: A Biographical Dictionary Down to 1550*. London, Batsford.

Harvey, J., 1978. *The Perpendicular Style, 1330-1485*. London, Batsford.

Hasted, E., 1798. *The History & Topographical Survey of Kent*. Canterbury, Bristow.

Hatcher, J. and Bailey, M., 2001 *Modelling the Middle Ages: The History and Theory of England's Economic Development*. Oxford, Oxford University Press.

Hauser, M., 2008. *An Archaeology of Black Markets: Local Ceramics and Economies in Eighteenth-Century Jamaica*. Gainesville, University Press of Florida.

Hawkes, J., 1967. God in the machine. *Antiquity* 41, 174-80.

Henderson, M., 2007. *An Archaeological Watching Brief and Historic Building Record during work at Stone Court, Green Court, and the Orangery Roof, Knole, Sevenoaks, Kent*. ASE Report 2335. Unpublished report, Archaeology South-East, available in National Trust archives, Knole.

Henley, J., 2010. How the National Trust is finding its mojo. *The Guardian Online*, available: http://www.guardian.co.uk/, accessed 17th June 2010.

Heritage Lottery Fund, 2015. *20 Years in 12 Places*. Online publication. Available: http://www.hlf.org.uk/about-us/research-evalaution/20-years-heritage.

Hermon, S. and Fabian, P., 2000. Virtual reconstruction of archaeological sites: Avdat Roman Military Camp as a case-study. In F. Niccoluci (ed.) *Virtual Archaeology: Proceedings of the VAST Euroconference, Arezzo 24-25 November 2000.* Oxford, Archaeopress, 103-8.

Hetherington, P., 2006. Safe as houses, *The Guardian online*, available: http://www.theguardian.com/society/2006/jul/12/voluntarysector.guardiansocietysupplement1 [accessed 17th June 2010].

Hillier, B. and Hanson, J., 1984. *The Social Logic of Space*. Cambridge, Cambridge University Press.

Hinton, D., 1990. *Archaeology, economy and society: England from the fifth to the fifteenth century.* London, Routledge.

Hodder, I., 1982. *Symbols in Action: Ethnoarchaeological Studies of Material Culture.* Cambridge, Cambridge University Press.

Hodder, I. (ed.), 1987. *The Archaeology of Contextual Meanings.* Cambridge, Cambridge University Press.

Hodder, I., 2012. *Entangled: An Archaeology of the Relations between Humans and Things.* Oxford, Blackwell.

Hodder, I. and Hutson, S., 2003. *Reading the Past: Current Approaches to Interpretation in Archaeology.* Cambridge, Cambridge University Press.

Hodder, I., Shanks, M., Alexandri, A., Buchli, V., Carman, J., Last, J. and Lucas, G. (eds), 1995. *Interpreting Archaeology: Finding Meaning in the Past.* London, Routledge.

Hohler, C., 1966. Kings and castles: court life in peace and war. In J. Evans and L.C.N. Brooke (eds), *The Flowering of the Middle Ages.* London, Bonanza Books, 133-78.

Holland, B., 2011. *How Extensive was John 'Mad Jack' Fuller's Landscaping at Bodiam Castle? How does this Landscaping Relate to his Brightling Estate and the Sociopolitical Context in which it Lies?* Unpublished BA thesis University of Southampton, Available at http://sites.northwestern.edu/medieval-buildings/.

Holt, R., 1988. *The Mills of Medieval England.* Oxford, Blackwell.

Honess, D., 2009. *New Pumping Station, Bodiam Castle, East Sussex: Geophysical Survey Report.* ASE Report 2009005. Unpublished report, Archaeology South-East, available at ESRO R/R/36/14451.

Hoskins, W G., 1955. *The Making of the English Landscape.* London, Hodder & Stoughton.

Hunt, J., 1965. Byzantine and early medieval. In H. Hayward (ed.), *World Furniture: An Illustrated History.* London, Paul Hamlyn, 12-23.

Impey, I. (ed.), 2008. *The White Tower.* New Haven, Yale University Press.

Ingold, T., 1992. Perception of the environment. In E. Croll and D. Parkin (eds), *Bush Base: Forest Farm -- Culture, Environment and Development.* London, Routledge, 39-56.

Ingold, T., 1993. The temporality of the landscape. *World Archaeology* 25(2), 152-74.

Ingold, T., 2000. *The Perception of the Environment: Essays on Livelihood, Dwelling and Skill.* London, Routledge.

Ingold, T., 2005. Comments on Christopher Tilley: The Materiality of Stone: Explorations in Landscape Phenomenology. *Norwegian Archaeological Review* 38(2), 122-9.

Ingold, T., 2010. Footprints through the weather-world: walking, breathing, knowing. *Journal of the Royal Anthropological Institute*, 121-40.

ISO (International Standards Organization). 2008. *Acoustics — Measurement of room acoustic parameters — Part 2: Reverberation time in ordinary rooms. ISO.* Online resource, available: https://www.iso.org/obp/ui/#iso:std:iso:3382:-2:ed-1:v1:en.

James, R., 2001. *Bodiam Castle, East Sussex: Summary Report of a Watching Brief during Drainage Works.* ASE. Report 1437. Unpublished report, Archaeology South-East.

James, R. and Whittick, C., 2008. *Archaeological and Historic Landscape Survey: Land South of Bodiam Castle, East Sussex.* ASE Project Report 2007201, Document: 2737. Unpublished report, Archaeology South-East, available at ESRO R/R/36/14405 and R/R/24/5/4.

James, S., Marshall, A. and Millett, M., 1984. An early medieval building tradition. *Archaeological Journal* 141, 182-215.

Janssen, C.R., 1969. Alnus as a disturbing factor in pollen diagrams. *Acta Botanica. Neerlandica* 8, 55-8.

Johnson, C., 1999. *An Archaeological Watching Brief at Bodiam Castle, East Sussex (Trees and Shrub Planting).* ASE Report 1062. Unpublished report, Archaeology South-East.

Johnson, C., 2002. *An Archaeological Watching Brief at Bodiam Castle, East Sussex.* Unpublished report, Archaeology South-East.

Johnson, C., 2003. *An Archaeological Watching Brief during Drainage Works at Bodiam Castle, East Sussex.* Unpublished report, Archaeology South-East.

Johnson, C., Martin, D. and Whittick, C., 2000. *Archaeological and Historic Landscape Survey, Bodiam Castle, East Sussex.* ASE Project Report P7. Unpublished report, available at ESRO R/R/36/14944, R/R/36/14944B and R/R/24/5/2.

Johnson, E., 2013. *A Moated Order: Space, Movement, and the Production of Authority in the Medieval Landscape.* Unpublished senior thesis, Northwestern University.

Johnson, E., 2015. Moated sites and the production of authority in the eastern Weald of England. *Medieval Archaeology* 59, 133-54.

Johnson, M.H., 1993. *Housing Culture: Traditional Architecture in an English Landscape.* London, University College London.

Johnson, M.H., 1996. *An Archaeology of Capitalism.* Oxford, Blackwell.

Johnson, M.H., 2002. *Behind the Castle Gate: From Medieval to Renaissance.* London, Routledge.

Johnson, M.H., 2007. *Ideas of Landscape.* Oxford, Blackwell.

Johnson, M.H., 2010a. *Archaeological Theory: An Introduction*, second revised edition. Oxford, Blackwell.

Johnson, M.H., 2010b. *English Houses 1300-1800: Vernacular Architecture, Social Life.* London, Longman.

Johnson, M.H., 2010c. A visit to Down House: some interpretive comments on evolutionary archaeology. In A. Gardner and E. Cochrane (eds), *Evolutionary and Interpretive Archaeologies.* Walnut Creek, Left Coast Press, 307-24.

Johnson, M H., 2011. On the nature of empiricism in archaeology. *Journal of the Royal Anthropological Institute* 17(4), 764-87.

Johnson, M.H., 2012a. Phenomenological approaches to landscape archaeology. *Annual Review of Anthropology* 41, 269-84.

Johnson, M.H., 2012b. What do medieval buildings mean? *History and Theory* 52, 380-99.

Johnston, S.A., Campana, D. and Crabtree, P., 2009. A Geophysical Survey at Dún Ailinne, County Kildare, Ireland. *Journal of Field Archaeology* 34, 385-402.

Jones, A.M., 2007. *Memory and Material Culture.* Cambridge, Cambridge University Press.

Jones, J., 2007. *Nocturnal Territories: Sleeping and the Construction of Gender 1350-1750 AD.* Unpublished Masters thesis, University of Southampton.

Jones, R., 1999. Castles and other defensive sites. In K. Leslie and B. Short (eds), *An Historical Atlas of Sussex.* London, Phillimore, 50-1.

Jones, R. and Page, M., 2006. *Medieval Villages in an English Landscape: Beginnings and Ends.* Oxford, Windgather Press.

Judkins, R.R., 2013. The game of the courtly hunt: chasing and breaking the deer in late medieval English literature. *The Journal of English and Germanic Philology* 112(1), 70-92.

Kantner, J., 2000. Realism vs reality: creating virtual reconstructions of prehistoric architecture. In J.A. Barcelo, M. Forte and D. Sanders (eds), *Virtual Reality in Archaeology. Computer Applications and Quantitative Methods in Archaeology.* BAR International Series 843. Oxford, British Archaeological Reports, 47-52.

Kellala, M. 2013, *Bodiam: In Search of the Classis Britannica River Port.* Unpublished Masters dissertation, University of Southampton.

Kenyon, J.R., 1981. Early artillery fortifications in England and Wales: a preliminary survey and reappraisal. *The Archaeological Journal* 138, 205-40.

Kilburne, R., 1659. *A Topographie or Survey of the County of Kent.* London, Atkinson.

Killingray, D., 1994. Rights, 'riot' and ritual: the Knole Park access dispute, Sevenoaks, Kent, 1883-5. *Rural History* 5, 63-79.

Killingray, D., 2010. Influences shaping the human landscape of the Sevenoaks area since c. 1600. *Archaeologia Cantiana* 130, 35-64.

King, D.J.C., 1983. *Castellarium Anglicanum.* London, Kraus.

Kleiner, M., Dalenback, B.-I. and Svensson, P., 1993. Auralization: an overview. *Journal of Audio Engineering Society* 41(November), 861-75.

Knocker, H.W., 1926. Sevenoaks: the manor, church, and market. *Archaeologia Cantiana* 38, 51-68.

Koerner, S. and Russell, I., 2010. *Unquiet Pasts: Risk Society, Lived Cultural Heritage, Re-designing Reflexivity.* Farnham, Ashgate.

Kosiba, S. and Bauer, A.M., 2013. Mapping the political landscape: toward a GIS analysis of environmental and social difference. *Journal of Archaeological Method and Theory* 20:1, 61-101.

Kuttruff, H., 2009. *Room Acoustics*, Fifth edition. Oxford, CRC Press.

Le Patourel, H.E.J., 1973. *The Moated Sites of Yorkshire*. SMA Monograph Series 5. London, Society for Medieval Archaeology.

Le Patourel, H.E.J. and Roberts, B.K., 1978. The significance of moated sites. In F.A. Aberg (ed.), *Medieval Moated Sites*. CBA Research Report 17. London, Council for British Archaeology, 46-55.

Leach, P.E., n.d.a. *Archaeological Report During Building Conservation of Ightham Mote, Vol. 1, North East Quarter 1989-1992 and Drawings*. Unpublished report, on file in National Trust archives, Ightham.

Leach, P.E., n.d.b. *Archaeological Report During Building Conservation of Ightham Mote, Vol. 2, Gate Tower & Clock Tower 1992-1993, Cottages, 1993-1994 and Drawings*. Unpublished report, on file in National Trust archives, Ightham.

Leach, P.E., n.d.c. *Archaeological Report During Building Conservation of Ightham Mote, Vol. 3, The East Range 1994-1995, The North West Quarter 1996-1997 and Drawings*. Unpublished report, on file in National Trust archives, Ightham.

Leach, P.E., n.d.d. *Archaeological Report During Building Conservation of Ightham Mote, Vol. 4, The South East Quarter 1998-2000; Laundry Cottage 1999-2000 and Drawings*. Unpublished report, on file in National Trust archives, Ightham.

Leach, P.E., n.d.e. *Archaeological Report During Building Conservation of Ightham Mote, Vol. 5, The Great Hall and Stair Hall 2000-1; West Lawn North Wall 2001*. Unpublished report, on file in National Trust archives, Ightham.

Leach, P.E., n.d.f. *Archaeological Report During Building Conservation of Ightham Mote, Vol. 7, The Great Courtyard & Fountain Garden 2005-6*. Unpublished report, on file in National Trust archives, Ightham.

Leach, P.E. and Rumley, P.J., n.d. *Archaeological Report During Building Conservation of Ightham Mote, Vol. 6, The South West Quarter 2002-4; Cottages 3 & 4*. Unpublished report, on file in National Trust archives, Ightham.

Lefebvre, H., 1991 [1974]. *The Production of Space*, translated by Nicholson-Smith, Oxford, Blackwell.

Leighton, M., 2015. Excavation methodologies and labour as epistemic concerns in the practice of archaeology: comparing examples from British and Andean archaeology. *Archaeological Dialogues* 22(1), 55-88.

Lemmon, C.H., 1960-61. The Rochester-Hastings Roman road. *Battle and District Historical Society Transactions* 10, 26-7.

Lemmon, C.H. and Darrell Hill, J., 1966. The Romano-British site in Bodiam. *Sussex Archaeological Collections* 104, 88-102.

Liddiard, R., 2005a. *Castles in Context: Power, Symbolism and Landscape, 1066-1500*. Macclesfield, Windgather Press.

Liddiard, R., 2005b. *Tutor's Guide to Teaching Medieval Castles*. London, Higher Education Academy.

Liddiard, R. and Williamson, T.M., 2008. There by design? Some reflections on medieval elite landscapes. *Archaeological Journal* 165, 520-35.

Linford, N. and Martin, L., 2008. *Shelford Manor, Shelford, Nottinghamshire: Report on geophysical survey, November 2007*. Unpublished EH report 031-2008. Portsmouth, English Heritage.

Little, B.J. and Zimmerman, L.J., 2010. In the public interest: creating a more activist, civically-engaged archaeology. In W. Ashmore, D. Lippert and B. Mills (eds), *Voices in American Archaeology*. Washington, DC, Society for American Archaeology, 131-59.

Llobera, M., 1996. Exploring the topology of mind: GIS, social space and archaeology. *Antiquity* 70, 612-22.

Long, A.J., 1992. Coastal responses to changes in sea level in the East Kent Fens and southeast England, U.K. over the last 7500 years. *Proceedings of the Geologists' Association* 103, 187-99.

Long, A.J. and Innes, J.B., 1993. Holocene sea-level changes and coastal sedimentation in Romney Marsh, southeast England, UK. *Proceedings of the Geologists' Association* 104, 223-37.

Long, A.J. and Scaife, R.G., 1995. Radiocarbon dates from Weatherlees Hill WTW - implication for relative sea-level movements. In C.M. Hearne, D.R.J. Perkins and P. Andrews (eds), *The Sandwich Bay Wastewater Treatment Scheme Archaeological Project, 1992-1994*. 320-2.

Long, A.J., Waller, M.P. and Plater, A.J. (eds), 2007. *Dungeness and Romney Marsh: Barrier Dynamics and Marshland Evolution*. Oxford, Oxbow.

Lozny, L.R., 2011. *Comparative Archaeologies: A Sociological View of the Science of the Past*. London, Springer.

Lucas, G., 2012. *Understanding the Archaeological Record*. Cambridge, Cambridge University Press.

Lynch, K., 1972. *'What Time is This Place?'* Massachusetts, MIT. Press.

Mackenzie, J.D., 1896. *The Castles of England, Their Story and Structure*. New York, The Macmillan Co.

Markham, G., 1625. *The Inrichment of the Weald of Kent: or a Direction to the Husbandman, for the True Ordering, Manuring, and Inriching of all the Grounds Within the Wealds of Kent and Sussex, and may Generally Serve for all the Grounds in England, of that Nature. Painfully Gathered for the Good of this Land, by a Man of Great Eminence and Worth*. London, G.P. for Roger Jackson.

Marquardt, W.H. and Crumley, C.L., 1987. *Regional Dynamics: Burgundian Landscapes in Historical Perspective*. San Diego, Academic Press.

Martin, D., 1973. *Bodiam Castle Medieval Bridges*. Hastings Area Archaeological Papers 1. Battle, Robertsbridge and District Archaeological Society.

Martin, D., 1989. Three moated sites in north-east Sussex, Part 1: Glottenham. *Sussex Archaeological Collections* 127, 89-122.

Martin, D., 1990. Three moated sites in north-east Sussex, Part 2: Hawksden and Bodiam. *Sussex Archaeological Collections* 128, 89-116.

Martin, D. and Martin, B., 2001. Westenhanger Castle - a revised interpretation. *Archaeologia Cantiana* 121, 203-36.

Martin, D. and Martin, B., 2004. *New Winchelsea, Sussex: A Medieval Port Town*. London, English Heritage.

Martin, D. and Martin, B., 2005. *An Archaeological Record and Overview of the Portcullis at Bodiam Castle, Bodiam, East Sussex*. ASE Report 1992. Unpublished report, Archaeology South-East. Available: ESRO R/R/36/14206.

Martin, D. and Martin, B., 2006. *Farm Buildings of the Weald 1450-1750: A Wood-Pasture Region in South-East England Once Dominated by Small Family Farms*. Kings Lynn, Heritage.

Martin, D., Martin, B. and Clubb, J., 2011. An archaeological interpretative survey of the Old Castle, Scotney, Lamberhurst: Part One - the medieval period. *Archaeologia Cantiana* 131, 321-44.

Martin, D., Martin, B. and Clubb, J., 2012. An archaeological interpretative survey of the Old Castle, Scotney, Lamberhurst: Part Two. *Archaeologia Cantiana* 132, 111-51.

Martin, D., Martin, B., Clubb, J. and Goulding, R., 2008. *An Archaeological Interpretive Survey of the Old Castle, Scotney, Lamberhurst, Kent*. ASE Project 3297. Unpublished report, Archaeology South East, available in National Trust archives, Scotney.

Martin, E., 1989. Medieval moats in Suffolk. *Medieval Settlement Research Group Annual Report* 4, 14.

Martinez-Jausoro, R., 2009. *The Orangery at Knole, Sevenoaks: Historic Building Recording and Investigation*. Unpublished report, Oxford Archaeology. Available at National Trust archive, Knole; also available at https://library.thehumanjourney.net/185/1/SEOKO08.pdfA.pdf.

Massey, D., 1994. *Space, Place and Gender*. Oxford, Polity.

Mate, M., 1998. *Daughters, Wives and Widows after the Black Death: Women in Sussex 1350-1535*. Woodbridge, Boydell.

Mate, M., 2010a. The economy of Kent, 1200-1500: the age of expansion, 1200-1348. In S. Sweetinburgh (ed.), *Later Medieval Kent 1220-1540*. Woodbridge, Boydell, 1-10.

Mate, M., 2010b. The economy of Kent, 1200-1500: the aftermath of the Black Death. In S. Sweetinburgh (ed.), *Later Medieval Kent 1220-1540*. Woodbridge, Boydell, 11-24.

Mathieu, J.R., 1999. New methods on old castles: generating new ways of seeing. *Medieval Archaeology* 43, 115-42.

Mawer, A., Stenton, F.M. and Gover, J.E.B., 1929-1930. *The Place-Names of Sussex*. Two volumes. English Place-Name Society 6-7. Cambridge, Cambridge University Press.

Mileson, S.A., 2007. The sociology of park creation in medieval England. In R. Liddiard (ed.), *The Medieval Park: New Perspectives*. Macclesfield, Windgather Press, 11-26.

Mileson, S.A., 2009. *Parks in Medieval England*. Oxford, Oxford University Press.

Miller, A.G., 2010. Knights, bishops and deer parks: episcopal identity, emasculation and clerical space in medieval England. In J.D. Thibodeaux (ed.), *Negotiating Clerical Identities: Priests, Monks and Masculinity in the Middle Ages*. New York, Palgrave MacMillan, 204-37.

Miller Tritton & Partners 2003. *Knole Stone Court*. Report 2148. Unpublished report, on file in National Trust archives, Knole.

Minihan, G., 2015. *Ightham Mote in the 14th Century: The Lived Experience of Sir Thomas Couen (d.1372)* Unpublished PhD thesis, University of Southampton.

Mlekuz, D., 2004. Listening to the landscapes: modelling soundscapes in GIS. *Internet Archaeology* 16. Available: http://intarch.ac.uk/journal/issue16/.

Moore, P.D. and Webb, J.A., 1978. *An Illustrated Guide to Pollen Analysis*. London, Hodder and Stoughton.

Moore, P.D., Webb, J.A. and Collinson, M.E., 1991. *Pollen Analysis*, Second edition. Oxford, Blackwell.

Moreland, J., 2001. *Archaeology and Text*. London, Duckworth.

Morgan, J. and Welton, P., 1994. The process of communication. In E. Hooper-Greenhill (ed.), *The Educational Role of the Museum*. London, Routledge, 27-36.

Morrill, J., 1984. The religious context of the English Civil War. *Transactions of the Royal Historical Society Fifth Series* 34, 155-78.

Morris, M., 2003. *Castle*. London, Macmillan.

Moser, S., 1992. The visual language of archaeology: a case study of the Neanderthals. *Antiquity* 66, 831-44.

Moser, S., 2001. Archaeological representation: the visual conventions for constructing knowledge about the past. In I. Hodder (ed.), *Archaeological Theory Today*. Cambridge, Polity, 292-322.

MovieMongerHZ, 2010. Toccata and Fugue in D Minor, [Video online], YouTube. Available: https://www.youtube.com/watch?v=ho9rZjlsyYY.

Mozart, W.A., 2011. Eine kleine Nachtmusik, [Video online], YouTube. Available: https://www.youtube.com/watch?v=o1FSN8_pp_o.

Munby, J. 2007. *Knole: An Archaeological Survey*. Unpublished report, Oxford Archaeology, available at National Trust archives, Knole.

Murray, S., 2008. The study of Gothic architecture. In C. Rudolph (ed.), *A Companion to Medieval Art: Romanesque and Gothic in Northern Europe*. Oxford, Blackwell, 382-402.

Myres, J.N.L., 1935. The medieval pottery at Bodiam Castle. *Sussex Archaeological Collections* 76, 222-30.

Nairn, I. and Pevsner, N., 1965. *The Buildings of England: Sussex*. Harmondsworth, Penguin.

National Co-ordinating Centre for Public Engagement, n.d. *NCCPE*. Online resource. Available: http://www.publicengagement.ac.uk/.

National Trust, 2009. *Scotney Conservation Management Plan*. Unpublished report, available in National Trust archives, Scotney.

National Trust 2015. *Playing Our Part. What Does the Nation Need from the National Trust in the 21st Century?* London, National Trust. Available at https://www.nationaltrust.org.uk/documents/national-trust-playing-our-part.pdf.

Neal, D.G., 2008. *The Masculine Self in Late Medieval England*. Chicago, University of Chicago Press.

Newman, J., 2012. *Kent: West and the Weald*, Pevsner Architectural Guides: The Buildings of England. New Haven, Yale University Press.

Nicolson, N., 2005 [1998]. *Ightham Mote*, Second revised edition. Swindon, National Trust.

Nigota, J.A., 2004. Fiennes, James, first Baron Saye and Sele (c.1390-1450). *Oxford Dictionary of National Biography* 19, 521-3.

O'Neil, B.H.S.J., 1960. *Castles and Cannon: A Study of Early Artillery Fortifications in England*. Oxford, Clarendon Press.

O'Halloran, S. and Woudstra, J., 2012. 'Keeping the garden at Knole': The gardeners of Knole in Sevenoaks, Kent, 1622-1711. *Garden History* 40(1), 34-55.

Olsen, B., 2003. Material culture after text: re-membering things. *Norwegian Archaeological Review* 36(2), 87-104.

Osiris Marine Services Limited. 2005. *Knole Underground Water Tank Diving Survey*. Unpublished report, on file in National Trust archives, Knole.

Overholtzer, L. and Robin, C. (eds), 2015. *The Materiality of Everyday Life*. Archaeological Papers of the American Anthropological Association 26. Washington, American Anthropological Association.

Page, W, 1907. Houses of Cistercian monks: Abbey of Robertsbridge. In W. Page (ed.), *A History of the County of Sussex: Volume 2.* London, Victoria County History, 71-4.

Parker Pearson, M.M. and Richards, C., 1994. *Architecture and Order: Approaches to Social Space.* New York, Routledge.

Peacock, B.Y., 2010. *The Role of Bodiam Castle in Popular Memory.* Unpublished Masters dissertation, University of Southampton.

Peacock, B. 2015. *The Future of Museum Communication: Strategies for Engaging Audiences on Archaeology.* Unpublished PhD thesis, University of Southampton. Available:

Pearce, B., 1930. The Roman site at Otford. *Archaeologia Cantiana* 42, 157-71.

Pearson, S., 1994. *The Medieval Houses of Kent: An Historical Analysis.* London, Her Majesty's Stationery Office.

Peyre, L., 2010. *An Archaeological Watching Brief at Knole House in Sevenoaks During Enabling Groundworks for Foul Water Separation Provision.* ASE Report 4150. Unpublished report, Archaeology South-East, available in National Trust archives, Knole.

Philip, B., 2002. The Anglo-Saxon cemetery at Polhill near Sevenoaks, Kent 1964-1986. West Wickham, Kent Archaeological Rescue Unit.

Phillips, C.J. 1923. *The History of the Sackville Family.* Two volumes. London, Cassell.

Phythian-Adams, C., 1992. Hoskins' England: a local historian of genius and the realisation of his theme. *Local Historian* 22, 170-83.

Pinterest, 2014. *About Pinterest.* Online resource, Available: https://about.pinterest.com/en-gb.

Platt, C., 1982. *The Castle in Medieval England & Wales.* London, Secker & Warburg.

Platt, C., 2007. Revisionism in castle studies: a caution. *Medieval Archaeology* 51, 83-102.

Platt, C., 2010a. The homestead moat: security or status? *Archaeological Journal* 167(1), 115-33.

Platt, C., 2010b. Review of Gilchrist, R. and Reynolds, A. (eds) *Reflections: 50 years of Medieval Archaeology. Medieval Archaeology* 54, 431-3.

Pollard, J. and Gillings, M., 1998. Romancing the stones: towards a virtual and elemental Avebury. *Archaeological Dialogues* 5(2), 143-64.

Pope, M., 2009. *A Geoarchaeological Watching Brief at the Rose Garden, Bodiam, Robertsbridge, East Sussex.* Unpublished Archaeology South-East report 2008254. Available at http://archaeologydataservice.ac.uk/archives/view/greylit/details.cfm?id=8228.

Pope, M., Maxted, A., Whittaker, J. and Scaife, R.G., 2009. *A Geoarchaeological Watching Brief at the Rose Garden, Bodiam, Robertsbridge, East Sussex.* ASE Project Report 2008254/3364. Unpublished report, Archaeology South-East. Available at http://archaeologydataservice.ac.uk/archives/view/greylit/details.cfm?id=8228.

Pope, M., Priestley-Bell, G. and James, R., 2011. *An Archaeological Watching Brief at Bodiam Castle Sewage Treatment Plant, Rose Garden, Bodiam, East Sussex.* ASE Project Report 2011218/4470. Unpublished report, Archaeology South-East.

Prager, B., 2007. *Aesthetic Vision and German Romanticism: Writing Images.* New York, Camden House.

Preucel, R. and Mrozowski, S. (eds), 2010. *Contemporary Archaeology in Theory: The New Pragmatism.* Oxford, Blackwell.

Priestley-Bell, G., 1995. *An Archaeological Watching Brief at Bodiam Castle, East Sussex.* ASE Report 310. Unpublished report, Archaeology South-East.

Priestley-Bell, G. and Pope, M., 2009. *An Archaeological and Geo-Archaeological Evaluation at the 'Rose Garden', Bodiam Castle, Kent. Portslade, East Sussex*: Archaeology South-East. Project Report 2009095/3765, Available: http://www.ucl.ac.uk/archaeologyse/resources/report-library/pdf-library-map-all and at ESRO R/R/36/14598.

Puckle, G.M., 1960. The Roman road near Bodiam Station. *Sussex Notes and Queries* 15, 6.

Rackham, O., 1986. *The History of the Countryside.* London, Dent.

Rackham, O., 1990. *Trees and Woodland in the British Landscape.* London, Dent.

Radulescu, R. and Truelove, A. (eds), 2005. *Gentry Culture in Late Medieval England.* Manchester, Manchester University Press.

Rardin, A., 2006 *Knole Park and Gardens - Historic Garden Assessment.* Unpublished report, available at National Trust archives, Knole.

Ravilious, K., 2016. The many lives of an English manor house. *Archaeology* 69(1), 44-9.

Ray, K., 2008. Transcending an archaeology of the visual: some spheres of implicated discourse in past material culture. In J. Thomas and V.O. Jorge (eds), *Archaeology and the Politics of Vision in a Post-Modern Context*. Cambridge, Cambridge Scholars Publishing, 13-29.

Recarte, J.M., Vincent, J.P. and Hewison, A.J.M., 1998. Flight responses of park fallow deer to the human observer. *Behavioral Processes* 44, 65-72.

Redwood, B.C. and Wilson, A.E., 1958. *Custumals of the Sussex Manors of the Archbishop of Canterbury*. Sussex Record Society 57. Lewes, Suffolk Records Society.

Reynolds, K.D., 1998. *Aristocratic Women and Political Society in Victorian Britain*. Oxford, Clarendon Press.

Rigold, S., 1968. Two types of court hall. *Archaeologia Cantiana* 83, 1-22.

Riccoboni, P., 2004. *Bodiam Castle Drainage Work (Phase 2)*. ASE report 1935. Unpublished report, Archaeology South-East, Available at ESRO R/R/36/14064.

Rippon, S., 2008. *Beyond the Medieval Village: The Diversification of Landscape Character in Southern Britain*. Oxford, Oxford University Press.

Robbins, P., 2012. *Political Ecology: A Critical Introduction*, Second edition. London, Wiley.

Roberts, B.K., 1964. Moats and mottes. *Medieval Archaeology* 8, 219-22.

Roberts, B.K., 2008. *Landscapes, Documents and Maps: Villages in Northern England and Beyond, AD900-1250*. Oxford, Oxbow.

Roberts, B.K. and Wrathmell, S., 2002. *Region and Place: A Study of English Rural Settlement*. London, English Heritage.

Roberts, E., 1988. The Bishop of Winchester's deer parks in Hampshire 1200-1400. *Proceedings of the Hampshire Field Club Archaeological Society* 44, 67-86.

Robin, C., 2013. *Everyday Life Matters: Maya Farmers at Chan*. Gainesville, University Press of Florida.

Rose, G., 1993. *Feminism and Geography*. Oxford, Polity.

Rumley, P.J., 2002. *The Archaeology of Selby Barn*. Unpublished report for the National Trust.

Rumley, P.J., 2006. *The Archaeological Watching Brief, Ightham Mote Water Treatment Plant*. Unpublished report, on file in National Trust archives, Ightham.

Rumley, P.J., 2007. *Ightham Mote, Ivy Hatch, Kent: Archaeological Assessment of the Garden*. Unpublished report, on file in National Trust archives, Ightham.

Rushton, N.S., 1999. Parochialisation and patterns of patronage in 11th century Sussex. *Sussex Archaeological Collections* 138, 133-52.

Russell, M., 2004. *Piltdown Man: The Secret Life of Charles Dawson*. Oxford, Tempus.

Sackville-West, V., 1922. *Knole and the Sackvilles*. London, Ernest Benn.

Salzman, L.F., 1952. *Building in England down to 1540: A Documentary History*. Oxford, Oxford University Press.

Samuel, R., 1994. *Theatres of Memory*. London, Verso.

Sands, H., 1903. Bodiam Castle. *Sussex Archaeological Collections* 46, 114-33.

Saul, N., 1984. Murder and justice medieval style: the Pashley case, 1327-8. *History Today* 34:8, 30.

Saul, N., 1986. *Scenes from Provincial Life: Knightly Families in Sussex 1280-1400*. Oxford, Oxford University Press.

Saul, N., 1995. Bodiam Castle. *History Today* 45(1), 16-21.

Saul, N., 1997. *Richard II*. New Haven, Yale University Press.

Saul, N., 1998. The rise of the Dallingridge family. *Sussex Archaeological Collections* 136, 123-32.

Saul, N., Mackman, J. and Whittick, C., 2011. Grave stuff: litigation with a London tomb-maker in 1421. *Historical Research* 84, 572-85.

Savery, J.C., 1868. On Bodiam manor and castle. *Journal of British Archaeological Association* 24, 352-61.

Sawyer, P.H., 1968. *Anglo-Saxon Charters. An Annotated Bibliography*. London, Royal Historical Society.

Scaife, R.G., 1980. *Late-Devensian and Flandrian Palaeoecological Studies in the Isle of Wight*. Unpublished PhD thesis, University of London, King's College.

Scaife, R.G., 2000. Holocene vegetation development in London. In J. Sidell, K. Wilkinson, R.G. Scaife and N. Cameron (eds), *The Holocene Evolution of the London Thames. Archaeological Excavations (1991-1998) for the London Underground Limited, Jubilee Line Extension Project*. London, Museum of London, 111-7.

Scaife, R.G., 2004. Pollen. In G. Keevil (ed.), *The Tower of London Moat: Archaeological Excavations 1995-9*. Oxford Archaeology and Historic Palaces Commission, 38-41; 79, 84-5,137-43; 182-85; 202.

Scaife, R.G. 2013. *Bodiam Castle: Stratigraphy and Pollen Analysis of the Soils and Sediments*. Unpublished report, University of Southampton.

Scaife, R.G. and Burrin, P.J., 1983. Floodplain development in, and the vegetational history of the Sussex High Weald and some archaeological implications. *Sussex Archaeological Collections* 121, 1-10.

Scaife, R G. and Burrin, P.J., 1985. The environmental impact of prehistoric man as recorded in the Cuckmere floodplain at Stream Farm, Chiddingly. *Sussex Archaeological Collections* 123, 27-34.

Scaife, R.G. and Burrin, P.J., 1987. Further evidence for the environmental impact of prehistoric cultures in Sussex as evidenced from alluvial fill deposits in the eastern Rother valley. *Proceedings of the Sussex Archaeological Society* 125, 1-6.

Scaife, R.G. and Burrin, P J., 1992. Archaeological inferences from alluvial sediments: some findings from southern England. In S. Needham and M. Macklin (eds), *Alluvial Archaeology in Britain*. Oxford, Oxbow, 75-91.

Scaife, R.G. and Copeland, P., 2015. *Bodiam Castle, Bodiam, East Sussex: Report on Coring in and around Bodiam Castle Permitted under Scheduled Monument Consent S00044985*. Unpublished report, University of Southampton, available at http://sites.northwestern.edu/medieval-buildings/.

Sclater, A.A., 1989. *Knole - Parkland and Garden Improvement Consultants: Vol 1-2*. Unpublished report, on file in National Trust archives, Knole.

Scollar, I., 1990. *Archaeological Prospecting and Remote Sensing*. Cambridge, Cambridge University Press.

Sidell, J., Wilkinson, K., Scaife, R.G. and Cameron, N., 2000. *The Holocene Evolution of the London Thames. Archaeological excavations (1991-1998) for the London Underground Limited, Jubilee Line Extension Project*, London, Museum of London.

Simpson, W.D., 1931. The moated homestead, church and castle of Bodiam. *Sussex Archaeological Collections* 72, 69-99.

Simpson, W.D., 1946. 'Bastard feudalism' and the later castles. *Antiquaries Journal* 26, 145-71.

Smith, A.T., 2003. *The Political Landscape: Constellations of Authority in Early Complex Polities*. Berkeley, University of California Press.

Smith, R.D. and Brown, R.R., 1989. The Bodiam mortar. *Journal of the Ordnance Society* 1, 3-22.

Speed, L., 1996. *An Archaeological Watching Brief at Bodiam Castle, East Sussex*. ASE Report 494. Unpublished report, Archaeology South-East. Available at ESRO R/R/36/14131.

Spencer, C. and Woodland, W., 2002. Palaeoenvironmental changes during the last 4000 years at Scotney Marsh, Romney Marsh, Kent: a multiproxy approach. In A. Long, S. Hipkin and H. Clarke (eds), *Romney Marsh: Coastal and Landscape Change Through the Ages*. Oxford, Oxford University Committee for Archaeology, 58-74.

Spencer, D. 2014. Edward Dallingridge: builder of Bodiam Castle. *Ex Historia* 6, 81-98. Available online at http://humanities.exeter.ac.uk/history/research/exhistoria/archive/volume6/.

Stace, C., 1992. *New Flora of the British Isles*. Cambridge, Cambridge University Press.

Statton, M., 2009. *An Archaeological Assessment of Bodiam Castle, Rother, East Sussex*. Archaeology South-East. Report 2009055.

Steane, J.M., 2001. *The Archaeology of Power*. Stroud, Tempus.

Stevens, S., 1995. *Bodiam Castle Moat Bank Protections Scheme*. ASE Report 147. Unpublished report, Archaeology South-East.

Stevens, S., 1999. A section through the moat bank at Bodiam Castle. *Sussex Archaeological Collections* 137, 182-3.

Stocker, D., 1992. The shadow of the General's armchair. *The Archaeological Journal* 149, 415-20.

Stocker, D. and Stocker, M., 1996. Sacred profanity: The theology of rabbit breeding and the symbolic landscape of the warren. *World Archaeology* 28(2), 265-72.

Strutt and Parker 1989. *The Restoration of Knole Park: A Landscape Report for The Trustees of the Knole Estate*. Unpublished report, on file in National Trust archives, Knole.

Sykes, N., 2007. Animal bones and animal parks. In R. Liddiard (ed.), *The Medieval Park: New Perspectives*. Macclesfield, Windgather Press, 49-62.

Tauber, H., 1965. Differential pollen dispersion and the interpretation of pollen diagrams. *Danmarks Geologiske Undersogelse II* 89, 1-69.

Tauber, H., 1967. Investigation of the mode of pollen transfer in forested areas. *Review of Palaeobotany and Palynology* 3, 277-87.

Taylor, C., 1972. Medieval moats in Cambridgeshire. In P.J. Fowler (ed.), *Archaeology and the Landscape: Essays for L.V. Grinsell*. London, 237-49.

Taylor, C., 1973. *The Cambridgeshire Landscape*. London, Hodder and Stoughton.

Taylor, C., 1984. *Village and Farmstead: A History of Rural Settlement in England*. London, George Philip.

Taylor, C., 2004. Ravensdale Park, Derbyshire, and medieval deer coursing. *Landscape History* 26(1), 37-57.

Taylor, C., Everson, P. and Wilson-North, R., 1990. Bodiam Castle, Sussex. *Medieval Archaeology* 34, 155-57.

Taylor, K., 2003. The development of the Park and Gardens at Knole. *Archaeologia Cantiana* 123, 153-84.

Thackray, C. and Bailey, G., 2007. *Bodiam Castle, Robertsbridge, East Sussex: Conservation Statement (v. 6.0)*. Bodiam, East Sussex: The National Trust. Unpublished report for the National Trust.

Thackray, D., 1991. *Bodiam Castle*. London, National Trust.

Thomas, J., 1999. *Time, Culture and Identity: An Interpretative Archaeology*. London, Routledge.

Thomas, J., 2001. Archaeologies of place and landscape. In I. Hodder (ed.), *Archaeological Theory Today*. Oxford, Blackwell, 167-86.

Thomas, J. and Jorge, V.O., 2008. *Archaeology and the Politics of Vision in a Post-Modern Context*. Cambridge, Cambridge Scholars Publishing.

Thompson, A.H., 1912. *Military Architecture in England during the Middle Ages*. Oxford, Oxford University Press.

Thompson, F.H., 1986. The Iron Age hillfort of Oldbury, Kent: Excavations 1983-4. *Antiquaries Journal* 66, 267-86.

Thompson, M.W., 1995. *The Medieval Hall: The Basis of Secular Domestic Life 600-1600*. Aldershot, Scolar Press.

Thompson, M.W., 2003. Hedging power in the European tradition: function, finery or fear? *Antiquity* 77, 620-24.

Tilley, C. (ed.), 1990. *Reading Material Culture*. Oxford, Blackwell.

Tilley, C., 1994. *A Phenomenology of Landscape*. London, Routledge.

Tilley, C., 2004. *The Materiality of Stone: Explorations in Landscape Phenomenology*. Oxford, Berg.

Tilley, C., 2008. *Body and Image: Explorations in Landscape Phenomenology*. Walnut Creek, Left Coast Press.

Timbs, J. and Gunn, A., 1872. *Abbeys, Castles and Ancient Halls of England and Wales Vol.1*. London, Frederick Warne.

Tipping, H.A., 1921. *English Homes: Period 1 Volume 1*. London, Country Life.

Town, E., 2010. *A House 'Re-edified' - Thomas Sackville and the Transformation of Knole 1605-1608*. Unpublished PhD thesis, University of Sussex, available at http://sro.sussex.ac.uk/6893/.

Toy, S., 1953. *The Castles of Great Britain*. London, Heinemann.

Turner, D.J., 1986. Bodiam, Sussex: true castle or old soldier's dream house? In W.M. Ormrod (ed.), *England in the 14th Century: Proceedings of the 1985 Harlaxton Symposium*. Woodbridge, Boydell, 267-77.

Turner, J., 1962. The Tilia decline: an anthropogenic interpretation. *New Phytologist* 61, 328-41.

Turner, T.H. and Parker, J.H., 1859. *Some Account of Domestic Architecture in England Vol. 3*. Oxford, Oxford University Press.

Verhaeghe, F., 1981. Medieval moated sites in coastal Flanders. In F.A. Aberg and A.E. Brown (eds), *Medieval Moated Sites in North-West Europe*. BAR International Series 121. Oxford, British Archaeological Reports 127-72.

Vigran, T.E., 2008. *Building Acoustics*. New York, Taylor & Francis.

Vivian, S.P. (ed.), 1953. *The Manor of Etchingham cum Salehurst*, Sussex Records Society 53. Lewes, Suffolk Records Society.

Vorländer, M., 2007. *Auralization: Fundamentals of Acoustics, Modelling, Simulation, Algorithms and Acoustic Virtual Reality*. New York, Springer.

Walker, S., 1983. Lancaster v. Dallingridge: a franchisal dispute in 14th century Sussex. *Sussex Archaeological Collections* 112, 87-94.

Waller, M., 1993. Flandrian vegetational history of south-eastern England. Pollen data from Pannel Bridge, East Sussex. *New Phytologist* 124, 345-69.

Waller, M., 1994a. Flandrian vegetation history of south-eastern England. Stratigraphy of the Brede valley and pollen data from Brede Bridge. *New Phytologist* 126, 369-92.

Waller, M., 1994b. Paludification and pollen representation: the influence of wetland size on Tilia representation in pollen diagrams. *The Holocene* 4, 430-4.

Waller, M., Burrin, P.J. and Marlow, A., 1988. Flandrian sedimentation and palaeoenvironments in Pett Level, the Brede and lower Rother valleys and Walland Marsh. In J. Eddison and C. Green (eds), *Romney Marsh, Evolution, Occupation, Reclamation*. Oxford.,Oxford University Committee for Archaeology, 3-30.

Ward, C.P., 1990. *The Romano-British Cremation Cemetery at Frog Farm, Otford, Kent in the context of contemporary funerary practices in South-East England*. Available at http,//www.kentarchaeology.org.uk/Research/02/ODAG/01/00.htm.

Watkeys, D., 2011. Roves Farm, Swindon, Wiltshire, Archaeological Evaluation Report. Oxford: Oxford Archaeological Unit. Report 5/11/0327, Document: 5174. Available at http://archaeologydataservice.ac.uk/archives/view/greylit/details.cfm?id=24578

Weideger, P., 1994. *Gilding the Acorn: Behind the Façade of the National Trust*. London, Simon & Schuster.

Weiss, G., 2008. *Refiguring the Ordinary*. Bloomington, Indiana University Press.

Weiss, K.M., 2011. The weald of Kent: Darwin hesitated to Ussher in a better date. *Evolutionary Anthropology: Issues, News, and Reviews* 20(4), 126-30.

Whistler, H., 1940. Cinerary Urn found at Bodiam. *Sussex Notes and Queries* 8: 25.

White, L., 1962. *Medieval Technology and Social Change*. Oxford, Clarendon Press.

Whitney, K.P., 1976. *The Jutish Forest. A Study of the Weald of Kent from 450 to 1370 AD*. Athlone Press.

Whittick, C., 1993. Dallingridge's bay and Bodiam Castle millpond: elements of a medieval landscape. *Sussex Archaeological Collections* 131: 119-23.

Whyte, N., 2009. *Inhabiting the Landscape: Place, Custom, and Memory, 1500-1800*. Oxford, Oxbow.

Wilkinson, K.N., Scaife, R.G. and Sidell, J.E., 2000. Environmental and sea-level changes in London from 10,500 BP to the present: a case study from Silvertown. *Proceedings of the Geologists' Association* 111, 41-54.

Williamson, T., 2004 *Shaping Medieval Landscapes: Settlement, Society, Environment*. Oxford, Windgather Press.

Williamson, T., Liddiard, R. and Partida, T., 2013. *Champion: The Making and Unmaking of the English Midland Landscape*. Liverpool University Press.

Wilson, D., 1985. *Moated Sites*. London, Shire Publications.

Winchester, S., 2001. *The Map that Changed the World: William Smith and the Birth of Modern Geology*. London, Viking.

Witney, K.P., 1990. The woodland economy of Kent, 1066-1348. *Agricultural History Review* 38, 20-39.

Wittur, J., 2013. *Computer-Generated 3D-Visualisations in Archaeology: Between Added Value and Deception*. Oxford, Archaeopress.

Wood, M., 1965. *The English Mediaeval House*. London, Bracken Books.

Woolf, V., 1928. *Orlando: A Biography*. New York, Crosby Gage.

Woolgar, C.M., 1999. *The Great Household in Late Medieval England*. New Haven, Yale University Press.

Woolgar, C.M., 2006. *The Senses in Late Medieval England*. New Haven, Yale University Press.

Worrall, S., 2003. *An Archaeological Watching Brief during Drainage Works at Bodiam Castle, East Sussex*. Archaeology South-East Report 1752. Available at ESRO R/R/36/13954 and R/R/24/5/1.

Worthen, S., 2006. Of mills and meaning. In S.A. Walton (ed.), *Wind and Water in the Middle Ages: Fluid Technologies from Antiquity to the Renaissance*. Tempe, Arizona Center for Medieval and Renaissance Studies, 259-82.

Wrigglesworth, M., 2009. Memories of place: Bronze Age rock art and landscape in west Norway. In M. Georgiadis and C. Gallou (ed.), *The Past in The Past: The Significance of Memory and Tradition in The Transmission of Culture*. BAR International Series 1925. Oxford, Archaeopress, 43-56.

Wright, D., 2008. *Knole Park Estate, Kent: Archaeological Earthwork Survey*. Unpublished report, Wessex Archaeology, on file at National Trust archives, Knole.

Index

A
A21 syndrome 7
Abbott, Daisy 153
Acoustics xiii, 144, 151-6
Affordance, concept 159-61, 168-70, 188, 202, 220
Agency, definition 162-8, 185, 192-9, 222
Allen, Charlotte and Davy 176
Amberley 46
Anglo-Saxon Chronicle 163
Anglo-Saxon period: see early medieval
Arts and Humanities Research Council (AHRC) xii, 6-7
Archaeology South-East xiv, 4, 21-4, 207-10, 221
Arundel 189
Arundel, Lord 148, 194
Ashburnham, Roger 6, 95, 97, 100-4, 110, 162, 192-3, 196
Ashdown Forest 8, 56, 126, 184, 194
Assarting 164, 187-8, 220

B
Bailey, George xii, 4, 19, 210
Ball, John 95
Bannister, Nicola 97-8, 100-3, 131-4
Barker, Dominic xiv, 6, 51, 56, 87, 106, 115, 214, 218
Barnes, Ian xii, xvi
Base or lower courts 18-19, 46, 132, 139, 166-7, 198
Basing, Margaret 168
Battle 20
Battle Abbey 15, 190, 206
Battle and District Historical Society 63
Battle Museum 207, 209-10
Beatles, The 113
Bewl, river and reservoir 97-8, 101-3, 192
Black Death 170, 188-9
Bolton 26, 45-6, 49
Bodiam 2-6, 9-97, 101-4, 106, 126, 136, 140, 143-54, 158-62, 166-7, 171-8, 180-1, 184, 188-95, 197-201, 203, 212-8
    Approach routes 16-17, 21, 45, 51, 53, 60, 67, 71-3
    Barbican 16, 18, 37, 44
    'Battle for Bodiam' 3-4, 7, 10, 51
    'Bodiam Bombard' xii, 206-10
    Bridge [across Rother] 4, 20, 51, 53, 55-6, 65, 74, 174, 206
    Bridges to castle 14-18, 20, 22, 32, 71, 85, 167, 208
    Canoe 206-7

Car park 14-15, 17, 21, 53, 56, 60, 65, 67, 71, 76, 80, 88, 93-4, 174, 209, 218
Castle Inn xii, 21, 23, 53, 68
'Cascade' 53, 65, 68, 71-2
Cattle yard, possible 71, 76, 82-3
Chapel, sacristy 26, 32, 36, 39-41, 43-5, 47, 203
Church 15-16, 53, 63
Court Lodge 15, 18-20, 36, 53, 63, 71, 208
Cricket field 53-6, 59-60, 67-9, 73-4, 216-7
Curzon's cricket pitch 74, 200
Demesne 15, 19
Dog walkers 174
Dokes Field 14, 53, 56, 59-63, 68, 71-4, 171, 209, 215, 218
Dovecot 48-9, 53
Gun Garden: see 'viewing platform'
Finds 22-3, 65, 206-11 Fireplaces 23, 32, 35-7, 39, 41-2, 46-50
Floodplain 10-15, 19, 51-6, 58-61, 75, 82, 90-4
Flote: see harbour
Gatehouses, north and south 19-22, 27, 35-9, 41, 43-50, 199
Frerens Meade 208
Gunports 4, 10, 47
Hall 22-3, 26, 32, 35-6, 43-8, 63, 209
Harbour 15-17, 21-22, 51, 53, 60, 67-8, 80, 93-4, 197, 210
Heraldry 38, 192, 194-5
Homestead moat 15, 159, 207, 210
Kilns 59, 65, 67
Kitchen, service area 26, 42-50, 145
Leafy boss 37-8
Lodgings 26, 39
Manor 160, 163, 45, 47, 49, 198
Masons, masons marks 39, 42-5, 197
Mill, mill pond, mill leat 10, 16-17, 19-22, 51, 53, 65, 67-8, 71, 74, 76, 80, 82-5, 87, 93-4, 190, 195, 197-200
Moat 4, 16-24, 32, 35, 40, 44, 46, 49, 51, 53, 56, 59, 67-8, 71-3, 75-7, 79-80, 83, 85, 87, 93-4, 208-10, 218
Octagon 16, 18, 167
Park 16, 19, 72, 74, 88, 126
Pillbox 17, 20, 23, 74, 174-5
Place-name 190
Plinths 32, 35, 38, 42, 46
Portcullis 22, 24, 36, 47, 49, 207
Public house: see Castle Inn

241

'Private apartments' 7, 36, 40-1, 44-5, 47, 143, 145-51
Roman road 11, 14, 16, 20, 51, 60, 65, 71-3, 175, 197, 207-10, 218
Roman settlement 14, 59
Rose Garden 12, 15, 21-4, 67, 93, 209
Sewage plant 12, 21-3, 209-10
Stairs 53, 74
'Tilt yard': see mill pond
Towers 26, 32, 35-45, 47-9, 77-9, 198-9
'Viewing platform' 16, 18, 46, 53, 77
Village 16, 46, 51-3, 60, 63, 65, 67, 71, 74-5, 94
Wharf: see harbour
Bodiam family 63
Bourchier, Archbishop 106, 110-1, 123-4, 126, 191-3, 197
Bramber 189
Brightling 19, 73, 200
Bronze Age 21-2, 53, 56, 59, 69, 75, 82, 90-1, 94, 109, 120, 190, 206-7, 220
Burrin, Paul 13, 56, 59, 90-1, 210

C
Caldicot 47
Canterbury 191
    Archbishop 7, 106, 110
    Cathedral 124
    Christ Church 189
    Westgate 47
Castle Toll 190
Catlin, Kathryn A xiii-iv, 6, 51, 55, 75, 147, 206, 209, 212, 215-6, 218
Chichester 98, 189
Church, Dora xii
Cinderella Castle 175
Civil War, English 18, 36, 63, 112, 204
Clanchy, Michael 187
Clifford, Lady Ann 116
Cohen, Nathalie xii, 109, 143
Couen, Thomas 6-7, 132, 147-8, 192-3
Cole, James xiii, 51
Conan Doyle, Arthur 186-8
Connerton, Paul 176
Cooling 19, 44-6
Cooper, Catriona xii-iv, 6-7, 25-7, 41, 47, 143, 149, 196, 200
Copeland, Penny xiii-iv, 6, 25-6, 35-44, 46, 48-50, 75-6, 87, 145, 218
Coppicing, pollarding 63, 77, 93, 103, 187, 220, 222
Coring xii, 6, 56, 71, 75-7, 80, 87, 105, 134, 190, 218
Cubitt, George (Lord Ashcombe) 19-20, 32, 35, 48, 74
Couen, Thomas 6-7, 132, 147-8, 192-3
Coulson, Charles 3, 9, 16, 25-6, 37, 104, 160, 194
Cranmer, Archbishop 11, 106, 126

Creighton, Oliver 10, 18, 97, 103, 134, 140-2, 145-6, 160, 167, 202
Cronon, William 185, 189
Curry, Anne xii, 204
Curzon, Lord 11, 17-20, 32, 35-6, 40, 42-4, 48, 53, 63, 66, 68, 71, 72, 74, 76, 78-80, 145, 175, 206-8, 210-11
    As Vicerory of India 200-1

D
Dallingridge, Sir Edward 3, 6, 15-16, 18-20, 44-7, 67-8, 71, 74, 93, 95, 97, 100, 104, 126, 162, 190-5, 197-8
Dallingridge, Sir John 18, 190-1, 195
Dallingridge, Phillipa 19
Darent valley 109
Darrell family 101
Dartington Hall 19, 46
Darwin, Charles 184-5
Dawson, Charles 185
Debate between the Heralds 123
Deer parks: see parks
Demesne lands 141, 164, 166, 199, 220; see also Bodiam
'Dens', -den place-name 187
'Designed landscapes', concept 6, 11, 17-20, 52-4, 74, 102-4, 129-31, 140-2, 198-204
Digital approaches and techniques 7, 25, 143-57, 196
Disneyland 175
Domesday Book 60, 164-5
Douglas Simpson, W. 26, 45
Dover 149
Down House 185
Downs 7, 109-10, 184-6, 189, 202
Drove roads 187-8, 191
Drury, Paul xii, 4, 15, 22, 27, 37, 39-40, 44, 59-60, 63, 65, 67-8, 71-3, 93, 206-8, 211

E
Earl, Graeme xii, 43, 146
Earle, Timothy 194
Early medieval period 15, 60, 93-4, 98, 109-10, 117, 140, 145, 186-90
Earth resistance (resistivity) survey: see survey techniques
East Sussex Record Office 21, 23
Edward III 26, 45, 123
Electrical resistivity tomography (ERT): see survey techniques
Emery, Anthony 19, 26, 46, 111, 132, 145
Empiricism 3, 144, 221
English Channel 20, 178, 189-90, 197
English Heritage, also Historic England xii, 5, 17, 27, 53, 76, 179, 181

Epping Forest   116
Etchingham   104, 162
Etchingham family   100, 104. 162, 192
Everson, Paul   3, 16-17, 67, 97, 103
Everitt, Alan   109-10, 132, 187-9, 191
Ewhurst manor   14-15, 63
Ewhurst Green   52, 56, 188
Ewhurst Place   36

F
Farleigh Hungerford   46
Faulkner, Patrick   26-7, 49, 145
Fiennes, James   110, 189, 191-3, 195
Fiennes, William   106, 126
Fleming, Peter   164, 168
Ford, Adam   xii, 140, 204
Fox, Cyril   183-4, 186
France   145, 18-19, 193-6, 221, 190
French raids   3, 9, 52, 74, 100, 190, 193
Fuller, John ('Mad Jack')   11, 19-20, 32, 35-6, 41, 72-4, 200, 205, 207, 210
    Ownership of slaves   200
Furnace Farm   159

G
Gascoigne, Alison   xii, 143
Geographic Positioning System (GPS)   53-4, 213, 221
Geology   11, 56, 109, 114-6, 125, 161-3, 183-6, 189, 216
Ghost of Roman soldier   175
Gilchrist, Roberta   2, 47, 123, 143-4,167
Gillings, Mark   143-4, 146, 161, 204
Gillow, Bernadette   xii
Glass production   124, 179, 188
Glottenham   159, 162
Goodall, John   3, 9-10, 26, 36
Goudhurst   44-5, 47
Great Chalfield   48
Greensand, sandstone   22-3, 44, 56, 109-10, 131; 134, 136, 184-5, 188, 190-2, 202
Gregory, Alden   51, 194
'Grey literature'   iii, 1, 3-4, 6, 9, 23, 56, 95-8, 106, 129-30, 136, 201-4, 221
Grovehurst family   100, 102, 110
Ground Penetrating Radar (GPR): see survey techniques

H
Hachure survey: see survey techniques
Halnaker House   46
Harvey, John   45, 47, 146
Hasted, Edward   103, 111
Hastings   14, 20, 53, 100
Hastings Area Archaeological Research Group   60, 207, 209

Hastings Museum   207, 210
Hastings, Rape of   16, 104, 164, 189,
Hauser, Mark   xiii
Hawkes, Jacquetta   9
Henry VIII   106, 111, 126-7
Henry Yevele   45, 47, 104
Heraldry   194
Herstmonceux   193
Hesdin   46, 221
Hetherington, Nigel   172
Hever Castle   93
Highland and Lowland Zones: see Fox, Cyril
Historic England: see English Heritage
Hodder, Ian   144, 161
Holland, Brittany   19, 32, 73, 200, 208
Holocene   12-13, 59, 90, 218, 221-2
Hops, hop picking   94, 176, 222
Hoskins, W.G.   7-8, 177, 186
Haute family   6, 140
Hunting: see parks
Hussey, Edward   97, 101

I
Ice Age   184, 188, 221
Iden, Alexander   195
Iden, The Mote   9, 46, 102, 159, 163, 166-7, 187, 210
Ightham Mote   xiii, xvi, 1-2, 6-7, 11, 19, 21, 48, 72, 106, 129-43, 145, 147-8, 151-8, 179-81, 188-93, 197-201, 203-5, 212-3
    Approaches   132, 137-141, 200
    Bridges to house   132, 139
    Car park   132
    Chapel   132, 141
    Conservation programme   134, 136, 204
    Gatehouse   133, 136, 140
    Great Hall   132, 151, 153-7
    Ightham church   191, 193
    Mill, mill pond   133-4, 138, 140, 179, 190
    Minstrels   151, 153, 157
    Moat   129, 132-6, 139-41
    Mote Stream   130, 134, 136
    Orchard   130-3, 135-7, 180
    Park pale, possible   131, 134, 140, 142
    Scathes Wood   133, 138-9
    Stables   131, 133
Industrial Revolution   172, 183
Ingold, Tim   144, 161, 196, 199
Iron Age   14, 221
Iron production and transport   13-14, 46, 60, 187-8, 197-8

J
Jack Cade rebellion   110, 126, 195
James, Richard   xiv, 9, 23, 53, 93

John of Gaunt   126, 194
Johnson, Casper   xiii, xiv, 3-4, 6, 9, 59
Johnson, Eric D.   xiv, 6, 95, 158, 160, 215
Johnson, Matthew   iii, xiv, 1, 9, 25-7, 37, 47, 51-2, 55-6, 75, 95-8, 100, 106-7, 111, 115, 125, 129-30, 133-4, 136, 139, 143, 158, 172-4, 176, 183, 191-3, 202, 212, 215-6.
Jones, Jude   147-8

K

Kellala, Meya   xii, 59, 215
Kent&East Sussex Railway   56, 60
Knocker, Group Captain   110
Knole   xii, xvi 1-2, 6-7, 11, 21, 72, 106-28, 131, 136, 143, 158, 171, 178-81, 185, 188-93, 195, 197, 199, 201, 203, 205, 212, 216
    Approaches   115, 120
    Bowling greens   107, 112, 118, 178
    'Birdhouse'   110-2
    Car park   113, 115
    Chapel   111
    Echo Mount   109, 113, 115-8, 120
    Engravings   112-3, 116, 118, 121
    Gatehouse   107
    Green Court   107-8, 111-12, 118-20
    Glassworks   125
    Golf course   113, 125, 178
    Ha-ha, possible   118
    Orangery   112
    Park   7, 106-28
    Pheasant Court   111
    Stable Court   111, 119
    Standing   123
    Stone Court and cisterns   111, 119-20, 179
    The Dranes   124
    Water Court   111
Knole family   110

L

Lamberhurst   97-8, 100-1, 192, 199
Lash, Ryan   xiv, 6, 106-7, 123-4, 129-30
Lay Subsidy Returns   192
Le Patourel, Jean   158, 160, 162, 164, 168, 170
Leach, Peter   129, 131-2, 134, 136, 204
Leeds castle and priory   46, 100, 201
Lennard, John   11, 116, 125
Lewes   189
Lewknor family   19, 36
Licences to crenellate   3, 16, 44, 46, 67, 100, 102, 104, 163-4, 167, 194, 221
LiDAR survey: see survey techniques
Liddiard, Robert   10, 18, 25, 130, 140, 145-6, 202
Little Ice Age   188
Lived experience, definition   1-2, 192-7

London   4, 7, 74, 113, 148, 178, 184, 190, 192-3, 195
Lowden   159
Lower courts: see base courts
Luttrell Psalter   197-9
Lynch, Kevin   174

M

McPhee, Kayley   68, 108, 130-3
Machicolations   44, 104, 222
Magnetic susceptibility: see survey techniques
Magnetometry: see survey techniques
Maps
    Ordnance Survey   8, 101, 103, 133, 138, 222
    Tithe   71, 133, 222
Markham, Gervase   185
Martin, Barbara   xiii, 3-4, 22, 37, 163-7
Martin, David   xiii, 3-4, 9, 22, 37, 44, 53, 101, 158, 163-7, 207-8
Martin, Edward   163
Masculinity   9, 123, 165, 192
Mate, Mavis   19, 164, 168, 187-8
Mesolithic   12, 14, 21, 90, 109, 131, 207, 209, 222
Midlands   16, 132, 188, 193-4
Miles, James   xiii, 25-6, 60, 87, 218
Minihan, Gemma   xii, 7, 132, 193
Miroir Historial   150
Moats   158-70, 220, 223; see also Bodiam, Ightham, Scotney
Moated Sites Research Group, later Medieval Settlement Research Group   158, 160
Mood boards   147, 150-2
Moore, Henry   200
Morrill, John   204
Moser, Stephanie   151
Mozart, Wolfgang A.   155
Murray, Stephen   144
Myres, J.N.L.   65, 207-8, 211

N

National Trust   iii, xii-iii, xvi, 1, 3-4, 6-7, 10, 14, 20-1, 51-3, 56, 60, 65, 68, 71, 74, 77, 95, 97-101, 106-8, 113, 128-31, 134, 136, 172, 174-80, 199-203, 205-8, 210, 221
    Volunteers xii-vi, 7, 128, 171-3, 176-182, 203
Northwestern University   iii, xii-vi, 1, 6, 8-10, 17, 26-7, 43, 51-3, 56, 73, 75, 95-6, 99, 106, 113, 130, 136, 156, 158, 171-2, 176, 203, 209
Neolithic   14, 80, 82, 90-1, 94, 109, 222
Norman Conquest   165, 189

O

Old Conghurst   159
Old Soar Manor   192
Oldbury   131

INDEX

Oosthuizen, Susan xiii
Oswald, Alistair xii, 109, 115, 125, 128
Otford 109-11, 191
Outridge Base Camp 6

P

Packham, James 147
Palstre Court 159
Pannage 110, 125, 187
Parks
    Deer parks 7, 72, 106-9, 111, 118, 121-3, 128, 131, 133-4, 140, 142, 167, 178, 190-3, 199, 204
    Hunting, meanings of 109, 122-5
    Pales, palings 111, 115-6, 125-6
    Park-breaking, trespass, poaching 122, 124-7, 142, 194
Parliament 126, 193, 200
Pashley, Edmund 163-4, 167-8
Peacock, Becky xiv, 7, 171-6, 179, 209
Peasants' Revolt 126, 195
Penshurst 48, 127, 156
Pevensey 188-9, 193
Phebus, Gaston 123
Piltdown 185
Pilgrims Way 191
Pinterest 146
Phenomenology 143-4, 196, 222
Platt, Colin 3, 10, 145-6, 158, 160, 163, 165, 170, 204
Peat 11, 13, 21-2, 45, 56, 59, 67, 69, 73, 78, 80, 82-5, 87, 90-1, 94, 190, 206, 216, 218-9, 222
Pevsner, Nikolaus 26, 47, 145
Pilgrims Way 191
'Pleasaunces' 18
Political economy and ecology 2, 8, 107, 125, 205
Pollard, Josh 144, 204
Pollarding: see coppicing
Pollen analysis xii, 68, 75-94, 218-9
Pope, Matt xv, 9, 12, 15, 21-2, 24, 67, 82, 90, 93, 207, 209-10
Powell, Nathaniel 36, 73
Pragmatist philosophy 203
Public engagement 2, 7, 171-82, 203

R

Rabbits, rabbit warrens 122-5, 167
Radiocarbon dating 22, 47, 76, 80, 82, 87, 90, 218, 223
Radynden family 195
Rape of Hastings 164
Renaissance 197, 199
Reverberation time 150, 154-6
'Revisionism' 3, 204
Richard II 126, 193-4

Robbins, Paul 205
Robin, Cynthia xii
Royal Artillery Museum xii, 206-8, 210
Robertsbridge 11, 13, 20, 53, 90
Robertsbridge Abbey 19, 72, 190, 197
Robertsbridge and District Archaeological Society 15
Robin, Cynthia xii
Rochester 14, 98
Romans, Roman period 11, 13-16, 20-22, 51, 56, 59-60, 65, 71-3, 75, 77, 91, 93-4, 109, 175, 186, 187, 197, 207-10
Romanticism 175, 199
Romney Marsh 10-11, 56, 59, 74, 188, 190, 192-3
Royal Commission on Historical Monuments (England) (RCHME) 3-5, 10, 16, 18, 46, 53, 63-7, 71-2
Rother, river and valley 10-16, 19-20, 51, 53-6, 58-9, 61, 63, 65, 67-8, 71, 75, 90-1, 93-4, 167, 184, 190, 197, 206-7, 210
Rye 13, 20, 59, 74, 100, 189-90, 197
Rumley, Peter 131, 133-4, 139-40, 204

S

Sackville, family and estate xii, 7, 106-8, 111-12, 114, 116, 127-8, 178-9, 189
Sackville-West, Vita 110, 125, 178
Saint Eustace 124
Sandstone: see greensand
Scaife, Rob xv, 13, 32, 59, 67, 75-7, 90-1, 210, 218
Scrope, Lord 45
Scrope vs Grosvenor case 195
Scotney iii, xii, xvi, 1-2, 6, 8, 11, 19, 21, 44-6, 72, 95-106, 110, 140, 158-9, 162, 166, 171, 177-80, 185, 188-93, 196, 199-203, 210, 212
    1630s rebuilding 96
    Approaches 95-8, 101-4
    Towers 96, 100-1, 104
    Base Camp 6
    Bridge to castle 95
    Car park 95
    Castle 95-9, 101, 103, 189
    Chapel 100, 102
    Gatehouse 100, 103
    Hall 96
    Henry Allen map 100, 105
    Mill 6, 97-8, 100, 103-5
    Moat 95, 97-8, 100-104
    New House, also New Castle 95, 97, 177, 200
    Park 96, 100
    Picturesque landscape 95, 97, 101, 103, 200-1, 210
    William Clout maps 98, 101-2, 105
Scott, Sir Walter 186
Sediment analysis 13-15, 75-80, 82, 85, 87-8, 90-4, 218
Selborne, Hampshire 814

Sevenoaks   106, 109-13, 117, 124, 126, 128, 131, 155, 178
Sheriff Hutton   45-6
Slocombe, Emma   xii
Sly, Timothy   xv, 6, 51, 95-6, 129-30, 136, 213-4
Smith, Adam T   141, 161, 167
Smith, Les   xii
Southampton, Medieval Merchants House   149
Southampton, University of   xii-vi, 1, 6-11, 26-7, 51, 53, 56, 76-7, 80, 95-6, 99, 113-4, 130, 136, 149, 154-5, 171-3, 176, 209, 212, 218-9
Spencer, Dan   193-5, 206
Stevenson, Victoria   87
Strutt, Kristian   xv, 6, 27, 51, 60, 106, 212-3
Survey techniques
    Earth resistance   53-4, 56-7, 60, 62-7, 69-70, 72-3, 107, 112, 114-5, 117-9, 212-4
    Electrical resistivity tomography (ERT)   54, 56, 58-9, 214-5
    Ground-penetrating radar (GPR)   26-7, 33-7, 39, 41-2, 46-8, 54, 56-7, 66-71, 80, 107-8, 114-5, 118-20, 135-7, 173, 79, 212-3, 216-7
    Hachure   4-5, 10, 16, 53, 65, 204
    LiDAR   11, 15, 59, 74, 104, 128, 130, 221
    Magnetic susceptibility   54, 56, 61, 216
    Magnetometry (gradiometry)   20, 53-66, 68-9, 72-4, 107, 114-8, 212, 215-6
    Topographic   1, 4, 6, 10-11, 17, 51, 53, 56, 58-60, 63, 65, 72-4, 82, 96-7, 99-104, 106-8, 113-8, 129-37, 200, 204, 212-3, 223
Sussex 'rapes'   189, 194
Sweetbourne, river   97-8, 100-1, 105

T
Tavernor Perry   32, 35-6
Taylor, Christopher   3, 5, 10, 15-16, 25, 53, 63, 65, 67, 71, 97, 140, 158, 160, 162-5, 170, 204, 207-8
Taylor, Kristina   111, 115-6, 123-5
Teise, river   97-8, 100
Thackray, Caroline   xii, 4, 6, 143
Thackray, David   xii, 26, 47
Thanet, Earls of   36
Thewlis, Patrick   114
Thompson, Michael   3, 152
Tilley, Christopher   143-4, 161, 196
Time Team   136, 177, 197
Tolkein, J.R.R.   186

Tolly, Peter   114
Topographic survey: see survey technique
Toy, Sydney   4, 146
Triangulated Irregular Network (TIN)   56-8, 223

U
Underhill, David   51
University College London   xii, 21, 218

V
Van der Weyden, Rogier   148-9
Van Eyck, Jan   148

W
Wardedieu, Elizabeth   16, 47, 63, 67, 190, 195
Warham, Archbishop   109, 111, 191
Warkworth   46
Wars of the Roses   206
Watercress Line   182
Weald   2, 6-8, 11-14, 17, 20, 44, 56, 59, 75, 90, 94-5, 104, 109-10, 131-4, 139, 158-170, 183-195, 198, 202, 223
Weald and Downland Museum   149
Weideger, Paula   172
Wessex Archaeology   115, 125
Westenhanger   19, 45-6
Wheeler, Mortimer   200
White, Gilbert   184
Whittick, Chris   xiii, xv, 4, 6, 9-10, 16-17, 19, 25, 44, 67-8, 93, 163-7, 195, 208
Willis, Carrie   xiii-iv, 129-30, 135, 137
Winchelsea   20, 100, 189-90, 193, 197
Windsor   26, 45, 122
Wingfield, Ross   xii
Woodland   7-8, 14, 20, 59, 75, 77-8, 82-3, 87-8, 90-1, 93-4, 103, 105, 109-10, 123, 125, 131-3, 137-8, 162, 164, 185, 187-8, 198, 223
Woodland clearance 88-91, 164, 186; see also assarting
Woolf, Virginia   178. 201
Woolgar, Chris   xii, 143, 145, 150, 156
World War II   113, 174-5, 178; see also Bodiam, pillbox
Wressle   45-6

Y
Yeomen   110, 126, 168, 188, 195, 223
Yevele, Henry   45, 47, 104